LENIENCY IN ASIAN COMPETITION LAW

In response to cartel formation, competition lawyers and policymakers in nine Asian jurisdictions have experimented with leniency programmes. This mechanism allows firms to come forward with information in relation to their illegal cartel participation in return for a reduction of or immunity from a sanction. The experimentation plays out across three different dimensions: the revision of early adopted leniency programmes, the introduction of newly written leniency programmes, and the decision – deliberate or otherwise – not to create a leniency programme. This volume is the first to analyse the empirical evidence across a number of countries to determine how effective these measures have been, and how they have been amended in response to problems encountered. In this volume, local experts from key Asian jurisdictions, together with international experts, offer an introduction to this fast-developing field, and explore the theoretical, international and regulatory contexts of leniency programmes.

STEVEN VAN UYTSEL is Professor of International Business Law at the Graduate School of Law, Kyushu University, Japan.

MARK FENWICK is Professor of International Business Law at the Graduate School of Law, Kyushu University, Japan.

YOSHITERU UEMURA is a Professor of Competition Law at the Faculty of Economics, Hannan University, Japan.

LENIENCY IN ASIAN COMPETITION LAW

Edited by

STEVEN VAN UYTSEL

Kyushu University

MARK FENWICK

Kyushu University

YOSHITERU UEMURA

Hannan University

CAMBRIDGE
UNIVERSITY PRESS

CAMBRIDGE
UNIVERSITY PRESS

University Printing House, Cambridge CB2 8BS, United Kingdom

One Liberty Plaza, 20th Floor, New York, NY 10006, USA

477 Williamstown Road, Port Melbourne, VIC 3207, Australia

314–321, 3rd Floor, Plot 3, Splendor Forum, Jasola District Centre, New Delhi – 110025, India

103 Penang Road, #05–06/07, Visioncrest Commercial, Singapore 238467

Cambridge University Press is part of the University of Cambridge.

It furthers the University's mission by disseminating knowledge in the pursuit of education, learning, and research at the highest international levels of excellence.

www.cambridge.org
Information on this title: www.cambridge.org/9781009152709
DOI: 10.1017/9781009152693

First published 2022

A catalogue record for this publication is available from the British Library.

ISBN 978-1-009-15270-9 Hardback

CONTENTS

TABLES AND BOXES

Tables

Boxes

CONTRIBUTORS

BASKARAN BALASINGHAM is an assistant professor in the department of International and European Law at the Utrecht University School of Law. His main research focus is on competition law and digitalisation. Baskaran completed his PhD at King's College London. While completing his doctoral research, he briefly worked at the UK Competition and Markets Authority. Before starting his PhD, he completed a traineeship at DG Competition of the European Commission. He has been a visiting researcher at Georgetown Law School, the Max Planck Institute for Innovation and Competition and Hannan University. His recent publications include 'Exclusionary Innovation in the European Commission's Decisions Against Google', European Competition Journal (accepted/in press); 'Digital Platforms and Journalism in Australia: Analysing the Role of Competition Law' (2022) 45 World Competition and Economics Review 295–318 (with Tai Neilson) and 'Super-dominant and Super-problematic? The Degree of Dominance in the Google Shopping Judgement', European Competition Journal (2022), DOI: 10.1080/17441056.2022.2059962 (with Alessia D'Amico).

YING BI is an associate professor of law at Zhejiang University in Hangzhou (China). She holds an LLB and LLM from Tsinghua University in Beijing, China, an LLD from Kyushu University in Fukuoka, Japan, and previously worked for the Japanese law firm Soga Uryu & Itoga in Tokyo and researched at Waseda University. Her major research interest covers global governance of state-owned enterprises, international trade law and competition law and regional trade agreements. She has published *Regulating Fintech in Asia* (Springer, 2020, co-edited with Steven Van Uytsel and Mark Fenwick), *Coordination of Competition and Antidumping Rules in China-Japan-South Korea FTA* (China Law Press, 2016), *Dumping: Antidumping Law or Competition Law* (Intellectual Property Publishing House, 2011) and a series of papers in well-known academic law reviews including *Social Science Japan Journal*, *Journal of East Asia and International Law*, *Journal of World Investment & Trade*, *Manchester Journal of*

International Economic Law, *China and WTO Review* and *Contemporary Social Sciences*. She also serves as an editorial board member of *China and WTO Review* and was selected as an expert for the Antimonopoly Expert Steering Committee of Zhejiang Province.

ANDY C. M. CHEN is professor of law in the Department of Financial and Economic Law at Chung Yuan Christian University (Taiwan) and was the dean of its law school from 2019 to 2021. He is currently on leave to serve as the vice chairperson of the Taiwan Fair Trade Commission. His familiarity with international competition laws and policies has made him a regular speaker on related topics to government agencies, private companies and leading academic institutions and professional organizations, such as Yale University, University of Southern California, National University of Singapore, Korea University, National Law University (Delhi, India), Jindal Global University (Delhi, India). Andy earned his law degrees from National Taiwan University (LLB), Soochow University (Taiwan, LLM), Duke University (LLM) and Northwestern University (Doctor of Juridical Science). He has published extensively on antitrust and regulatory issues in both Chinese and English, mainly from the perspective of economic analysis. His most recent English publications include 'Due Process and Transparency Requirements for Investigating Competition Cases in Taiwan', in *Antitrust Procedural Fairness*, edited by D. Daniel Sokol and Andrew T. Guzman (Oxford University Press, 2019), 'Political, Economic and Legal Driving Forces Shaping the Developmental Contours of Competition Law: the Experience of Taiwan', in *Research Handbook on Asian Competition Law*, edited by Steven Van Uytsel, Shuya Hayashi and John O. Haley (Edward Elgar, 2020) and 'Setting Sail on a Sea of Doubt Again?: Antitrust Review of Data-Driven Non-Horizontal Mergers', in *The Evolution of Antitrust in the Digital Era: Essays on Competition Policy*, vol. 1, edited by David S. Evans (Competition Policy International, 2021).

YO SOP CHOI is a professor of law at the Graduate School of International and Area Studies, Hankuk University of Foreign Studies (Seoul). He specialises in competition law, European Union (EU) law and public policy. His research interest lies mainly at the field of a comparative study of economic regulation and competition law. Professor Choi received his BA from Hankuk University of Foreign Studies, MA in economics from the State University of New York at Buffalo and LLM degrees from Erasmus University Rotterdam and Durham University. He also obtained a PhD in law from the University of Glasgow. Professor Choi has been a visiting scholar at several universities in Asia and Europe. He is a member of the

Academic Society of Competition Law (ASCOLA) and the Korean Competition Law Association. His articles have appeared in the peer review journals, including *IIC-International Review of Intellectual Property and Competition Law*, *European Competition Law Review*, *European Business Organization Law Review*, *Queen Mary Journal of Intellectual Property*, and *World Competition: Law and Economics Review*.

SCOTT CLEMENTS is a competition law specialist with more than fourteen years of experience in Singapore. He has extensive experience in relation to contentious and non-contentious competition law matters. Scott was involved in the first set of appeals made to the Competition Appeal Board in respect of a cartel matter and the appeal of the first ever abuse of dominance case. Scott has assisted on multiple leniency filings made to the Competition and Consumer Commission of Singapore. Scott graduated with a degree in economics from Victoria University of New Zealand and holds a postgraduate degree in economics for competition law from King's College London. He is qualified as an advocate and solicitor of Singapore, and a barrister and solicitor of the High Court of New Zealand. Scott was a contributing author to *Lim & Bull, Competition Law and Policy in Singapore* (2nd ed., Academy Publishing Singapore, 2015).

SANDRA MARCO COLINO is an associate professor at the Faculty of Law of the Chinese University of Hong Kong, and a former director of its Centre for Financial Regulation and Economic Development. She is the Director of the Summer Schools on EU Competition Law for Asian officials at the College of Europe in Bruges, and a member of the Academic Board of the law firm Dictum. Her publications include the monograph *Vertical Agreements and Competition Law* (Hart, 2010, 2nd ed. forthcoming) and the textbook *Competition Law of the EU and UK* (8th ed., Oxford University Press, 2019). She was previously a lecturer at the University of Glasgow and has been a visiting scholar at the University of California at Berkeley, the University of Melbourne, the University of Birmingham and the University of Wisconsin at Madison. She was also a fellow of Stanford University's Transatlantic Technology Law Forum from 2009 until 2011. She has been working on cartel detection and leniency since 2014.

ALIZEDNEY M. DITUCALAN is a professor of law and currently the University Chancellor of the Mindanao State University – Iligen Institute of Technology. He is among the few Filipino academics and lawyers who specialise in competition law. His most recent publication is 'The Philippine Competition Dilemma: US-EU Fusion to Tension?', in *Research*

Handbook on Asian Competition Law, edited by Steven Van Uytsel, Shuya Hayashi and John O. Haley (Edward Elgar, 2020). He was the former law dean of the Mindanao State University. He is currently a visiting professor at the Graduate School of Law of San Beda University, teaching competition law subjects.

MARK FENWICK is a professor of international business law at the Graduate School of Law, Kyushu University. His primary research interests are in the field of business regulation in a digital age. His recent publications include *International Business Law: Emerging Fields of Regulation* (Hart, 2018, co-authored with Stefan Wrbka), *Regulating Fintech in Asia* (Springer, 2020, co-edited with Steven Van Uytsel and Bi Ying) and *Smart Contracts: Technological, Business, and Legal Perspectives* (Hart, 2021, co-edited with Marcelo Corrales Compagnucci and Stefan Wrbka). He has been a visiting professor at Duke University, the University of Hong Kong, the National University of Singapore and Tilburg University, and he has conducted research for the EU, the Organisation for Economic Co-operation and Development (OECD) and the World Bank.

JUHI HIRANI is a legal associate with Touchstone Partners (New Delhi, India). She is currently working in the mergers and acquisition, private equity and corporate team of the firm assisting on varied cross-border transactions. Her research interests include antitrust economics and law.

NIKITA KORADIA is an assistant professor at the Institute of Law, Nirma University (Ahmedabad, India). She has completed a double master's in international corporate governance and financial regulation from the University of Warwick (United Kingdom) and Pennsylvania State University. Her recent publications include 'Algorithmic Collusion and Indian Competition Act: Suggestions to Tackle Inadequacies and Naivety', co-authored with Kiran Manokaran and Zara Saeed, in *The Digital Economy and Competition Law in Asia*, edited by Steven Van Uytsel (Springer, 2021); 'The Hyundai Model: A Quasi Leviathan in the Making' 15 *National Law School Journal* 34 (2019–2020); (co-authored with Rohan Dembani), 'Can Non-Dominant Entities Behave Dominantly: Revisiting the Grey Areas of Predatory Pricing During the Curious 5 Years' Growth of Jio' 11(2) GNLU Journal of Law, Development & Politics (2021).

CASSEY LEE is a senior fellow and coordinator of the Regional Economic Studies Programme at ISEAS, Yusof Ishak Institute (Singapore). Prior to joining ISEAS, Dr Lee held academic appointments at the University of Wollongong, Nottingham University Business School (Malaysia) and University of Malaya.

Lee received his PhD (economics) from the University of California, Irvine. Lee specialises in industrial organisation. He has published in peer-reviewed journals such as *Computational Economics*, *Journal of Economic Dynamics and Control*, *Kyklos*, *Journal of Economic Surveys* and *Economic Modelling*. Lee is currently the co-managing editor of the *Journal of Southeast Asian Studies* and associate editor of *Journal of Economic Surveys*, *Asian Economic Journal* and *Asian Economic Policy Review*.

KIRAN MANOKARAN is an attorney practising in India. He is currently associated with Lakshmikumaran and Sridharan Attorneys (Chennai) as a Senior Associate and also with Nishimura and Asahi (Tokyo) as an Associate-Secondee. He pursued his bachelor's in law from SASTRA University (Thirumalaisamudram, India), and his master's in law from Pennsylvania State University. His recent publications include 'Algorithmic Collusion and Indian Competition Act: Suggestions to Tackle Inadequacies and Naivety', co-authored with Nikita Koradia and Zara Saeed, in *The Digital Economy and Competition Law in Asia*, edited by Steven Van Uytsel (Springer, 2021).

PLOYKAEW PORANANOND is a lecturer at the Faculty of Law, Chiang Mai University (Thailand). Her research interest centres around regional competition law especially that of the Association of South-East Asian Nations (ASEAN), as well as competition law in developing countries. Ploykaew has some experience as a legal consultant to a number of public sector organisations, most notably the Energy Regulatory Commission of Thailand in 2017. She has published *Competition Law in the ASEAN Countries: Regional Law and National Systems* (Kluwer International, 2018). She is currently conducting research projects for the Thailand Research Fund and the National Research Council of Thailand focussing on the application of Thailand competition law to the digital market.

DAREN SHIAU is a corporate lawyer and is Co-Head of Allen & Gledhill LLP's Corporate & Commercial Department and the firm's competition and antitrust practice. He is a regional competition law specialist whose practice covers antitrust litigation, international cartels, monopolies and dominance, and global merger control. Daren has worked in London and Brussels competition practices on European Commission and Office of Fair Trading matters, and he is a non-practising solicitor in England and Wales. Daren graduated from the National University of Singapore in 1996 and was awarded the *Malayan Law Journal* Book Prize. He is District Councilor of the Central Singapore District.

YOSHITERU UEMURA is a professor of competition law at the Faculty of Economics, Hannan University (Osaka, Japan), where he has been teaching Japanese competition law since 2004. He has been a visiting scholar at Melbourne Law School, where he researched the regulation of resale price maintenance under Australian competition law. He also conducted research on US laws at Fordham Law School and Northwestern Law School and was a visiting researcher at the Competition Policy Research Center, Japan Fair Trade Commission. Before joining Hannan University, Yoshiteru worked for TMI Associates (Tokyo, Japan) as a researcher focussing on the Antimonopoly Act of Japan while studying in a doctoral course of business laws at Hitotsubashi University. He holds a Master's degree in International Economic Law from Yokohama National University and a Bachelor of Laws from Tohoku University (Japan). He is a member of the Academic Society for Competition Law (ASCOLA).

STEVEN VAN UYTSEL is a professor of international business law at the Graduate School of Law, Kyushu University (Japan). His primary research interest is competition law and innovation and law. His recent publications include *Research Handbook on Asian Competition Law* (Edward Elgar, 2020, co-edited with Shuya Hayashi and John O. Haley), *Regulating FinTech in Asia: Global Contexts, Local Perspectives* (Springer, 2020, co-edited with Mark Fenwick and Ying Bi), *The Digital Economy and Competition Law in Asia* (Springer, 2021). Steven has cooperated on various competition law issues with the Australian Competition and Consumer Commission, the Competition and Consumer Commission of Singapore, the Japan Fair Trade Commission, Thai Fair Trade Commission and the Thai Office of the Judiciary. He is a member of Academic Society for Competition Law (ASCOLA).

PREFACE AND ACKNOWLEDGEMENTS

This edited volume aims to bring together scholars and practitioners working in the field of competition law and white-collar crime in Asia. Our aim in developing this collection is to show how Asian jurisdictions are experimenting with leniency programmes to enforce the anti-cartel provisions of their respective competition laws. We can see three categories of experimentation in Asia. First, early adopters of the leniency programme in Asia are confronted with design flaws or shortcomings. These countries have recently extensively revised their respective leniency programme. Second, Asian countries without a leniency programme are convinced that such a programme can make their enforcement policy more effective. These countries have recently adopted a leniency programme. Third, there are some Asian countries that have no leniency programme. Among these countries, there is one, Thailand, that has made a deliberate choice not to implement a leniency programme.

The ideas developed in this volume have been explored in the symposium Leniency Policies in Asian Competition Laws, held in Kyushu University, Fukuoka, Japan on 5–6 October 2018. The conference and this volume have benefitted from a grant from Kyushu University's Progress 100 – Research Hub for the Humanities, Social Sciences, and Interdisciplinary Knowledge.

The editors owe a word of gratitude to Yuko Matsumura, whose help was instrumental in the organisation of the symposium. Thanks also go to Alizedney M. Ditucalan and Oliver Posani, doctoral students at Kyushu University, for their help either during the symposium or in the editing of this volume. We would also like to express our gratitude to Joe Ng and his colleagues at Cambridge University Press for their support in bringing this project to fruition. Finally, we would like to acknowledge the decision and feedback of the two anonymous referees who approved this volume.

ABBREVIATIONS

1MDB	1Malaysia Development Berhad
AAEC	Appreciable adverse effect on competition
ACPERA	Antitrust Criminal Penalty Enforcement and Reform Act
AEC	ASEAN Economic Community
AMA	Antimonopoly Act
AMC	Anti-Monopoly Commission
AMEA	Anti-Monopoly Enforcement Authority
AML	Antimonopoly Law
ANA	American Bar Association
ASEAN	Association of South-East Asian Nations
Bafia	Banking and Financial Institutions Act
BN	Barisan National
BRICS	Brazil, Russia, India, China and South Africa
CA	Competition Act
CCA	Competition Commission Act
CCCS	Competition and Consumer Commission of Singapore
CCI	Competition Commission of India
CCP	Code of Criminal Procedure
CCS	Competition Commission of Singapore
CEO	Chief Executive Officer
CLRC	Competition Law Review Committee
CPC	Communist Party of China
CPTPP	Comprehensive and Progressive Trans-Pacific Partnership Agreement
DG	Director General
DOJ	Department of Justice
EAEUSFTA	Eurasian Economic Union-Singapore Free Trade Agreement
EU	European Union
FAQ	Frequently Asked Question
FBI	Federal Bureau of Investigation
FCA	Financial Conduct Authority
FCR	First Conduct Rule
FTA	Free Trade Agreement
FTP	Fast-track procedure

GAO	Government Accountability Office
GCI	Global Competition Initiative
HKCC	Hong Kong Competition Commission
HKCO	Hong Kong Competition Ordinance
HKCT	Hong Kong Competition Tribunal
HKHA	Hong Kong Housing Authority
HLDSK	Hitachi-LG Data Storage Korea Inc.
ICN	International Competition Network
ICPAC	International Competition Policy Advisory Committee
IMF	International Monetary Fund
IPP	Independent power producer
IT	Information technology
JFTC	Japan Fair Trade Commission
KFTC	Korean Fair Trade Commission
LDP	Liberal Democratic Party
LPR	Competition Commission of India (Lesser Penalty) Regulation
MACC	Malaysian Anti-Corruption Commission
MENA	Middle East and North Africa
MITI	Ministry of International Trade and Industry
MOC	Memorandum of Cooperation
MOFCOM	Ministry of Commerce
MOU	Memorandum of Understanding
MR	Merger Rule
MRFTA	Monopoly Regulation and Fair Trade Act
MRTPA	Monopolies and Restrictive Trade Practices Act
MyCC	Malaysia Competition Commission
NCA	National competition authority
NCLAT	National Company Law Appellate Tribunal
NDRC	National Development and Reform Commission
NFC	National Feedlot Corporation
NGO	Non-governmental organisation
OECD	Organisation for Economic Co-operation and Development
OFC	Office for Competition
PAMR	Provincial Administration for Market Regulation
PARC	Policy Affairs Research Council
PCA	Philippine Competition Act
PCC	Philippine Competition Commission
PID	Proposed Infringement Decision
PLDS	Philips & Lite-On Digital Solutions Corporation
RCA	Regional Cooperation Agreement
RCEP	Regional Comprehensive Economic Partnership
RM	Malaysian ringgit

SAIC	State Administration for Industry and Commerce
SAMR	State Administration for Market Regulation
SAV	Significant added value
SCAP	Supreme Command of Allied Powers
SCR	Second Conduct Rule
SII	Structural Impediments Initiative
SME	Small and medium-sized enterprise
SO	Statements of Objections
SPC	State Planning Commission
TA	Telecommunication Authority
TFEU	Treaty on the Functioning of the European Union
TFTA	Taiwan Fair Trade Act
TFTC	Taiwan Fair Trade Commission
TGRN	Transgovernmental regulatory network
TSSTK	Toshiba-Samsung Storage Technology Korea Corporation
UK	United Kingdom
UMNO	United Malay National Organisation
UNCTAD	United Nations Conference on Trade and Development
US	United States
WPA	Whistleblower Protection Act

PART I

Introduction

1

Leniency in Asian Competition Law

STEVEN VAN UYTSEL, MARK FENWICK
AND YOSHITERU UEMURA

There is an international consensus that cartels[1] should be eradicated from society.[2] The Organisation for Economic Co-operation and Development (OECD) expressed this view in 1998 by considering that 'cartels are the most egregious violations of competition law'[3] in its recommendation on effective actions against hard-core cartels. A similar formulation can be found in the documents of the International Competition Network (ICN). The ICN holds that '[c]artels are generally among the most serious competition infringements'.[4] National enforcement agencies often use more colourful language to convey a similar message. Mario Monti, the European Union (EU) Commissioner for Competition between 1999 and 2004, for example, expressed it in this way: '[c]artels are cancers on the

[1] Cartels could be understood as 'an anticompetitive agreement, anticompetitive concerted practice, or anticompetitive arrangement by competitors to fix prices, make rigged bids (collusive tenders), establish output restrictions or quotas, or share or divide markets by allocating customers, suppliers, territories or lines of commerce.' See OECD Council, 'Recommendation of the OECD Council Concerning Effective Action against Hard Core Cartels' (1998), p. 2, para. A2(a). Retrieved from www.oecd.org/daf/competition/2350130.pdf. Some other definitions focus on the secret nature of cartels but are expressing the same message. See Argenton, C., Geradin, D. and Stephan, A., *EU Cartel Law and Economics* (Oxford: Oxford University Press, 2020), p. 5 (proposing the following definition: 'Cartels are instances of formal, often secret, cooperation between competing firms with a view to suppressing or softening the rivalry between them by reaching an agreement on outputs, sales, prices or other commercial variables').

[2] Harding, C. and Joshua, J., *Regulating Cartels in Europe* (Oxford: Oxford University Press, 2010, 2nd ed.), p. 1.

[3] OECD, 'Recommendation of the Council Concerning Effective Action against Hard Core Cartels', C(98)35/FINAL (25 March 1998). Retrieved from https://legalinstruments.oecd.org/public/doc/193/193.en.pdf.

[4] ICN Working Group on Cartels, 'Building Blocks for Effective Anti-Cartel Regimes' (2005), p. 1.

open market economy'.[5] In the United States (US), enforcement officials started to speak of the 'war against international cartels'.[6] The US Supreme Court added to this list with the view that collusion is the 'supreme evil of antitrust',[7] which was repeated by Thomas O. Barnett, an assistant attorney general at the Antitrust Division of the US Department of Justice (DOJ), in 2007.

The international consensus is built around the idea of consumer protection. The OECD phrases the problem of cartels in terms of an injury to consumers caused 'by raising prices or restricting supply, thus making goods and services completely unavailable to some purchasers and unnecessarily expensive for others'.[8] The ICN stated that '[c]onsumers benefit from competition through lower prices and better products and services'.[9] Consumers are deprived of these benefits if competitors start to collude. Joel Klein, the Assistant Attorney General at the Antitrust Division of the DOJ, bluntly stated that 'cartel behavior ... is bad for consumers'.[10] As a justification for this statement, he held that 'cartels are the equivalent of theft by well-dressed thieves'.[11] Monti taught us that the consumer will pay the bill for the fact that cartels produce less and earn higher profits.[12] Neelie Kroes, the EU Commissioner for Competition between 2010 and 2014, repeated the linkage of theft and cartels. The breaking-up of cartels, she says, 'is to stop money being stolen from customers' pockets'.[13]

Against this background, it should not come as a surprise that 'deterring, detecting and prosecuting cartel conduct is a high priority for

[5] Monti, M., 'Fighting Cartels Why and How? Why Should We Be Concerned with Cartels and Collusive Behaviour?' (Presentation at 3rd Nordic Competition Policy Conference, Stockholm, 11–12 September 2000). Retrieved from http://europa.eu/rapid/press-release_SPEECH-00-295_en.htm.

[6] Klein, J. I., 'The War against International Cartels: Lessons from the Battlefront' (Presentation at Fordham Corporate Law Institute 26th Annual Conference on International Antitrust Law & Policy, 14 October 1999). Retrieved from www.justice.gov/atr/speech/war-against-international-cartels-lessons-battlefront.

[7] *Verizon Communications* v. *Law Offices of Curtis* v. *Trinko*, 540 U.S. 398, 408 (2004).

[8] OECD, 'Recommendation of the Council' (n. 3 above), p. 5.

[9] ICN Working Group on Cartels, 'Building Blocks' (n. 4 above), p. 1.

[10] Klein, 'War against International Cartels' (n. 6 above).

[11] Ibid.

[12] Monti, 'Fighting Cartels' (n. 5 above).

[13] Kroes, N., 'Taking Competition Seriously – Anti-Trust Reform in Europe' (Presentation at the International Bar Association/European Commission Conference Anti-trust Reform in Europe: A Year in Practice, Brussels, 10 March 2005). Retrieved from http://europa.eu/rapid/press-release_SPEECH-05-157_en.htm.

competition agencies worldwide'.[14] However, because of the illegal nature of cartel conduct, participants will go to great lengths to keep their conduct secret. Participants will do whatever is necessary either not to create documents that could serve as proof of illegal conduct or, if these documents come into existence at any point, endeavour to ensure they are hidden or destroyed. Such behaviour, therefore, makes it extremely difficult for the relevant competition agencies to produce the necessary evidence in order to convict cartel participants.[15]

To deal with the problem of secrecy, in 1978 the DOJ developed a new enforcement tool, the leniency programme, to trigger the reporting of illegal cartel conduct. The aim of the programme was to offer immunity to a cartel participant reporting the existence of a cartel. In other words, the reporting cartel participant would not have to pay any monetary fine, nor would any employee be sent to jail for their involvement. The details of the programme were outlined in the DOJ's Corporate Leniency Policy.[16]

The initial experimentation with leniency programmes was not very successful, however.[17] It was only when the DOJ altered the incentive structure for reporting that major successes were achieved. And many of these enforcement successes involved international cartels. For example, the Lysine cartel, one of the earliest successful detections that was attributed to the leniency programme, operated internationally, and comprised American, European, Korean and Japanese corporations.[18] Closely following the developments on the other side of the Atlantic and Pacific Ocean, the EU and the Republic of Korea (Korea) rolled out their respective leniency programmes in 1996.[19]

The early implementers of the leniency programmes started to share their experience on an international level in the hope of convincing others to follow their lead. The OECD, the ICN and later the United Nations Conference on Trade and Development (UNCTAD) all endorsed this new approach.[20] International guidelines and best practices, all based on the

[14] Beaton-Wells, C., 'Leniency Policies: Revolution or Religion', in Beaton-Wells, C. and Tran, C. (eds.) *Anti-Cartel Enforcement in a Contemporary Age: Leniency Religion* (Oxford: Hart Publishing, 2015), 3, p. 3.

[15] Van Uytsel, S., 'A Comparative US and EU Perspective on the Japanese Antimonopoly Law's Leniency Program' (2008) 75(3) *Hosei Kenkyu* F1.

[16] For an explanation, see Balasingham, Chapter 2 in this volume.

[17] Ibid.

[18] See Van Uytsel, Chapter 5 in this volume.

[19] See O'Brien, A., 'Leadership of Leniency', in Beaton-Wells and Tan, *Anti-Cartel Enforcement* (n. 14 above), 17, p. 19.

[20] Van Uytsel, Chapter 3 this volume.

experience of the early implementers, soon developed. The international advocacy for the leniency programme also led to a gradual proliferation of this enforcement tool. Since mid-2018, there are more than sixty jurisdictions that have adopted some form of leniency programme.[21] Among these sixty jurisdictions are several Asian countries. Most of the leniency programmes in Asia were adopted between 2010 and 2020, with Korea (1996),[22] Japan (2005)[23] and Singapore (2006)[24] as exceptions.[25]

It is the aim of this book to critically review the turn to leniency programmes in Asian competition law. The choice of jurisdictions is as follows: Hong Kong, India, Japan, Malaysia, People's Republic of China (China), Republic of China (Taiwan), Korea and Singapore.[26] The choice of these jurisdictions is justified because the majority of them have actively used their respective leniency programme for the enforcement of competition law. The book also discusses the Philippines and Thailand. The Philippine leniency programme has only been adopted recently and has not yet rendered any substantive decision. Yet the unique conceptualisation, especially institutionally, makes a detailed discussion worthwhile.[27] Thailand is interesting because it does not have a leniency programme and this was a deliberate choice. This begs the question of why a country would opt not to create a leniency programme, and, eventually, how cartel enforcement might be advanced without utilising this innovative new enforcement tool.[28]

This introductory chapter to the book is structured as follows. Section 1.1 provides an overview of the origins of the leniency programme. Both the practical necessity of a leniency programme and the first use of the

[21] OECD, 'Challenges and Co-Ordination of Leniency Programmes – Background Note by the Secretariat', DAF/COMP/WP3(2018)1 (2018), pp. 3–4. Retrieved from https://one.oecd.org/document/DAF/COMP/WP3(2018)1/en/pdf.

[22] Choi, Chapter 7 this volume.

[23] Van Uytsel, Chapter 5 this volume; Van Uytsel and Uemura, Chapter 6 this volume.

[24] Clements and Shiau, Chapter 10 this volume.

[25] The Indian Competition Act of 2002 provided for the possibility of lenient treatment, but the Competition Commission of India (CCI) only created the guidelines in 2009. See Koradia, Manokaran and Hirani, Chapter 13 this volume.

[26] The choice to leave out other jurisdictions is based on various reasons. Vietnam adopted a leniency programme in 2018. However, the Vietnamese enforcement has, so far, not focused on cartel formation. The main enforcement focus is on unfair trade practices, which do not fall under the leniency programme. Indonesia, in contrast, has not adopted a leniency programme yet. A draft leniency programme has been elaborated in the framework of a broader review of its competition law.

[27] Ditucalan and Van Uytsel, Chapter 14 this volume.

[28] Porananond, Chapter 15 this volume.

leniency programme in the US will be highlighted. In Section 1.2, the focus will shift to Asia. We will indicate that competition law in Asia is a relatively recent phenomenon, which, in turn, has an impact on the implementation of the leniency programme in Asia. Section 1.3 gives an overview of how the literature in relation to leniency has developed and how this book fills the gap in the literature by providing a comprehensive regional study on the use of leniency programmes.

1.1 The Leniency Programme and Its Origin

1.1.1 The Leniency Programme: The Concept and Its Use

A leniency programme is situated in the realm of law enforcement, for the purpose of this book competition law enforcement. Within competition law enforcement, a leniency programme is designed to assist enforcement of anti-cartel provisions. A leniency programme does so by incentivising cartel participants to defect and report a cartel. This incentive is either immunity for or reduction of the sanction prescribed for infringing the relevant anti-cartel provisions.[29]

The need to rely on cartel participants for the enforcement of the anti-cartel provisions relates to the character of a cartel. Having engaged in prohibited conduct, participants of a cartel will go to extreme lengths to hide the existence of the cartel and their involvement. Everything needs to happen in secrecy and any paper trail revealing the existence of a cartel needs to be avoided as it would provide a road map for regulators.[30] Consequently, letters, emails and faxes will not be the primary means of communication for a cartel. At least historically, telephone communications were much safer. However, as more and more jurisdictions allow telephone tapping and other surveillance, cartel participants will prefer meetings in person and this would either be difficult to trace or not trigger any suspicion. A coincidental meeting in the lobby of an airport when transiting in the same country, a friendly talk during a round of golf or

[29] Barlund, I. M. H., *Leniency in EU Competition Law* (Alphen aan de Rijn: Wolters Kluwer, 2020), pp. 3–4; Salemme, E., *Enforcing European Competition Law through Leniency Programmes in the Light of Fundamental Rights: With an Overview of the US Leniency Programme* (Baden-Baden: Nomos, 2019), p. 85; Balasingham, B., *The EU Leniency Policy: Reconciling Effectiveness and Fairness* (Alphen aan de Rijn: Wolters Kluwer, 2017), p. 2.

[30] If, for one reason or another, paper documents were to be created, these documents would be destroyed or kept at secret places outside the premises of the firms participating in the cartel.

an organised meeting in a backroom during an official trade association meeting, for example, provide the favourite communication channels for organising a cartel.[31]

This makes it very difficult for competition law enforcement agencies to precisely determine that a cartel exists and, if they can find the existence of a cartel, to gain enough evidence to sustain a case against the participants of the cartel. In this context, relying on inside information to detect cartels becomes a rational strategy for the enforcement agencies.

To explain the willingness of cartel participants to defect, scholars have often referred to the prisoner's dilemma, whereby it is claimed that confessing is the dominant strategy if one does not know what the other parties to the cartel are doing.[32] Thus, the leniency programme presupposes that the cartel participants act rationally within the premises of a prisoner's dilemma. Baskaran Balasingham will, in Chapter 2 of this volume, further explain the details of how the prisoner's dilemma functions to activate this desired result.[33]

One should be aware, however, that not all cartel participants are caught within the rationale of a prisoner's dilemma. There will be cartel participants who are, for whatever reason, not responsive to the risk of being caught and punished. First, an 'overconfidence bias' could exist, whereby there is a tendency to 'overestimate the probability of good things happening to them, and underestimate the probability of bad things happening to them',[34] which builds trust among cartel participants. It is this trust among the cartel participants that prevents a cartel from internally disintegrating. Second, a change of management might also trigger leniency

[31] Van Uytsel, S., 'Leniency under the Japanese Antimonopoly Law: Towards the End of the Cartel Archipelago?' in Cheng, T., Marco Colino, S. and Ong, B. (eds.), *Cartels in Asia* (Hong Kong: Wolters Kluwer Law & Business, 2015), pp. 75–76.

[32] Barlund, *Leniency in EU Competition Law* (n. 29 above), pp. 36–37; Salemme, *Enforcing European Competition Law* (n. 29 above), pp. 96–101; Zingales, N., 'European and American Leniency Programmes: Two Models towards Convergence' (2008) 5(1) *Competition Law Review* 5, pp. 8–12; Leslie, C. R., 'Antitrust Amnesty, Game Theory, and Cartel Stability' (2006) 31 *Journal of Competition Law* 453.

[33] Balasingham, Chapter 2 this volume.

[34] Sharot, T., 'The Optimism Bias' (2011) 21(23) *Current Biology* R941–R945. For application in legal scholarship, see Van Uytsel, S., 'The Hybridization of Competition Law Enforcement: Some Lessons from Japan's Introduction of the Leniency Program' (ASLI Working Paper Series No. 027, 2012), pp. 23–26; Stucke, M. E., 'Am I a Price Fixer? A Behavioral Economics Analysis of Cartels', in Beaton-Wells, C. and Ezrachi, A. (eds.), *Criminalising Cartels: Critical Studies of an International Regulatory Movement* (Oxford: Hart Publishing, 2011), 263, p. 271.

applications.[35] This has been exemplified by the Sotheby's–Christie's cartel, whereby the new management of Christie's sought to end the cartel and applied for leniency. Third, some leniency applications are not motivated by the existence of a leniency programme itself, but by investigations of the same cartel elsewhere in the world. Fourth, several studies have indicated that many leniency applications are submitted when the cartel is already disbanded and has no future, in which case the application seems to be driven by strategic considerations rather than by deterrence.[36]

1.1.2 *The Leniency Programme First Develops in the United States*

The first competition agency to experiment with a leniency programme was the DOJ. In 1978, the DOJ issued the Corporate Leniency Policy (1978 Leniency Policy),[37] a programme in which immunity was offered to the first cartel participant defecting from the cartel and providing with candour and completeness previously unknown information.[38] However, even though the defecting cartel participant complied with all the other conditions attached to the 1978 Leniency Policy, the DOJ had the final decision on whether to grant immunity. The DOJ could refuse immunity if it had a reasonable expectation that it could have discovered the reported cartel conduct by itself. This uncertainty of outcome made cartel participants ignore the existence of the 1978 Leniency Policy. Staff of the DOJ have reported that it only received, on average, one leniency application per year.[39]

35 Interview by Steven Van Uytsel (Professor, Kyushu University) with Miriam Driessen-Reilly (Cartel Section, European Commission Directorate-General for Competition), in Brussels (26 March 2012). See Van Uytsel, 'The Hybridization of Competition Law Enforcement' (n. 34 above), p. 26.

36 For a popular account of the cartel, Mason, C., *The Art of the Steal* (New York: Berkeley Publishing Group, 2005).

37 Further discussion, Balasingham, Chapter 2 this volume.

38 It is said that the US DOJ started to discuss the implementation of a leniency programme as early as 1976.

39 Hammond, S. D., 'The Evolution of Criminal Antitrust Enforcement: Over the Last Two Decades' (Presentation at the ABA Criminal Justice Section and the ABA Center for Continuing Legal Education, 2010), p. 2. Retrieved from www.justice.gov/atr/file/518241/download. Bruce Kobayashi reports that seventeen corporations applied for leniency between 1978 and 1993. Six requests were denied and ten corporations qualified for amnesty. Only four out of these ten corporations qualified for amnesty before 1987, the year in which a leniency programme for individuals started. At the time of revision of the 1978 Leniency Policy in 1993, there was still one request pending. Kobayashi also concedes that the initial 1978 Leniency Policy had an average of approximately one leniency application per year. See Kobayashi, B. H., 'Symposium: Antitrust Agency and Amnesty: An Economic Analysis of the Enforcement of Antitrust Laws against Corporations' (2001) 69 *George Washington*

Despite the low detection rate of the 1978 Leniency Policy, Vivek Ghosal and Daniel Sokol point out that there was a general increase of prosecuted cartel cases in the US after 1978.[40] Between 1978 and 1980, there were about twenty cartel cases per year prosecuted and the number rose to an average of sixty cartel cases from 1981 onwards.[41] This result was made possible by focusing on the prosecution of one specific type of cartel: bid rigging.[42] It seems that for public procurement projects, the enforcement agencies had enough instruments to successfully make their case and this goal could be achieved without relying on a good cartel story from an inside participant. But even the prosecution of bid rigging started to diminish as the DOJ's motive became 'hands-off markets, irrespective of the nature of the violations' under the George H. W. Bush administration.[43]

Things changed, however, with the Clinton administration. At the start of this administration in 1993, the Federal Investigation Bureau had, via a large undercover operation in the lysine sector, an indication that price fixing was as prevalent as bid rigging.[44] The enforcement agencies realised that price fixing had been neglected, probably because of the belief that setting up successful cartels was as good as impossible.

To rectify the situation, the DOJ started to revise the 1978 Leniency Policy. In August 1993, the DOJ issued its new Corporate Leniency Policy (1993 Leniency Policy). By making immunity automatic for a leniency application prior to the start of an investigation, making leniency available to corporations even after an investigation had begun, and extending immunity to all officers, directors and employees who came forward with the corporations, the DOJ improved the incentive structure. These changes proved to be successful. The 1993 Leniency Policy, being more transparent and predictable, attracted on average two leniency applications per month.[45]

Law Review 715, pp. 728–31. This number is more or less confirmed by Christopher Leslie, who, by referring to James Griffin, speaks of an average of three per month. See Leslie, C. R., 'Editorial: Antitrust Leniency Programmes' (2011) 7 *Competition Law Review* 175. Ann O'Brien further reports that there was not a single` international or large domestic cartel revealed by the 1978 Leniency Policy: O'Brien, 'Leadership of Leniency' (n. 19 above), p. 18.

40 Ghosal, V. and Sokol, D. D., 'The Rise and (Potential) Fall of U.S. Cartel Enforcement' (2020) 2 *University of Illinois Law Review* 471, p. 478.

41 Ghosal, V. and Sokol, D. D., 'The Evolution of U.S. Cartel Enforcement' (2014), p. 7. Retrieved from https://papers.ssrn.com/sol3/papers.cfm?abstract_id=2345983.

42 Ghosal and Sokol, 'The Rise and (Potential) Fall of U.S. Cartel Enforcement' (n. 40 above), p. 477.

43 Ibid., p. 485.

44 Ibid., pp. 480 and 498.

45 Ibid., pp. 479–80.

Canada did not wait for the success of the leniency programme to be proven in practice when its Competition Bureau created some form of leniency programme in 1991.[46] The EU and Korea were inspired by the immediate success of the 1993 Leniency Policy and implemented a leniency programme in 1996.[47] Both EU and Korean leniency programmes suffered from shortcomings.[48] Without being transparent and predictable, these leniency programmes did not offer sufficient incentives for the cartel participants to defect and report the existence of the cartel conduct. It is only with subsequent revisions that the latter two became more effective.

Leaving aside the Korean leniency programme, Ann O'Brien observed that the leniency programmes in the US and the EU have moved towards each other. She even goes as far as suggesting that these two leniency programmes underwent substantial convergence.[49] This substantial convergence, she further claims, has been 'based initially on the US DOJ Antitrust Division's experience, followed closely by the experience of the European Commission and other jurisdictions, and reflected in the approach endorsed by international and regional organisations such as the Organisation for Economic Co-operation and Development, the International Competition Network and the European Competition Network'.[50] As the basic principles for leniency programmes have been set out by the US and the EU, and then further spread by the OECD and the ICN, both aspects are covered in this book.[51] Since the OECD and ICN are not the only international organisations dealing with the proliferation of competition law institutions,

46 O'Brien, 'Leadership of Leniency' (n. 19 above), p. 19.

47 Ibid.

48 For Europe: Stephan, A. and Nikpay, A., 'Leniency Theory and Complex Realities' (CCP Working Paper 14-8, 2014). Retrieved from http://papers.ssrn.com/sol3/papers.cfm?abstract_id=2537470; Stephan, A. 'An Empirical Assessment of the 1996 Leniency Notice' (CCP Working Paper 05-10, 2005). Retrieved from http://papers.ssrn.com/sol3/papers.cfm?abstract_id=911592. For Korea: Han, K. J., 'Cartel Leniency Program and Cartel Enforcement in South Korea' (2015) MPA/MPP Capstone Projects 225, p. 3. Retrieved from https://uknowledge.uky.edu/mpampp_etds/225; Nayoung, K. and Yungsan, K., 'Who Confesses for Leniency: Evidence from Korea' (2016) 12(2) *Journal of Competition Law & Economics* 351, p. 353.

49 O'Brien, 'Leadership of Leniency' (n. 19 above), p. 19, noting that '[a]fter Canada issued its Immunity Bulletin in 2000 and the European Commission issued its revised Leniency Notice in 2002, the "Big Three" corporate leniency policies –those of the United States, the European Union and Canada – underwent substantial convergence.'

50 Ibid., p. 16 (abbreviations added).

51 Balasingham, Chapter 2 this volume; Van Uytsel, Chapter 3 this volume.

the efforts of the UNCTAD and Association of Southeast Asian Nations (ASEAN) are covered as well.

1.2 Leniency Programmes in Asian Competition Law

1.2.1 Competition Law in Asia, a Relatively Recent Phenomenon

Competition law has been, for a long time, a legal instrument foreign to most Asian jurisdictions. With the exception of the Philippines, Japan, India, Korea and Taiwan, most Asian countries adopted competition law around, or just after, the year 2000.[52]

The Philippines enacted its first competition law, Act No. 3247, in 1925.[53] Japan did so in 1947, when it adopted the Act to Prohibit Monopolies and Combinations in Restraint of Trade.[54] India approved its first competition law, the Monopolies and Restrictive Trade Practices Act (MRTPA), in 1969. The MRTPA was replaced by the Competition Act of 2002.[55] Korea enacted the Monopoly Regulation and Fair Trade Act (MRFTA) in 1980.[56] The Taiwanese Fair Trade Law was adopted in 1992. Thailand endorsed a comprehensive competition law, the Trade Competition Act, in 1999.[57] The Singaporean Competition Act was enacted in 2004.[58] China, Malaysia and Hong Kong

[52] Van Uytsel, S., 'The Proliferation of Competition Law in Asia: From Forced Adoption to an Integration Project', in Van Uytsel, S., Hayashi, S. and Haley, J. (eds.), *Research Handbook on Asian Competition Law* (Cheltenham: Edward Elgar, 2020), 25, p. 25.

[53] See, e.g., Ditucalan, A. M., 'Institutional Design of Philippine Competition Law' (2018) 8 *KLRI Journal of Law and Legislation* 29; Aldaba, R. M. and Sy, G. S., 'Designing a Cooperation Framework for Philippine Competition and Regulatory Agencies' (Discussion Paper Series No. 2014-31, 2014). Retrieved from https://pidswebs.pids.gov.ph/CDN/PUBLICATIONS/pidsdps1431.pdf.

[54] See Gerber, D., *Global Competition: Law, Markets, and Globalization* (Oxford: Oxford University Press, 2010), p. 208, indicating that 'Japan's competition law experience may have been the most extensive of any other country outside the US and Europe'.

[55] Monopolies and Restrictive Trade Practices Act, 1969. Retrieved from www.mca.gov.in/Ministry/actsbills/pdf/The_Monopolies_and_Restrictive_Trade_Practices_Act_1969.pdf; Competition Act, 2002. Retrieved from www.cci.gov.in/sites/default/files/cci_pdf/competitionact2012.pdf.

[56] Monopoly Regulation and Fair Trade Act. Retrieved from www.ftc.go.kr/eng/cop/bbs/selectBoardList.do?key=2835&bbsId=BBSMSTR_000000003631&bbsTyCode=BBST11; Fair Trade Law. Retrieved from https://law.moj.gov.tw/ENG/LawClass/LawAll.aspx?pcode=J0150002.

[57] Trade Competition Act B.E. 2542 (1999). Retrieved from http://web.krisdika.go.th/data/outsitedata/outsite21/file/TRADE_COMPETITION_ACT_B.E._2542.pdf. Thailand had a price control law from 1979.

[58] Competition Act (Chapter 50B) (Original Enactment: Act 46 of 2004) rev. ed. 2006. Retrieved from https://sso.agc.gov.sg/act/ca2004.

introduced their respective competition laws in 2007 (Antimonopoly Law),[59] 2010 (Malaysian Competition Act)[60] and 2012 (Competition Ordinance).[61]

The shift towards the adoption of a competition law was triggered by various factors. The earliest proliferation of competition law in the Asian region can be linked with the political control of the US over the Philippines and Japan. The Philippines came under the control of the US after Spain had lost the Spanish-American War in 1898. As part of its colonial rule, the US gradually started to integrate the Philippine economic system into its own. As a result, the US required the Philippine ruler to introduce the equivalent of the Sherman Act.[62] The situation in Japan was slightly different. After the defeat in World War II, Japan was put under the control of the Supreme Command of Allied Powers (SCAP). The actual control of SCAP, though, was performed by the US. Under the influence of the US, SCAP eventually embraced the idea that also Japan needed to adopt a competition law as part of a policy to deconcentrate the economy. A highly concentrated industrial sector was regarded as a contributing factor in the militarisation of Japan.[63] While the early competition law in the Philippines never rooted,[64] Japan slowly embraced most aspects of a modern competition law.[65]

The end of World War II created a different political reality, whereby the dependency of Asian countries on the goodwill of foreign governments ended. Being independent, Asian countries had to develop their own economic systems and thus their position towards competition law shifted.

[59] Anti-Monopoly Law of the People's Republic of China, adopted at the 29th Meeting of the Standing Committee of the National (30 August 2007). For a text in Chinese and English, see Harris, H., Wang, P. J., Zhang, Y., Cohen, M.A. and Evrard, S. J., *Anti-Monopoly Law and Practice in China* (Oxford: Oxford University Press, 2011), pp. 373–94.

[60] Laws of Malaysia, Act 712 Competition Act 2010. Retrieved from www.mycc.gov.my/sites/default/files/Competition%20Act%202010%20-%2022092020.pdf.

[61] An ordinance to prohibit conduct that prevents, restricts or distorts competition in Hong Kong; to prohibit mergers that substantially lessen competition in Hong Kong; to establish a Competition Commission and a Competition Tribunal; and to provide for incidental and connected matters. Retrieved from www.elegislation.gov.hk/hk/cap619.

[62] Van Uytsel, S., 'Adopting Competition Law in Asia: An Increasingly Complex Reality', in Van Uytsel, Hayashi and Haley, *Research Handbook on Asian Competition Law* (n. 52 above), 2, p. 2.

[63] Ibid., p. 4.

[64] Ditucalan, 'Institutional Design of Philippine Competition Law' (n. 53 above), pp. 245–48.

[65] Vande Walle, S., 'Competition and Competition Law in Japan: Between Skepticism and Embrace', in Dowdle, M. W., Gillespie, J. and Maher, I. (eds.), *Asian Capitalism and the Regulation of Competition: Towards a Regulatory Geography of Global Competition Law* (Cambridge, UK: Cambridge University Press, 2013), 123, p. 123.

India chose a planned economy, with an emphasis on government-led industries. This strict government control of industrial life led to the formation of big business houses, potentially preventing the equitable distribution of wealth. With this observation of the Committee on Distribution of Income and Levels of Living, or the Mahalanobis Committee, the Indian government appointed a Monopolies Inquiry Commission in 1964. This Commission was the predecessor of two more commissions that all came to the same conclusion: India needed to adopt a law to bend economic power in the hands of a few. For this reason, India adopted the MRTPA in 1969. As this law was insufficient for dealing with cartels, a revision of the law was suggested in 1999. It took three more years, however, before India passed the Competition Act of 2002.[66]

Korea's choice for its economic system was focused on industrialisation. The path to industrialisation was characterised by fostering industrial conglomerates. When these industrial conglomerates, called *chaebols*, attained too much power, the Korean government was asked to intervene by adopting a competition law. Even though the first initiative was launched in 1964, it took another two decades to adopt the MRFTA in 1980.[67]

Excessive power of industry was also one of the reasons that Thailand decided to transform its price law into a full-fledged competition law. This excessive power was shown by automobile manufacturers, who decided to ban exports of cars to Thailand. It was uncertain whether this kind of conduct could fall under the application of the Price Control and Monopoly Prevention Act BE 2522, thus initiating talks within the government to adopt a competition law. Government instability caused a delay in the bill passing the legislative process, and it was only in 1999, after the financial crisis, that the parliament enacted the Thai Trade Competition Act.[68]

The liberalisation of the economy has often been the start for discussing the need for a competition law. When Taiwan made the decision to turn away from a government-led economy and favour private initiatives – under the framework of 'Liberalisation, Internationalisation and

[66] Parthasarathy, S., *Competition Law in India* (Alphen aan de Rijn: Wolters Kluwer Law & Business, 2011), pp. 20–38.

[67] Choi, Y. S., 'The Evolution of Fair and Free Competition Law in the Republic of Korea', in Van Uytsel, Hayashi and Haley, *Research Handbook on Asian Competition Law* (n. 52 above), 65, p. 65.

[68] Thanitkul, S., 'Competition Law in Thailand: In Transition to an Operational Law', in Van Uytsel, Hayashi and Haley, *Research Handbook on Asian Competition Law* (n. 52 above), 118, p. 118.

Institutionalisation of the Economy' – proposals for the introduction of a competition law were also discussed. Parallel to this internal drive to liberalise the market, the US was also pressuring Taiwan to further open its market. This would be facilitated by a competition law, which Taiwan adopted in 1992.[69]

A similar story can be observed in Singapore. Liberalisation efforts in various sectors of the economy led to the adoption of sector-specific competition laws. Plans to stimulate private entrepreneurship alongside government-run enterprises sparked a debate within the government about the need for a competition law. With the US requesting Singapore to adopt a general competition law during the negotiations for a free trade agreement between the two countries, the final impetus was given for adopting a competition law. The Singapore Competition Act was adopted in 2004.[70]

The initiation of economic reforms has been another trigger for adopting a competition law. Malaysia, for example, first discussed the adoption of a comprehensive competition law in the framework of the Eight Malaysia Plan (2001–2005), an instrument to set out the future development of the Malaysian economy. The plan to adopt a competition law was finalised during the accession negotiations to the World Trade Organization (WTO). Note that by the time Malaysia opted for trade liberalisation within the framework of the WTO, ASEAN had also formulated its plan to form the ASEAN Economic Community (AEC). For the concretisation of the AEC, a form of trade liberalisation among ASEAN member states, the adoption of a competition law was seen as one of the essential pillars.[71] Similarly, China, as Grace Li and Angus Young have indicated, started to work on a competition law as part of the transformation from a planned economy to a market economy. However, internal power struggles among regulatory agencies caused a delay in the adoption of the final version of the Antimonopoly Law.[72]

69 Chen, A. C. M., 'Political, Economic and Legal Driving Forces Shaping the Developmental Contours of Competition Law: The Experience of Taiwan', in Van Uytsel, Hayashi and Haley, *Research Handbook on Asian Competition Law* (n. 52 above), 81, p. 81.

70 Ong, B., 'Competition Law in Singapore: The First Decade', in Van Uytsel, Hayashi and Haley, *Research Handbook on Asian Competition Law* (n. 52 above), 151, p. 151.

71 Cheong, M. F., Teoh, J. B. C. and Khoo, E. L. E., 'Legal Transplant: Giving Life to Malaysia's Competition Regime', in Van Uytsel, Hayashi and Haley, *Research Handbook on Asian Competition Law* (n. 52 above), 181, p. 181.

72 Li, G. and Young, A., 'Competition Laws and Policies in China and Hong Kong: A Tale of Two Regulatory Journeys' (2002) 7 *Journal of International Trade Law and Policy* 186, p. 189.

Hong Kong is difficult to categorise under any of the above reasons for adopting a competition law. The idea for a competition law was launched when Hong Kong was still under United Kingdom (UK) rule. However, China protested. The debate about a competition law did not revive under the first Chief Executive of Hong Kong, Tung Chee-hwa. The government of this former business tycoon sided with the business sector, defying any attempt to talk seriously about a competition law. As this left the business sector without any restraints, it led to excesses in pricing policy. Public outcry over these practices thus created a favourable political climate for the adoption of a competition law in 2005. However, deliberations over the precise form of the law took another five years. Concerns formulated by small and medium-sized enterprises delayed the adoption of the law by another two years and the Competition Ordinance was only finally adopted in 2012.[73]

ASEAN further inspired several of its member states that already had a competition law in place to rework their respective competition laws. As mentioned above, it was agreed within ASEAN that competition law would be a necessary element for the creation of an economic community among member states. Rather than adopting a supranational competition law, ASEAN recommended that its member states adopt a domestic competition law by 2015. Guidelines for the development of a competition law were also provided by the ASEAN secretariat. This call for developing a competition law inspired countries like the Philippines and Thailand to revise their existing competition laws. Whereas the changes in the Thai Competition Trade Act of 2017 were only minor,[74] the Philippines seized the opportunity to overhaul its existing competition regime and adopted a full-fledged competition law in 2015.[75]

1.2.2 The Proliferation of Leniency Programmes in Asia

At the time that the US vision of anti-cartel enforcement shifted and started to crack down on (international) price-fixing cartels, several Asian countries, namely Japan, India, Korea and Taiwan, had a competition law

[73] Cheng, T. K., 'Hong Kong Competition Law and Legal Transplant', in Van Uytsel, Hayashi and Haley, *Research Handbook on Asian Competition Law* (n. 52 above), 168, p. 168.

[74] Thanitkul, 'Competition Law in Thailand' (n. 68 above), p. 118.

[75] Ditucalan, A. M., 'The Philippine Competition Law Dilemma: US-EU Fusion to Tension', in Van Uytsel, Hayashi and Haley, *Research Handbook on Asian Competition Law* (n. 52 above), 233, p. 233.

in place. However, this evolution was not reflected in the enforcement record of any of these countries. Such a phenomenon may be explained by the fact that cartels were not given priority in the enforcement policies of the various countries.

Japan had for a long time had an industrial policy in which the Antimonopoly Act (AMA) was downplayed. Ever since Japan regained its independence after the end of the US occupation in 1952, it had undertaken efforts to minimise the effect of its competition law. This changed in the 1970s, when Japanese society was confronted with a cartel in the oil sector. This led to a revision of the AMA, whereby the powers of the Japan Fair Trade Commission (JFTC) to investigate and punish cartels were greatly expanded. Despite these improvements, the AMA's enforcement activities remained dormant throughout the 1980s. Enforcement of the AMA became better in the 1990s, in the aftermath of the Structural Impediments Initiative (SII). During the SII, which was a series of bilateral trade talks between the US and Japan to tackle the trade deficit with Japan, the US raised the issue of the omnipresence of anti-competitive conduct in the Japanese market, which was not being addressed by the JFTC. The increased efforts of the JFTC mainly focused on domestic bid-rigging cases. The international cartels that were being exposed by the US and EU enforcement agencies cannot be found in the enforcement records of the JFTC. One of the reasons, it is claimed, was the absence of a leniency programme. This frustrated the JFTC and therefore it started to lobby the legislator to also introduce this enforcement instrument in the AMA.[76]

The situation was different in Korea. Even though Korean firms were also involved in various international cartels that were investigated during the 1990s, another element seems to have been more important in the adoption of a leniency programme in Korea. The MRFTA was adopted with the idea of preventing the business conglomerates, the *chaebols*, from gaining too much market power. Since its inception, monitoring the power of the *chaebols* has been the most important purpose of the Korean enforcement policy. The focus started to shift in the aftermath of the Asian financial crisis, which hit Korea in 1997.

A bailout by the International Monetary Fund (IMF) followed.[77] Together with the bailout, the IMF formulated various conditions. One of

[76] Van Uytsel, 'Leniency under the Japanese Antimonopoly Law' (n. 31 above), pp. 69–76.

[77] Jung, Y. and Chang, S. W., 'Korea's Competition Law and Policies in Perspective: Symposium on Competition Law and Policy in Developing Countries' (2005–2006) 26 *Northwestern Journal of International Law & Business* 687, p. 693.

them was to amend the competition law to 'restructure its economy into one based on market competition'.[78] This required the legislator to also develop elements that could focus on anti-competitive conduct rather than those related to the excessive power of the *chaebols*. The inclusion of a leniency programme might be understood in this regard, as it would bring the MRFTA closer to western competition law models. The legislative changes did not remain a dead letter, however. With more budget to tackle cartels, the Korean Fair Trade Commission (KFTC) made some landmark decisions against cartels. This led Korean scholars to state that the 1997 amendments meant that a 'transformation of the KFTC from chaebol regulator to traditional competition authority had begun in earnest'.[79]

India has a somewhat similar experience to Korea. Its original competition law, the MRTPA, was designed to control investments in the market and prevent the power of big business houses growing excessively. When India shifted its economy towards liberalisation and globalisation, it became obvious that the MRTPA was not suitable for dealing with conduct that is generally regulated by a competition law: abuse of dominance and cartels. Even though attempts were made to interpret the MRTPA to include this kind of conduct, the Raghaven Commission investigated the suitability of the MRTPA and concluded that these interpretations were often contradictory and thus not appropriate as guidelines for business. Therefore, the suggestion was made to create a completely new competition law, which became the Competition Act of 2002. With the Competition Act of 2002, the Indian legislator created the possibility for lenient treatment in Section 46. Constitutional issues, however, prevented the Competition Act of 2002 from ever entering into force. Only after settling these issues in 2009 did the Competition Act of 2002 became operational.[80] It is also in that year that the Competition Commission of India (Lesser Penalty) Regulation was issued.

Taiwan also had a competition law in place by the time the US and the EU started to implement their leniency programmes. Taiwan's response

[78] Ibid., p. 687.

[79] Yi, S.-S. and Jung, Y., 'A New Kid on the Block: Korean Competition Law, Policy, and Economics' (2007) 3(2) *Competition Policy International* 153, p. 160. Retrieved from www.researchgate.net/profile/Sang-Seung-Yi/publication/227387454_A_New_Kid_on_the_Block_Korean_Competition_Law_Policy_and_Economics/links/0046351d02a6080bb1000000/A-New-Kid-on-the-Block-Korean-Competition-Law-Policy-and-Economics.pdf.

[80] Bhattacharjea, A. and De, O., 'Cartels and the Competition Commission' (2012) 47(35) *Economic and Political Weekly* 14.

to this new instrument was slower than the other three countries, which had had a relatively long history with competition law. It took until 2008 before the Taiwan Fair Trade Commission (TFTC) saw the need to implement a leniency programme. This shift in policy occurred subsequent to a decision of the DOJ and the European Commission to impose fines on the main producers of thin film transistor liquid crystal displays (LCDs) for their involvement in a price-fixing scheme related to LCDs. The main producers were all Asian firms, several of whom had their headquarters in Taiwan.[81] The appreciation for the LCD case was mixed, both on the side of the enforcement agency and in the business community. The enforcement agencies got to learn that the cartel had organised more than sixty meetings in Taiwan to sustain the cartel between 2001 and 2006, showing that the business community was not fearful of any enforcement action. This is probably linked to the observation that the standard of proof in Taiwan for a cartel, requiring the actual implementation of the agreement, is higher than elsewhere. Such a high standard of proof makes it particularly difficult for the TFTC to adopt an assertive enforcement policy if it is not able to secure the necessary information to meet this high burden. The business community had to observe that the fines for cartel activity abroad could be much higher than what is prescribed in Taiwan itself. Furthermore, the use of leniency by the Korean firm Samsung confronted the Taiwanese business community for the first time with the aggressive business reality of international cartels, which were more than ever subject to extraterritorial enforcement of competition laws as well. Besides the increased interest in competition law issues, especially among businesses that are active internationally, it is generally accepted that this case triggered a more aggressive enforcement policy, which is best exemplified by the enactment of a leniency programme.[82]

The above discussion highlights a similar pattern in the adoption of a leniency programme in Japan, Korea, India and Taiwan, namely a shortcoming in the legislation that did not allow the enforcement agency to respond adequately to behaviour that was increasingly considered as

[81] Taiwanese firms AU Optronics, Chimei InnoLux Corporation, Chunghwa Picture Tubes and HannStar Display Corporation. See European Commission, 'Antitrust: Commission Fines Six LCD Panel Producers €648 Million for Price Fixing Cartel' (2010). Retrieved from https://ec.europa.eu/commission/presscorner/detail/es/IP_10_1685.

[82] Chen, A. C. M., 'The LCD Cartel: Impacts and Implications for the Competition Policy of Taiwan', in Charbit, N., Pavlik, A. and Rebarber, J. (eds.), *William E. Kovacic Liber Amicorum: An Antitrust Tribute Volume II* (New York, Institute for Competition Law, 2014), 325, p. 325.

undesirable. It should be noted, however, from the moment the shortcoming is noticed and the moment of introducing a leniency programme there is often a time gap. In some countries this lag can be explained by the lack of readiness to implement an enforcement tool that might potentially undermine the status quo in the relationship between the business community and enforcement agencies. Whether this lack of readiness is based on a business culture that cultivates cooperation rather than competition and betrayal or on the purely rational selfishness of the business community to lobby for a delayed implementation is a question that is difficult to answer. For the moment, however, it suffices to state that the former opinion has often been expressed in an Asian context,[83] but that whenever a leniency programme was implemented properly it has been used without hesitation.[84] Chapter 16 of this volume delves a little deeper into this important issue.

Connected to this is that Indonesia and Thailand – who both adopted a competition law in 1999 – and Vietnam – who adopted a competition law in 2004 – did not embark upon the same journey as the US and the EU, and thus did not implement a leniency programme at the time of adopting a competition law. For Indonesia, the explanation can be found in the fact that they were essentially forced to adopt a competition law by the IMF in return for the loans necessary to survive the Asian financial crisis of 1997.[85] In such a process, the necessity was created of complying with the foreign demand. Thailand, although also suffering from the crisis, was already contemplating an amendment to its price law to transform it into a competition law prior to the crisis. The Asian crisis just accelerated this process. In retrospect, it is possible to say that the Thai Competition Trade Act of 1999 was captured by the business community. This broadly explains why this law had no tools for being harsh towards business interests.[86] A leniency programme simply did not fit with the law.

[83] See, e.g., Uesugi, A., 'How Japan Is Tackling Enforcement Activities against Cartels' (2005) 13 *George Mason Law Review* 349, p. 362; Wu, S., Hsieh, Y. and Wu, W.-H., 'Leniency Programme in Taiwan: The Impact of a "Whistle-Blower" System in Eastern Culture' (2013). Retrieved from www.leeandli.com/Att/Profile/Euromoney%20-%20Taiwan%20competition.pdf.

[84] Van Uytsel, 'A Comparative US and EU Perspective' (n. 15 above), pp. F3 and F8.

[85] Wahyuningtyas, S. Y., 'Indonesian Competition Law: Up for Renewal', in Van Uytsel, Hayashi, and Haley, *Research Handbook on Asian Competition Law* (n. 52 above), 100, p. 100.

[86] Poapongsakorn, N., 'The New Competition Law in Thailand: Lessons for Institution Building' (2002) 21(2) *Review of Industrial Organization* 185.

Vietnam adopted its competition law in 2004, also without a leniency programme. Drawing on enforcement practice, it could be said that Vietnam did not have the intention to focus on dealing with cartels.[87] Of these three countries, only Vietnam has incorporated a leniency programme when the competition law was recently revised. Yet the implementation rules still need to be written. Once this is done, it remains to be seen whether the leniency programme will be used actively.[88] Indonesia has written a draft leniency programme but has not been able to implement it.[89] Thailand has made a deliberate decision not to employ a leniency programme.[90]

Other Asian countries took a completely different approach and, when designing their respective competition laws, these countries included contemporary instruments, like leniency programmes, for the enforcement of their competition laws. India, when writing its new competition law in 2002, included Section 46 of the Indian Competition Act, allowing for reducing the sanction applicable to cartel activity.[91] Singapore adopted its competition law with a leniency programme included in 2006.[92] China incorporated the possibility for a leniency programme in its 2007 Antimonopoly Law.[93] Malaysia provided for the possibility of lenient treatment in its Malaysian Competition Act, which went into

[87] Tuan, N. A., 'A Review of Ten Years of Enforcement: Challenges and Prospects of the Vietnamese Cartel Regime', in Cheng, Marco Colino and Ong, *Cartels in Asia* (n. 31 above), 211, p. 211.

[88] Mayer Brown, 'Vietnam Competition Law: Key Changes in 2019' (2018), p. 70. Retrieved from www.mayerbrown.com/-/media/files/perspectives-events/publications/2019/02/vietnam_competition_law_key_changes_in_2019.pdf. The scope of the Vietnamese leniency programme is broader than many others. The programme does not apply only to cartel agreements, but also to various horizontal cooperation agreements and vertical price and non-price agreements. Hence, it is conceivable that the leniency programme could be used to escape liability from the competition law. This will be especially so if Article 112 of the Vietnamese Competition Law (VCL) is interpreted as not giving any discretion to the enforcement agency to grant leniency or not. See the difference in wording in para. 1 of Article 112 VCL (might receive) and para. 3 of Article 112 VCL (shall be granted).

[89] On the desire to have a leniency programme, Wahyuningtyas, S. Y., 'Challenges in Combating Cartels, 14 Years after the Enactment of Indonesian Competition Law' (2014) 7(10) *Yearbook of Antitrust and Regulatory Studies* 279.

[90] Poranonond, Chapter 15 this volume.

[91] Koradia, Manokaran and Hirani, Chapter 13 this volume.

[92] Clements and Shiau, Chapter 10 this volume.

[93] Bi and Van Uytsel, Chapter 9 this volume. Note that the guidelines for its implementation were only developed two and four years later. The leniency programme for non-price violations of the Chinese Antimonopoly Law were developed in 2009, while those applicable to price violations were only released in 2011.

force in 2012.[94] Hong Kong pronounced its leniency programme together with its Competition Ordinance in 2015.[95] This was also the year in which the Philippines endorsed the development of a leniency programme by adopting its competition law.[96]

Despite the inclusion of rules on leniency in the respective competition laws, the details of the leniency programme were often elaborated in the regulatory instruments of enforcement agencies. Singapore, Malaysia and Hong Kong issued their respective guidelines on leniency at the moment their competition laws entered into force, which was in 2006, 2014 and 2015, respectively. China and the Philippines first let their competition laws enter into force before elaborating the guidelines on leniency. The leniency guidelines for non-price violations of the Chinese Antimonopoly Law, which entered into force in 2008, were developed in 2009, while those applicable to price violations were only released in 2011. The Philippines published its respective leniency guidelines in 2018, three years after the Philippine Competition Act came into force.

1.3 The Literature on Leniency Programmes and This Book

1.3.1 The Literature on Leniency Programmes

The proliferation of the leniency programme in Asia took place when the academic literature on leniency programmes started to develop. This literature can be divided into four periods: the early economic studies, the first empirical studies, the critical studies from a holistic perspective, and the jurisdiction-focused studies.

Around the time that the DOJ started to update its leniency programme, economists began to develop models to predict what kind of leniency programmes would break the trust inside a cartel. The models had to allow us to draw conclusions on the optimal design of such programmes.[97] Many of

[94] Lee, Chapter 11 this volume.

[95] Marco Colino, Chapter 12 this volume.

[96] Ditucalan and Van Uytsel, Chapter 14 this volume.

[97] See, e.g., Bigoni, M., Fridolfson, S. O., Le Coq, C. and Spagnolo, G., 'Fines, Leniency, Rewards and Organized Crime: Evidence from Antitrust Experiments' (IFN Working Paper No. 738, 2008). Retrieved from www.ifn.se/wfiles/wp/wp738.pdf; Harrington, J. E., Jr, 'Optimal Corporate Leniency Programs' (2008) 56(2) *Journal of Industrial Economics* 215; Chen, J. and Harrington, J. E., Jr, 'The Impact of the Corporate Leniency Program on Cartel Formation and the Cartel Price Path' (2007) 282 *Contribution to Economic Analysis*

the economic studies relied on game theory and the tool of the prisoner's dilemma. Thus, these economic studies presume that it is possible to put a cartel in 'a "prisoner's dilemma" about whether to report a cartel and to increase the potential costs for cartelists who decide not to report or lose the race to apply for leniency, so as to obtain an increase in the number of cartels reported and a decrease in the number of cartels formed'.[98] Few of the economic studies were behavioural experiments, in which a group of students would act in a lab-designed model as if they were a corporate director who had to decide on a leniency application.[99] The main critique of these studies was that these models relied on unrealistic assumptions that did not reflect reality, or that a simple prisoner's dilemma does not reflect the kind of situation in which a leniency application will be typically made.[100]

Once the US and the EU started to have functioning and effective leniency programmes, the literature drawing conclusions from models could be complemented by real-life experiments. Comparisons were made between the early 1978 Corporate Leniency Policy and the 1993 version to conclude why the 1993 Corporate Leniency Policy was better in design.[101] Further studies contrasted the operation of the US 1993 Leniency Policy with the EU 1996 Leniency Policy, in order to find that the latter led only to a very low number of independent leniency applications.[102] This kind of empirical study was the predecessor of interpretational studies, whereby

59; Brisset, K. and Thomas, L., 'Leniency Program: A New Tool in a Competition Policy to Deter Cartel Activity in Procurement Auctions' (2004) 17 *European Journal of Law and Economics* 5; Motta, M. and Polo, M., 'Leniency Programs and Cartel Prosecution' (2001) 21 *International Journal of Industrial Organization* 347.

98 Jenny, F., 'Foreword' in Beaton-Wells and Tran, *Anti-Cartel Enforcement in a Contemporary Age* (n. 14 above), p. vi.

99 See, e.g., Hamaguchi, Y. and Kawagoe, T., 'An Experimental Study of Leniency Programs' (RIETI Discussion Paper Series 05-E-003, 2003). Retrieved from www.rieti.go.jp/jp/publications/dp/05e003.pdf; Apesteguia, J., Dufwenberg, M. and Selten, R., 'Blowing the Whistle' (2007) 31 *Economic Theory* 143.

100 See., e.g., Stephan, A. and Nikpay, A., 'Leniency Decision-Making from a Corporate Perspective: Complex Realities', in Beaton-Wells and Tran, *Anti-Cartel Enforcement in a Contemporary Age* (n. 14 above), 139, p. 139; Harding, C., Beaton-Wells, C. and Edwards, J., 'Leniency and Criminal Sanctions in Anti-Cartel Enforcement: Happily Married or Uneasy Bedfellows' in Beaton-Wells and Tran, *Anti-Cartel Enforcement in a Contemporary Age* (n. 14 above), 233, p. 233.

101 Kobayashi, 'Symposium: Antitrust Agency and Amnesty' (n. 39 above).

102 Stephan, 'An Empirical Assessment of the 1996 Leniency Notice' (n. 48 above); Brenner, S., 'An Empirical Study of the European Corporate Leniency Program' (2009) 27 (6) *International Journal of Industrial Organization* 639.

the terminology of a leniency programme was assessed against transparency and predictability.[103] The latter were two conclusions drawn from the early empirical studies.

Despite the early critics of leniency programmes, enforcement agencies, through their representatives, started to praise the use of leniency programmes. James Griffin, summarising the past ten years of the operation of the US leniency programme, claimed that the programme had led to an increase in the number of cartel prosecutions and the number of fines imposed.[104] Philip Lowe, detailing the history of European cartel enforcement, indicated that the real change in enforcement came with the adoption of the leniency programme.[105] Alexander Italianer, Director-General for Competition of the European Commission, writes in his article 'Fighting Cartels in European and the US: Different Systems, Different Goals' that 'the leniency programme has been highly successful in increasing the number of cartel decisions adopted by the Commission'.[106] Toshiyuki Nambu, the former Deputy Secretary General on International Affairs of the JFTC, has recalled the reasons for the success of the Japanese leniency policy. In his article 'A Successful Story: Leniency and (International) Cartel Enforcement in Japan', Nambu makes reference to the number of applications, the correlation between leniency applications and the number of cartel and bid-rigging cases, and the amount of surcharges.[107]

The simplicity with which the success of a leniency programme was claimed forced scholars to be more critical. They argued that a leniency programme should be assessed against other enforcement instruments

[103] See, e.g., Beaton-Wells, C., 'The ACCC Immunity Policy for Cartel Conduct: Due for Review' (2013). Retrieved from https://papers.ssrn.com/sol3/papers.cfm?abstract_id=2316556; Van Uytsel, 'A Comparative US and EU Perspective' (n. 15 above); Barlingen, B. and Barennes, M., 'The European Commission's 2002 Leniency Notice in Practice' (2005) 3 *Competition Policy Newsletter* 6.

[104] Griffin, J., 'The Modern Leniency Program after Ten Years – a Summary Overview of the Antitrust Division's Criminal Enforcement Program' (Presentation at the American Bar Association Annual Meeting, San Francisco, 2003). Retrieved from www.justice.gov/atr/public/speeches/201477.htm.

[105] Lowe, P. 'What's the Future for Cartel Enforcement' (Presentation at the Understanding Global Cartel Enforcement, Brussels, 2003), p. 11. Retrieved from http://ec.europa.eu/competition/speeches/text/sp2003_044_en.pdf.

[106] Italianer, A., 'Fighting Cartels in Europe and the US: Different Systems, Different Goals' (2013), p. 4. Retrieved from http://ec.europa.eu/competition/speeches/text/sp2013_09_en.pdf.

[107] Nambu, T., 'A Successful Story: Leniency and (International) Cartel Enforcement in Japan' (2014) 5(4) *Journal of European Competition Law & Practice* 158.

and called for much deeper empirical research.[108] Even though individual articles were written on these issues,[109] Caron Beaton-Wells and Christopher Tran's work *Anti-Cartel Enforcement in a Contemporary Age: Leniency Religion* was instrumental in breaking open the discussion on leniency programmes. The group of scholars gathered by Beaton-Wells and Tran: (1) challenged the positive claims made by enforcement agencies that leniency programmes were the panacea for cartel enforcement; (2) investigated how individuals within a firm may distort the rational logic behind leniency programmes for achieving higher goals of the firm; (3) questioned whether individuals should be incentivised to report cartels and so create a competition with leniency programmes; (4) held that criminal sanctions are a pre-condition for leniency programmes to work well; (5) researched whether claims for compensation could undermine the efficiency of leniency programmes; and (6) claimed that leniency programmes can be used to bolster the presence of compliance programmes that could raise awareness of the deployable character of cartels.[110] More recent empirical studies confirm the complexity with which leniency programmes operate, making it less possible to frame a leniency programme as a trust-breaking tool.[111] This kind of study further questions the success of leniency programmes.

Subsequent to the long-awaited contributions gathered by Beaton-Wells and Trans, the discussion gravitated towards critical reflections on leniency in one geographical region: Europe. Baskaran Balasingham approached the EU leniency programme with the question of whether it can reconcile effective enforcement with fairness.[112] Similarly, Emma

108 See, e.g., Van Uytsel, S., 'The International Competition Network, Its Leniency Best Practice and Legitimacy: An Argument for Introducing a Review System', in Fenwick, M., Van Uytsel, S. and Wrbka, S. (eds.), *Networked Governance, Transnational Business and the Law* (Berlin: Springer, 2014), 180, pp. 209–11; Sokol, D. D., 'Cartels, Corporate Compliance, and What Practitioners Really Think about Enforcement' (2012) 78 *Antitrust Law Journal* 201, pp. 213–14; Veljanovski, C., 'Cartel Fines in Europe – Law, Practice and Deterrence (2007). Retrieved from http://ssrn.com/abstract=920786.

109 See, e.g., Borrell, J.-R., Jiménez, J. L. and García, C., 'Evaluating Antitrust Leniency Programs' (2014) 10 *Journal of Competition Law and Economics* 107; Gärtner, D. L., Zhou, J., 'Delays in Leniency Application: Is There Really a Race to the Enforcer's Door?' (TILEC Discussion Paper DP 2012–044, 2012). Retrieved from http://ssrn.com/abstract=2187771.

110 Beaton-Wells and Tran, *Anti-Cartel Enforcement in a Contemporary Age* (n. 14 above).

111 See, e.g., Jaspers, J. D., 'Leniency in Exchange for Cartel Confessions' (2020) 17(1) *European Journal of Criminology* 106, pp. 115–20.

112 Balasingham, *The EU Leniency Policy* (n. 29 above).

Salemme investigated the EU leniency programme with questions of procedural fairness.[113] Ingrid Margrethe Halvorson Barlund researched the intersection of the EU leniency programme with other elements of public enforcement and with private enforcement to find out the most effective balance.[114]

1.3.2 Positioning This Book

With the last trend in the literature, the first steps were taken to combine the critical review of leniency programmes with the practice in a specific jurisdiction. The geographical focus, however, was limited to Europe. A critical study of the leniency programmes of another geographical region has not yet been done. By focusing on Asia, this book is a modest start on filling this gap. It covers research on the leniency programmes of nine Asian countries, Korea, Japan, Singapore, China, India, Taiwan, Malaysia, Hong Kong and the Philippines. For eight of these countries, experts contribute by describing the content of the respective leniency programmes, highlighting and explaining their enforcement results, and analysing their prospects and challenges. For one country, Thailand, an explanation is given as to why a leniency programme has not been conceptualised.

The book is divided into four parts. After this introductory Part I, Part II embarks on theoretical considerations regarding leniency programmes with an overview and analysis of the two oldest jurisdictions using leniency programmes, an introduction to the international effort to support the proliferation of leniency programmes, and a comment on how leniency programmes might reflect a number of broader trends in contemporary business regulation.

In Chapter 2, Baskaran Balasingham introduces pioneers of the leniency programme, the US and the EU. Balasingham's analysis start with an overview of the theory behind leniency programmes. This is followed by mapping out the different versions of the US's and the EU's respective leniency programmes, in order to then evaluate the most recent version of the leniency programmes against the theory behind leniency programmes. The chapter finishes with some thoughts on the similarities and differences between the two leniency programmes.

Steven Van Uytsel sheds light in Chapter 3 on the international organisations that have been active in proliferating leniency programmes.

[113] Salemme, *Enforcing European Competition Law* (n. 29 above).

[114] Barlund, *The EU Leniency Policy* (n. 29 above).

This contribution includes the efforts of the OECD, ICN, UNCTAD and ASEAN. For each of these organisations, Van Uytsel argues that they have a tendency to look for the common elements among existing leniency programmes and present them as an international guideline or best practice. When the existing leniency programmes diverge, the international guideline or best practice is to offer options. By not further clarifying these options, Van Uytsel holds, the international organisations do no more than summarise local practices and pull them outside of their context. As a result of this practice, convergence is unlikely to happen because, when the international guidelines or best practices are consulted, there will be an automatic reflex to also consult existing local practices and the existing literature regarding those practices.

In Chapter 4, Mark Fenwick situates the emergence of leniency programmes in competition law within the broader context of contemporary trends in business regulation. It is suggested that although leniency programmes are a distinctive form of regulatory intervention, they do exhibit a family resemblance with other regulatory mechanisms that have emerged in the last two decades in other fields of business regulation, and that similar trends, pressures and effects can be seen across different regulatory contexts. The four trends highlighted are a shift towards some form of negotiated justice, a new emphasis on regulatory experimentation, the creation of new forms of transnational legal risk, and the emerging importance of regulatory networks. The intention of Chapter 4 is not to blur the distinction between these different developments, but rather to suggest that by locating leniency within the context of these broader trends, we can deepen our understanding of the significance of these developments.

In Part III, experts on nine different Asian countries analyse the position of their respective country towards leniency programmes in competition law. The discussion is chronologically organised, first discussing the oldest leniency programme and closing with a country that rejects the idea of adopting a leniency programme.

In Japan, the JFTC saw the benefits of having a leniency programme very early. However, as Steven Van Uytsel highlights in Chapter 5, there was one element preventing the JFTC from successfully requesting that the legislator adopt this new enforcement tool. The JFTC was not able to show to Sadanori Yamanaka, the leading politician within the Liberal Democratic Party for competition law reform, that a leniency programme is essentially different from plea bargaining and that a leniency programme does not necessarily detract from the rigid characteristic of the surcharge, the financial remedy applicable to infringements of the AMA.

Van Uytsel indicates that, when Yamanaka passed away, the opposition to a leniency programme disappeared, partly because the JFTC was able to show the legislator the substantial difference between a leniency programme and plea bargaining and the possibility of introducing a leniency programme without its claiming any discretion. The leniency programme without discretion, so argues Van Uytsel, has led to unmeritorious leniency applications. Some did not enable the JFTC to pursue an investigation; others obliged the JFTC to grant lenient treatment without getting extra information. As the JFTC considered the latter problematic, the leniency programme was amended in 2019.

Steven Van Uytsel and Yoshiteru Uemura continue in Chapter 6 to investigate the 2019 amendment to the Japanese leniency programme. Their approach starts by observing that the old leniency programme may not have substantially contributed either to detecting or to deterring cartels. The question, therefore, is whether the new leniency programme, whereby the amount of reduction of leniency is drastically lowered for subsequent applicants, but which can be compensated for by entering a consultation process with the JFTC regarding the information to be submitted, is able to address the limitations of the old leniency programme. Van Uytsel and Uemura conclude that this may not be the case, since the changes to the leniency programme only address the potential of subsequent leniency applications. Nothing is done to attract better leniency applications from the start. To increase deterrence, Van Uytsel and Uemura therefore investigate whether there is still some possibility of tweaking the sanctions in order to compensate for what the leniency programme cannot yet achieve.

Korea, though the first country in Asia to adopt a leniency programme in 1996, initially had no effective leniency programme. This has changed, as Yo Sop Choi elaborates in Chapter 7. To date, the leniency programme has contributed to nearly 55 per cent of all detected cartels. For the other 45 per cent, the Korean enforcement agency can rely on other means, such as the informant reward system, to guarantee active and continuous enforcement, which is necessary to keep the leniency programme attractive. Choi informs us further that the leniency programme offers the right incentives to apply for leniency. The leniency programme is conceptualised in such a way as to offer high rewards for only a limited number of firms and its conditions are transparent and predictable. Furthermore, Choi claims that private actions and criminal sanctions are not necessarily detrimental to a leniency application in Korea. Both are very rare and, in case of criminal sanctions, there is a court judgment that leniency applicants should be excluded from the indictment. To improve the leniency programme, Choi suggests weakening the ineligibility of recidivists to apply for leniency and to introduce penalty plus, whereby the sanction increases if a firm refrains from disclosing participation in another cartel, and an omnibus question, whereby a leniency applicant is asked to report information on other forbidden practices it is aware of.

Andy C. M. Chen assesses the Taiwanese leniency programme in Chapter 8. Taiwan incorporated a leniency programme in the Taiwan Fair Trade Act (TFTA) in 2011. Since it became operational in 2012, the leniency programme has been used fifteen times. Out of these fifteen leniency applications, four applications have led to a decision. Noting that financial rewards are not really assisting the leniency applications, Chen investigates whether the low number of decisions could be attributed to the design of the leniency programme. This is done based upon the checklist of effective leniency programmes created by the ICN. The main conclusion Chen draws from comparing the Taiwanese leniency programme with the ICN's checklist is that the leniency programme may be only moderately effective. Chen then further examines practising lawyers' perspective on the leniency programme. Their concern is that the risk of private enforcement, uncertainty about the calculation of the fines, access to the leniency dossier by third parties, and uncertainty on how the Fair Trade Commission deals with cartel cases in general deter firms from applying for leniency. Except for private enforcement, which is as good as non-existent in Taiwan, Chen substantiates, and thus confirms, each of the other concerns. Despite these concerns, Chen identifies the underlying reason for several of these concerns. The TFTA does not provide for a suspension of the statute of limitations from the moment the TFTC starts the investigation. This may invite strategic leniency applications, whereby the time for the TFTC to finalise its investigations is limited. Such time limitations may cause hasty decisions, which contribute to the concerns the lawyers have identified. Another concern that Chen ascertains is the lack of awareness in Taiwan about the disputable character of cartels. To address this, leniency for individuals may offer a solution.

Ying Bi and Steven Van Uytsel argue in Chapter 9 that the Chinese legislator has infused a dose of trust and predictability into its leniency programme. Trust was necessary because not all enforcement agencies in China, the National Reform and Development Commission specifically, applied due process during their investigations. Predictability was required because the existing leniency programmes, one for price-related cartels and one for non-price-related cartels, gave too much discretion to the enforcement agencies. As a result of the lack of due process or predictability, the outcomes of investigations were uncertain. Chapter 9 will show that, by reconfiguring the enforcement structure and adopting a single leniency programme, both elements are addressed. There is one condition, though, to make the new leniency programme effective: the new enforcement agency, the State Administration for Market Regulation, should ensure transparency by consistently publicising its decisions.

The Singaporean leniency programme is examined by Scott Clements and Daren Shiau in Chapter 10. After briefly introducing the anti-cartel provisions in the Singaporean Competition Act, Clements and Shiau provide a detailed description of the leniency programme. Originally created in 2006, it was revised in 2009 and 2016. The latest revision has created a leniency programme whereby immunity is guaranteed for a leniency applicant prior to an investigation, immunity could be obtained by the first leniency applicant once an investigation has started, and granting leniency to subsequent leniency applicants is at the discretion of the Singaporean enforcement agency, the Competition and Consumer Commission of Singapore (CCCS). Furthermore, leniency plus, whereby extra reduction can be obtained for revealing participation in another cartel, and the fast track procedure, whereby extra reduction can be obtained for admitting to the fact, has been introduced as well. It is now also possible for a cartel to be exposed through a reward or whistleblowing scheme, though this scheme is not available for persons active in the infringement. By 2020, Clements and Shiau report, the leniency programme has contributed to several of the fifteen cartel infringement decisions. Eight of these fifteen cases were supported by a leniency application. These eight cases could be further divided into three cases involving an international cartel and five cases involving a domestic cartel. Clements and Shiau point out that the sanctions for the international cartels were a record high for Singapore, notwithstanding the application of reductions. Among the domestic cases, it is noteworthy that the CCCS is silent about the degree of reduction for the first leniency applicant subsequent to the start of an investigation, and that the CCCS actively solicited for cartel participants to apply for leniency. Another point worth mentioning, according to Clements and Shiau, is whether reduction for leniency and cooperation can be applied cumulatively.

The leniency programme in Malaysia is researched by Cassey Lee in Chapter 11. The Malaysian leniency programme has been implemented since 2014. However, it has been scarcely used. Of all seven cartel cases that have been investigated by the Malaysian Competition Commission

(MyCC), only one case has been linked with a leniency application, and this leniency application was rejected. Lee investigates whether this low rate of usage could be attributed to the design of the leniency programme. In this respect, Lee points out that the MyCC retains a high degree of discretionary power. Other elements that could contribute to the unattractiveness of the leniency programme could be the generosity towards the number of eligible leniency applicants, exclusion of the ringleader as an eligible leniency applicant, or the possibility of facing private damages actions. Yet, Lee does not exclude that the effectiveness of the leniency programme is affected by the distrust of the business community in government institutions. To substantiate this view, Lee draws parallels with the acceptance of whistle-blowing and business's perception that government institutions are independent.

Sandra Marco Colino reports in Chapter 12 that the leniency programme in Hong Kong was promulgated at the same time that the Hong Kong Competition Ordinance went into full effect in 2015. This leniency programme has been successfully used once. The Hong Kong Competition Commission (HKCC) reached a leniency agreement in 2020, despite its strong focus on tackling cartels. Six out of the seven cases the HKCC has brought to the Hong Kong Competition Tribunal are cartel related. These enforcement successes are attributable to market studies by the HKCC itself. Marco Colino argues that this situation should not be misinterpreted. She indicates that with the arrival of Brent Snyder, a former employee of the Antitrust Division of the DOJ, as the Chief Executive Officer in 2017, steps were taken to reform the leniency system in Hong Kong. Lenient treatment remained limited to immunity, but also became available once an investigation has started. Two new schemes were introduced: leniency for individuals and leniency plus. A leniency applicant is given immunity from damages claims. Further, reduction of sanctions was made possible through the introduction of a cooperation policy. These recent changes should contribute to enforcement and supplement the successfully concluded ex officio investigations, which Marco Colino details at the beginning of her contribution.

Nikita Koradia, Kiran Manokaran and Juhi Hirani suggest in Chapter 13 that the Indian Competition Act of 2002 already had the possibility of offering lenient treatment to a firm that reports the existence of a cartel. However, the details for offering lenient treatment were only elaborated for the first time in 2009, in the Lesser Penalty Regulation. A revision followed in 2017. Koradia, Manokaran and Hirani inform us that leniency has been sought in thirteen decisions of the Competition Commission of

India (CCI). This low number may be explained by the discretion the CCI has to judge leniency applications and the uncertainty that leniency applicants face in relation to damages claims. Koradia, Manokaran and Hirani recommend addressing these issues, but also increasing the incentives to apply for leniency by introducing individualised sanctions on directors or immunising successful leniency applicants against debarment from procurement projects. Koradia, Manokaran and Hirani further advise that the government should take the existence of the leniency programme into consideration when suggesting changes to the Competition Act.

In Chapter 14, Alizedney M. Ditucalan and Steven Van Uytsel introduce one of the more recent leniency programmes in Asia. Due to the dual enforcement structure, the Philippines has developed two different leniency programmes, one administered by the Philippine Competition Commission (PCC) and one by the Office for Competition of the Department of Justice (DOJ-OFC). Whereas the latter is only applicable in criminal proceedings, the former applies to administrative, criminal and civil proceedings. Ditucalan and Van Uytsel argue that both leniency programmes are generous. However, the discretionary powers of the enforcement agencies and the possibility of carving employees out of the leniency application diminish the attractiveness of leniency programmes. Uncertainty about the outcome of a leniency application has, in general, not been well accepted by cartel participants. It can therefore be predicted that, no matter how generous the leniency programmes are, there will be no race to the enforcement agencies' doors.

Ploykaew Porananond describes in Chapter 15 how the Thai government modernised its Trade Competition Act of 1999 in 2017. The so-created Trade Competition Act of 2017 (2017 Act) was implemented to change a situation in which the enforcement agency only investigated but did not adjudicate on any case. After detailing the institutional design of the 2017 Act, Porananond introduces part of the debate on its drafting to show that there was a desire to introduce a leniency programme. The leniency programme would be applied to the criminal sanctions that the bill prescribed for hard-core cartels, such as price fixing or bid rigging. However, the Office of the Attorney General objected, with the reason that giving immunity from a sanction is the constitutional prerogative of the court. In order not to jeopardise the creation of a leniency programme, the drafting committee was willing to limit the lenient treatment to just a reduction in the sanction or to the cartels for which only an administrative sanction would apply. But these initiatives were not incorporated into the 2017 Act. Instead, as described by Porananond, the 2017 Act gave tremendous flexibility to the enforcement agency by only prescribing maximum sanctions. This might allow a similar result to a leniency programme to be achieved, albeit without a well-defined formal framework. Hence, firms are potentially subject to a greater degree of discretionary behaviour on the part of the enforcement agency.

Part IV gives a comparative overview of the leniency programmes in Asia to identify the potential for convergence.

Steven Van Uytsel, Mark Fenwick and Yoshiteru Uemura argue in Chapter 16 that Asian leniency programmes only converge on the core elements of a leniency programme. These core elements are the building blocks of a leniency programme. However, the composition of these blocks is often different. Some of the differences are subtle. Other differences make the respective leniency programme distinct from the others. Some of the distinctive elements even give a unique character to the particular leniency programme. Chapter 16 further claims that these differences can be explained by either the political economy of a country or experimentation due to prior negative enforcement results, achieving better enforcement results or foreign influence. Since the result of experimentation cannot always be predicted, Van Uytsel, Fenwick and Uemura estimate that further amendments will be made to the Asian leniency programmes.

PART II

Leniency in Historical, International and Theoretical Context

2

The Development of the Leniency Programmes of the United States Department of Justice and the European Commission

BASKARAN BALASINGHAM

2.1 Introduction

Leniency programmes have fundamentally changed cartel enforcement around the world. Two of the oldest leniency programmes in the world are the leniency programmes of the United States (US) Department of Justice's (DOJ) Antitrust Division and the European Commission. In light of the track records of the Antitrust Division and the European Commission in detecting and punishing international cartels, these leniency programmes are also two of the most important ones. While they are very successful now, this has not always been the case. Both leniency programmes have been subject to substantial revisions and are to some extent continuously evolving. Moreover, their development also shows that they are not simply standalone tools of cartel detection, but have over time become more embedded in the wider (international) cartel enforcement system. With the benefit of hindsight gained from their respective, unsuccessful predecessors, and particularly the Antitrust Division's 1978 Corporate Leniency Policy (1978 Leniency Policy) as the world's first leniency programme, those revisions focused on what have come to be understood as the three pre-requisites for an effective leniency programme. However, practice has also shown that concentrating on those pre-requisites alone is not enough. The framers of a leniency programme must also pay attention to any adverse effects that criminal and private enforcement may have on the incentives to apply for leniency.

The purpose of this chapter is to shed light on the development of the US and European Union (EU) leniency programmes. The chapter is organised as follows: Section 2.2 briefly sets out the theoretical underpinning of leniency programmes. Sections 2.3 and 2.4 analyse the evolution of the US and EU leniency programmes, respectively, and in doing so primarily deal with the pre-requisites for effectiveness. Section 2.5 then examines the main similarities and differences between the two leniency programmes. Section 2.6 draws some conclusions.

2.2 Theory

To fully understand competition authorities' reliance on leniency programmes, it is necessary to first set out the theoretical foundation of the concept of leniency in cartel enforcement and identify the factors that make leniency programmes effective.[1]

2.2.1 *Race for Confession*

The theoretical foundation for the concept of leniency in cartel enforcement is the prisoner's dilemma. This game-theoretical model describes a situation where players achieve a sub-optimal outcome because they pursue their individual interests and act in a selfish manner instead of collaborating in pursuit of their collective interest.[2] The rationale of a leniency programme is to lure at least one member of the cartel into confessing in exchange for a reduction of the penalty or even complete immunity, while all other co-conspirators will be subject to penalties. A leniency programme thus applies a 'carrot-and-stick' approach. Importantly, the highest reward is offered only to the firm that comes forward first. However, unlike in the theoretical prisoner's dilemma, confession is not the dominant strategy in most real-life cartel situations, since prosecutors do not have leverage over a secret cartel. Although the cartel would be better off if it collectively agreed to remain silent, the existence of a leniency programme stokes distrust among the cartel members and increases the chances that one of them defects from the cartel.[3] Since each cartel member has an incentive to be the first to blow the whistle, a leniency programme creates what is called a 'race for confession'.

[1] For a current overview of the various cartel and leniency policies in the world see, e.g., Buretta, J. and Terzaken, J. (eds.), *The Cartels and Leniency Review* (London: Law Business Research, 2018).

[2] Leslie, C. R., 'Antitrust Amnesty, Game Theory, and Cartel Stability' (2006) 31 *Journal of Corporation Law* 453, p. 455.

[3] See Zingales, N., 'European and American Leniency Programmes: Two Models Towards Convergence?' (2008) 5 *Competition Law Review* 5, pp. 8–9; Harding, C. and Joshua J., *Regulating Cartels in Europe*, 2nd ed. (Oxford: Oxford University Press, 2010), p. 235.

2.2.2 *Pre-requisites for Effectiveness*

Although the functioning of a leniency programme can be explained based on the prisoner's dilemma, competition authorities have been influenced more directly by practical and empirical insights.[4] The success of a leniency programme has traditionally been attributed to three main pre-requisites. According to Scott Hammond, the former Deputy Assistant Attorney General for Criminal Enforcement of the Antitrust Division, the cornerstones of any effective leniency programme are (1) the threat of severe sanctions if a cartel is detected and prosecuted, (2) a high risk of detection of a cartel, and (3) a high degree of transparency and predictability in relation to the award of leniency.[5] These three pre-requisites were derived retrospectively from the experience of the unsuccessful first US corporate leniency programme, the 1978 Leniency Policy, and are also indirectly based on the insights from the prisoner's dilemma. Moreover, as briefly discussed below, these pre-requisites also help to explain the interaction between public, criminal and private enforcement. While these three 'traditional' pre-requisites have likely played the most important role in designing new leniency programmes and reforming existing ones, recent competition scholarship has identified other factors that may also be relevant for the effectiveness of a leniency programme. The discussion of those other factors is beyond the scope of this chapter.[6]

[4] Caron Beaton-Wells recently wrote: 'There is a large body of theoretical and empirical economic research that has sought to establish the "optimal" design of leniency policies and test for their success in cartel detection, prosecution and deterrence .... [T]he economic literature does not reveal how a leniency policy is actually perceived by the business sector in general, by leniency applicants or prospective applicants and their advisers and by competition authorities and their political masters. The economic research has also not explored the role and impact of leniency policies in a broader policy setting, in which other interconnected aspects of enforcement are at work and in which general considerations of agency governance are relevant': Beaton-Wells, C., 'Leniency Policies: Revolution or Religion?' in Beaton-Wells, C. and Tran, C. (eds.), *Anti-Cartel Enforcement in a Contemporary Age: Leniency Religion* (Oxford: Hart Publishing, 2015), p. 4.

[5] Hammond, S. D., 'An Update of the Antitrust Division's Criminal Enforcement Program' (Presentation at the ABA Section of Antitrust Law Cartel Enforcement Roundtable, Washington, DC, 16 November 2005), p. 3. This was affirmed by the current Deputy Assistant Attorney General Richard Powers at the 13th International Cartel Workshop (San Francisco, 19 February 2020). *See also* Spratling, G. R., 'Detection and Deterrence: Rewarding Informants for Reporting Violations' (2001) 69 *George Washington Law Review* 798, pp. 799 and 806–23; O'Kane, M., *The Law of Criminal Cartels: Practice and Procedure* (Oxford: Oxford University Press, 2009), p. 6.

[6] For a discussion of these other factors, see, e.g., the various contribution in Beaton-Wells and Tran, *Anti-Cartel Enforcement in a Contemporary Age* (n. 4 above).

2.2.2.1 Threat of Severe Sanctions

A leniency programme is generally considered to be more effective if the threat of sanctions has a sufficiently high deterrent effect.[7] This criterion is the first and foremost one. Generally, the greater the penalty (and the likelihood of detection) is, the higher the deterrent effect will be, and therefore the more appealing it will be for cartel members to come forward.[8] Reversely, the greater the offered discount from the otherwise applicable penalty is, the stronger the incentive to defect will be.[9] For any cartel member it is therefore advisable to apply for leniency if the ensuing benefits outweigh the risks and consequences of detection. The penalties imposable on cartel members that choose to remain silent should be of such severity that would make it very difficult for the relevant corporations and their executives to treat them as a mere cost of doing business.[10] Since cartel participation might yield higher profits for the corporations involved, as well as higher bonuses for their executives, the benefit of leniency (i.e. collaborative payoff) should outweigh the imposable sanction (i.e. collusive payoff). The penalties that are waived or reduced could be any sanctions that are applicable in the jurisdiction concerned, such as fines against the corporation, fines against individuals, director disqualification or even imprisonment.[11]

The prisoner's dilemma can help to illustrate how the threat of severe sanctions or the prospect of leniency respectively may influence a cartel participant's decision to come forward or not. Each player is less likely to trust the other not to come forward when the reward for confessing is relatively high. Similarly, players are more likely to distrust one another the more they stand to lose because of their co-conspirator's betrayal. In the absence of confession as the dominant strategy, cartel members have less reason to distrust that any one of them will cooperate with the authorities. However, the threat of severe sanctions can render the cost of guessing wrong as to the other cartel members' behaviour unacceptably high.

[7] Barnett, T., 'Criminal Enforcement of Antitrust Laws: The U.S. Model', in Hawk, B. E. (ed.), *Annual Proceedings of the Fordham Competition Law Institute: International Antitrust Law & Policy* (New York: Fordham University Press, 2007), 1, p. 3.

[8] Ibid., p. 3; Crampton, P. and Reynolds, G., 'Leniency Programmes in Competition Law', in Dhall, V. (ed.), *Competition Law Today – Concepts, Issues, and the Law in Practice* (Oxford: Oxford University Press, 2007), 113, pp. 114–15.

[9] Wils, W. P. J., 'Leniency in Antitrust Enforcement: Theory and Practice' (2007) 30 *World Competition* 25, p. 43.

[10] Albrecht, S., *Die Anwendung von Kronzeugenregelungen bei der Bekämpfung internationaler Kartelle* (Baden-Baden: Nomos, 2008), p. 133.

[11] Wils, 'Leniency in Antitrust Enforcement' (n. 9 above), p. 25.

Even if the chances that another cartel member will confess are low, provided that the penalty imposed for guessing wrong is sufficiently high, corporations are more likely to confess to avoid the high cost of confessing second. Thus, the threat of severe sanctions can lead to more distrust among cartel members and intensify the race for confession.

2.2.2.2 High Risk of Detection

Another important criterion of an effective leniency programme is that cartel members must fear an imminent risk of detection of their cartel. Detection might either be the result of a leniency application from a co-conspirator (or sometimes even a former employee) or might come at the hands of a competition authority using its inspection powers such as dawn raids.[12] Yet, if cartel members are relatively certain that competition authorities will not detect the cartel, nor that any of their co-conspirators will defect, then even the threat of severe sanctions is not likely to induce them to blow the whistle. Competition authorities must therefore institute an environment in which cartel members sense a material risk of detection.[13] It is important to note that a leniency programme will only start attracting applications if the competition authority has succeeded in generating sufficient credibility as to its capacity to detect and prosecute cartels on its own (i.e. without the assistance of leniency applications).[14] Furthermore, the risk of detection should not solely depend on a competition authority's leniency programme. Detection efforts through the leniency programme should ideally be supplemented by other enforcement and inspection powers. The more effective those powers are, the more pressure cartel members will feel to be the first to blow the whistle.

2.2.2.3 High Degree of Transparency and Predictability

Thirdly, a leniency programme will be more effective if it provides a high degree of transparency and predictability about the prospect and outcome of applying for leniency.[15] A cartel member is less likely to blow the whistle

[12] Ibid., p. 47.

[13] Hammond, 'An Update of the Antitrust Division's Criminal Enforcement Program' (n. 5 above), p. 6.

[14] Wils, 'Leniency in Antitrust Enforcement' (n. 9 above), pp. 47–48. Hence, there is a virtuous circle or a vicious circle depending on the effectiveness of the leniency programme.

[15] Barnett, 'Criminal Enforcement of Antitrust Laws' (n. 7 above), p. 3; Crampton and Reynolds, 'Leniency Programmes in Competition Law' (n. 8 above), pp. 119–20; O'Brien, A., 'Leadership of Leniency', in Beaton-Wells and Tran. *Anti-Cartel Enforcement in a Contemporary Age* (n. 4 above), 17, pp. 24–31. See also OECD, 'Report on Leniency Programs to Fight Hard Core Cartels' Document DAFFE/CLP 2001 (27 April 2001), p. 13.

if the leniency programme is opaque and offers little certainty.[16] As prospective applicants come forward in direct proportion to the certainty of whether they will qualify for leniency, it is important that competition authorities limit their discretion in awarding leniency to a minimum.[17] Apart from clearly setting out the conditions for obtaining immunity and any other lenient treatment, a leniency programme must also provide clear rules on the procedure as well as other important aspects such as confidentiality.[18]

2.2.2.4 Interdependence of the Pre-requisites

The above three pre-requisites are not only indispensable for creating an effective leniency programme, they are also interdependent. Deterrence, which is the trigger of the race to confession, is the product of the threat of sanctions and the risk of detection.[19] Without severe sanctions the pressure to apply for leniency (i.e. the risk of detection) will be low; and when there is only little risk of detection, the pressure will remain low even if severe penalties were to be imposed. To increase the risk of detection through a competition authority's leniency programme the latter needs to be transparent. Finally, due to the interdependence between leniency and sanctions, a competition authority should also provide clear rules on cartel sanctions.

2.3 Interplay between Competition Law Enforcement Types

The elements of the carrot-and-stick approach mostly stem from the public administrative side of competition law enforcement. However, in some jurisdictions competition law enforcement also comprises criminal and private enforcement. In those jurisdictions the interplay between the different competition enforcement mechanisms can either reinforce the

[16] Albrecht, *Die Anwendung von Kronzeugenregelungen* (n. 10 above), p. 135. See also Hammond, S. D., 'Detecting and Deterring Cartel Activity through an Effective Leniency Program' (Presentation at the International Workshop on Cartels, Brighton, 21–22 November 2000).

[17] Hammond, 'An Update of the Antitrust Division's Criminal Enforcement Program' (n. 5 above).

[18] See Crampton and Reynolds, 'Leniency Programmes in Competition Law' (n. 8 above), p. 119.

[19] Landes, W. M., 'Optimal Sanctions for Antitrust Violations' (1983) 50 *University of Chicago Law Review* 652, pp. 666–68; Lande, R. and Davis, J., 'Comparative Deterrence from Private Enforcement and Criminal Enforcement of the U.S. Antitrust Laws' (2011) 37 *Brigham Young University Law Review* 315, pp. 319–20.

incentive for a leniency application or diminish it, and can therefore be crucial in how effective a leniency programme will be.

In terms of criminal enforcement and its interplay with public administrative enforcement, criminal penalties, particularly prison sentences for corporate actors, are considered the most deterrent form of punishing cartel infringements. For this deterrent effect to have a positive impact on the effectiveness of leniency, the immunity that is granted to the corporation also needs to be extended to the individuals who run the corporation (and were ultimately responsible for the corporation's cartel activity or are at least accountable). If this is not the case, the fear of a prison sentence will almost certainly discourage the corporation from blowing the whistle. Furthermore, investigative powers of enforcement authorities are typically more intrusive under criminal enforcement and therefore generate a higher risk of detection.

The interplay between public and private enforcement is more complex than that between public administrative and criminal enforcement. Private enforcement can have both a compensatory and a deterrent function. Private actions brought by victims after the conviction of a cartel (i.e. 'follow-on actions') to recover their losses as a result of the cartel may serve as an additional cartel penalty besides corporate fines (and possibly criminal penalties in certain jurisdictions) and therefore further increase the threat of severe sanctions. Secondly, when a competition authority cannot or will not prosecute a cartel, private actions (i.e. 'standalone actions') may offer the only recourse to go after cartelists.[20] For optimal cartel enforcement, public and private enforcement should complement each other.[21] In the leniency context, two specific issues need to be addressed: (1) the rules on access to file to the national competition authority's documents including corporate leniency statements, and (2) the rules on joint and several liability of cartelists. On the one hand, by allowing access to file, a higher number of successful follow-on actions might be possible and cartel members would be exposed to greater civil liability. However, leniency applicants might incur a greater risk than their co-conspirators. If private litigants gain access to corporate leniency statements, an immunity recipient is more likely to be the easiest target of private actions. In the worst-case scenario, if all co-conspirators are insolvent under the 'ordinary' rules of joint and several liability, the

[20] Cf. Weber Waller, S., 'Towards a Constructive Public–Private Partnership to Enforce Competition Law' (2006) 29 *World Competition* 367, p. 370.

[21] OECD, 'Private Remedies' (2011) 11(2) *OECD Journal: Competition Law and Policy* 11, p. 12.

immunity recipient might even have to bear liability for the entire damage caused by the cartel.[22] These risks might discourage potential leniency applicants from blowing the whistle and damage the effectiveness of the leniency programme. On the other hand, the threat of even more severe penalties than in the absence of leniency might incentivise cartel members to cooperate with the authorities.

2.4 Development of the US Leniency Programme

The Antitrust Division of the DOJ was the first competition authority to establish a leniency programme. It had a rather slow start and it was not until the revision of the Corporate Leniency Policy that the concept of leniency in cartel law enforcement gained worldwide traction.

2.4.1 The 1978 Corporate Leniency Policy

The first version of the Corporate Leniency Policy was introduced in 1978 as an attempt to detect more cartels. It offered complete amnesty from prosecution for the first cartel member to come forward and cooperate with the Antitrust Division. However, the 1978 Leniency Policy did not produce the desired result and was widely considered a failure.[23] On average the Antitrust Division received only about one leniency application per year, none of which was in relation to an international or large domestic cartel.[24]

The 1978 Leniency Policy suffered from three key problems. The first one was in relation to the threat of severe sanctions. Even though in 1974 committing a cartel offence under the Sherman Act was changed from a misdemeanour to a felony with a maximum term of imprisonment of one year (the maximum fine was increased to US$1 million for corporations and US$100,000 for individuals), the leniency programme did not extend immunity from criminal prosecution to the corporate actors of the corporation that applied for leniency. This was undoubtedly a huge disincentive for corporations to apply for leniency. Possibly the level of these

[22] Howard, A., 'The Draft Directive on Competition Law Damages – What Does It Mean for Infringers and Victims?' (2014) 35 *European Competition Law Review* 51, p. 54.

[23] Hammond, 'An Update of the Antitrust Division's Criminal Enforcement Program' (n. 5 above).

[24] OECD, 'Roundtable on Challenges and Co-ordination of Leniency Programmes – Note by the United States', DAF/COMP/WP3/WD(2018)33 (23 May 2018), p. 2.

penalties was not high enough to create sufficient deterrence.[25] Between 1984 and 1990 the level of sanctions was therefore ratcheted up a couple of times, reaching a maximum fine of US$10 million for corporations and US$350,000 for individuals, and a maximum of three years of imprisonment. While this steady increase of the level of sanctions may have been adequate to generate deterrence, the risk of detection was insufficient. The Antitrust Division had not built up a sufficiently strong reputation for detecting cartels, partly owing to the lack of tools in its arsenal and partly due to the ineffectiveness of its leniency programme itself. Another shortcoming of the original leniency programme was the lack of transparency and predictability. The award of immunity was not automatic, and the Antitrust Division retained substantial prosecutorial discretion. Importantly, leniency was not available after the Antitrust Division had already received any information about the activity being reported from another source. Furthermore, the transparency was significantly compromised since there was no written policy.

2.4.2 *Revision of the Leniency Programme*

The Antitrust Division completely revamped its Corporate Leniency Policy in 1993 (1993 Leniency Policy). Several features were added to the revised leniency programme over time.

2.4.2.1 The 1993 Corporate Leniency Policy

Under the revised 1993 Leniency Policy, the Antitrust Division substantially increased the transparency and predictability in relation to the award of leniency. In addition to issuing a written policy, the Antitrust Division has further clarified the application of its leniency policy by publishing several speeches to address questions that have arisen in relation to it, including a Frequently Asked Questions paper.[26] An important amendment to enhance predictability was the creation of an alternative leniency for corporations that come forward after an investigation has begun. Under 'Type A Leniency', which applies before an investigation has begun, leniency is automatic if the applicant can meet the following

[25] Since 1984, fines in excess of the statutory maximum may be imposed according to 18 U.S.C. § 3571(d), which provides for a fine of up to twice the gain derived by, or twice the loss caused by, the cartel.

[26] OECD, 'Roundtable on Challenges and Co-ordination of Leniency Programmes' (n. 24 above), p. 5.

six objective criteria:[27] (1) at the time the corporation comes forward to confess criminal behaviour, the Antitrust Division has not yet received information about the cartel from any other source; (2) upon the corporation's discovery of the cartel, the corporation took prompt and effective action to terminate its participation in the activity; (3) the corporation reports the wrongdoing with candour and completeness and provides full, continuing and complete cooperation to the Antitrust Division throughout the investigation; (4) the confession of wrongdoing is truly a corporate act, as opposed to isolated confessions of individual corporate actors; (5) where possible, the corporation makes restitution to the injured parties; and (6) the corporation did not coerce another party to participate in the cartel and clearly was not the ringleader or originator of the cartel. Under Type A Leniency the Antitrust Division has virtually no discretion and in addition has developed a long record of honouring leniency agreements, which provides potential applicants with comforting certainty.[28]

If an applicant cannot qualify for Type A Leniency, it may seek the alternative 'Type B Leniency', which is available to the first corporation to come forward after an investigation has already been initiated. It requires many of the same conditions as in Type A Leniency, with the additional requirements that (1) at the time of the corporation's application, the Antitrust Division does not yet have evidence against the corporation that is likely to result in a sustainable conviction; and (2) the Antitrust Division determines that granting leniency would not be unfair to others, considering the nature of the cartel activity, the confessing corporation's role in the activity, and the time at which the corporation comes forward.

The more important novelty of the Corporate Leniency Policy was the granting of immunity from criminal prosecution for corporate actors. If a corporation qualifies for leniency, all current directors, officers and employees of the corporation who admit their involvement in the cartel activity as part of the corporate confession will also receive leniency (under Type A) or be considered for leniency (under Type B) if they admit their wrongdoing and cooperate with the Antitrust Division. Senior officials of the Antitrust Division touted the threat of a prison sentence as the 'single greatest incentive' for individuals involved in a

[27] Ibid.

[28] Lynch, N. E., 'Immunity in Criminal Cartel Investigations: A US Perspective' (Latham & Watkins LLP white paper, 2011), p. 3. Retrieved from www.lw.com/presentations/immunity-in-criminal-cartel-investigations-us-perspective.

cartel activity to self-report through a leniency application and thereby escape penalties.[29]

In relation to the threat of severe punishment, the constant ratcheting-up of the level of sanctions and the added positive impact of the revised leniency programme marked the beginning of record penalties decade after decade.[30] In the 1980s the total of the criminal antitrust corporate fines was US$188 million; a decade later it was already US$1.6 billion. The number of individuals prosecuted and the length of prison sentences imposed for antitrust crimes saw an equally dramatic increase. The increase in the level of sanctions is also due to the Antitrust Division's reallocation of resources to focus on international cases involving larger volumes of commerce, and the change in perception by judges as to the seriousness of antitrust crimes.[31] Yet, the increase is mostly attributable to the increase in maximum penalties for antitrust crimes. In 2004, the US Congress enacted the Antitrust Criminal Penalty Enforcement and Reform Act (ACPERA) to further increase the deterrence and incentives for cartel offenders to self-report illegal conduct through the Antitrust Division's leniency programme.[32] This Act increased the maximum fine for antitrust violations to US$100 million for corporations and US$1 million for individuals and increased the maximum jail time to ten years.[33] In the 2011–2020 period the total corporate fines amounted to over US$9.6 billion. The average prison sentence in the past two decades was nineteen months, compared to only eight months in the 1990s.[34]

With respect to generating a higher risk of detection in order to boost the effectiveness of the revised leniency programme, the Antitrust Division availed itself of every investigative means possible, including the use of grand jury investigations, informants, consensual monitoring, audio and video tape recordings, wiretapping[35] and search warrants.

[29] Werden, G., 'Deterrence and Detection of Cartels: Using All the Tools and Sanctions' (Presentation at the ABA Center for Continuing Legal Education, Miami, 1 March 2012), p. 7.

[30] Buretta, J. and Terzaken, J., 'United States', in Buretta and Terzaken, *The Cartels and Leniency Review* (n. 1 above), 346, pp. 385–86.

[31] Hammond, S. D., 'The Evolution of Criminal Antitrust Enforcement over the Last Two Decades; (Presentation at the 24th Annual Institute on White Collar Crime, Miami, 25 February 2010), pp. 4–5.

[32] Antitrust Criminal Penalty Enhancement and Reform Act, Pub. L. No. 108–237, 118 Stat. 661 (2004). On 1 October 2020, the US Congress extended ACPERA permanently.

[33] Retrieved from www.justice.gov/atr/criminal-enforcement-fine-and-jail-charts.

[34] Ibid.

[35] In 2006, US Congress amended the wiretapping statute to include antitrust violations.

The Antitrust Division's criminal investigations are also supported by other government agencies such as the Federal Bureau of Investigation (FBI).[36] Moreover, the private bar was credited for promoting antitrust compliance programmes, which proved to play an important role in detecting cartels.[37]

2.4.2.2 Leniency Policy for Individuals

Leniency for corporate actors under the 1993 Corporate Leniency Policy only applies to current employees of a corporation. In 1994, the Antitrust Division introduced the Leniency Policy for Individuals, which expanded the scope of leniency to also cover former employees who come forward on their own behalf and not as part of a corporate confession. To qualify for leniency, (1) the Antitrust Division must not have received information about the cartel; (2) the individual leniency applicant is required to admit his or her wrongdoing and cooperate with the Antitrust Division; and (3) the individual must not have coerced another party to participate in the cartel and was not the ringleader. As a result of extending leniency to former employees, the race for confession is not just between the members of the cartel any more but also between the corporations and their former employees. Deterrence and the likelihood of detection are thus greater, and the overall leniency policy more effective.

2.4.2.3 Marker System

In the race for confession, time is of the essence. Since corporations sometimes need additional time to prepare their leniency application, the Antitrust Division has established a marker system. A marker affords an applicant the opportunity to save its place in line for leniency ahead of other applicants while gathering the necessary information to support its application. To obtain a marker, an applicant has to (1) report that it has uncovered some information or evidence indicating that it is involved in a cartel; (2) disclose the general nature of the cartel conduct discovered; and (3) identify the industry, product or service involved in terms that are specific enough to allow the Antitrust Division to

[36] Werden et al., 'Deterrence and Detection of Cartels' (n. 29 above), p. 13.

[37] Spratling, G. R., 'Making Companies an Offer They Shouldn't Refuse' (Presentation at the 35th Annual Symposium on Associations and Antitrust, Washington, DC, 16 February 1999).

determine whether leniency is still available.[38] The possibility to secure a marker increases both the incentive and predictability in the leniency process.

2.4.2.4 Leniency Plus

In 1999, the Antitrust Division introduced a 'leniency plus' provision as an additional feature to the 1993 Leniency Policy. Under this provision, a corporation that loses out to a co-conspirator in the race for confession in relation to a cartel is nonetheless encouraged to denounce its participation in another undetected cartel, as it will be rewarded with more favourable treatment in relation to the former cartel in addition to receiving immunity in relation to the second cartel. The rationale for introducing leniency plus was the realisation that half of the Antitrust Division's international cartel investigations were launched after immunity recipients in an ongoing cartel investigation had unveiled information on their cartel activities in other markets.[39] Also empirical studies have shown that in certain industries companies are more frequently involved in multiple, unrelated cartels than in other industries.[40] Moreover, from a theoretical perspective a corporation that participates in one cartel is more likely to also participate in at least one other cartel.[41] Such a corporation has upon its first cartel participation already surpassed the moral barrier, which would inhibit law-abiding corporations from engaging in any illegal activity. The corporation may have also gained valuable experience in how cartels operate that could be useful for potential subsequent cartel activities.[42] According to the Antitrust Division, the leniency plus programme has been a powerful source of investigation, since many of the Division's investigations result from evidence developed during an investigation of a completely separate conspiracy.[43]

The US corporate leniency programme also features a 'penalty plus' provision, which is the mirror image of leniency plus. If in the course of

[38] Department of Justice, 'Frequently Asked Questions about the Antitrust Division's Leniency Program and Model Leniency Letters' (19 November 2008, updated 26 January 2017), Question 2.

[39] Jephcott, M., 'The European Commission's New Leniency Notice –Whistling the Right Tune; (2002) 23(8) *ECLR* 378, p. 381.

[40] See, e.g., Stephan, A., 'An Empirical Assessment of the European Leniency Notice' (2008) 5 *Journal of Competition Law & Economics* 537, p. 537.

[41] Wils, 'Leniency in Antitrust Enforcement' (n. 9 above), p. 59.

[42] Ibid., pp. 59–60.

[43] Department of Justice, 'Frequently Asked Questions about the Antitrust Division's Leniency Program and Model Leniency Letters' (n. 38 above), Question 8.

an investigation the Antitrust Division discovers an earlier conspiracy to which the immunity applicant was party and which the latter has not disclosed, the Antitrust Division will argue strongly in court that this conduct amounts to an aggravating factor and that the company's punishment in relation to the second cartel should therefore be towards the upper end of the range set out in the Sentencing Guidelines.[44]

Despite the absence of a formal leniency provision for subsequent applicants (barring plea bargaining) under the 1993 Leniency Policy, leniency plus can be considered to compensate for this. The prospect of immunity in relation to a second cartel and an additional fine reduction in relation to the first cartel serve as a 'consolation prize' for those beaten in the race for immunity in the first cartel. Leniency plus may enhance the effectiveness of the leniency programme by increasing the incentive to come forward. This can again be explained by the insight of the prisoner's dilemma that players are more distrusting if they would suffer greatly in response to any betrayal of their trust.[45] A corporation that is involved in multiple cartels simultaneously has reason to be more suspicious of a corporation that only participates in a single cartel. The impact of leniency plus on deterrence is further enhanced by penalty plus. Leniency plus and penalty plus thus perfectly illustrate the carrot-and-stick approach that is firmly embraced in US antitrust enforcement.

2.4.2.5 More Lenient Treatment under Private Enforcement

US antitrust law ordinarily allows for automatic treble damages in all successful private antitrust actions, with each member to the infringement being jointly and severally liable (with no right of contribution).[46] Although the 1993 Leniency Policy produced remarkable results, the civil exposure of potential immunity recipients was considered a limiting factor.[47] In order to overcome the disincentives posed by private actions, the abovementioned ACPERA offers potential immunity applicants a reduction of their civil liability. Under what is termed the 'de-trebling provision', an immunity recipient can confine its civil liability to the harm actually inflicted by its conduct (i.e. single damages instead of treble damages), if

44 Utton, M., *Cartels and Economic Collusion: The Persistence of Corporate Conspiracies* (Cheltenham: Edward Elgar, 2011), p. 136.

45 See Leslie, 'Antitrust Amnesty, Game Theory, and Cartel Stability' (n. 2 above), p. 475.

46 See *Texas Industries Inc* v *Radcliff Materials Inc* 451 US 630 (1981).

47 Simmons, I. and O'Rourke, K., 'Reflections on Cartel Enforcement' (2012) 27(1) *Antitrust* 33, p. 33.

it provides civil plaintiffs with timely, satisfactory cooperation.[48] In addition, the immunity recipient is not jointly and severally liable for the cartel damage. Satisfactory cooperation includes providing a full account of all facts known to the immunity recipient in relation to the private action and furnishing all relevant documents in its possession.[49]

By de-trebling the immunity recipient's damages and removing joint liability in return for its cooperation with private claimants, the ACPERA offers an additional incentive for cartel members to come forward while ensuring that cartel victims have recourse to compensation, since access to file is facilitated.[50] It has a positive impact on private enforcement and overall cartel enforcement, as it enhances the likelihood of more successful private actions with higher damages amounts. As argued by Daniel Crane, the ACPERA is an example of how the legislator can structure certain aspects of the private litigation system to increase both deterrence and compensation, and that leniency does not necessarily have to be inconsistent with pursing a compensation goal.[51] Although a report by the Government Accountability Office (GAO) in 2011 showed that the de-trebling provision of the ACPERA had only a minor impact on the number of immunity applications,[52] it has nonetheless been positively received overall by the plaintiffs' bar.[53] Plaintiffs' lawyers state that information they had obtained through cooperation under the ACPERA both reinforced and streamlined their cases.[54] The American Antitrust Institute expressed the view that the GAO Report supports the conclusion that the ACPERA's de-trebling provision is instrumental in incentivising leniency applicants.[55]

[48] Antitrust Criminal Penalty Enhancement and Reform Act, Pub. L. No. 108–237, tit. II, 118 Stat. 661 (2004), Section 213(b) & (c), 15 U.S.C. § 1 note.

[49] Ibid., Section 213(b).

[50] Kon, S. and Barcroft, A., 'Aspects of the Complementary Roles of Public and Private Enforcement of UK and EU Antitrust Law: An Enforcement Deficit?' (2008) 1(1) *Global Competition Litigation Review* 11, p. 17.

[51] Crane, D., 'Why Leniency Does Not Undermine Compensation', in Beaton-Wells and Tran, *Anti-Cartel Enforcement in a Contemporary Age* (n. 4 above), 263, p. 269.

[52] Government Accountability Office, 'Criminal Cartel Enforcement: Stakeholder Views on Impact of 2004 Antitrust Reform Are Mixed, But Support Whistleblower Protection' (Report to Congressional Committees, GAO-11-916, July 2011), pp. 15–17 (GAO Report).

[53] Ibid., p. 26.

[54] Ibid., p. 27; Lynch, N. E. and Fox, K., 'How ACPERA Has Affected Criminal Cartel Enforcement' (11 August 2011). Retrieved from https://m.lw.com/thoughtLeadership/how-acpera-affects-criminal-cartel-enforcement.

[55] American Antitrust Institute, 'Comments of the American Antitrust Institute Prepared for the Antitrust Division Roundtable on the Antitrust Criminal Penalty Enhancement and Reform Act' (31 May 2019), p. 4. Retrieved from www.justice.gov/atr/page/file/1168666/download.

2.4.3 Evaluation

The 1993 Leniency Policy removed the shortcomings of its predecessor and set the blueprint for what an effective leniency programme could look like. A crucial change in comparison to the unsuccessful 1978 Leniency Policy was the automatic award of immunity, the possibility to qualify for immunity even after the Antitrust Division had launched an investigation, and the extended scope of immunity for corporate actors of the applicant. The plaintiffs' bar initially had reservations about the revised leniency programme, and in particular the idea of an otherwise guilty offender getting off scot-free. Over time, however, this reservation made room for a continually growing recognition of the programme's merits.[56]

The effectiveness of the current Corporate Leniency Policy is clearly premised on a carrot-and-stick approach. Since 1993 the incentives have got larger as the first corporation to break ranks can qualify for (1) immunity from corporate fines; (2) de-trebled damages and no joint and several liability; and (3) immunity from criminal prosecution for the directors, officers and employees. On the flip side, the penalties have got larger too. Following every legislative amendment corporate fines tend to get higher and prison sentences longer. And then there are also private actions, which could take the form of class actions. The 1993 Leniency Policy has been a resounding success. According to the GAO Report, the Antitrust Division filed a total of 173 criminal cartel cases between 2004 and 2010, 129 of which involved a successful leniency applicant (i.e. 75 per cent of all cases).[57]

2.5 Development of the EU Leniency Programme

The European Commission formally established its leniency programme in 1996 under the first Leniency Notice.[58] This Leniency Notice served the purposes of experimenting as well as codifying the Commission's informal leniency practice, which it had operated since 1994.[59] The 1996

[56] Spratling, G. R., 'The Corporate Leniency Policy: Answers to Recurring Questions' (Presentation at the ABA Antitrust Section Spring Meeting, Washington, DC, 1 April 1998).

[57] See Government Accountability Office, 'Criminal Cartel Enforcement' (n. 52 above), pp. 59–63.

[58] European Commission, 'Commission Notice on Non-imposition or Reduction of Fines in Cartel Cases', O.J. C207/4 (1996) (1996 Leniency Notice).

[59] Hölzel, N., *Kronzeugenregelungen im Europäischen Wettbewerbsrecht: Ermittlungsinstrument unter Reformzwang* (Halle: Universitätsverlag Halle-Wittenberg, 2011), p. 106.

Leniency Notice was modelled on the successful US and Canadian leniency policies, but was adjusted to suit the specific European situation.[60]

2.5.1 *The 1996 Leniency Notice*

The 1996 Leniency Notice set out three degrees of leniency. The first and highest degree involved a 'very substantial reduction' of the fine by at least 75 per cent, and possible immunity to the first corporation to adduce decisive evidence of the cartel's existence. This leniency award was subject to the condition that the Commission had not started an investigation ('Section A leniency') or had not already collected sufficient information to establish the existence of the alleged cartel ('Section B leniency'). In addition to this main condition, the leniency applicant also had to fulfil three other cumulative conditions, namely (1) to cease its involvement in the cartel; (2) to provide the Commission with all the relevant information; and (3) to maintain continuous and complete cooperation throughout the investigation. To be eligible for this largest leniency award, the applicant must not have acted as the cartel instigator or ringleader.

A corporation that was the first to cooperate with the Commission after the latter had already undertaken an investigation could qualify for the second degree of leniency, which consisted of a 'substantial reduction' of the fine by 50–75 per cent ('Section C Leniency'). This degree of leniency involved the same three cumulative conditions as under Section B. If a corporation was not eligible for the first two degrees of leniency it could qualify for the third degree, which involved a 'significant reduction' of the fine by 10–50 per cent ('Section D Leniency'). This reduction was available in two situations. A corporation had to provide the Commission with evidence that could materially contribute to establishing the existence of the cartel before the statement of objections had been sent to the corporations involved in the cartel. Alternatively, if statements of objections had already been sent out, a corporation could inform the Commission that it did not substantially contest the facts on which the Commission based its allegations.

The 1996 Leniency Notice had a number of major shortcomings, and therefore failed to spark a race for confession. The most glaring flaws of the 1996 Leniency Notice were the lack of incentives and the lack of

[60] European Commission, *XXVIth Report on Competition Policy 1996* (Brussels: Office for Official Publications of the European Communities, 1997), para. 34.

transparency.[61] Even when a corporation had won the race for confession, immunity was not automatically guaranteed.[62] Practice showed that it was not enough for a corporation to blow the whistle before an investigation had been initiated, but the cooperation also had to be entirely spontaneous; that is, before the Commission had sent out a request for information.[63] In the majority of cases, the first corporation to confess only received a very substantial fine reduction instead of immunity. In addition, the 1996 Leniency Notice contained only sparse explanations of the Commission's leniency procedure.[64] The Commission would determine whether an applicant satisfied the conditions of any of the three degrees of leniency only on the adoption of a prohibition decision.[65] Thus, there was no certainty for corporations until the end of the administrative procedure.[66] In addition, the term 'decisive evidence' was unclear and rather subjective.[67] Another significant shortcoming was that the Commission's cartel fines at that time not only lacked severity but also foreseeability, due to a lack of transparency in their calculation.[68] The cumulative effect of a lack of automatic immunity and hardly foreseeable amounts of fines had a very negative effect on deterrence.

During the five and a half years in which the 1996 Leniency Notice was in force the Commission received 188 applications. Only three undertakings received immunity and two others received a very substantial fine reduction. These awards were at the higher end of the scale and were awarded towards the end of the 1996 Leniency Notice's tenure, which was a period when the Commission did not follow it very strictly any more and instead was more generous in giving out lenient treatment to cartel

[61] Utton, *Cartels and Economic Collusion* (n. 44 above), p. 138; O'Kane, *The Law of Criminal Cartels* (n. 5 above), p. 12; Jephcott, 'The European Commission's New Leniency Notice' (n. 39 above), p. 380; Bloom, M., 'Despite Its Great Success, the EC Leniency Programme Faces Great Challenges', in Ehlermann, C.-D. and Atanasiu, I. (eds.), *European Competition Law Annual 2006: Enforcement of Prohibition of Cartels* (Oxford: Hart Publishing, 2007), 546, p. 546; Harding and Joshua, *Regulating Cartels in Europe* (n. 3 above), p. 242.

[62] Swaak, C. and Arp, D., 'A Tempting Offer: Immunity from Fines for Cartel Conduct under the European Commission's New Leniency Notice' (2003) 24 *European Competition Law Review* 9, p. 11.

[63] Albrecht, *Die Anwendung von Kronzeugenregelungen* (n. 10 above), pp. 631–32.

[64] Levy, N. and O'Donoghue, R., 'The EU Leniency Programme Comes of Age' (2004) 27 *World Competition* 75, p. 78.

[65] 1996 Leniency Notice, Section E, para. 2.

[66] Jephcott, 'The European Commission's New Leniency Notice' (n. 39 above), p. 380; Levy and O'Donoghue, 'The EU Leniency Programme Comes of Age' (n. 64 above), p. 78.

[67] Jephcott, 'The European Commission's New Leniency Notice' (n. 39 above), p. 380.

[68] Harding and Joshua, *Regulating Cartels in Europe* (n. 3 above), p. 242.

members.[69] In light of these shortcomings, it should not come as a surprise that a race for confession did not materialise under the 1996 Leniency Notice. In the Commission's view, on the other hand, the leniency programme was an indisputable success.[70] Commission officials stated that statistical data showed a very significant increase in the Commission's cartel enforcement activity and that the 1996 Leniency Notice had been a decisive factor.[71] However, the majority of leniency applications were derivative,[72] often stemming from investigations by the DOJ's Antitrust Division with respect to the same cartels.[73] Furthermore, almost half of the cartels revealed through the 1996 Leniency Notice concerned closely related infringements in the chemicals industry, and in all those cases leniency applications were made after the cartel had ceased to operate.[74] This suggests that those cartels had unravelled for reasons other than the EU leniency programme.[75] Thus, even from a statistical point of view the 1996 Leniency Notice was not as successful as the Commission likes to claim.

2.5.2 *Revision of the Leniency Programme*

Motivated to fix some of the abovementioned shortcomings, the Commission overhauled the 1996 Leniency Notice and published a revised version in February 2002. The Commission largely held on to the core principles, but acknowledged that the 'effectiveness would be improved by an increase in the transparency and certainty of the conditions on which a reduction of fines will be granted'.[76] The changes that were made were far-reaching. Less than five years after the 2002 Leniency Notice was published, the Commission replaced it with the current 2006 Leniency Notice.[77]

69 Jephcott, 'The European Commission's New Leniency Notice' (n. 39 above), p. 380.
70 Arbault, F. and Peiró, F., 'The Commission's New Notice on Immunity and Reduction of Fines in Cartel Cases: Building on Success' (2002) 2 *Competition Policy Newsletter* 15, p. 15.
71 Ibid.
72 Riley, A., 'The Modernisation of EU Anti-Cartel Enforcement: Will the Commission Grasp the Opportunity?' (CEPS Special Report, 2010), p. 4.
73 Stephan, 'An Empirical Assessment of the European Leniency Notice' (n. 40 above), pp. 540–41.
74 Ibid., pp. 545–46.
75 See Reynolds, M. and Anderson, D., 'Immunity and Leniency in EU Cartel Cases: Current Issues' (2006) 27 *European Competition Law Review* 82, p. 82.
76 Commission Notice on the Non-imposition and Reduction of Fines in Cartel Cases (2002), OJ C45/03, para. 5 (2002 Leniency Notice).
77 Commission Notice on Immunity from Fines and Reduction of Fines in Cartel Cases (2006), OJ C298/17 (2006 Leniency Notice).

2.5.2.1 The 2002 Leniency Notice

Compared to the 1996 Leniency Notice, the 2002 Leniency Notice made a clearer distinction between immunity ('Section A Leniency') and reductions in fines ('Section B Leniency').[78] The Commission granted immunity in two situations. A corporation could qualify for immunity if it was the first to submit evidence sufficient to enable the Commission to carry out an investigation into the alleged cartel.[79] Alternatively, in case the Commission had already started an investigation, immunity was still available if a corporation was the first corporation to submit evidence that could enable the Commission to find a cartel infringement.[80] The common denominator of both situations was that the immunity applicant must have been the first to provide the Commission with evidence that the latter did not otherwise have and that enabled it to initiate an investigation and/or prove an infringement.[81] In addition, the immunity applicant had to satisfy three cumulative criteria: (1) the applicant had to cooperate fully, continuously and expeditiously throughout the Commission's administrative procedure;[82] (2) the applicant must have immediately ended its involvement in the cartel;[83] and (3) the applicant must not have taken steps to coerce other corporations to participate in the cartel.[84]

The Commission held on to the model of awarding subsequent applicants. To qualify for a fine reduction a corporation had to provide the Commission with evidence that constituted 'significant added value' (SAV) with respect to the evidence already in the Commission's possession.[85] In assessing SAV the Commission considered the extent to which the evidence strengthened its ability to prove the infringement. The Commission also adjusted the leniency bands for reductions of the fine. The first successful subsequent leniency applicant (i.e. the second-in confessor) would benefit from a reduction of 30–50 per cent, while the third-in confessor would enjoy a reduction of 20–30 per cent. All other

[78] Jephcott, 'The European Commission's New Leniency Notice' (n. 39 above), p. 383; Albrecht, *Die Anwendung von Kronzeugenregelungen* (n. 10 above), p. 211; Schroll, G., *Der Einfluss interner und externer Faktoren auf die Effektivität der Kronzeugenprogramme der EU-Kommission und des Bundeskartellamtes* (Bern: Peter Lang, 2012), p. 68.

[79] 2002 Leniency Notice, para. 8(a).

[80] Ibid., para. 8(b).

[81] Swaak and Arp, 'A Tempting Offer' (n. 62 above), p. 10.

[82] 2002 Leniency Notice, para. 11(a).

[83] Ibid., para. 11(b).

[84] Ibid., para. 11(c).

[85] Ibid., para. 21.

subsequent leniency applicants would receive a reduction of up to 20 per cent.[86] The exact percentage within each of those leniency bands depended on the timing, the quality of the information, as well as the extent and continuity of the applicant's cooperation. The Commission also formally introduced the concept of partial immunity. This concept sets out that an applicant who discloses evidence proving that the cartel had started earlier, or ended later, or was more harmful than the Commission was previously aware of, will not be penalised with an increase in its fine that would account for the longer duration or higher gravity of the infringement. In other words, information and evidence submitted by an applicant will not be used against it.

Lastly, the Commission also amended the procedure for obtaining leniency. Conditional immunity has been offered since the 2002 Leniency Notice. An immunity applicant will now be immediately informed in writing that immunity will be granted if the conditions set out in the Leniency Notice are met.[87] The revised Leniency Notice has also introduced the possibility of making a hypothetical leniency application. A corporation can now present evidence in hypothetical terms by submitting a list describing the nature and content of the evidence it proposes to reveal at a later stage.[88]

2.5.2.2 The 2006 Leniency Notice

Despite the relative success of the 2002 Leniency Notice, the Commission acknowledged the need to further increase the effectiveness of its leniency policy.[89] In revising the 2002 Leniency Notice, the Commission retained the key elements and focused on further enhancing transparency and predictability.[90] A new key feature in that respect was the introduction of the marker system, similar to the one known from the US.

The Commission also made changes to two of the conditions for immunity. The 2006 Leniency Notice now states that the immunity applicant has to be the first corporation 'to submit information and evidence which,

[86] Ibid., para. 23(b).

[87] Ibid., para. 14.

[88] Ibid., para. 13(b).

[89] Suurnäkki, S. and Tierno Centella, M., 'Commission Adopts Revised Leniency Notice to Reward Companies That Report Hard-Core Cartels' (2007) 1 *Competition Policy Newsletter* 7, p. 7.

[90] Utton, *Cartels and Economic Collusion* (n. 44 above), p. 139; Billiet, P., 'How Lenient Is the EC Leniency Policy? A Matter of Certainty and Predictability' (2009) 30 *European Competition Law Review* 14, p. 14.

in the Commission's view, will enable it to carry out a targeted inspection in connection with the alleged cartel'.[91] The Commission explains this amendment by arguing that an immunity applicant should be in a position to provide the Commission with 'insider' knowledge on the cartel that would allow it to conduct an inspection with more specific information in terms of the type and location of the evidence sought after by the investigators.[92]

The other change relates to the immunity applicant's termination of its cartel activity. Under both previous leniency notices, a corporation must have ended its participation in the cartel by the time of its leniency application. Under the 2006 Leniency Notice, the Commission will not mandate the applicant to terminate its cartel participation if this would put the Commission's inspection at risk. If a corporation ceases its cartel activities abruptly, the other cartel members might take this as a sign that it might have blown the whistle. They might then destroy potential incriminating evidence before the Commission launches a dawn raid, and hence make it more difficult to prosecute the cartel. The new condition on an immunity applicant's cartel termination therefore safeguards the effectiveness of the Commission's enforcement activities.

The most important changes, apart from the marker system, were not in relation to the leniency programme itself, but rather changes that supported the operation of the leniency programme. First, Regulation 1/2003 entered into force in 2004 – right in between the two revisions of the leniency programme. It abolished the cumbersome notification of agreements to the Commission and freed up resources so that the Commission could focus on detecting and prosecuting hard-core cartels.[93] Regulation 1/2003 expanded the Commission's arsenal of investigative powers to include inter alia search warrants for private homes.[94] The Commission's broader inspection powers increase the risk of detection and therefore deterrence. Secondly, the

91 Emphasis added.

92 European Commission, 'Competition: Revised Leniency Notice – Frequently Asked Questions', MEMO/06/469 (7 December 2006).

93 O'Kane, *The Law of Criminal Cartels* (n. 5 above), p 14; see also European Commission, 'White Paper on Modernisation of the Rules Implementing Articles 85 and 86 of the EC Treaty', OJ C132/1 (1999); Lowe, P., 'Setting Enforcement Priorities at European and National Level Post Modernization' (Presentation at VIII Treviso Conference, Treviso, 22 May 2008). Retrieved from http://ec.europa.eu/competition/speeches/text/sp2008_17_en.pdf.

94 Council Regulation (EC) No 1/2003 of 16 December 2002 on the Implementation of Rules on Competition Laid Down in Articles 81 and 82 of the Treaty (2003), OJ L1/1, Recital 26.

Commission published the 2006 Fining Guidelines.[95] These guidelines succeeded the 1998 Fining Guidelines, which were criticised for the lack of transparency in how the Commission calculated antitrust fines. The 2006 Fining Guidelines have not only enhanced transparency but more importantly have led to significantly higher fines. While the total amount of cartel fines in the 1990s was only €615.2 million, the total amount was over €11 billion in the 2000–2009 period and over €15.8 billion in the 2010–2019 period.[96]

2.5.2.3 More Lenient Treatment under Private Enforcement

The 2006 Leniency Notice expressly states that cooperation under the Notice does not provide cartel members with any immunity from the civil law consequences of their cartel participation. Since private enforcement has become more popular in certain EU Member States, private claimants have started to seek access to the file of national competition authorities (NCAs) and the Commission through various avenues. In the Pfleiderer case,[97] the Court of Justice of the EU established a controversial balancing test, which granted access to corporate leniency statements on a case-by-case basis. Acknowledging the potentially negative repercussions on the effectiveness of leniency of this approach in particular and private actions generally, the EU's Damages Directive addresses this issue with two measures. The first measure is the categorisation of leniency-related material that can or cannot be disclosed. While corporate leniency statements enjoy absolute protection, NCAs and the Commission may disclose pre-existing information (i.e. evidence that exists independently of the proceedings of a competition authority) at any time. Documents prepared for the purpose of cartel investigations may be disclosed by court order only after an NCA or the Commission has taken a decision in the case or closed its file. The second measure is the removal of joint and several liability for the immunity recipient. While all members of the cartel are jointly and severally liable for the

[95] Guidelines on the Method of Setting Fines Imposed Pursuant to Article 23(2)(a) of Regulation No 1/2003 (2006), OJ C210.

[96] See European Commission, 'Fines Imposed (Adjusted for Court Judgments) – Period 1990–2020' (July 2021). Retrieved from https://ec.europa.eu/competition-policy/cartels/statistics_en. According to one study, there was a 107 per cent increase in the level of fines after the implementation of the 2006 Fining Guidelines: see Connor, J. and Miller, D., 'Determinants of EC Antitrust Fines for Members of Global Cartels' (6 March 2013). Retrieved from http://papers.ssrn.com/sol3/papers.cfm?abstract_id=2229358.

[97] Case C-360/09 *Pfleiderer* v. *Bundeskartellamt*, EU:C:2011:389.

entire harm caused by the cartel,[98] the immunity recipient is only liable to its direct and indirect purchasers.[99] The other injured parties may only seek redress from the immunity recipient where full compensation cannot be obtained from any of its co-conspirators.[100]

The two leniency-related measures introduced in the Damages Directive are meant to safeguard the incentives of potential leniency applicants. At the same time, access to the file can help claimants to bring more substantiated private actions, which in turn would increase the civil liability of cartel members and thus lead to an increase in deterrence. Although immunity recipients remain liable for the damages of their direct and indirect purchasers, they at least enjoy some protection from joint and several liability, provided other co-conspirators are solvent. As this benefit is only available to immunity recipients, this should have a positive effect on the race for confession.[101] At least in theory the two measures protect the effectiveness of leniency without unduly impairing claimants' right to full compensation. Whether this is true in practice remains to be seen.

2.5.3 *Evaluation*

The 2002 and 2006 Leniency Notices constituted a clear improvement of the original leniency programme. Compared to the latter the priorities have clearly shifted since the 2002 version. In hindsight, the 1996 Leniency Notice was an instrument to facilitate the investigation of detected cartels. Pursuant to Commission officials it had 'proved to be particularly effective when combined with the Commission's other investigative powers, in particular dawn raids. Nevertheless, experience of its day to day implementation has revealed a number of factors which prevented it from fully developing its potential effectiveness concerning the detection of new

98 Directive 2014/114/EU of the European Parliament and of the Council of 26 November 2014 on Certain Rules Governing Actions for Damages under National Law for Infringements of the Competition Law Provisions of the Member States and of the European Union (2014), OJ L349/1, Art. 11(1) (Damages Directive).

99 Ibid., Article 11(4)(a).

100 Ibid., Article 11(4)(b) and recital 38.

101 Cf. Centre for European Policy Studies (CEPS), Erasmus University Rotterdam (EUR) and Luiss Guido Carli (LUISS), 'Making Antitrust Damages Actions More Effective in the EU: Welfare Impact and Potential Scenarios', Report for the European Commission – Contract DG COMP/2006/A3/012 (2007), p. 524 Retrieved from http://ec.europa.eu/competition/antitrust/actionsdamages/files_white_paper/impact_study.pdf.

cartels and the collection of the evidence required for the adoption of final decisions'.[102]

The 2002 Leniency Notice was therefore designed to become an instrument to uncover cartels and subsequently initiate investigations.[103] This revised leniency programme rebalanced the public policy interest of detecting cartels on the one hand, and sanctioning cartel members on the other hand, recognising that the uncovering of a larger number of cartels is the main objective of a leniency programme.[104] The Commission had realised that immunity must be guaranteed from the outset in clear and achievable circumstances, subject to as little discretion as possible. Apart from introducing the marker system, which enhances predictability for potential applicants, the 2006 Leniency Notice brought only minor changes compared to its predecessor. Probably more noteworthy in terms of the pre-requisites for success of a leniency programme were the legislative changes that led to the risk of higher corporate fines and higher likelihood of detection. Furthermore, the incentive for immunity has become greater than ever. The latest substantive changes introduced by the Damages Directive were made to protect that incentive.

According to Wils, the introduction of the leniency programme has led to a significant increase in the number of cartels detected and punished by the Commission. In comparing the statistics for the 1996–2000 and the 2001–2005 periods, he argues that the number of cartel decisions tripled following the introduction of the leniency programme.[105] However, as argued above, this significant increase is largely attributable to the 2002 Leniency Notice rather than the 1996 version. This tripling of the number of cartel decisions has also substantially enhanced the level of deterrence.[106] In addition, Wils shows that between 1996 and 2010 the EU leniency programme has contributed to a growing number of cartels having broken down earlier than they would have in the absence of the leniency

[102] Arbault and Peiró, 'The Commission's New Notice' (n. 70 above), p. 17. See also Van Barlingen, B., 'The European Commission's 2002 Leniency Notice after One Year of Operation' (2003) Summer (2) *Competition Policy Newsletter* 16, p. 17.

[103] Hölzel, *Kronzeugenregelungen im Europäischen Wettbewerbsrecht* (n. 59 above), p. 113; Schroll, *Der Einfluss interner und externer Faktoren* (n. 78 above), pp. 70–71.

[104] Sandhu, J. S., 'The European Commission's Leniency Policy: A Success?' (2007) 28(3) *ECLR* 148, p. 149.

[105] Wils, W. P. J., 'The Use of Leniency in EU Cartel Enforcement: An Assessment after Twenty Years' (2016) 39 *World Competition* 327, p. 338.

[106] Ibid.

programme.[107] In the 1996–2000 period only one cartel broke down early, while this figure rose to seven in the 2001–2005 period, and a record of fifteen cartels in the 2006–2010 period.[108] Finally, Wils also shows that the number of cartel decisions involving immunity has increased from 10 per cent (one out of ten) in the 1996–2000 period to over 61 per cent (twenty out of thirty-three) in the 2001–2005 period, 81 per cent (twenty-five out of thirty-one) in the 2006–2010 period and 91 per cent (twenty-one out of twenty-three) in the 2011–2015 period.[109] In the 2016–2020 period the figure was 100 per cent (sixteen out of sixteen).[110] These statistics show that the EU leniency programme has clearly become a crucial instrument in the Commission's enforcement arsenal. At the same time, some scholars have warned about 'leniency inflation', 'a trend towards possibly excessive use of leniency as a substitute for investigative effort'.[111]

2.6 Similarities and Differences between the US and EU Leniency Programmes

A number of similarities and differences can be identified in comparing the development of and experience with the leniency programmes of the Antitrust Division and the European Commission. This chapter limits itself to the most important similarities and differences.

2.6.1 Similarities

The similarities in the development of the US and EU leniency programmes can mainly be traced back to the three pre-requisites for

[107] Wils does so by counting the number of Commission decisions in cases in which the cartel was detected exclusively through leniency and the cartel was still ongoing at the time of the first leniency application (ibid.). However, it is important to note that it is unknown how effective leniency programmes have been in inducing cartels to collapse, let alone deterring them from forming in the first place; see Harrington, J., 'Optimal Corporate Leniency Programs; (2008) 56 *Journal of Industrial Economics* 215, p. 238.

[108] Wils, 'The Use of Leniency in EU Cartel Enforcement' (n. 105 above), p. 338.

[109] Ibid., p. 335.

[110] This figure excludes re-adopted decisions and is calculated based on the information on the Commission cartel website: https://ec.europa.eu/competition/cartels/cases/cases.html.

[111] See Marvão, C. and Spagnolo, G., 'Leniency Inflation, Cartel Damages and Criminalization' (29 June 2021), p. 8. Retrieved from https://ssrn.com/abstract=3180685. Leniency inflation is not unique to the EU leniency programme. Van Uytsel suggests that a similar problem exists in Japan: see Van Uytsel, S., 'Anti-Cartel Enforcement in Japan: Does Leniency Make the Difference?' in Beaton-Wells and Tran, *Anti-Cartel Enforcement in a Contemporary Age* (n. 4 above), p. 81.

effectiveness. First, both the 1993 Leniency Policy and the 2002 Leniency Notice significantly enhanced the transparency and predictability in relation to obtaining leniency. Under the original leniency programmes of both jurisdictions, the main condition for the award of immunity was that the first leniency applicant came forward before any investigation had begun. And even then, the respective competition authorities retained considerable discretion. Under the revised versions of those leniency programmes, immunity is automatically awarded when at the time of the application no investigation into the cartel activity in question has been launched already. In addition, immunity is now also available after an investigation has begun.

Secondly, the revisions of the leniency programmes in both jurisdictions were supported by a significant upward trend in the level of sanctions. In the US, it was the Antitrust Amendments Act of 1990, shortly before the revision of the Antitrust Division's leniency policy in 1993, that significantly raised the level of sanctions compared to the previous penalty structure.[112] Although the level was topped once more when Congress passed the ACPERA in 2004, judging from the penalties imposed and the number of leniency applications the 1990 amendment clearly had a positive impact on the effectiveness of the US leniency policy. In the case of the EU, it was primarily the 2006 Fining Guidelines, which were published around the same time as the 2006 Leniency Notice, that led to higher fines.

Thirdly, the respective revisions were also supported by more intrusive investigative tools. Around the time when the 1993 and 2006 revisions were made, both competition authorities had at their disposal tools and resources that were not available when the original leniency programmes were in operation.

2.6.2 *Differences*

Barring criminal antitrust enforcement, which does not exist at the EU level,[113] the most significant differences between the US and EU leniency policies pertain to the treatment of subsequent leniency applicants and the lenient treatment in relation to private actions for damages.

112 Ghoshal, V. and Sokol, D. D., 'The Evolution of U.S. Cartel Enforcement' (2014) 57 *Journal of Law & Economics* S51, p. S57.

113 Criminal enforcement exists under the national competition law of some EU Member States.

2.6.2.1 Leniency for Subsequent Applicants

At first sight, the treatment of subsequent leniency applicants appears to be the starkest difference between the US and EU leniency programmes. The US leniency programme formally applies a 'winner-takes-all' approach – only the first confessor can receive immunity and all subsequent leniency applicants go away empty-handed. The EU leniency programme, on the other hand, grants leniency to more than one confessor – only the first confessor will be awarded immunity, but all subsequent applicants can at least qualify for a fine reduction. The degree of the fine reduction depends on the applicant's rank in the race for leniency and its level of cooperation. While the US 1993 Leniency Policy does not formally reward subsequent applicants, it may be argued that plea bargaining arrangements between latecomers and the Antitrust Division can to some extent function as a 'consolation prize'.[114] Yet, unlike under a leniency programme, where fine reductions are expressly provided for in the Leniency Notice, plea bargains are entirely at the discretion of the prosecutor and therefore clouded in more legal uncertainty. The other 'consolation prize' for subsequent applicants, as mentioned above, is leniency plus. Considering plea bargains and leniency plus, the difference in the treatment of subsequent leniency applicants between the US and EU leniency programmes is not quite as significant in practice.

As it only takes one confessor to break up a cartel, it is not necessary to give out more leniency than to just one cartel member. Under this leniency model the penalty level is not unnecessarily reduced.[115] This model also comes closer to the traditional prisoner's dilemma. Since the competition authority only rewards one cartel member, more deterrence is instigated and the race for confession leads to faster break-ups of cartels. Nonetheless, the leniency model chosen by the EU is not entirely unwarranted. A justification to reward at least the second confessor is that its statement can be used to corroborate the first confessor's testimony. A cartel may therefore be prosecuted with more certainty and more rapidly. Considering the enormous harm caused by hard-core cartels and the intricacy of their detection with traditional methods, the granting of immunity for the first applicant and a fine reduction for one subsequent

[114] O'Brien, 'Leadership of Leniency' (n. 15 above), pp. 28–29.

[115] Albrecht, *Die Anwendung von Kronzeugenregelungen* (n. 10 above), pp. 137–39; *see* Wils, 'Leniency in Antitrust Enforcement' (n. 9 above), p. 46.

applicant appears to be justified.[116] However, offering leniency to any subsequent applicant after the second confessor leads to further reductions of the penalty level and is more difficult to justify. In general, a penalty reduction only seems to be acceptable if a leniency applicant's cooperation advances an ongoing investigation substantially.

2.6.2.2 Leniency and Private Enforcement

A common problem that arose in both jurisdictions after the latest revision of the respective leniency programmes was the concern that potential leniency applicants would be discouraged by the potential exposure to civil liability. In the US this concern was alleviated by the 2004 ACPERA, and in the EU it was the 2015 Damages Directive. Under both leniency programmes immunity recipients remain liable for the specific cartel damage that they caused as a result of their cartel activity but are generally shielded from joint and several liability. While the concept is very similar, the incentives under the US leniency policy are far greater than under the EU equivalent. In the US, the damages the immunity recipient would be liable for are de-trebled, whereas all other co-conspirators remain liable for treble damages. Thus, the relative incentive under private enforcement is three times higher in the US. This relative incentive might be even greater considering that private actions, particularly class actions, are much more common in the US than in the EU. Possibly the more striking difference between the US and EU is that immunity recipients in the US, pursuant to the de-trebling provision of the ACPERA, are required to cooperate with private claimants. From a retributive justice perspective, the justification for protecting immunity recipients from private actions is therefore larger compared to the EU measure.[117]

2.7 Conclusion

The operation and success of a leniency programme are premised on a carrot-and-stick approach that is expected to lead to a race for confession, as the highest and sometimes only reward – depending on the design of the leniency programme – is for the first cartel member to defect and cooperate with the authorities. The main pre-requisites to instigate this race for

[116] Hölzel, *Kronzeugenregelungen im Europäischen Wettbewerbsrecht* (n. 59 above); Schroll, *Der Einfluss interner und externer Faktoren* (n. 78 above), p. 37.

[117] Balasingham, B., *The EU Leniency Policy: Reconciling Effectiveness and Fairness* (Alphen aan de Rijn: Kluwer Law International, 2017), pp. 181–87.

confession are the threat of severe sanctions if a cartel is caught, a high risk of detection of a cartel, and a high degree of transparency and predictability in relation to leniency. When the Antitrust Division and the European Commission revised their original, unsuccessful leniency programmes they did so with those pre-requisites in mind, which were developed in hindsight based on the experience of the unsuccessful predecessors. Firstly, in terms of predictability, both the 1993 Corporate Leniency Policy and the 2002/2006 Leniency Notices have made the award of immunity automatic. An applicant will qualify for immunity if it comes forward before any investigation into the cartel has started. Immunity is now also available after an investigation has been launched, as long as the Antitrust Division has not yet received information about the cartel from any other source, or if the applicant is the first to submit evidence that could enable the European Commission to find a cartel infringement. Predictability under both leniency programmes has also been enhanced by setting out the conditions for leniency more clearly and by introducing a marker system (in the EU since the 2006 Leniency Notice). Secondly, cartel penalties under both systems have become much more severe over time and the incentives have, therefore, become more appealing. Immunity recipients in the US and EU may also qualify for more lenient treatment in relation to private actions for damages. Deterrence under both revised leniency programmes has also been raised, as the likelihood of detection has been enhanced by investigative tools that were not available when the original leniency programmes were in force. A crucial incentive introduced under the 1993 Corporate Leniency Policy is the immunity from criminal prosecution for corporate actors. Apart from the absence of immunity from criminal prosecution for corporate actors under the EU leniency programme, the biggest difference between the two programmes is that the benefits in relation to US private enforcement are higher and immunity recipients in the US must cooperate with private claimants in order to qualify for those benefits.

3

International Guidelines and Best Practices on Leniency Programmes

Decontextualised Summaries of Local Practices

STEVEN VAN UYTSEL

3.1 Introduction

The development of leniency programmes in competition law has gained significant impetus from the experiments in the United States (US) and the European Union (EU).[1] The US has shown that the enforcement of anti-cartel provisions may require a leniency programme.[2] The EU has further shown how a leniency programme can be conceptualised in a different format than that developed by the US. More specifically, the EU showed that a leniency programme should not be restricted to the first applicant. Subsequent applicants could also be decisive in mapping out the full extent of the illegal cartel activity.[3] The more cartels were revealed through leniency programmes, the more this new enforcement tool attracted the interest of other countries and international organisations.

Several international organisations decided to research the conceptualisation and use of leniency programmes. This research led to international guidelines and best practices (international guidelines). The Organisation for Economic Co-operation and Development (OECD) issued its first

[1] The international literature mainly discusses the leniency programmes of the US and the EU, despite the fact that Canada was earlier in its adoption of a leniency programme and that the Republic of Korea (Korea) enacted its first leniency programme only one year after the EU. The US implemented the first leniency programme in 1978 and updated it in 1993. Canada followed in 1995. The EU adopted its first leniency programme in 1996. Korea followed one year later, when a leniency programme became part of its Monopoly Regulation and Fair Trade Act (MRFTA). See O'Brien, A., 'Leadership of Leniency', in Beaton-Wells, C. and Tran, C. (eds.), *Anti-Cartel Enforcement in A Contemporary Age: Leniency Religion* (Cambridge, UK: Cambridge University Press, 2015), 17, p. 19.

[2] Balasingham, Chapter 2 this volume.

[3] Ibid.

report on leniency in 2002, which included some abstractly formulated guidelines in its summary.[4] The International Competition Network (ICN) finalised its first research on leniency programmes in 2009, when its best practices on leniency programmes were published.[5] These best practices were updated in 2014.[6] Other documents with useful information to write leniency programmes have supplemented the best practices.[7] Within the context of developing countries, the United Nations Conference on Trade and Development (UNCTAD) gave its view on leniency programmes in 2016.[8] Geographically more limited, but nevertheless important for discussions on Asia, the Association of Southeast Asian Nations (ASEAN) has included elements on leniency programmes in its 2010 document giving guidance to its Member States on how to write a comprehensive competition law.[9]

This chapter will give an overview of the international guidelines developed by OECD, ICN, UNCTAD and ASEAN. In doing so, it will show that nearly all the international guidelines represent decontextualised experiences of various domestically applied leniency programmes. This is manifested in different ways. First, the conceptualisation has been done through deducting common elements from locally applied leniency programmes. Second, no explanation has been added on why these common

[4] OECD, 'Fighting Hard Core Cartels: Harm, Effective Sanctions and Leniency Programmes' (2002). Retrieved from www.oecd.org/competition/cartels/1841891.pdf (OECD Report).

[5] ICN, 'Anti-Cartel Enforcement Manual' (2009) (on file with the author).

[6] ICN, 'Anti-Cartel Enforcement Manual' (2014). Retrieved from www.internationalcompetitionnetwork.org/wp-content/uploads/2018/05/CWG_ACEMLeniency.pdf (ICN Leniency Guidelines).

[7] ICN, 'Checklist for Efficient and Effective Leniency Programmes' (2017). Retrieved from www.internationalcompetitionnetwork.org/wp-content/uploads/2018/09/CWG_LeniencyChecklist.pdf (ICN Checklist); ICN, 'Good Practices for Incentivising Leniency Applications' (2019). Retrieved from www.internationalcompetitionnetwork.org/wp-content/uploads/2018/09/CWG_LeniencyChecklist.pdf (ICN Practices on Incentivising Leniency); ICN, 'Guidance on Enhancing Cross-Border Leniency Cooperation' (2020). Retrieved from www.internationalcompetitionnetwork.org/wp-content/uploads/2020/07/CWG-Leniency-Coordination-Guidance.pdf (ICN Cross-Border Leniency Guideline).

[8] Brusick, P., 'Competition Guidelines: Leniency Programmes' (2016). Retrieved from https://unctadmena.org/wp-content/uploads/2018/12/Competition-Guidelines_Leniency-Programmes_EN.pdf (UNCTAD Leniency Guidelines).

[9] ASEAN, *ASEAN Regional Guidelines on Competition Policy* (Jakarta: ASEAN Secretariat, 2010). Retrieved from www.asean.org/wp-content/uploads/images/2012/publications/ASEAN%20Regional%20Guidelines%20on%20Competition%20Policy.pdf (ASEAN Regional Guidelines).

elements have been incorporated. Third, exceptional conceptualisations are barely included, and if they are, are not further explained. Fourth, there is a bias towards the earliest adopted leniency programmes, meaning either the one from the US or that from the EU.

Considering the fact that the international guidelines aim to assist other countries in developing their respective leniency programmes, the above-mentioned characteristics may result in convergence. However, the convergence may only be partial. Due to decontextualisation, convergence is likely to happen only on the level of the common elements. Thus, the international guidelines leave room for divergence in the details, thus still allowing for unique characteristics in building a leniency programme.

This chapter is structured as follows. Section 3.2 will highlight the international organisations that are especially influential in relation to the conceptualisation of leniency programmes. This section will also list the international guidelines that were developed by these organisations. In Section 3.3, it will be indicated that the international guidelines share their understanding of what a leniency programme is. Further, this section will also highlight what the international guidelines consider the pre-requisites for an effective leniency programme. The content of the international guidelines will be detailed in Section 3.4. In Section 3.5, I will address the likely consequences of decontextualised international guidelines. The emphasis will be on the extent to which convergence can be achieved by the international guidelines. Section 3.6 will conclude that the international guidelines could form the basis for conceptualising a leniency programme, but to understand the consequences of some choices, a detailed study of domestic experiences will be required.

3.2 International Organisations Summarising Locally Created Leniency Programmes

3.2.1 The OECD and Leniency Programmes

The OECD has been active in the field of competition law since 1961, when the Committee of Experts on Restrictive Business Practices was established.[10] This Committee of Experts, now called the Committee on

[10] Zisler, A, 'The Work of the OECD Committee of Experts on Restrictive Business Practices' (1974) 19 *Antitrust Bulletin* 289, p. 289. The OECD itself was founded in 1960 as the successor to the Organisation for European Economic Cooperation: Kennedy, K. C., *Competition Law and the World Trade Organisation: The Limits of Multilateralism* (London: Sweet & Maxwell, 2001), p. 96.

Competition Law and Policy (Competition Committee),[11] was to 'protect and promote competition as an organising principle of modern economies, based on the knowledge that vigorous market competition boosts growth and employment and makes economies more flexible and innovative'.[12] The Competition Committee adopts various methods, often complementary, to achieve this goal. The practices of national competition laws will be monitored to find new developments.[13] Appropriate competition law and policy issues will be subjected to a closer examination.[14] To enhance competition law enforcement, the Competition Committee will also issue best practice, non-binding guidelines and recommendations.[15]

Leniency-related recommendations have not yet been issued by the OECD,[16] but a study was undertaken around 2000. The results of this study were published in 'Fighting Hard Core Cartels: Harm, Effective Sanctions and Leniency Programmes' (OECD Report).[17] This report maps out the difficulties an enforcement agency experiences in detecting and punishing cartels. A substantial part of the OECD Report, though, is focused on reviewing the main characteristics of existing leniency programmes and so providing a type of international guidelines.[18] Since the format is one of a report, abstract guidelines are barely formulated. Abstractly formulated guidelines are only to be found in the Executive Summary.[19] Each of these guidelines is further elaborated in the report itself with reference to examples of various countries. In this sense, the OECD Report is the least decontextualised document among the international guidelines discussed in this chapter.

[11] Kennedy, *Competition Law and the World Trade Organisation* (n. 10 above), p. 96.

[12] OECD, 'Resolution of the Council Concerning the Committee of Experts on Restrictive Business Practices and Amending Its Name and Terms of Reference', C(87)138(Final) (2020), Article A, I, 1. Retrieved from https://oecdgroups.oecd.org/Bodies/ShowBodyView.aspx?BodyID=1673&Lang=en.

[13] Kennedy, *Competition Law and the World Trade Organisation* (n. 10 above), p. 96.

[14] Ibid., p. 96.

[15] Ibid., p. 106.

[16] See the list of recommendations in OECD, 'Recommendations and Best Practices on Competition Law and Policy'. Retrieved from www.oecd.org/daf/competition/recommendations.htm.

[17] OECD Report.

[18] Ibid., pp. 7–30.

[19] Ibid., pp. 7–10.

The OECD Report has been supplemented with several Roundtable Best Practices.[20] The topics covered were leniency for subsequent applicants,[21] the use of the marker[22] and challenges of leniency programmes.[23] Each of these topics is discussed in a series of documents, ranging from a Note by the Secretariat to an Executive Summary, Detailed Summary of the Discussion, and Contributions by the Member States. The Executive Summary most closely resembles the abstractly formulated guidelines. Context is provided in the Note by the Secretariat, while further explanations can be consulted in the Contributions by Member States. The latter also mean that the discussion on these topics is not decontextualised.

3.2.2 *The ICN and Leniency Programmes*

The ICN has grown out of a recommendation of the US's International Competition Policy Advisory Committee (ICPAC) that was established to investigate 'new tools, tasks and concepts that will be needed to address the competition issues that are just arising on the horizon of the global economy'.[24] The recommendation of ICPAC was to establish a Global Competition Initiative (GCI) that could act as a forum 'for sharing views and experiences, for close cooperation, and for exploration of common issues that could lead to convergence or harmonization'.[25] Inspired by the proposal of setting up a GCI, Joel Klein called for an initiative at the global level, something that may eventually pave the way for multilateralism within the field of competition law.[26] Once it became clear that enough enforcement authorities would back this initiative, the Fordham

20 OECD, 'Best Practice Roundtables on Competition Policy' (2021). Retrieved from www.oecd.org/daf/competition/roundtables.htm.

21 OECD, 'Policy Roundtables: Leniency for Subsequent Applicants' (2012). Retrieved from www.oecd.org/daf/competition/Leniencyforsubsequentapplicants2012.pdf (OECD Subsequent Applicants).

22 OECD, 'Competition and the Use of Markers in Leniency Programmes' (2014). Retrieved from www.oecd.org/daf/competition/markers-in-leniency-programmes.htm (OECD Markers).

23 OECD, 'Challenges and Co-ordination of Leniency Programmes' (2018). Retrieved from www.oecd.org/daf/competition/challenges-and-coordination-of-leniency-programmes.htm (OECD Challenges of Leniency Programmes).

24 See Fox, E., 'Linked-In: Antitrust and the Virtues of a Virtual Network', in Lugard, P. (ed.), *The International Competition Network at Ten: Origins, Accomplishments and Aspirations* (Antwerp: Intersentia, 2011), 105, p. 113.

25 Ibid., p. 113.

26 Ibid., p. 114.

International Antitrust Conference of 2001 was used to launch it.[27] The name given to the initiative was the International Competition Network.

From its establishment, the ICN has aimed at 'addressing antitrust enforcement and policy issues of common interest and formulat[ing] proposals for procedural and substantive convergence through a result-orientated agenda and structure'.[28] The idea of convergence has been complemented with the encouragement of 'the dissemination of antitrust experiences and best practices'[29] and promoting the 'advocacy role of the antitrust agencies'.[30] This initial aim has been restated in the Operational Framework that the Steering Committee formulated in 2012.[31] The ICN's website incorporates a short restatement of this mission statement. In what it calls its mission statement at the top of its website, the ICN advocates 'the adoption of superior standards and procedures in competition policy around the world, formulat[ing] proposals for procedural and substantive convergence, and seek[ing] to facilitate effective international cooperation to the benefit of member agencies, consumers and economies worldwide'.[32]

One of the areas in which the ICN performed this role was anti-cartel enforcement. This task was given to the Cartel Working Group. It was decided in 2004 in Sydney that the Cartel Working Group should shed light on the leniency programme as an instrument to enforce anti-cartel provisions and formulate best practices as to what elements are important for an effective leniency programme. The Cartel Working Group finalised its first analysis in 2009 and issued 'Drafting and Implementing an Effective Leniency Policy' as part of the Anti-Cartel Enforcement Manual.[33] This document was updated in 2014 (ICN Leniency Guidelines).[34]

[27] Van Uytsel, S., 'The International Competition Network, Its Leniency Best Practice and Legitimacy: An Argument for Introducing a Review System', in Fenwick, M., Van Uytsel, S. and Wrbka, S. (eds.), *Networked Governance and the Law* (Singapore: Springer, 2014), 185, p. 190.

[28] ICN, 'ICN's Vision for Its Second Decade' (2011), p. 1. Retrieved from www.internationalcompetitionnetwork.org/wp-content/uploads/2018/07/ICN2dDecade2011.pdf.

[29] Ibid.

[30] Ibid.

[31] Ibid.

[32] ICN, 'About the ICN' (2018). Retrieved from www.internationalcompetitionnetwork.org/about. See also Maher, I. and Papadopoulos, A., 'Competition Agency Networks around the World', in Ezrachi, A. (ed.), *Research Handbook on International Competition Law* (Cheltenham: Edward Elgar, 2012), 60, p. 74.

[33] ICN, 'Anti-Cartel Enforcement Manual' (2009) (on file with the author).

[34] ICN Leniency Guidelines.

Other documents complemented the ICN Leniency Guidelines, one with a focus on a quick reference tool for conceptualising leniency programmes,[35] another with an emphasis on how to deal with cross-border leniency applications,[36] and still another explaining how to create an appropriate and effective incentive structure.[37]

3.2.3 UNCTAD and Leniency Programmes

UNCTAD, an intergovernmental body established in 1964,[38] aims at providing 'support [to] developing countries to access the benefits of a globalised economy more fairly and effectively'.[39] It entered the field of competition law in 1980.[40] UNCTAD did so by organising a conference on restrictive business practices, which yielded the document 'Set of Multilaterally Agreed Equitable Principles and Rules for the Control of Restrictive Business Practices' (UNCTAD Principles).[41] The UNCTAD Principles were guidelines for developing countries to create protective measures against the restrictive business practices of multinational firms.[42] These Principles and Rules were reviewed in 1985, 1990, 1995, 2000 and 2005. UNCTAD also adopted a Model Law on Competition. In addition, UNCTAD offers technical cooperation and training activities.[43]

In its attempt to review all aspects of the Principles and Rules, the UNCTAD Secretariat issued a note on how to use leniency programmes as an enforcement tool against hard-core cartels in developing countries.[44] However, a more systematic approach followed in 2016, when, in the framework of training sessions for the Sweden-sponsored Middle

[35] ICN Checklist.

[36] ICN Cross-Border Leniency Guideline.

[37] ICN Practices on Incentivising Leniency.

[38] UNCTAD, 'About UNCTAD: History' (2021). Retrieved from https://unctad.org/about/history.

[39] UNCTAD, 'About UNCTAD' (2021). Retrieved from https://unctad.org/about.

[40] Dabbah, M. M., *International and Comparative Competition Law* (Oxford: Oxford University Press, 2010), p. 144.

[41] 'Set of Multilaterally Agreed Equitable Principles and Rules for the Control of Restrictive Business Practices', UN Doc. TD/RBP/CONF/10 (22 April 1980).

[42] Kennedy, *Competition Law and the World Trade Organisation* (n. 10 above), p. 118.

[43] Dabbah, *International and Comparative Competition Law* (n. 40 above), p. 148.

[44] UNCTAD, 'Sixth United Nations Conference to Review All Aspect of the Set of Multilaterally Agreed Equitable Principles and Rules for the Control of Restrictive Business Practices' (2010). Retrieved from https://unctad.org/meeting/sixth-united-nations-conference-review-all-aspect-set-multilaterally-agreed-equitable.

East and North Africa (MENA) Programme,[45] UNCTAD published 'Competition Guidelines: Leniency Programmes' (UNCTAD Leniency Guidelines).[46] The recipients of the MENA Programme were countries in the MENA region,[47] but the information in the UNCTAD Leniency Guidelines is of a general nature, so that it can be a useful document for other countries, especially developing countries.

3.2.4 ASEAN and Leniency Programmes

ASEAN, established in 1967, is a latecomer in the field of competition law. It was initially established to 'prevent conflicts in the region, build mutual confidence, and promote regional stability and security so as to lay the regional foundation for the pursuit of economic development'.[48] The focus on economic cooperation only took off about a decade after its establishment.[49] When it became apparent that China and India were gradually attracting more investment, ASEAN began to think about deeper economic integration.[50] The vision for deeper economic integration was laid down in the Declaration of ASEAN Concord II made in Bali in 2003 (Bali Declaration). The main message of the Bali Declaration was to establish the ASEAN Economic Community (AEC). That the Bali Declaration was different to any of the previous declarations could be deduced from the fact that the High Level Task Force had also elaborated recommendations for its implementation.

The original idea was to build the AEC by 2020, but the date was advanced to 2015.[51] This occurred during the 13th ASEAN Summit in

[45] UNCTAD, 'About UNCTAD-MENA' (2018). Retrieved from https://unctadmena.org/about. The 'UNCTAD MENA programme was launched in 2015, aims to boost regional economic integration, among other topics, by strengthening markets through improved competition and consumer protection policies in the Middle East and North Africa region'.

[46] The guidelines were written by Brusick in his capacity as UNCTAD-MENA expert.

[47] UNCTAD, 'UNCTAD MENA Programme 1st Annual Review Meeting' (2017). Retrieved from http://unctad.org/en/pages/MeetingDetails.aspx?meetingid=1386.

[48] Porananond, P., *Competition Law in the ASEAN Countries: Regional Law and National Systems* (The Hague: Wolters Kluwer, 2018), p. 3; Wanandi, Y., 'ASEAN's Past and the Challenges Ahead: Aspects of Politics and Security', in Tay, S. S. C., Estanislao, J. P. and Soesastro H. (eds.), *Reinventing ASEAN* (Singapore: ISEAS, 2001), 25, p. 25.

[49] The ASEAN Summit of heads of state in 1976 was the start of closer economic cooperation. In 1977, the Preferential Trading Arrangement was adopted. Eventually in 1992, the ASEAN Free Trade Area was adopted. The ASEAN Framework Agreement on Services followed in 1995 and the agreement on the ASEAN Investment Area in 1998.

[50] Pelkmans, J., *The ASEAN Economic Community: A Conceptual Approach* (Cambridge, UK: Cambridge University Press, 2016), pp. 12, 63 and 191.

[51] In 2007, ASEAN settled on its vision for 2015: the ASEAN Economic Community.

Singapore in 2007, when the ASEAN Charter was signed. This Charter serves as the legal and institutional framework as well as the constitution for the AEC. The AEC is premised on a single market 'via a free flow of goods, service, foreign direct investment, skilled labor, and a freer flow of capital'.[52]

Before all ASEAN Member States had even adopted a competition law, ASEAN established the ASEAN Expert Group on Competition (Expert Group) in 2007. The Expert Group is an official body of ASEAN composed of representatives from the competition enforcement authorities or other relevant bodies within the governments of ASEAN Member States. To facilitate the other Member States in their process of enacting a competition law, the Expert Group released the ASEAN Regional Guidelines on Competition Policy (ASEAN Regional Guidelines) in 2010.[53] The Expert Group worked on these Regional Guidelines for a period of two years and drew inspiration from the experience of some of the Member States and other mature competition law regimes.[54] The Regional Guidelines are a guidebook for writing a competition law. The Regional Guidelines address and detail the possible goals of competition law, the scope of competition law, the institutional structure and its enforcement powers.[55] The leniency programme was included in the latter part.

3.2.5 *Decontextualised Summaries of Local Leniency Programmes*

The work of the OECD, ICN, UNCTAD and ASEAN on leniency programmes followed the experiments of several countries with this new enforcement tool.

Some of the international guidelines explicitly indicate which local leniency programmes constitute their basis. The OECD Report is a compilation of the practices originating in the US, the EU, Canada, the United

52 Chia, S. Y., 'The ASEAN Economic Community: Progress, Challenges, and Prospects' (ADBI Working Paper 440, 2013), p. 4. Retrieved from www.adb.org/publications/asean-economic-community-progress-challenges-and-prospects.

53 Ong, B., 'Competition Law and Policy in the ASEAN Region: Origins, Objectives and Opportunities', in Ong, B. (ed.), *The Regionalisation of Competition Law and Policy within the ASEAN Economic Community* (Cambridge, UK: Cambridge University Press, 2019), 1, pp. 8–9. For the guidelines, see ASEAN Regional Guidelines.

54 Ong, 'Competition Law and Policy in the ASEAN Region' (n. 53 above), p. 9; Porananond, *Competition Law in the ASEAN Countries* (n. 48 above), p. 67.

55 ASEAN Regional Guidelines, pp. 3–44.

Kingdom, Korea and Italy.[56] The guidelines in the OECD Executive Summaries on subsequent applicants and challenges to the leniency programme are excerpted from the contributions of several Member States.[57] The OECD Note by the Secretariat on markers is drawn from scholarly writings.[58] The UNCTAD Guidelines are written by an expert, Philippe Brusick. His bibliography shows that inspiration was derived from the leniency programmes of Austria, France, the US, and the EU.[59] In relation to the latter, Brusick states that he has also been using the European Competition Network's Model Leniency Programme as revised in 2012.

Other international guidelines do not make any explicit reference to their sources. This is the case with the ICN Leniency Guidelines and the ASEAN Regional Guidelines. In case of the ICN, it could be said that it is not necessary to give any reference. Theoretically, the information was drawn from all Member States through a process of learning from diversity. However, it should not be neglected that well-established enforcement agencies have been more vocal, due to which their experiences have been given more weight.[60] In more recent documents on leniency, the ICN has chosen to reveal the sources of its information. The origin of the ASEAN Regional Guidelines is also not explicitly mentioned in the document. However, large parts of the Regional Guidelines are based upon the competition law and practice of the EU. The leniency programme is no exception to this.[61]

The broad approach to locally developed leniency programmes by the international organisations is similar. OECD, ICN, UNCTAD and ASEAN look at the common elements of the leniency programmes they use as their sources. These elements are eligibility, incentive structure

[56] More specifically, the following documents were used: the US 1993 Corporate Leniency Policy (1993 Leniency Policy), the US 1994 Individual Leniency Policy, the European Commission Notice on the non-imposition or reduction of fines in cartel cases of 1996, the Canadian Immunity Program under the Competition Act of 2000, the UK Office of Fair Trading guidance as to the appropriate amount of a penalty (both the draft version of 1999 and the adopted version of 2000), the Korean Monopoly Regulation and Fair Trade Act as changed in 1997, and the Italian practice of granting lenient treatment without a formal policy. See OECD Report, pp. 12–14.

[57] OECD Subsequent Applicants, pp. 21–164; OECD Challenges of Leniency Programmes.

[58] OECD Marker, pp. 30–32.

[59] UNCTAD Leniency Guidelines, p. 17.

[60] Van Uytsel, 'The International Competition Network' (n. 27 above), p. 215.

[61] Van Uytsel, S., 'Adopting Competition Law in Asia: An Increasingly Complex Reality', in Van Uytsel, S., Hayashi, S. and Haley, J. (eds.), *Research Handbook on Asian Competition Law* (Cheltenham: Edward Elgar, 2020), 2, p. 22.

for reporting, conditions to receive leniency, procedure and confidentiality. For each of these elements, the international organisations summarise the main points and leave out the details. Whereas this is done in a well-structured manner in the guidelines of the OECD, UNCTAD and ASEAN, the structuring of the summary of the main points in the ICN Leniency Guidelines is more random. Some of the international guidelines go further than summarising the main characteristics. The intersection between leniency and private enforcement is discussed by OECD, ICN and UNCTAD. The ICN also provides information on the intersection between leniency and sector regulators.

The summaries of OECD, ICN and UNCTAD are sometimes linked to the sources from which they draw their inspiration. This kind of information is increasingly available in more recent documents from OECD and ICN. ASEAN does even not provide this kind of information. This means that, in principle, there is no context explaining either why a specific country has conceptualised its leniency programme the way it has done or what kind of theoretical foundations are underlying the inclusion of some concepts. Equally, when a guideline indicates that certain elements do not work well in a leniency programme, no clarification is added on the reason. The absence of clarifying information qualifies the international guidelines as decontextualised. The sole sporadic reference to the source of the inspiration for formulating the international guidelines does not abrogate this qualification.

Before analysing how decontextualisation impacts convergence, the different guidelines of OECD, ICN, UNCTAD and ASEAN will be highlighted.

3.3 A Common Understanding on Leniency Programmes and Their Pre-requisites

3.3.1 *Leniency Programmes Defined or Described*

Of all the international guidelines discussed in this chapter, there is only one that defines a leniency programme. The ICN Leniency Guidelines define a leniency programme as 'a system of partial or total exoneration from the penalties that would otherwise be applicable to a cartel participant in return for reporting its cartel membership and supplying information or evidence related to the cartel'.[62] All other ICN documents concur

[62] ICN Leniency Guidelines, p. 4.

with this definition.[63] None of the other international guidelines provides this kind of succinct definition of a leniency programme. The OECD Report,[64] the UNCTAD Leniency Programme[65] and the ASEAN Regional Guidelines[66] merely give a description of what a leniency programme could be. The message, however, is similar to what can be found in the definition provided by the ICN.

The OECD Report adds a specific section in relation to terminology.[67] The OECD Report notes that the literature uses two different terms: leniency and amnesty programmes. Leniency programmes include 'all programs that provide for any reduction in sanction in exchange for information and co-operation'.[68] The reduction could be partial or complete reduction of the sanction. In case the programme promises no penalty, thus complete reduction of the sanction, it is possible to use the term amnesty programme.[69]

63 ICN Checklist, p. 1, n. 1; ICN Practices on Incentivising Leniency, p. 5, n. 1; ICN Cross-Border Leniency Guideline, p. 3, n. 1.

64 OECD Report, p. 11. A leniency programme is understood to 'encourage violators to tell … secrets, to confess and implicate their co-conspirators with first-hand, direct "insider" evidence that provides convincing proof of conduct parties want to conceal. The programs uncover conspiracies that would otherwise go undetected. They elicit confessions, direct evidence about other participants, and leads that investigators can follow for other evidence too. … To get this information the parties who provide it are promised lower fines, shorter sentences, less restrictive orders, or even complete amnesty.'

65 UNCTAD Leniency Guidelines, p. 1. These guidelines state that '[l]eniency programmes are designed to give incentives to cartel members to take the initiative to approach the competition authority, confess their participation in a cartel and aid the competition law enforcers. The aim is to drive a wedge at the heart of a cartel through its trust and mutual benefit. The reward for the first whistleblower is generally a large (or total) reduction in penalties and other incentives can be offered to the second whistleblower and to those who come after, if they bring forward decisive evidence. Effective leniency programmes are aimed at creating a race among conspirators to disclose their conduct to enforcers, in some instances, even before an investigation has begun, and to quickly crack cartels that may have otherwise gone undetected.'

66 ASEAN Regional Guidelines, pp. 30–31. The ASEAN Regional Guidelines introduce the idea that leniency programmes may be created to assist the enforcement of anti-cartel provisions. A clear definition of a leniency programme is not given. The ASEAN Regional Guidelines describe the situation that may lead to the necessity of a leniency programme. Reference is made to undertakings that have participated in a cartel and want to come clean. The fear for serious penalties will disincentivise these undertakings from reporting the cartel to the enforcement agency. A leniency programme could provide this incentive.

67 OECD Report, p. 11. See also OECD Marker, p. 6.

68 OECD Report, p. 11.

69 Ibid.

3.3.2 *A Well-Functioning Enforcement Regime as the Pre-requisite for an Effective Leniency Programme*

Leniency programmes will only be successful if they function in the right environment. The ICN Leniency Guidelines set out, in a fairly systematic way, the basic conditions for this environment: a high risk of detection followed by the actual imposition of sanctions, the need for the sanctions to be significant, and transparent and consistent application of the leniency programme.[70]

The OECD Report elaborates the first two issues.[71] The 'seriousness of the possible penalties ... is an important factor'[72] for the success of a leniency programme. Penalties are serious if they are not weak or are applied frequently. Only in such cases does a leniency programme provide a sufficient incentive for applying for leniency. The basis for this conclusion is the presumption that corporations engage in a cost–benefit analysis, in which the benefits of continuing the violation are weighed against the costs of getting caught.[73] These costs, as the OECD Report recognises, are not only determined by penalty but also by the frequency with which this penalty is applied.[74]

The high risk of detection and the seriousness of the sanctions need to be backed up by a leniency programme that does not give rise to an unexpected outcome. This requires that a leniency programme is 'clear, comprehensive, regularly updated, well publicised, coherently applied, and sufficiently attractive'.[75] It could be understood that, if these pre-requisites are not present, there may only be interest in applying for leniency once an investigation has started.[76]

70 ICN Leniency Guidelines, p. 5.

71 OECD Report, p. 9; OECD Challenges of Leniency Programmes, pp. 7–8. See also OECD, 'Executive Summary of the Roundtable on Challenges and Co-ordination of Leniency Programmes' (2019). Retrieved from https://one.oecd.org/document/DAF/COMP/WP3/M(2018)1/ANN2/en/pdf (OECD Executive Summary on Challenges).

72 OECD Report, p. 9. See also ICN Leniency Guidelines, p. 5 (the enforcement must lead to sanctions that are higher than the actual gains of the cartel. If necessary, sanctions should extend to individuals to achieve sufficient high sanctions).

73 OECD Report, p. 9. The cost–benefit analysis could be corrupted, though. If a corporation's position is asymmetrical compared to the position of the other corporations, defecting from the cartel may become a rational strategy even though the penalty is not high. See OECD Report, p. 25.

74 OECD Report, p. 9. See also ICN Leniency Guidelines, p. 5 (high risk of detection can only be shown when an enforcement agency has robust investigatory powers, which are then really used).

75 ICN Leniency Guidelines, p. 6.

76 Ibid., p. 5.

The UNCTAD Leniency Guidelines carry the same message as described above, but add that there are several elements that could indicate that competition law enforcement is not a priority.[77] Developing countries may invest in controlling market power rather than anti-cartel enforcement.[78] The limited financial and human resources of the enforcement agency will then be used for screening mergers and acquisitions or controlling monopolies. A high degree of state intervention or the exclusion of state monopolies from competition law could also be a sign that the enforcement of anti-cartel provisions is not a must.[79] Equally, when the Ministry of Commerce has been given an important voice in the decision-making process, other goals, such as 'employment security, competitiveness of domestic industry or … industrial policy',[80] may trump any serious attempt to set up an anti-cartel enforcement policy. Sectoral regulators often deny the competence of a competition agency in their sector, favouring and defending policies that stimulate cooperation in their sector. Cooperation with the competition agency over cartel enforcement is generally unthinkable.[81]

Business culture is another aspect that the UNCTAD Leniency Guidelines pursue to indicate that a leniency programme may not be feasible. Business culture that is built on 'trust and personal relations … and where business circles are relatively small and familiar'[82] may not facilitate the implementation of a leniency programme. In such an environment a leniency applicant may experience the backlash of social or informal penalties. Such social penalties could range from a boycott from business to social exclusion or even physical harm.[83] Going one step further, if the business in its entirety operates in the informal economy, which, according to the UNCTAD Leniency Guidelines, seems often to be the case in developing countries, the unwillingness to report on secret agreements may even be greater.[84] The leniency applicant may enjoy leniency for its violations of competition law, but potentially face serious sanctions for violating other laws.

The ASEAN Regional Guidelines are basically quiet on the pre-requisites. The only clue that is given to ASEAN Member States is that there is

77 UNCTAD Leniency Guidelines, p. 4.

78 Ibid.

79 Ibid.

80 Ibid.

81 Ibid.

82 Ibid.

83 Ibid.

84 Ibid.

a need to investigate whether imposing penalties outweighs the need to attract confessions regarding cartel infringement and thus whether leniency programmes should be part of a country's enforcement strategy.[85]

3.4 International Guidelines for a Leniency Programme

3.4.1 Eligibility Criteria to Apply for Leniency

Sanctioning cartel infringements may differ depending on the jurisdiction. Some jurisdictions may focus on sanctioning the corporation, other jurisdictions may also focus on individuals.[86] By recognising this difference, the international guidelines underscore that leniency programmes may vary in scope. The general trend among the international guidelines is to recommend extending the leniency programme if individual liability exists in the country's respective competition law.[87] The OECD Report adds some nuance by indicating that individual liability is not a necessity to have a more efficient leniency programme.[88]

Some of the international guidelines give more context on why leniency programmes should extend to individuals.[89] Individual liability, it is held, creates extra deterrence against forming a cartel.[90] If a country choses to extend the liability for cartels to individuals, the common view is that it is more efficient for a leniency programme to also extend to the individual.[91] The individual may not be willing to cooperate with the leniency application if no protection can be claimed by him or her. Such a situation may be troublesome for the corporation, especially if the individual has substantial knowledge of the cartel.[92]

85 ASEAN Regional Guidelines, p. 31.

86 OECD Report, p. 9; ICN Leniency Guidelines, pp. 5–6; UNCTAD Leniency Guidelines, pp. 2 and 6.

87 OECD Report, p. 9; ICN Checklist, p. 1; ICN Practices on Incentivising Leniency, pp. 13–17; UNCTAD Leniency Guidelines, p. 6. The OECD Challenges of Leniency document links this debate with criminal sanctions. This document further indicates that having criminal sanctions is not always beneficial for a leniency programme. Three reasons are put forward. First, the individual may shield him- or herself from the corporation. Second, criminal sanctions may be a deterrent to applying for leniency if one is not sure if one is eligible. Third, in countries with criminal sanctions, the leniency programme is usually limited to the first applicant. See OECD Challenges of Leniency, pp. 10–12.

88 OECD Report, p. 9.

89 ICN Practices on Incentivising Leniency, pp. 13–14.

90 UNCTAD Leniency Guidelines, p. 2; ICN Practices on Incentivising Leniency, p. 13.

91 ICN Practices on Incentivising Leniency, p. 13.

92 Ibid.,

A leniency programme can protect the individual in various ways. Corporate leniency can extend to individuals who are current and former employees.[93] The extension can be linked to the condition that the individuals cooperate with the enforcement authority.[94] The extension can be automatic, at the request of the corporation or at the request of the individual.[95] In any case, just like in the case of corporate leniency programmes, the position of the individual in the leniency application process should be transparent, reliable and predictable.[96] The latter is especially important in the relationship between corporate and individual leniency applications. It is further held that corporate leniency should not be precluded when an individual applies for leniency.[97]

The discussion on eligibility based upon the legal status of the leniency applicant – corporation or individual – is supplemented with a discussion on who should be ineligible. The four discussed international guidelines envision three categories of cartel participants: coercer, instigator and ringleader.[98] The ICN Leniency Guidelines state that these participants should not be eligible for immunity, which is more specific than leniency.[99] A similar view is taken by the UNCTAD Leniency Guidelines, albeit they use the concept of originator.[100] The OECD Report emphasises that 'the' coercer, instigator or ringleader should be excluded from leniency in general. It further adds that, if only two corporations have formed a cartel, none of the cartelists should be eligible for leniency.[101] The ASEAN Regional Guidelines has no specification included.[102]

The context that is given to exclude some cartel participants from a leniency programme is fairness.[103] It could be regarded as unfair to let cartel participants who had a central role to play in the cartel escape liability. This may be especially so when other cartel participants may, due to their minor role in organising the cartel, not be able to apply for leniency.

[93] Ibid., pp. 14–15.
[94] Ibid.
[95] Ibid., p. 15.
[96] ICN Practices on Incentivising Leniency, pp. 16–17. See also ICN Leniency Guidelines, p. 12.
[97] ICH Checklist, p. 1.
[98] OECD Report, p. 9; ICN Leniency Guidelines, pp. 9 and 12; UNCTAD Leniency Guidelines, pp. 11 and 15; ASEAN Regional Guidelines, p. 31.
[99] ICN Leniency Guidelines, p. 12.
[100] UNCTAD Leniency Guidelines, p. 11. The concept of the originator is mentioned through incorporating the text of the 1993 Leniency Policy.
[101] OECD Report, p. 18.
[102] ASEAN Regional Guidelines, p. 31.
[103] OECD Report, pp. 9–10.

3.4.2 *The Incentive Structure of a Leniency Programme*

It is most common for leniency programmes to offer immunity from and/or a reduction of the sanction prescribed for a cartel infringement. This practice has been copied into the international guidelines. However, some leniency programmes offer extra incentives. Therefore, the international guidelines refer to these extra incentives as a possible option to include in a leniency programme as well.

3.4.2.1 Immunity from and Reduction of the Sanction

An application for leniency does not happen automatically. Cartel participants need to be incentivised. The international guidelines all believe that the incentive structure needs to relate to lowered sanctions. Three issues are elaborated. First, there is discussion on when an incentive should be offered. Second, there is discussion on how much incentive should be offered. Third, there is discussion on who should be incentivised. As this links to who should be eligible for leniency, this discussion has been addressed above.

The international guidelines take the position that an incentive to apply for leniency should be given both before and after the start of an investigation. The OECD Report says that providing leniency after an investigation has begun was one of the major changes to the US 1993 Corporate Leniency Policy (1993 Leniency Policy) and that it had a positive effect. Therefore, it is included as an illustration of best practice, albeit that the incentive after the start of an investigation could be lower than before the start.[104] The ICN Leniency Guidelines state that leniency should be made available 'in circumstances where the competition agency is unaware of the cartel and where the competition agency is aware of the cartel, but the competition agency does not have sufficient evidence to proceed to adjudicate or prosecute the cartel'.[105] The latter may indicate that leniency could be made available after an investigation has started. There are other elements that seem to confirm this view. First, when discussing the full and frank disclosure requirement, the guiding text notes that leniency may also be available after an investigation has commenced.[106] However, the guiding text limits this possibility only to the first eligible applicant.[107] Second, the best practice on subsequent applicants does not exclude the

104 OECD Report, p. 9.

105 ICN Leniency Guidelines, p. 7.

106 Ibid., p. 8.

107 Ibid.

possibility that a leniency programme extends to more than one applicant. Whether the subsequent applicants defect before or after a dawn raid is a question that is not answered.[108] The UNCTAD Leniency Guidelines, by quoting the 1993 Leniency Policy, confirm the view that immunity could at least be offered before or after the start of an investigation.[109] The ASEAN Regional Guidelines do not provide substantial information on this issue.

There is also a common understanding in relation to how much incentive should be given. Immunity from a penalty prescribed for a cartel infringement is put forward as the best incentive in the ICN Leniency Guidelines.[110] The ICN Checklist adds that immunity should only be given to applicants enabling a targeted inspection or establishing the full extent of the infringement.[111] The OECD Report does not go that far, but indicates that the immunity should be conceptualised as the best deal inside a leniency programme.[112] This is also how the UNCTAD Leniency Guidelines think about immunity.[113] The ASEAN Regional Guidelines add a little more information. These Guidelines state that '[t]o encourage a "rush to the door" to contact the competition regulatory body or other law enforcement body, the first eligible applicant (before an investigation has begun) may be granted automatic and complete immunity'.[114]

There is also a common message in the international guidelines that a reduction of the penalty prescribed for a cartel infringement would be a good option when designing a leniency programme. The ICN Checklist recognises that reduction, especially for subsequent applicants, could be part of the incentive structure to report a cartel.[115] The ICN Checklist also stresses that it is necessary to have an incentive structure among the applicants for reduction in order to keep a race to the enforcement authority. This could be by imposing an evidentiary threshold for the reduction of fines, limiting the number of eligible applicants, tweaking the levels of reduction, or granting immunity if previously unknown information can

[108] Ibid., p. 9.

[109] UNCTAD Leniency Guidelines, p. 11.

[110] OECD Report, p. 14; UNCTAD Leniency Guidelines, pp. 1–12. The ICN is not that outspoken. Immunity may be given. It is, however, essential for a leniency programme to provide a higher incentive to cooperate than the sanction. ICN Leniency Guidelines, p. 6.

[111] ICN Checklist, p. 2.

[112] OECD Report, p. 14.

[113] UNCTAD Leniency Guidelines, p. 11.

[114] ASEAN Regional Guidelines, p. 31.

[115] ICN Checklist, p. 2.

be provided.[116] The OECD Report states that reduction is only a secondary option and should therefore be much lower than immunity.[117] As an example, a reduction between 75 per cent and 50 per cent, between 50 per cent and 10 per cent or up to 5 per cent could be considered depending on the value of the information. The order of application does not seem to be that valuable according to the OECD Report.[118] The UNCTAD Leniency Guidelines express a similar message, but in a more abstract way. These guidelines state that if more than one applicant could be granted leniency, the difference between immunity and reduction should be substantial.[119] The ASEAN Regional Guidelines would add conditions to accepting leniency applicants for reduction. Second, and any subsequent, leniency applicants should only be given lenient treatment if they provide evidence that adds significant value to the investigation.[120] How much reduction should be given is left unanswered, as long as the reduction reflects 'the actual contribution of the company, in terms of quality and timing, to the establishment of the infringement'.[121]

3.4.2.2 Extra Incentives to Apply for Leniency

The international guidelines inform us that there are other incentive structures for cartel participants to report a cartel. These incentive structures are leniency plus and penalty plus.[122] The UNCTAD Leniency Guidelines also mention the omnibus question.[123] Leniency plus allows cartel participants under investigation to disclose another cartel and so obtain leniency for the first and second cartel infringements.[124] Penalty plus will aggravate the sentencing factor for cartels for which the investigated cartel participant failed to report its existence under leniency plus.[125]

116 ICN Checklist, p. 3.
117 OECD Report, p. 19.
118 Ibid.
119 UNCTAD Leniency Guidelines, p. 11.
120 ASEAN Regional Guidelines, p. 31.
121 Ibid.
122 For the purpose of the book, we use leniency plus instead of amnesty plus. Several of the international guidelines use the latter: OECD Report, p. 21 (only mentioning leniency plus); ICN Leniency Guidelines, p. 9 (mentioning both leniency plus and penalty plus); ICN Checklist, p. 4 (mentioning both leniency plus and penalty plus); UNCTAD Leniency Guidelines, p. 12 (mentioning both leniency plus and penalty plus).
123 UNCTAD Leniency Guidelines, p. 12.
124 ICN Leniency Guidelines, p. 9; ICN Checklist, p. 4 (mentioning both leniency plus as the equivalent of amnesty plus and penalty plus); UNCTAD Leniency Guidelines, p. 12.
125 ICN Leniency Guidelines, p. 9; ICN Checklist, p. 4; UNCTAD Leniency Guidelines, p. 12.

The omnibus question focuses on cartel witnesses, who are asked under oath whether they have knowledge of other cartels than the one that is being investigated. The incentive to comply with this question is the perjury sanction.[126]

Besides mentioning and defining these incentives, there is no information given on when to include them in a leniency programme. The OECD Report and the UNCTAD Leniency Guidelines only account for the fact that these incentive structures have been deployed in the US.[127] It is indicated that these extra incentives may have been created to make up for the absence of leniency for subsequent applicants.[128]

3.4.3 Requirements and Conditions to Receive Leniency

A leniency programme should not provide lenient treatment without conditions attached to the application. Disregarding the small differences in language to spell out these conditions, there is general agreement on how leniency applicants need to behave. On one element there is some disagreement, and that is the kind of information that needs to be submitted.

3.4.3.1 Information Requirements

The international guidelines are clear about one thing: information needs to be given in return for lenient treatment. However, there is a lot of difference in how the information requirement is treated across the international guidelines. A distinction is made between the information requirement for immunity applicants and for applicants for reduction.

The general trend is that immunity applicants should submit relevant or sufficient information.[129] Despite the use of this general term in some of the international guidelines, more precise terminology is used more frequently. Relevant information could be understood as evidence enabling a conviction to be sustained.[130] The relevant information could be information that allows a targeted inspection or establishes the full extent of a

126 UNCTAD Leniency Guidelines, p. 12.

127 OECD Report, p. 21; UNCTAD Leniency Guidelines, p. 12.

128 OECD Report, p. 21.

129 OECD Report, p. 15; ICN Leniency Guidelines, pp. 7–8.

130 OECD Report, pp. 22 (calling it decisive evidence of the cartel's existence); UNCTAD Leniency Guidelines, p. 11.

cartel infringement.[131] It is also mentioned that information helping the investigation to progress could be seen as relevant.[132] The OECD Report explicitly adds that it is important for leniency applicants to submit information that is unknown to the enforcement authority.[133] The UNCTAD Leniency Guidelines add to this by stating that unknown information could be one way to secure immunity.[134]

When a reduction is made available in a leniency programme, the international guidelines also emphasise the quality of the information. The OECD Report and the ICN Leniency Guidelines do not further specify what such quality should be.[135] The only statement that is made is that subsequent leniency applicants should offer more than just a tip about the cartel.[136] The ICN Checklist and the UNCTAD Leniency Guidelines demand that the information should have significant added value to the evidence already in the possession of the enforcement authority.[137] The justification for the extra burden is that this extra information strengthens the ability to prove the existence of the cartel.[138] However, the UNCTAD Leniency Guidelines warn that enforcement agencies can face difficulties in judging the strength of the added value and thus this results in the question of whether weak value-added evidence should be taken into consideration.[139]

The approach in the ASEAN Regional Guidelines is slightly different. No distinction is made between applicants for immunity and for reduction. The ASEAN Regional Guidelines just demand that a leniency applicant should submit 'all the information, documents and evidence available to it regarding the cartel activity'.[140]

131 ICN Checklist, p. 2, where it is stated that this information could include 'name/address of entities involved; name/position/address of individuals involved; product scope; known duration; type of conduct, means; foreseeable meetings or contacts (if the cartel is ongoing); information on other agencies with whom they have filed or plan to file similar submissions'; UNCTAD Leniency Guidelines, p. 11.

132 OECD Report, pp. 9 and 14.

133 Ibid. The ICN Leniency Guidelines report that this is a less frequent characteristic in leniency programmes: ICN Leniency Guidelines, p. 10.

134 UNCTAD Leniency Guidelines, p. 11.

135 OECD Report, p. 9 (stating that the information requirement for reduction applicants may need to be more stringent); ICN Leniency Guidelines, p. 12.

136 OECD Report, p. 15.

137 ICN Checklist, p. 3, giving more detail on what significant added value can be: 'direct evidence vs. indirect or circumstantial evidence; stand-alone evidence vs. evidence that requires corroboration; written, contemporaneous evidence vs. oral statement at the time of the procedure'. See UNCTAD Leniency Guidelines, p. 13.

138 UNCTAD Leniency Guidelines, p. 13.

139 UNCTAD Leniency Guidelines, p. 15.

140 ASEAN Regional Guidelines, p. 32.

3.4.3.2 Behavioural Requirements

Subsequent to submitting information to the enforcement agencies, the international guidelines suggest relying on a set of behavioural requirements to guarantee that the leniency applicant does not hamper or sabotage the investigation.

The ICN Leniency Guidelines rely on the following behavioural requirements: (1) full and frank disclosure, (2) full and continuous cooperation with the enforcement authorities and (3) terminating participation in the cartel infringement.[141] The ICN Checklist adds to this (1) not destroying, falsifying or concealing evidence, (2) keeping the leniency application confidential towards third parties and (3) identifying participation in the cartel.[142]

These behavioural requirements are found in other international guidelines.[143] However, the OECD Report is silent on keeping the application confidential and admitting participation in the cartel.[144] This is also the case for the UNCTAD Leniency Guidelines and the ASEAN Regional Guidelines.[145] The UNCTAD Leniency Guidelines also do not mention that terminating the infringement would be a good guideline.[146] The OECD Report and the UNCTAD Leniency Guidelines add that it could be beneficial if the leniency applicant undertakes good faith efforts to remedy the damage. Both documents allow this to be linked to good practice with one of the leniency programmes applicable in the US.[147]

3.4.4 Procedure for a Leniency Application

The procedure for applying for leniency can be broken down into four stages. The first stage is pre-application, when a potential leniency applicant needs accurate information on the extent to which the cartel is known by the enforcement agency. The second stage, after a decision has been made to apply, relates to securing the best position within the leniency programme. The third stage is the actual application and deals with the conceptualisation of the method of applying. The fourth stage concludes the leniency application.

141 ICN Leniency Guidelines, p. 9.

142 ICN Checklist, p. 3.

143 OECD Report, pp. 16–19; UNCTAD Leniency Guidelines, p. 9.

144 OECD Report, pp. 16–19.

145 UNCTAD Leniency Guidelines, p. 9. Note, however, that the issue of secrecy is addressed at the level of problems in the enforcement and that actions of the enforcement agency may even reveal a leniency application. See UNCTAD Leniency Guidelines, p. 15.

146 OECD Report, p. 18; UNCTAD Leniency Guidelines, p. 9.

147 UNCTAD Leniency Guidelines, p. 11.

Prior to investigation, cartel participants may want to secure information regarding the availability of leniency. The ICN Leniency Guidelines therefore recommend, and this is repeated by the ICN Checklist,[148] that an anonymous consultation with the enforcement authority should be available to estimate the authority's knowledge about the cartel and the possible position in the leniency queue if an application were to be made.[149] The UNCTAD Leniency Guidelines side with this observation by stating that an anonymous check with the enforcement authorities is available in many leniency programmes.[150] The OECD Report does not make any direct reference to anonymity, but indirectly suggests it by stating that contact can be made by telephone.[151] The OECD Report, however, puts more emphasis on the submission of a hypothetical proffer of information. On the condition that an undertaking can provide what is suggested in the proffer, it could lead to lenient treatment. At the time of writing the OECD Report, this system was linked to the US.[152] However, more recent international guidelines indicate that creating a hypothetical leniency application system could be good practice.[153]

The submission of a hypothetical proffer or a hypothetical application is already one step towards securing the first position in a leniency queue. However, these systems may not necessarily be included in all leniency programmes. In order to still offer a way to secure the first position in a leniency queue, even though the potential applicant has not collected all the information, the ICN Leniency Guidelines, the UNCTAD Leniency Guidelines and the ASEAN Regional Guidelines suggest the creation of a marker.[154] A marker allows a cartel participant to declare the intention to defect, after which time is given to collect and submit the information.[155] If necessary, the ICN Leniency Guidelines state that an extension

148 ICN Checklist, p. 4.
149 ICN Leniency Guidelines, p. 8.
150 UNCTAD Leniency Guidelines, p. 8.
151 OECD Report, p. 21
152 Ibid., pp. 21–22. It is important that a leniency programme provides clarity and certainty on how this hypothetical proffer is assessed.
153 ICN Leniency Guidelines, pp. 8–9; ICN Checklist, p. 4.
154 ICN Leniency Guidelines, pp. 8, 11–12 and 22; UNCTAD Leniency Guidelines, p. 8; ASEAN Regional Guidelines, p. 32.
155 ICN Leniency Guidelines, p. 11. A marker, so the UNCTAD Leniency Guidelines inform us, is a mechanism to secure a provisional position within the leniency queue. This position is secured by submitting some information, after which the corporation gets a deadline by which it must submit all information requested by the leniency programme. See UNCTAD Leniency Guidelines, p. 8.

of the marker period could be good practice. During this process, the undertaking needs to comply with the conditions of the respective leniency programmes.[156] The content of the information necessary to secure a marker may vary among different jurisdictions, but the UNCTAD Leniency Guidelines generalise that 'the company must declare its name and address, and provide clear information about the specific products and the geographical market covered by the cartel, identity [sic] the other members of the cartel, the nature of the agreement and its estimated duration, as well as all the leniency applications the company has, or intends to submit to other competition authorities'.[157] None of the other international guidelines provides this kind of information. An alternative to the marker would be a system in which a leniency application is made based upon the available information, after which an addendum can be added to the original application.[158]

Moving ahead to the actual application procedure, the ICN Leniency Guidelines make it clear that there are two forms of leniency application: written and oral.[159] In principle, it is best practice that a leniency application is made in writing. However, 'due to fear of private damages actions, including class actions, arising out of the application or a fear that any documents supplied may be discoverable by parties in private civil actions in the jurisdiction leniency is sought and/or in other jurisdictions',[160] leniency programmes should allow for oral applications.[161] This best practice, put forward in the ICN Leniency Guidelines, would still require leniency applicants to 'provide all pre-existing documents'.[162] However, this should only be so if the legal framework can sufficiently protect sensitive information. The ICN Leniency Guidelines are brief in mentioning that oral application could be good practice and indicates that it requires a person responsible for leniency in an enforcement agency.[163] This person should handle the oral leniency application.

The next step is closing the leniency application. It is made clear that not all leniency applications lead to an investigation. Several options are

156 ICN Leniency Guidelines, p. 11.

157 UNCTAD Leniency Guidelines, p. 8. These guidelines, besides this general statement, also make reference to the US marker system.

158 OECD Report, pp. 22–23.

159 ICN Leniency Guidelines, p. 13. See also ICN Checklist, p. 4.

160 ICN Leniency Guidelines, p. 13.

161 Ibid., p. 13.

162 Ibid.

163 Ibid., p. 15.

suggested when this occurs. The options range from upholding the leniency application to granting final immunity, to withdrawing the leniency application. If an investigation follows the leniency application, the enforcement agency will need to take a decision on this application. This decision can be done in one or two steps. The one-step option is to inform the leniency applicant that the leniency application has been received and, if everything is complied with, this application becomes final with issuing the cease-and-desist or fining order. The two-step option is to notify the leniency applicant that all requirements for leniency are fulfilled and grant him or her conditional leniency. Upon complying with these conditions during the investigation, the leniency will become final. This will either be through a leniency letter or the final decision of the enforcement agency in relation to the investigation.

3.4.5 *Keeping the Leniency Application Confidential*

Confidentiality has been one of the key elements of a leniency programme since the first international guidelines were issued. Whereas initially confidentiality mainly related to issues of access by private parties, it gradually expanded to include other enforcement agencies and sectoral regulators.

3.4.5.1 Private Enforcement and Confidentiality

A leniency application reveals the presence of a cartel. Victims of that cartel may want to obtain damages and therefore 'rely on the infringement decision's findings in relation to leniency applicants'.[164] The leniency applicants risk being sued first and held liable for the full amount of the cartel damages. If there is a disclosure of self-incriminating statements in the leniency application, this risk is even aggregated.[165] Therefore, active private enforcement may disincentivise leniency applications.[166] To diminish this risk, enforcement agencies have devised rules to either limit or exclude the liability of leniency recipients or tackle the disclosure of documents obtained by the enforcement agencies.

Among all the international organisations discussed, the ICN has been the most prolific in suggesting rules to limit the liability for private

164 ICN Practices on Incentivising Leniency, p. 8.

165 Ibid.

166 Ibid., pp. 8–9. See also OECD Report, pp. 20–21; ICN Leniency Guidelines, pp. 14–15; UNCTAD Leniency Guidelines, p. 15; OECD Challenges on Leniency, pp. 8–10.

damages.[167] The suggestions made include limiting the scope of liability for the immunity recipient to its direct and indirect purchasers,[168] changing treble damages to single damages for a successful leniency applicant,[169] not making leniency recipients jointly and severally liable,[170] and excluding immunity recipients from liability.[171]

An alternative to limiting the liability of leniency recipients is to protect the confidentiality of the documents that leniency applicants submit to the enforcement agencies.[172] To name a few of the international guidelines in this respect, it has been recommended that enforcement agencies oblige themselves to ensure the non-disclosure of sensitive documentation,[173] courts are prohibited from ordering the disclosure of voluntarily provided statements,[174] or the law provides provisions stating that disclosure can be refused if the interests of third parties could be harmed.[175]

3.4.5.2 Other Enforcement Agencies and Confidentiality

Cartel participants may be deterred from applying for leniency not only by damages claims under private lawsuits, but also by the risk of an investigation in a country other than the one in which the leniency application is being considered.[176] It is therefore essential that a leniency application in one country remains confidential to the enforcement agencies.[177] In this respect, several international guidelines call for confidentiality for both the identity of the leniency applicants and the information and evidence that they have submitted.[178] Only the consent of the leniency applicant should

167 ICN Checklist, p. 4.

168 ICN Practices on Incentivising Leniency, pp. 11–12.

169 OECD Report, p. 21; ICN Practices on Incentivising Leniency, p. 12.

170 ICN Practices on Incentivising Leniency, p. 12.

171 Ibid.

172 Ibid. See also OECD Report, p. 10 (even though most emphasis is put on confidentiality towards other enforcement agencies. This issue is also prominently present in the ICH Checklist, p. 5); UNCTAD Leniency Guidelines, p. 15.

173 ICN Practices on Incentivising Leniency, p. 12.

174 Ibid.

175 Ibid.

176 UNCTAD Leniency Guidelines, p. 5, stipulating that high sanctions or an unreliable leniency programme could be a reason for seeing the other country as a risk. See also ICN Cross-Border Leniency Guideline, pp. 4–5.

177 ICN Cross-Border Leniency Guideline, p. 4

178 OECD Report, p. 24; ICN Leniency Guidelines, pp. 14–15; ICN Cross-Border Leniency Guideline, pp. 9–10; UNCTAD Leniency Guidelines, p. 5; ASEAN Regional Guidelines, p. 32. The latter also informs us that law may override a waiver and oblige the disclosure of information.

be taken into consideration to waive confidentiality. These international guidelines should be understood against the background of the absence of a single leniency programme for cartels that operate across borders. Such an absence confronts a cartel defector with different leniency programmes, thus less transparency and predictability. This may require extra time to prepare leniency applications. Any actions of the enforcement agencies to jeopardise this process should be avoided. The ICN, having paid special attention to cross-border leniency applications, provides further information on how to conceptualise the waiver, including templates.[179]

Some of the international guidelines, in particular those from OECD and ICN, call for cautiousness on the part of leniency applicants.[180] The confidentiality requirement has limitations. It will be limited to the identity of the leniency applicant and the information and evidence he or she submitted. Enforcement agencies will be able to communicate about the cartel as long as the identity and the evidence of the leniency application are not revealed. Because of this possibility, the international guidelines indicate that a leniency programme could create an incentive to apply for leniency elsewhere. Therefore, it is good practice to ask in which other jurisdictions leniency has been applied for.[181]

Having information on which enforcement agencies have received a leniency application may be important for another reason. Some competition regimes have special procedures in place to exchange information without having obtained consent. These information gateways are supported by international agreements. Despite these information gateways, the ICN Cross-Border Leniency Guideline still cautions the enforcement agencies to be vigilant with information sharing.[182]

3.4.5.3 Sector Regulators and Confidentiality

Leniency applications may also be affected by the presence of sector regulators. Sector regulators may impose obligations, such as an obligation to report infringements. The duty to disclose this information to the sector regulator may conflict with the conceptualisation of a leniency programme, which often requires confidentiality. This will pose a conundrum for the corporation willing to apply for leniency: forsaking leniency to comply with the sector regulator's reporting duty or applying for

[179] ICN Cross-Border Leniency Guideline, pp. 9–11.

[180] OECD Report, p. 24; ICN Cross-Border Leniency Guideline, pp. 7–9.

[181] ICN Leniency Guidelines, p. 14.

[182] ICN Cross-Border Leniency Guideline, pp. 11–14.

leniency and breach the obligation to report.[183] It is possible that infringing competition law may also lead to sanctions by the sector regulator. These sanctions are often related to licences that are withdrawn. If sanctions are imposed, the incentive for applying for leniency diminishes.[184]

The Cartel Working Group notes that the reporting obligation is barely a problem.[185] However, a competition law infringement, especially in relation to bid rigging, often has implications for participation in future bid-rigging projects. In many jurisdictions, the revelation that one has participated in bid rigging will result in disqualification from the next public procurement project.[186]

Because of this observation, one of the main lessons to be drawn for the conceptualisation of a leniency programme is to connect 'full protection or discounts from debarment from future procurement projects'[187] to all or some of the leniency recipients. Therefore, it may also be worthwhile to set up communication channels between the competition enforcement authority and the sector regulator.[188] This will also prevent the latter hampering competition law–related investigations by the competition enforcement authority. Another good practice is involving the sector regulators in detecting infringements and so raising the risk of detection.[189] A higher risk of detection will contribute to more instability and thus a swifter use of leniency programmes.

3.4.6 *Increased Concern for Multi-jurisdictional Leniency Applications*

The discovery of international cartels, cartels operating across borders, has shown the difficulty of upholding different leniency programmes across the world. This has prompted several cases with multi-jurisdictional leniency applications. The international guidelines are increasingly paying attention to this phenomenon, because this kind of leniency application creates a greater burden on the leniency applicants.[190]

[183] ICN Practices on Incentivising Leniency, p. 18.

[184] Ibid., p. 19.

[185] Ibid.

[186] Ibid., p. 20.

[187] Ibid., p. 21.

[188] Ibid., pp. 21–22. See also ICN Cross-Border Leniency Guideline, pp. 24–26.

[189] ICN Practices on Incentivising Leniency, p. 21.

[190] Obsteiner, T., 'International Antitrust Litigation: How to Manage Multijurisdictional Leniency Applications' (2013) 4(1) *Journal of European Competition Law & Practice* 16.

To lessen that burden, the ICN Cross-Border Leniency Guideline makes suggestions on how enforcement agencies can coordinate their investigations. Some of this coordination may directly involve elements of the leniency programme. The ICN Cross-Border Leniency Guideline state, for example, that it may be possible for the enforcement agencies to coordinate the proffer of the marker or the interviews with the leniency witnesses.[191]

Other recommendations are more useful for the enforcement agencies than for the leniency applicant and include, among others, discussions on how to interpret the evidence submitted in a leniency application and taking into consideration differences in interrogation practices.[192] In relation to the case outcome, the ICN Cross-Border Leniency Guideline recommends an exchange of views on the ranking of the leniency applicants as well as the percentage of the reduction they could obtain.[193]

None of the international guidelines makes the explicit proposition of harmonising leniency programmes,[194] suggests creating a one-stop shop for multi-jurisdictional leniency applications, or advocates for extending the international agreements between enforcement agencies so as to reciprocally recognise decisions on lenient treatment.[195]

3.5 Decontextualised Summaries and Their Challenge for Convergence

3.5.1 The Process towards Convergence

Convergence can be defined as 'the voluntary adoption of widely-accepted norms of competition policy, substantive standards, procedures and levels of institutional capacity'.[196] Underlying the ideal of convergence is the understanding that the currently applied competition policies, substantive standards, procedures and institutions are diverging. This may be explained by the socio-political and economic background of the different countries.

[191] ICN Cross-Border Leniency Guideline, p. 16. A flexible, though predictable, approach is also advocated in the ICN Checklist, p. 5.

[192] ICN Cross-Border Leniency Guideline, pp. 18–19.

[193] Ibid., pp. 19–20.

[194] But see ASEAN Regional Guidelines, p. 32, requesting consistency among leniency programmes in cases of cross-border cartels.

[195] Obsteiner, 'International Antitrust Litigation' (n. 190 above), pp. 28–30.

[196] ICN, 'ICN's Vision for Its Second Decade' (n. 28 above), p. 5.

Divergence is crucial for development towards convergence. It allows for experiments,[197] which in turn will enable us to see which policies, standards, procedures or institutional capacities are more effective. The information and experiences from these experiments can then be shared. This part will facilitate the identification of best practices, which could be put forward as the benchmark for convergence.[198] Eventually, individual countries may decide to adopt the benchmark. At this point, a consensus has been reached on what the best possible solution is for a specific problem.[199]

This process from divergence to the 'voluntary adoption of widely-accepted norms'[200] requires 'editors, filters, interpreters and clue-givers, as well as "evaluators" in distilling power for the plenitude of information'.[201] The practice of the ICN, especially the ICN Leniency Guidelines, has been explicitly hailed as a good example of how an organisation can fulfil this role.[202] By studying leniency programmes of different origins, OECD, UNCTAD and ASEAN, each within their own methodology, equally represent this role of collecting and distilling information from relevant experiments.

Despite this positive note on the role these organisations have played in collecting, distilling and evaluating different leniency programmes, there is also a need to look beyond the process. It is necessary to look at the content of the international guidelines to assess how the organisations are accomplishing their role as collector, distiller and evaluator. This assessment will be important to see to what extent convergence can be attained.

3.5.2 The International Guidelines as Decontextualised Summaries

When looking at the content of the international guidelines, there are some elements that are common. These elements can be considered as the core of leniency programmes. This chapter has identified the following

197 Stucke, M. E., 'Greater International Convergence and the Behavioral Antitrust Ambit', in Ezrachi, *Research Handbook on International Competition Law* (n. 32 above), 158, p. 158.

198 Hollman, H. M., Kovavic, W. E. and Robertson, A. S., 'Building Global Antitrust Standards: The ICN's Practicable Approach', in Ezrachi, *Research Handbook on International Competition Law* (n. 32 above), 89, p. 92.

199 ICN, 'ICN's Vision for Its Second Decade' (n. 196 above), pp. 5–6.

200 Ibid., p. 5.

201 Keohane, R. and Nye, J.S., Jr, *Power and Independence: World Politics in Transition* (Boston: Little Brown, 1977), p. 89.

202 Stucke, 'Greater International Convergence' (n. 197 above), p. 158.

common elements: pre- and post-investigation leniency, immunity, reduction, extra application incentives, providing information regarding the infringement, behavioural conditions, informal contact with the enforcement agency, marker, written applications, oral applications and confidentiality. The international guidelines do not offer much explanation on why these elements are considered essential for leniency programmes. Furthermore, the detailed elaboration of the common elements often differs among the international guidelines. Most of these differences are usually not explained in the international guidelines. The lack of explanation renders the international guidelines decontextualised. The degree of decontextualisation is exemplified below.

Leniency could be provided prior to the start of an investigation or after. The strength behind this guideline is a reference to the US, which has incorporated this possibility in its 1993 Leniency Policy. This guideline is not supported by any reference to research showing a positive cost–benefit analysis explaining why having both options is better.[203] Indeed, the more relevant information is gathered, the faster an investigation can be concluded. This of course demands that the introduction of both options is linked to the quality of information the enforcement agency should require from leniency applicants. Further, the international guidelines do not enlighten us as to what the scope of leniency should be once an investigation has started. The international guidelines leave it open on whether immunity can be provided or only reduction.

Immunity is considered the best incentive to convince corporations to defect from a cartel. There is also agreement that immunity should be limited to the first applicant. Some issues remain unsettled. Should the first applicant submit information of a certain quality? Should immunity be available after an investigation has started? Statements are made in favour of one or the other, but no international guidelines are given on what solution is best in what kind of circumstances. One possible consideration

[203] See, e.g., Chen, J. and Harrington, J. E., 'The Impact of the Corporate Leniency Program on Cartel Formation and the Cartel Price Path' (Center for International Research on the Japanese Economy, Working Paper No. CIRJE-F-358, 2005), p. 12. Retrieved from https://repository.upenn.edu/cgi/viewcontent.cgi?article=1155&context=bepp_papers; Feess, E. and Walzl, M., 'Corporate Leniency Programs in the EU and the USA' (German Working Papers in Law and Economics, Working Paper No. 24, 2003), pp. 7–8 and 17. Retrieved from http://papers.ssrn.com/sol3/papers.cfm?abstract_id=384740; Ellis, C. J. and Wilson, W. W., 'What Doesn't Kill Us Makes Us Stronger: An Analysis of Corporate Leniency Policy' (2001), pp. 17–18. Retrieved from www.researchgate.net/publication/2498536_What_Doesn't_Kill_us_Makes_us_Stronger_An_Analysis_of_Corporate_Leniency_Policy.

could be fairness, whereby it is not opportune to still provide immunity for an infringement that has already been detected.

The international guidelines also put forward that giving reduction to leniency applicants subsequent to the first could be good practice. This reduction should be substantially less than immunity. Reduction should be available both before and after the start of an investigation. Other than an example of how the reduction is conceptualised in one jurisdiction, no further international guidelines are provided. Should the reduction be set as an exact percentage? Or should the enforcement agency be given discretion within a band of reduction? Equally, should the information leniency applicants need to submit to obtain reduction be qualified? What happens if reduction can be obtained by submitting just a general cartel story? There is no instruction to have alternatives, such as plea bargaining, in place if reduction is not offered.

Several of the international guidelines state it is good practice to offer extra incentives to report cartel activity, such as leniency plus or penalty plus. In some of the documents it is made clear that such incentives were introduced in the US. The US's leniency programme is specific and may warrant the introduction of these extra incentives. There is indeed no room for subsequent leniency applicants within the 1993 Leniency Policy. If these special incentives are introduced in a leniency programme that also grants leniency to subsequent leniency applicants, how should the reduction be combined with these extra incentives?

The international guidelines are firm in that lenient treatment needs to be compensated with information regarding the infringement. There is agreement that the information may need to be different between an applicant for immunity and for reduction. However, within these two categories there is ample agreement on what the right criteria are to qualify the information. When is it appropriate to just require the submission of a good cartel story? Is this the same as requiring information that allows an investigation to be started? Why would it be better to ask for information leading to a sustainable conviction or to fully reveal the extent of the cartel? What is the difference between unknown information and information that has a significant added value? How can enforcement agencies deal with the interpretational problems that may arise from the use of these concepts?

Informal contact with the enforcement agency has been put forward as a best practice. Some of the international guidelines just limit this to having anonymous telephone contact with the enforcement agency.

Other international guidelines extend it to the possibility of submitting hypothetical leniency applications. The advantages and disadvantages of both systems have not been explained. The positive effect of hypothetical leniency applications is also not explained. Equally, no information is given on the relationship between a hypothetical leniency application and other instruments in a leniency programme, such as a marker. The only context that has been given in the international guidelines is the need to have either of them to secure a specific position within the order of applications.

Related to securing a specific position within the order of applications is the marker. The marker has been conceptualised to provide the first applicant with time for gathering the necessary information after a rapid initial reporting of the infringement. Even though there is unanimity on the need for having a marker system, the international guidelines are not informative on the conceptualisation of the marker system. Based on the OECD Marker document, it is possible to show what kind of context is uncovered by the international guidelines.[204] Should the leniency applicant be given some flexibility regarding the information he or she submits in order to obtain a marker?[205] Or is it better that the leniency applicant gets some guidance? In other words, it is better that the marker system prescribes the information the enforcement agency needs to grant the marker.[206] The absence of information for either system also explains why the international guidelines do not explain what kind of information a prescriptive system should ask for.[207] The international guidelines also do not indicate the advantages and disadvantages of a flexible or prescriptive marker system. It is also not indicated, if a choice is made for either of these marker systems, what the implication is for the further conceptualisation of the leniency programme, such as the inclusion of anonymous contact with the enforcement agency. The international guidelines are mute on when the right to a marker becomes obsolete or whether the applicant should submit a list of possible evidence he or she will be able to submit.[208] It is also not clear to what extent a marker should be offered to subsequent applicants.[209] In terms of perfecting the marker, the international guidelines remain silent on

204 OECD Marker.
205 Ibid., pp. 15–16.
206 Ibid., pp. 16–18.
207 Ibid., pp. 16–17.
208 Ibid., pp. 19–20.
209 Ibid., p. 20.

what the ideal time frame is. However, extending the period for perfection may be good practice.[210]

There are three exceptions to the decontextualised summary: the eligibility criteria, the behavioural conditions and confidentiality.

The international guidelines share knowledge on why and when a leniency programme should extend to individuals and why some cartel participants should be excluded. Despite this context, none of them explains the difficulty of applying the criteria for ineligibility on the basis of originator, leader or coercer.[211]

The behavioural conditions for obtaining leniency are more or less the same across the different international guidelines. The aim of these behavioural conditions is to make sure the leniency applicants stop infringing the law and cooperate with the enforcement agencies. Some context is provided regarding the termination of the infringement, as this is not always beneficial for the investigation into the cartel. In relation to cooperation, the international guidelines indicate that it could be good practice for corporations to give access to computer data, make telephone records available, let current employees be interviewed or assist in locating former employees.[212]

Confidentiality is another element on which the international guidelines give more context, especially when it relates to private damages actions. For countries in which private enforcement of competition law is well advanced, the international guidelines stipulate that leniency information should be treated as confidentially as possible. In this respect, the international guidelines elaborate extensively on the need to organise oral leniency applications.

3.5.3 A Great Opportunity for Divergence within the Common Elements of a Leniency Programme

Convergence is, in principle, a voluntary process whereby a norm is adopted by several countries. These countries adopt that norm because they believe there is general acceptance of its effectiveness. With more

210 Ibid., pp. 21–23.

211 See, e.g., Balasingham, B., *The EU Leniency Policy: Reconciling Effectiveness and Fairness* (Alphen aan de Rijn: Wolters Kluwer, 2017), p. 141; Van Uytsel, S., 'A Comparative US and EU Perspective on the Japanese Antimonopoly Law's Leniency Program' (2008) 75(3) *Hosei Kenkyu* F1, p. F49.

212 OECD Report, pp. 16–17; ICN Leniency Guidelines, p. 16; UNCTAD Leniency Guidelines, p. 9.

than sixty countries having adopted a leniency programme, a trend is noticeable towards convergence on having this enforcement tool against cartel infringements. This trend is most likely triggered by the positive stance towards this enforcement tool by enforcement agencies that have adopted it. Critical voices regarding the leniency programme did not negatively impact that trend.

Whether there is also convergence on the content of the leniency programmes will depend on how the leniency programmes are conceptualised. As has been indicated above, convergence will only be the case if there agreement has been reached on the different elements of the leniency programme. By looking closely at different leniency programmes, the international guidelines reveal that such an agreement has only been reached on a limited number of elements. Many of these elements constitute the core for operating a leniency programme. The visibility that is given to these elements in the international guidelines mean that convergence is likely, even for elements that do not necessarily belong to the core. As no further information is added to these common elements, the international guidelines will not be the cause of 'disruptive innovation in antitrust implementation strategies'.[213]

When discussing how the common elements need to be implemented, the international guidelines reveal divergent approaches. There is no agreement yet on what the best solution is for dealing with the common elements. It is at that point that the international guidelines do not look like a solution well suited to a specific problem, but rather resemble a collection of experiences, substantive or procedural, that work for a specific problem.[214] It is often the case that these experiences reflect the practice of financially well-resourced enforcement agencies,[215] and thus constitute a minoritarian bias.[216] Less mature enforcement agencies may not have

[213] Svetiev, Y., 'Partial Formalization of the Regulatory Network' (2010), p. 35. Retrieved from http://papers.ssrn.com/sol3/papers.cfm?abstract_id=1564890&download=yes.

[214] Ibid., p. 35.

[215] Fox, 'Linked-In' (n. 24 above), p. 126.

[216] Neil Komesar has pointed out that the more agencies participate and the more complex the issue at stake, there is an 'enhanced possibility of minoritarian bias and the prospect of "rent-seeking"'. The ideas or interest of the majority risk being underrepresented. See Komesar, N. K., *Law's Limits: The Rule of Law and the Supply and Demand of Rights* (Cambridge, UK: Cambridge University Press, 2001), p. 153. Another point of critique on participation within the ICN is on the bias towards maturer and richer competition jurisdictions. The financially restrained agencies will face difficulties in organising workshops or the Annual Conference. This in turn may jeopardise their chances of being a member or chair of the Steering Group or the chair of a Working Group. With less chance of being

enough skills to discuss and evaluate the proposed experiences and thus do not counteract that bias.

The implementation experiences are presented in the form of an abstract guideline, nudging their users to further explore what would work in their respective jurisdiction. In other words, users should still look at different leniency programmes in order to distil experiences that suit the task and the local environment in which they are supposed to operate. Therefore, the international guidelines will not lead to a 'broad dissemination, and improvement, of practices actually useful to the participating authorities in their day-to-day work'.[217] Convergence on the details is much less likely than on the core elements.

3.6 Conclusion

Various international organisations, such as OECD, ICN, UNCTAD and ASEAN, have embarked on research into leniency programmes to formulate international guidelines. Their research revealed that leniency programmes only converge on core elements. The details of implementing these core elements, however, show great divergence. This has resulted in international guidelines mapping out the core elements and providing different choices to implement these elements. In doing so, the international guidelines are no more than summaries of existing leniency programmes. Moreover, little information, either from practice or theory, is added to explain the different choices. In this sense, this chapter holds that the summaries are decontextualised. The more recent international guidelines seem to deviate from this pattern and include more context.

The consequence of putting forward decontextualised summaries of existing leniency programmes is that potential users of the international

a member of the Steering Group, these financially restrained agencies will have less power to influence the agenda setting of the ICN. Further, due to the fact that they will most likely not be chairing a Working Group, these agencies will also not be the ones holding the pen when the first drafts of the recommended practices are written. See Hollman, H. M. and Kovavic, W. E., 'The International Competition Network: Its Past, Current and Future Role', in Lugard, *The International Competition Network at Ten* (n. 24 above), 51, p. 58 (without support of the wealthy agencies, the ICN will collapse).

217 Svetiev, 'Partial Formalization of the Regulatory Network' (n. 213 above), p. 35. Studies of specific jurisdictions thus remain important for deciding how leniency programmes should be conceptualised. An example of such a study is Zingales, N., 'European and American Leniency Programmes: Two Models Converge?' (2008) 5(1) *Competition Law Review* 5, pp. 26–60.

guidelines only receive limited elements on which there is general agreement. It is likely that these elements are taken into consideration when creating new leniency programmes, with convergence as a result. As to the details of a leniency programme, the potential user only receives options without context. This will require the user of the international guidelines to revert to existing leniency programmes or scholarly writings. Divergence among the details of leniency programmes will be the result. It may even be that, if nothing suitable can be found among what exists, innovative legislative developments might arise.

4

Situating Leniency

MARK FENWICK

4.1 Introduction

The essence of a leniency programme in a competition law context is that individuals or companies that cooperate with the authorities in a formal proceeding – by disclosing verifiable information on the existence of unlawful activities, specifically cartels – are granted immunity or mitigation from formal sanction. At the centre of a leniency programme, therefore, is an agreement between a regulatory authority and a natural or legal person involving a transfer of relevant information in exchange for preferential, or at least different, treatment from that which might ordinarily be expected in the absence of such disclosure and cooperation. The justification for such programmes seems to be primarily utilitarian. Detecting and proving competition law violations are difficult – participants have a strong incentive to keep their conduct secret – and the administrative costs of successfully pursuing a cartel case, for example, can be significantly reduced if those with relevant information are offered a clear and predictable incentive – in the form of immunity or mitigation – to cooperate with authorities by disclosing that information. Over the last few decades, leniency programmes have come to be regarded as an effective mechanism to provide such an incentive and tackle anti-competitive behaviour, specifically the different forms of cartel, and, as a result, they have proliferated globally, including – as evidenced by this volume – in many jurisdictions in Asia.

The purpose of this chapter is to situate the emergence of this new regulatory form – the leniency programme in competition law – in the broader context of contemporary trends in transnational business regulation. It will be suggested that although leniency programmes are a distinctive type of regulatory intervention, they do exhibit a family resemblance with other regulatory mechanisms that have emerged in the last two decades in other fields of business law and that similar trends, pressures and effects can be seen across these different regulatory settings. The intention of this chapter is not to blur the distinction between these different developments, but rather to suggest that by linking leniency with these broader trends, we might deepen our understanding of the distinctive character and broader significance of these initiatives.

The chapter identifies four general trends in business regulation that are relevant in this context, which are discussed in turn. First, there is a trend towards what will be characterised here as negotiated justice (Section 4.2). In this context, negotiated justice refers to procedural mechanisms that address alleged unlawful (and possibly criminal) behaviour by a company or individuals within that company via some form of negotiated settlement between the regulator and the company, rather than allowing the administrative or judicial process to play out as it ordinarily would do in the absence of such an agreement. The character of this agreement varies depending on the specific form of negotiated justice, but all such negotiated justice can be characterised as a form of diversion that seeks to increase the effectiveness of law enforcement, while at the same time minimising the collateral effects of initiating a formal proceeding against a company. This trend towards negotiated justice originated in the United States (US) in the late 1990s but now – as with leniency programmes – has expanded to Asia and Europe.

The second trend is the emergence and normalisation of what is described here as regulatory experimentation (Section 4.3). In this context, what is particularly important is that regulators and policy-makers increasingly adopt new and more dynamic policy interventions in which regulatory structures and schemes are not thought of as final events to be made for all time or even the foreseeable future. Rather, we should think of regulatory action as open-ended, ongoing, and highly contingent selections that are merely one step or stage in a longer process and not the final word on a particular issue. One consequence of this new emphasis on contingent experimentation is that regulatory interventions are constantly being made and then remade based on experience. This emphasis on feedback – acting, collecting data, learning and then iterating – can be seen in many of the examples of leniency programmes discussed in this volume and offers a good example of this more general trend towards more dynamic or responsive forms of regulatory action.

The third trend concerns what Gralf-Peter Callies and Peer Zumbansen refer to as the 'rough consensus' in transnational business regulation

(Section 4.4).[1] Their suggestion is that contemporary business law is characterised by a broad agreement on the desirability of a particular regulatory intervention, such as a leniency programme. However, this agreement is typically 'rough' in the sense that minor, yet potentially important differences emerge between specific instantiations. Again, the chapters in this volume provide multiple illustrations of this rough consensus. On the one hand, there seems to be a broad agreement among competition policymakers in Asia that a leniency programme adds value (the moment of 'consensus') and yet there are many subtle but important differences in how such a scheme is implemented in different jurisdictions (the 'rough' moment). From the point of view of companies, rough consensus creates a significant degree of legal risk, especially for any business that operates transnationally, and this risk needs to be managed via the compliance function within a firm.

The final trend discussed here concerns coordination between regulatory agencies (Section 4.5). The transnational character of business and business regulation creates the need for greater regulatory cooperation between national regulators to ensure the effective implementation of any regulatory action, such as a leniency agreement. Again, this is evidenced by the international character of many cartels and creates a need for greater cooperation between competition authorities. Similarly, the trend towards experimentation and identification of best practice creates a similar pressure to coordinate in the sharing of information. This trend towards regulatory cooperation can be seen across many fields of business regulation (securities regulation, financial services regulation and anti-corruption regulation), as well as competition law. Crucially, this new form of cooperation involves bottom-up agency-to-agency coordination, what is characterised here as networked governance, rather than more traditional forms of international cooperation.

By situating the proliferation of leniency programmes in Asia and elsewhere in the broader context of these four trends in contemporary business regulation, the chapter hopes to facilitate a better understanding of the significance and character of leniency programmes today, both in Asia and elsewhere.

4.2 The Rise of Negotiated Justice

The rise of leniency programmes can be understood as an example of a more general shift towards what will be characterised here as negotiated

[1] Callies, G.-P. and Zumbansen, Z., *Rough Consensus and Running Code: A Theory of Transnational Private Law* (Oxford: Hart Publishing, 2010).

justice in contemporary transnational business regulation. Initially this trend started in the US, but similar developments have occurred elsewhere.[2] The background to this shift is the perceived failure of, or at least limitations in, traditional regulatory mechanisms to deal effectively with corporate wrongdoing and the need for more innovative thinking and new instruments for regulators in responding to such wrongdoing.

The first set of considerations driving this perception of regulatory failure and the need for a different response concerns the administrative costs of law enforcement in cases involving corporations, especially large corporations.[3] Detecting, investigating and prosecuting cases of corporate wrongdoing are notoriously difficult, given the complex fact patterns, highly motivated and competent defence strategies that such corporations employ, and the limited resources and capacities of regulators. Information asymmetries – specifically the informational disadvantages that regulators experience – create prohibitively high costs in all but the simplest cases.

Compounding these practical difficulties is minoritarian bias on the part of regulators – specifically regulatory capture, in which regulators are too closely connected to the firms that they ostensibly regulate – which distorts regulatory choices, resulting in an inadequate level of enforcement. Such issues can be found across all fields of business regulation, including in a competition law context.

And even when a case is successful and enforcement action is brought against a corporation, there is a significant body of research that questions the capacity of fines – the primary sanction in such cases – to provide an effective deterrent for any firms contemplating unlawful activities.[4] Many commentators have criticised fines as being ineffective in either preventing or deterring corporate wrongdoing. In particular, it is often suggested that fines have traditionally been set far too low in the case of corporate wrongdoing and that, consequently, they come to be seen by the business community as the price or cost of engaging in unlawful, but economically lucrative, behaviour. It has also been suggested that fines are ineffective because a company can transfer the burden of the fine to innocent third

[2] See, generally, Fenwick, M., 'The New Corporate Criminal Law and Transnational Legal Risk', in Fenwick, M. and Wrbka, S. (eds.), *Flexibility in Modern Business Law* (Singapore: Springer, 2016), 149.

[3] See, generally, Ayres, I. and Braithwaite, J., *Responsive Regulation* (Oxford: Oxford University Press, 1996).

[4] See Simpson, S., *Corporate Crime, Law and Social Control* (Cambridge, UK: Cambridge University Press, 2002).

parties, such as customers, shareholders or employees. If the effects of the fine can be mitigated in this way, then the threat of the fine is significantly reduced and increasing the level of the fines – the obvious response – would merely mean imposing a greater burden on these innocent third parties.

Of course, fines are not the only formal sanctions that are available in cases of corporate wrongdoing. Other sanctions might be imposed – such as loss of licence or shaming – but, depending on the nature of a corporation's business, these alternatives to the fine can have unpredictable or possibly disastrous consequences for a company. Such uncertain effects illustrate a more general problem, so-called collateral damage. This is the idea that a successful enforcement action can cause unintended harm to innocent third parties and has greatly influenced regulatory thinking on the best response to corporate wrongdoing.[5]

The most widely cited example of collateral damage involved the conviction of the financial services provider Arthur Andersen for obstruction of justice in June 2002 for its role in the Enron accounting scandal. Because federal regulations bar convicted persons from auditing public companies, the conviction had a catastrophic effect on Arthur Andersen. Although the Supreme Court ultimately overturned the conviction because of improper jury instructions, it was too late to save the company. The US Department of Justice was heavily criticised for the harm caused to the mostly blameless 25,000 plus employees who lost their jobs because of the conviction and collapse of the firm, and the market lost an important service provider.

On this type of account, therefore, traditional regulatory responses to corporate wrongdoing have come to be seen as inadequate in how they impact upon the incentives of relevant actors. Either they are too ineffective or weak to have any chilling effect in preventing corporate wrongdoing or they are too unpredictable and excessive in their effects, as occurred in the Arthur Andersen case.

The response to this perceived failure in existing regulatory schemes has been regulatory innovation. At the core of this shift has been the emergence of regulatory mechanisms that suspend the law's normal operations and adopt some form of negotiated settlement as an alternative.

The obvious and most important example of such negotiated justice has been the increased use of pre-trial diversion in a US context, in

[5] See Bucy, P.H., 'Civil Prosecution of Health Care Fraud' (1995) 30 *Wake Forest Law Review* 720, p. 723.

particular the emergence and use of deferred prosecution agreements in cases involving corporate defendants in criminal proceedings.[6] The rise of such agreements is among the most significant post-2000 developments in how corporate wrongdoing is managed.

A deferred prosecution agreement involves a settlement between law enforcement and a corporate defendant. Common provisions in such agreements include an admission of wrongdoing by the company; a commitment to cooperate with the government in ongoing investigations, including those in which corporate agents and employees are targeted; payment of a nominal 'fine' agreed between the regulator and the company; an undertaking to improve compliance programmes, usually under the scrutiny of a 'monitor', hired and paid for by the company; a waiver of the statute of limitations; and a provision stating that if the company breaches the agreement, it will be subject to prosecution, and that the agreement's statement of facts, which constitutes an admission of guilt, will be admissible. However, if the company complies with the terms of the agreement (a determination made by prosecutors based on advice from the independent monitor), the case will not proceed.[7] Interestingly, this approach has now been copied, with slight modifications, by several jurisdictions in Asia and Europe.

A second example of negotiated justice can be seen in the response to the global financial crisis of 2008–09, specifically alleged fraud in the sale of highly risky derivatives by large banks. Although the unravelling of such transactions was a central cause of the crisis and there is a lot of evidence that the sale of such securities was possibly fraudulent in many cases, no criminal cases were brought against either the responsible individuals or financial service providers.[8] Instead, various forms of pre-trial diversion – notably consent orders – were employed that allowed structurally important financial institutions to preserve the fiction that they had done nothing wrong, while imposing some obligations on them to improve their behaviour. Again, this response was motivated by a recognition of limits in traditional regulatory tools and traditional forms of

[6] On the rise of the deferred prosecution agreement in the context of corporate criminal law and procedure, see Garrett, B. L., *Too Big to Jail: How Prosecutors Compromise with Corporations* (Cambridge MA: Belknap Press, 2014).

[7] Warin, F. J. and Jaffe, P. E., 'The Deferred-Prosecution Jigsaw Puzzle: A Modest Proposal for Reform' (2005) 19 *Andrews Litigation Report* 3, p. 5.

[8] See, generally, Tett, G., *Fool's Gold: The Inside Story of J.P. Morgan and How Wall St. Greed Corrupted Its Bold Dream and Created a Financial Catastrophe* (New York: Free Press, 2010).

enforcement, as well as a fear of collateral damage if criminal cases were employed against structurally important financial institutions.

What we can see, therefore, from the examples of deferred prosecution agreements and the response to the 2008–09 financial crisis is a broader policy shift in how businesses, and particularly large businesses, are regulated. This shift has been driven by regulatory concerns over the high administrative costs and uncertainties of pursuing enforcement actions against economically powerful entities, as well as the risks of collateral damage. These new regulatory forms – and deferred prosecution agreements in particular – have spread to other countries in a similar way to leniency programmes. In this respect, we can see the emergence of what we might call a new post-2000 corporate criminal law and procedure.[9]

Clearly, the abovementioned mechanisms are different in form and purpose from a leniency agreement, and it is not the intention of this chapter to blur this distinction. However, the suggestion is that there is some 'family resemblance' between these new measures. First, and most obviously, leniency programmes are a response to a perceived regulatory failure, namely a recognition of the difficulties for regulators in pursuing a formal investigation and enforcement in complex cartel cases. In addition, this new approach involves the incentivisation of cooperation via some form of preferential – or at least different – treatment that is offered in exchange for this cooperation. Although there is little to suggest that a fear of collateral damage has played a significant role in the proliferation of leniency programmes, a perception of regulatory failure – specifically recognition of the administrative costs of enforcement and the limits of traditional sanctions – has played a crucial role in their adoption. And this new mechanism involves the granting of discretion to regulators and diversion from traditional process and negotiated justice. Even if this discretion is constrained to various degrees by the law, some degree of negotiation and agreement between participants in a leniency programme and regulators seems inevitable, as is the fact of preferential treatment (in the form of immunity or mitigation) for successful applicants.

The recent trend in a US context is for leniency to be used in combination with pre-trial diversion. The Antitrust Division of the US Department of Justice, for example, was historically not keen on using

[9] See Fenwick, M., 'The Multiple Uncertainties of Corporate Criminal Law', in Fenwick, M. and Wrbka, S. (eds.), *Legal Certainty in a Contemporary Context* (Singapore: Springer, 2016), 148.

deferred prosecution agreements to resolve criminal antitrust violations.[10] However, the Division began to change its approach in July 2019, when then Assistant Attorney General Makan Delrahim announced the Division's new policy of using deferred prosecution in such cases. Since that announcement, the Division has entered into nine such agreements in combination with leniency. Delrahim announced that, going forward, the Division would consider and credit effective compliance programmes at the prosecution stage and would be willing to resolve such cases with a deferred prosecution, rather than a criminal conviction.[11]

This general trend towards negotiated justice is controversial. There seem to be conflicting or, at least, ambiguous policy objectives – most obviously, the tension between holding offenders to account for their wrongdoing and avoiding the collateral damage and other uncertainties that may result from upholding the rule of law. Furthermore, the executive-administrative appropriation of judicial authority seems to undermine traditional understandings of the separation of powers in the legal system, notably the distinction between executive and judicial branches. Moreover, a public perception of 'going soft' on corporate offenders means that the broader legitimacy of the legal system is potentially undermined. Finally, differences between national implementation of these measures creates legal risk for firms and requires a greater degree of international regulatory cooperation, an issue we will come back to in Section 4.4.

As such, these new procedural mechanisms need to be treated cautiously, particularly in the case of serious allegations of corporate wrongdoing. The legitimacy of the legal system more general can be undermined by the lack of transparency in the use of such measures. Although several of these concerns are relevant in a discussion of leniency programmes, the rather modest form of negotiated justice adopted in a competition law context, at least in Asia, seems preferable. From this perspective, leniency can be seen as a pragmatic adjustment to the complexities of investigating cartels, rather than a more fundamental shift in how cases of serious corporate wrongdoing are treated.

[10] On the use of deferred prosecution agreements in an antitrust context in the US, see Geverola, A. and Rigburg, K., 'A Changing Landscape: The DOJ Antitrust Division's Use of Deferred Prosecution Agreements', *Arnold & Porter, Enforcement Edge Blog* (12 August 2021). Retrieved from www.arnoldporter.com/en/perspectives/blogs/enforcement-edge/2021/08/doj-antitrust-division-use-of-deferred.

[11] Delrahim, M., 'Winds of Change: A New Model of Incentivizing Antitrust' (July 11, 2019). Retrieved from https://www.justice.gov/opa/speech/assistant-attorney-general-makan-delrahim-delivers-remarks-new-york-university-school-l-0.

4.3 Regulatory Experimentation

The second general trend in contemporary business regulation that seems relevant in the context of leniency programmes is a trend towards more dynamic or responsive regulatory interventions, or what is characterised here as regulatory experimentation.[12] Over the last few decades, the theory and practice of regulation have focused on improving the ability of regulators to respond to changing industry practices and on improving relationships between regulators and regulated entities.[13] So-called dynamic or responsive regulation responds to changing industry practices through feedback effects and enhanced information for developing regulatory forms.[14]

What is particularly important is that that within the framework of these more dynamic regulatory models, regulatory decisions should not be thought of as 'final events' that are made once and for all time and from which we then all move on. Rather, we should think of regulatory choice as a form of what Michel Callon has called 'measured decision-making'; that is, regulation involves open-ended and highly contingent selections that are merely one stage or moment in a longer process and not the final word on a particular issue.[15] As such, regulators abandon a fixation on finality and legal certainty and embrace contingency, flexibility and an openness to learning. The justification for this new openness derives from the contingency of the fast-moving business environment in which regulators now must operate. Any regulatory choice ultimately remains

[12] In a competition law context, see Svetiev, Y., *Experimentalist Competition Law and the Regulation of Markets* (Oxford: Hart Publishing, 2020).

[13] See Black, J., Hopper, M. and Bland, C., 'Making a Success of Principles-Based Regulation' (2007) 1 *Law & Financial Markets Review* 191; Black, J., 'Forms and Paradoxes of Principles-based Regulation' (LSE Working Papers, 2009). Retrieved from http://eprints.lse.ac.uk/23103/1/WPS2008-13.pdf.

[14] Fenwick, M., Kaal, W. A. and Vermeulen, E. P. M., 'Regulation Tomorrow: What Happens When Technology Is Faster Than the Law' (2017) 6 *American University Business Law Review* 561. This regulatory innovation can be seen as a response to technological innovation and organisational innovation within business. See Fenwick, M. and Vermeulen, E. P. M., 'The New Firm: Staying Relevant, Unique & Competitive' (2015) 16 *European Business Organization Law Review* 595; Fenwick, M., McCahery, J. A. and Vermeulen, E. P. M., 'Fintech and the Financing of SMEs and Entrepreneurs: From Crowdfunding to Marketplace Lending', in Cumming, D. and Hornuf, L. (eds.), *The Economics of Crowdfunding: Startups, Portals and Investor Behavior* (London: Palgrave Macmillan, 2016), 103; Fenwick, M. and Vermeulen, E. P. M., 'The Future of Finance: Why Regulation Matters', in Liaw, K. T. (ed.) *The Routledge Handbook of Fintech* (New York: Routledge, 2020), 38.

[15] Callon, M., Lasoumes, P. and Barthe, Y., *Acting in an Uncertain World: An Essay on Technical Democracy* (Cambridge, MA: MIT Press, 2009).

open-ended, leaving space to incorporate new knowledge, discoveries and claims. The need for finality, Callon argues, is usually overstated, more the product of expediency and habit than actual necessity.

This new emphasis on contingency and iteration in regulation is a function of the environment, specifically globalisation and technological change. This complex new operating environment creates a challenge for policymakers. One response has been a willingness to innovate in regulatory schemes and remove the temporal horizon that has traditionally defined decision-making. Under such circumstances, policy experimentation – that is, testing different regulatory schemes and then comparing the results – becomes attractive. But such experimentation poses a problem for regulators. Too often, regulators define success in negative terms, as in the avoidance of catastrophe and avoiding criticism, which can result in an overly cautious approach, often referred to as the 'precautionary principle'. Moreover, it risks undermining, or at least changing the meaning of, legal certainty in the contemporary legal order.[16]

One influential example of such experimentation is the recent emergence of the regulatory sandbox.[17] The Financial Conduct Authority (FCA), the financial regulatory body in the United Kingdom (UK), is widely accredited with first introducing this approach to regulation.[18] In April 2016, the FCA announced the introduction of the sandbox, which allowed start-up and established companies to test new ideas, products and business models in financial services. The aim of the sandbox was to create a 'safe space' (hence the sandbox metaphor) in which businesses can test innovative products, services, business models and delivery mechanisms without immediately incurring all the normal regulatory obligations of engaging in the activity in question.

The idea behind the sandbox is for the regulatory authority to approve a firm-specific, deregulated space for the testing of innovative products and services without that firm being forced to comply with the applicable set of existing rules and regulations. With the sandbox, the regulator aims to foster innovation by lowering regulatory barriers and costs for testing disruptive innovative technologies, while ensuring that consumers will not be negatively affected.

[16] See Fenwick, M., Siems, M. and Wrbka, S. (eds.), *The Changing Meaning of Legal Certainty in Contemporary Comparative and Transnational Law* (London: Hart Publishing, 2019).

[17] See Zetzsche, D. A., 'Regulating a Revolution: From Regulatory Sandboxes to Smart Regulation' (2017) 23 *Fordham Journal of Corporate and Financial Law* 31.

[18] See Financial Conduct Authority, *Regulatory Sandbox* (2015). Retrieved from www.fca.org.uk/publication/research/regulatory-sandbox.pdf.

The individualised suspension of existing regulation within the sandbox is justified on the grounds of fostering innovation, but an additional advantage of sandboxes is that they offer opportunities to generate information and data relevant for future regulatory design and iterations in existing regulatory models. This allows all participants in the ecosystem – that is, regulators, incumbent companies, start-ups, investors, consumers – to learn about new technologies. In this way, the sandbox can create a dialogue that helps regulators better understand new technologies and reduce information asymmetries in the marketplace between regulators and business. As such, it comes as no surprise that regulatory sandboxes have been adopted by other regulators, such as the Australian Securities and Investment Commission, Singapore's Monetary Authority and Abu Dhabi's Financial Services Regulatory Authority.[19]

The key point about a sandbox for a discussion of leniency is that it entails the flexible application and suspension of the law's normal operations in favour of a more dynamic process that brings additional benefits in the form of attracting innovation and empowering regulators.

Moreover, the experience of leniency programmes offers many examples of this ongoing process of gathering data, learning and adjustment to ensure better outcomes. The most famous example of such a learning process, at least in the context of leniency programmes, is in the US and the adjustments made to the leniency version 1.0 of the late 1970s.[20] By making immunity automatic for a leniency application prior to the start of an investigation, making leniency available to corporations even after an investigation had begun and extending immunity to all officers, directors and employees who came forward with the corporation, the US Department of Justice significantly improved the incentive structure and effectiveness of the scheme. The 1993 Corporate Leniency Policy (1993 Leniency Policy) offered better and more predictable incentives and began to attract several leniency applications every month. More generally, it provides for an illustration and model for the process of experimentation, learning and iterating that characterises contemporary business regulation.

Crucially, once the US and the European Union (EU) started to implement functioning and effective leniency programmes, a body of literature that was previously built on abstract economic models was

[19] See, generally, Fenwick, M., Van Uytsel, S. and Ying, B., *Regulating Fintech in Asia: Global Context, Local Perspectives* (Singapore: Springer, 2020).

[20] See, generally, Ghosal, V. and Sokol, D. D., 'The Rise and (Potential) Fall of US Cartel Enforcement' (2020) 2 *University of Illinois Law Review* 471.

supplemented by empirical data. Real-world comparisons could thus be made between the earlier 1978 Corporate Leniency Policy and the 1993 version.[21] Again, further studies could be developed when other jurisdictions adopted such schemes, for instance contrasts between the operation of the 1993 Leniency Policy and the 1996 EU Leniency Notice.[22] Finally, this kind of empirical study was supplemented by what were termed 'interpretational studies', in which leniency programmes could then be evaluated based on more abstract metrics, such as accountability and transparency.[23]

In an age of global markets and fast-paced technological innovation, knowing what, when and how to structure regulatory interventions has become much more difficult. Against this background, experimentation, contingent action and a process of institutionalising feedback and learning have become important elements of business regulation across multiple jurisdictions and fields of regulation.[24]

4.4 'Rough Consensus' and New Legal Risk

The third general trend in contemporary business regulation relevant to a discussion of leniency concerns what Callies and Zumbansen refer to as 'rough consensus'.[25] The basic idea of this concept is that contemporary business regulation is increasingly characterised by a broad agreement on the desirability of a particular regulatory intervention, such as a leniency programme, but this agreement is always 'rough' in the sense that minor, yet potentially important differences remain between specific instantiations, and these divergences have important implications for all stakeholders. As such, rough consensus is both a corollary of regulatory experimentation and a form of regulatory competition.

21 Kobayashi, B. H., 'Symposium: Antitrust, Agency, and Amnesty: An Economic Analysis of the Enforcement of Antitrust Laws against Corporations' (2001) 69 *George Washington Law Review* 715.

22 Brenner, S., 'An Empirical Study of the European Corporate Leniency Program' (2009) 27 (6) *International Journal of Industrial Organization* 639.

23 See, e.g., Beaton-Wells, C., 'The ACCC Immunity Policy for Cartel Conduct: Due for Review' (2013). Retrieved from https://papers.ssrn.com/sol3/papers.cfm?abstract_id=2316556; Van Barlingen, B. and Barennes, M., 'The European Commission's 2002 Leniency Notice in Practice' (2005) 3 *Competition Policy Newsletter* 6.

24 Fenwick, Kaal and Vermeulen, 'Regulation Tomorrow' (n. 14 above); Kaal, W. A. and Vermeulen, E. P. M., 'How to Regulate Disruptive Innovation: From Facts to Data' (2017) 57 *Jurimetrics: The Journal of Law, Science, and Technology* 169.

25 Callies and Zumbansen, *Rough Consensus and Running Code* (n. 1 above).

The chapters in this volume provide multiple illustrations of such a rough consensus in leniency programmes. On the one hand, there is a clear consensus among competition policymakers in Asia that such a programme adds value (the 'consensus' element) and yet there are many subtle but important differences in how such a scheme is implemented (the 'rough' element). Points of difference include the following. First is the issue of whether a leniency programme should be restricted to the first applicant or offered to multiple applicants. Experience has shown how subsequent applicants can also be decisive in mapping out the full extent of the illegal cartel activity and some sort of incentive needs to be provided for them. Second, an important distinction in any leniency programme is that between the 'pre' and 'post' investigation phase. All countries discussed in this volume – except for Korea – make such a distinction. A key question in navigating leniency thus becomes the point of division between the two phases. However, if one considers the specific criteria, the start of an investigation is interpreted very differently across different Asian jurisdictions. For example, the investigation phase may start from the 'dawn raid' (in Japan) or the moment the investigator becomes aware of the cartel (in China, Taiwan and Malaysia). Similar local differences exist in the implementation of the marker system, which is designed to ensure that the first to come forward receives the most favourable treatment. A final set of differences revolve around the type of information that needs to be submitted to ensure leniency and – crucially – immunity from prosecution and sanction.

One significant consequence of this rough consensus is that it creates a new degree and form of legal risk. From the point of view of companies, rough consensus creates a greater level of legal risk, at least for any business that operates transnationally, and this risk needs to be managed via the compliance function within a firm. After all, these minor distinctions can have enormous implications and managing the resulting risk takes on even greater significance in a fast-moving regulatory environment characterised by experimentation.

There are several aspects to the claim that legal risk has expanded, and that this risk has an indeterminable character that requires continued management. First, the number of legal norms confronting a firm has massively increased since the second half of the twentieth century and the complex range of issues that they cover has similarly increased. An irony of the rise of the neoliberal, financially driven corporations post 1980 is that it coincided with a massive expansion in the amount of regulation, so-called net widening.[26] Competition law is one layer affecting firm activities, but there are also substantive norms in fields such as company law, labour law, health and safety law, environmental law and many other sector-specific regulatory rules, depending on the type of business that a firm engages in. The effect of this enormous expansion in the amount of regulation and the subject matter of legal risk is to greatly increase compliance costs for any business.

Part of the reason for this proliferation of new laws is that law reform – enacting new laws – has become the default political response to scandals involving corporate wrongdoing. In a US context, for instance, Sarbanes–Oxley and Dodd–Frank function as shorthand for these swathes of legal rules introduced in the shadow of corporate wrongdoing (the Enron scandal in 2001 and the financial crisis in 2008–09), but such a trend can be seen in other jurisdictions. It is important to acknowledge the potential negative effects of introducing more layers of regulation. Despite the populist appeal of such an approach, there are concerns that the new regulations do not work in the way that policymakers hope or intend. After all, the number, scale and effects of corporate scandals and economic failures do not appear to be diminishing, despite the proliferation of such regulation.

A second complication is that for corporations, economic globalisation and the expansion in transnational legal risk add to this normative uncertainty and complexity. Not only do firms need to consider the laws of any jurisdiction in which they operate but, increasingly, they need to be aware of the laws of jurisdictions where they have any sort of presence.

Take as an example of this form of expanding legal risk the increased extraterritorial application of many regulatory offences in fields such as environmental law or labour law. In its most basic sense, this simply refers to the fact that the substantive norms of a particular jurisdiction are applied to corporate conduct that has occurred overseas. More recently, however, the territorial reach of corporate criminal laws has extended even further. The law of a particular jurisdiction may also apply to any corporation that issues securities or simply conducts part of its business in that jurisdiction, irrespective of where that corporation was established, where the firm's centre of operations is located or where the alleged

[26] See Cohen, S., *Visions of Social Control* (Cambridge, UK: Polity, 1991).

wrongdoing took place.[27] A company that has been established and has its centre of operations in one jurisdiction, but issues shares on a UK-based stock exchange, for example, may be exposed to liability in the UK for conduct occurring in either the UK, the company's home jurisdiction or a third country.

A final complication, implicit in the above but nevertheless worth noting, is that the regulatory environment – and legal risk – is constantly changing as a function of the policy experimentation described. New laws are continually being made and older laws revised. The profile of legal risk for companies is rendered highly unstable, and the uncertainties created by the fact of the relentless speed of law reform itself become an additional source of legal risk. The instability of contemporary business regulation – the fact that, at any moment, the law somewhere is being revised or reviewed – also has a transnational aspect. Add to this the changing form of regulation, for example the proliferation of so-called soft law, and the 'undecidability' of the contemporary legal environment becomes apparent.[28]

As a result, companies are obliged to spend more time and money on managing the rising costs associated with navigating the mosaic of overlapping legal rules that constitutes the contemporary regulatory landscape. Corporations need to manage this undecidable legal risk and the result has been a massive expansion in the compliance function within firms. This is an issue for all firms, but for larger, publicly listed corporations that conduct a significant part of their activities across multiple jurisdictions and in different sectors of the economy, managing transnational and cross-sectoral legal risk can become a debilitating burden.

Take the example of financial service providers. Estimates put the governance, risk and compliance costs at around 15–20 per cent of the total running costs of a bank, after the financial crisis. A *Financial Times* 2015 investigation into rising compliance costs post 2000 revealed the scale of the expansion in

[27] See Fenwick, 'The New Corporate Criminal Law' (n. 2 above), p. 149. It is worth noting here, for example, that the US leniency programme was first developed in a policy statement of the Antitrust Division of the Department of Justice and the European Commission incorporated its first leniency programme in a notice. Both a 'policy' and a 'notice' are non-binding legal instruments and might be described as typical examples of soft law. As evidenced in the chapters of this book, however, leniency programmes in an Asian context have all been embedded in the respective competition laws. A complicating factor is that procedural rules are often found in soft law instruments.

[28] Callies and Zumbansen, *Rough Consensus and Running Code* (n. 1 above).

compliance.[29] In 2013, JP Morgan added 4,000 employees to its compliance team and spent an additional US$1 billion on controls. Citigroup reported that of the US$3.4 billion in costs that it had saved in the past year through greater efficiency, 59 per cent of that was then being consumed by new compliance spending. HSBC expanded its compliance department from 2,000 to 5,000 in 2013 alone, and it currently employs 7,000.

The entrepreneurial spirit that made a firm effective can be hollowed out by more bureaucratic corporate practices that are forced on companies by the need to comply with rules and regulations, while also striving to meet business targets. As such, a disconnect arises between the regulatory-driven structures and the resulting organisational culture of corporations, on the one hand, and the capacity to meet various business challenges, on the other. Too often, fear and negativity, rather than vision and creativity, come to drive the internal agenda within an organisation, and such negativity inevitably has a corrosive effect on a firm's capacity to motivate stakeholders or act creatively and decisively. Firms inevitably get bogged down in the resulting regulatory thicket created by corporate governance that surrounds all aspects of a modern corporation's operations.[30]

When considering such costs, it is important to stress that it is not the direct compliance costs (which include fees paid to consultants and intermediaries) that are the only problem. For many large firms, there are also the indirect costs that arise because of the adoption of a bureaucratic one-size-fits-all corporate culture, which is based on risk-averse behaviour and an overemphasis on formalistic compliance. A process of seepage occurs, as more cautious forms of behaviour spread throughout the different divisions and departments of the firm, with a culture of compliance taking over.

The result? In large, well-established organisations, compliance tends to be defensive in character – it is about protecting the firm's legal interests – and, given the dominance of lawyers in compliance departments, this typically involves strategies concerned with minimising exposure to legal risk. In practice, this means minimal communication and public disclosure of information regarding the internal structure, operations and decision-making processes of the firm. The internal logic of a legalistic

[29] Noonan, L., 'Banks Face Pushback over Surging Compliance and Regulatory Costs', *Financial Times* (28 May 2015). Retrieved from www.ft.com/content/e1323e18-0478-11e5-95ad-00144feabdc0#axzz3jN2kPKMc.

[30] Chen, C. and Soltes, E., 'Why Compliance Programs Fail—and How to Fix Them', *Harvard Business Review* (March 2018), p. 116. Retrieved from https://hbr.org/2018/03/why-compliance-programs-fail.

approach seems clear: why take any chance of disclosing information to the public (crucially, potential plaintiffs) that increases potential exposure to lawsuits and damage to the market value of the firm?

In a competition law context, this new legal risk will inform how leniency applications are managed and has the potential to create awkward problems for any business considering making such an application. For example, a leniency programme application will often intersect with, and be affected by, the presence of sector-specific regulations and the involvement of sector-specific regulators, as well as antitrust regulators. The sector-specific regulators – for example, health and safety, labour or environmental agencies – may impose obligations, such as a reporting obligation on infringements, that push a firm in a different direction from that demanded by leniency. Most obviously, an obligation to disclose the facts of a substantive violation to the sector regulator may come into conflict with the need to maintain confidentiality in a leniency application.

As such, meeting the demands of antitrust authorities may come into conflict with the demands of the sector-specific authorities, and the resulting tension creates a complicated dilemma for any corporation looking to apply for leniency. Either the company abandons the leniency application to comply with the sector regulator's reporting duty or applies for leniency and entrenches the obligation to report. The involvement of multiple agencies across multiple jurisdictions merely adds to the compliance challenge of navigating a complex, interconnected and undecidable legal environment.

4.5 Regulatory Cooperation

The fourth and final general trend in business regulation that seems relevant in a discussion of leniency in competition law is regulatory cooperation. Recent decades have seen a rapid expansion in routinised purposive interaction between public officials from government agencies of different countries that share a common sphere of authority and expertise (such as competition, banking, securities, public health, anti-terrorism, policing, fisheries or the environment), a phenomenon that we shall refer to here as transgovernmental regulatory networks (TGRNs).[31] In the context of economic and business law, relatively developed examples of TGRNs

[31] By way of a caveat, it is worth noting that TGRNs often entail the participation of quasi-public and non-state actors, such as non-governmental organisations (NGOs), trade associations etc., and, as such, are not the exclusive preserve of public authorities, although this is not an issue explored here. Moreover, such networks often blur the public–private distinction.

include cooperation between securities regulators – the International Organization of Securities Commissions (IOSC); environmental agencies – the International Network for Environmental Compliance and Enforcement (INECE); and, most relevant here, antitrust regulators – the International Competition Network (ICN).[32] Cooperation of this kind has facilitated cross-border investigations and coordination in enforcement actions, policy development and standard setting, as well as information exchange and capacity building.

Although examples of TGRNs can be found from the early decades of the twentieth century (in the field of drug controls, for example),[33] such networks have developed rapidly in the last three decades and their proliferation connects with several trends noted above, notably regulatory innovation, experimentation and rough consensus. The environment in which regulators operate has also changed drastically. For example, there is an increase in normative uncertainty and complexity created by legal globalisation and the expansion in transnational legal risk.[34] An important effect of this change is to create new pressures on regulators to coordinate their activities.[35]

The ICN example was the result of an initiative of the US International Competition Policy Advisory Committee (ICPAC) that was established to investigate 'new tools, tasks and concepts that will be needed to address the competition issues that are just arising on the horizon of the global economy'.[36] The recommendation of ICPAC was to establish a Global Competition Initiative (GCI) that could act as a forum 'for sharing views and experiences, for close cooperation, and for exploration of common issues that could lead to convergence or harmonization'.[37] As such, the aim of ICN is 'addressing antitrust enforcement and policy issues of

[32] See, generally, Lugard, P. (ed.), *The International Competition Network at Ten: Origins, Accomplishments and Aspirations* (Antwerp: Intersentia, 2011); Van Uytsel, S., 'The International Competition Network, Its Leniency Best Practice and Legitimacy: An Argument for Introducing a Review System', in Fenwick, M., Van Uytsel, S. and Wrbka, S. (eds.), *Networked Governance, Transnational Business and the Law* (Heidelberg: Springer, 2014), 185, p. 190.

[33] For example, the 1936 Convention for the Suppression of the Illicit Traffic in Dangerous Drugs facilitated the creation of new national agencies to coordinate international efforts at drug control.

[34] See Fenwick, 'The New Corporate Criminal Law' (n. 2 above), p. 149.

[35] Baldwin, R., Cave, M. and Lodge, M., *Understanding Regulation* (Oxford: Oxford University Press, 2012), p. 160.

[36] See Fox, E., 'Linked-In: Antitrust and the Virtues of a Virtual Network', in Lugard, *The International Competition Network at Ten* (n. 32 above), 113, p. 113.

[37] Ibid, p. 113.

common interest and formulate proposals for procedural and substantive convergence through a result-orientated agenda and structure'.[38]

TGRNs have been praised and described as a 'blueprint for the international architecture of the twenty first century'.[39] In a situation where complex regulatory problems often require a coordinated response from assorted state and non-state actors, TGRNs are widely regarded as an effective means of improving governance. Defined in this way, the concept of TGRNs describes a broad range of contemporary cooperation occurring at an international level across multiple fields.

Since the publication of Robert Keohane and Joseph Nye's seminal paper on these regulatory networks in 1974, an extensive academic literature in legal and political science has also developed examining the emergence, structure and legitimacy of TGRNs.[40] Well-known work in this area – at least in an Anglo-American context – is associated with writers such as Benedict Kingsbury, Nico Krisch and Richard B. Stewart,[41] Charles Sabel and Jonathan Zeitling,[42] and Anne-Marie Slaughter.[43] Moreover, there are several writers who have drawn upon contemporary sociology – for example, the work of Niklas Luhmann[44] and Michel Foucault[45] – to advance our understanding of TGRNs.

In this literature, a network metaphor has often been used to characterise the distinctive form of cooperation that is utilised by these organisations. TGRNs are regarded as networks in the sense that coordination is usually based on loosely structured, horizontal ties developed over time

[38] ICN, 'Memorandum on the Establishment and Operation of the International Competition Network' (2001), p. 1. Retrieved from www.internationalcompetitionnetwork.org/wp-content/uploads/2019/07/ICNMemo_on_Establishment.pdf.

[39] Slaughter, A.-M., 'The Real New World Order' (1997) 47 *Foreign Affairs* 183, p. 197.

[40] Keohane, R. O. and Nye, J. S., 'Trans-Governmental Relations & International Organizations' (2004) 27 *World Politics* 39.

[41] See, for example, Cassese, S., 'Administrative Law without the State? The Challenge of Global Regulation' (2005) 37 *New York University Journal of International Law and Politics* 663; Kingsbury, B., Krisch, N. and Stewart, R. B., 'The Emergence of Global Administrative Law' (2005) 68 *Law and Contemporary Problems* 15. For a collection of essays, see Anthony, G. (ed.), *Values in Global Administrative Law* (Oxford: Hart Publishing, 2011).

[42] See, for example, Sabel, C. and Zeitlin, J., 'Learning from Difference: The New Architecture of Experimentalist Governance in the EU' (European Governance Papers No. C-07-02, 2002).

[43] See, for example, Slaughter, A.-M., *A New World Order* (Princeton: Princeton University Press, 2004).

[44] See, generally, Kjaer, P., *Between Governing and Governance: On the Emergence, Function and Form of Europe's Post-National Constellation* (Oxford: Hart Publishing, 2010).

[45] See, for example, Braithwaite, J. and Drahos, P., *Global Business Regulation* (Cambridge, UK: Cambridge University Press, 2000); Burris, S., Drahos, P. and Shearing, C., 'Nodal Governance' (2005) 30 *Australian Journal of Legal Philosophy* 1.

through repeat interaction among multiple players, rather than via centrally coordinated, hierarchical, ex ante formal agreement.[46] The network metaphor is adopted to suggest that the relationships between the various stakeholders are best viewed in heterarchical rather than hierarchical terms; that is, there has been a 'flattening' of relationships.

The organisational hubs that have emerged in the context of relatively developed TGRNs – for example, the ICN – are often characterised by relatively small secretariats that possess relatively few substantive powers and instead focus on capacity building. The most important function of the ICN, for instance, has been to research and identify best practice across different fields of competition law, including leniency. The ICN finalised its first research on leniency programmes in 2009, when its best practices on leniency programmes were first published. This account was updated in 2014.[47] A significant feature of these guidelines has been a greater awareness of the increasing importance of multi-jurisdictional investigations and the need for deeper and more effective cooperation efforts.[48]

Finally, regulatory cooperation within TGRNs is commonly structured – when it is formally structured at all – by informal or non-legally binding agreements (e.g. memorandums of understanding), and primarily involves routinised peer-to-peer cooperation between participating agencies that is primarily trust based and forged over time. Such cooperation often occurs in the absence of direct control by the executive of the respective governments. The metaphor of a network is thus used in the context of a narrative of de-juridification that describes a shift from hierarchical legal forms ('government') to more flexible, responsive, 'post-legal' institutional forms ('governance').

4.6 Conclusion

Writing in the mid-1980s, the legal theorist Gunther Teubner identified a 'regulatory trilemma' facing all regulators and policymakers in late capitalism.[49] Teubner argued that any regulatory intervention faces three

[46] See Fenwick, M., Van Uytsel, S. and Wrbka, S. (eds.), *Networked Governance and the Law* (Singapore: Springer, 2014).

[47] ICN, 'Anti-Cartel Enforcement Manual' (2014). Retrieved from www.internationalcompetitionnetwork.org/wp-content/uploads/2018/05/CWG_ACEMLeniency.pdf.

[48] See Obsteiner, T., 'International Antitrust Litigation: How to Manage Multi-Jurisdictional Leniency Applications' (2013) 4(1) *Journal of European Competition Law & Practice* 16.

[49] Teubner, G., *Dilemmas of Law in the Welfare State* (London: De Gruyter, 1986).

different and often competing risks: the risk of the regulatory intervention not working (i.e. the regulation misses the target or is otherwise ineffective); the risk of breaking the thing that the regulation seeks to regulate (i.e. the regulation removes any incentive to engage in the activity that is being regulated); and the risk of undermining the law (i.e. the regulation undermines the doctrinal integrity of the law and legal system more generally). The 'trilemma' that Teubner described can be reformulated as a question: how can we ensure that any regulatory intervention is effective, responsive and legally coherent?

Navigating this regulatory trilemma – and managing these competing pressures – has become increasingly complex in the context of contemporary business regulation because of the ongoing processes of globalisation and the digital revolution. More specifically, in the context of a book on leniency programmes, the trilemma manifests itself in terms of a tension between the goal of eradicating an undesirable economic and social problem, namely cartels, while maintaining a commitment to traditional legal principles, notably due process and equal treatment. On one account, the challenge of overcoming information asymmetries in the investigation and detection of cartels has driven a regulatory innovation that has initiated a limited compromise or suspension of those legal principles, at least as they have traditionally been understood. One of the central claims of this chapter is that this tradeoff can be seen across multiple fields of contemporary regulation and that this kind of complex policy choice has become the new normal.[50]

The more general question raised by this trend is whether a compromise of the kind evidenced by leniency risks undermining the law in the long term. This would seem to be a particularly pressing question in legal and political systems that have a history of instability or a less settled relationship with the rule of law. The traditional belief that universal principles – either formal or substantive – can provide an enduring foundation for modern law no longer seems credible. From this point of view, leniency programmes can appear justified, given the practical benefits that they deliver. Such an approach seems reasonable when balanced against the problem that they address, namely cartels, and the real economic harm that cartels cause, both at a structural and an individual level. Nevertheless, we should not be blind to the risks and problems that are potentially created by such schemes.

[50] For a theoretical account of this blurring of the distinction between the rule of law and the law's suspension, see Agamben, G., *The State of the Exception* (Chicago: University of Chicago Press, 2003).

A second concluding question concerns the process of regulatory experimentation described above and the new forms of risk – for companies and regulators – that have emerged. The basis of contemporary business regulation is a contingent understanding of a social problem and the effectiveness (or otherwise) of a particular regulatory scheme. Crucially, this contingent understanding of a problem and the existing regulatory framework is constantly evolving in response to both the experience of stakeholders and the political and economic demands of the public more generally. In the context of political modernity, it has always been the case that the validity of law is temporary, subject to the countervailing wishes of the people as articulated through the legislature. However, under contemporary conditions there is a rapid acceleration in the temporal instability of the validity of the law as legislators and policymakers struggle to manage the complex, competing expectations of various constituencies. The result is that laws are constantly being made and remade. Again, the chapters in this book provide multiple examples of this new structural instability, and the question that it raises is whether such adjustments can be justified as a mature process of learning, iteration and improvement or whether they risk becoming something altogether costlier, notably the introduction of a permanent instability into the legal order that jeopardises the coherence and stability of that order.

PART III

Leniency Programmes in Selected Asian Jurisdictions

5

The Original Leniency Programme of Japan

Law Making in the Shadow of Lobbying, Political Pressure and Legal Constraints

STEVEN VAN UYTSEL

5.1 Introduction

Japan introduced leniency into its Act on Prohibition of Private Monopolisation and Maintenance of Fair Trade (AMA)[1] in 2005. In Article 7(2) of the AMA, the Japan Fair Trade Commission (JFTC) was given the option to reduce the administrative surcharge, a sanction aimed at taking away the illegal profits from a cartel, in exchange for information received from a cartel participant (2005 Leniency Programme).[2] In doing so, Japan followed the example of the United States (US) and the European Union (EU).[3]

The US and EU experiments generated a great deal of information for conceptualising properly functioning leniency policies. Nevertheless, Japan chose a slightly different path. Though the Japanese 2005 Leniency Programme has features of the US and EU leniency policies, Japan has set its own emphasis. This chapter will

[1] Law No. 54 of 1974, shiteki dokusen no kinshi oyobi kousei torihiki no kakuho ni kan suru houritsu [Law Concerning the Prohibition of Private Monopolies and the Assurance of Fair Trade] (AMA). This chapter will refer to the '2005 AMA' when discussing the leniency programme as adopted in 2005. Later revisions of the AMA have changed the articles in which the leniency programme was elaborated. When we just use AMA, this refers to the AMA in its latest revised version, i.e. the one of 2019.

[2] 2005 AMA, Article 7(2). This chapter will use the term leniency programme in the Japanese context, because the conceptualisation is mainly developed in the AMA itself. For the US and the EU, this chapter will use leniency policy. Leniency is in these jurisdictions elaborated in soft law instruments.

[3] See Balasingham, Chapter 2 this volume.

argue that this distinct path can be attributed to the political economy of Japan.

Keidanren, Japan's Business Federation, argued that Japan did not need a leniency programme and sought political support for its viewpoint.[4] A key politician in the Liberal Democratic Party (LDP) sided with industry, albeit for different reasons. These reasons had to do with the Japanese legal environment, which would not allow the adoption of a programme allowing firms to come forward with information in relation to their illegal cartel participation in return for a reduction of or immunity from a sanction.[5] These legal concerns still found resonance within the political elite when the 2005 Leniency Programme was drafted. The politicians would only settle for a leniency programme that was transparent and would not attribute any decision power to the JFTC. Eventually, this resulted in a culmination of 'dormant' and unmeritorious leniency applications.[6]

The chapter is structured as follows. Section 5.2 illustrates the slow route towards adopting leniency in Japan. More specifically, this section will familiarise the reader with the gradually growing desire in Japan to develop a smooth enforcement infrastructure and the fact that this desire was hampered by lobbying and politics. Section 5.3 elaborates on two beliefs that political actors used to prevent a leniency programme from coming into being: the belief that the administrative surcharge was an inflexible sanction not eligible for changes and the belief that plea bargaining could not be introduced through competition law. The legacy of these beliefs further impacted the actual drafting of the 2005 Leniency Programme, which is explained in Section 5.4. This section also illustrates that the programme was transparent and objective. The consequence of this conceptualisation, a culmination of 'dormant' and unmeritorious leniency applications, is described in Section 5.5. Section 5.6 concludes.

[4] See Nippon Keidanren, Press Release, 'Proposal of Nippon Keidanren Regarding Revision of the Antimonopoly Act Enforcement Systems' (5 September 2005). Retrieved from www.keidanren.or.jp/english/policy/2003/088.html.

[5] Van Uytsel, S., 'A Comparative US and EU Perspective on the Japanese Antimonopoly Law's Leniency Programme' (2008) 75 *Hosei Kenkyu* F1, p. F2.

[6] Van Uytsel, S., 'Anti-Cartel Enforcement in Japan: Does Leniency Make the Difference?' in Beaton-Wells, C. and Tran, C. (eds.), *Anti-Cartel Enforcement in a Contemporary Age: Leniency Religion* (Oxford: Hart Publishing, 2015), p. 81.

5.2 The Difficult Road towards the Adoption of a Leniency Programme in Japan

5.2.1 *The Shift away from Japan as Cartel Archipelago*

Cartels have been so pervasive in the Japanese economy that the country has been referred to as a 'cartel archipelago'.[7] Even though this reference is often made in the English literature, the term was probably first coined by a former JFTC official. Patricia Maclachlan reports that Takahashi Toshihide,[8] who became the Chairman of the JFTC in 1972, appealed to this concept to emphasise that he wanted to develop a policy that would shift Japan away from being a cartel haven.[9]

Identifying Japan as a cartel archipelago had its origin in the widespread prevalence of cartels, many of which were organised at the instigation of the Ministry of International Trade and Industry (MITI). MITI's influence had developed along three different lines. First, MITI allowed recession or depression cartels (*fukyou karuteru)* and rationalisation cartels (*gourika karuteru*).[10] These types of cartels, it was argued, would facilitate economic growth, which in turn could benefit consumers.[11] Second, MITI enacted several special statutes to exempt various forms of cartels.[12] These bypass statutes regulated, among others, cartels among small and medium-sized enterprises, import cartels and export cartels.[13] Third, when MITI found overcapacity in an industry,

7 Van Uytsel, S., 'Leniency under the Japanese Antimonopoly Law: Towards the End of the Cartel Archipelago?' in Cheng, T., Marco Colino, S. and Ong, B. (eds.), *Cartels in Asia* (Hong Kong: Wolters Kluwer Law & Business, 2015), p. 67.

8 Maclachlan, P. L., *Consumer Politics in Postwar Japan: The Institutional Boundaries of Citizen Activism* (New York: Columbia University Press, 2002), p. 160.

9 Beeman, M. L., *Public Policy and Economic Competition in Japan: Change and Continuity in Antimonopoly Policy, 1973–1995* (Oxford: Routledge, 2002), pp. 40–68.

10 Schaede, U., *Cooperative Capitalism: Self-Regulation, Trade Associations, and the Antimonopoly Law in Japan* (Oxford: Oxford University Press, 2000), pp. 80–81. See also Nakazawa, T. and Weiss, L. W., 'The Legal Cartels of Japan' (1989) 34 *Antitrust Bulletin* 641.

11 Johnson, C. A, *MITI and the Japanese Miracle – the Growth of Industrial Policy, 1925–1975* (Stanford: Stanford University Press, 1982), p. 215.

12 Yoshikawa, S., 'Fair Trade Commission vs. MITI: History of the Conflicts between the Antimonopoly Policy and the Industrial Policy in Post War Period of Japan' (1983) 15 *Case Western Reserve Journal of International Law* 489, p. 492.

13 See, e.g., Uesugi, A., 'Japan's Cartel System and Its Impact on International Trade' (1986) 27 *Harvard International Law Review* 389, pp. 400–8 (providing a detailed list of the bypass statutes).

MITI would recommend a reduction of the output (*kankoku soutan*) to all entrepreneurs.[14] These ministerial recommendations, commonly referred to as 'administrative guidance' or *gyousei shidou*, often had no formal legal standing or basis.[15]

The JFTC was not in a position to counter MITI's influence over market regulation. Two events, exogenous to the JFTC, changed the situation. First, a public backlash over price explosions caused by cartels during the oil crisis in the 1970s enabled the JFTC to demand a stronger application of the AMA. The JFTC initiated its first criminal case since the end of the US occupation in 1952.[16] Courts followed by declaring the cartels supported by administrative guidance illegal.[17] The legislator strengthened the sanctions and introduced a new one: the administrative surcharge.[18] Second, in its demand to have access to the Japanese market, the US urged for a stronger application of the AMA during the Structural Impediments Initiative (SII).[19] The response to the SII was gradual. Over a period of a decade, the sanctions further increased.[20] The position of the JFTC was upgraded, allowing it to expand its human resources and budget.[21] The number of exemptions from the AMA was drastically reduced.[22] Last, an injunctive relief system was created in 2000.[23]

Against the backdrop of all these reforms, the JFTC stepped up its cartel investigations. Whereas the average number of decisions in relation to cartels was about twenty every year throughout the 1990s, it reached an

[14] Schaede, *Cooperative Capitalism* (n. 10 above), p. 82.

[15] Haley, J. O., 'Japanese Antitrust Enforcement: Implications for United States Trade' (1991) 18 *Northern Kentucky Law Review* 335, p. 348.

[16] Schaede, *Cooperative Capitalism* (n. 10 above), p. 98.

[17] Beeman, *Public Policy and Economic Competition in Japan* (n. 9 above), pp. 44–45.

[18] Murakami, M., *The Japanese Antimonopoly Act* (Tokyo: Shouji Houmu, 2003), p. 76.

[19] Morita, M. K., 'Structural Impediments Initiative: Is it an Effective Correction of Japan's Antimonopoly Policy' (1991) 12 *University of Pennsylvania Journal of International Business Law* 742.

[20] Soon after the SII talks in 1992, the government raised the amount of the sanctions provided in the AMA. The administrative surcharge increased to four times the previous rate, with a maximum of 6 per cent. Criminal sanctions were multiplied twentyfold to the amount of ¥100 million. See Matsushita, M., 'The Antimonopoly Law of Japan', in Graham, E. M. and Richardson, J. D. (eds.) *Global Competition Policy*, Washington, DC: Institute for International Economics, 151, pp. 155–56.

[21] Wakui, M., *Antimonopoly Law: Competition Law and Policy in Japan* (Bury St Edmunds: Arima Publishing, 2008), p. 32.

[22] Ibid.

[23] Ibid.

average of thirty by the early 2000s.[24] Yet concluding that these reforms were sufficient to tackle the image of Japan as a cartel archipelago may be premature. The JFTC's investigation mainly focused on domestic bid-rigging cases related to public procurement projects. There was barely any investigation into pure price-fixing cases, this at a time at which the US and the EU were successfully detecting and punishing international price-fixing cartels. Among these cartels were the Lysine cartel, the Citrus cartel, the Graphite Electrodes cartel and the Vitamins cartel.[25]

The resurgence of interest in prosecuting cartels, and especially ones with an international dimension, was not seen in Asia. It is reported that '[o]nly two global cartels were prosecuted by any Asian antitrust authorities: the Vitamins and Graphite Electrodes were surcharged by the KFTC [Korean Fair Trade Commission] in 2002'.[26] The JFTC only issued warnings.[27] Yet this does not mean that these cartels had weak links with Japan. Aijinomoto Co. and Kyowa Hakko Kogyo, cooperating with the Lysine cartel, are two Japanese firms.[28] The Graphite Electrodes cartel had the Japanese firms Tokai Carbon Co. Ltd, Showa Denko K.K., SEC

24 Van Uytsel, S., 'Am I a Bid Rigger? How Bureaucrats Came within the Focus of Regulating Bid Rigging in Japan' (Presentation at the 13th Asian Competition Forum, Hong Kong, 11–12 December 2017), slide 3.

25 John M. Connor and C. Gustav Helmers inform us that 'since the mid 1990s there has been a resurgence of interest in economic and legal studies of cartels, particularly cartels with international dimensions'. See Connor, J. M. and Helmers, C. G., 'Statistics on Modern Private International Cartels, 1990–2005' (American Antitrust Institute AAI Working Paper No. 07-0, 2007), p. 3. Retrieved from https://papers.ssrn.com/sol3/papers.cfm?abstract_id=944039.

26 Connor, J. M., 'Global Antitrust Prosecutions of International Cartels: Focus on Asia' (2008). Retrieved from https://editorialexpress.com/cgi-bin/conference/download.cgi?db_name=IIOC2008&paper_id=13.

27 Warnings (*keikoku*) are usually issued when the JFTC believes that the enterprise could have violated the AMA but has not sufficient evidence to sustain a formal decision. See Kurita, M., 'Effectiveness and Transparency of Competition Law Enforcement – Causes and Consequences of a Perception Gap between Home and Abroad on the Anti-Monopoly Act Enforcement in Japan' (2004) 3 *Washington University Global Studies Law Review* 387, p. 391 (further indicating that the warning is a 'informal instructions not to repeat the offense, only to Japanese participants in international cartel cases'). See also Connor, 'Global Antitrust Prosecutions of International Cartels' (n. 26 above), p. 390; Iwase, K., 'The Role of Competition Policy in Economic Partnership Agreements' (Lecture at the 12th Technical Training Course on the Antimonopoly Act and Competition Policy, Osaka and Tokyo, 22 September–22 August 2005), slide 16. Retrieved from www.jftc.go.jp/eacpf/05/jicatext2/0916Rol.pdf.

28 European Commission, 'Press Release: Commission Fines ADM, Ajinomoto, Others in Lysine Cartel' (7 June 2000). Retrieved from https://ec.europa.eu/commission/presscorner/detail/en/IP_00_589.

Corporation, and Nippon Carbon Co. Ltd among its members.[29] Daiichi Pharmaceutical Co. Ltd, Eisai Co. Ltd, Takeda Chemical Industries Ltd, Kongo Chemical Co. Ltd, Sumitomo Chemical Co. Ltd, Sumika Fine Chemicals Ltd and Tanabe Saiyaku Co. Ltd were the Japanese firms active in the Vitamins cartel.[30]

One of the main reasons behind the failure of the JFTC to take legal action in the abovementioned cases was the inability to obtain information on the impact of these cartels on the Japanese market.[31] Unlike the US and the EU, Japan had limited means to properly investigate a price-fixing cartel. More specifically, the JFTC pointed to the absence of a leniency programme within the context of the AMA.[32]

There is a strong belief among the officials of the JFTC that a leniency programme would have given them more information, enabling them to start litigating the Graphite Electrode cartel and the Vitamin cartel. Kazuyuki Funahashi, then Deputy Director General of the Investigation Bureau of the JFTC, claimed:

> what is essential to make the cooperation agreements work best is that each of the countries involved in agreements has adopted a leniency programme, if the agreements are to work fully. Generally speaking, it is paramount that, when companies or individuals involved in an international cartel attempt to make application leniency programmes, they apply to the competition authorities in all related countries and regions for eligibility under the same programme and receive reductions in or exemptions from fines.[33]

A similar message was expressed by Yuichi Terakawa, then Director of the Special Investigation Division of the JFTC. Terakawa stated that '[w]e especially expect the introduction of the leniency programme that provides important measures in cases without enough evidence. And we

29 European Commission, 'Press Release: Commission Fines Eight Companies in Graphite Electrode Cartel' (18 July 2001). Retrieved from http://europa.eu/rapid/press-release_IP-01-1010_en.htm?locale=en.

30 European Commission, 'Press Release: Commission Imposes Fines on Vitamin Cartels' (21 November 2001). Retrieved from http://europa.eu/rapid/press-release_IP-01-1625_en.htm.

31 Another reason mentioned is the period of prescription. In the 1990s, Japan had to bring a legal action against a cartel within one year after the violation ceased. It is claimed that, even with a leniency programme in place, a legal action against the Vitamins cartel would have been impossible. The period of prescription of one year had elapsed.

32 Funahashi, K., 'International Cooperation to Crack International Cartels – Japanese Successes and Failures' (2004). Retrieved from www.jftc.go.jp/en/policy_enforcement/speeches/2004_files/internationalcartel1.pdf.

33 Ibid., p. 8.

expect that the cooperative relationships with other countries' competition authorities pressure the violators to offer leniency.'[34]

Despite the desire for a leniency programme, the implementation proved to be difficult. Industry started to lobby against it and found a partner in Sadanori Yamanaka, the politician in charge of competition law issues within the LDP. His support for the 'argument' against a leniency programme blocked a change to the AMA for several years.

5.2.2 *Industry Lobbying and Law Making in Japan*

Lobbying is a widespread technique to influence law making.[35] Japan is no exception to that.[36] One of the reasons politicians are open for lobbying in Japan is the organisation of the funding for politicians. Brian Woodall informs us about the cost of being a politician in Japan:

> Some first-term MPs assume their seats bearing over a million dollars in debt .... A candidate's major expenses include salaries for administrative assistants and clerical staff, gifts for constituents on ceremonial occasions, and costs of mailing and office supplies. In addition, a candidate is expected to pay for festive gatherings, outing to resorts, and a host of other activities involving *kōenkai* members .... A typical backbencher spends about ... 120 million [yen] a year, and as much as eight times that amount in an election year.[37]

To cover these amounts, a politician can rely on some public financing and party support.[38] This financial support may be supplemented by contributions of a leader of a faction within a party and its senior members.[39] However, this way of financing is rather small. For more than half of the required finances, politicians will have to secure donations. These donations come from firms, trade associations and labour unions.[40]

[34] Terakawa, Y., 'International Exchange of Information between Competition Authorities: Update on Recent Bilateral Developments in Japan' (Presentation at 5th International Cartels Workshop, Brussels, 1–3 October 2003), p. 5. Retrieved from https://dl.ndl.go.jp/view/download/digidepo_1254664_po_terakawa_icw_031003.pdf?contentNo=1&alternativeNo=.

[35] See, e.g., Lane, E., *Lobbying and the Law* (Los Angeles: University of California Press, 1964), p. 3.

[36] Nakano, M., *The Policy-Making Process in Contemporary Japan* (London: Palgrave Macmillan, 1997).

[37] Woodall, B., *Japan under Construction: Corruption, Politics, and Public Works* (Berkeley: University of California Press, 1996), pp. 94–95.

[38] Ibid., p. 95.

[39] Ibid.

[40] See, e.g., Misawa, M., 'An Overview of Problems Concerning Political Donations in Japan' (2008) 21(2) *Columbia Journal of Asian Law* 161, pp. 163–64.

When politicians depend on donations from the private sector, 'there is a considerable incentive to barter political influence, in the form of constituency services, for financial support from corporate donors. For many candidates, the construction industry represents a lucrative and convenient source of such support'.[41] The incentive for the construction industry to support these politicians is rooted in a complex system of public procurement that balances construction firms, bureaucrats involved in public works and politicians.[42] The politicians were not necessarily needed to influence the public procurement process, but their support was necessary to funnel public money to construction projects and to make sure that the projects relevant for their donors were approved.

The politicians receiving support from the construction industry are grouped in the *kensetsu zoku*, the construction tribe.[43] A *zoku* has no formal status within the ruling political party in Japan, the LDP. It is just a term to identify a group of politicians that are aligned with a specific interest group. The *zoku* would defend the interests of that group. This happened in the wake of the intended adoption of a leniency programme.[44]

When the JFTC intended to adopt a leniency programme in the aftermath of the failed attempts to tackle international cartels that were discovered in the US and the EU, the construction industry felt that its interests could be harmed.[45] Indeed, a leniency programme would enable a better investigation into bid rigging, one specific form of cartel to which the construction industry often resorted to do business. The construction industry advocated that bid rigging was an expression of harmony among construction firms. The need for this harmony has been justified with various reasons. The construction firms would operate a system to guarantee post-retirement jobs

41 Woodall, *Japan under Construction* (n. 37 above), p. 95.

42 Public procurement projects in Japan were used to guarantee post-retirement jobs for bureaucrats; see ibid., pp. 51–80. In a system advocating seniority-based promotion and lifetime employment, a solution has to be found for seniors who cannot be promoted, simply because there are not enough promotion posts, and who have to be guaranteed a job. Japan developed the practice of *amakudari*, literally meaning 'descent from heaven', which reflects the practice that retired bureaucrats are rehired by private firms. See ibid., pp. 68–75. For further information, see Colignon, R. A. and Usui, C., *Amakudari: The Hidden Fabric of Japan's Economy* (Ithaca, NY: Cornell University Press, 2003).

43 See Woodall, B., 'The Logic of Collusive Action: The Political Roots of Japan's Dangō System' (1993) 25(3) *Journal of Comparative Politics* 297, p. 300.

44 Interview with Sadaaki Suwazono, Former Director of International Affairs, JFTC, in Tokyo, Japan (25 January 2019).

45 Ibid.

for bureaucrats, also known as *amakudari*.[46] Cooperation in the construction industry has also been justified as a form of compensation for the willingness to help during natural disasters.[47] Maintaining a high standard of quality in public procurement projects is another reason the construction industry has forwarded to justify cooperation.[48]

It is not the case that only the construction industry had its doubts about a leniency programme. Keidanren, the Japanese Business Federation, also fiercely objected to leniency within the context of the AMA. Similar to the construction industry, underlying Keidanren's formal objections was a fear that leniency could lead to a better detection of cartels. This in turn could increase the fines for the firms whose interests Keidanren was seeking to protect.[49]

5.2.3 *Sadanori Yamanaka Puts the Leniency Programme on Hold*

To be successful in their lobbying, the *kensetsu zoku* and Keidanren had to convince one person: Sadanori Yamanaka. Yamanaka had advanced himself to be 'the' competition law expert within the LDP. That Yamanaka was in such a position in the late 1990s dates back to the oil crisis of the 1970s.[50] During the oil crisis, it became apparent that cartels were pushing the prices higher and that the JFTC was not able to react. Supported by the public, the JFTC demanded a reinstatement of the AMA to power. This made the LDP realise that it needed a more official body in its party structure to deal with competition law issues. Therefore, the LDP established the Anti-Monopoly Act Examination Committee (Examination Committee).[51] The Examination Committee was positioned in the Policy Affairs Research Council (PARC) of the LDP.[52] Yamanaka was appointed

[46] Wakui, M., 'Bid Rigging Initiated by Government Officials: The Conjuncture of Collusion and Corruption in Japan', in Cheng, Marco Colino and Ong, *Cartels in Asia* (n. 7 above), 41, p. 41.

[47] Ibid.

[48] Ibid.

[49] Uesugi, A., 'A Leniency Programme à la Japonnaise – How It Is Going to Be Enforced' (2005), p. 4. Retrieved from www.jftc.go.jp/en/policy_enforcement/speeches/2005_files/051116uesugi_aba.pdf.

[50] Mogaki, M., *Understanding Governance in Contemporary Japan: Transformation and the Regulatory State* (Manchester: Manchester University Press, 2019), p. 92.

[51] This Examination Committee was given a dual task. On the one hand, it had to function as the forum to debate competition-related issues and so formulate the official LDP's view. On the other hand, it had to examine bills amending the AMA.

[52] Mogaki, *Understanding Governance* (n. 50 above), p. 92.

head of the Examination Committee.[53] As such, Yamanaka had to prepare the LDP's vision on the reforms necessary to restore the trust in the AMA in the 1970s.

Yamanaka prepared himself well for this job. He would seek advice from JFTC officials and study competition law issues together with them. The knowledge so gained was put to use when he had to decide on the best way forward for the AMA. Seldom or never, indicates Masahiro Mogaki, has this decision been made dependent on the demands of interest groups, not even the JFTC.[54] In this regard, Mogaki quotes an interview with a retired senior civil servant of the JFTC: 'When Yamanaka's Examination Committee worked well, it gave civil servants a sense of trust. Probably to other government ministry officials too, for he wasn't a mere JFTC sponsor. In short, he happened to be the chairman of the AMA Examination Committee, but wasn't "the supporter of the JFTC: Sadanori Yamanaka".'[55]

Yamanaka's independence was further combined with a dictatorial flavour. In this respect, Mogaki recites an interview with an official from Keidanren. This official noted that '[t]he LDP's AMA Examination Committee was a very mysterious organization; it's only an organization under the PARC, but under Mr Yamanaka's dictatorial influence … Mr Yamanaka dictatorially decided AMA [related affairs] during the period of the Yamanaka Examination Committee'.[56] Mogaki further suggests that this position was supported by Yamanaka's extensive expertise in the field of competition law and his seniority within the LDP. The latter probably also explains why no other politicians responsible for competition-related matters, in particular the chief Cabinet secretary who in reality supervised the JFTC on behalf of the Prime Minister, strongly intervened in how things were administered by the JFTC. Mogaki goes even so far as to state that the 'chief Cabinet secretary was titular and negligible under the LDP/LDP-led Coalition governments'.[57]

Despite the minimal control of other politicians, Yamanaka did not stretch his dictatorial influence to the edge. He was not the person to determine the long-term vision for the JFTC. The JFTC was independent and thus had the ability to develop its own enforcement policy and even

[53] Ibid.

[54] Ibid., p. 106 (see, e.g., 'with his confident idea on how the AMA should be, Yamanaka rejected things against it, even if from the Prime Minister').

[55] Ibid., pp. 105–6.

[56] Ibid., p. 107.

[57] Ibid.

make suggestions for new legislation.[58] Especially in relation to the latter, Yamanaka did not take an active role. He was more an arbitrator, judging whether the proposals made by the JFTC were good or not and thus worthwhile to pursue or not. In this respect, a senior JFTC official pointed out that 'Mr Yamanaka didn't actively give concrete instructions. Rather, we said "we want this", "we want that", and he sometimes rejected saying "you can't do that", or sometimes said "that's good. Interesting, do it". It's up to the cases.'[59]

One of the issues Yamanaka had to decide upon was the implementation of a leniency programme. Desired by the JFTC but disguised by the LDP's *kensetsu zoku*, Yamanaka had to make a choice on whether to go ahead with an amendment of the AMA that included a leniency programme. He listened to the arguments and, unfortunately for the JFTC, came to the conclusion that a leniency programme could not be implemented in Japan. Two arguments convinced Yamanaka. First, he could not be persuaded that the leniency programme was not an expression of plea bargaining.[60] As will be discussed later, at the time that the adoption of a leniency programme was being discussed, plea bargaining was foreign to the Japanese legal system. It was generally believed that plea bargaining should not be indirectly introduced to the Japanese legal system through the AMA. Second, Yamanaka also shared the opinion that the administrative surcharge was a non-flexible sanction.[61] The JFTC should thus not be given the power to adjust the surcharge according to changing circumstances. This meant a deadlock for the adoption of a leniency programme. It was clear that as long as Yamanaka was in power, the much-desired leniency programme could not be realised. When Yamanaka passed away in 2004, the JFTC officials lobbied once more for a leniency programme.[62] Even though this time the political elite went along with the JFTC's desire, they insisted in not discarding the sensitivities that were emphasised by Yamanaka. The non-flexible status of the administrative surcharge should not be affected and the leniency programme should not contain elements of bargaining.

[58] Ibid., pp. 107–9.

[59] Mogaki, M., 'The Transforming Japanese State and Governance in Antimonopoly Regulation' (2014), p. 13. Retrieved from www.psa.ac.uk/sites/default/files/conference/papers/2014/201404%20PSA%20Conference%20(Mogaki).pdf.

[60] Interview with Suwazono (n. 44 above).

[61] Ibid.

[62] Ibid.

5.3 The Conceptualisation of the Leniency Programme Constrained by Rigid Beliefs on the Scope of the Law

5.3.1 *The Administrative Surcharge Is Not Flexible*

When the AMA was adopted in 1947, the remedies available to the JFTC were limited. In relation to price fixing or cartels, the JFTC could only order entrepreneurs to terminate the infringement.[63] This limited power of the JFTC was in line with the aim of the General Headquarters of the Supreme Command of Allied Powers (SCAP) to limit the possibility of administrative agencies imposing administrative fines.[64] If harsher punishments were deemed appropriate, the JFTC had to rely on the judicial system. This required the JFTC to file an accusation with the Prosecutor General.[65] The actual decision to proceed to court is taken by the Prosecutor General's office. During the US occupation, the option of a criminal sanction was used three times.[66] Once Japan regained sovereignty in 1952, the criminal sanction was not used any more until the oil cartel in 1974.[67]

With criminal sanctions as the only remedy in the law books, the JFTC was effectively toothless. It was only in the 1970s that this situation changed. The economic slowdown, triggered by the oil shock, made the JFTC's advisory body, the Antimonopoly Conference, call for a revival

[63] Iyori, H., 'A Comparison of U.S.-Japan Antitrust Law: Looking at the International Harmonization of Competition Law' (1995) 4 *Pacific Rim Law & Policy Journal* 59, p. 84, citing in this respect the following: 'In Japan, until the early 1970s, the thought with respect to violations of the Antimonopoly Law was that eliminating the illegal act was sufficient. Therefore, violations were handled by administrative cease and desist orders.'

[64] See interview with Suwazono (n. 44 above). The legacy of not allowing an administrative agency to impose an administrative fine has played a role in the conceptualisation of the administrative surcharge. The JFTC did not want to create an administrative fine. Instead, it aimed for just taking away the profits obtained from the illegal conduct in order not to take the form of a fine or sanction. Therefore, the JFTC did not refer to *karyou* (non-penal fine or administrative fine), but created a new name, *kachoukin* (administrative surcharge). See also Suwazono, S., *The 2005 Amendments of the Antimonopoly Law – An Article-by-Article Commentary of the New Surcharge System and the Hearing/Criminal Investigation System* (Tokyo: Shojihoumu, 2005), pp. 9–10 (in Japanese).

[65] Iyori, 'A Comparison of U.S.-Japan Antitrust Law' (n. 63 above), p. 84.

[66] Ariga, M. and Rieke, L. V., 'The Antimonopoly Law of Japan and Its Enforcement' (1964) 39 *Washington Law Review* 437, p. 477 ('However, in 16 years experience under the act, only three indictments have been brought, and all of these were during the occupation period. Only one, after appeal to the Supreme Court, resulted in a fine').

[67] Vande Walle, S., 'The Saitama Saturday Club Case: Political Meddling, Public Opinion, and Antitrust Enforcement in Japan at a Turning Point' (2013) 36 *Journal of Japanese Law* 143, p. 144, n. 13.

of the power lost in the 1953 AMA revision.[68] This call was supported by the then newly appointed chairman, Takahashi. In the end, the economic downturn drove firms to further cartelise, with an inflation of consumer prices as a result, and the JFTC had no proper means to tackle these cartels.[69] In the light of this general dissatisfaction with the state of the AMA, Chairman Takahashi announced in 1973 that the strengthening of the AMA would be subject to a study group.[70]

The strong impression that Takahashi left during his interventions in the Diet, the Japanese Parliament,[71] and the public anger towards cartels, which were perceived by consumers as the cause of the 'insufferable price explosion',[72] created a climate in which calls for revision could no longer be ignored, not even within the LDP. Consumers were, in the end, the ones who would cast votes and the 1974 elections were already not favourable for the ruling party.[73] Therefore, Prime Minister Takeo Miki urged the government to strengthen its grip on business excesses.[74]

Despite the agreement to work on a revision of the AMA, it still took another three years to finalise this first reform of the AMA since 1953. One of the major changes in this reform was the introduction of a new remedy: the administrative surcharge.[75] By allowing the JFTC to impose a financial burden on infringers of the AMA, it may be seen that the Japanese legislator shifted away from the policy imposed by SCAP not to allow administrative agencies to levy fines. To avoid this impression, the surcharge was not conceptualised to punish. The administrative surcharge was supposed to take away the profit made while infringing the AMA. It operated as a rigid system, whereby a certain percentage would be multiplied with the total sales of the good or service of which the price was fixed. The law prescribed which percentage had to be used in what kind of circumstances. The JFTC was not given the power to adjust these percentages according to its own judgement of the facts.

Because leniency has the possibility of adjusting the rigidly determined percentages of the administrative surcharge, Yamanaka resisted

[68] Beeman, *Public Policy and Economic Competition in Japan* (n. 9 above), p. 70.

[69] Ibid.

[70] Ibid., pp. 70–71.

[71] Ibid., pp. 71–72.

[72] Schaede, *Cooperative Capitalism* (n. 10 above), p. 100.

[73] Maclachlan, *Consumer Politics in Postwar Japan* (n. 8 above), pp. 160–62.

[74] Iyori, H. and Uesugi, A., *The Antimonopoly Laws and Policies of Japan* (Washington, DC: Federal Legal Publications, 1994), p. 52.

[75] Wakui, *Antimonopoly Law* (n. 21 above), pp. 25–26.

the adoption of a leniency programme. However, the rigidity remained a problem when the legislator decided to proceed with the creation of a leniency programme. The political elite was of the opinion that nothing in the leniency programme should affect the rigidity. This could be reached by not conceptualising a leniency programme in which the amount of reduction could vary based upon an interpretation by the JFTC of various elements related to the leniency application. This could be to make the degree of reduction dependent on a judgement of the value of the submitted information or the continued cooperation of the leniency applicant. In summary, the preference was that the amounts of reduction should be fixed in the law.

5.3.2 Plea Bargaining Is Not Part of the Japanese Legal System

Another reason why a leniency programme was rejected by the industry was, according to Funahashi, that 'there is no reason to introduce a plea bargaining programme into formal procedure when there is, as yet, no such programme in place within the Japanese criminal procedure'.[76] To understand the fear of anything that looked like plea bargaining, we have to go back to the Lockheed scandal.

Though the Lockheed scandal was not limited to Japan, it was the first Japanese corruption case that caught the attention of the western press.[77] This should not come as a surprise, because the Lockheed scandal involved the then Prime Minister of Japan, Kakuei Tanaka, and six other politicians, among whom were the former Transport Minister, Tomisaburo Hashimoto, and the former Vice Transport Minister, Takayuki Sato.[78] Without going into the detail of the case, the Japanese part of the Lockheed scandal involved a bribe of US$2.1 million to influence All Nippon Airways' decision on buying Lockheed's Tristar aircraft.[79] According to Didrick Castberg, '[t]he bribe first came to light in the U.S. in 1976 when

[76] Funahashi, 'International Cooperation to Crack International Cartels' (n. 32 above), p. 9. Plea bargaining was introduced in Japan in 2018. See Baker & McKenzie, 'Introduction of a Bargaining System to Japanese Criminal Procedure' (2018). Retrieved from www.bakermckenzie.co.jp/wp/wp-content/uploads/ClientAlert_180921_Japanese_Plea_Barganing_System_E.pdf.

[77] Castberg, A. D., 'Prosecutorial Independence in Japan' (1997) 16(1) *Pacific Basin Law Journal* 38, p. 75.

[78] Ibid.

[79] See ibid.

A. Carl Kotchian, a vice-president of Lockheed Aircraft Corporation, testified before Senator Frank Church's sub-committee of the Senate Foreign Relations Committee, that Lockheed paid ¥500 million ($1.4 million) to bribe various Japanese officials to facilitate the purchase of the Tristar'.[80] More information was provided by the same person to the Department of Justice in a plea agreement.

Takeo, the politician succeeding Tanaka as Prime Minister, requested Gerald Ford to provide information on the Senate hearings and the plea agreement to the Japanese government. Ford, according to Castberg, 'agreed, providing that the information would remain confidential and be used for investigative and trial purposes only. An agreement was signed to that effect and shortly thereafter the material was supplied to Japanese officials and relayed to the Tokyo District Prosecutor's office'.[81] This information, supplemented by information seized in Japan, led to the indictment of, among others, former Prime Minister Tanaka. He was found guilty in 1983.[82] Tanaka appealed the Tokyo District Court's decision. The Tokyo High Court rejected this appeal in 1987 and an appeal to the Supreme Court followed.[83] The Supreme Court upheld the conviction of Tanaka in 1995, but explicitly stated that the testimonies given in a plea bargaining proceeding could not be used in court.[84]

With its 1995 decision, the Supreme Court confirmed somehow the stance it had already taken in 1966 in a case related to a taxpayer bribing a tax office employee. In this case:

> The taxpayer involved in the case had an attorney who had a meeting with the prosecutor. At the meeting the prosecutor stated that if the defendant quit lying and showed some remorse, the prosecution would seriously consider suspending the prosecution of the case. The attorney for the taxpayer and the defendant's attorney went to meet with the defendant while he was being confined. At the meeting the taxpayer's attorney relayed what the prosecutor had said, and advised him to accept the prosecutor's offer. The defendant did so; he confessed, and expected to have his case dismissed.[85]

80 Ibid.

81 Ibid.

82 Ibid., p. 76.

83 Ibid., pp. 76–77.

84 Johnson, C., *Japan: Who Governs? The Rise of the Developmental State* (New York: W. W. Norton, 1995), p. 200.

85 Cleary, W. B., 'The Law of Criminal Procedure in Contemporary Japan (2)' (1991) 41(4) *Hokkaido Law Review* 512, p. 477.

The Supreme Court held that a confession in return for a promise of a reduced sanction could not be considered in court, as it is not considered a 'voluntarily given' confession.[86]

With these decisions in mind, it was not immediately clear how a leniency programme in the AMA could operate. Indeed, on a superficial level, a leniency programme has features of plea bargaining. A leniency programme, just like plea bargaining, aims to reduce the sanction for an infringement in return for information on the infringement. If, based on this observation, leniency is considered equal to plea bargaining, the JFTC would run into problems when the information obtained in a leniency application was used in a criminal case. Based upon the settled case law at that time, none of the information obtained in the leniency application would be admissible in court. Thus, the JFTC would not be able to pursue a criminal case for the most serious cartels, if it was detected through a leniency application.

The superficial understanding of what a leniency programme is paralysed the legislative process surrounding the leniency programme. It was only after a visit to the European and German enforcement authorities that the JFTC realised that a leniency programme is substantially different from plea bargaining.[87] Plea bargaining requires that the defendant pleads guilty.[88] In return for the guilty plea, the prosecutor commits, in a charge bargaining case, to drop, reduce or refrain from bringing additional charges.[89] Sentence bargaining, on the contrary, offers the defendant a prosecutorial recommendation of sentencing concessions.[90] No matter which type of plea bargaining is implemented, it has a dual function.[91] First, plea bargaining facilitates the investigative process by obtaining evidence. Second, the enhanced way of obtaining evidence leads to closure of the case in a more resource-efficient way. It is the latter point that makes the difference to a leniency programme. A leniency programme is pre-eminently an investigative tool. Cartel participants are induced to defect and provide

[86] See ibid. The author also mentions that the decision was based on an early high court judgment dealing with the same issue, wherein it was held that a confession based upon a promise could not have been given voluntarily.

[87] Interview with Suwazono (n. 44 above).

[88] Fine, R. A., 'Plea Bargaining: An Unnecessary Evil' (1987) 70 *Marquette Law Review* 615, p. 616.

[89] Jolly, R. L. and Prescott, J. J., 'Beyond Plea Bargaining' (2020), p. 106. Retrieved from https://ssrn.com/abstract=3579226. Recently there is also fact bargaining, 'in which the parties stipulate to the version of facts consistent with the charges that will be presented to the court'; ibid.

[90] Ibid.

[91] Fine, 'Plea Bargaining' (n. 88 above), p. 616.

information on the cartel. This information will relate both to their activities within the cartel and to the activities of others. At no point, however, is there a requirement to plead guilty. Hence, a leniency programme is thus solely an investigative tool. It is in no way a case-closing tool.

Once knowledgeable about the substantive difference between plea bargaining and leniency, Akinori Uesugi acknowledged that the JFTC still 'had to try to make people understand the nature of a leniency programme'.[92] Uesugi also discussed their success in doing so.[93] Yet, no matter how convincing the JFTC may have been with its arguments, the impact of the debate on whether leniency is just another name for plea bargaining was tremendous. This debate meant that the drafters of the leniency programme for the AMA had to avoid any decision-making power for the JFTC in the leniency application process.

5.4 The 2005 Leniency Programme Devoid of Any Discretionary Power for the JFTC

5.4.1 Yamanaka's Legacy

The Japanese government, more specifically the law makers in the LDP, gave the green light to think of implementing leniency in the context of the AMA in 2004. However, the law makers did not want to simply reject the objections of Yamanaka.[94] Yamanaka emphasised that the JFTC should not have the power to change the percentages of the administrative surcharge. Also, based on his idea that leniency and plea bargaining are similar in nature, Yamanaka indirectly pointed out that he did not want the JFTC to bargain with violators of the AMA on a reduction of their administrative surcharge. The impact of these considerations was twofold. First, the law makers considered that the leniency programme should be conceptualised within the AMA and not as a soft law instrument.[95] Second, the law makers should set out the parameters against which a reduction of the administrative surcharge could be granted. In other words, the JFTC should only be the recipient of a leniency application and should check whether the eligibility criteria are met.[96]

92 Uesugi, 'A Leniency Programme à la Japonnaise' (n. 49 above), p. 4.

93 Ibid. Uesugi makes the comment that 'most people accepted our [the JFTC's] arguments that a leniency programme is quite different from a plea-bargaining', p. 4.

94 Interview with Suwazono (n. 44 above).

95 Ibid.

96 Ibid.

5.4.2 *The Scope of the 2005 Leniency Programme*

The leniency programme in Japan was implemented through a change in the AMA, more specifically Article 7(2) of the 2005 AMA. This article dealt with the administrative surcharge.[97] After elaborating on the surcharge that can be levied on infringers of the cartel provision of the AMA, Article 7(2) of the 2005 AMA allowed for a reduction of the administrative surcharge on the condition that an entrepreneur violating the AMA comes forward with information regarding that illegal cartel activity.[98] The incorporation of leniency in this article has as a consequence that the leniency programme could not be applied to criminal sanctions or private damages.

The 2005 Leniency Programme was only available to a maximum of three entrepreneurs.[99] The leniency could be applied for before or after the

[97] For a discussion on the leniency programme, see, e.g., Irie, G. and Matsushima, T., *Cartel Regulation and Leniency: Research on and Practical Use of the Reduction and Immunity of the Surcharge System* (Tokyo: Sankyouhouki, 2014) (in Japanese); Shinagawa, T. and Iwanari, H., *Reduction and Immunity from the Surcharge under the Antimonopoly Law* (Tokyo: Koutori Kyoukai, 2010) (in Japanese); Inoue, A., *The Leniency Practice: Protect Your Company against the Rough Seas of Competition* (Tokyo: Lexis Japan, 2006) (in Japanese). For an explanation of the administrative surcharge, see Wakui, *Antimonopoly Law* (n. 75 above), pp. 233–34. The amount of the surcharge is calculated by multiplying the amount of the sales of the relevant products or services during the period in which the unreasonable restraint of trade was implemented (the maximum period is three years) by the surcharge calculation rate of the specific industry. The general category of surcharge is 10 per cent. This can be increased to 15 per cent if the entrepreneur has been subject to a surcharge payment during the last ten years or has played a major role in the unreasonable restraint of trade. The surcharge can be increased to 20 per cent if both aggravating factors are present. The surcharge can be mitigated on the condition that the company ceases its infringement one month prior to the investigation by the JFTC. In this case, the surcharge will be 8 per cent. The surcharge rate differs for retailers and wholesalers. The former has a general rate of 3 per cent, an aggravated rate of 4.5 per cent or 6 per cent and a mitigated rate of 2.4 per cent. The latter has a general rate of 2 per cent, an aggravated rate of 3 or 4 per cent, and a mitigated rate of 1.6 per cent.

[98] This chapter adopts the terminology used in the AMA. Accordingly, 'entrepreneur' is used to indicate the actor that infringes the AMA. 'Firm' will be used when legal entities are addressed outside the scope of the AMA.

[99] See Van Uytsel, 'A Comparative US and EU Perspective' (n. 5 above), pp. F6–F7. The original leniency programme only provided for leniency for up to three entrepreneurs. Experts within a study group under the Cabinet Office, the *dokusen kinshi hou kihon mondai kohandai* (Round Table Conference on the Fundamental Problems of the Antimonopoly Law), recommended the programme be extended to allow up to five entrepreneurs to apply for leniency. This study group comprised academics, business people, the private bar and consumer organisations. JFTC officials were not members of the group, but the JFTC decided to support the recommendation and took it over in the bill changing the AMA in 2009. Interview with Takujiro Kono, Senior Officer for Immunity from or Reduction of Surcharges, JFTC, Tokyo, 17 February 2012. For a change in the number of entrepreneurs eligible for leniency, see Van Uytsel, 'Anti-Cartel Enforcement in Japan' (n. 6 above), p. 83.

JFTC started an investigation. The criteria for determining whether the JFTC began an investigation was the dawn raid.[100] Any leniency application that arrived before the dawn raid would be an application prior to a JFTC investigation. In contrast, any leniency application that arrived once a dawn raid had been initiated was considered a leniency application done after the JFTC investigation started.

Prior to an investigation, the first entrepreneur that reported its participation in a cartel and met the relevant conditions was eligible for immunity.[101] The two remaining spots in the leniency programme offered only partial reductions. The highest partial reduction was 50 per cent, which could be granted to the second applicant that met the relevant conditions.[102] The third entrepreneur that came forward with information and met the relevant conditions was offered a reduction of 30 per cent.[103] Any other applicant beyond the third entrepreneur was not eligible for a reduction.

Once the JFTC commenced with a dawn raid, a maximum of three entrepreneurs could have been granted leniency provided that not a single entrepreneur was granted leniency prior to the dawn raid.[104] The number of entrepreneurs eligible for leniency at this stage would reduce proportionally to the number of successful applicants prior to the start of the investigation. And at this stage, an entrepreneur had twenty business days from the day of the dawn raid to submit a leniency application,[105] and if successful, the applicant would only be eligible for a 30 per cent reduction of the surcharge.[106] In terms of deadlines and the potential size of the reduction, there was thus no distinction drawn based on the order in which the entrepreneurs come forward with information.[107]

In order to enjoy immunity from or a reduction of a surcharge, a leniency applicant had to submit reports providing detailed information regarding the illegal cartel.[108] The process for submitting reports

[100] 2005 AMA, Article 7-2 (7)–(9).
[101] Ibid., Article 7-2 (7).
[102] Ibid., Article 7-2 (8).
[103] Ibid.
[104] Ibid., Article 7-2 (9).
[105] JFTC, 'Rules on Reporting and Submission of Materials Regarding Immunity from or Reduction of Surcharges' (Fair Trade Commission Rule No. 7 of 2005), p. 5. Retrieved from www.jftc.go.jp/en/legislation_gls/antimonopoly_rules_files/immunityH21.pdf (Leniency Rules).
[106] 2005 AMA, Article 7-2 (9).
[107] Ibid., Article 7-2 (9).
[108] Ibid., Article 7-2 (7) (i), (8) (i), and (9) (i).

to the JFTC was described in the Rules on Reporting and Submission of Materials Regarding Immunity from or Reduction of Surcharges (Leniency Rules).[109] It differed depending upon the timing of the application. Applicants reporting before a dawn raid had to submit Form 1[110] and Form 2.[111] Those applying after a dawn raid had to submit Form 3.[112]

The application process was quite rigid. Applicants in the pre-investigation period needed to fax Form 1 to a centrally established fax number.[113] The submission of this report secured the position of the applicant. The receipt of the fax thus functioned as a kind of marker,[114] but the order was only provisionally secured. Failing to submit Form 2 and the required evidentiary materials within the time period stipulated by the JFTC (usually two weeks) resulted in the automatic revocation of the applicant's previously secured position in the order of applications.[115] After the dawn raid, a marker was not available. This was logical, as the amount of reduction

109 See Leniency Rules.

110 Form 1 required the leniency applicant to submit the following information: an outline of the infringement, a description of the cartel conduct and the duration of the infringement. The outline of the infringement required information about the goods and services in order to define any relevant markets. The description of the cartel conduct included a typology of the cartel conduct as price fixing, output restriction, bid rigging or any other form of collusive conduct. The leniency applicant also had to identify the other cartel members and the involvement, if any, of trade associations. Depending on the type of cartel, conduct-specific information had to be provided. For price fixing, this related to the setting of prices. For bid rigging, this could be the public agency deciding to whom the bid should be granted. To determine the duration of the infringement, the leniency applicant had to count from the date when the applicant was certain there was an implementation of the infringing act.

111 Form 2 was more detailed than Form 1. Besides a repetition of the information already provided in Form 1, Form 2 also required the identification of individuals active in the cartel and an indication of the materials that evidenced the infringement. The former meant that the names and titles of the conspiring employees of the applicant and the co-conspirators had to be provided. The guideline in the Leniency Rules further stipulated that all employees involved in the illegal activity – executives and others, current and past – be listed in Form 2. The evidence of the infringement could include memoranda of meetings, business reports, correspondence between cartel members and written reports bearing the signatures or seals of executives or employees. All information had to be submitted in Japanese or accompanied by Japanese translations.

112 Form 3 was essentially as detailed as Form 2. However, Form 3 required extra information regarding the relevant goods or services or the situation surrounding the implementation of the infringing act.

113 Leniency Rules, Section 1(2). The fax number was 03-3581-5599 (for faxes from outside Japan the number was +81-3-3581-5599). Note that fax has been replaced by email in the newly adopted leniency programme of 2019. See Van Uytsel and Uemura, Chapter 6 this volume.

114 Leniency Rules, Section 7.

115 2005 AMA, Article 7-2 (17) (ii).

was the same for all applicants. Therefore, the entrepreneurs were not given a period of grace to gather necessary documents and evidence. The entrepreneurs, at this stage, had to submit a full application, including evidence, in the format of Form 3.

It was common practice for Form 2 and Form 3 to be submitted by writing.[116] However, the JFTC also accepted oral statements.[117] The oral statement had to be made before the Senior Officer for Immunity from or Reduction of Surcharges at the premises of the JFTC. The Leniency Rules did not specify the reasons for substituting the written procedure with oral statements. Two lawyers have indicated that the threat of discovery procedures in follow-on actions for damages could constitute an exceptional circumstance justifying oral statements.[118]

All three forms had to be submitted in Japanese. The language requirement also applied to the documents submitted as evidence. This meant that a Japanese translation had to be provided for any documentary evidence in a foreign language. Leniency applicants had to keep the application secret from third parties.[119] Once it had been reported, the applicant had to terminate the illegal conduct[120] and provide additional information if requested by the JFTC.[121] The information provided could not be false.[122] Further, the applicant should not have coerced other entrepreneurs to participate in the leniency programme nor prevented an entrepreneur from ceasing such conduct.[123] Similar conditions applied to the applicants applying for a reduction.[124]

An applicant who successfully submitted the reports and evidence was promptly informed by the JFTC about the receipt of those documents.[125] This notice of acceptance did not legally guarantee the grant of immunity

[116] See Leniency Rules, Section 6. Form 2 could either be directly delivered or sent by registered mail to the Senior Officer for Immunity from or Reduction of Surcharges or transmitted in facsimile. Section 4 (2) stipulates that Form 3 has to be transmitted in facsimile.

[117] Ibid., Section 3(2).

[118] Ishida, H. and Hara, E., 'Japan: Cartels' (2014) *Asia-Pacific Antitrust Review* 110, p. 112.

[119] Leniency Rules, Section 8. Under that section, the applicant may disclose the application if it has a 'justifiable reason' for doing so.

[120] 2005 AMA, Article 7-2 (7) (ii).

[121] Ibid., Article 7-2 (11).

[122] Ibid., Article 7-2 (12) (i). Bunka Shutter Co. Ltd has seen its leniency status revoked for submitting false information. See Suzuki, M., 'Japan' (2010) 32(2) *Antitrust* 37, p. 38.

[123] 2005 AMA, Article 7-2 (12) (iii).

[124] Ibid., Articles 7-2 (8) (i) and (ii) and (9) (i) (report and evidence); Articles 7-2 (8) (iii) and (9) (ii) (termination of the illegal conduct); Articles 7-2 (11) (continued assistance) and Article 7-2 (12) (false information and coercion).

[125] Ibid., Article 7-2 (10).

or reduction.[126] Leniency, whether in the form of immunity or fine reduction, only became official when the JFTC issued the surcharge payment order against the other AMA violators.[127]

5.4.3 A Transparent and Objective Leniency Programme

With the above-described leniency programme, the Japanese legislator showed that much had been learned from the US and EU early leniency programmes. This manifested itself in the inability of the JFTC to second-guess a leniency application, in a substantial incentive to apply by providing immunity, and in a clarification of the order of application.[128]

However, the special environment in which the leniency programme was made forced the JFTC to ensure that the leniency programme would be 100 per cent transparent and objective. The leniency programme should not only need to be, but also be seen to be, transparent and objective.[129] Therefore, the leniency programme avoided concepts requiring interpretation and decision-making. The former led to the avoidance of concepts such as value-added information or originator and leader of a cartel. The latter manifested itself in a fixed degree of reduction depending on the timing of submitting a leniency application.

The just-mentioned observations meant that the practice of the 2005 Leniency Programme offset itself from the (failing) practice in the US and the EU.

The JFTC cannot, for whatever reason, disregard a leniency application. When an entrepreneur submits a leniency application that fulfils all requirements set forth by the law, the JFTC has to grant immunity or reduction at the moment a surcharge order is issued. Making the granting of leniency automatic is a lesson learned from the US. The Antitrust Division of the Department of Justice, in its earliest leniency programme, had the right to reject a leniency application if it was of the opinion that a similar result could have been achieved without a leniency application. This kind of second-guessing was considered detrimental to smooth

[126] Koma, F., Inoue, A. and Ae, J., 'Japan', in Mobley, S. J. and Denton, R. (eds.), *Global Cartels Handbook: Leniency: Policy and Procedure* (Oxford: Oxford University Press, 2011), 317, p. 322.

[127] 2005 AMA, Article 7-2 (13).

[128] See Van Uytsel, 'A Comparative US and EU Perspective' (n. 5 above).

[129] Berzins, M., 'Wrestling with Cartels: The Emergence of Competition Laws, Anti-Cartel Enforcement and a Leniency Programme in Japan' (2008) 8(1) *International Journal of Knowledge, Culture & Change Management* 15, p. 20.

operation. Second-guessing a leniency application was not included in the revised 1993 US Leniency Policy.[130]

The EU never considered second-guessing leniency applications.[131] However, the EU started to test another form of uncertainty for leniency applicants. Rather than giving a leniency applicant certainty on the amount of leniency, the European Commission was allowed to reconsider the granting of immunity. The first leniency applicant could be given a reduction instead of immunity because of considerations related to the cooperation of the leniency applicant and the value of the information provided.[132] As this affected the number and quality of leniency applications, the European Commission decided to erase this discretionary power from 2002.[133] This lesson was obvious to the Japanese legislator. The first applicant was, if complying with all conditions, automatically given immunity.

Japan went even further in terms of fixing the degree of reduction. Japan introduced the possibility of giving reduction to leniency applicants subsequent to the first applicant. This practice is similar to that in the EU. However, the EU never fixed the degree of reduction for subsequent leniency applicants. It only provided a band of reduction, with upper and lower bounds. It was the task of the European Commission to choose the exact degree of reduction based upon the value of the information and the applicant's cooperation.[134] The Japanese legislator did not follow this example, but fixed the degree of reduction and linked it automatically to the order of applications.[135]

In relation to the order of applications, the JFTC could only mechanically accept the order based upon the arrival of a fax. There is nothing that allowed the JFTC to lift one leniency applicant over another and so give more beneficial treatment. Again, this approach is different than that in the EU, where the original leniency programme allowed a switch in the order of applications based upon the degree of cooperation or value of information.

Linked with the two previous issues, the JFTC was not given the competence to judge the evidentiary value of the information of a leniency application. Together with the general information of Forms 1, 2 and 3, the entrepreneurs had to submit evidence of the infringement. Some of

[130] Van Uytsel, 'A Comparative US and EU Perspective' (n. 5 above), pp. F32–F35.
[131] Ibid., pp. F34–F35.
[132] Ibid.
[133] Carle, J., Lindeborg, P. and Segenmark, E., 'The New Leniency Notice' (2002) 23 *ECLR* 265.
[134] Balasingham, Chapter 2 this volume.
[135] 2005 AMA, Article 7-2(8) and (9).

the evidence could have greater value to conclude that an infringement occurred or to evaluate the extent of the infringement. The JFTC could take notice of this fact, but could not advantage an applicant based upon the quality of the evidence.[136]

Still linked to information, the JFTC had to accept any leniency application even if the information contained in the application was already known to the JFTC either through ex officio investigations or through another leniency application.[137] This stance is very generous and deviates from both the US and the EU leniency programmes. A leniency applicant in the US needs to submit unknown information if he or she wants to obtain immunity. In the EU, a leniency applicant for immunity is required, depending on whether an investigation has started or not, to submit information sufficient to start an investigation or to establish an infringement.[138] If the application is for a reduction, the information needs to significantly add value to the already known information.

The Japanese legislator also did not allow for discretion in relation to the conditions attached to the leniency programme. Among the much-contested concepts in early US and EU leniency programmes were those of originator, coercer and leader.[139] Since this requires an in-depth judgement of the facts, almost none of these concepts was repeated in the Japanese leniency programme. Only one concept was retained: coercer.[140] If an entrepreneur had coerced other entrepreneurs to enter a cartel or prevented them from leaving a cartel, that entrepreneur would not be eligible for leniency. When considering whether to retain the concept of coercer, the legislator immediately clarified the concept. An entrepreneur would only be considered as coercer if that entrepreneur exerted physical violence towards employees of other entrepreneurs.[141]

5.5 The Race to the JFTC: Ran by Too Many, Aborted Too Early

With no power for the JFTC to change elements of a leniency application, the 2005 Leniency Programme was one of the most transparent

[136] Van Uytsel, 'A Comparative US and EU Perspective' (n. 5 above), pp. F51–F54.

[137] Van Uytsel, 'Anti-Cartel Enforcement in Japan' (n. 6 above), p. 88.

[138] Balasingham, Chapter 2 this volume.

[139] Ibid.

[140] 2005 AMA, Article 7-2 (12).

[141] See Shiraishi, T., *Dokusen Kinshi Hou [The Antimonopoly Law]* (Tokyo: Yuhikaku Publishing, 2006), pp. 500–1; Inoue, A., 'The Recent Amendment of the Japanese Antimonopoly Law' (2006) 1(1) *Japan Business Law Review* 4, p. 8.

and objective leniency programmes. Further, combining immunity with reduction, the 2005 Leniency Programme was also very generous.[142] The combination of transparency, objectivity and generosity should, according to economic experimental studies, result in a substantial number of leniency applications.[143] This was the case. In an early study, Akinori Uesugi observed that the 2005 Leniency Programme had triggered a high number of leniency applications, giving way to a smooth decision-making process by the JFTC.[144] Toshiyuki Nambu, a former official of the JFTC writing in his personal capacity, repeated this observation nearly ten years later.[145]

Indeed, the 2005 Leniency Programme attracted an immense number of leniency applications from the start. By the time of its first revision in 2009, the Leniency Programme had been used by 323 leniency applicants. By 2020, the year in which a major revision of the Japanese leniency programme went into force, 1343 leniency applicants had been registered. It is very difficult to put these data into perspective. There are very few countries that reveal how many leniency applications their respective leniency programmes attract. In Table 5.1, the total number of leniency applications is given. The total number is further broken down into the number of leniency applications for each fiscal year (FY).[146]

Leaving aside any explanation for the waves in the number of applications,[147] the total number of leniency applications takes on a different complexion if it is compared to the total number of decisions and the total number of successful leniency applicants. The 1343 leniency applications led to 153 decisions supported by leniency applications. The total of 153 decisions was further supported by 391 leniency applicants. Table 5.2

[142] Van Uytsel, 'Anti-Cartel Enforcement in Japan' (n. 6 above), pp. 85–91.

[143] Van Uytsel, 'A Comparative US and EU Perspective' (n. 5 above), pp. F9–F15.

[144] Uesugi, A., 'The Japanese Leniency Programme – One Year In' (2007) 21 *Antitrust* 79, pp. 83–84.

[145] Nambu, T., 'A Successful Story: Leniency and (International) Cartel Enforcement in Japan' (2014) 5 *Journal of European Competition Law & Practice* 158.

[146] The fiscal year in Japan starts on 1 April in a given year and ends on 31 March of the next year. Fiscal year 2006, for example, covers the period from 1 April 2006 to 31 March 2007.

[147] The JFTC did not have an official explanation on the decline of the number of applications between 2011 and 2015, but acknowledged that one of the reasons could be that the follow-on applications of international cartels, and then specifically the cartels related to car parts, had come to an end. Email from Toshiyuki Nambu, Deputy Secretary General for International Affairs, JFTC, to Steven Van Uytsel, Associate Professor, Faculty of Law, Kyushu University (September 22, 2014) (on file with the author). Another possible factor in the decline could have been entrepreneurs' familiarisation with the practice of the JFTC towards the leniency programme, due to which the entrepreneurs are more selective in the decision to apply for leniency. See Ishida and Hara, 'Japan: Cartels' (n. 118 above), p. 113.

Table 5.1 *Number of leniency applications based on the original leniency programme*

FY	2006	2007	2008	2009	2010	2011	2012	2013	2014	2015	2016	2017	2018	2019	2020	Total
No.	79	74	85	85	131	143	102	50	61	102	124	103	72	73	33	1343

Source: Van Uytsel, 'Anti-Cartel Enforcement in Japan: Does Leniency Make the Difference?' in Beaton-Wells, C. and Tran, C. (eds.), *Anti-Cartel Enforcement in a Contemporary Age: Leniency Religion* (Oxford: Hart Publishing, 2015), p. 92, supplemented with JFTC, 'Concerning the Enforcement Status of the Antimonopoly Law Infringement Cases of the Fiscal Year 2020' (5 May 2021). Retrieved from www.jftc.go.jp/houdou/pressrelease/2021/may/210526.html (in Japanese).

Table 5.2 *Total number of decisions supported by (a) leniency applications and (b) the total number of successful leniency applicants*

FY	2006	2007	2008	2009	2010	2011	2012	2013	2014	2015	2016	2017	2018	2019	2020	Total
(a)	6	16	8	21	7	9	19	13	4	7	9	11	7	9	8	153
(b)	16	37	21	50	10	27	41	33	10	19	28	35	21	26	17	391

Source: Van Uytsel, 'Anti-Cartel Enforcement in Japan: Does Leniency Make the Difference?' in Beaton-Wells, C. and Tran, C. (eds.), *Anti-Cartel Enforcement in a Contemporary Age: Leniency Religion* (Oxford: Hart Publishing, 2015), p. 92, supplemented with JFTC, 'Concerning the Enforcement Status of the Antimonopoly Law Infringement Cases of the Fiscal Year 2020' (5 May 2021). Retrieved from www.jftc.go.jp/houdou/pressrelease/2021/may/210526.html (in Japanese).

presents these data, wherein (a) stands for the JFTC decisions supported by leniency applications and (b) for the total number of successful leniency applicants.

If Tables 5.1 and 5.2 are compared with each other, it is immediately obvious that there is a discrepancy between the total number of leniency applicants and the total number of successful leniency applicants. There are 936 leniency applications that are not reflected in JFTC decisions. Nambu has reported that these applications were not investigated due to a lack of sufficient evidence.[148] They became so-called dormant leniency applications. However, the discrepancy between the successful and dormant leniency applications may highlight a potential shortcoming of the leniency programme.

Ishida and Hara have argued that the discrepancy can be attributed to the leniency conditions related to information and cooperation. Indeed, the 2005 Leniency Programme did not require the submission of relevant (let alone valuable) information.[149] Entrepreneurs went with whatever information they had at hand to the JFTC, as even the tiniest piece of information would make them eligible for immunity or reduction. The fact that these applications remained dormant could say a lot about the obligation to cooperate with the JFTC.

The obligation to cooperate with the JFTC is limited. Entrepreneurs are only required to respond to explicit requests of the JFTC.[150] As long as the JFTC does not formulate any question in relation to the dormant leniency applications, these applications remain without any consequence. But there is more. The obligation to cooperate with the JFTC also applies to the successful leniency applications. Sadaaki Suwazono, a former Director of International Affairs of the JFTC and once responsible for following up the drafting of the original 2005 Leniency Programme, expands on this issue in a short article, 'A Japanese View of Competition Law Enforcement'.[151] He informs us as follows:

> In many cases, the JFTC will repeatedly ask questions and request the submission of relevant documents concerning business details and the conduct of the applicants' cartel. The applicants, in order to secure an exemption or

[148] Nambu, 'A Successful Story' (n. 145 above). See also interview with Kono (n. 99 above).

[149] Ishida and Hara, 'Japan: Cartels' (n. 118 above), p. 113.

[150] Ibid.

[151] Suwazono, S., 'A Japanese View of Competition Law Enforcement' *InformaConnect* (21 November 2016). Retrieved from https://informaconnect.com/a-japanese-view-of-competition-law-enforcement.

> a reduction of sanctions, are required to continue to cooperate with the JFTC's requests for an extended period of time. This is not unique to the Japanese leniency programme (for example, the same requirements may apply throughout the leniency programmes in South Korea and China). In addition, the JFTC sets tight timelines for leniency applicants to submit documentation. Even in investigations concerning a large-scale cartel or an international cartel, the JFTC allows only three weeks for a leniency applicant to file a document called a Form 2 document after submitting the Form 1 document. Also, even after a leniency applicant submits the Form 2 document, the JFTC requests that the applicant continuously report additional information and submit additional evidence to the JFTC. To deal with these JFTC requests, foreign companies should retain local counsel who have a great deal of experience dealing with leniency applications with the JFTC, in order to make the filing process as smooth as possible. On the other hand, as some practitioners have pointed out, there *might be possibility* [sic] *that the applicants do not have any incentives to be cooperative to JFTC's investigation once they are guaranteed their status of leniency applicants by submitting application form* [sic] *accompanied by some evidence.*[152]

Suwazono's explanation may need more contextualisation. At the outset, the functioning of the requirement to cooperate with the JFTC may seem to be very rigid. That may be true for the submission of Forms 1 and 2, especially when it relates to the deadline of submitting the latter document. However, the continued cooperation upon the request of the JFTC is less rigid. In theory, the JFTC could communicate a formal request. In practice, such a formal request is seldom issued.[153] The JFTC prefers to informally engage with leniency applicants. Whereas this usually leads to the desired result, the JFTC has little room for manoeuvre when the leniency applicant informs it that the requested information is not at hand. A request for information will only be formalised, and thus create a ground for rejecting a leniency application if not complied with, when the leniency applicant's attitude is one of complete unwillingness to interact with the JFTC.[154] The question is, however, to what extent entrepreneurs should fear a formal request based upon Suwazono's statement . In other words, Suwazono seems to indicate that there are also unmeritorious leniency applications among the successful leniency applications, which are not really contributing to a smooth decision-making process.

152 Ibid. (emphasis added).

153 See email from Kentaro Hirayama, Associate Professor, Faculty of Law, Kyushu University, to Steven Van Uytsel, Professor, Faculty of Law, Kyushu University (8 January 2021) (on file with the author).

154 Ibid.

A transparent, objective and generous leniency programme thus carries a risk of swamping the enforcement agency with lots of leniency applications. Not all these applications will lead to decisions. A selection therefore has to be made on whether or not to proceed with a leniency application. The leniency applications that are not pursued by the JFTC become dormant. But again, there is more. The decision to proceed with an investigation may also have to be done based upon unmeritorious leniency applications. These are applications that provide information that does not contribute to handling the case. In other words, some of the eligible leniency applications may not give further insight into the full scope of the cartel agreement, due to the limited amount of new information these applications contain. It is therefore possible that the full extent of some cartels is not uncovered or, in cases where this did happen, it took more time.

5.6 Conclusion

When Japan was contemplating the enactment of a leniency programme, it could rely on considerable experience built up in the US and the EU. The political economy, though, first prevented the leniency programme from coming into being. When the obstacles to continuing with the drafting of a leniency programme disappeared, the same political economy prevented the legislator from adopting a leniency programme that was completely in line with one of the existing leniency policies. The bottom line was that the JFTC should not be given any power to decide on elements of the leniency application process. Combining this element with the lessons from the US and the EU, Japan drafted a leniency programme that was transparent, objective and generous.

The transparent, objective and generous leniency programme attracted a tremendous number of leniency applications. This led to a lot of unmeritorious leniency applications and had two dimensions. On the one hand, not all leniency applications were useful in terms of revealing a cartel. These are the so-called dormant leniency applications. On the other hand, not all leniency applications that revealed a cartel contributed to the facilitation of the investigation. Whereas the former did not lead to granting leniency, the latter did. To rectify the above-analysed situation, different changes may be required to a leniency programme. The JFTC chose to solve the latter issue.[155]

[155] Van Uytsel and Uemura, Chapter 6 this volume.

6

Negotiated Leniency in Japan Embedded in Ever-Increasing Sanctions

A Deterrence Perspective

STEVEN VAN UYTSEL AND YOSHITERU UEMURA

6.1 Introduction

In 2005, Japan followed the international trend of implementing a leniency programme to enforce the anti-cartel provision of its Act on Prohibition of Private Monopolization and Maintenance of Fair Trade (Antimonopoly Act or AMA).[1] With this new enforcement tool, the Japan Fair Trade Commission (JFTC) could offer, in return for information on a cartel, immunity from or reduction of the administrative surcharge. The surcharge is a kind of administrative sanction aimed at taking away the illegal profits from a cartel. The Japanese legislator made the first changes to its 2005 Leniency Programme[2] in 2009 (2009 Leniency Programme).[3]

The 2005 Leniency Programme, and the slightly amended version of 2009, attracted 1,345 leniency applications by the end of 2020.[4] These leniency applications have resulted in 153 decisions by the JFTC.[5] In an earlier study, one of us has argued that these numbers do not reflect the degree of

[1] Law No. 54 of 1974, shiteki dokusen no kinshi oyobi kousei torihiki no kakuho ni kan suru houritsu [Law Concerning the Prohibition of Private Monopolies and the Assurance of Fair Trade] (AMA). This chapter will refer to the '2005 AMA' when discussing the leniency programme as adopted in 2005. The '2009 AMA' will be used when discussing the leniency programme after the revision in 2009. This distinction is made because the article in which the leniency programme has been laid down varies depending on the timing of when the adjustments were made. When we just use AMA, this refers to the AMA in its latest revised version, i.e. the one of 2019.

[2] 2005 AMA, Article 7 (2). This chapter will use the term leniency programme in the Japanese context, because the conceptualisation is mainly developed in the AMA itself. For the United States (US) and the European Union (EU), this chapter will use leniency policy. Leniency is in these jurisdictions elaborated in soft law instruments.

[3] 2009 AMA, Article 7-2 (10).

[4] See Table 5.1, Van Uytsel, Chapter 5 this volume.

[5] See Table 5.2, Van Uytsel, Chapter 5 this volume.

deterrence that the leniency programme has brought about.[6] In 2019, the Japanese legislator decided to amend the leniency programme. This revision did not only affect the different degrees of leniency a leniency applicant could enjoy; it also gave the JFTC the power to partially negotiate the degree of leniency. The so-created 2019 Leniency Programme represents a paradigm shift in this regard. Never before had the JFTC had so much discretion to negotiate with leniency applicants.

It remains to be seen whether the amendments will lead to better deterrence. This chapter will, therefore, ask whether the 2019 Leniency Programme addresses the problems of the 2005/2009 Leniency Programme. Of course, better detection, brought about by the leniency programme, is only one element of the deterrence equation. Sanctions are the other side of the equation. Therefore, this chapter will position the changes to the leniency programme against the background of changes made to the sanctions and the sanctioning system, in order to make an assessment of the likely overall deterrence.

The chapter proceeds as follows. Section 6.2 introduces the early leniency programmes of Japan and highlights the extent to which these programmes have contributed to deterrence. As there is doubt that the 2005/2009 Leniency Programme has fully contributed to deterrence, the Japanese legislator amended the leniency programme in 2019. These amendments are detailed in Section 6.3. Section 6.3 will also make a prediction on whether these amendments contribute to deterrence. With uncertainty on the effectiveness of these amendments to deterrence, Section 6.4 reflects on other parts of the deterrence equation: sanctions. This section will describe how the Japanese legislator gradually made the sanctions stricter, so that flaws in the leniency programme could be underscored. Section 6.5 concludes by stating that the Japanese competition law regime is gradually developing towards more deterrence, but that there is still room for optimisation.

6.2 Deterrence and the Early Japanese Leniency Programme

6.2.1 Deterrence through Leniency

Leniency programmes have to be situated within theoretical views on law enforcement. Influential in this regard was Nobel Prize Laureate

[6] Van Uytsel, S., 'Anti-Cartel Enforcement in Japan: Does Leniency Make the Difference?' in Beaton-Wells, C. and Tran, C. (eds.), Anti-Cartel Enforcement in a Contemporary Age: Leniency Religion (Oxford: Hart Publishing, 2015), 81.

Gary Becker and his article titled 'Crime and Punishment: An Economic Approach'.[7] In this article, Becker proposed that a criminal fine could be understood as a price attached to violating the law and can thus be seen as a potential cost for a person willing to engage in the undesirable conduct.[8] Becker further indicates that the fine is not the only element determining the cost. The cost is also influenced by the probability of detecting the violation of the law and whether actual punishment follows upon detection.[9] Presuming than that people act rationally, Becker holds that such costs will influence their behaviour.[10] High costs, either in the form of a high fine or a high degree of detection and punishment, will make people refrain from violating the law. Low costs, to the contrary, will inspire people to violate the law.

It has been claimed that Becker's view on 'criminal sanctions is most relevant for the enforcement of the cartel prohibition'.[11] 'Whereas the assumption of rational behaviour may be criticised with regard to irrational crimes (such as murder), calculating behaviour is a rather more realistic scenario for white-collar crimes. Antitrust violations generally result from calculating business decisions',[12] purport Roger Van den Bergh and Peter Camesasca. They further indicate that, if one applies Becker's view on competition law, '[f]irms will engage in price fixing if the gains derived from this activity are higher than the costs, both adjusted for the probability that they will materialise'.[13]

Law and economics have traditionally argued that the imposition of high fines is the most efficient choice for competition enforcement agencies.[14] This view was derived from the fact that enforcement agencies will not have the resources to control all kinds of behaviour. Very often, the enforcement budgets are limited and cannot easily be changed.[15] More recently, it has been suggested that detection should not be neglected. Without a sufficient rate of detection, people lose sight of the potential

7 Becker, G., 'Crime and Punishment: An Economic Approach' (1968) 76 *Journal of Political Economy* 169.

8 Ibid.

9 Ibid.

10 Ibid.

11 Van den Bergh, R. J. and Camesasca, P. D., *European Competition Law and Economics: A Comparative Perspective*, 2nd ed. (Cheltenham: Edward Elgar, 2006), p. 312.

12 Ibid., p. 312.

13 Ibid.

14 Ibid., p. 313.

15 Ibid.

high fines that can be imposed. Moreover, in a situation in which detection is low, fines may need to be of a magnitude beyond the capacity of a firm to pay. It goes without saying that leniency programmes are addressing this issue.[16] Without spending much of their own resources, competition agencies can increase the probability of detection by relying on information provided from the law infringers themselves. Of course, the parameters of the leniency programme need to be calibrated in an appropriate way to achieve deterrence through better detection.[17]

6.2.2 *The Early Leniency Programme in Japan: An Inflated Number of Decisions and Follow-On Investigations Affect Deterrence*

In Chapter 5, the early leniency programme of Japan has been explained.[18] Observers of the Japanese leniency programme have been quite positive on the correct conceptualisation of the 2005/2009 Leniency Programme. Toshiyuki Nambu, an official of the JFTC writing in a personal capacity, recently expressed this opinion in an article with the telling title 'A Successful Story: Leniency and (International) Cartel Enforcement in Japan'.[19] Former Chairman of the JFTC Kazuhiko Takeshima claimed 'that the leniency programme has produced significant results since its introduction'.[20] Akinori Uesugi, formulating his observations one year after the leniency programme went into effect in 2006, gave directions for drawing such conclusions. The leniency programme, he observed, had triggered a high number of leniency applications, giving way to a smooth decision-making process by the JFTC.[21]

While these observations are correct, there is a need for caution. The data to sustain the abovementioned conclusions refer either to the number of leniency applications or the total number of decisions taken. Yet

16 Beaton-Wells and Tran, *Anti-Cartel Enforcement in a Contemporary Age* (n. 6 above).

17 Jaspers, J. D., 'Leniency in Exchange for Cartel Confessions' (2020) 17(1) *European Journal of Criminology* 106, p. 108 (describing that the assumptions underlying a leniency programme are rationality, predictable benefits and likelihood of detection. The analysis of the assumptions is done to test the reliability of these assumptions).

18 Van Uytsel, Chapter 5 this volume.

19 Nambu, T., 'A Successful Story: Leniency and (International) Cartel Enforcement in Japan' (2014) 5 *Journal of European Competition Law & Practice* 158.

20 Takeshima, K., 'Leniency Programme and Bid Riggings in Public Sector – Enforcement Experiences in Japan' (2007). Retrieved from www.jftc.go.jp/en/policy_enforcement/speeches/2007/saicsymposium2007.html.

21 Uesugi, A., 'The Japanese Leniency Programme – One Year In' (2007) 21 *Antitrust* 79, pp. 83–84.

the number of leniency applications and the process of decision-making tell only a partial story, and they are insufficient measures for assessing the success or otherwise of a leniency programme. A leniency programme is an enforcement tool, aimed at facilitating both the deterrence and detection of cartels. To appreciate fully the effectiveness of a leniency programme, and to assess any overarching policy on cartel deterrence and detection, more information is required. In an earlier study, we have argued that the start of such information has to be the number of successful leniency applicants.[22]

The number of leniency applications has to be offset against the number of successful leniency applications. The latter is obtained by looking at how many enterprises have been granted leniency in decisions that are based upon those leniency applications.[23] The number so obtained needs to be broken down into domestic cartels and international cartels. International cartels should not be on the account of an enforcement agency that did not take the initial step towards uncovering these cartels.[24] In relation to the domestic cartels, an assessment needs to be done on whether all cartel decisions are separate cartels. If there is a tendency to split up cartels based upon large customers or product characteristics, not all cartel decisions should be considered as detecting separate cartels. The reason behind this observation is that the cartel-organising enterprises are identical.[25] Once this analysis has been done, information needs to be collected on the number of enterprises that obtain immunity and pre-investigation leniency. All the other leniency applications can be neglected, as they are submitted after the enforcement agency has done a dawn raid, due to which enterprises have received a wake-up call that their respective cartel has been detected.[26]

When applied to Japan, our study has revealed that the Japanese leniency programme attracted much fewer independent leniency applications than the total number of leniency applications would suggest. Our study's estimate is that out of the 775 leniency applications by 2015, there were only 22 truly independent leniency applications.[27] If we update the study to 2020, the most recent date for which the JFTC has released relevant

[22] Van Uytsel, 'Anti-Cartel Enforcement in Japan' (n. 6 above), pp. 91–102.
[23] Ibid., pp. 91–93.
[24] Ibid., pp. 93–95.
[25] Ibid., pp. 95–97.
[26] Ibid., p. 97.
[27] Ibid., pp. 98–99.

data, we estimate that the number of truly independent applications has risen to 58. In the meantime, the number of leniency applications has risen to 1,343.[28]

The data on truly independent leniency applications are, however, not directly available. They can only be obtained after meticulously analysing data available from the JFTC's website and comparing these data with those available on international enforcement actions. The constant focus on the high number of leniency applications, which are resulting in a substantially high number of decisions, allows the JFTC to obscure the reality. By obscuring this reality, the JFTC could contribute to deterrence. In the end, deterrence is created, among other things, by the perceived risk of being detected and punished.[29]

To counter the real effect on deterrence by publicising leniency-related cartel decisions, two elements need to be highlighted. On the one hand, the JFTC should reveal the real strength of the leniency programme. This strength is the increased detection of price-fixing agreements and agreements on bid rigging in private procurement projects.[30] Even though this information is sporadically available in the online reports of the JFTC, it could be argued that this feature of the leniency programme is highly underrated. To achieve better deterrence, more publicity on this feature may be necessary. On the other hand, many of the enterprises submitting truly independent leniency applications are listed companies. It is not possible to make a statement on each of these individual companies, but the JFTC has surveyed the compliance activities of the listed companies. Though the development of legal departments in Japan was a late phenomenon, most of these listed companies now have competition law compliance manuals and sessions. In other words, there should be an increased awareness of competition law, its sanctions and its enforcement among the enterprises applying for leniency. And yet, we still see several of these enterprises engaging in cartel agreements.[31]

[28] This is based on information drawn from JFTC, 'Concerning the Enforcement Status of the Antimonopoly Law Infringement Cases of the Fiscal Year 2020' (5 May 2021). Retrieved from www.jftc.go.jp/houdou/pressrelease/2021/may/210526.html (in Japanese). JFTC, 'Public Announcement Regarding Businesses to Which the System for Reduction of or Immunity from the Surcharge Applied' (2021). Retrieved from www.jftc.go.jp/dk/seido/genmen/kouhyou/index.html (in Japanese).

[29] Beaton-Wells, C., 'Immunity for Cartel Conduct: Revolution or Religion? An Australian Case Study' (2014) 2 *Journal of Antitrust Enforcement* 126, p. 151.

[30] Van Uytsel, 'Anti-Cartel Enforcement in Japan' (n. 6 above), pp. 104–5.

[31] Ibid., pp. 99–102.

Two observations could be made. First, the discrepancy between the number of leniency applications and the number of decisions creates a perception that the leniency programme is only effective in a few cases. Second, the enterprises may have a general perception that the sanctioning system of the AMA is too weak.

To curb some of the abovementioned issues, the leniency programme has recently been changed. The change mainly focused on the number of eligible leniency applicants, the degree of leniency and extra leniency for cooperating enterprises. This is not to say that the sanctioning system has been neglected. Together with the introduction of the leniency programme, several issues of the sanctioning system have been altered. The question is whether both changes could be considered sufficient to address deterrence.

6.3 Predicting the Deterrence Impact of Negotiated Leniency

6.3.1 Immunity Remains the Incentive, But the Reductions Are Substantially Decreased

The Japanese legislator amended the 2005/2009 Leniency Programme in 2019.[32] The amendments are substantial. Within the existing framework of allowing leniency applications before and after an investigation has started, the 2019 Leniency Programme has changed the total number of enterprises eligible for leniency. In a pre-investigation stage, the JFTC can grant leniency to, theoretically at least, an unlimited number of applicants.[33] The first applicant will receive immunity,[34] the second a reduction of 20 per cent,[35] the third to the fifth applicants a reduction of 10 per cent,[36] and from the sixth applicant onwards 5 per cent.[37] It is important to note that the immunity or reduction can only be obtained if the enterprise refrained from committing the violation from the date of the investigation by the JFTC.[38]

32 For documents discussing the amendments, see JFTC, 'Enactment of the Act to Amend the Antimonopoly Act' (2019). Retrieved from www.jftc.go.jp/en/pressreleases/yearly-2019/June/19061907.html.

33 Inoue, A., *Antitrust Enforcement in Japan – History, Rhetoric and Law of the Antimonopoly Act*, 2nd ed. (Tokyo: Dai-Ichi Hoki, 2019), p. 250; Dokei, T., Nakajima, H. and Onoki, T., 'New Bill: Expansion for Leniency and Fines under the Japan Anti-Monopoly Act; (2019). Retrieved from www.jdsupra.com/legalnews/new-bill-expansion-for-leniency-and-24551.

34 AMA, Article 7-4 (1) (i).

35 Ibid., Article 7-4 (2) (i).

36 Ibid., Article 7-4 (2) (ii).

37 Ibid., Article 7-4 (2) (iii).

38 Ibid., Article 7-4 (2) (v).

In the post-investigation stage, a maximum of three applicants can receive 10 per cent reduction on the condition that there are not more than five leniency applicants in total.[39] This means that for each extra leniency applicant in the pre-investigation stage, there will be one fewer eligible for the 10 per cent reduction in the post-investigation stage and the 10 per cent reduction will not be available any more if there are a total of five applicants in the pre-investigation stage. Any applicant not eligible for the 10 per cent reduction in the post-investigation stage may be eligible for a 5 per cent reduction.[40] Also in this stage, there is a requirement to stop the infringement when submitting the leniency application.[41]

Whether or not the leniency application is submitted prior to or after the dawn raid, the 2019 Leniency Programme, just like the 2009 Leniency Programme, allows joint applications.[42] This means that enterprises that are connected to each other can obtain the same degree of leniency. The connection is made when the enterprises belong to the same corporate group, for example as subsidiaries of the same parent company, or the enterprises have changed corporate structure, for example through an acquisition or a company split.

6.3.2 No Substantial Changes to the Information Requirement and Application Conditions

Unlike the number of eligible leniency applicants, the 2019 Leniency Programme does not alter much in relation to the information requirement and the other application conditions.

The 2005 Leniency Programme just required the submission of information related to an infringement of the unreasonable restraint of trade prong of Article 3 of the AMA. This information requirement was further operationalised in the Rules on Reporting the Facts and Submitting the Materials Regarding Immunity from or Reduction of Surcharges (Leniency Rules).[43] In the pre-investigation stage, information had to be provided in two stages. A short description of the cartel had to be submitted in Form 1. The submission of this report secured the position of the applicant and

39 Ibid., Article 7-4 (3).

40 Ibid.

41 Ibid., Article 7-4 (3) (iii).

42 Ibid., Article 7-4 (4).

43 JFTC, 'Rules on Reporting and Submission of Materials Regarding Immunity from or Reduction of Surcharges' (Fair Trade Commission Rule No. 7 of 2005, 2005), p. 5. Retrieved from www.jftc.go.jp/en/legislation_gls/antimonopoly_rules_files/immunityH21.pdf (Leniency Rules).

functioned as a kind of marker. To secure that position, Form 2 had to be submitted within a time period to be stipulated by the JFTC. The JFTC usually kept this period at two weeks. Leniency applicants submitting on or after a dawn raid had only one form to complete, Form 3. This form, including the accompanying evidence, had to be submitted within twenty days counting from the date of the investigation. In principle, Form 2 and Form 3 had to be submitted in writing. However, exceptional circumstances not specified in any of the documents may justify oral reporting to the Senior Officer for Immunity from or Reduction of Surcharges.[44] None of the information-related elements changed with the adoption of the 2019 Leniency Programme and the revision of the Leniency Rules in 2020.[45]

When amending the 2005 Leniency Programme in 2009, the legislator increased the number of eligible leniency applicants from three to five. With this change, the legislator also amended the information requirement for the fourth and fifth leniency applicants. Both leniency applicants were only eligible for leniency if they could submit information that had not yet been ascertained by the JFTC.[46] In other words, they had to submit new or unknown information. With the expansion of eligible leniency applicants in 2019, the requirement to submit new information applies beyond the fourth and fifth applicants and thus also to the sixth and subsequent leniency applicants.[47]

Information used to be submitted by facsimile.[48] This was to guarantee the order of the leniency applications. The revision of the Leniency Rules in 2020 changed the method. The main method is now email, even though facsimile applications are still allowed.[49] The submission through email applies to Form 1 and Form 3.[50]

44 See Van Uytsel, S., 'A Comparative US and EU Perspective on the Japanese Antimonopoly Law's Leniency Program' (2008) 75 *Hosei Kenkyu* F1.

45 JFTC, 'Rules on Reporting the Facts and Submitting the Materials Regarding Immunity from or Reduction of Surcharges (Fair Trade Commission Rule No. 3 of 2020)' (2020). Retrieved from www.jftc.go.jp/en/legislation_gls/201225001.pdf (Rule No. 3 of 2020).

46 2009 AMA, Article 7-4 (12).

47 AMA, Article 7-4 (2) (i)-(v).

48 See Van Uytsel, 'Anti-Cartel Enforcement in Japan' (n. 6 above), p. 84.

49 Rule No. 3 of 2020; JFTC, 'The Surcharge Leniency Programme'. Retrieved from www.jftc.go.jp/dk/seido/genmen/genmen_2.html (in Japanese). The order of receipt of the emails will determine the order of leniency applications. Note that an email may not arrive at the JFTC, for example when an email contains a virus or due to a glitch. Therefore, the JFTC recommends checking with the Senior Officer for the Leniency Programme by telephone to confirm the receipt of the email. See JFTC, 'A Summary of Rules and Guidelines (Proposal) Regarding Reduction System for Cooperation in Investigation' (2020). Retrieved from www.jftc.go.jp/en/pressreleases/yearly-2020/April/200402a6.pdf.

50 Rule No. 3 of 2020, Section 4 and Section 7.

Besides the information requirement, the 2005 Leniency Programme imposed certain conditions.[51] All of these conditions can be found in the 2019 Leniency Programme. Therefore, leniency applicants will have to respond to requests of the JFTC for further information.[52] Leniency applicants will have to submit reports and materials that are not false.[53] In order not to lose their eligibility, leniency applicants should not have coerced other enterprises to take part in the cartel or to prevent discontinuing participation in a cartel.[54] Without a justifiable reason, leniency applicants should also not disclose the application for leniency to other cartel participants.[55] A new condition added in 2019 is the one requiring that leniency applicants should not have blocked another enterprise from submitting a leniency application.[56]

6.3.3 *Negotiating a Better Leniency Deal under the Reduction System*

6.3.3.1 Consultation with the JFTC Subsequent to a Leniency Application

The 2019 Leniency Programme puts any of the first five leniency applicants who do not apply for immunity in a worse position than before. The leniency offered to these leniency applicants has been drastically reduced. On the other hand, enterprises that were not eligible to apply for leniency any more under the 2005/2009 Leniency Programme because the available slots were filled are treated slightly better under the 2019 Leniency Programme. These enterprises are now, in theory at least, eligible for a small degree of leniency.

To incentivise the enterprises in a worse position still to cooperate with the JFTC, the Japanese legislator has added an extra layer to the leniency programme. A leniency applicant can request a 'conference'[57] with

[51] Van Uytsel, 'Anti-Cartel Enforcement in Japan' (n. 6 above), pp. 84–85.

[52] AMA, Article 7-6.

[53] Ibid., Article 7-6 (1) (i)–(iii).

[54] Ibid., Article 7-6 (1) (iv).

[55] Ibid., Article 7-6 (1) (vi).

[56] Ibid., Article 7-6 (1) (iv).

[57] 'Conference' is used in documents of the JFTC. See, e.g., AMA, Article 7-5. Documents created by practitioners or professional data providers speak of 'consultation'. See, e.g., Ae, J., 'Japan: Draft Guidelines on Amendment to the Antimonopoly Act: Reduction System for Cooperation and Attorney–Client Privilege' (2020). Retrieved from https://globalcompliancenews.com/japan-draft-guidelines-released-on-amendment-to-the-antimonopoly-act-reduction-system-for-cooperation-and-attorney-client-privilege-20200504.

the JFTC in order to reach an agreement on a higher rate of reduction.[58] Whether this higher degree of reduction can be obtained depends on whether the leniency applicant requesting the conference can contribute to revealing the truth the investigation.[59]

In order to be eligible to request a conference with the JFTC, an enterprise needs to have applied for leniency.[60] This means that the enterprise needs to submit the reports and materials required by the leniency programme. Upon submitting that information, the JFTC has to notify the leniency applicant in writing of the submission. However, prior to issuing this notification, the JFTC may request additional information. Once the notification has been received by the leniency applicant, the leniency applicant has 10 days to request a conference.[61]

The enterprise requesting the conference shall explain the content of the information it can report to the JFTC. The information will relate to information that the leniency applicant has revealed in the course of the conference, to the information the leniency applicant has submitted in its leniency application dossier, and to information the JFTC has revealed in its investigation.[62]

The JFTC will judge the explanation of the information obtained from the enterprise requesting the conference. If the JFTC is of the opinion that the explanation contributes to revealing the truth of the case, the JFTC, and this is an independent decision of the JFTC, enters into an agreement with the consulting enterprise.[63] In this agreement, the JFTC will stipulate the extra reduction of the administrative surcharge to which the consulting enterprise is eligible on top of the reduction it has already obtained with its original leniency application. The extra reduction is referred to in the AMA as the 'specified rate'.[64] The specified rate needs to be below 40 per cent for leniency applicants of the pre-investigation stage and below 20 per cent for leniency applicants of the post-investigation stage.[65]

[58] AMA, Article 7-5.

[59] Ibid., Article 7-5 (1).

[60] Ibid., Article 7-5 (1).

[61] JFTC, 'Guidelines to Reduction System for Cooperation in Investigation (Proposal); (2020), p. 3. Retrieved from www.jftc.go.jp/en/pressreleases/yearly-2020/April/200402a2.pdf (Reduction Guidelines).

[62] AMA, Article 7-5 (1) (i) (a)–(c).

[63] Reduction Guidelines, p. 4.

[64] AMA, Article 7-5 (1) (ii).

[65] Ibid., Article 7-5 (1) (ii) (a) and (b).

It is possible, though, that, after the agreement on the specified rate is concluded, it may become apparent that the consulting enterprise can ascertain new facts or materials regarding the case. If the ascertaining of new facts or materials requires a period of time, the JFTC may request, during the conference, that the consulting enterprise makes an agreement. Such an agreement will also provide a reduction, which is called the 'after assessment rate'.[66] The after assessment rate is also limited by the upper limits mentioned above, but, besides that, it cannot be lower than the specified rate. In other words, the after assessment rate will be somewhere between the specified rate and 40 per cent or 20 per cent, depending on whether the leniency application was made at a pre- or post-investigation stage.[67]

The agreement closing the conference and thus stipulating the specific rate or the after assessment rate has to be in writing and sealed.[68] The agreement will contain the conditions with which the consulting enterprise needs to comply.[69] The conditions relate to the submission of evidence regarding the case. Non-compliance with the conditions will not only affect the extra reduction but also the original leniency application. The enterprise will be eligible neither for leniency nor for the negotiated reduction.[70]

The end result of an agreement will be an extra reduction of the administrative surcharge. This means that the reduction of either the specified rate or the after assessment rate will be added to the reduction to which the consulting enterprise is entitled under the leniency programme.[71]

Just in case no agreement is reached between the JFTC and the consulting enterprise, the AMA stipulates that the JFTC may not use the information it has become familiar with during the conference as evidence.[72]

6.3.3.2 Guidelines on Information and the Degree of Extra Reduction

The process to start the conference and its possible consequences are elaborated in the AMA. However, little substance has been given to the method for how the JFTC will judge the cooperation of the enterprise seeking the

[66] Ibid., Article 7-5 (2).
[67] Ibid., Article 7-5 (2) (ii).
[68] Ibid., Article 7-5 (4).
[69] Ibid., Article 7-5 (5).
[70] Ibid., Article 7-6 (1).
[71] Ibid., Article 7-5 (3).
[72] Ibid., Article 7-5 (7).

conference. The AMA is silent on two aspects. First, the AMA is vague on the kind of information that will be taken into consideration to give extra reduction. Second, the AMA is silent on how the degree of cooperation will be evaluated. Moreover, the AMA says that the JFTC should elaborate on these issues.[73] The JFTC has done so in the Guidelines to the Reduction System for Cooperation in Investigation (Reduction Guidelines).[74]

The Reduction Guidelines introduce, in an attachment, what kind of information could contribute to the truth of a case. The information is divided into eight different categories: (1) goods and services subject to the violation, (2) description of the violation, (3) participants in the violation, (4) time of the violation, (5) implementation of the violation, (6) other matters related to the violation (e.g. participation of outsiders, trade associations or officials, such as bureaucrats, etc.), (7) the basic amount for calculating administrative surcharges, and (8) the calculation rate of surcharges. For each of these categories, the Reduction Guidelines provide examples.[75]

The degree of reduction will be determined by the following three elements: (1) how detailed and concrete the information is, (2) how many of the eight categories can be ticked off, and (3) to what extent the information can be corroborated by materials (i.e. documents related to the violation).[76] When evaluating these three elements, the JFTC will also recognise to what extent the consulting enterprise could ascertain these elements given the degree of its involvement in the infringing act.[77] On the other hand, facts that have been ascertained by the JFTC, either in a voluntary interview or in an interrogation, will, in principle, not be considered as contributing to revealing the truth.[78]

The JFTC considers that a consulting enterprise is highly cooperating if it can satisfy all three elements mentioned just above. Two elements will lead to the conclusion of medium-level cooperation, and one element to low-level cooperation. High cooperation will lead to an extra 40 per cent reduction in the pre-investigation stage and an extra 20 per cent reduction in the post-investigation stage. Medium-level cooperation will lead to 20 per cent or 10 per cent extra reduction in the pre- and post-investigation stage, respectively. Low-level cooperation will entitle the consulting

73 Ibid., Article 7-5 (8).
74 Reduction Guidelines.
75 Ibid., pp. 8–12.
76 Ibid., p. 6.
77 Ibid.
78 Ibid.

enterprise to an extra reduction of 10 per cent or 5 per cent in the pre- and post-investigation stage, respectively.[79]

In an after assessment rate agreement, the exact content of the information remains unclear at the time of the agreement. However, as this kind of agreement always relates to new information, the JFTC is of the opinion that the rate of 40 per cent will in principle apply in a pre-investigation stage. The reduction rate will be 20 per cent in the case of a post-investigation conference. In both cases, the new information is presumed to contribute highly to revealing the truth of the case.

6.3.3.3 A Shift in Position towards the Attorney–Client Privilege by the JFTC

The JFTC has traditionally not recognised the attorney–client privilege. This meant that the correspondence between a client and his or her lawyer could be part of the evidence to prove that the client, an enterprise from the perspective of the JFTC, was engaged in illegal cartel behaviour.[80] The year 2019 meant a shift in the JFTC's policy towards the attorney–client privilege. With only a twenty-day deadline, enterprises do not only need to make decisions on a leniency application, but also on a conference to obtain extra reduction.[81] Enterprises thus need to make strategic decisions much more quickly than before. Hence, the assistance of a lawyer may be required more than before. This has been recognised in the AMA, where it is stated that the assistance of a 'special agent' for submitting the application for leniency and extra reduction is permissible.[82] To facilitate that issue, the JFTC has drafted Guidelines on Treatment of Objects Recording Confidential Communications between Enterprises and Attorney (Attorney–Client Privilege Guidelines).[83]

The Attorney–Client Privilege Guidelines detail the scope of the attorney–client privilege for the purpose of leniency applications. They document what kind of information falls under the privilege and to whom the privilege applies. One caution should be mentioned here. The JFTC

[79] Ibid., pp. 6–7.

[80] Matake, Y., 'Recent Developments Regarding Attorney–Client Privilege' (2019). Retrieved from www.noandt.com/ja/publications/2019/documents/competitionandantitrust_no11.pdf.

[81] Ae, 'Japan: Draft Guidelines' (n. 57 above), p. 4.

[82] AMA, Article 7-5 (6).

[83] JFTC, 'Guidelines on Treatment of Objects Recording Confidential Communication between an Enterprise and Attorney' (2020). Retrieved from www.jftc.go.jp/en/pressreleases/yearly-2020/June/20062602 (Attorney–Client Privilege Guidelines).

makes it clear that the shift in attorney–client privilege will only apply to confidential communication between a lawyer and a client regarding legal advice on an unreasonable restraint of trade.[84] Hence, the privilege will not apply to anything else than cartels and bid rigging. Moreover, it will only apply to the administrative investigation and not to the compulsory investigation of criminal cases.[85]

The attorney–client privilege will apply to confidential communication between an enterprise and its attorney.[86] The confidential communication is, however, limited in scope. It only contains documents reflecting consultations between the enterprise and the attorney and reports stating legal advice that is based on internal investigations by the attorney. If these documents and reports are discussed with an attorney and minutes have been made of this meeting, these minutes will also be covered by the privilege.[87] Anything that is created outside the communication with the attorney, even though that kind of information is the basis of communication with an attorney, falls outside of the privilege. This could be materials directly related to the cartel or bid rigging and thus containing facts in relation to the case.

Only communication with the attorney falls under the privilege. An attorney is anyone who can 'engage in legal practices independently from the enterprise'[88] and this in accordance with the Attorney Act (Act No. 205 of 1949).[89] The Attorney–Client Privilege Guidelines further stipulate that in-house attorneys could be included on the condition that they 'get out of the directions, orders and supervision … from the enterprise who is the employer and that the attorneys will engage in legal practice independently'.[90] Since foreign attorneys, including the ones registered in Japan, will only give consultations on foreign competition laws, the AMA does not, in principle, allow the JFTC to order the submission of documents related to these consultations.[91] However, this statement in the guidelines does not clarify whether the communication of these attorneys could fall under the privileged communication.

[84] Ibid., p. 2.
[85] Ibid., p. 1.
[86] Ibid., p. 2.
[87] Ibid., p. 3.
[88] Ibid., p. 2 note 4.
[89] Ibid., p. 2 note 4.
[90] JFTC, 'Treatment of Confidential Communication between an Enterprise and Attorney' (2019), p. 2. Retrieved from www.jftc.go.jp/en/pressreleases/yearly-2019/March/190312_3.pdf.
[91] AMA, Article 47.

Whether or not the attorney–client privilege applies is subject to an application procedure. An enterprise has to request this kind of privileged treatment. For that purpose, the enterprise has to identify the documents and reports to which it should apply.[92] The documents and reports have to be appropriately labelled and sealed.[93] The documents and reports will be stored with the determination officer, who is an officer belonging to the JFTC but not with the status of investigator.[94] The determination officer has to verify the content of these documents and reports.[95] The idea behind this process is to see that the enterprise does not attempt to interfere with the investigation. If documents and reports outside of the scope are found by the determination officer, the content will be reported to the JFTC.[96] If not, the documents and reports will be returned to the enterprise.[97]

6.3.4 *Negotiated Leniency, Attorney–Client Privilege and Deterrence*

The JFTC has heavily relied on the leniency programme to enforce the anti-cartel provisions of the AMA. However, as has been indicated above, there may be a perception that the 2005/2009 Leniency Programme was only effective in a small number of cases. A much larger number of leniency applications were not used at all to open investigations. One of the reasons put forward was the lack of appropriate information in these leniency applications.[98] Allowing the JFTC to negotiate with the leniency applicants could be a solution to this problem on the condition that the focus of the negotiation is the building-up of the cartel story. The 2019 Leniency Programme is, however, different in focus.

To pinpoint the focus of the 2019 Leniency Programme, it is important to distinguish possible information failures. Leniency applications could be unmeritorious in two different ways. First, a leniency application may not contain enough information to start an investigation, due to which the application becomes a dormant one. This kind of application is not considered by the JFTC and does not result in granting any form of leniency. Second, a leniency application, though leading to a reduction of the administrative surcharge, may not have contributed to the investigation

92 Attorney–Client Privilege Guidelines, p. 5.
93 Ibid., pp. 5–6, II. 3–4.
94 Ibid., p. 6, IV.
95 Ibid., p. 7, IV. 2
96 Ibid., p. 7.
97 Ibid., p. 9, V.
98 Van Uytsel, 'Anti-Cartel Enforcement in Japan' (n. 6 above), p. 92.

because no new information was revealed or no elements were added to already known information.

A reduction of the first type of unmeritorious leniency application can only be achieved by imposing requirements on the information to be submitted for immunity. Such a requirement could be to submit information that could lead to an investigation. These extra requirements will make it necessary to seek legal advice, due to which leniency applications with just a story will most likely no longer be submitted. The 2019 Leniency Programme has, however, no specific information requirement for the immunity applicant. The duty to respond to requests of the JFTC will not necessarily help. The JFTC can only formulate requests if it has the slightest idea of what it needs to ask.

It is not the case that submitting just a story needs to be considered as something bad. However, in such a case, the enforcement agency should have the power to actively engage with the leniency applicant to build up the cartel story. Nevertheless, the negotiation process is not conceptualised for that reason.

Consequently, the 2019 Leniency Programme will not rectify the number of unmeritorious leniency applications that end up as dormant leniency applications. There is even a risk that this kind of leniency application will increase in the future. To incorporate the consultation process, the legislator has significantly lowered the reduction for the leniency applicants subsequent to the immunity applicant. As long as the legal community is still familiarising itself with the new 2019 Leniency Programme, enterprises and their advisers may seek to be on the safe side and submit an application much earlier than that they would have done under the incentive structure of the 2005/2009 Leniency Programme. It has indeed been an important insight of the law and economics literature that the greater the difference is between the immunity and the degree of leniency of the subsequent applicant, the greater the 'race' will be to the enforcement agency.[99]

What, then, is the value of according negotiating power to the JFTC? The 2005 Leniency Programme had not only no specific information requirements for the immunity applicant, but also none for reduction applicants. As long as the leniency applicant submitted the necessary documents and complied with the conditions, leniency would be granted. This means that even leniency applicants submitting the same information as an immunity applicant, or as that which was already known by the JFTC, could enjoy lenient treatment. The investigation process was, however, not furthered

[99] Van Uytsel, 'A Comparative US and EU Perspective' (n. 44 above), p. F27.

by these applications. The 2009 Leniency Programme rectified this situation only partly by imposing a requirement to submit information that was not yet ascertained by the JFTC on the fourth and fifth leniency applicants. Such new information has been submitted in several investigations, indicating that there is actually a need for deeper cooperation by the cartel participants with the investigation process. It is obvious that, by limiting the negotiation with the JFTC to leniency applicants subsequent to the immunity applicant, the 2019 Leniency Programme is focusing on the leniency applications unmeritorious to an investigation.

How would these conclusions relate to deterrence? The negative impact on deterrence of the discrepancy between dormant leniency applications and the actually used leniency applications may remain. The 2019 Leniency Programme does not solve the origin of that problem. However, by increasing the potential information flow on cartels under investigation, the JFTC could speed up the decision process and so handle more cases. If that is not the consequence, the information flow may give a deeper insight into the scope of the cartel and so lead to a higher basis for calculating the administrative surcharge. These two elements may positively contribute to deterrence. If this could be combined with a faster race to the JFTC, cartel-destabilising factors will increase. This will also contribute to deterrence.

6.4 A Broader Perspective on the Deterrence Equation

6.4.1 Detection Stands Next to Sanctions

The introduction of the leniency programme has been a lengthy process, in which key figures in the political world had to be convinced of the suitability of this enforcement tool within the Japanese legal system.[100] The origin of this process lies in the fact that the JFTC has little discretion in relation to the administrative surcharge and sanctions it can apply to violations of the AMA. As a result, any change to the fines and the sanctions needs to be part of the AMA.

As changing the AMA requires the completion of the legislative process, it should not come as a surprise that the introduction of the leniency programme was done with other revisions to the AMA. Some of the other revisions sided with the leniency programme in the deterrence equation and should increase detection. Other revisions were on the opposite side of the deterrence equation and improved the sanctioning system. Hence,

[100] Van Uytsel, Chapter 5 this volume.

statements about the deterrence of the leniency programme should be made in connection to the revisions of the sanctioning system of the AMA.

During the nearly twenty years that leniency has been operating in Japan, the Japanese legislator has made the following revisions. In 2005, when the leniency programme was introduced, the legislator also increased the rate of the administrative surcharge, clarified the scope of unreasonable restraint of trade and introduced a compulsory investigative power for the JFTC. The amendment of the leniency programme in 2009 also introduced an increased administrative surcharge for ringleaders, revised the upper limit of the criminal sanctions and clarified to whom cease-and-desist and administrative surcharge orders should be directed. In 2019, the calculation of the administrative surcharge was amended.

6.4.2 *The 2005 Amendments to the Administrative Surcharge and Sanctioning System*

6.4.2.1 A Move towards a More Severe Administrative Surcharge

In an attempt to make the toolkit of the JFTC better equipped to deal with cartels and bid rigging, the administrative surcharge was inscribed in the AMA in 1977.[101] The basic calculation rate applied to large manufacturers was merely 2 per cent of the amount of sales from the relevant goods or services affected by their violating acts.[102] The amendment of the AMA in 1991 tripled the basic calculation rate to 6 per cent of the sales from the relevant goods or services affected.[103]

Together with the introduction of the leniency programme in Japan, the basic calculation rates used for calculating the administrative surcharge were raised for the first time since 1991. The 2005 amendment increased

[101] See Schaede, U., *Cooperative Capitalism: Self-Regulation, Trade Associations, and the Antimonopoly Law in Japan* (Oxford: Oxford University Press, 2000), p. 117.

[102] Kameoka, E., *Competition Law and Policy in Japan and the EU* (Cheltenham: Edward Elgar, 2014), p. 132. For a discussion of why the surcharge was inscribed, see, e.g., Van Uytsel, S., 'Leniency under the Japanese Antimonopoly Law: Towards the End of the Cartel Archipelago?' in Cheng, T., Marco Colino, S. and Ong, B. (eds.), *Cartels in Asia* (Hong Kong: Wolters Kluwer Law & Business, 2015), 67, p. 67; Vande Walle, S., 'Competition and Competition Law in Japan: Between Skepticism and Embrace', in Dowdle, M., Gillespie, J. and Maher, I. (eds.), *Asian Capitalism and the Regulation of Competition: Towards a Regulatory Geography of Global Competition Law* (Cambridge, UK: Cambridge University Press, 2013), 123, pp. 131–32.

[103] Kameoka, *Competition Law and Policy in Japan and the EU* (n. 102 above), p. 132.

the basic calculation rate applicable to large manufacturers from 6 per cent to 10 per cent.[104]

In addition, the 2005 amendment took a more severe stance towards reoffenders. The JFTC must levy a 50 per cent extra charge against reoffenders. Reoffenders are considered enterprises that had been subject to an administrative surcharge in the ten years preceding the newly levied administrative surcharge.[105]

6.4.2.2 Clarification and Expansion of the Scope of Administrative Surcharge

Before the amendment in 2005, Article 7-2(1) of the AMA provided that agreements falling under the unreasonable restraints of trade prong of Article 3 of the AMA could be the target of the administrative surcharge as long as those agreements related to the price of goods or services, or substantially restrained the volume of supply of goods or services and thereby affected their price. Although this provision may be interpreted to include hard-core cartels such as those pursuing market division and customer allocation, the enterprises engaged in those violating acts once argued that they would not be subject to the administrative surcharge. This was because those types of cartels were not written explicitly in the wording of the relevant article.[106]

The 2005 AMA amendment clarified the coverage of the administrative surcharge. The amendment pointed out that market division and customer allocation between competitors are the target violations of the administrative surcharge under the AMA. In the same way, agreements that may affect the price of goods or services by substantially restricting

[104] Ibid. Likewise, the basic calculation rate for small and medium-sized enterprises was raised by 1 per cent from the previous rate of 3 per cent.

[105] Takeshima, K., 'Leniency Programme and Bid Riggings in Public Sector – Enforcement Experiences in Japan' (2007). Retrieved from www.jftc.go.jp/en/policy_enforcement/speeches/2007/saicsymposium2007.html. On the other hand, a 20 per cent lower calculation rate is applied to enterprises that stopped engaging in violations by the day one month prior to the date on which JFTC commenced investigations, as long as the period of implementation for the violations is less than two years (2005 AMA, Article 7-2(6)). This 'earlier withdrawal' from violations was introduced in the AMA for the sake of encouraging enterprises to stop violating acts in their earlier stages and differs from the leniency programme in which enterprises can be rewarded by reporting their violation facts to the JFTC. Therefore, there could be a case in which both 'leniency' and 'earlier withdrawal' are applied. Wakui, M., *Antimonopoly Law: Competition Law and Policy in Japan* (Bury St Edmunds: Arima Publishing, 2008), p. 287.

[106] Iyori, H. and Uesugi, A., *The Antimonopoly Laws and Policies of Japan* (New York: Federal Legal Publications, 1994), pp. 85–86, 257.

the volume of purchase were proclaimed as a clear target of the administrative surcharge. Prior to the amendment, only cartels restraining the volume of supply were deemed to have a noticeable amount of sales on which the JFTC could levy the monetary penalty and this was written in the AMA. Given the economic similarity between supply cartels and purchase cartels in which purchasers restrict competition to buy goods or services, however, the amended law added purchase cartels to Article 7-2(1) of the AMA. In purchase cartels, the JFTC imposes a surcharge based on the purchase amount of the goods or services.[107]

6.4.2.3 Extension of the Statute of Limitations for Cease-and-Desist Orders

As for the JFTC's administrative measures against cartels and bid rigging, the amendment of the AMA in 2005 extended the period within which the JFTC could issue appropriate cease-and-desist orders to eliminate the violations and recover competition in the relevant market. Before the amendment, the AMA enabled the JFTC to issue a cease-and-desist order against price fixing, for example, even if the violating act had already ceased to exist. However, the period during which the JFTC could issue such an order was only one year from the last day of the violating act. In the past, there were cases in which the JFTC could not take appropriate measures because the statute of limitations for its administrative order had elapsed.[108] The amended law in 2005 extended the short statute of limitations up to three years in order to increase the ability of the JFTC to take action and issue appropriate orders against cartels and bid-rigging activities that were abandoned before the commencement of the JFTC's investigations.[109]

[107] AMA, Article 7-2 (1).

[108] Suwazono, S., *The 2005 Amendments of the Antimonopoly Law – An Article-by-Article Commentary of the New Surcharge System and the Hearing/Criminal Investigation System* (Tokyo: Shojihoumu, 2005), p. 97 (in Japanese).

[109] 2005 AMA, Article 7-2 (21). See also Wakui, *Antimonopoly Law* (n. 105 above), p. 288; JFTC, 'Summary of the Amendment to the Antimonopoly Act' (2009), slide 10. Retrieved from www.jftc.go.jp/en/pressreleases/yearly-2009/jun/090603-1_files/090603-2.pdf (indicating the situation in 2005 and 2009). Regarding the period for the JFTC to issue an administrative surcharge payment order even after the termination of unlawful conduct, it had already been three years from the last day of the violating act before the 2005 amendment. This was because surcharge payment orders by the JFTC had to follow its cease-and-desist orders under the AMA at that time. Due to the amendment in 2005, which enabled the JFTC to issue a cease-and-desist order and a surcharge payment order at the same time, the statute of limitations for the two types of the JFTC's administrative order became the same.

6.4.2.4 Compulsory Investigative Powers for the JFTC

Since the publication of the policy on criminal accusations against hard-core cartels in 1990, the JFTC had been relatively active in seeking criminal penalties in serious cases where the influence of the relevant violations was widespread throughout Japan.[110] The JFTC's stringent attitude towards vicious hard-core cartels was welcoming in terms of strengthening deterrence. However, there were several problems at that time with regard to criminal prosecution under the AMA.

First of all, the JFTC's investigative power was merely an administrative one and was not to be construed under the AMA as being granted for conducting a criminal investigation. When the JFTC sought to conduct an on-site inspection, for example, the officials from the Japanese competition agency had to wait at the gate or the front door until the persons concerned agreed to accept the inspection, as the JFTC did not have any direct compulsory investigative power. It only had the power to force the persons concerned not to refuse, obstruct or evade the inspection against a backdrop of criminal punishment. At that time, the criminal penalty for refusing, obstructing or evading an on-the-spot inspection by the JFTC was either imprisonment with labour for not more than six months or a fine of not more than ¥200,000.[111] Having only such indirect compulsory investigative power, the JFTC had great difficulty collecting substantial evidence for prosecuting hard-core cartels. There was always a risk that important evidence would be destroyed while the officials from the JFTC were requesting the persons investigated to accept their on-the-spot inspection. The 2005 AMA amendment entitled the JFTC to use direct compulsory power in a criminal investigation.[112] With the new investigative power, the JFTC may conduct an on-site inspection, search or seizure based on a warrant issued in advance by a judge of a court having appropriate jurisdiction.[113] Also, after receiving

[110] Kameoka, *Competition Law and Policy in Japan and the EU* (n. 102 above), p. 128, making reference to the Guidelines on criminal prosecution against AMA infringements of 20 June 1990. These Guidelines were amended in 2005 and 2009. The latest revision is of 2020. JFTC, 'The Fair Trade Commission's Policy on Criminal Accusation and Compulsory Investigation of Criminal Cases Regarding Antimonopoly Violations (Tentative translation)' (2020). Retrieved from www.jftc.go.jp/en/legislation_gls/210312.pdf.

[111] Kameoka, *Competition Law and Policy in Japan and the EU* (n. 102 above), p. 129. The maximum penalty for obstructing the JFTC's on-site inspection was raised by the AMA amendment in 2005 to either one year's imprisonment with labour or a fine of ¥300,000.

[112] For a full explanation of this procedure, see Kameoka, *Competition Law and Policy in Japan and the EU* (n. 102 above), pp. 129–30.

[113] 2005 AMA, Article 102 (1) and (2)

a warrant from a court, the Japanese competition agency may seize postal items, correspondence or documents related to telegrams that were sent by or to a criminal suspect.[114] With a proper warrant from a court, the JFTC may seize even postal items and so on that are not sent by or to a criminal suspect, to the extent that there are sufficient grounds to suspect the postal matters and so on are related to a criminal case.[115] In the case of an on-site inspection, search or seizure, officials from the JFTC have the power to open locks, break seals and take other necessary measures.[116] Furthermore, the JFTC officials may prohibit any person from entering or leaving the site without permission while conducting such an investigation.[117] The JFTC's officials engaging in on-site inspection, search or seizure may also request the assistance of police officials if necessary in order to accomplish their investigative activities in full.[118] These kinds of strong investigative power are equivalent to those usually permitted in criminal investigations by the police or the prosecution. Therefore, it can be said that the amendment in 2005 equipped the JFTC with powerful weapons to investigate hard-core cartels.

Secondly, cooperation between the JFTC and the prosecutor was not efficient to handle the same case in the past. For instance, a written statement recorded by the JFTC was for the competition agency to take appropriate administrative measures and not for criminal punishment. The prosecutor in charge could not use the written statement in the subsequent criminal procedures, even after the JFTC filed an accusation with the Prosecutor General.[119] Accordingly, the prosecutor had to take and record similar statements from scratch, spending enormous amounts of time and energy. In this regard, the amended law obliges the JFTC to hand over any retained or seized objects when the competition agency files an accusation with the Prosecutor General. After an object retained or seized by the JFTC has been ceded to the prosecution in accordance with the amended law, the object is deemed to have been seized under the provisions of the Code of Criminal Procedure.[120] In doing so, the amendment certainly reduced the burden that the prosecution must bear in the process of a criminal investigation under the AMA.

114 Ibid., Article 103 (1).

115 Ibid., Article 103 (2).

116 Ibid., Article 107 (1).

117 Ibid., Article 108.

118 Ibid., Article 110.

119 According to Article 74 (1) of the 2005 AMA, whenever it is convinced that a criminal offence has taken place, the JFTC must file an accusation with the Prosecutor General.

120 2005 AMA, Article 106 (3).

Thirdly, from the perspective of due process, the system of criminal accusation under the AMA had been widely criticised, as the JFTC was able to file an accusation based on the result of its administrative investigation, which was usually not aimed at leading to a criminal punishment. For the person concerned, it was not easy to recognise whether the investigation he or she was suffering was for an administrative order or for a criminal accusation. Regarding the requirement of due process, the abovementioned investigative power was newly introduced in the AMA apart from the JFTC's existing power to investigate AMA violations for administrative measures. Therefore, it is fair to say that the amended law aimed to achieve complete separation of the JFTC's criminal procedures from the agency's administrative procedures.[121]

6.4.3 *The 2009 Amendments Focus on Ringleaders and Suspended Criminal Sanctions*

6.4.3.1 Ringleaders of Cartels up for a Higher Administrative Surcharge

The amendment of the AMA in 2009 allowed the JFTC to impose a 50 per cent increased surcharge against ringleaders of a cartel or bid rigging. For example, a large-scale manufacturer that planned to engage in illegal price fixing of a product and caused other enterprises to engage in or not to discontinue the violation would be forced to pay 15 per cent of the sales from the relevant product affected. Given that the normal basic calculation rate applicable to large manufacturers is 10 per cent, the basic calculation rate will be 1.5 times higher for manufacturers who played a leading role in the price fixing.[122]

As mentioned before, the 2005 amendment had already increased the basic calculation rate for reoffenders. Reoffenders already faced a 1.5 times higher basic calculation rate. Then, what if a reoffender played a leading role in a cartel case? Theoretically speaking, the basic calculation rate should be 2.25 times higher. However, Article 7-2 (9) of the 2009 AMA stated that the basic calculation rate applicable to such a ringleader should be twice as high as the rate provided under Article 7-2 (1) of the 2009

[121] Article 101 (1) of the 2005 AMA makes it clear that the JFTC can use the criminal investigative power against the limited number of crimes provided in Articles 89–91 of the 2009 AMA. Among such crimes, hard-core cartels and private monopolisation, both of which are prohibited under Article 3 of the AMA, are included.

[122] Kameoka, *Competition Law and Policy in Japan and the EU* (n. 102 above), p. 132.

AMA. This means that the JFTC would use the 20 per cent basic calculation rate if the reoffending ringleader was a large-scale manufacturer.[123]

6.4.3.2 Creating a Way to Limit Suspended Criminal Sanctions

Before the AMA amendment of 2009, a criminal penalty against individuals who violated the unreasonable restraint of trade provision could either be imprisonment with labour for not more than three years or a criminal fine of not more than ¥5 million.[124] In order to secure effective deterrence against individuals who engage in cartels or bid rigging, the 2009 amendment has increased the maximum jail term up to five years[125] while the maximum amount of fine applicable to individuals has remained unchanged.[126]

Raising the upper limit of the jail term to five years has a significant meaning regarding the suspension of execution of sentence by criminal courts. In Japan, the Criminal Code provides that criminal courts may grant a suspension of execution of the sentence only when a person is sentenced to imprisonment for not more than three years.[127] After the amendment, criminal courts cannot suspend execution of sentences if they pronounce imprisonment with labour exceeding three years. Since all the criminal cases in Japan were treated so far with suspension of execution of the sentences, the extension of the maximum jail term for individuals engaged in cartels or bid rigging can be an effective deterrent to those infringements, as well as a sufficient reason for enterprises to utilise the leniency programme in Japan. In addition, the increase in maximum jail term has resulted in the extension of the statute of limitations for the cartel or bid-rigging offence. According to the Code of Criminal Procedure in Japan, a cartel offence whose maximum imprisonment with labour is five years under the current AMA, for example, is subject to the five-year statute of limitations.[128] This is a longer statute of limitations compared to the three-year period[129] applied to criminal offences under the AMA prior to the amendment in 2009.

123 2009 AMA, Article 7-2 (9).

124 Ikeda, 'Introduction to the Antimonopoly Law' (n. 106 above), slide 30.

125 Since the enactment of the AMA in 1947, the maximum jail term against individuals engaged in cartels or bid rigging had been three years, until the amendment in 2009.

126 2009 AMA, Article 89 (1).

127 Act No. 45 of April 24, 1907 (Criminal Code), Article 25 (1). Translation available at www.cas.go.jp/jp/seisaku/hourei/data/PC.pdf.

128 Act No. 131 of July 10 1948 (Code of Criminal Procedure), Article 250 (v). Translation available at www.japaneselawtranslation.go.jp/en/laws/view/2056/en.

129 Code of Criminal Procedure, Article 250 (vi).

6.4.3.3 The Responsible Enterprise in Case of Merger, Split or Business Transfer

The 2009 amendment has also made it clear who would be the enterprise to whom the JFTC can address a cease-and-desist order even when the violator of Article 3 of the 2009 AMA, for example, ceased to exist because of a merger, a company split or a transfer of a business, as enumerated in Article 7(2) of the 2009 AMA.[130] At the same time, the amended law stipulated that an administrative surcharge payment order could be issued to the enterprise that took over the violating business from the violator within the same company group, as provided in Article 7-2(25) of the 2009 AMA.[131] By securing the administrative measures against business-succeeding companies, the amendment aimed to block any circumvention, by violators of the AMA, of the JFTC's administrative orders through mergers and acquisitions.

6.4.4 The 2019 Amendments Revise the Administrative Surcharge Drastically

The 2019 amendment, which altered the leniency programme drastically, made changes to the administrative surcharge system as well. Besides some adjustments to the basic calculation rate of the surcharge, the most important amendment for the purpose of deterrence is the broadening of the calculation base of the surcharge.

The amount of the administrative surcharge was, until 2020, calculated based upon the sales turnover of the product subject to an infringement and this for up to three years. Furthermore, the statute of limitations was five years.[132] This meant that the JFTC could not issue a surcharge order for violations that ceased more than five years ago. From 2020 onwards, these terms have been extended. The JFTC will be able to take the ten-year sales turnover of the product subject to an infringement into consideration. The ten years will be counted backwards from the year in which the JFTC initiated its investigation.[133] The statute of limitations has been

130 2009 AMA, Article 7-2.

131 Ibid., Article 7-2 (25).

132 Wakui, *Antimonopoly Law* (n. 105 above), p. 288; JFTC, 'Summary of the Amendment to the Antimonopoly Act' (n. 109 above), slide 10.

133 JFTC, 'The Outline of the Antimonopoly Act Amendment – The Direction of the Revision of the Surcharge System' (2019), p. 3. Retrieved from www.jftc.go.jp/en/pressreleases/yearly-2019/June/190619071.pdf.

extended to seven years.[134] The extension of the period of sales turnover may have as a consequence that not all relevant information is available when the JFTC initiates an investigation. To overcome that problem, the AMA allows the JFTC to estimate the basis for calculating the surcharge.[135]

In order to better take away the gains obtained with a cartel violation, the 2019 amendment improved the basis for calculating the surcharge. The basis was extended to the 'financial gains as a reward for not supplying the goods or services to cartels, the amount of sales of business related to goods or services subject to cartels (e.g. subcontract), [and] the amount of sales of the [sic] certain enterprises that belong to the same group as the violators and receive the instructions or information of the violators'.[136]

The revision of the surcharge system also dealt with some issues in relation to the percentage for calculating the surcharge. The 2019 amendment brought a unification of the percentages to calculate the surcharge. This was done by abolishing the different percentages applicable for retailers and wholesalers, who were enjoying lower percentages (respectively 3 and 2 per cent) to calculate the surcharge. In the future, all businesses will thus be subject to 10 per cent of the total sales turnover of a specific period of time.[137] Equally, a lowered percentage for enterprises that have withdrawn early from an infringement will be dropped.[138] This means that enterprises withdrawing from an infringing act no later than a month before the JFTC started an investigation into that conduct will no longer be granted a 20 per cent discount from the surcharge. Besides abolishing several percentages, one new percentage was introduced. The surcharge for small and medium-sized enterprises (SMEs) will be calculated by multiplying the relevant sales turnover by 4 per cent.[139] Note that this percentage will also be used if the SME is part of a corporate group.[140]

The percentage for calculating the surcharge can be increased when the violating enterprise is found to be the ringleader. This possibility was inscribed in 2009. The categories to which this increase of 50 per cent applies have been broadened. For example, an enterprise obstructing the JFTC investigation by providing incorrect information will face an

134 AMA, Article 7-8 (6).
135 Ibid., Article 7-2 (3). See also JFTC, 'The Outline of the Antimonopoly Act Amendment' (n. 134 above), p. 3.
136 JFTC (n. 134 above), p. 3.
137 Ibid.
138 Ibid.
139 Ibid.
140 Ibid.

increase of 50 per cent.[141] On the contrary, the 50 per cent increase will not apply any more to a second infringement, on the condition that the enterprise has ceased to participate in the second infringement before the JFTC issued a surcharge payment order for the first infringement.[142]

6.4.5 *A More Severe Surcharge, Better Investigation Procedures and Deterrence*

Leniency programmes are introduced to increase the probability of detection. Increased detection should contribute to deterrence. The deterrence equation does indeed hold that 'the total sanction imposed for violations of antitrust law' should equal 'the harm of the violation to society, multiplied by the inverse probability of a sanction being imposed'.[143] A detailed analysis of the Japanese leniency programme has revealed that there are some issues affecting its impact on the deterrence equation. It may be that, unlike what is commonly held, the 2005/2009 Leniency Programme does not have the anticipated result of really increasing detection. The amendments of 2019 may have a positive effect on deterrence. However, due to not addressing the issue of unmeritorious leniency applications, there may still be a perception that only a few leniency applications lead to detection. Indeed, by not addressing the stream of leniency applications that do not lead to an investigation, the discrepancy between the number of applications used in a decision and the actual number of leniency applications may continue to be very high.

An argument could be made that such a deficiency may be countered by addressing problems in the sanctioning system. The Japanese legislator seems to follow that reasoning. Every revision of the AMA since the implementation of the leniency programme has included some changes to the sanctioning system. Many of these changes relate to the administrative surcharge. Some changes related to the increase of the basic calculation rate of the surcharge, others related to the broadening of the basis for calculating the surcharge. The revision also broadened the categories of infringers that should receive, for some objective reason, a severer sanction. Another important change was to give the JFTC better investigation powers, even for administrative investigations. The criminal sanctions of

141 Ibid.

142 Ibid.

143 Vande Walle, S., 'Deterrence of Antitrust Violations: Do Actions for Damages Matter in Japan?' (2012) 2 *Asian Journal of Law and Economics* 3.

the AMA have received much less attention. Besides facilitating the criminal investigation procedure, the criminal sanctions have only been raised once over the last twenty years.

All the abovementioned evolutions show that the JFTC is gradually, with small but incremental steps, trying to achieve a more optimal degree of deterrence. An important step was taken in 2019. The basic calculation rate for the administrative surcharge system was made uniform at 10 per cent. For several categories of enterprises, this meant an increase of the basic calculation rate. At the same time, the 2019 amendments abolished several favourable regimes, giving away special reductions of the administrative surcharge. Only for SMEs was a special regime kept. This evolution is epitomising a trend towards moving away from proportional justice towards deterrence. Proportional justice is called for when the high fines are, for several reasons, not socially accepted. With all the favourable regimes, the Japanese legislator has been adjusting sanctions so that they become proportionate 'to the degree in which society disapproves of the harm caused'.[144]

Despite these improvements, there are still various indicators that the Japanese legislator and the JFTC are not prioritising deterrence. At two points, proportional justice takes the upper hand in the enforcement policy of the AMA. These points make it difficult to fully balance out, in the deterrence equation, the extent of failed detection by the respective Japanese leniency programmes.

First, the administrative surcharge is determined based on the turnover. Van den Bergh and Camesasca point out that turnover is 'not a sound basis for calculating the fine if it does not allow for the reversal of the gains of the infringement'.[145] It is thus important that the height of the fine exceeds the gains of the infringement. Even though there may be issues with the identification of the gains,[146] there have been studies that point out that the average gain of a cartel in Japan ranges from 15 per cent to 30 per cent.[147] Taking into consideration that Japan has increased

144 Van den Bergh and Camesasca, *European Competition Law and Economics* (n. 11 above), p. 311.

145 Ibid.

146 Ibid. (indicating that 'The gain equals the mark-up times the volume of the affected trade. Figures on sales are not difficult to obtain given the broad availability of market studies. It is more difficult to determine the mark-up, since this requires either econometric calculation or the identification of a benchmark of the competitive price in the absence of collusion').

147 McMillan, J., '*Dango:* Japan's Price Fixing Conspiracies' (1991) 3(3) *Economics and Politics* 201; Woodall, B., *Japan under Construction* (Berkeley: University of California Press, 1996), p. 48.

the basic calculation rate for the surcharge to 10 per cent of turnover, the amount is still too small to achieve optimal deterrence. The fact that the administrative surcharge has not yet increased up to a level that might be regarded as the profit of a cartel may again reveal that proportional justice has been one of the motives driving the enforcement policy.

Second, incarceration is considered to be one of the better types of sanctions to obtain deterrence, because it makes the individual decision-makers accountable.[148] It is also important not to limit the criminal sanctions to monetary ones, as the firm can compensate the employees ex ante.[149] With both jail sentences and criminal fines, the AMA should score well in terms of deterrence. However, criminal accusations are still few in Japan. If there are criminal accusations, the individuals still end up with a suspended sentence despite recent developments to avoid such an evolution. The deterrence that should be achieved by the criminal sanctions could thus be regarded as jeopardised. Due to the weakening of the criminal sanctions, this part of the JFTC's enforcement policy is still reflecting more proportional justice than deterrence.

6.5 Negotiated Leniency, A Higher Surcharge and Deterrence

Leniency is an enforcement tool aimed at facilitating the detection of illegal cartels. Economic theory suggests that increased detection could contribute to deterrence. Of course, this requires the leniency programme to achieve the goal for which it should be designed. A nuanced conclusion has been drawn about the 2005/2009 Leniency Programme. Despite the analysis that only a minority of leniency applications are genuinely independent, the JFTC partly curbs this impression by systematically stressing the total number of decisions based on leniency applications. The discrepancy between the number of decisions and the total number of leniency applications may negatively affect the impression that leniency applications are taken seriously by the JFTC. Furthermore, the JFTC could, more than ever, stress the increased enforcement of the AMA against some types of cartels, such as price fixing and bid rigging in private procurement projects, which were less often discovered before the introduction of the leniency programme.

With the introduction of the 2019 amendments to the leniency programme, the prediction is that not much will change to the analysis made

148 Van den Bergh and Camesasca, *European Competition Law and Economics* (n. 11 above), p. 311.

149 Ibid.

for the 2005/2009 Leniency Programme. The reason? The 2019 Leniency Programme does not address the impression that a relatively large number of leniency applications are not meritorious in the sense that they do not lead to an investigation. The way the 2019 Leniency Programme is conceptualised, the prediction is that investigations will be smoother and deeper. More information may be revealed in a shorter period of time. If this leads to a capacity increase at the JFTC to investigate more cases or to higher surcharges, an extra dimension could be added to the deterrence of the 2005/2009 Leniency Programme.

If the leniency programme itself is not conceptualised to attract valuable independent leniency applications, severer sanctions may do the job.[150] Indeed, economic studies have pointed out that the incentive for applying for leniency rises the higher the cost is of infringing the law. If the sanction is high, an enterprise will gain significantly from applying for leniency. Defecting from a cartel will become a rational strategy. Yet even with the incremental steps to a more optimal sanctioning system, too many problems remain to conclude that the sanctions could compensate for the deficiencies in the power of the leniency programme to deter. Above, we have already mentioned two reasons why the sanctions are not able to do so despite their recurrent revision. On the one hand, the calculation of the surcharge does not allow the real profit of the illegal activity to be considered. On the other hand, criminal sanctions are still not frequently used and, if they are used, they are always suspended.

Despite these observations, the implementation of negotiated leniency could lead to a better understanding of the full scale and duration of an illegal cartel. Together with the enactment of the extended base for calculating the surcharge and an increased basic calculation rate for most types of enterprises, the negotiated leniency could result in a higher absolute surcharge. It is only in this way that the interaction between these new amendments of the AMA positively contributes to deterrence.

6.6 Conclusion

The 2019 amendment to the AMA marked a significant turn in the conceptualisation of the leniency programme in Japan. Leniency became available for an unlimited number of enterprises, but the degree of leniency

150 Theoretically speaking, this could also be done by prioritising domestic cartels. However, this could create the impression that Japan is cartel heaven for international cartels.

was drastically lowered. To provide an incentive for enterprises to participate in the programme, an extra reduction is offered for their cooperation on submitting valuable information to discover the truth of the case. This kind of amendment, we suggest, will contribute to a smoother investigation process and so better reveal the full picture of the cartel. With a better understanding of all facets of the cartel, the JFTC will be better placed to calculate the surcharge. Since the 2019 amendment also revised the basis for the calculation of the surcharge, it is likely that this further contributes to the calculation of a higher surcharge. If this leads to a higher surcharge on average, a higher degree of deterrence may be achieved. However, since the newly designed leniency programme is not aimed at getting better applications for immunity and the increase of sanctions is not sufficient to take away the profits of the illegal activity in all cases, the overall deterrent effect of the 2019 amendments may still be relatively low.

7

The Law and Policy on Cartels and Leniency in Korea

YO SOP CHOI*

7.1 Introduction

Cartels are the major target of antitrust law, and the rules against cartels lie at the heart of competition policy. However, only a small number of cartels are ever detected, particularly at the international level,[1] because several practical difficulties exist in detecting illegal collusion, such as high investigation costs, different legal frameworks and culture, and dissimilar levels of public and private enforcement among countries.[2] Despite the obstacles, competition authorities across the globe have tried to establish a robust system for effective enforcement by providing various legal measures to identify cartels. One of the key legal techniques of cartel detection and deterrence is obviously a leniency programme.[3]

The dictum 'there is no honour among thieves' highlights the success of leniency policy.[4] Leniency programmes can destabilise undisclosed collusions by providing various incentives for cartel participants, such

* English translations of the Korean works are the author's own and are unofficial.

1 Williams, M., 'Cartel Prohibition and the Search for Deterrent Penalties: The United States, the European Union, Australia and China Compared', in Healey, D., Jacobs, M. and Smith, R. (eds.), *Research Handbook on Methods and Models of Competition Law* (Cheltenham: Edward Elgar, 2020), 116, p. 116.

2 Choi, Y. S., 'Competition Laws and Policies against International Cartels in Northeast Asia: International Cooperation for Effective Enforcement', in Cheng, T., Marco Colino, S. and Ong, B. (eds.), *Cartels in Asia: Law & Practice* (Hong Kong: Wolters Kluwer Law & Business, 2015), 133, p. 147.

3 The high percentage of cartel cases uncovered by leniency programmes indicates the importance of leniency policy. See OECD, 'Challenges and Co-ordination of Leniency Programmes – Background Note by the Secretariat' (5 June 2018), p. 4. Retrieved from https://one.oecd.org/document/DAF/COMP/WP3(2018)1/en/pdf.

4 Borrell, J.-R., Jiménez J. L. and Ordóñez-de-Haro, J. M., 'The Leniency Programme: Obstacles on the Way to Collude' (2015) 3 *Journal of Antitrust Enforcement* 149.

as immunity or a reduction in sanctions, which trigger a race towards competition agencies.[5] In effect, leniency programmes in many countries have induced cartelists to disclose their secret agreements and provide essential information and evidence of the violation of cartel laws, because the benefit of full immunity and the reduction of heavy penalties that come from a grant of leniency are very attractive to them.[6]

The United States (US) Department of Justice (DOJ) and the European Commission adopted their leniency programmes in 1978 and 1996, respectively, and the successful implementations of these programmes have resulted in 'a standard feature of cartel enforcement regimes' in the world.[7] South Korea has also developed leniency law and policy to achieve the goal of preventing hard-core cartels. The Korean competition regime adopted a leniency provision in 1996, which became effective in 1997.[8] This shows its feature of being an early adopter that accepts various competition law methods, including leniency programmes.[9] Over the last twenty-five years, the Korean regime has revised its leniency rules in the Monopoly Regulation and Fair Trade Act (MRFTA)[10] and the supplementary soft law provisions,[11] such as the Notification on the Implementation of the Leniency Programme (Leniency Notice).[12] Its several amendments

[5] Whelan, P., 'Criminal Cartel Enforcement in the EU: Avoiding a Human Rights Trade-Off', in Beaton-Wells, C. and Ezrachi, A. (eds.), *Criminalising Cartels: Critical Studies of an International Regulatory Movement* (Oxford: Hart Publishing, 2011), 217, p. 231.

[6] OECD, 'Challenges and Co-ordination of Leniency Programmes' (n. 3 above), p. 4.

[7] Ibid., p. 4. However, some argue that it is not certain whether the current leniency policy is successful because it is not possible to find out how many cartels are discovered. See Utton, M. A., *Cartels and Economic Collusion: The Persistence of Corporate Conspiracies* (Cheltenham: Edward Elgar, 2011), p. 150.

[8] See, generally, Kwon, O. and Seo, J., *Antitrust Law*, 3rd ed. (Paju: Bobmunsa, 2018), p. 354 (in Korean).

[9] In 1997, only the US, the EU and Korea had leniency programmes. See Park, S., 'Key Issues and Implications of the Leniency Policy' (2018) 116 *Justice* 301 (in Korean).

[10] Law No. 17799, amended 29 December 2020 (effective 30 December 2021). English materials on Korean competition law and policy, including statutory provisions, are available at the Korean competition agency's website. Retrieved from www.ftc.go.kr/eng/index.do.

[11] See also Kum, C. H., Yoon, H. and Park, Y. J., 'In Brief: Cartel Immunity and Leniency Programmes in South Korea' Lexology (28 November 2020). Retrieved from www.lexology.com/library/detail.aspx?g=620d0f61-bf8c-4f79-b45b-a457c1330018.

[12] KFTC, 'Public Notification on the Implementation of the Leniency Programme Including Corrective Measures for Voluntary Reporters, etc. of Illegal Cartel Conduct' (Notification No. 2021-72, amended 10 June 2021) (Leniency Notice). The Supreme Prosecutors' Office

to the leniency provisions reveal notable efforts by the Korea Fair Trade Commission (KFTC) to strengthen its cartel enforcement.

Commentators assert that the Korean leniency programme appears to be effective in preventing hard-core cartels.[13] A total of 626 cartel cases were detected in the period between 1999 and 2018; of these, 339 (54.2 per cent) were detected within the framework of the leniency programme. In particular, over the past ten years, the Korean leniency programme has demonstrated its pivotal role in effective enforcement against cartels.[14] In this period, the highest percentage of cartel cases caught by leniency was 82.9 per cent.[15]

The Korean competition regime shares common features with leniency programmes in other regimes. For example, full immunity is offered to the first informant who voluntarily reports a cartel.[16] There are also similar conditions and requirements for leniency, such as the honest disclosure of information and evidence and full and continuous cooperation with the KFTC.[17] However, the Korean regime has distinctive provisions that are somewhat different from other countries, such as a benefit, albeit less than full immunity, to the second applicant,[18] the immunity exception for the coercer in a cartel, the immunity exception for a recidivist, the absence of penalty plus and the omnibus question. In particular, there are critical issues related to private litigation for

also provides the Leniency Guidelines (Guidelines No. 1275, effective 28 March 2022). Retrieved from www.spo.go.kr/site/spo/ex/board/View.do?cbIdx=1304&bcIdx=1026858 (in Korean).

13 See, e.g., Lee, H. W. and Choi, Y. J., 'How Does the New Leniency Program in Korea Affect Cartel Formation and Cartel Detection?' (2014) 32(2) *Journal of Korean Economic Studies* 99 (in Korean); Kwon, N., 'An Economic Analysis of Leniency in Korea' (2010) 18(4) *Korean Journal of Industrial Organization* 41 (in Korean).

14 Since the KFTC revised leniency provisions for improving transparency and predictability in 2005, the number of cartel cases detected by leniency has been noteworthy in its increase. See Lee, K. J., 'Measures to Enhance the Effectiveness of Leniency Programs' (2018) 31(4) *Commercial Cases Review* 249, p. 250 (in Korean).

15 KFTC, '2019 White Paper' (24 October 2019), pp. 292–93. Retrieved from www.ftc.go.kr/www/cop/bbs/selectBoardList.do?key=191&bbsId=BBSMSTR_000000002318&bbsTyCode=BBST01 (in Korean).

16 Supreme Court of Korea Judgment 2010 *Du*28915, 30 June 2011.

17 OECD, 'Challenges and Co-ordination of Leniency Programmes' (n. 3 above), p. 4.

18 The leniency conditions for subsequent applicants are often different among competition regimes. For instance, the EU and Japanese regimes grant more than two applicants, while the US agency offers full immunity only to the first leniency applicant. See, e.g., Van Uytsel, S., 'Leniency under the Japanese Antimonopoly Law: Towards the End of the Cartel Archipelago?' in Cheng, Marco Colino, and Ong, *Cartels in Asia* (n. 2 above), 67, pp. 77–78.

damages in follow-on cases from the KFTC decisions and to criminal sanctions related to the leniency policy.[19]

In effect, dissimilar leniency programmes may cause negative effects on cartel enforcement. Moreover, the lack of cooperation between competition authorities across countries and a one-stop-shop of leniency notification weaken law enforcement against international cartels;[20] multinational enterprises need to apply leniency in multiple jurisdictions, which generates considerable cost and burden when they have to comply with divergent and contradictory leniency requirements.[21] Considering the practical problems, enforcement agencies in many countries have shown efforts to improve the effectiveness of leniency programmes and the convergence of those programmes,[22] and it is timely to assess the current leniency programme in Korea.

This chapter aims to examine competition law and policy on cartels and leniency in Korea and to discuss the recent issues with respect to the leniency programme. The chapter consists of five sections and is structured as follows. Section 7.2 explains the Korean law and policy on cartel and leniency, which covers the provisions in the MRFTA, the Enforcement Decree of the MRFTA[23] and the Leniency Notice. Section 7.3 assesses the present leniency programme and suggests proposals for a better policy. Section 7.4 examines the issue of harmonising other competition policies related to private litigation and criminal sanctions. Lastly, Section 7.5 provides a summary and conclusion.

7.2 Korean Law and Policy on Cartel and Leniency

7.2.1 Substantive Provisions of the Cartel and Leniency Programme under the MRFTA

Each competition regime has its own distinctive objectives, and the Korean regime is no exception. Article 1 of the MRFTA articulates its purpose, which is to promote *fair* and *free* competition and to thereby encourage

[19] See, e.g., Park, 'Key Issues and Implications of the Leniency Policy' (n. 9 above).

[20] Choi, N., 'Problems of Leniency Programs in International Cartels and the Direction to Improve the Programs' (2013) 28 *Journal of Korean Competition Law* 85, p. 110 (in Korean).

[21] OECD, 'Executive Summary of the Roundtable on Challenges and Co-ordination of Leniency Programmes' (5 June 2018), p. 4. Retrieved from https://one.oecd.org/document/DAF/COMP/WP3/M(2018)1/ANN2/en/pdf.

[22] See, e.g., OECD, 'Challenges and Co-ordination of Leniency Programmes' (n. 3 above), p. 5.

[23] Enforcement Decree No. 32274, amended 28 December 2021 (effective 30 December 2021).

creative business activities, protect consumers and improve balanced economic growth through the prohibition of various anti-competitive and unfair trade conduct that includes cartels.[24] This statement reflects the fact that the objective of the Korean regime broadly deals with diverse socio-political values. This background is often crucial for implementing competition rules on unilateral conduct and merger control. However, the goal of cartel law is somewhat different from that of unilateral conduct provisions.[25] Most competition regimes treat hard-core cartels as 'a supreme evil' of society,[26] and thus this type of conduct is generally prohibited by a per se or quasi per se rule. The Korean regime also provides a stringent rule against cartels.[27] The MRFTA has four substantive provisions,[28] one of which is Article 40, which prohibits anti-competitive agreements.[29]

Article 40(1) of the MRFTA provides a non-exhaustive list of illegal agreements by undertakings[30] and widely prohibits various types of hard-core cartels, including price fixing, output restriction, market sharing, bid rigging and so on.[31] There is no individual exemption in Article 40 as there is in Article 101(3) of the Treaty on the Functioning of the European Union (TFEU). However, Article 40(2) includes an exemption rule that is based on a notification-and-authorisation method,[32] and the implementation of

[24] Choi, Y. S., 'The Evolution of Fair and Free Competition Law in the Republic of Korea', in Van Uytsel, S., Hayashi, S. and Haley, J. (eds.), *Research Handbook on Asian Competition Law* (Cheltenham: Edward Elgar, 2020), 65, p. 68.

[25] However, in some jurisdictions cartel law also covers non-economic goals. For instance, one of the important goals of the EU competition rule of anti-competitive agreement is market integration. See Ibáñez Colomo, P., 'Article 101 TFEU and Market Integration' (2016) 12(4) *JCLE* 749.

[26] *Verizon Communications* v. *Law Offices of Curtis V. Trinko*, 540 U.S. 398, 408 (2004).

[27] See also KFTC, 'Policy Area: Competition – Cartel' (n. d.). Retrieved from www.ftc.go.kr/eng/contents.do?key=502.

[28] The four substantive provisions are the prohibitions against abuses of market dominance, anti-competitive agreements, unfair trade practices and merger control. See, e.g., Choi, 'The Evolution of Fair and Free Competition Law' (n. 24 above), pp. 70–73.

[29] See, generally, Lee, M. H., 'Recent Developments in the Treatment of Collusion by Korean Courts' (2005) 4(2) *Journal of Korean Law* 115.

[30] Article 2 of the MRFTA paragraph 1 defines an undertaking as 'a person who conducts a manufacturing business, service business or any other business. Any executive, employee, agent or any other person who acts in the interest of the undertaking shall be deemed an undertaking in the application of the provisions pertaining to business associations.'

[31] The KFTC also provides the Guidelines of Assessments of Anti-Competitive Agreements (Guidelines No. 390, amended 28 December 2021).

[32] Choi. 'The Evolution of Fair and Free Competition Law' (n. 24 above), p. 71. The criteria for exemption include industrial rationalisation, research and development improvement, economic depression, industrial restructure and improvement of trading conditions and of small and medium-sized enterprises' competitiveness.

cartel law is close to Section 1 of the Sherman Act,[33] although the MRFTA does not have a per se rule, even on hard-core cartels.[34] Articles 42 and 43 of the MRFTA then, respectively, clarify corrective measures[35] and an administrative surcharge of up to 20 per cent of the yearly turnover[36] as the consequences of an Article 40(1) violation.

The Korean competition regime also provides a leniency rule in the MRFTA that has a binding effect, while the regimes of the US and the European Union (EU) provide leniency programmes in their soft laws.[37] Article 44(1) of the MRFTA states that corrective measures and surcharges under Articles 42 and 43 may be mitigated or exempted for leniency applicants; it ensures full immunity or reduction of penalties. Moreover, it articulates an immunity from criminal sanctions: leniency applicants are exempted from the KFTC's filing of a complaint with the Prosecutor General pursuant to Article 129 of the MRFTA.[38] Article 44(1) sets out general leniency criteria as follows. First, it offers leniency benefits to a person who voluntarily reports a cartel or cooperates in the investigation by providing evidence or other means.[39] In addition, to prevent strategic use of the leniency provision, Article 44(2) proscribes a recidivist's

[33] Other substantive provisions in the MRFTA are closer to the EU competition rules, i.e. the prohibition of abuses of market dominance. See, e.g., Furse, M., *Antitrust Law in China, Korea and Vietnam* (Oxford: Oxford University Press, 2009), p. 24.

[34] Yang, M.-C., 'Competition Law and Policy of the Republic of Korea' (2009) 54(3) *Antitrust Bulletin* 621, p. 633; Williams, 'Cartel Prohibition and the Search for Deterrent Penalties' (n. 1 above), p. 119.

[35] Article 42 states that the KFTC may order the undertaking to cease the anti-competitive agreement, to publish the fact that the undertaking was ordered to correct such an agreement or to take other necessary corrective measures.

[36] At the time of writing in July 2021, the amount of surcharge is up to 10 per cent, but it will be increased to 20 per cent when the revised provision becomes effective in December 2021. See KFTC, 'Press Release: Amendment to the MRFTA Was Passed by the Congress' (9 December 2020). Retrieved from www.ftc.go.kr/www/selectReportUserView.do?key=10&rpttype=1&report_data_no=8868 (in Korean).

[37] US DOJ, 'Corporate Leniency Policy' (1993). Retrieved from www.justice.gov/atr/corporate-leniency-policy; US DOJ, 'Individual Leniency Policy' (1994). Retrieved from www.justice.gov/atr/individual-leniency-policy; European Commission, 'Commission Notice on Immunity from Fines and Reduction of Fines in Cartel Cases', O.J. C298/17 (2006).

[38] Article 129 provides that any penalty offence shall be prosecuted by a public action after a complaint is filed by the KFTC; the KFTC shall file its complaint with the Prosecutor General when the violation may substantially impede competition and the degree of infringement is obvious and serious from the objective point of view.

[39] The amendment to the MRFTA in 2001 included a leniency benefit for undertakings that reported or cooperated in the cartel investigation. See Kum, Yoon, and Park, 'Cartel Immunity and Leniency Programmes in South Korea' (n. 11 above).

application for leniency. It articulates that if a person for whom a corrective measure or surcharge is mitigated or exempted pursuant to Article 44(1) violates Article 40(1) again within five years from the date of mitigation or exemption, the applicant cannot receive a leniency benefit.

Article 44(3) articulates that the KFTC can withdraw the immunity or reduction of penalties if the leniency applicants, who received exemption benefits, make a statement to the court different from that during the KFTC investigation. Article 44(4) then stipulates the protection of leniency information by stating that the KFTC should not disclose information or materials related to leniency applicants, such as the applicants' identity and details of the information,[40] except in cases prescribed by the Enforcement Decree of the MRFTA. Article 44(5) also states that the Enforcement Decree provides the measures on conditions and criteria necessary for deciding whether the applicants are entitled to immunity and a reduction of the surcharge, and the details regarding the disclosure of critical information. Therefore, the MRFTA sets out rough guidelines for the leniency programme, and the Enforcement Decree provides clearer criteria for implementing the leniency provisions.

7.2.2 Criteria and Conditions of Mitigation and Immunity under the Enforcement Decree

The Enforcement Decree and the Leniency Notice set out details of the exemption criteria pursuant to Article 44 of the MRFTA. Article 51(1) (formerly Article 35(1))[41] of the Enforcement Decree contains an important standard of mitigation and exemption based on the applicants' rank. First, Article 51(1) subparagraph 1 states that a person who has filed a leniency application before KFTC's investigation commenced[42] can receive

[40] Protection of applicants is one of the priorities of the leniency system. See, e.g., Lee, H., Kim, K.-W., and Ha, M.-H., 'Needs and Devices to Protect Statements of Cartel Leniency Applicants from U.S. Discovery' (2010) 22 *Journal of Korean Competition Law* 338 (in Korean).

[41] At the time of writing in July 2021, there is a discussion on the amendment to the Enforcement Decree, and there will be a renumbering. This chapter follows the renumbering of the draft. Retrieved from www.ftc.go.kr/www/selectReportUserView.do?key=10&rpttype=1&report_data_no=9101 (in Korean).

[42] Article 3 of the Leniency Notice states that the commencement of investigation refers to the time at which the KFTC requests one or more undertakings to submit documents or verbal evidentiary proof by telephone, in a written form or in any other manner; or makes inquiries about relevant facts of such undertakings; or the KFTC requests such undertakings to be present at the KFTC; or conducts an on-site investigation on suspicion of the

full immunity when the following conditions are met: (a) the applicant is the first who provides evidence necessary to substantiate a cartel; (b) the applicant has filed a voluntary report of a secret cartel under circumstances in which the KFTC fails to obtain information about the cartel or sufficient evidence necessary to substantiate the cartel; (c) the applicant has faithfully cooperated with the KFTC until it completes the investigation by stating all facts about the cartel and submitting relevant materials; and (d) the applicant has ceased to engage in the cartel.[43]

Second, subparagraph 2 articulates that a person who cooperates in an investigation after the KFTC's commencement of an investigation also receives full immunity from surcharge and a reduction or exemption from corrective measures if the following conditions are met: (a) the applicant has cooperated in the investigation under circumstances in which the KFTC fails to obtain information about the cartel or sufficient evidence for substantiating the cartel; and (b) the applicant is eligible for exemption when he or she satisfies the conditions in subparagraph 1(a), (c) and (d) above.

Third, subparagraph 3 stipulates that the surcharge will be reduced by 50 per cent and the corrective measure may be mitigated for a person who has filed a leniency application before the KFTC has commenced an investigation or who cooperates in the investigation if the following conditions are met: (a) the person is the second applicant who provides evidence necessary to substantiate the existence of a cartel[44], except when two undertakings engage in a cartel and the applicant is one of the cartel members; (b) the person is eligible under subparagraph 1(c) and (d) above; and (c) the applicant files a report within two years starting from the first applicant's report. To summarise, the status of the second applicant cannot be secured when there are only two participants in the cartel or when two years have elapsed since the first applicant reported a cartel or cooperated in the investigation.[45]

cartel. In addition, if a request for submission of documents is made in a written form, the time at which the KFTC sends the written notification is deemed the time at which the investigation commences.

[43] Most pre-requisites for immunity qualification in the Enforcement Decree are almost identical to those of other competition regimes like the EU. See, e.g., Kecsmar, K. and Keidel, A., 'Shaping the EU Leniency Programme: The Recent Approach Adopted by EU Courts' (2015) 6(8) *Journal of European Competition Law & Practice* 556, pp. 559–60.

[44] The Supreme Court of Korea seems to broadly accept the probative value of supplementary or additional evidence in assessing the rank of second applicant. See Supreme Court of Korea Judgment 2012 *Du*8724.

[45] Kum, Yoon, and Park, 'Cartel Immunity and Leniency Programmes in South Korea' (n. 11 above).

Table 7.1 *Standard of immunity and mitigation under the MRFTA and the Enforcement Decree*

	Before the KFTC's commencement	After the KFTC's commencement
Surcharge (Art. 43 of the MRFTA)	Compulsory immunity for the first applicant	Compulsory immunity for the first person who cooperates with the KFTC
	Compulsory reduction of 50 per cent of surcharge for the second applicant	Compulsory reduction of 50 per cent of surcharge for the second person who cooperates with the KFTC
Corrective Measure (Art. 42 of the MRFTA)	Compulsory immunity for the first applicant	Compulsory immunity or mitigation for the first person who cooperates with the KFTC
	Discretionary mitigation for the second applicant	Discretionary mitigation for the second person who cooperates with the KFTC

The features of immunity and the reduction of the surcharge and corrective measures based on the applicant's rank are stated in Table 7.1.

Moreover, subparagraph 4 provides amnesty plus when the applicant satisfies the provisions of subparagraphs 1 and 2 above. Article 51(2) then limits an exemption benefit for the applicant who coerces another party to participate in the cartel or when the person repeatedly violates Article 40(1) of the MRFTA within a certain period of time.[46]

7.2.3 *The Soft Law Provisions of the Leniency Notice*

In addition to the Enforcement Decree, the KFTC provides the Leniency Notice, which articulates the details of the process of the leniency

[46] See, generally, Harris, S., 'Korea', in Sokol, D. D., Crane, D. A. and Ezrachi, A. (eds.), *Global Antitrust Compliance Handbook* (Oxford: Oxford University Press, 2014), 465, pp. 485–86.

application and the guidelines for immunity and mitigation for leniency applicants.[47] The Leniency Notice comprises seven chapters and eighteen articles.[48] Chapter 2 of the Leniency Notice provides the criteria for decisions on leniency, which is the most important part and should be reviewed. Moreover, the marker provision in Chapter 3 and amnesty plus in Chapter 5 also need to be discussed in this section.

First of all, Chapter 2 of the Leniency Notice widely covers various requirements for deciding whether to grant leniency. Article 4 states that the KFTC examines whether the submitted evidence satisfies the eligibility criteria according to Article 51(1) (formerly Article 35(1)) of the Enforcement Decree. The leniency applicant may receive leniency benefits where he or she provides evidence that can directly substantiate details of a cartel or its formation and implementation, such as a written agreement, minutes of meetings or internal reports of cartel participants. The evidence should include materials that describe specific facts of the cartel that have been discussed or conducted, such as letters of confirmation or affidavits written by undertakings or employees who have participated in the cartel.[49]

One of the important elements of a leniency decision is the requirement of the applicant's continuous and sincere cooperation.[50] Article 5(1) of the Leniency Notice stipulates that the KFTC considers the following factors in leniency decisions: (1) whether the applicant has reported all facts about the cartel without delay; (2) whether the applicant has promptly submitted all materials relating to the cartel that are in his or her possession or can be collected; (3) whether the applicant has promptly responded to the KFTC's requests and cooperated as necessary for the verification of facts; (4) whether executive officers and employees have made efforts to continuously and honestly cooperate with the KFTC in investigations and deliberations, including attendance at the court and so on; and (5) whether the applicant has not destroyed, fabricated, mutilated or concealed any evidence and information related to the cartel. These criteria are essential for an effective investigation, which has been confirmed by

[47] Leniency Notice, Article 1.

[48] The chapters include the general provisions, criteria for decisions of leniency, leniency application, determination of qualification for leniency, additional voluntary report (amnesty plus), supplementary provisions and administrative matters.

[49] There is no limit on the form or type of evidence; a written form, audio record or computer file can be considered as evidence.

[50] Competition regimes in other countries normally require full and continuous cooperation. See Stephan, A., 'The EU Method of Antitrust Enforcement', in Healey, Jacobs, and Smith, *Research Handbook on Methods and Models of Competition Law* (n. 1 above), 391, p. 404.

the Supreme Court of Korea.[51] The Court held that where the applicant has destroyed evidence prior to the commencement of the investigation or the leniency application, the individual should not be considered as a faithful applicant.

Article 5(2) of the Notice further states that when the applicant divulges the fact of a leniency application to a third party without the consent of the KFTC prior to the termination of its deliberation, the applicant is deemed to have not cooperated sincerely,[52] except when it is mandatory to disclose the fact of filing a leniency application under other Korean laws or when a notification is provided to a foreign government. Article 6 also articulates that the applicant should cease the cartel immediately after filing a leniency application. However, where an official specifies a certain period of time for investigations, the applicant needs to cease the cartel instantly after the end of that period. Lastly, Article 6-2 provides the criteria for a coercer in the cartel by examining whether the undertaking has exercised a physical force over, threatened or committed acts against others or imposed any sanction on or committed any relevant act against others to maintain the cartel.

Chapter 3 of the Leniency Notice contains the leniency application procedure, and Article 8-2 provides the verbal leniency application, which includes a marker system. It states that when there is a difficulty in filing a written form of leniency application with the KFTC, the applicant may file a verbal application. However, a leniency application by telephone is excluded. Upon receipt of a verbal application, the public official in charge of investigations should verbally ask questions about the matters and record and preserve answers by an audio or video recording device.

Chapter 5 of the Notice provides amnesty plus, which is designed to mitigate or revoke sanctions against cartelists that are under KFTC's investigations; the target of amnesty plus is often multimarket cartelists.[53] When a cartelist provides important information or evidence relating to another cartel as a first applicant, the informant may get the benefit of surcharge reduction.[54] Article 13 of the Notice states that the

[51] Supreme Court of Korea Judgment 2017 *Du*30788, 20 July 2018; Supreme Court of Korea Judgment 2016 *Du*46458, 11 July 2018.

[52] Supreme Court of Korea Judgment 2016 *Du*45783, 26 July 2018; Supreme Court of Korea Judgment 2016 *Du*48010, 26 July 2018; Supreme Court of Korea Judgment 2017 *Du*46912, 26 July 2018. Leaking information about a leniency application can be considered as an infringement of the faithful cooperation requirement.

[53] Martyniszyn, M., 'Leniency (Amnesty) Plus: A Building Block or a Trojan Horse?' (2015) 3(2) *Journal of Antitrust Enforcement* 391, p. 392.

[54] KFTC, 'Policy Area: Competition – Cartel' (n. 27 above).

Table 7.2 *The standard of amnesty plus reduction*

Comparison of sizes of the subsequently and initially disclosed cartels	Percentage of additional reduction for the initially disclosed cartel
The size of the subsequently disclosed cartel is the same or less than that of the first cartel	Up to 20 per cent
The size of the subsequently disclosed cartel is more than but less than twice the size of the first cartel	30 per cent
The size of the subsequently disclosed cartel is more than twice but less than four times the size of the first cartel	50 per cent
The size of the subsequently disclosed cartel is more than four times the size of the first cartel	100 per cent

Source: Kwon, O. and Seo, J., *Antitrust Law*, 3rd ed. (Paju: Bobmunsa, 2018).

KFTC may additionally fully or partially exempt the applicant from the surcharge when he or she satisfies the amnesty plus provision in Article 51(1) subparagraph 4 of the Enforcement Decree. The amount of amnesty plus reduction is determined by the size relation between the initially and subsequently disclosed cartels.[55] The surcharge for the first cartel can be fully or partially exempted pursuant to amnesty plus as follows: (1) if the size of the subsequent cartel is the same as or less than the size of the initially disclosed cartel, the surcharge can be reduced by up to the baseline of 20 per cent; (2) if the size of the subsequent cartel is more than the size of the first cartel but less than twice its size, the surcharge can be reduced by 30 per cent; (3) if the size of the subsequent cartel is more than twice but less than four times the size of the first cartel, the surcharge can be reduced by 50 per cent; and (4) if the size of the subsequent cartel is more than four times the size of the first cartel, the surcharge should be fully exempted.

The percentage criteria for additional reduction in Table 7.2 are not legally binding, but the Supreme Court confirmed their binding effect by stating that the standard set out in the Notice implies notable discretion for the KFTC, which does not go beyond what is necessary.[56]

[55] Martyniszyn, 'Leniency (Amnesty) Plus' (n. 53 above), p. 404.

[56] Supreme Court of Korea Judgment 2011 *Du*28783, 14 November 2013.

7.3 Current Issues Relating to Leniency Policy and Practice in Korea

7.3.1 Assessments of Cartel Enforcement and the Leniency Programme in Korea

Critics assert that the main goal of cartel enforcement is to detect and punish hard-core cartels. An effective implementation of leniency can increase the possibility of catching and punishing cartel members, and leniency is an important tool for deterring cartels. Rational undertakings normally abstain from participating in a cartel if the expected penalty is higher than the gain from the cartel.[57] Furthermore, where there is a high probability of detection by competition agencies, undertakings are unlikely to form a cartel.[58] Therefore, the carrot of rewards from leniency applications and the stick of severe penalties are the important bases for the detection and deterrence of cartels.[59] In addition, leniency programmes may save administrative costs in detecting cartels. Without the full cooperation of leniency applicants, competition agencies bear significant costs because cartel investigations often require substantial time and human resources.[60] Therefore, agencies can reduce the burdens and costs of obtaining important evidence for enforcement by implementing leniency programmes.[61]

According to the OECD,[62] it is necessary to ensure some conditions for cartel detection, deterrence and efficient enforcement; the prerequisites for these conditions include (1) a high possibility of detection; (2) severe sanctions; and (3) the transparency and predictability of leniency

[57] In particular, the US model of leniency focuses on 'the design of the irresistible offer'. See Harding, C. and Joshua, J., *Regulating Cartels in Europe*, 2nd ed. (Oxford: Oxford University Press, 2010), p. 232.

[58] OECD, 'Challenges and Co-ordination of Leniency Programmes (n. 3 above), p. 6. Leniency programmes generate a 'prisoner's dilemma', which explains a cartel participant's fear of any confession of other participants. See also Varian, H. R., *Intermediate Microeconomics*, 9th ed. (New York: W. W. Norton, 2020), pp. 547–49; Stephan, A. and Nikpay, A., 'Leniency Theory and Complex Realities' (CCP Working Paper 14-8, 2014). Retrieved from https://papers.ssrn.com/sol3/papers.cfm?abstract_id=2537470.

[59] See, e.g., Marco Colino, S., 'The Perks of Being a Whistleblower: Designing Efficient Leniency Programs in New Antitrust Jurisdictions' (2017) 50 *Vanderbilt Journal of Transnational Law* 5.

[60] Wils, W. P. J., 'The Use of Leniency in EU Cartel Enforcement: An Assessment after Twenty Years' (2016) 39(3) *World Competition* 327, pp. 336–37.

[61] OECD, 'Challenges and Co-ordination of Leniency Programmes' (n. 3 above), p. 7; Stephan and Nikpay, 'Leniency Theory and Complex Realities' (n. 58 above).

[62] OECD, 'Challenges and Co-ordination of Leniency Programmes' (n. 3 above), p. 7.

provisions.[63] Firstly, leniency programmes can function properly where a competition agency has proven its effective detection and punishment of hard-core cartels because the agency's capability makes cartelists perceive a high risk of detection. In other words, an effective ex officio investigation is important for improving leniency programmes.[64]

It is beyond doubt that the KFTC's cartel law enforcement satisfies this requirement, as the number of cartel cases from 1999 to 2018 is 626, which is remarkable.[65] A significant percentage of ex officio cases during this time reveals its high capability in cartel investigations.[66] Moreover, the MRFTA provides various tools to detect cartels beyond ex officio investigations, such as the informant reward pursuant to Article 91(1) of the Enforcement Decree subparagraph 2. The total number of reward cases from 2002 to 2018 is 94,[67] and this demonstrates successful enforcement against hard-core cartels.[68] Therefore, the current approach of the KFTC does not indicate an over-reliance on leniency programmes.

Secondly, significant sanctions are essential for the functioning of leniency programmes, and this often includes criminal sanctions. Many believe that significant fines are important not only to punish and deter cartels, but also to make undertakings comply with competition law in the future.[69] We have seen a global trend of increasing criminal sanctions, including jail terms and fines against undertakings and individuals.[70] The KFTC also maintains its discretionary power to bring a criminal complaint with the Prosecutors' Office. In other words, an undertaking is prosecuted by a public action after a complaint is filed by the KFTC under Article 129(1) of the MRFTA.[71]

63 Hammond, S. D., 'Cornerstones of an Effective Leniency Program' (Presentation at the ICN Workshop on Leniency Programs, Sydney, 22–23 November 2004). Retrieved from www.justice.gov/atr/speech/cornerstones-effective-leniency-program.

64 It is often difficult for developing countries to have successful ex officio detection of cartels. See Cheng, T., K., *Competition Law in Developing Countries* (Oxford: Oxford University Press, 2020), p. 513.

65 KFTC, '2019 White Paper' (n. 15 above), p. 293.

66 Park, 'Key Issues and Implications of the Leniency Policy' (n. 9 above), pp. 328–29.

67 KFTC, '2019 White Paper' (n. 15 above), p. 294.

68 See, e.g., Stephan, A., 'Is the Korean Innovation of Individual Informant Rewards a Viable Cartel Detection Tool?' in Cheng, Marco Colino and Ong, *Cartels in Asia* (n. 2 above), p. 109.

69 Stephan, 'The EU Method of Antitrust Enforcement' (n. 50 above), p. 404.

70 OECD, 'Challenges and Co-ordination of Leniency Programmes' (n. 3 above), p. 7.

71 Article 129(3) and (4) of the MRFTA states that the Prosecutor General, the Chairperson of the Board of Audit and Inspection, the Minister of SMEs and Start-ups and the Head of Public Procurement Service may request the KFTC to file a complaint with the prosecutor. However, in practice, the KFTC does not file a complaint with the prosecutor in the case of leniency applicants. See Kwon and Seo, *Antitrust Law* (n. 8 above), p. 372.

The existing provision of criminal sanctions and the recent amendment to the surcharge provision, which increased the surcharge from 10 per cent to 20 per cent, can be considered as sanctions sufficient to ensure an effective leniency policy.

Thirdly, the transparency and predictability of leniency are important for potential applicants. Without a sufficient level of transparency and predictability, leniency programmes cannot help applicants predict the consequences of a leniency application. Therefore, a competition agency needs to provide a standard that is 'clear, comprehensive, regularly updated, well publicised, coherently applied, and sufficiently attractive for the applicants'.[72] In effect, the US DOJ and the European Commission have revised leniency provisions to clarify their leniency policies. Similarly, the KFTC has provided various legal measures that clearly set out the standards and requirements for the grant of leniency. In effect, the Korean competition regime favours legal certainty, which is one of the characteristics of a civil law system[73]; as shown in Section 7.2 above, the leniency provisions in the MRFTA and the Enforcement Decree confirm this feature. Furthermore, the Leniency Notice contains details about the rank of applicants, the amount of the reduction of the surcharge and so on, and this increases the transparency and predictability of the leniency programme.[74]

7.3.2 Recent Discussions on the Leniency Programmes in Korea: Some Suggestions

Notwithstanding the robust foundation for its effective implementation, some critics have discussed several issues related to the Korean leniency policy. It is worth reviewing some of these arguments, such as the immunity exception for a recidivist and the absence of penalty plus and the omnibus question. These issues are based on the divergence problem of

[72] OECD, 'Challenges and Co-ordination of Leniency Programmes' (n. 3 above), p. 7.

[73] Choi, Y. S., 'The Rule of Law in a Market Economy: Globalisation of Competition Law in Korea' (2014) 15 *EBOR* 419, p. 430.

[74] Yun, S.-U. and Song, J.-H., 'Practical Issues of the Current Leniency Program' (2009) 20 *Journal of Korean Competition Law* 263, p. 294 (in Korean); Kwon and Seo, *Antitrust Law* (n. 8 above), p. 354. The authors argue that the major amendments to the leniency provisions in the MRFTA in 2001, 2005 and 2013 improved the transparency and predictability of the leniency programme by reducing the KFTC's discretion in leniency. See also Billiet, P., 'How Lenient Is the EC Leniency Policy? A Matter of Certainty and Predictability' (2009) 30(1) *ECLR* 14.

legal requirements that conflict with those of other countries. In effect, the Korean leniency programme has parallel legal requirements with some countries while it is different from others. Therefore, it is meaningful to examine these issues to provide proposals for a better implementation of the leniency programme in Korea.

Firstly, a strategic use or exploitation of leniency is a widely discussed problem;[75] the MRFTA prevents recidivism due to misuse of leniency programmes. One of the examples of possible exploitation of leniency is a case in which cartelists take turns to apply for leniency whenever one of their cartels is about to be detected and when they repeatedly form and then report a cartel.[76] To prevent this strategic behaviour, the MRFTA prohibits a recidivist's application for leniency for a five-year period following an earlier grant of immunity under an earlier leniency action.[77] In effect, a moral dilemma lies behind this five-year rule. Many believe that large undertakings use leniency programmes to drive out smaller competitors from the market. In 2011, several large undertakings received full immunity by applying for leniency while smaller firms received significant sanctions. After discussion on this case, the five-year rule was adopted in 2016.[78] Furthermore, the law prohibits an exemption benefit for the second applicant where there are only two participants in the cartel.[79] There was a case that influenced the adoption of this provision: the KFTC found an agreement between leniency applicants to share the surcharge imposed on the second applicant, and the two-participant rule was eventually created in 2013.[80] Overall, the toolbox for blocking strategic use of leniency explains the evolution in implementing various leniency techniques in Korea.

However, some allege that recidivists' applications should not be prohibited because they can better provide important information and evidence than other participants. Moreover, excluding recidivists from granting leniency

75 Wils, 'The Use of Leniency in EU Cartel Enforcement' (n. 60 above), p. 341.

76 OECD, 'Challenges and Co-ordination of Leniency Programmes' (n. 3 above), p. 19.

77 Beaton-Wells, C., 'Criminal Sanctions for Cartel Conduct: The Leniency Conundrum' (2017) 13(1) *JCLE* 125, p. 145. Some argue that there were concerns about the unfair use of leniency programmes by large multinational undertakings because they repeatedly applied for immunity benefits.

78 Park, 'Key Issues and Implications of the Leniency Policy' (n. 9 above), pp. 314–16.

79 However, some argue that in a similar way to the five-year rule, the limit of a leniency application when there are two cartel participants may strengthen existing cartels. See Park, S. B., 'Practical Issues and Proposed Solutions for the Current Leniency Program' (2012) 26 *Journal of Korean Competition Law* 3, p. 20.

80 Park, 'Key Issues and Implications of the Leniency Policy' (n. 9 above), p. 324.

may embolden recidivism.[81] According to those who take this view, the existing Korean provisions may reinforce secret cartels within the five years for which a participant has already received immunity or when only two undertakings take part in cartels. It is possible that the limit of the functioning of leniency programmes may cause ineffective deterrence of cartels. Therefore, Korean policymakers need to consider a possible amendment to the five-year rule and the two-participant rule. The KFTC may offer partial immunity: for example, it may impose a 50 per cent reduction of surcharge with full immunity from criminal sanctions for recidivists and two participants.

Second, some critics argue for the adoption of a provision of penalty plus and an omnibus question. The KFTC indicates that its leniency and amnesty plus are established to mitigate or revoke sanctions for a violation of law when a cartelist voluntarily reports other cartels[82]; it considers both leniency and amnesty plus as important tools for effective enforcement.[83] However, it is also possible that leniency applicants use amnesty plus strategically. Importantly, amnesty plus is 'an integral part of the leniency programme' and is also one of the elements of the US 'tripartite plus package'; that is, amnesty plus, penalty plus and the omnibus question.[84] Penalty plus is understood as 'a flip side of amnesty plus':[85] if an undertaking pleads guilty to a cartel offence but fails to disclose another cartel in which it participates, not only will the undertaking lose potential benefits from leniency, but the US DOJ will impose a stricter punishment against it.[86] In addition, the US DOJ provides an omnibus question; that is, a question that asks whether the undertaking has any information about other cartels.[87] The omnibus question strengthens the effectiveness

[81] Harrington, J. E., Jr, *The Theory of Collusion and Competition Policy* (Cambridge, MA: MIT Press, 2017), p. 105; Park, S. B., 'Practical Issues in the Enforcement of Leniency Program in Korea' (2015) 15 *Journal of Korean Law* 73, pp. 85–86; Park, "Key Issues and Implications of the Leniency Policy' (n. 9 above), p. 316; Wils, 'The Use of Leniency in EU Cartel Enforcement' (n. 60 above), pp. 346–47.

[82] KFTC, 'Policy Area: Competition – Cartel' (n. 27 above).

[83] There are a number of successful enforcements using amnesty plus, e.g., KFTC Decision 2008-269, 24 September 2008; KFTC Decision 2008-268, 25 September 2008; KFTC Decision 2008-267, 25 September 2008, etc. See also Kwon and Seo, *Antitrust Law* (n. 8 above), p. 375.

[84] Martyniszyn, 'Leniency (Amnesty) Plus' (n. 53 above), pp. 397–98.

[85] Ibid., p. 397.

[86] US Department of Justice, 'Frequently Asked Questions about the Antitrust Division's Leniency Program and Model Leniency Letters' (2017), p. 11. Retrieved from www.justice.gov/atr/page/file/926521/download.

[87] US Department of Justice, *Antitrust Division Manual*, 5th ed. (2014), p. III–103. Retrieved from www.justice.gov/atr/file/761166/download.

of amnesty plus by preventing cartelists from maintaining undetected cartels. Therefore, commentators explain that the additional advantages from amnesty plus and the further disadvantages from an extra penalty, along with the measure preventing the possible dilemma of cost and benefit by using an omnibus plus, can effectively improve the functioning of leniency programmes.[88] As shown by the success in the US, it is necessary to consider an adoption of the US-style plus package for preventing any misuse of amnesty plus in Korea.[89]

7.4 Challenges in the Leniency Programme and Proposals

7.4.1 Challenges in Coordination of Leniency Programmes with the Competition Policy of Private Litigation

The OECD paper provides a discussion about 'challenges in coordination of leniency programmes with other cartel enforcement policies' that contain private and criminal liabilities.[90] The task of balancing leniency programmes with these two areas has become crucial in many jurisdictions, including Korea. Analogous to the EU and northeast Asian countries, Korea adopts a framework that focuses on administrative enforcement. At the same time, the Korean regime provides criminal sanctions and treble damages that are not adopted in other Asian countries or the EU, but are actively implemented in the US. This indicates the Korean regime's effort to provide various instruments for improving the detection and deterrence of cartels.[91] In sum, the Korean leniency programme is founded on a mixture of legal techniques, mainly from the EU and the US.[92] The current approach of the KFTC is its emphasis on harmonising leniency programmes with private litigation and criminal sanctions, which needs to be discussed.

Private enforcement is one of the challenges in effective leniency programmes. Similar to other competition regimes, the Korean regime has shown its enthusiasm to improve a private litigation framework. Many believe that public and private enforcement are interrelated. Private

[88] Martyniszyn, 'Leniency (Amnesty) Plus' (n. 53 above), p. 398.

[89] Park, 'Key Issues and Implications of the Leniency Policy' (n. 9 above), p. 322.

[90] See OECD, 'Challenges and Co-ordination of Leniency Programmes' (n. 3 above), pp. 8–13.

[91] To compare the civil law–based competition law system, such as in the EU and China, with the common law–based antitrust law system, as in the US, see Williams, 'Cartel Prohibition and the Search for Deterrent Penalties' (n. 1 above), pp. 126–27.

[92] Park, 'Key Issues and Implications of the Leniency Policy' (n. 9 above), p. 309.

actions against cartels can complement public enforcement by improving deterrence effects.[93] To strengthen private enforcement, the Korean regime adopted a treble-damages provision in 2018.[94] The provision of treble damages may eventually improve private litigation, but it is hard to find any relevant case at this moment. In Korea, private litigation involving damages is mostly triggered by follow-on actions after a successful KFTC decision because of the absence of a discovery system.

Some assert that follow-on actions against leniency applicants may cause negative effects on leniency programmes, and the disadvantages to the applicants from private enforcement may become a major motivation for cartelists not to come forward to the KFTC.[95] Regardless, private litigation is not popular, possibly because of Korean legal culture or the absence of discovery rules, which differ from those in the US.[96] Therefore, the assertion of the negative effects of follow-on cases against leniency may be correct for international cartel cases, but only when cartelists are caught in a jurisdiction in which private litigation is active, such as in the US. However, when private litigation is not common, leniency programmes are rarely influenced by follow-on cases. As shown in Korea, despite the increase of damages to up to three times, private enforcement is not popular. In addition to treble damages, the Korean competition regime tries to increase civil liability. As discussed earlier, the increase in the surcharge for the violation of Article 40(1) is notable as it is high enough to outweigh the gain from a cartel, which can destabilise collusion.[97]

Overall, the optimal sanctions as an important incentive can make undertakings report their cartels and the KFTC had to examine the possible effects of greater damages on leniency applicants. Commentators argued for an amendment to the treble-damages provision to protect leniency applicants by limiting their liabilities to single damages,[98] which was analogous to the US amendment to the Antitrust Criminal Penalty

[93] OECD, 'Challenges and Co-ordination of Leniency Programmes' (n. 3 above), p. 8. Private enforcement to recover damage from cartels is rare in many countries except the US, where private litigation is active.

[94] Article 109(2) of the MRFTA.

[95] See, e.g., OECD, 'Challenges and Co-ordination of Leniency Programmes' (n. 3 above), p. 9; Walsh, D. J., 'Carrots and Sticks – Leniency and Fines in EC Cartel Cases' (2009) 30(1) *ECLR* 30.

[96] See, e.g., OECD, 'Challenges and Co-ordination of Leniency Programmes' (n. 3 above), p. 8.

[97] Stephan and Nikpay, 'Leniency Theory and Complex Realities' (n. 58 above).

[98] Kwon and Seo, *Antitrust Law* (n. 8 above), p. 374; Lee, 'Measures to Enhance the Effectiveness of Leniency Programs' (n. 14 above), pp. 273–74.

Enhancement and Reform Act of 2004.[99] The amendment to the treble-damages rule in Article 109(2) of the MRFTA now confirms a leniency applicant's single damages. The limit of damages can offer further incentive for leniency applicants, because administrative sanction becomes sufficiently high to induce leniency.

7.4.2 *Challenges in Coordination of Leniency Programmes with the Competition Policy of Criminal Sanction*

Criminal offences are another challenge in leniency programmes as the number of competition regimes that adopt criminal sanctions seems to be increasing around the globe.[100] In effect, the adoption of criminal sanctions in Korea may influence the effectiveness of leniency programmes. Under the MRFTA, when an undertaking's leniency application is accepted by the KFTC, the applicant will be exempted from criminal prosecution. Nevertheless, the Prosecutor General may ask the KFTC to file a complaint with the Prosecutors' Office when the infringement of law is objectively obvious and so serious as to significantly impede competition.[101] The problem of uncertainty relating to the immunity from criminal prosecution arose in a case in which the KFTC filed a criminal complaint against cartel members other than leniency applicants. In this case, the Prosecutors' Office indicted all cartel participants, including the applicant undertakings and their two executives. The lower court dismissed the prosecutor's indictments against the leniency applicants and executives because of the lack of appropriate criminal referrals from the KFTC. This judgment was upheld by the Supreme Court,[102] which confirmed an immunity for leniency applicants from criminal prosecution.[103]

99 OECD, 'Challenges and Co-ordination of Leniency Programmes' (n. 3 above), p. 9. The benefit of single damages without joint and several liability in the US is based on the condition that the leniency applicants cooperate with the plaintiffs in private litigation. See also Hovenkamp, H., *Federal Antitrust Policy: The Law of Competition and Its Practice*, 6th ed. (St Paul, MN: West Academic, 2020), p. 196.

100 OECD, 'Challenges and Co-ordination of Leniency Programmes' (n. 3 above), p. 10.

101 Article 129(3) of the MRFTA; Kum, Yoon and Park, 'Cartel Immunity and Leniency Programmes in South Korea' (n. 11 above).

102 Supreme Court of Korea Judgment 2008*Do*4762, 30 September 2010.

103 Kum, Yoon and Park, 'Cartel Immunity and Leniency Programmes in South Korea' (n. 11 above); Kwon and Seo, *Antitrust Law* (n. 8 above), pp. 372–73. There has been an ongoing discussion about the effective cooperation between the KFTC and the Prosecutors' Office relating to the cartel investigations. See Lee, 'Measures to Enhance the Effectiveness of Leniency Programs' (n. 14 above), pp. 275–80; Kang, W., 'Fully Rethinking Cartel Offence

Despite clearer exemptions from the case law, there are some criticisms of cartel criminalisation.[104] In effect, there are two opposite views on the role of criminal sanctions relative to the effectiveness of leniency programmes. Some argue that the blend of sufficient sanctions, particularly on individuals, and the high possibility of detection are important to deter hard-core cartels.[105] Forming and maintaining cartels are unreasonable and completely unprofitable when the risk of not only a significant penalty from damages actions but also of criminal sanctions with active public enforcement is notable.[106] Based on these arguments, competition agencies should improve legal techniques for both private and criminal liabilities.

In contrast, others assert that cartel criminalisation causes a chilling effect on leniency programmes.[107] They argue that cartel criminalisation may hinder cartel members from reporting cartels where it is uncertain that they satisfy conditions of immunity. It is also possible that cartel criminalisation may reduce the predictability of the consequences of a leniency application, especially when each country has different procedural requirements for immunity from criminal sanctions.[108] For example, leniency applicants are often reluctant to come forward to a competition agency that does not impose criminal sanctions when they can be caught by prosecutors in other countries because of their leniency application in the former jurisdiction.[109] Moreover, some assert that leniency does not go well with cartel criminalisation: the significant benefits for applicants may undermine the criminal nature of punishing hard-core cartels, because leniency systems may weaken people's perceptions of cartels as a great offence.[110]

in Terms of Substantive and Constitutional & Procedural Law' (2020) 176 *Justice* 113 (in Korean); Son, Y.-H., 'Discussion over Abolishment of Exclusive Complaint Right under the Monopoly Regulation and Fair Trade Act' (2018) 32(4) *Business Law Review* 225, pp. 248–49 (in Korean).

104 Beaton-Wells, 'Criminal Sanctions for Cartel Conduct' (n. 77 above), p. 125.

105 See, e.g., Furse, M., *The Criminal Law of Competition in the UK and in the US* (Cheltenham: Edward Elgar, 2012), pp. 48–49.

106 Stephan, 'The EU Method of Antitrust Enforcement' (n. 50 above), p. 400.

107 Beaton-Wells, 'Criminal Sanctions for Cartel Conduct' (n. 77 above), p. 134.

108 See, e.g., Whelan, P., *The Criminalization of European Cartel Enforcement: Theoretical, Legal, and Practical Challenges* (Oxford: Oxford University Press, 2014), p. 237.

109 See, e.g., OECD, 'Challenges and Co-ordination of Leniency Programmes' (n. 3 above), p. 11.

110 Williams, R., 'Cartels in the Criminal Law Landscape', in Beaton-Wells, C. and Ezrachi, A. (eds.), *Criminalising Cartels: Critical Studies of an International Regulatory Movement* (Oxford: Hart Publishing, 2011), 311, p. 311.

With respect to the concerns about the negative effects of cartel criminalisation, some critics have stressed that civil liability rather than a criminal sanction is more effective to deter hard-core cartels.[111] However, in jurisdictions like Korea, criminal sanctions and private litigation are rare in practice. The toolbox of treble damages and a higher surcharge, without criminal liability, may be sufficient to detect and punish hard-core cartels. Nonetheless, at this moment it appears difficult to withdraw the provision for criminal sanctions. Korean commentators seem to believe that criminal sanctions are necessary to deter harmful business conduct, because many cartels are formed by employees without the knowledge of their superiors. In this case, an imposition of criminal liability is more effective than that of civil liability.

7.5 Conclusion

Critics points out that leniency programmes explain the characteristics of competition law enforcement[112] and that the Korean leniency programme highlights its distinctive features. The Korean competition regime has revised its leniency programme several times by adopting the approaches in other countries. Importantly, the Korean regime has effectively raised the stakes on the range of carrots and sticks in leniency programmes. On the carrot side, the Korean regime has provided generous benefits for leniency applicants, especially for amnesty plus.[113] On the stick side, it has imposed severe punishment by designing a framework of notable surcharge, private liability of treble damages and criminal sanctions. Moreover, the KFTC introduced a five-year rule to prevent recidivists from strategic misuse of leniency. The recent developments of the leniency programme in Korea, with the new legal techniques of informant reward and cartel screening, reveal the progressive evolution of the leniency programme and policy on cartel enforcement.[114] Furthermore, the Korean regime has discussed a possible harmonisation of various competition goals within certain rules, such as private and public enforcement.[115]

[111] Williams, 'Cartel Prohibition and the Search for Deterrent Penalties' (n. 1 above), p. 117.
[112] Stephan, 'The EU Method of Antitrust Enforcement' (n. 50 above), p. 403.
[113] Martyniszyn, 'Leniency (Amnesty) Plus' (n. 53 above), p. 404.
[114] Lee, 'Measures to Enhance the Effectiveness of Leniency Programs' (n. 14 above), pp. 269–70; Park, 'Key Issues and Implications of the Leniency Policy' (n. 9 above), pp. 304–5.
[115] Park, 'Key Issues and Implications of the Leniency Policy' (n. 9 above), p. 302.

In effect, each competition regime has distinctive characteristics based on its own socio-political goals, which may result in the introduction of new leniency instruments. However, we have seen a notable convergence relating to cartel enforcement among competition regimes; that is, a localised harmonisation of per se or quasi per se rules against hard-core cartels and a grant of immunity for cartel informants. Notably, the KFTC has developed its legal techniques not only from other regimes, but also from its own experience and study.[116] Localised harmonisation in leniency programmes may mitigate the problems of possible clashes in cartel enforcement between competition agencies and reduce the potential costs of compliance with cartel laws for multinational undertakings.[117] It seems almost impossible to have an identical leniency provision for competition regimes because of their dissimilar legal backgrounds and cultures. Therefore, the best way to reduce possible conflicts in leniency policy is to set a lowest common denominator. The lack of cooperation between competition authorities across countries and one-stop-shop leniency applications also cause serious problems of enforcement against international cartels. However, the localised harmonisation of leniency programmes may solve these problems.

To conclude, leniency programmes were originally designed to assist with effective enforcement against hard-core cartels, and they should not be a substitute but a complement to successful enforcement.[118] In addition to the improvement of ex officio investigations, each regime needs to consider the value of increasing convergence in leniency programmes and effective coordination with competition agencies in other countries, thereby ensuring incentives for leniency application.[119] Hard-core cartels are considered to be 'Public Enemy Number 1'.[120] To prevent hard-core cartels in domestic and global markets, it is important to balance leniency policy not only with other competition policies like private and criminal liabilities in Korea's own regime, but also with various techniques in the leniency programmes of other regimes.

116 See, e.g., Borrell, Jiménez and Ordóñez-de-Haro, 'The Leniency Programme' (n. 4 above), p. 150.

117 Choi, Y. S. and Heinemann, A., 'Competition and Trade: The Rise of Competition Law in Trade Agreements and Its Implications for the World Trading System' (2020) 43(4) *World Competition* 521, p. 524.

118 Wils, 'The Use of Leniency in EU Cartel Enforcement' (n. 60 above), p. 350; Whelan, 'Criminal Cartel Enforcement in the EU' (n. 5 above), p. 231.

119 OECD, 'Executive Summary of the Roundtable' (n. 21 above), p. 4.

120 Choi, Y. S., 'The Issue of Information Exchanges Regarding Price under Competition Law: Comments on the Supreme Court's Judgment on the *Ramen* Cartel from a Comparative Perspective' (2016) 35 *Soongsil Law Review* 1, p. 2.

8

The Leniency Programme in Taiwan

Enforcement Experience, Effectiveness Assessment and Future Challenges

ANDY C. M. CHEN

8.1 Introduction

The leniency programme was incorporated into the Taiwan Fair Trade Act (TFTA), the competition law in Taiwan, in 2011. In its statement of legislation, legislators expressed their concern that as the competition enforcement agency, the Taiwan Fair Trade Commission (TFTC), gained experience over the years, cartel members have also become savvier in concealing direct and incriminating evidence, making cartel prosecution more challenging than ever for the agency. The legislators therefore suggested that a mechanism similar to the Corporate Leniency Program of the United States (US) be implemented to enhance the incentive to report violations.[1] During the ten years since the introduction of the programme, fifteen cases were reported to have applied for this programme, but only four of them succeeded in persuading the TFTC to grant fine exemptions or reductions for their cooperation. Statistically, they may not have been fully successful and it is interesting to know why. We begin this chapter in Section 8.2 by briefly introducing the legal framework for applying the leniency programme in Taiwan. In Section 8.3, we review the enforcement experience of the TFTC. We then proceed, in Section 8.4, to assess the effectiveness of the leniency programme and, in Section 8.5, to outline the future challenges needing to be addressed by the TFTC. Section 8.6 concludes.

[1] Relevant documents for Fourteenth Meeting of Fifth Session, Seventh Session of the Legislative Yuan, Yuan-Chung-Zi No. 1375.

8.2 Legal Framework for Enforcing the Leniency Programme in Taiwan

The legal framework for enforcing the leniency programme consists of several layers of law and regulations. The founding provision was stipulated in Article 35 of the TFTA. Under this Article, leniency applicants are divided into two general types: the investigation-initiating and investigation-assisting applicants. According to Paragraph 1, Item 1 of Article 35 of the TFTA, an enterprise that 'files a complaint or informs the competent authority in writing about the concrete illegal conduct of the concerted action in which it has partaken and also submits the evidence and assists the investigation before the competent authority is aware of the said illegal conduct or initiated an investigation in accordance with this Act' is qualified as a leniency applicant. Alternatively, an enterprise that 'reveals the concrete illegal conduct as well as submits the evidence and assists the investigation during the period in which the competent authority investigates the said illegal conduct in accordance with this Act' is also eligible for leniency application pursuant to Item 2 of the same paragraph. Paragraph 2 of Article 35 of the TFTA further authorises the TFTC to enact administrative regulations to specify the requirements for granting a fine exemption or reduction. The TFTC then promulgated 'Regulations on Immunity and Reduction of Fines in Illegal Concerted Action Cases' (Leniency Regulations) in 2012, which were most recently revised in 2015.[2] The pertinent parts of the Leniency Regulations can be summarised as follows.

8.2.1 *Disqualified Applicants*

Applicants who engage in the following activities are not eligible for filing the application (Article 2 of the Leniency Regulations):

1. compelling other enterprises to join or restricting them from exiting the cartel;
2. destroying, forging, altering, or concealing relevant material or evidence before the competent authority initiates its investigations;
3. directly or indirectly revealing the fact that they are going to file the application or any content that is going to be submitted to the competent authority.

[2] The Traditional Chinese version of the Regulations can be retrieved from www.ftc.gov.tw/internet/main/doc/docDetail.aspx?uid=1404&docid=12145.

8.2.2 *Formats of Application*

In its original version, Article 10 of the Leniency Regulations required a written application. The applicant needed to complete an application form prepared by the TFTC together with the submitted materials and evidence. The TFTC soon changed this requirement in its subsequent revision in 2012. The revised Article 10 of the Leniency Regulations allowed for oral application. In addition to the submitted materials and evidence, enterprises opting for oral application need to dispatch personnel to make statements on the information specified in Paragraph 1 of Article 10 of the Leniency Regulations (the name of the enterprise, the product or service involved, the form of the concerted action, the geological areas affected, the duration of the action, etc.) before the TFTC and sign on behalf of the enterprise on the minutes of the statements (Paragraph 2 of Article 10 of the Leniency Regulations).

8.2.3 *Sufficiency of Evidence*

In summary, investigation-initiating applicants must provide a concrete description of their involvement in the cartel and present evidence not yet in the possession of the TFTC, which could potentially enable the TFTC to acquire information regarding the skeleton of the cartel, the time and place a collusive agreement was made, and the contents of that agreement to initiate an investigation (Article 4 of the Leniency Regulations). Alternatively, in addition to providing a concrete description of their involvement, investigation-assisting applicants must provide any evidence already in their possession upon application that could prove the culpability of the cartel (Article 5 of the Leniency Regulations).

8.2.4 *Conditions for Granting Approvals*

The TFTC may impose conditions on the applicants upon its approvals. The conditions shall contain the following requirements (Article 6 of the Leniency Regulations):

1. after filing the application, the applicant shall immediately, or from the time designated by the TFTC, cease participating in the cartel;
2. before the completion of the investigated cases, the applicants shall cooperate fully, honestly, and continually with the TFTC during investigations, including: (1) providing in a timely fashion existing or future materials and evidence relating to the investigated cartel; in fine-reducing applications, the materials and evidence provided must

be useful for investigation or could enhance the probative value of the acquired evidence; (2) following the instructions of the TFTC and providing a prompt description or cooperation to help the investigation on related facts capable of proving the existence of the concerted actions in question; (3) allowing its staff members or representatives having participated in activities related to the concerted action in question to be questioned by the TFTC; (4) the content of the statement, information, or evidence provided may not contain any untruthfulness and no destruction, forgery, alteration, or concealment of any information or evidence related to the concerted action in question shall be tolerated; (5) without the consent of the competent authority, the applicant may not disclose to any other parties about filing the application or any content of the application before the case is concluded.

8.2.5 *Fine Exemption and Reduction*

According to Article 7 of the Leniency Regulations, full exemption of fines will be granted to the first applicant who meets the requirements set by the TFTC. This Article 7 is applicable to both investigation-initiating and investigation-assisting applications. For investigation-assisting applicants who do not qualify for full immunity, the TFTC has the discretion to reduce the fine by between 30 per cent and 50 per cent for the first applicant, 20 per cent and 30 per cent for the second applicant, 10 per cent and 20 per cent for the third applicant, and up to 10 per cent for the fourth applicant (Article 8 of the Leniency Regulations). Unlike the US antitrust authorities' leniency policy,[3] the Leniency Regulations allow cartel initiators or instigators to file for exemption or fine reductions. This difference in legislation might partly be attributable to the difficulty in practice of verifying the role an applicant played in a cartel. Moreover, it is also likely that initiators or instigators are the parties who possess and can provide information and evidence with a higher probative value to the TFTC.

8.2.6 *The Marker System*

A candidate applicant who intends to apply but currently has no sufficient evidence to qualify for fine exemption may present a written or

[3] US Department of Justice, Corporate Leniency Policy (10 August 1993), para. A6. Retrieved from www.justice.gov/sites/default/files/atr/legacy/2007/08/14/0091.pdf.

oral statement containing the information prescribed by the Leniency Regulations to the TFTC and request a marker, a preservation of the priority status for the fine exemption that they may be granted. Enterprises that have been granted the preservation shall provide the information and evidence specified in Articles 4 and 5 of the Leniency Regulations within the specified period or they shall lose the priority status preserved.

8.2.7 *Confidentiality Protection*

Under Article 20 of the Leniency Regulations, the TFTC has the obligation to maintain the confidentiality of the identity of an applying enterprise unless the enterprise agrees otherwise in advance. To avoid this identifying information being revealed or inferred from the disposition that contains the imposed fines for each individual cartel member and that is required by law to be sent to each one of them, the TFTC indicates in Article 18 of the Leniency Regulations that the formats for its final dispositions or other written documents could be completed, subject to the TFTC's discretion, in the following manner: (1) with the consent of the applying enterprise, indicate the name of the enterprise, the fine imposed, and the amount of fine reduced and the reasons; (2) without the consent of the applying enterprise, use codes and other confidential means to indicate the identity of the enterprise in question; (3) establish a disposition for each offender and the main text regarding the fine referring only to the enterprise in question and containing no information about other offenders involved in the same case; (4) other means that might be useful in maintaining identity confidentiality.

8.2.8 *The Antitrust Fund*

To supplement the enforcement of the leniency policy and to enhance the incentive to report violations, the TFTC introduced into Article 47-1 of the TFTA in its 2015 Amendments a programme that authorises it to establish an antitrust fund to facilitate its enforcement against cartels. The source of the fund comes from 30 per cent of the fines imposed in violating cases, interest accrued on the fund, government budget allocations and other relevant incomes of the TFTC. The fund is to be used in part as a reward for reporting illegal concerted actions. To implement the enforcement of Article 47-1 of the TFTA, the TFTC promulgated the Regulations on Payment of Rewards for Reporting of Illegal Concerted Actions in October 2015. Article 5 of the Regulations put forward the criteria for granting rewards. For applications that provide materials and evidence helpful for initiating investigation, the rewards will be 5 per cent of the total amount of the penalties imposed on the illegal concerted actions, not exceeding NT$1,000,000 (approximately US$34,000). Applications that provide evidence and materials to assist the TFTC in proving indirectly the existence of collusion will be granted a reward of 10 per cent of the total amount of penalties, not exceeding NT$10,000,000 (approximately US$340,000). Applications that provide evidence and materials to assist the TFTC in proving directly the existence of collusion will be granted a reward of 20 per cent of the total amount of penalties, not exceeding NT$20,000,000 (approximately US$680,000). In cases involving total penalties imposed exceeding NT$200,000,000 (approximately US$6,700,000) but less than NT$500,000,000 (approximately US$16,800,000), the rewards could be raised to twice the maximal amounts. In cases involving total penalties imposed exceeding NT$500,000,000, the rewards could be raised to five times the maximal amounts.[4]

8.3 Enforcement Experience of the TFTC

For the past ten years since its introduction, there have been fifteen cases applying for the leniency programme, but only four that succeeded in convincing the TFTC to grant a fine exemption for their cooperation. Similarly, there were only six cases to which the rewards were granted from the antitrust fund to reporters of violations. Given the unavailability of detailed data and information related to leniency reviews in these cases, the following commentary offers only background information for reference purposes. Moreover, due to confidentiality restrictions, only two of the four cases are reported here.

8.3.1 The CD-ROM Cartel (2012)[5]

This was the first case involving a leniency application in Taiwan. The parties under investigation in this case were four global CD-ROM producers: HLDSK, PLDS, TSSTK and Sony Optiarc Inc. According to the TFTC, the four companies had engaged in bid-rigging activities in the international markets for computer CD-ROMs from 2006 to 2009. They exchanged information regarding individual submitted prices and company capacities and outputs, subsequently agreeing on the winning bidders for several

[4] The Traditional Chinese version of the Regulations can be retrieved from www.ftc.gov.tw/internet/main/doc/docDetail.aspx?uid=1477&docid=14243.

[5] Kong-Tsu-Zi No. 101127, 101130, 101131, 101132.

overseas bids proposed by Dell and Hewlett-Packard. In its decision, the TFTC found that the four defendants held a market share of more than 75 per cent in the CD-ROM market. Dell and Hewlett-Packard controlled approximately 10 per cent of the market for personal or desktop computers in Taiwan and 90 per cent of their demands for computer CD-ROMs were met through biddings. Based on those statistics, the TFTC concluded that the cartel had affected the function of the CD-ROM market in Taiwan. The evidence in this case was provided by a participating member through the leniency programme. The applicant was later granted full immunity from all administrative fines.[6]

8.3.2 *The Aluminium and Tantalum Capacitor Cartels (2015)*[7]

This case originated from an ex officio investigation by the TFTC of collusion among major suppliers of capacitors. Relying on the meeting notices, meeting materials, emails, notes, reimbursement invoices and receipts, and oral statements provided by the participating member, the TFTC was able to confirm, after cross-referencing those materials, that major aluminium and tantalum capacitor companies[8] had initiated and convened a number of meetings from the 1980s in which they exchanged information about prices, quantities, capacities and responses to buyers' price offers. The TFTC further concluded that exchanging those pieces of sensitive information in the meetings had constituted agreements of collusion and affected supply and demand conditions in the Taiwanese market.

As far as the antitrust fund is concerned, there were also only six cases in which rewards had been granted. These include collusion on fixing loading and storage fees by storage companies,[9] prices for hand-made thin noodles,[10] commission and services fee for brokerage of foreign fishermen,[11] fees for harbour warehousing and stevedoring,[12] service charges

[6] However, the case was appealed by one of the cartel members and was rescinded based on reasons *not related to the leniency programme* by the Supreme Administrative Court in 2015. Pan-Zi No. 212 (2015).

[7] Kong-Tsu-Zi No. 104133, 104134, 104135, 104137.

[8] They included Sanyo HK, Rubycon, NCC HK, NCC TW, ELNA, NICHICON HK, NICHCON TW, SANYO, FMD, HAIC (aluminum); VISHAY, NEC TOKIN and MATSUO (tantalum).

[9] Kong-Tsu-Zi No. 105034.

[10] Kong-Tsu-Zi No. 105054.

[11] Kong-Tsu-Zi No. 105101.

[12] Kong-Tsu-Zi No. 107027.

for securities by the securities industry association[13] and prices for drugs treating colon cancer.[14] The total rewards amounted to approximately NT$1,230,000 (approximately US$42,000).

8.4 Assessment of the Effectiveness of the Leniency Programme in Taiwan

Systematic study of the effectiveness of the leniency programme in Taiwan is still rare. A recent research project commissioned by the TFTC attempted to apply the 'checklist' proposed by the International Competition Network (ICN) for that purpose,[15] whose findings will be summarised in Section 8.4.1. However, the study was conducted by taking the leniency programme as given, without providing an initial review of the degree of contribution that the programme might make marginally to cartel prosecution in Taiwan and its inherent costs. Conceptually, the effectiveness of the leniency programme can be assessed from the following two perspectives. First, it requires a general evaluation of the costs and benefits of the programme, particularly when compared with other cartel-detecting mechanisms within the enforcement regime. Second, it should involve an examination of the factors that could influence the success of the programme and can be further classified into those related to the *predictability*, *profitability* and *probability* of administering leniency. Admittedly, it is notoriously difficult to conduct credible empirical tests regarding this effectiveness issue and even more so in Taiwan due to the very limited availability of case information and the small case sample. Therefore, we focus primarily on providing a *qualitative* description of the likely benefits and costs from introducing the leniency programme in Taiwan in Section 8.4.2 and the factors that could influence its success in Section 8.4.3.

8.4.1 The ICN Checklist

In 2017, the ICN Cartel Working Group produced a concise document that lists the legal and enforcement pre-requisites to an effective and

[13] Kong-Tsu-Zi No. 108044.

[14] Kong-Tsu-Zi No. 110032.

[15] Shi-Hao Shi and Chun-Fa Chuang, 'The Study on the Implementation Effectiveness of Leniency Policy of Other Countries' (Research Project Report Commissioned by the TFTC, November 2017), pp. 271–87.

efficient leniency programme. According to the ICN, the purpose of the checklist is to provide useful guidelines for young competition authorities that plan to elaborate on their leniency regimes.[16] In the recently commissioned project by the TFTC, the checklist was used to evaluate the effectiveness of the leniency programme and its findings are listed as follows. In summary, if the ICN Checklist is viewed as an ideal template to test the effectiveness of a leniency policy, then the leniency programme in Taiwan might be ranked as moderately effective.

8.4.1.1 Leniency Can Be Applicable to Both Corporations and Individuals under Civil, Administrative and Criminal Competition Legal Regimes

In principle, leniency applies only to corporations in Taiwan. However, if an individual within the violating firm is to be jointly punished according to the Administrative Penalty Act, the TFTC could also exempt or reduce the fines for that individual if he or she cooperated with the TFTC throughout the investigation. In Taiwan, the leniency programme applies only to the exemption and reduction of administrative fines.

8.4.1.2 Types of Infringements Covered by Leniency

According to Article 15 of the TFTA, concerted action is defined as including only agreements among horizontal competitors. Therefore, the leniency programme does not apply to vertical arrangements.

8.4.1.3 Bifurcated Leniency Systems

As was described earlier in Section 8.4.1.1, the leniency programme applies only to corporations. Although other legislation, such as the Government Procurement Act, also prohibits and sanctions bid rigging, the leniency programme is not applicable in those cases.

8.4.1.4 No Less of an Advantageous Position

Under the current leniency programme, the TFTC has the legal obligation to maintain the confidentiality of the identity of the applicants, and of the statements and documents provided by the applicants, and to request that the court does not have an open trial of the cases. However, the TFTC is still unclear about whether an applicant can withdraw its application and

[16] ICN, 'Checklist for Efficient and Effective Leniency Programmes' (2017). Retrieved from www.internationalcompetitionnetwork.org/portfolio/leniency-program-checklist.

how the statements and documents provided by an applicant will be handled. Therefore, whether the applicant will not be placed into a less advantageous position by cooperating with the TFTC remains to be assessed on a case-by-case basis.

8.4.1.5 Immunity and/or Reduction of Fines

As was described earlier, the leniency programme involves both immunity and reduction of fines, depending on the timing of the application and the evidence and materials provided.

8.4.1.6 Behavioural Conditions for Awarding Leniency

The Leniency Regulations stipulate a number of behavioural conditions, including fully and continuously cooperating with the TFTC, truthful statements and non-disclosure duties as the requirements for awarding leniency. Although the Leniency Regulations do not specifically require the applicant to admit his or her participation in an alleged cartel, the application itself might be deemed as an implied admission of participation.

8.4.1.7 Discretionary Reward System

The leniency programme provides clear requirements for exemption and reduction of administrative fines. However, the Leniency Regulations do not require the applicant to compensate for the harms of the victims or return ill-gotten gains. Nor do they require the applicant to cooperate in private litigation and/or other related investigations.

8.4.1.8 Procedural Aspects of Successful Leniency Programmes

According to the ICN Checklist, a successful leniency programme may include the following procedural elements:

a. availability of anonymous approaches/hypothetical applications;
b. availability of a marker (protection of an applicant's place in the queue for immunity or reduction of fines);
c. procedures for revoking leniency if necessary;
d. summary applications;
e. form of applications (written or oral, ability to make oral submissions known as proffers);
f. protection to private plaintiffs from disclosure of self-incriminating statements provided under leniency;

g. procedures for handling information on closely related leniency applications; and
h. handling information in the case of withdrawal/refusal of the application.

Among those elements, elements c, d, f, g and h are not covered in the Leniency Regulations.

8.4.1.9 Incentives for Cooperation (Leniency Plus or Penalty Plus)

No leniency plus or penalty plus programmes have been instituted under the current leniency programme in Taiwan.

8.4.1.10 Protection of Confidentiality

The accomplishments and limits of the current leniency programme in this regard are highlighted in the discussion in Sections 8.4.1.4 and 8.4.1.8.

8.4.1.11 Leniency in the Global Competition Law Environment

The TFTC is a member of both the Organisation for Economic Co-operation and Development (OECD) Competition Committee and the ICN. These are the two major venues through which the TFTC can exchange opinions and information with other competition jurisdictions concerning the operation and improvements of leniency policy in general. In the case of dealing with international cartels, however, the TFTC may still need to propose relevant rules and regulations to handle the issues of cross-border exchange of confidential information obtained from leniency applications and how to harmonise the disparity of application requirements among various enforcement regimes.

8.4.1.12 Non-Legislative Supportive Measures

For the past decade, the TFTC has hosted a number of domestic and international conferences, seminars, experience-sharing workshops by Taiwanese companies and keynote speeches by experts to enhance public awareness of the leniency programme.

8.4.2 A Preliminary Assessment of the Benefits and Costs from the Introduction of the Leniency Programme in Taiwan

The implementation of the leniency programme will create net social gains if the benefits from its reduction of the number of cartels outweigh 'the deadweight losses that it generates in the form of wasteful administration, prosecution, and litigation activities'.[17] In theory, the primary benefit of the leniency programme is the destabilising and deterrent effects it generates by incentivising cartel members to report violations and by raising the probability of detection.[18] One of the frequently used indicators to support this assertion is the increase in the number of prosecuted cartel cases after the introduction of the leniency programme. For example, in response to criticism from Congress for its ineffective enforcement, the TFTC in 2015 argued that in comparison with Korea, who from 1996 to 2004 had only five cases within an enforcement period of eight years, the TFTC already had three successful cases in four years.[19] Obviously, this approach could be controversial and misguided: it establishes only the correlation but not causation between the leniency programme and its effectiveness in deterring cartel formation. In fact, the change in the number of cartel cases that were prosecuted after the implementation of the leniency programme in Taiwan further calls the validity of this approach into question. The number of prosecuted cartel cases rose significantly in 2012, the year immediately following the implementation of the programme, from eight to eighteen cases, but dropped consecutively in 2013 (seven cases) and 2014 (six cases). The number rose again to twelve cases in 2015, but was then followed by significant drops in 2016 (four cases), 2017 (one case) and 2018 (one case).[20] It would be difficult to infer from this pattern of changes a plausible explanation that the observed drop in enforcement activities was attributable to the deterrent effects brought about by the programme and that it is not the result of cartelists being more vigilant when forming cartels.[21] Similarly, an increase in the

[17] Marvão, C., 'What Do We Know about the Effectiveness of Leniency Policies? A Survey of the Empirical and Experimental Evidence', in Beaton-Wells, C. and Tran, C. (eds.) *Anti-Cartel Enforcement in a Contemporary Age: Leniency Religion* (Oxford: Hart Publishing, 2015), 57, p. 57.

[18] Borrell, J.-R., Jiménez J. L. and Ordóñez-de-Haro, J. M., '25 Years of Leniency Programs: A Turning Point in Cartel Prosecution' (2019) 1(2) *Competition Policy International Antitrust Chronicle* 1. Retrieved from http://diposit.ub.edu/dspace/bitstream/2445/154157/1/693856.pdf.

[19] Shry-Hau, S., 'A Comparison of the Effectiveness and Efficacy of the Leniency Program: What Can Taiwan Learn from the Success Stories of the USA, Germany and Korea?' (2018) 26 *Fair Trade Quarterly* 115, pp. 134–35 (citations omitted).

[20] TFTC Statistics. Retrieved from www.ftc.gov.tw/upload/583a6488-ee2a-4517-b728-0336e8db5e50.pdf.

[21] Bell, R. B. and Millay, K., 'The Corporate Leniency Program: Did the Antitrust Division Kill the Goose That Laid the Golden Eggs?' (2018) 33 *Antitrust* 80, p. 82.

number of convicted cases may be due to the increase in the overall number of cartels formed.[22]

Economists have designed sophisticated and mostly game-theoretical models to investigate leniency effectiveness with specific evaluation parameters.[23] However, those models may not be very helpful for jurisdictions with limited case numbers and enforcement experience. To gauge the effectiveness of the leniency programmes in those jurisdictions, it may be necessary for researchers to rely on indirect but more available data. Holding constant all other cartel enforcement mechanisms in a jurisdiction, for example, the change in the number of cases applying for cartel exemptions[24] or requiring clarification of the law against cartels from the enforcement authority after the introduction of a leniency programme may reflect enhanced public awareness caused by the implementation of the leniency programme of the legal risk of organising cartels. Applying this observation to Taiwan, as the 2011 TFTA revisions were predominantly concerning its leniency programme,[25] we might conclude in general and with a certain degree of confidence that if any changes in cartel enforcement activities occurred after 2011, they are highly likely to be the result of the implementation of the leniency programme. With respect to the number of cases applying for exemption, it increased from four cases in 2011 to nine cases in 2012, but dropped to zero cases in 2013 and three cases in 2014, and rose to eight cases in 2015.[26] However, the applying cases appeared to be those requesting extensions of the previously approved exemptions and did not involve new applications.[27] In fact, the two peaks of application in 2012 and 2015 further support this observation because the typical exemption period granted by the TFTC is three years. The

[22] Marvão, C., 'Challenges and Co-ordination of Leniency Program – Note by Catarina Marvão – Background Materials for the Meeting of OECD Competition Committee' (2018). Retrieved from https://one.oecd.org/document/DAF/COMP/WP3/WD(2018)32/en/pdf.

[23] For a summary of those studies, see Marvão, 'What Do We Know about the Effectiveness of Leniency Policies?' (n. 17 above), pp. 59–67.

[24] Cartel exemptions are provided in Article 15 of the TFTA, which authorises the TFTC to approve after review of the cartels that could increase efficiency, promote exports, soothe the impacts from economic downturn or advance technical developments.

[25] In addition to the leniency programme, the other two revisions were the amendments of endorsement advertisement (Article 21 of the TFTA) and the increase of cartel fines to 10 per cent of the total business turnover of the cartel members (Article 41 of the TFTA). The latter was also closely related to the leniency programme in terms of its effect on enhancing the cartel members' willingness to report violations.

[26] TFTC Statistics.

[27] Ibid.

change in the number of cases requesting clarification of the law is more interesting. From 55 cases in 2011 to 58 cases in 2012, they then increased dramatically to 266 cases in 2013 and 337 cases in 2014.[28] Unfortunately, the TFTC's statistics showed only the total number, but did not indicate how many of those cases were related to the leniency programme.

Similar to all newly incorporated legal systems, a leniency programme incurs additional administrative costs from enforcement. Whether these costs are worth undertaking depends on their tradeoffs with the enhanced rates of cartel convictions the programme generates compared with the rates produced under the same cost structure but without the programme. Conversely, the assessment should also include comparison of the administrative costs before and after the implementation of the programme, holding constant the rates of conviction. Scholarly discussions have raised the concern that a leniency programme might induce the enforcement agency to eagerly rely on the programme to maximise the number of prosecuted cases and fines, because they are frequently used indicators to measure agency performance.[29] As the percentage of successful leniency applications is not particularly high (four out of a total of fifteen cases or 27 per cent) in Taiwan, it may still be far-fetched to assert that the leniency programme has caused this type of governance-distortion effect to occur inside the TFTC.

8.4.3 *Factors Affecting the Success of the Leniency Programme*

Even though the benefits gained from having a leniency programme outweigh the associated costs, there are various factors that can diminish the incentive for business to apply and thereby render ineffective the operation of the programme in practice. According to a recent survey of thirty practitioners with extensive leniency experience, 83 per cent of the participants indicated that they sensed a decline of interest in applying for leniency from their clients.[30] The underlying reasons for this lack of interest include (1) concern about exposure to civil damages (36 per cent);

[28] Ibid. The case numbers for the years after 2014 are 267 cases in 2015, 252 cases in 2016, 216 cases in 2017 and 247 cases in 2018. However, as the TFTA was significantly revised in 2015, those numbers may reflect requests for clarification on non-leniency issues.

[29] See Kovacic, W. E., 'A Case for Capping the Dosage: Leniency and Competition Authority Governance' in Beaton-Wells, C. and Tran, C. (n. 17 above), 123, pp. 128–30.

[30] Ysewyn, J. and Kahmann, S., 'The Decline and Fall of the Leniency Program in Europe' (2018) 1 *Concurrence* 44, p. 45 n. 8 (citing the survey conducted by Brussels Matters for its meeting 'The European Antitrust Leniency c. 2016: Still Worth It?').

(2) uncertainty resulting from the publication of parallel enforcement proceedings (26 per cent); (3) uncertainty about how authorities will grant leniency reductions (19 per cent); (4) uncertainty about how authorities will calculate fines (14 per cent); and (5) uncertainty about how authorities will deal with requests for access to file for leniency submissions (12 per cent).[31]

In assessing how private enforcement changes the incentive to file a leniency application, in particular the treble damages rule, Daniel Sokol's study established that results were minimal in the US.[32] If the study were conducted in Taiwan, the result could be trivial or irrelevant, as private enforcement against cartels is extremely rare, even though the system is provided for in Chapter 5 of the TFTA. Therefore, the impact on the incentive to apply for leniency protection from follow-on private litigation could be reasonably neglected. With respect to the costs from enforcement uncertainty, the most frequently mentioned cost is that the ways fines for cartel violations are calculated and the factors that are taken into account for the total amounts are frequently opaque.[33] Article 36 of the Enforcement Rules of the TFTA authorises the TFTC to consider broadly 'all circumstances' when determining fines, with particular attention paid to the numerous factors specified in that Article.[34] In practice, the TFTC enjoys a near-exclusive discretion over the priorities and weight given to each individual factor. Only after the fines are imposed and announced can the investigated parties know the amounts of their penalties and then have them controverted in appeal proceedings.

With regard to requests to access files for leniency submissions, Paragraph 3 of Article 20 of the Leniency Regulations prohibits the TFTC from providing these files to organisations, groups or individuals other than to investigation or trial agencies unless the laws provide otherwise. Therefore, whether the TFTC can disclose information gathered from leniency applications depends on whether there are other laws mandating

[31] Ibid.

[32] Sokol, D. D., 'Cartels, Corporate Compliance, and What Practitioners Really Think about Enforcement' (2012) 78 *Antitrust Law Journal* 201, p. 235.

[33] Wang, M-Y., 'Analysis and Review of Leniency Policy and Reward Programs' (2016) 25 *Fair Trade Quarterly* 127, pp. 161–62.

[34] These factors include (1) motivation, purpose and expected improper benefit of the act; (2) the degree of the act's harm to market order; (3) the duration of the act's harm to market order; (4) benefits derived on account of the unlawful act; (5) scale, operating condition and market position of the enterprise; (6) types of, number of and intervening time between past violations and the punishment for such violations; and (7) remorse shown for the act and attitude of cooperation in the investigation.

disclosure. For example, Article 46 of the Administrative Procedure Act of Taiwan entitles the investigated parties or the interested third parties to apply to an administrative authority for examining, transcribing, copying or taking photographs of relevant materials or records. Based on the same reviewing criteria set forth in Article 46, the TFTC further promulgated a Notice for Access of Files and Documents. To make the reviewing process more transparent, the TFTC in Attachment II of the Notice specifies the types, the accessibility and the legal basis for approving or denying access. Although the TFTC can deny the application for access by an interested third party based on confidentiality considerations or on the grounds that open access will impede the function of the TFTC's duties in maintaining public interest, most applications are approved.[35]

Finally, uncertainty about the sufficiency of submitted materials and the interpretation of the requirements for establishing cartel violations are other major sources of costs that might deter leniency application. For example, the potential applicants typically are not aware of the progress of investigation by the TFTC when considering the filing of a leniency application, and are unable to predict whether the information they provide will inform the TFTC of secret collusion or will only assist the TFTC in further proving the culpability of a cartel already under investigation. Application in pursuance of the antitrust fund system may be the other source of unpredictability, because the information provided by a leniency applicant might have already been submitted by prior application for rewards from the antitrust fund. The 'collateral damage' from miscalculation of application outcomes may be to alert the TFTC of a potential cartel case that the TFTC has not yet investigated.

Divergent interpretations of the legal requirements for establishing cartels between leniency applicants and the TFTC, or between the TFTC and the courts, add to this list of uncertainty costs for leniency applications. The courts may not fully embrace the determination by the TFTC on the probative value of the evidence provided by leniency applicants. For example, in the CD-ROM cases, the higher administrative court of Taipei treated the statements and evidence gathered from the leniency programme as simply a 'complaint' and considered that the TFTC had failed to review its probative value to establish violations. Discrepancies could occur not only in widespread and notorious issues, such as inferring a collusive agreement from parallel behaviour among competitors, but

[35] See Chen, A. C. M., 'Due Process and Transparency Requirements for Investigating Competition Cases in Taiwan', in Sokol, D. D. and Guzman, A. T. (eds.), *Antitrust Procedural Fairness* (Oxford: Oxford University Press, 2019), 88, pp. 89–90 and p. 96.

also in those related to the fundamental questions concerning the characterisation of a cartel. For example, in a recent case involving independent power producers (IPPs) in Taiwan,[36] the IPPs argued that even though they had entered this *partially* deregulated market for power supply through a bidding process posted by the government, they were no longer a 'competitor' as defined under Article 4 of the TFTA to include only businesses that 'compete for trading opportunities in the same market with one or more enterprises through offering a more favourable price, quantity, quality, service, or any other terms', because each bid-winning IPP could only sell its electricity to the government on the price and quantity terms specified in the bidding agreement after entering the market. That is, the post-entry price or non-price competition for business opportunities among bid-winning IPPs had been excluded and, as a result, they should not be governed by the TFTA.[37] In its decision against the alleged boycott by the bid-winning IPPs, the TFTC held that bidding was a competition 'for the market' in which IPPs were competitors. However, the administrative courts disagreed with the TFTC on this characterisation assertion and the case is still pending in the courts.

8.5 Future Challenges

In its submission to the 2018 OECD Competition Committee Policy Roundtable on the leniency programme, the TFTC summarised the challenges it encountered when dealing with leniency applications as follows.[38]

First, as the applicants are primarily multinational enterprises that have filed applications to various competition authorities in different jurisdictions simultaneously, coordination with other competition authorities will be more important than ever. This implies that laws and rules aiming to administer international cooperation will also be more urgently needed.

[36] For a summary and comment on this case, see Chen, A. C. M., 'The Taiwan Fair Trade Commission Imposes Record Fines on Independent Power Producers for Collectively Refusing to Adjust the Rate for Wholesale Electricity' (2013), e-Competitions – National Competition Laws Bulletin No. 52501.

[37] The TFTA limits concerted actions to agreement among horizontal competitors. Paragraph 1 of Article 14 of the TFTA provides that the rules on concerted actions apply only to '*competing* enterprises at the same production and/or marketing stage'.

[38] OECD Competition Committee, 'Roundtable on Challenges and Co-ordination of Leniency Programmes – Note by Taiwan' (5 June 2018). Retrieved from https://one.oecd.org/document/DAF/COMP/WP3/WD(2018)20/en/pdf.

Second, the statutes of limitations for concerted actions and legislation on search and seizure vary in different countries. This may lead to inconsistent investigation results among jurisdictions. Furthermore, the TFTC's investigation will not stop the statutes of limitations for sanctions from running. The TFTC is frequently under time pressure to evaluate the materials and evidence provided by leniency applicants and to engage in coordination with other competition authorities.

In addition, there are other challenges arising from the *strategic* application of the leniency programme, which might affect its effectiveness in practice.[39] For example, the problems with statutes of limitations have given potential applicants the incentive to opportunistically use the programme by filing an application near the completion of the statute of limitations. The TFTC could thereby be under pressure to make hasty decisions based on inadequate evidence, increasing the possibility of its decisions being reversed on appeal. Similarly, the disparity in legal requirements and the ease of obtaining an exemption or reduction of fines have also incentivised cartel members to engage in a sort of 'forum shopping' when making application decisions. That is, applicants may try to influence or press the TFTC to grant approvals by arguing that their applications have been granted in other jurisdictions, while the evidence they provide may be quite different from that submitted to the TFTC. Furthermore, in some cases materials and evidence furnished by later applicants could have a much more probative value than those provided by the earlier applicants. It is also likely that the later application may expose the insufficiency of the evidence or materials provided by the first applicant. However, they would not be qualified for exemption or increases in fine reductions due to late application.

Several of the effectiveness issues and challenges discussed in the competition literature have also been experienced in Taiwan. For example, despite the efforts by the TFTC in advocating for the value of market competition and the benefits of the leniency programme, the public awareness of cartels seems to be low in Taiwan, except in cases involving bid rigging of government projects. This might be a common phenomenon around Asia, but could reduce the costs of participating in a cartel and lessen the incentive to report violations.[40] Moreover, as Sokol has described, an effective leniency programme requires the understanding of not only firm

[39] I am indebted to my former colleague at the TFTC Ms Lin Shin-Wen for kindly sharing the following points with me.

[40] Sokol, 'Cartels, Corporate Compliance' (n. 32 above), p. 238.

behaviour but also the incentive of individuals within the firm.[41] Even if a company has instituted a compliance programme within a firm, its implementation still hinges on whether and to what extent the managers could be protected when things go wrong. To bridge the gap of incentive disparity between company and managers, the legal framework for individual leniency in Taiwan still leaves much to be desired.

8.6 Concluding Remarks

Although Taiwan is an experienced jurisdiction with regard to competition law in Asia, it is still in the process of improving its leniency programme. With respect to the programme itself, it needs to be amended, particularly to include individual leniency and related protection measures to enhance the incentive to report violations. From a policy perspective, the TFTC should continue its competition advocacy to raise public awareness of cartels and revise the laws and regulations related to the legal mechanisms for prosecuting cartels, including but not limited to the rules for bringing in private enforcement. Still, meaningful improvements in the leniency programme in the future depend on knowledge of its enforcement effectiveness in the past. Due to the small number of successful cases and rather limited availability of data, empirical and critical studies on the leniency programme in Taiwan have yet to be conducted. It is therefore highly advisable that the TFTC seeks to delineate the objective criteria through empirical effectiveness studies for designing a functional roadmap to improve its current programme.

[41] Ibid., p. 223.

9

The State Administration for Market Regulation and Its Leniency Programme

Infusing a Dose of Trust and Predictability

YING BI[*] AND STEVEN VAN UYTSEL

9.1 Introduction

Monopoly agreements, the concept referring to cartels in the People's Republic of China's (China) Antimonopoly Law (AML),[1] have been barely detected with the use of a leniency programme. Nearly all of the leniency applications in China were submitted after one of the enforcement agencies, the National Development and Reform Commission (NDRC) or the State Administration for Industry and Commerce (SAIC),[2] had started its investigation and thus detected the existence of the monopoly agreement.[3]

* This chapter has benefited from the Zhejiang Philosophy and Social Science Planning Project 'Belt & Road Initiative and Innovation of International Trade Rules on State-owned Enterprises' (19NDJC176YB).

1 Anti-Monopoly Law of the People's Republic of China, adopted at the 29th Meeting of the Standing Committee of the National People's Congress (30 August 2007). For a text in Chinese and English, see Harris, H. S. Jr, Wang, P. J., Zhang, Y., Cohen, M. A., and Evrard, S. J., *Antimonopoly Law and Practice in China* (Oxford: Oxford University Press, 2011), pp. 373–94.

2 NDRC took competence over price-related monopoly agreements. SAIC decided in relation to non-price-related monopoly agreements. See Wang, X., 'Retrospectives and Prospects of China's Anti-Monopoly Law', in Van Uytsel, S., Hayashi, S. and Haley, J. (eds.) *Research Handbook on Asian Competition Law* (Cheltenham: Edward Elgar: 2020), 209, pp. 218–23. Monopoly agreements is the term used in the Chinese AML to refer to horizontal agreements. The second paragraph of Article 13 of the AML exemplifies hard-core agreements or cartels. Vertical agreements, which are also qualified as monopoly agreements, are dealt with in Article 14 of the AML. See Ng, W., *The Political Economy of Competition Law in China* (Cambridge, UK: Cambridge University Press, 2018), pp. 64–65; Xu, S. and Tao, T., 'Monopoly Agreements, Trade Associations and Competition Culture in China', in Cheng, T., Marco Colino, S. and Ong, B, (eds.) *Cartels in Asia: Law and Practice* (Hong Kong: Wolters Kluwer Law & Business, 2015), pp. 255, 262–63.

3 Deng, F. and Zhang, Y., 'Interview with Xu Kunlin, Director General of the Bureau of Price Supervision and Anti-monopoly under the National Development and Reform

Why has there been such a delay in submitting leniency applications? The unpredictable and non-transparent conceptualisation of the leniency programme has often been understood as the cause. Neither the NDRC's leniency programme[4] nor the SAIC's leniency programme[5] made it possible to guess what the outcome would be. Immunity from sanctions was not guaranteed. The order of application was not fixed. Everything was made contingent on the value of the evidence that the undertaking had to submit together with its leniency application. This prompts another question. Why would an undertaking apply after an investigation had started? The secrecy in which these cartel-like monopoly agreements are veiled may prevent an enforcement agency from discovering the full extent of the wrongdoing, even when an investigation has started.[6] There must have been something else to convince some participants in the monopoly agreement to apply for leniency. It has often been said that pressure from NDRC – SAIC was far less active in enforcing cartel-like monopoly agreements – has been this 'something else'.[7]

Things changed in 2018. The National People's Congress (Congress), the highest legislative body of China, decided to take away the AML-related enforcement powers from NDRC and SAIC and hand them over to a newly created agency, the State Administration for Market Regulation (SAMR).[8] In this chapter, we will claim that the establishment of a new agency allowed the Congress to signal a new way forward. First, by positioning SAIC officials at key positions in the AML section of SAMR, due process considerations could be introduced into the investigation process.[9] Second, squeezing the enforcement powers

Commission of the People's Republic of China' (2014) 13 *Antitrust Source* 1, p. 3. Retrieved from www.edgewortheconomics.com/media/publication/61_Fei_Deng_Interview_with_DG_Xu_Kunlin_of_Chinas_NDRC.pdf.

4 See Harris, *Antimonopoly Law and Practice in China* (n. 1 above), pp. 461–69.

5 See Linklaters, 'Order of the State Administration for Industry and Commerce No. 53' (2010). Retrieved from www.linklaters.com/pdfs/mkt/london/1a.pdf.

6 Mason, C., *The Art of the Steal* (New York: Berkley Publishing Group, 2004).

7 Williams, M., 'Leniency Policy with Chinese Characteristics', in Beaton-Wells, C. and Tan, C. (eds.), *Anti-Cartel Enforcement in a Contemporary Age: Leniency Religion* (Oxford: Hart Publishing, 2015), 33, pp. 49–51.

8 Ma, J., *Competition Law in China: A Law and Economics Perspective* (Heidelberg: Springer, 2019), pp. 20–21.

9 Brumfield, N. A., Gidley, J. M., Zhang, Z. A. and Ying, Y., 'China Merges Antitrust Enforcement Agencies into One, as Its Anti-Monopoly Law Approaches 10th Anniversary' (2018). Retrieved from www.whitecase.com/sites/whitecase/files/files/download/publications/china-merges-antitrust-enforcement-agencies-into-one-samr.pdf.

of several enforcement agencies into a single agency opened the way to creating new guidelines. SAMR did so for leniency in 2019.[10] Despite the new opportunities, we will also argue that some details could still hamper the implementation of a better due process culture or the predictability of the outcome of leniency applications.

This chapter is structured as follows. Section 9.2 will, after briefly introducing the early Chinese leniency programmes, articulate the main critique of these programmes. The unpredictability and non-transparency prevented the leniency programmes from attracting many leniency applications, especially leniency applications that were detecting new cartels. Despite this, we will also show that, due to the neglect of due process, the enforcement agencies, and especially NDRC, have tried to circumvent the critique of unpredictability and non-transparency. In Section 9.3, we will explain that the change of the enforcement structure may be the first step towards rectifying the complex environment in which the leniency programme is operating in China. This will be done by specifying how the new enforcement agency, SAMR, relies more on the enforcement culture of SAIC than of NDRC. However, a situation in which more attention could be paid to due process is only half the solution. The unpredictability and non-transparency need to be addressed as well. Section 9.4 will show that SAMR took the opportunity to do so when issuing a new leniency programme in 2019. Section 9.5 will conclude that there are still some minor issues that may cause the continuation of delayed leniency applications.

9.2 Pressure to Apply for Unpredictable and Non-transparent Leniency Programmes

9.2.1 NDRC's and SAIC's Discretion in Handling Leniency Applications

When China adopted its AML in 2007, it provided in Article 46 (2) of the AML that '[i]f the business manage [sic], on its own initiative, reports to the authority for enforcement of the Anti-monopoly Law about the monopoly agreement reached, and provides material evidence, the said

[10] Antimonopoly Commission of the State Council, 'Guidelines for the Application of the Leniency Programme to Horizontal Monopoly Agreement Cases' (2019). Retrieved from http://gkml.samr.gov.cn/nsjg/fldj/202009/t20200918_321856.html (in Chinese) (Leniency Guidelines).

authority may, at its discretion, mitigate, or exempt the undertaking from, punishment'.[11] Generally stated, Article 46 (2) of the AML formed the basis for lenient treatment of undertakings that decided to report their participation in an illegal monopoly agreement. It has been generally understood that lenient treatment could be provided for both horizontal and vertical monopoly agreements.[12]

Two leniency programmes were elaborated based on Article 46 (2) of the AML. NDRC elaborated its leniency programme in Article 14 of its Procedural Rules on Administrative Enforcement of Anti-price Monopoly (NDRC Leniency Programme).[13] The NDRC Leniency Programme would apply to price-related monopoly agreements. SAIC adopted its leniency programme in Articles 11, 12 and 13 of the Procedural Rules for Prohibition by Administrative Authority for Industry and Commerce against Monopoly Agreements (SAIC Leniency Programme).[14] The SAIC Leniency Programme would apply to non-price-related monopoly agreements.

[11] Article 46 (1) of the AML was the provision on sanctions. It read as follows: 'Where an undertaking, in violation of the provisions of this Law, concludes and implements a monopoly agreement, the authority for enforcement of the Anti-monopoly Law shall instruct it to discontinue the violation, confiscate its unlawful gains, and, in addition, impose on it a fine of not less than one percent but not more than 10 percent of its sales achieved in the previous year. If such monopoly agreement has not been implemented, it may be fined not more than RMB 500,000 yuan.'

[12] For a detailed discussion on the use of leniency in a vertical context, see Cai, J., 'Public Antitrust Enforcement of Resale Price Maintenance in China: A Crusade or Discrimination?' (2016) 42 *Brooklyn Journal of International Law* 1, pp. 41–45. Even though generally accepted as possible, the extension of the scope of the leniency policy to vertical agreements has been criticised as leading to perverse results, whereby the imposer of a vertical restriction walks away freely after self-reporting something over which it had full control. See Williams, 'Leniency Policy with Chinese Characteristics' (n. 7 above), p. 37. Note, however, that the need for a leniency programme in a vertical context may arise when it is sustaining a horizontal agreement. This has been explicitly accepted in the leniency programme of the United Kingdom. See Whish, R. and Bailey, D., *Competition Law*, 10th ed. (Oxford: Oxford University Press, 2021), p. 437. A vertical agreement sustaining a horizontal agreement has been found in cases where algorithms are implemented. See Bauer, G. and Wagner, R., 'Resale Price Maintenance in the Digital Age' (2018). Retrieved from http://competitionlawblog.kluwercompetitionlaw.com/2018/08/23/resale-price-maintenance-digital-age. It has been pointed out, though, that not leniency but cooperation has been key to solving such cases. See Voss, K., 'Between Enforcement and Regulation: A Study of the System of Case Resolution Mechanisms Used by the European Commission in the Enforcement of Articles 101 and 102 TFEU' (Doctoral Thesis, Stockholm University, 2019), pp. 176 and 183.

[13] Order No. 8.

[14] Order No. 53.

When comparing the two leniency programmes, the following can be said:

- The NDRC Leniency Programme provided that the first applicant could be granted immunity.[15] The second applicant could be offered at least a 50 per cent reduction.[16] Once these two slots were occupied, an unlimited number of subsequent applicants could obtain a maximum of a 50 per cent reduction.[17] The programme did not indicate how an applicant could assure its position in the order of applications. The programme did also not indicate when the order could be confirmed to the applicant. The SAIC Leniency Programme made a slightly different categorisation: immunity or reduction.[18] Immunity was available for the first applicant who, after confessing, fully cooperated with the investigation.[19] There was some discussion on whether the first applicant may or should be given immunity. The majority indicated that the literal interpretation of the text requires that SAIC should give automatic immunity.[20] Subsequent applicants could receive a reduction, but the level of reduction was not specified.[21]
- The text of the NDRC and the SAIC Leniency Programmes was silent on when a leniency application could be submitted, leaving it an open question as to whether a leniency application could only be made before or also after an investigation had started. It was, however, clear that there was no explicit prohibition for an application after the start of an investigation.[22] The absence of such a prohibition eventually led to the conclusion that a leniency application could be submitted both before and after an investigation.[23]

[15] Order No. 8, Article 14.

[16] Ibid. Case law did not necessarily indicate how different levels of leniency were granted. See Zhang, C., and Sun, S., 'What Determines Antitrust Fines in China?' (2019) 40 *ECLR* 47, p. 57, where the authors refer to the second applicant in two different cases whereby one only received a 60 per cent reduction and the other 90 per cent.

[17] Order No. 8, Article 14.

[18] Order No. 53, Article 11.

[19] Ibid., Article 12.

[20] Harris, *Antimonopoly Law and Practice in China* (n. 1 above), p. 293; Xue, Q. and Yang, X., 'Anti-Cartel Law and Enforcement in China: A Survey', in Emch, A. and Stallibras, D. (eds.), *China's Anti-Monopoly Law: The First Five Years* (The Hague: Wolters Kluwer, 2013), 83, pp. 83–94.

[21] Order No. 53, Article 12.

[22] Order No. 8, Article 14 and Order No. 53, Articles 11–13.

[23] Despite this being confirmed in several cases, such as the Baby Formula case and the Zhejiang Insurance Industry case. See Cai, 'Public Antitrust Enforcement of Resale Price Maintenance' (n. 12 above), p. 41. Todd Liao and Bonnie Li argue that a leniency application could not be submitted once a dawn raid was done. The reason? They claim that the

- Essential to both the NDRC and the SAIC Leniency Programmes was the submission of material evidence.[24] According to the NDRC Leniency Programme, material evidence is evidence that can ascertain the existence of the monopoly agreement.[25] The rules were silent on whether different applicants could submit the same evidence, or each applicant had to provide fresh evidence. It was also not stipulated that the information should not be false. However, one could infer that false information could not constitute material evidence.[26] The SAIC Leniency Programme was a little more elaborate. Evidence would be material when it facilitated the initiation of an investigation or it could contribute to the finding of an agreement. Such evidence could include the parties to the agreement, the products subject to the agreement, the form and the content of the agreement, and details about the implementation of the agreement.[27]
- The NDRC and SAIC Leniency Programmes did not expand on the need to fulfil certain conditions.[28] It was not clear whether the leniency applicant had to terminate its illegal behaviour, even though, in the case of the SAIC Leniency Programme, voluntary termination could be a contributory factor in the decision process of granting lenient treatment.[29] The rules did not stipulate whether the leniency applicant had to continue cooperation with the enforcement agencies. The rules were also silent on whether the leniency applicant had to keep its submission secret to third parties.[30]

start of an investigation indicates the presence of material evidence. Their understanding implies that that no further material evidence could be submitted. See Liao, T. and Li, B., 'Antitrust Dawn Raids in China: On the Tenth Anniversary of Chinese Antitrust Enforcement' (2018) 10 *China Antitrust Law Journal* 1, p. 11.

[24] This chapter uses the wording 'material evidence'. This is the official translation of the law given by the Ministry of Commerce, see MOFCOM, 'Anti-monopoly Law of the People's Republic of China' (2008). Retrieved from http://english.mofcom.gov.cn/article/policyrelease/Businessregulations/201303/20130300045909.shtml. The majority of the literature, however, refers to 'important evidence'. For the purposes of this chapter, the two concepts are interchangeable and have the same meaning.

[25] Order No. 8, Article 14.

[26] Van Uytsel, S. and Ying, B., 'Delayed Leniency Applications – the Unfortunate But Predictable Outcome of the Flexible Leniency Policies under the Chinese Antimonopoly Law', in Fenwick, M. and Wrbka, S. (eds.), *Flexibility in Modern Business Law: A Comparative Assessment* (Singapore: Springer, 2016), 91, p. 101.

[27] Ibid., pp. 101–2.

[28] Order No. 53, Article 10. See also Harris, *Antimonopoly Law and Practice in China* (n. 1 above), p. 292.

[29] As such, this lenient treatment seemed to be available for undertakings that had not applied for leniency. See Order No. 53, Article 10.

[30] Van Uytsel and Ying, 'Delayed Leniency Applications' (n. 26 above), pp. 100–2.

- The NDRC and SAIC Leniency Programmes had different views on the eligibility of organisers of a monopoly agreement. The NDRC Leniency Programme did not exclude the organiser of a monopoly agreement from its leniency programme.[31] The leniency applicant under the SAIC Leniency Programme, to the contrary, could not be an organiser of the monopoly agreement.[32] There seemed to be an understanding that the organiser included both the originator and the leader.[33] In other words, SAIC would neither provide leniency to the undertaking establishing the illegal agreement nor to the undertaking that was responsible for operating the agreement.[34]

Both NDRC and SAIC had a lot of discretion in relation to their respective leniency programmes.[35] NDRC did not, unlike SAIC, guarantee automatic immunity for the first successful applicant. Instead, NDRC could choose between immunity, reduction or no lenient treatment at all. Subsequent leniency applicants had to face uncertainty about their level of reduction, because this was made dependent on the discretion of NDRC and SAIC, respectively. The lack of any rules on determining the order of applications made it possible for NDRC and SAIC to make the order dependent on the value of the material evidence. Equally, however, the lack of any prefixed conditions opened the door for NDRC and SAIC to arbitrarily proceed with any of the leniency applications.

9.2.2 NDRC Lures Undertakings to Apply for Leniency

Leniency programmes with uncertainty are prone to being ineffective. When looking at the numbers of the respective NDRC and SAIC Leniency Programmes, China seems to confirm this conclusion.[36]

31 See Oded, S., 'Leniency and Compliance: Towards an Effective Leniency Policy in the Chinese Anti-Monopoly Law', in Faure, M. and Zhang, X. (eds.), *Competition Policy and Regulation: Recent Developments in China, the US and Europe* (Cheltenham: Edward Elgar, 2011), 142, p. 156.

32 See Order No. 53, Article 20.

33 See Harris, *Antimonopoly Law and Practice in China* (n. 1 above), p. 293; Xue and Yang, 'Anti-Cartel Law and Enforcement in China' (n. 20 above), p. 88.

34 Van Uytsel and Ying, 'Delayed Leniency Applications' (n. 26 above), pp. 101–2.

35 Ibid., pp. 91–118.

36 An alternative explanation for this could be that investigations mainly resulted from sector investigations. See Dodoo, N., 'A New Dawn for Cartel Enforcement in China', in Emch, A. and Ng, W. (eds.), *Wang Xiaoye: The Pioneer of Competition Law in China – Liber Amicorum* (New York: Institute for Competition Law, 2019), 67, p. 77.

The NDRC Leniency Programme was only supporting 19 decisions out of the 183 decisions by 2020.[37] SAIC was only able to link one of its 23 decisions to a leniency application.[38] NDRC leniency applications were primarily linked to domestic monopoly agreements, both cartels and vertical price-fixing agreements.[39] What could explain this apparently irrational use of leniency programmes?

An answer may be found in the fact 'that companies have sought leniency and received it after cooperating with NDRC's investigation, but only after the investigation had been initiated'.[40] However, this reaction has prompted further research. Most outspoken was Michael Martina. In various articles for Reuters, Martina outlined stories he heard from lawyers and business people.[41] Most of these stories originated either because of

[37] Yu, X., Jiang, H. and Ling, Z., 'How Does the Leniency Program Apply to Monopoly Agreement Cases? Highlights of the Relevant Antitrust Guidelines' (2020). Retrieved from www.sohu.com/a/415223549_120051855 (in Chinese). Whether these data are correct is difficult to ascertain. NDRC has never had the practice of consistently publishing its decisions and, if they were published, they were far from transparent enough to get a proper understanding of what led to the decision. See Deng and Zhang, 'Interview with Xu Kunlin' (n. 3 above), p. 9 (where Mr Xu is avoiding the question of whether all decisions have been published. He rather speaks of an effort to do so – a limited list of references to cases can be found in Ng, *The Political Economy of Competition Law in China* (n. 2 above), pp. 319–31). In terms of publicising the decisions, the following can be said: 'Since 29 July 2013, the SAIC has launched a publication platform for antitrust enforcement decisions, where the final penalty decisions of all cases that have been closed will be published on the SAIC's website, including 23 cartel cases as of 10 December 2016. As regards the NDRC, according to an announcement made by a senior NDRC official in November 2014, the agency is aiming to gradually publish the full text of all its enforcement decisions. As of 10 December 2016, the NDRC has published the full administrative penalty decisions of seven cases, of which one is an abuse of dominance case, one is a vertical monopoly agreement case and the other five are cartel cases.' See Ning, S., Yin H. and Peng, K., 'China', in Varney, C. A. and Terzaken, J. (eds.), *The Cartels and Leniency Review* (London: Law Business Research, 2017), 57, p. 69.

[38] Ning, Yin and Peng, 'China' (n. 37 above), p. 77.

[39] Deng and Zhang, 'Interview with Xu Kunlin' (n. 3 above), p. 3.

[40] Ibid.; see also Editorial Board, 'China's NDRC Uses Leniency Program to Uncover and Punish Cartel Members' (2012). Retrieved from http://blogs.orrick.com/antitrust/2012/12/03/chinas-ndrc-uses-leniency-program-to-uncover-and-punish-members-of-cartel.

[41] Martina, M., 'EU Lobby Piles in on Foreign Criticism of China's Antitrust Enforcement', *Reuters* (9 September 2014). Retrieved from www.reuters.com/article/uk-china-antitrust-eu/eu-lobby-piles-in-on-foreign-criticism-of-chinas-antitrust-enforcement-idUKKBN0H40SB20140909; Martina, M. and Miller, M., '"Mr. Confession" and His Boss Drive China's Antitrust Crusade', *Reuters* (15 September 2014). Retrieved from www.reuters.com/article/us-china-antitrust-ndrc-insight-idUSKBN0HA27X20140915; Martina, M., 'Exclusive: Tough-Talking China Pricing Regulator Sought Confessions from Foreign Firms', *Reuters* (22 August 2013). Retrieved from https://jp.reuters.com/article/idINL4N0GK18M20130822.

attendance at information sessions of NDRC or because of investigations conducted by NDRC. Martina's journalistic research has been widely quoted by lawyers,[42] some of whom are employed in prestigious law firms in Beijing, and by scholars[43] and chambers of commerce.[44] Not all scholars, though, reach a similar conclusion on Martina's research.[45]

One of the stories relates to a training session of NDRC, SAIC and the Ministry of Commerce (MOFCOM) held on 24 and 25 July 2013, purportedly to celebrate the fifth anniversary of the AML. Martina reports that in-house lawyers of more than thirty firms, often foreign firms,[46] attended the event. Some of the attendees testified anonymously about what was said during the event. None of the testimonies related to what SAIC or MOFCOM officials had said, but all focused on the speech of Xu Xinyu, a senior official within NDRC. It is said that Xu emphasised the need to confess the infringement of the AML when an undertaking is under investigation. To facilitate such a confession, some officials showed

[42] Foster, A. L., 'Navigating the Unique Features of China's Competition Landscape' (2017) 31(2) *Antitrust* 79, p. 83.

[43] See, e.g., Zhang, A. H., *Chinese Antitrust Exceptionalism: How the Rise of China Challenges Global Regulation* (Oxford: Oxford University Press, 2021), p. 42; Chen, R., 'Legal Informality and Human Capital Development in China', in Liebman, B. L. and Milhaupt, C. J. (eds.), *Regulating the Visible Hand? The Institutional Implications of Chinese State Capitalism* (Oxford: Oxford University Press, 2016), 151, p. 174; Williams, 'Leniency Policy with Chinese Characteristics' (n. 7 above), pp. 49–50; Epstein, R. A., 'Curbing the Abuses of China's Anti-Monopoly Law: An Indictment and Reform Agenda' (Center for the Protection of Intellectual Property Law, 2014). Retrieved from https://sls.gmu.edu/cpip/wp-content/uploads/sites/31/2014/04/Curbing-the-Abuses-of-Chinas-Anti-Monopoly-Law.pdf.

[44] European Chamber of Commerce in China, 'Press Release: European Chamber Releases Statement on China AML-Related Investigations' (13 August 2014). Retrieved from www.europeanchamber.com.cn/en/press-releases/2132/european_chamber_releases_statement_on_china_aml_related_investigations.

[45] Zhang, A. H., 'Bureaucratic Politics and China's Anti-Monopoly Law' (2014) 47(3) *Cornell International Law Journal* 671, p. 678. She states that '[t]o make matters worse, enforcement agencies such as NDRC often artificially create a race among firms under investigation by applying generous leniency or complete immunity to those who readily admit their guilt and satisfy the agency's demands'. This conclusion seems to be drawn from the Infant Formula case.

[46] Martina, 'Tough-Talking China Pricing Regulator' (n. 41 above), in which he provides a list of firms present at the meeting: 'The two sources said the following companies were at the hotel: GE, Siemens, Samsung Electronics, Microsoft, Volvo, IBM Corp, Michelin, Swedish packaging giant Tetra Pak, Intel Corp, Qualcomm, Dumex, a subsidiary of France's Danone and U.S. cable equipment maker Arris Group Inc. Tetra Pak confirmed it was there but declined to comment further. Samsung and Volvo said they were not aware of any meeting. IBM, Intel, GE and Microsoft declined to comment. Siemens, Arris, Michelin and Dumex did not respond to questions while Reuters was unable to immediately reach Qualcomm.'

examples of how to write what Martina described as 'self-criticism letters'.[47] It is said that Xu conveyed that no confession could lead to more serious sanctions. Further, it was advised that the use of 'external' lawyers was not appreciated.[48] A reason for this statement was not given. But an antitrust lawyer admitted that NDRC cannot prohibit an undertaking from hiring a lawyer. However, afraid of the power of NDRC, the same lawyer testified that some undertakings gave up counsel.

Another of Martina's stories describes the tactics of NDRC used in its investigations. Based upon interviews with attorneys, executives and other experts, Martina together with Matthew Miller reported that a culture of intimidation was characteristic of NDRC. The allegations go quite far and include 'behind-the-scenes tactics – from personal threats to forced apologies and brow beatings'.[49] It is further stated that the interrogations occurred in the presence of Xu Kunlin, the director of the bureau's second division. His tactics were to bring the interrogated representatives of undertakings to a confession.[50] Because of this, his nickname became Mr Confession among some lawyers. Also problematic is that the hastily produced reports of the interrogation in the Chinese language had to be reviewed and signed off before leaving the place of interrogation.[51]

[47] Ibid.

[48] Ibid. But see Ma, J. and Sokol, D. D., 'Procedural Fairness in Chinese Antitrust', in Sokol, D. D. and Guzman, A. T. (eds.), *Antitrust: Procedural Fairness* (Oxford: Oxford University Press, 2019), 71, p. 78 (where the authors claim that foreign counsel could attend investigations of NDRC and SAIC).

[49] Martina and Miller, '"Mr. Confession"' (n. 41 above). This allegation is made despite the hearings being filmed and photographed. Martina and Miller do not indicate how the rough interrogation tactics combine with the fact that all is registered. They only mention that '[s]essions at the NDRC "hearings" are filmed and photographed, and companies under investigation are required to review and sign off on hastily produced Chinese-language transcripts of the meetings before leaving the building.' Zhang refers extensively to Martina and Miller. However, she seems to add information when she writes that an interviewed lawyer compared NDRC's way of handling things with the Red Guard tactics used during the Cultural Revolution. See Zhang, *Chinese Antitrust Exceptionalism* (n. 43 above), p. 49.

[50] In order to extract the confession, it seems that threats have been made to executives and other employees to hold them personally responsible for the AML infringements. Jail sanction was also mentioned in this context. Mark Williams suggests that the basis for this sanction could be Article 52 of the AML, even though it is difficult to state with certainty. See Williams, 'Leniency Policy with Chinese Characteristics' (n. 7 above), p. 50.

[51] Martina and Miller, '"Mr. Confession"' (n. 41 above). It is reported that the foreign critique was barely heard in China itself. Zhang, A. H., 'The Role of Media in Antitrust: Evidence from China' (2018) 41 *Fordham International Law Journal* 473, p. 503. It is also reported that Xu Kunlin would use the media to push a case forward. See Zhang, A. H., 'Strategic Public Shaming: Evidence from Chinese Antitrust' (2017), p. 4. Retrieved from https://papers.ssrn.com/sol3/papers.cfm?abstract_id=2943268.

As a result of all this, Mark Williams purports that undertakings under investigation have board meetings to decide which board member will be sent to NDRC interviews in order to minimise the risk of an adverse outcome. Some undertakings go even further and decline the request to send any executives for a meeting with NDRC.[52]

Still another of Martina's stories related to pressure put on Chinese-registered lawyers not to excessively defend their foreign clients. This pressure is known as the 'two-warning system'.[53] Under this system, a Chinese-registered lawyer will receive a warning if his or her efforts to defend a multinational are too aggressive. If such a warning was given twice, the lawyer would be barred from representing his or her client again in front of NDRC.[54] However, when publicising the decision on the Zhejiang Insurance Industry case, NDRC explicitly mentioned that the defence counsel raised arguments against the case and further explained why NDRC rejected the case.[55] Hence, more transparency on the part of NDRC could be a way to attain more due process.

Another account of forcing undertakings into self-reporting is NDRC's weak understanding of how to properly enforce the AML.[56] Wendy Ng states that, in this respect, '[s]ome commentators speculate that the NDRC's frequent application of the leniency policy is due to its limitations in resources, competition law knowledge, legal analytical capabilities and enforcement capabilities'.[57]

9.2.3 NDRC's Aggressive Enforcement in Its Ambition to Become the Sole Enforcement Agency

Much of the criticism towards the leniency programmes in China has focused on NDRC and its neglect of due process. To use the words of Williams,

[52] Williams, 'Leniency Policy with Chinese Characteristics' (n. 7 above), p. 50.

[53] Martina and Miller, '"Mr. Confession"' (n. 41 above).

[54] Ibid.

[55] Gu, M. and Yu, S., 'Better Late Than Never: NDRC Publishes Full Decisions on Zhejiang Car Insurance Cartel Case – Analysis of NDRC's Antitrust Law Enforcement Approach' (2014), p. 6. Retrieved from www.chinalawvision.com/2014/09/competition-law-anti-monopoly-law/better-late-than-never-ndrc-publishes-full-decisions-on-zhejiang-car-insurance-cartel-case-analysis-of-ndrcs-antitrust-law-enforcement-approach.

[56] Anecdotal in this respect is the story that Xu Kunlin expressed his view on why vertical monopoly agreements should also be covered by a leniency programme. See Cai, 'Public Antitrust Enforcement' (n. 12 above), p. 43. Ng indicates that this is speculation. See Ng, *The Political Economy of Competition Law in China* (n. 2 above), p. 77.

[57] Ng, *The Political Economy of Competition Law in China* (n. 2 above), p. 77.

> lurid allegations have been well publicised in the international press recently and have fuelled allegations that China's AML enforcement policies and practices are highly politicised. … the foreign chambers of commerce denounced allegedly high-handed, aggressive and discriminatory enforcement policies and practices that they said disregarded due process and fuelled a culture of intimidation where 'confessions' were extracted illegitimately and leniency was used inappropriately to create a climate of fear.[58]

Andrew L. Foster similarly alludes that compelling undertakings into using the leniency procedure, and thus soliciting the target undertakings to self-report and submit material evidence, could be explained by pressure on NDRC officials to close the investigations as soon as possible.[59] This pressure, according to Williams, was 'to bolster the claim of NDRC to be seen as the leading AML enforcement agency'.[60] Being seen as the leading enforcement agency could help NDRC to realise its original ambition: 'to administer all competition matters, displacing the SAIC and the MOFCOM'.[61] It has been said that '[t]his was NDRC's ambition a decade ago, prior to the adoption of the AML, and almost certainly remains its strategic objective'.[62]

The ambition to position itself as the sole enforcement agency has a longer history. NDRC is a government agency that saw its origin in the 1950s as the State Planning Commission (SPC). The market liberalisation process in the wake of the accession to the World Trade Organization made the Chinese government reorganise SPC in order to serve the reform and development of a market economy. The more this market economy became realised, the more the power of NDRC was tainted.[63] With the adoption of the AML, NDRC saw its chance to regain a part of its former power.[64]

[58] Williams, 'Leniency Policy with Chinese Characteristics' (n. 7 above), pp. 50–51.

[59] Foster, 'Navigating the Unique Features' (n. 42 above), p. 83.

[60] Williams, 'Leniency Policy with Chinese Characteristics' (n. 7 above), p. 53. Zhang gives the impression, though, that it may have been the personal ambition of Xu rather than of the NDRC as a whole. She reports that 'all these cases were brought during the tenure of Xu Kunlin …, who served as the Director General of the antitrust bureau during from December 2009 to February 2015. Xu, a veteran in charge of price monitoring and supervision in China, is a highly ambitious and resourceful technocrat.' Zhang, 'The Role of Media in Antitrust' (n. 51 above), p. 5.

[61] Williams, 'Leniency Policy with Chinese Characteristics' (n. 7 above), p. 53.

[62] Ibid.

[63] Ng, *The Political Economy of Competition Law in China* (n. 2 above), p. 139.

[64] Zhang, 'Bureaucratic Politics and China's Anti-Monopoly Law' (n. 45 above), pp. 694–99.

SAIC has never displayed the same ambition as NDRC. Its investigations were also far less aggressive. This may explain why he SAIC's investigations have been devoid of any due process concerns.[65]

9.3 SAIC Taking the Lead When the Tripartite Enforcement Structure Ends

9.3.1 Towards a Single Enforcement Agency: SAMR

For almost a decade, China has had a tripartite enforcement structure. The enforcement of the AML has been divided among three different agencies: NDRC, SAIC and MOFCOM. NDRC, SAIC and MOFCOM were all ministerial agencies.[66] NDRC was the enforcement agency in charge of price-related anti-competitive conduct, including among others price-related monopoly agreements (cartels), resale price maintenance and price-related abuses of dominance.[67] SAIC, as an enforcement agency, was dealing with non-price-related anti-competitive conduct, whether it is implemented as an agreement or unilateral conduct.[68] NDRC and SAIC also dealt with administrative monopolies,[69] which are 'the distortion of market competition by public power'.[70] It was often held, and criticised, that this division between price- and non-price-related monopoly agreements could be murky, as monopoly agreements would often have elements of both.[71] MOFCOM was the sole enforcement agency in charge of merger control.[72]

[65] Foster, 'Navigating the Unique Features' (n. 42 above), p. 84.

[66] Wang, 'Retrospectives and Prospects' (n. 2 above), pp. 215–23.

[67] Williams, Leniency Policy with Chinese Characteristics' (n. 7 above), p. 39.

[68] Ibid.

[69] Zhang, Z. and Wu, B., 'Governing China's Administrative Monopolies under the Anti-Monopoly Law: A Ten-Year Review (2008–2018) and Beyond' (2018), pp. 3–4. Retrieved from https://papers.ssrn.com/sol3/papers.cfm?abstract_id=3294291.

[70] Ibid., p. 1.

[71] That this division could become murky is obvious. See Van den Bergh, R. and Faure, M., 'Critical Issues in the Enforcement of the Anti-monopoly law in China: A Law and Economics Perspective', in Faure and Zhang, *Competition Policy and Regulation* (n. 31 above), 54, p. 58; Zhang, X. and Zhang, V. Y., 'New Developments in China's Competition Policy against Monopolistic/Collusive Agreements', in Faure, M. and Xu, G. (eds.), *Economics and Regulation in China* (Abingdon: Routledge, 2013), pp. 123–26. Without any jurisdictional rules in the AML or its implementation guidelines, the division of jurisdiction was done on the basis of the first-mover advantage. The enforcement agency that starts the investigation over a complex cartel first, whether ex officio or based on a leniency application, would have jurisdiction. See Wang, X. and Su, J., *Competition Law in China* (Alphen aan de Rijn: Wolters Kluwer, 2012), pp. 68–69.

[72] Wang, 'Retrospectives and Prospects' (n. 2 above), p. 215.

This tripartite enforcement structure reflected the enforcement of competition-related laws existing prior to the AML.[73] However, at first it was not clear whether the three existing agencies would remain responsible for enforcement of their respective areas within competition law. It was more of a compromise following a power struggle to be the single enforcement agency.[74] Ng succinctly describes the difficult struggles between the different agencies.[75] She notes that SAIC and MOFCOM were the two ministerial agencies most heavily involved in the drafting process of the AML from the beginning.[76] Whereas these two agencies initially intended to collaborate with each other, 'over time they undertook the drafting work separately, including submitting separate drafts of the AML to the State Council, where they each nominated themselves as the sole government agency responsible for enforcing the AML'.[77] The issue became even more complex when NDRC entered the scene. This was only around 2003, at the moment that the AML drafting was already being discussed at the State Council level.[78] Despite NDRC entering the drafting process at a late stage, it was the most powerful ministerial agency of the three[79] and it 'fought tenaciously … to obtain a role in the administration of the AML'.[80] This impasse led to the delay in appointing the actual enforcement agency. Article 9 of the AML stated that the enforcement would be left to an Anti-Monopoly Enforcement Authority (AMEA).[81] As a matter of compromise, the State Council eventually decided that

[73] The historical powers of the respective AML enforcement agencies are explained by Ng as follows. NDRC was an agency that had control over the price laws. SAIC had been focusing on unfair competition practices, but also on 'anti-competitive conduct of enterprises in monopoly industries such as telecommunications, post, insurance, banking, electricity supply'. Moreover, SAIC also handled mergers and acquisitions between domestic, thus Chinese, firms and foreign firms. It did so together with MOFCOM. See Ng, *The Political Economy of Competition Law in China* (n. 2 above), pp. 138–47.

[74] Wang, X., *The Evolution of China's Anti-Monopoly Law* (Cheltenham: Edward Elgar, 2014), pp. 230–60. In this section, Wang discusses in detail how scholars saw the enforcement structure, with reference to the European Union and the US.

[75] Ng, *The Political Economy of Competition Law in China* (n. 2 above), pp. 215–19.

[76] Ibid., p. 215.

[77] Ibid.

[78] Ibid., p. 216.

[79] Zhang, 'Bureaucratic Politics and China's Anti-Monopoly Law' (n. 45 above), p. 694.

[80] Williams, 'Leniency Policy with Chinese Characteristics' (n. 7 above), p. 39.

[81] Emch, A. and Hao, Q., 'The New Chinese Anti-Monopoly Law – an Overview', eSapience Center for Competition Policy (2007), p. 3. Retrieved from www.sidley.com/~/media/files/publications/2007/11/the-new-chinese-antimonopoly-law--an-overview/files/view-pdf/fileattachment/newchineseantimonopolyenglish.pdf.

the tasks of the AMEA would be taken care of by the three competing agencies: MOFCOM, NDRC and SAIC.

Yane Svetiev and Lei Wang inform us that the tripartite enforcement structure had some advantages:

> First, it prevents delayed enforcement by alleviating the resource and staff constraints that a wholly new agency would face immediately after it is established. Existing authorities can use already established mechanisms for monitoring markets and disciplining companies to enforce the new law. Second, the local authorities' familiarity with the underlying principles of a transplanted law may facilitate effective enforcement. Third, the existing ministerial authorities are already well-embedded in the political system and have channels of communication with industry and other market stakeholders, including foreign companies. Therefore, they may be seen as powerful and credible regulators.[82]

Despite this positive analysis, Svetiev and Wang warn that there is a risk attached to attributing agencies with enforcement responsibilities over an area in which they had prior mandates. The agencies 'may continue to follow the rules, public policy goals, or decision-making routines under their former mandate, without adjusting to the novel goals'.[83] This issue has been extensively researched by Angela Zhang, who holds that the main objective of each of the enforcement agencies has been

> to maximize their departments' policy control, which is directly tied to their factional interests and hence their career prospects. As each Chinese enforcement agency is nested within a different ministry, their divergent responsibilities and political missions shape their enforcement priorities, as amply demonstrated in the case of NDRC's attempt to use the AML as a tool to maintain price stability and fulfill industrial policy goals.[84]

The capture of the enforcement agencies did not only occur internally, by the ministry to which the agencies belonged, but also externally, by other government departments, often in a superior position to the competition law enforcement agencies.[85] Though Wang has categorised this as capture,[86] Zhang describes this intervention as a process of

[82] Svetiev, Y. and Wang, L., 'Competition Law Enforcement in China: Between Technocracy and Industrial Policy' (2016) 79(4) *Law and Contemporary Problems* 187, pp. 195–96. Retrieved from https://scholarship.law.duke.edu/cgi/viewcontent.cgi?article=4807&context=lcp.

[83] Ibid., p. 196.

[84] Zhang, 'Bureaucratic Politics and China's Anti-Monopoly Law' (n. 45 above), p. 706.

[85] Wang, 'Retrospectives and Prospects' (n. 2 above), pp. 227–28.

[86] Ibid., p. 227.

consensus building within the government.[87] Whether capture or consensus building, it has been argued that the process itself jeopardises the predictability of the AML. The enforcement agencies are not able to develop a consistent enforcement policy. That could only be guaranteed by a single independent enforcement agency.[88]

Even though there has been a scholarly argument for a single independent enforcement agency, the Communist Party of China (CPC), at its 18th National Congress, revealed that it was aware that the government structure related to market supervision had to be revised. Therefore, a commission for reform, known as the Central Comprehensively Deepening Reforms Commission (Reform Commission), was set up in 2013 and positioned as a sub-division of the Politburo of the CPC. It was led by President Xi Jinping.[89] The aim of this Reform Commission was, among others, to improve the market system and so facilitate the creation of a fair, open and transparent market, in which competition rules would have a central role.[90] Another aim was to streamline the government structure in order to embrace a rationalisation of the competences of different ministries and agencies.[91]

[87] Ibid.

[88] Ibid., pp. 227–28.

[89] Li, C., *Chinese Politics in the Xi Jinping Era: Reassessing Collective Leadership* (Washington, DC: Brookings Institution Press, 2016), p. 12.

[90] Wang, K., Yang, M. and Zhang, D., 'China's New State Administration for Market Regulation: What to Know and What to Expect', *Ropes & Gray Alert* (2018). Retrieved from www.ropesgray.com/en/newsroom/alerts/2018/04/Chinas-New-State-Market-Regulatory-Administration-What-to-Know-and-What-to-Expect. Restoring the trust in the market meant that responsibilities had to be merged into the SAMR. SAMR 'will merge and undertake the responsibilities previously held by the State Administration for Industry and Commerce (SAIC), General Administration of Quality Supervision, Inspection and Quarantine (AQSIQ), the Certification and Accreditation Administration (CAC), the Standardization Administration of China (SAC) and the China Food and Drug Administration (CFDA). The restructuring will also assimilate the antitrust and price supervision functions of certain regulators, including the Anti-monopoly and Anti-unfair Competition Enforcement Bureau of the SAIC (as part of the broader absorption of the SAIC into the SAMR), Price Supervision and Anti-monopoly Bureau of the National Development and Reform Commission, the Anti-monopoly Bureau of the Ministry of Commerce (MOFCOM), and the Anti-monopoly Commission of the State Council. Finally, it will govern a newly formed State Intellectual Property Office (SIPO) to regulate intellectual property rights.' For a detailed summary of all the areas of this reform, see USC US-China Institute, 'Decision of the Central Committee of the Communist Party of China on Some Major Issues Concerning Comprehensively Deepening the Reform, November 12, 2013' (2013). Retrieved from https://china.usc.edu/decision-central-committee-communist-party-china-some-major-issues-concerning-comprehensively.

[91] USC US-China Institute, 'Decision of the Central Committee' (n. 90 above).

The work of the Reform Commission resulted in one of the biggest government reshuffles since the introduction of the 'Open Door' policy in the 1970s,[92] whereby a new agency for supervising the market was established: the State Administration for Market Regulation.[93]

SAMR has been given a broad range of competences. The agency is supposed to oversee 'everything from drug safety supervision, quality inspection, fair competition and commercial bribery, issuance of business registrations, certifications and accreditations, management of intellectual property rights and comprehensive supervision and management of the market order'.[94] SAMR has thus become the 'single most powerful market regulator',[95] with the enforcement of the AML as just one of its tasks.[96]

The functions of the Price Supervision and Anti-Monopoly Bureau of NDRC, the Anti-Monopoly and Anti-Unfair Competition Bureau of SAIC and the Anti-Monopoly Bureau of MOFCOM were thus transferred to SAMR. This transfer, however, did not have an impact on the existence of NDRC and MOFCOM as agencies under the State Council.[97] SAIC, on the other hand, no longer exists. The entire agency was integrated into SAMR.[98]

9.3.2 *More Due Process with SAIC Officials Taking Leading Positions within SAMR*

The integration of SAIC into the structures of SAMR had an important consequence. Former SAIC members were able to take leading positions within SAMR. Jingyuan Ma reports that '[t]he former minister of the SAIC, Mr Zhang Mao, became the minister of SAMR, and the former vice minister of the SAIC, Ms. Gan Lin, became the vice minister of the Anti-monopoly Bureau of the SAMR'.[99] Besides, and this

92 Wang, Yang and Zhang, 'China's New State Administration' (n. 90 above).
93 Ma, *Competition Law in China* (n. 8 above), p. 171.
94 Wang, Yang and Zhang, 'China's New State Administration' (n. 90 above).
95 Ibid.
96 Ma, *Competition Law in China* (n. 8 above), p. 21.
97 Ibid., p. 172.
98 Zhang, *Chinese Antitrust Exceptionalism* (n. 43 above), p. 50.
99 Ma, *Competition Law in China* (n. 8 above), p. 179. This is also confirmed by other sources, such as Wang, Yang and Zhang, 'China's New State Administration' (n. 90 above); Zhang, *Chinese Antitrust Exceptionalism* (n. 43 above), p. 50. Note that the two later sources state that Mao Zhang became the Deputy Communist Party Secretary and Director of the SAMR.

is reported by Zhang, four other SAIC officials got a position with the leadership board of SAMR. They held respectively the third, fourth, fifth and twelfth positions within the board.[100] These appointments put an end to rumours that NDRC officials would be in charge of the Anti-Monopoly Bureau.[101] In fact, none of the members of the Price Supervision and Anti-Monopoly Bureau of NDRC has received a leading position within SAMR. The same is true for the Anti-Monopoly Bureau of MOFCOM.

What the consequence of this evolution is for law enforcement is still speculative. However, lawyers at White & Case have suggested that the appointment of SAIC personnel at key positions within the Anti-Monopoly Bureau of SAMR could be a political sign in favour of a more modest approach to the enforcement of the AML.[102] In the end, SAIC's enforcement has always been depicted as less aggressive. The less aggressive character of SAIC's enforcement is due to two reasons.[103] First, SAIC has been much more restrained in approaching anti-competitive conduct by multinational firms. It is only towards the end of its ten-year existence that SAIC started to investigate foreign-based multinational firms.[104] Second, SAIC has built a better reputation when it comes to following investigation procedures. Leaving aside the former understanding of its aggressiveness, SAIC has never been blamed for the due process excesses of which NDRC has been accused. To use the words of Andrew Foster, Counsel in the Beijing and Hong Kong offices of Skadden, Arps, Slate,

[100] Zhang, *Chinese Antitrust Exceptionalism* (n. 43 above), p. 50. She points out that the other members of the leadership board came from the former General Administration of Quality Supervision Inspection and Quarantine and the former Food and Drug Administration. Other seats in the board were taken by the newly established State Intellectual Property Office and the Central Party Discipline Committee.

[101] Brumfield, 'China Merges Antitrust Enforcement Agencies into One' (n. 9 above).

[102] Ibid. See also DavisPolk, 'Update on Establishment of Single Antitrust Agency in China', *Client Memorandum* (2018), p. 4. Retrieved from www.davispolk.com/sites/default/files/2018-10-24_china_consolidates_antitrust_powers_into_single_agency.pdf.

[103] In relation to NDRC, aggressive has also been understood in terms of the height of the fine applied. This can be deduced from the statement that '[t]he NDRC has been well recognized as the most aggressive antitrust enforcer in China. One example of its comparatively aggressive posture was the agency's record breaking fine (approximately USD 975 million) against Qualcomm in 2015.' Brumfield, 'China Merges Antitrust Enforcement Agencies into One' (n. 9 above).

[104] Liao and Li, 'Antitrust Dawn Raids in China' (n. 23 above), p. 3 (referring to Tetra Pak and Microsoft in 2013 and 2014, respectively).

Meagher & Flom LLC, 'SAIC's investigations (especially of multinationals) tend to be have [sic] a much longer duration and have largely been devoid of any reported due process concerns'.[105]

Zhang agrees with the vision that '[t]here is no doubt that former SAIC leadership and staff will maintain a prominent role and are expected to more directly influence SAMR for the foreseeable future within SAMR'.[106] To use her words, she predicts that SAMR will become more '"legalized" and professional'[107] and that 'the agency will be more cognizant of requirements under Chinese administrative law and the requirement to observe the due process requirements'.[108]

Despite this optimism, a few additional elements need to be highlighted. It has been reported that legal representation is possible for undertakings that are facing an investigation by SAMR.[109] The legal representation does not, however, extend to being present during interrogations by SAMR officials of employees for undertakings that have applied for leniency. Even though the absence of a lawyer during such interrogations is not limited to China,[110] it may allow for psychological pressure by the investigation team on the employees.

The psychological pressure, or, much more broadly, nudging undertakings to apply for leniency, may not be regarded as problematic from a due process perspective.[111] However, the due process principles applicable in western countries are not necessarily similar in China. With reference to Randall Peerenboom, Zhang concludes that bureaucrats will not be

105 Foster, 'Navigating the Unique Features' (n. 42 above), p. 84. He states that '[f]or example, the SAIC opened its investigation into the rebating and discounting practices of Tetra Pak in July 2013, spending more than three years collecting data and engaging in hearings and bilateral meetings before fining the company nearly RMB 668 million (US$ 97 million) in a decision that Tetra Pak says it will not appeal. Similarly, the SAIC's investigation of Microsoft, first opened in 2014, is still ongoing today, signalling the SAIC's decision to proceed with thoroughness and caution in its high-profile investigations.'

106 Wang, Yang and Zhang, 'China's New State Administration' (n. 90 above).

107 Zhang, *Chinese Antitrust Exceptionalism* (n. 43 above), p. 51.

108 Ibid.

109 Liang, D., 'China', in Campbell, N. (ed.), *Cartel Regulation 2021* (London: Law Business Research, 2021), 74, p. 87.

110 Hayashi, S., 'The 2013 Amendment to the Antimonopoly Act – Procedural Fairness under Japanese Competition Law' (2015) 39 *Journal of Japanese Law* 89, p. 106. He states that 'Similarly, there are no regulations regarding the presence of legal counsel during witness interrogation and, in practice, it is not accepted either.'

111 This point has been confirmed to the authors through email interview with several lawyers.

inclined to cede what is best for the public if politics has other priorities defined or if superiors dictate them to act differently.[112]

Furthermore, SAMR will not conduct all the investigations by itself. SAMR is centrally organised and only has a limited number of staff.[113] To facilitate investigations, SAMR has delegated parts of its enforcement powers in relation to monopoly agreements to the Provincial Administration for Market Regulation (PAMR). These PAMRs can institute and conduct investigations autonomously from the central bureaucracy.[114] It is uncertain to what extent the culture of SAIC trickles down to these autonomous provincial administrations. One of them, the one in Jiangsu, for example, has already actively called upon undertakings to apply for leniency.[115] It is to be seen whether these encouragements will lead to actively pressuring parties into further confessions. There is no real protection built into the AML to prevent this, except for the fact that a PAMR has to report the investigation to SAMR within seven days after the start of the investigation.[116]

112 Zhang, *Chinese Antitrust Exceptionalism* (n. 43 above), p. 53. Zhang also explains this in another article, where she states that 'This regulatory inertia continued until Ant Group's IPO debacle, when the antitrust regulator received a clear signal from China's top leadership to rein in the tech giants.' See Zhang, A. H., 'Commentary: Why did China Wait So Long to Crack Down on Alibaba?' (2021). Retrieved from www.channelnewsasia.com/commentary/chinese-tech-giant-alibaba-jack-ma-regulation-ant-300791. Bo Zhiyue explains this phenomenon in an article where he writes that 'Alibaba decided to accept the SAMR ruling and pay the fine without any argument. In a country that has yet to establish the primacy of law with a genuine due process, Alibaba did its best to protect its own interests. By accepting the fine, it could close this issue and move on. Alibaba knows it is not a good idea to push the envelope in a year of great importance for the ruling party in China.' See Zhiyue, B., 'Commentary: Why China's US$2.8 Billion Fine Is a Huge Relief for Alibaba' (2021). Retrieved from www.channelnewsasia.com/commentary/china-fine-alibaba-billions-monopoly-behaviour-jack-ma-215146.

113 It is mentioned that only 50 persons out of the 805 work for the 10 divisions related to the AML. See Ma, *Competition Law in China* (n. 8 above), p. 171.

114 Heng, J. and Ping, L., 'China's Anti-Monopoly Law and the Role of Economics in Its Enforcement', (2020) 6(3) *Russian Journal of Economics* 219, p. 221. Retrieved from https://rujec.org/article/56362.

115 Han, M., Huang, C., van Opstal, C., Wong, J., Seet, J. and Liang, X., 'Antitrust China 2020 Annual Review' (2020). Retrieved from www.fangdalaw.com/wp-content/uploads/2021/01/ANTITRUST-CHINA-2020-ANNUAL-REVIEW.pdf.

116 Liang, 'China' (n. 109 above), p. 79. Note that a PAMR can also communicate the start of an investigation to SAMR. Dodoo informs us that the scope of investigation can be very broad, including the premises of third parties (such as auditors), bank accounts or even employees' homes. However, she also communicates that the investigation teams have been professionalised. A dawn raid requires at least two officials present, who can identify themselves. Further, the investigation teams now also comprise lawyers, IT specialists and forensic accountants. Lawyers can be present during the dawn raid, but there is no attorney client privilege. Dodoo, 'A New Dawn for Cartel Enforcement in China' (n. 36 above), pp. 82–83.

9.4 One Enforcement Agency, One Leniency Programme

9.4.1 NDRC's Mandate to Draft New Guidelines

The shift to one enforcement agency also calls for a revision of the existence of two different leniency programmes. Since the division between price-related and non-price-related monopoly agreements had become redundant with SAMR taking the role of enforcement agency of the AML, it would also be logical that SAMR would issue its own leniency programme and repeal the ones developed by NDRC and SAIC. However, the idea of implementing a single leniency programme already grew as early as 2015. To achieve this, the Anti-Monopoly Commission (AMC) under the State Council entrusted the Price Supervision and Antimonopoly Bureau of NDRC to elaborate a new leniency programme. This leniency programme was 'expected to unify the difference between the NDRC and the SAIC programmes'.[117]

By 2 February 2016, the NDRC drafted the Guidelines for Application of the Leniency Regime to Cases of Horizontal Agreements (Draft Leniency Guidelines). The Draft Leniency Guidelines were presented to the public for comments and feedback. Despite the fact that the period for comments and feedback was only one month, the whole of February 2016, it did not lead to new rules.[118] Friction between the enforcement agencies has been put forward as one reason.[119] More likely, however, is that the preparation of a sweeping government reform, which had to put an end to the rivalry between the competition agencies, had already made great progress, meaning it was better to stop the transformation of the different leniency programmes into one. The transformation of the Draft Leniency Guidelines into real guidelines was thus put on hold.[120]

The government reform was finally approved on 17 March 2018 by the Congress. As mentioned above, the establishment of SAMR was one of the results of the reform. With a single integrated agency in charge of the AML, there was also a need to unify the regulations implementing the AML. One of the earliest documents released by SAMR was the Guidelines for the Application of the Leniency Programme to Horizontal

117 Ning, Yin and Peng, 'China' (n. 37 above), p. 68.

118 Wang, P., Zhang, Y. and Xue, Q., 'Combination of China's Three Antitrust Enforcement Agencies May Bring More Aggressive Enforcement over Long Run' (June 2018), p. 3. Retrieved from www.jonesday.com/en/insights/2018/06/combination-of-chinas-three-antitrust-enforcement.

119 Wang, Zhang and Xue, 'China's New State Administration' (n. 90 above), p.3.

120 Ibid.

Monopoly Agreements (SAMR Leniency Guidelines).[121] The speed with which the SAMR Leniency Guidelines were adopted, half a year after being established, was made possible by the preparatory work of NDRC. Indeed, the content of the Draft Leniency Guidelines was the basis for the SAMR Leniency Guidelines.

9.4.2 SAMR Adopts the Leniency Guidelines Prepared by NDRC

SAMR picked up the work done by NDRC in relation to creating a new leniency programme.[122] NDRC's work was the basis for the creation of the SAMR Leniency Guidelines. As the SAMR Leniency Guidelines were almost an exact copy of the Draft Leniency Guidelines, this chapter will only discuss the content of the former.

One of the biggest changes that is implemented by the SAMR Leniency Guidelines is to limit leniency to horizontal monopoly agreements.[123] This implies that the SAMR Leniency Guidelines only apply to Article 13 of the AML. With upcoming reforms of the AML, the monopoly agreements covered by Article 13 of the AML will also include hub-and-spoke cartels.[124]

Another important issue that is clarified by the SAMR Leniency Guidelines is that leniency can be applied for both before and after SAMR initiates a case or launches an investigation.[125] Note, however, that the leniency application needs to be submitted before the issuance of a Prior Notice for the Administrative Penalty.[126]

[121] SAMR issued six guidelines. Editorial Board, 'Interview with Wu Zhenguo, Director General, Anti-Monopoly Bureau of the State Administration for Market Regulation (SAMR), People's Republic of China', *The Antitrust Source* (2021), pp. 2–3 and 8. Retrieved from www.samr.gov.cn/xw/zj/202107/P020210707589294998827.pdf. At the end of 2019, SAMR published, among other things, 'the Interim Provisions for Prohibiting Eliminating and Restricting Competition by Abuse of Administrative Power, the Interim Provisions for Prohibiting Monopolistic Agreements, and the Interim Provisions for Prohibiting Abuse of Market Dominance'. See Heng and Ping, 'China's Anti-Monopoly Law' (n. 114 above), p. 225. It was also indicated that these 'legal documents supersede the early regulations issued by NDRC and SAIC and provide unified and consistent guidelines towards monopoly agreements, abuse of dominance, and administrative monopolies, respectively'. Ibid., p. 226.

[122] Dodoo, 'A New Dawn for Cartel Enforcement in China' (n. 36 above), p. 79.

[123] Leniency Guidelines, Article 3.

[124] Liang, 'China' (n. 109 above), p. 74.

[125] Leniency Guidelines, Article 4.

[126] Liang, 'China' (n. 109 above), p. 86.

The timing of submission is important for the undertaking that will be ranked as the first leniency applicant. A first-ranked leniency applicant who submitted the application before the initiation of a case or launching an investigation will be eligible for immunity or reduction.[127] The reduction will be no less than 80 per cent.[128] The SAMR Leniency Guidelines hold that if the application is made before the start of an investigation, the first applicant will receive immunity as long as the applicant did not act as originator or coercer.[129] The second-ranked leniency applicant, whether before or after an investigation, will be eligible for a reduction of the fine by between 30 per cent and 50 per cent.[130] For the third-ranked leniency applicant, the reduction will be between 20 per cent and 30 per cent.[131] Any other successful leniency applicant may be granted a reduction of no more than 20 per cent.[132] Even though the SAMR Leniency Guidelines give the impression that an unlimited number of undertakings can apply for leniency,[133] Article 12(2) of the SAMR Leniency Guidelines limits, in principle, the number of undertakings eligible for leniency to three.[134] Only in high-profile and complex cases can the SAMR decide to grant leniency to more than three undertakings.[135]

As the order of application is important to determine the level of leniency, one could expect a rigid system to fix the order. Article 11 of the SAMR Leniency Guidelines stipulates that this needs to be done according to the timing of application. In principle, SAMR will issue a written receipt when the necessary documents are received.[136] It is not clear whether this is also done for oral applications.[137] However, an undertaking can only keep its position in the order of submission if all conditions of the SAMR Leniency Guidelines are complied with.[138] If, for whatever reason, an undertaking loses its position, the undertaking next in position can move up one place.[139] However, the possibility to move up in

127 Leniency Guidelines, Article 6.

128 Ibid., Article 13(1).

129 Ibid.

130 Ibid., Article 13(2).

131 Ibid.

132 Ibid.

133 Ibid. (this article states that leniency applicants subsequent to the third one may be granted a reduction of up to 20 per cent).

134 Leniency Guidelines, Article 12(2).

135 Ibid.

136 Ibid., Articles 7 and 8.

137 Ibid., Article 9 (only mentioning the that audio recordings and written records will be made).

138 Ibid., Article 11(2).

139 Ibid.

the order does not apply when the first-ranked applicant's immunity submission is cancelled.[140]

Securing the first position in the order of applications is by no means easy. The information that needs to be gathered is enormous. SAMR requires the leniency applicant to submit:

> (1) The basic information on the participants of the monopoly agreement ...; (2) The stage of the monopoly agreement ...; (3) The main content of the monopoly agreement ...; (4) The geographical scope affected and market size; (5) The duration of the implementation of the monopoly agreement; (6) Explanation of evidence materials; (7) Whether the undertaker applies for leniency to any other law enforcement authorities; (8) Other relevant documents and materials.[141]

If the information is complete, the applicant gets informed about the receipt of the leniency application and the documents submitted. When the first leniency applicant cannot provide all this information at the time of applying, or information is missing, SAMR will give the undertaking 30 days, extendable to 60 days, to gather the necessary evidence.[142] This period, for which the undertaking gets a written message, is considered to be the marker system.

The evidence necessary for immunity differs depending on the timing of the application. If SAMR did not yet initiate a case or launch an investigation, the evidence needs to enable SAMR to do so.[143] It is understood that this kind of evidence will be unknown to SAMR. When an investigation has started, the leniency applicant needs to submit evidence that allows SAMR to determine the existence of a monopoly agreement.[144] In case an undertaking is not able to provide this kind of evidence within the specified time, the registration will be cancelled.[145] If no other leniency applicants turn up, a reapplication for immunity is possible, but without going through the marker procedure.[146] In case other undertakings applied for leniency, the undertaking whose application is disqualified for immunity could eventually consider applying for a reduction.[147]

140 Ibid., Article 11.
141 Ibid., Article 6. See also Liang, 'China' (n. 109 above), p. 85.
142 Leniency Guidelines, Article 7(3).
143 Ibid., Article 6(3)(1).
144 Ibid., Article 6(3)(2).
145 Ibid., Article 7(3).
146 Ibid., Article 7(4) (indicating that the process of Article 7(1) is open for reapplication and not Article 7(3)).
147 Liang, 'China' (n. 109 above), p. 86.

To obtain a reduction of a fine, the SAMR Leniency Guidelines are slightly different than for immunity. Leniency applicants aiming for a reduction cannot enjoy a marker system. They need to submit a report that includes the participants to the monopoly agreement, the products or services involved, and the time and location of reaching and implementing the agreement.[148] Besides this report, the leniency applicant needs to submit evidence. SAMR will only accept evidence that has either a greater probative effect in relation to how the monopoly agreement has been reached or a 'supplementary probative value in terms of the content of the monopoly agreement, the time of its being reached and implemented, the scope of products or services involved, the participating member, etc.'.[149] In addition, SAMR will also accept other evidence that can prove the monopoly agreement or take away the uncertainty about the probative value of other evidence.[150]

In order to maintain the order of applications, the leniency applicants need to comply with certain conditions.[151] Non-compliance with any of the following conditions will render a leniency applicant ineligible for leniency and thus the cancellation of the acquired position in the order of leniency applications. The leniency applicant shall terminate immediately the illegal activity, unless otherwise required by SAMR. Prompt, continuous, full and sincere cooperation is required of the leniency applicant. A leniency applicant is required to promptly preserve the evidence and other information and thus refrain from concealing, destroying or transferring it. The available information, as long as it is not falsified, should be provided to SAMR. The leniency application should not be disclosed to anyone else, unless SAMR gives permission to do so. Lastly, the leniency applicant should refrain from engaging in conduct that can hinder the investigation.[152] Coercing a competitor to enter or stay in a monopoly agreement does not affect the eligibility to apply for a reduction.[153] The same applies to undertakings that acted as the organiser of the monopoly agreement.[154]

148 Leniency Guidelines, Article 8(2).

149 Ibid., Article 8(3); Liang, 'China' (n. 109 above), p. 85.

150 Leniency Guidelines, Article 8(3)(3).

151 Ibid., Article 10(1)(1)–(5).

152 Liang, 'China' (n. 109 above), p. 86.

153 Leniency Guidelines, Article 10(2).

154 Ibid. Liang also notes that coercion and taking a leading role are aggregating factors and will increase the initial sanction for monopoly agreements by 1 per cent. Liang, 'China' (n. 109 above), p. 83.

The SAMR Leniency Guidelines oblige SAMR to explicitly state that it has given leniency and provide the reasons for granting leniency. Furthermore, a decision involving leniency needs also to be promptly published on SAMR's website.[155] The publication of the decision in which leniency is granted does not have any impact on the confidentiality of the documents and information that has been submitted as evidence. SAMR will keep these documents and information confidential, even from other agencies, organisations and individuals. The confidential treatment of documents and information is identical for applicants receiving immunity and reduction.[156]

9.4.3 SAMR Retains a Small Amount of Discretion to Judge the Quality of the Evidence

The newly created leniency programme has addressed many of the unpredictable and non-transparent elements that existed in the respective leniency programmes of NDRC and SAIC. By reducing the number of leniency programmes to only one, there is no longer any uncertainty as to which programme will apply. It has further been settled that leniency can be obtained before and after the start of an investigation. The amount of reduction has been fixed in four different bands: 80 per cent to 100 per cent; 30 per cent to 50 per cent; 20 per cent to 30 per cent; and up to 20 per cent. The order of application is fixed by giving a notice to the leniency applicants. Failure to observe the conditions will, of course, lead to the withdrawal of the secured position in the queue. Further, eligibility criteria that could be open to interpretation, such as originator and coercer, have only been retained in relation to the first leniency applicant applying before the start of an investigation.

Despite the great effort in limiting unpredictability and non-transparency, SAMR has still discretional powers in relation to one element: the quality of the evidence. For each stage of the leniency application, SAMR will have to analyse the evidence and ascertain its value. The value of the evidence will determine the level of reduction.

Retaining some discretion over the evidence has advantages. SAMR will be able to abstract information with higher probative value than the evidence it has already found or received. In doing so, the SAMR Leniency Guidelines can prevent the submission of unmeritorious leniency applications. Such applications would grant lenient treatment without

155 Leniency Guidelines, Article 15.

156 Ibid., Article 16. Liang, 'China' (n. 109 above), p. 86.

advancing the case. Undertakings can anticipate this system by having prior communication with SAMR, whether anonymously or not.[157]

The disadvantage of this discretion over the evidence is the potential to discriminate between different leniency applications and thus the undertakings applying for leniency. This discrimination can take two forms. On the one hand, evidence could be dismissed as not having any added value. On the other hand, in judging the evidence low value could be attributed, due to which a low level of leniency would be granted. There are mechanisms installed in SAMR that could prevent this kind of negative outcome. Undertakings can use the communication with SAMR prior to submitting the evidence to check the value of their evidence. If the undertaking appears to have valuable evidence, it can proceed to submit it. Once it is submitted, SAMR is under the obligation to provide a receipt stating the timing of application and the documents that joined the application. After granting leniency, and this happens when the final decision is being issued, SAMR has a duty to explain why it has granted leniency to the applicant. And SAMR is also under a duty to finally publicise the decision and so reveal to the public how it has decided.[158]

The SAMR Leniency Guidelines seem to have all necessary checks and balances in place to prevent any negative outcome. However, more detailed information could have been given in relation to how SAMR will appreciate evidence. This is also something that has been done in Europe since 2002. Of course, undertakings and their legal teams may work by analogy and reason that the required evidence is similar to what applies in the European Union.

9.5 Conclusion

To facilitate the enforcement of the monopoly agreements provision of the AML, the Chinese enforcement agencies, NDRC and SAIC, employed leniency programmes from an early stage. These leniency programmes were fraught with elements making their application unpredictable and non-transparent. This resulted in delayed leniency applications,

[157] Leniency Guidelines, Article 5; Liang, 'China' (n. 109 above), p. 87.

[158] For an example of a recently published decision, which is the first one in which the leniency programme has been used in a bid-rigging case, see Zhejiang Provincial Market Supervision Administration Bureau, Administrative Penalty Decision, Zhejiang City Supervision Case (2021), No. 5. Retrieved from www.samr.gov.cn/fldj/tzgg/xzcf/202111/t20211118_336968.html (in Chinese).

whereby the participants in the monopoly agreements only reported their participation after the enforcement agencies had started their investigation. The argument goes that, especially in relation to NDRC, many of these leniency applications were made under pressure.

During the last three years, different changes materialised in relation to the enforcement of the AML. A single enforcement agency, SAMR, was established. As the single enforcer, SAMR also repealed the different leniency programmes in order to replace them by a new one.

This evolution is important in two ways. The establishment of SAMR meant that NDRC lost its competence over the AML, preventing it from exercising undue power over it. Moreover, as SAIC officials took important positions within SAMR, especially in relation to the AML, it is believed that the future enforcement culture will align more with procedures laid down in the law. However, decentralisation of the enforcement powers and the absence of lawyers during investigatory interviews may leave room for SAMR to pressure or nudge monopoly agreement participants into applying for leniency. Furthermore, the new leniency programme has put an end to many elements that made a leniency application unpredictable and non-transparent. However, by being given discretionary power to judge the value of evidence, SAMR could take a negative stance towards some leniency applicants. Only transparency would be a remedy against this danger.

10

Leniency Policy in Singapore

SCOTT CLEMENTS AND DAREN SHIAU

10.1 Introduction

Cartel activities are considered to have the object of preventing, restricting or distorting competition within Singapore, and are prohibited by Section 34 of the Competition Act (Chapter 50B) of Singapore (Singapore Competition Act).[1] The Competition and Consumer Commission of Singapore (CCCS), the authority tasked with enforcing the Singapore Competition Act, recognises cartel agreements (such as price fixing, output limitation, bid rigging and market sharing) to be the most serious type of infringement under Section 34 of the Singapore Competition Act and had issued sixteen cartel infringement decisions as of 30 June 2021. Given that the detection of cartels is inherently difficult and costly due to the clandestine nature of cartels, a leniency programme was introduced by the CCCS to incentivise undertakings participating (or which may have participated in) cartels to blow the whistle by voluntarily providing the CCCS with evidence of their cartel activities and by cooperating with the CCCS in its investigation. The incentive to cooperate ranges from full indemnity from financial penalties to reduction of financial penalties – depending on the position of the undertaking in the leniency queue, and in each case subject always to the applicant's adherence to the conditions and requirements imposed by CCCS in its leniency guidelines.

This chapter will provide a brief overview of cartel regulation and enforcement in Singapore (Section 10.2), and will then focus on the general framework of Singapore's leniency programme (Section 10.3) and its details (Sections 10.4 and 10.5). Thereafter, Section 10.6 discusses the leniency applications made in previous cartel infringement decisions issued by CCCS. Section 10.7 then considers the vital role of counsel in leniency applications in Singapore, and Section 10.8 touches on Singapore's

[1] Competition Act (Chapter 50B), Original Enactment: Act 46 of 2004, Revised Edition 2006. Retrieved from https://sso.agc.gov.sg/Act/CA2004 (Singapore Competition Act).

cooperation arrangements (or agreements) with other countries or agencies in respect of cartel investigations. Section 10.9 discusses the reform of the country's leniency programme.

10.2 Overview of Cartel Regulation and Enforcement in Singapore

The Singapore Competition Act is the principal statute governing the competition law regime in Singapore. The Singapore Competition Act is closely modelled on the United Kingdom (UK) Competition Act[2] and was enacted to ensure the efficient functioning of Singapore's markets via the protection of the process of competition.[3] To achieve this objective, the Singapore Competition Act regulates anti-competitive agreements and/or practices that may have an appreciable adverse effect on competition within Singapore,[4] abuses of dominance[5] and mergers[6] that may result in the substantial lessening of competition within Singapore.

Cartel enforcement falls within the scope of Section 34 of the Singapore Competition Act, which prohibits agreements between undertakings, decisions by associations of undertakings or concerted practices that have, as their object or effect, the prevention, restriction or distortion of competition within Singapore, unless excluded by the Third Schedule to the Singapore Competition Act or a block exemption (the 'Section 34 Prohibition'). The types of agreements caught by the Section 34 Prohibition include hardcore agreements such as price fixing, output limitation, bid rigging and market sharing (where the appreciability of their negative effects on competition is presumed), and other types of agreements such as fixing trading conditions, joint purchasing or selling, sharing information, exchanging price information, exchanging non-price information, restricting advertising and setting technical or design standards. The Section 34 Prohibition is closely modelled on Chapter 1 of the UK Competition Act 1998 and Article 101 of the Treaty of the Functioning of the European Union (formerly

[2] UK Competition Act 1998, Chapter 41 (UK Competition Act 1998).

[3] Parliament of Singapore, 'Competition Bill', Vol. 78 *Official Report, Parliamentary Debates* (19 October 2004) Cols. 863–890 (Dr Vivian Balakrishnan, Senior Minister of State for Trade and Industry). Retrieved from https://sprs.parl.gov.sg/search/topic?reportid=035_20041019_S0004_T0006.

[4] Singapore Competition Act, Section 34.

[5] Ibid., Section 47.

[6] Ibid., Section 54.

Article 81 of the European Community Treaty). Accordingly, decisions from the UK and European Union are generally highly persuasive when interpreting the Section 34 Prohibition.[7]

The CCCS, formerly known as the Competition Commission of Singapore (CCS), is the authority tasked with enforcing the Singapore Competition Act, and was established on 1 January 2005 as a statutory body under the arm of the Ministry of Trade and Industry.

The CCS was renamed the CCCS (with effect from 1 April 2018) after taking on the additional function of administering the Consumer Protection (Fair Trading) Act (Chapter 52A). This reform brings Singapore in line with jurisdictions such as Australia, Japan, South Korea and the UK, where the protection of fair trading, antitrust and competition is carried out by a single agency.

Additionally, the Competition (Amendment) Act came into effect on 16 May 2018. This amendment follows a public consultation on the proposed changes to the Singapore Competition Act, which was conducted by the CCCS between 21 December 2017 and 11 January 2018. The key aims of the amendments are to provide the CCCS with appropriate enforcement tools in line with international best practices and to streamline existing processes. Some key amendments include amendments to Sections 60A and 60B of the Singapore Competition Act to allow the CCCS to accept binding and enforceable commitments for cases involving anti-competitive agreements under the Section 34 Prohibition. The investigative powers of the CCCS have also been streamlined under Sections 64 and 65 of the Singapore Competition Act.

As of 30 June 2021, the CCCS had issued sixteen cartel infringement decisions, with the highest financial penalties imposed in the CCCS cartel infringement decision on 12 September 2018 concerning fresh chicken distributors.[8]

Out of the sixteen cartel infringement decisions, three infringement decisions were issued against international cartels. In 2014, the CCCS issued its first two infringement decisions against international cartels.[9]

[7] See *Re Pang's Motor Trading* v. *Competition Commission of Singapore, Appeal No. 1 of 2013* [2014] SGCAB 1, para. 33.

[8] CCCS 500/7002/14: Notice of Infringement Decision in relation to the sale and distribution of fresh chicken products in Singapore (12 September 2018).

[9] See CCS 700/002/11, Infringement of the Section 34 Prohibition in relation to the supply of ball and roller bearings, and CCS 700/003/11 (27 May 2014), Infringement of the Section 34 Prohibition in relation to the provision of air freight forwarding services for shipments from Japan to Singapore (11 December 2014).

Table 10.1 *Financial penalties imposed by the CCCS: 1 January 2006–30 June 2021*

International cartel cases	*Fines (millions)*
Aluminium electrolytic capacitors cartel	S$19.55 (US$ 14.47)
Ball bearings cartel	S$9.31 (US$ 6.89)
Freight forwarders cartel	S$7.15 (US$ 5.29)
Domestic cartel cases	*Fines (millions)*
Fresh chicken distributors cartel	S$20.11 (US$14.79)[10]
Express bus operators cartel	S$1.70 (US$1.25)
Hotel room accommodation cartel	S$1.52 (US$1.12)
Financial advisers cartel	S$0.91 (US$0.67)
Electrical services and asset tagging services cartel	S$0.63 (US$0.46)
Swimming pools and other water features maintenance services cartel	S$0.42 (US$0.31)
Modelling agencies cartel	S$0.36 (US$0.27)
Ferry operators cartel	S$0.29 (US$0.21)
Pest control operators cartel	S$0.26 (US$0.19)
Electric works cartel	S$0.19 (US$0.14)
Motor vehicle traders cartel	S$0.18 (US$0.13)
Employment agencies cartel	S$0.15 (US$0.11)
Building, construction and maintenance contractors cartel	S$0.03 (US$0.02)

More recently, in January 2018, the CCCS issued a third infringement decision regarding an international cartel, involving manufacturers of aluminium electrolytic capacitors.[11] A full list of financial penalties imposed by the CCCS in cartel cases is set out in Table 10.1.

10.3 The Singapore Leniency Programme

The detection of cartels is an inherently difficult and costly exercise.[12] In practice, enforcement of the Singapore Competition Act against cartels that are, by their very nature, secretive and discreet is both demanding

[10] See Consent Order (8 August 2019) between Kee Song Food Corporation (S) Pte. Ltd. and CCCS and [2020] SGCAB 1: Decision of the Competition Appeal Board (4 December 2020). Penalties imposed by CCCS on some of the undertakings were reduced upon their appeals before the Competition Appeal Board, and the total fines were reduced from circa S$26.95 million to circa S$20.11 million.

[11] See CCS 700/002/13, Notice of Infringement Decision issued by CCS in relation to the market for sale, distribution and pricing of Aluminium Electrolytic Capacitors in Singapore (5 January 2018).

[12] PLC Cross-Border Handbooks, *Competition: Volume 2 – Leniency* (Toronto: Practical Law Company, 2008), p. 9.

and challenging for an Asian (but global) city like Singapore. In particular, Singapore's high density of corporate headquarters and concentration of foreign subsidiaries arguably make it a gateway between the East and the West, thus heightening the risk of international cartel activity via local proxy. The CCCS, tasked with administering and enforcing the Singapore Competition Act, recognises cartel agreements to be the most serious type of infringement of the Section 34 Prohibition. Due to the clandestine nature of cartels, the CCCS decided that incentives should be given to undertakings participating (or which may have participated) in cartels to come forward and out the cartel activity. In the CCCS's view, the policy of granting leniency to undertakings that cooperate with the CCCS 'outweighs the policy objectives of imposing financial penalties on such cartel participants'.[13]

In order to provide proper incentives for such undertakings to come forward with information on cartel activities, a leniency programme was introduced in 2006 (and was subsequently revised in 2009 and 2016). The CCCS's leniency programme is detailed in its Leniency Guidelines 2016, which were issued pursuant to Section 61 of the Singapore Competition Act.

The changes in the Leniency Guidelines 2016, which represent a distinct departure from the CCCS's past leniency policy, include the following:

1. Leniency applicants must unconditionally admit to the cartel conduct.
2. Leniency applicants must grant an appropriate waiver of confidentiality to the CCCS in respect of any jurisdiction where the applicant has also applied for leniency or any other regulatory authority that it has informed of the conduct.
3. An undertaking that has initiated or coerced another undertaking to take part in the cartel activity is now eligible for leniency for up to a 50 per cent reduction in the financial penalty.

Singapore's leniency programme shares many key features with the leniency programmes of long-established competition jurisdictions. Similar leniency programmes have been found to be effective in other competition law regimes. These include, inter alia, the following:

1. A sliding scale where the reduction of financial penalties depends on the position of the applicant in the leniency queue.

[13] See CCCS, 'CCCS Guidelines on Lenient Treatment for Undertakings Coming Forward with Information on Cartel Activity Cases 2016' (2016), para. 1.5 (Leniency Guidelines 2016).

2. A marker system for the applicant to retain its place in the leniency queue while it gathers the necessary information and evidence to perfect the marker and qualify for leniency or immunity.
3. The requirement of full and frank disclosure and an ongoing obligation to cooperate with the CCCS.
4. The requirement for the applicant to cease all existing cartel activity unless instructed to do otherwise by the CCCS.

The above features are designed to incentivise cartel members to voluntarily provide the CCCS with incriminating evidence of their cartel activities. Under the sliding scale, the maximum reduction of financial penalties granted to subsequent applications is capped at 50 per cent. This creates a strong incentive for cartel members to voluntarily provide the CCCS with evidence of cartel activity early, rather than adopting a wait-and-see approach. This redefines the dynamic of the cartel, from a cooperative collusive understanding to that of a competitive zero-sum interaction.

10.3.1 Conditions for Leniency

The Leniency Guidelines 2016 set out the conditions to be satisfied before an undertaking or leniency applicant can receive the benefit of leniency. Specifically, all leniency applicants must satisfy the conditions set out below:

1. Provide the CCCS with all the information, documents and evidence available to the leniency applicant regarding the cartel activity immediately. The information, documents and evidence must provide the CCCS with sufficient basis to commence an investigation.
2. Grant an appropriate waiver of confidentiality to the CCCS in respect of any jurisdiction where the applicant has also applied for leniency or any other regulatory authority that the leniency applicant has informed of the conduct.
3. Unconditionally admit to the conduct for which leniency is sought and detail the extent to which this had an impact in Singapore by preventing, restricting or distorting competition within Singapore.
4. Maintain continuous and complete cooperation throughout the investigation and until the conclusion of any action by the CCCS arising as a result of the investigation.
5. Refrain from further participation in the cartel activity from the time of disclosure of the cartel activity to the CCCS (except as may be directed by the CCCS).

10.3.1.1 Total Immunity from Financial Penalties

Full immunity from administrative penalties is available in Singapore. An applicant stands to benefit from full immunity from financial penalties if the applicant is the first in line to provide the CCCS with evidence of the cartel activity before an investigation has commenced, provided that the CCCS does not already have sufficient information to establish the existence of the alleged cartel activity, and subject to the satisfaction of the general conditions for applicants set out in the Leniency Guidelines 2016, and as outlined above.

10.3.1.2 Reduction of up to 100 Per Cent in the Level of Financial Penalties

Where the undertaking is the first to come forward but only after an investigation has commenced, the undertaking may nevertheless benefit from a reduction of up to 100 per cent of the financial penalty if:

1. The applicant is still the first to provide the CCCS with evidence of the cartel activity.
2. The information is provided to the CCCS after the CCCS has started an investigation but before the CCCS has sufficient information to issue a Proposed Infringement Decision (PID) pursuant to Section 68(1) of the Singapore Competition Act.
3. The information adds significant value to the CCCS's investigation.
4. The applicant has not initiated or coerced another undertaking to take part in the cartel activity.
5. The applicant satisfies the general conditions set out in the Leniency Guidelines 2016.

10.3.1.3 Reduction of up to 50 Per Cent in the Level of Financial Penalties

If an applicant is not the first to come forward, but (1) provides useful evidence before the CCCS issues a PID that the Section 34 Prohibition has been infringed; or (2) the applicant has initiated or coerced another undertaking to take part in the cartel activity, the applicant may still be granted a reduction of up to 50 per cent of the financial penalty.[14]

Any reduction in the level of the financial penalty under these circumstances is discretionary and the CCCS will take into account (1) the stage at

[14] Leniency Guidelines 2016, para. 4.

which the applicant came forward; (2) the evidence already in the CCCS's possession; and (3) the quality of the information provided.

10.3.1.4 Leniency Plus System

The CCCS also employs a leniency plus system to encourage cartel members cooperating with an investigation by the CCCS in one market (the first market) to report their involvement (if any) in a completely separate cartel activity in another market (the second market). Under leniency plus, an applicant may be granted a further reduction in the financial penalties imposed on it in relation to the first market, in addition to the reduction that it would have received for its cooperation in the first market alone.

An applicant can qualify for leniency plus if the CCCS is satisfied that both the following are the case:

1. The evidence provided by the applicant relates to a completely separate cartel activity.
2. The applicant would qualify for full immunity or a reduction of up to 100 per cent in the amount of the financial penalty for its activities in the second market.

The leniency applicant is not required to have applied for or received leniency in the first market, and can benefit from leniency plus as long as it is receiving a reduction in the first market by way of cooperation as a mitigating factor.[15] In the CCCS Guidelines on the Appropriate Amount of Penalty 2016, cooperation is described as a mitigating factor that enables the enforcement process to be more efficacious and concluded more speedily.

The leniency plus system was used in the Fresh Chicken Distributors cartel decision. Some of the leniency applicants provided evidence relating to separate cartel activity for which conditional leniency was granted. Accordingly, the leniency applicant was granted a further undisclosed reduction under the leniency plus system.

10.3.1.5 Leniency Submissions and the Fast-Track Procedure

Leniency applicants are also eligible for the fast-track procedure (FTP). Under the FTP, a leniency applicant is eligible to an additional discount on top of leniency. For example, if a leniency applicant is granted a 40 per cent reduction in financial penalties due to leniency, the leniency applicant can receive a

[15] Ibid., para. 6.3.

further 10 per cent reduction due to the fast-track procedure. Overall, the leniency applicant will receive a reduction of 50 per cent in financial penalties.[16]

The FTP was applied for the first time in the recent Swimming Pools and Other Water Features Maintenance Services decision. Some of the leniency applicants signed a fast-track agreement with CCCS in which they, among other things, agreed to cooperate throughout CCCS's investigation and confirmed that they will not make extensive written representations or request to inspect the documents and evidence in CCCS's file. Accordingly, each of the leniency applicants was granted a further 10 per cent reduction under the FTP.

10.3.1.6 The CCCS's Reward/Whistle-Blowing Scheme

The leniency programme is not the only tool the CCCS has at its disposal to incentivise parties to come forward with critical information regarding cartels. Another tool that the CCCS uses to incentivise whistleblowers is its Reward/Whistle Blowing Scheme. The CCCS's Reward/Whistle Blowing Scheme provides financial rewards to informants for providing information about competition infringements. Under the CCCS Reward/ Whistle Blowing Scheme, rewards of up to S$120,000 (approximately US$88,000) can be paid out to parties who come forward with information regarding competition infringements.[17]

The reward is not available for individuals or business owners directly involved in competition infringements; the applicable regime for such approaches would be the leniency programme. Moreover, the reward will not be awarded if the subject matter of the complaint and/or information provided is already under investigation by the CCCS.

The actual amount paid out is determined at the sole discretion of the CCCS and the CCCS can reject offers of information without giving any reasons. The CCCS can only assess the value of the information given just before the issuance of the infringement decision; accordingly, the exact quantum of reward available is usually not available until the value of the information is assessed.

The CCCS relied on information provided by a secret informant in the Fresh Chicken Distributors cartel decision. The sum of the reward given to the secret informant was not publicly disclosed.

16 See CCCS, 'CCCS Practice Statement on the Fast Track Procedure for Section 34 and 47 Cases 2016' (2016), para. 5.3.

17 See CCCS, 'FAQ: Approach CCCS for Leniency or Reward' (2018). Retrieved from www.cccs.gov.sg/faq/approaching-cccs-for-leniency-or-reward.

10.4 Application Procedure

Leniency applications must be submitted to the CCCS. Any person contacting the CCCS on an undertaking's behalf must have power to represent the undertaking.

10.4.1 Informal and Confidential Guidance

The CCCS allows for initial contact or 'feelers' to be made anonymously by potential applicants, or their authorised representatives (for example, external legal counsel), to ascertain if immunity or leniency is available. This would usually be made by way of a without prejudice telephone call. The CCCS will typically require a brief description of the market concerned, the conduct involved and the relevant time period before it can respond on whether immunity or leniency is available.

10.4.2 Form of Application

There are four ways to submit a leniency application to the CCCS:

1. By submitting online (however, the online forms do not support attachments),
2. By emailing the complete CCCS leniency application form together with the supporting documents to the CCCS.
3. By posting the complete CCCS leniency application form together with the supporting documents directly to the CCCS.
4. By arranging to meet the CCCS in person by calling the CCCS's hotline to set up an appointment.

10.4.3 Marker System

The CCCS marker system for leniency applications is based on the 'first-in' principle. If a first-in applicant is not able to, at the time of the application, provide the CCCS with all the evidence relating to the suspected infringement available to the applicant, the applicant may apply for a marker to secure its position in the leniency queue. This marker system encourages applicants to come forward early by giving them the assurance that their position in the queue will be secure even if they need time to gather the information and evidence needed.

The following rules apply in relation to markers:

1. A marker protects the first-in-line applicant's place in the queue for a limited period of time specified by the CCCS to allow it to gather the necessary information and evidence to perfect the marker. The CCCS will grant markers to subsequent leniency applicants to secure their rank so long as first-in-line immunity or leniency (i.e. total immunity or a reduction of up to 100 per cent in financial penalties) is still available.
2. For an applicant to secure a marker, it must provide its name and a description of the cartel conduct in sufficient detail to allow the CCCS to determine that no other applicant has applied for immunity or a reduction of up to 100 per cent for such similar conduct. Additionally, the CCCS now requires, in accordance with the Leniency Guidelines 2016, that an applicant define the market in which the cartel activity occurred and detail the impact of the conduct on the identified relevant markets in Singapore.[18]
3. If the first-in-line applicant fails to perfect the marker, the next applicant in the marker queue will be allowed to perfect its marker to obtain immunity or a reduction of up to 100 per cent in financial penalties.
4. To perfect a marker, the applicant must provide information, documents and evidence that meet the requirements for a grant of conditional immunity or leniency.
5. There are no set deadlines in the Leniency Guidelines 2016 for the perfection of a marker. At the point when a first-in-line marker is granted, the applicant will discuss the timing and the process of perfecting the marker with the CCCS. The length of time given by the CCCS can range from two weeks to one month, and varies on a case-by-case basis. The CCCS has stated that it will work with leniency applicants who genuinely cooperate with the CCCS to set reasonable time frames for providing information and evidence in relation to the reported cartel.

The CCCS retains discretion over the grant of a marker. However, the CCCS notes that granting of a marker is expected to be the norm rather than the exception.[19] This is in line with past practice and observed precedent thus far.

[18] See Leniency Guidelines 2016, para. 5.5.

[19] Ibid., para. 5.7.

10.4.4 Oral Statements

The CCCS can accept leniency statements made orally. Information provided to the CCCS by a leniency applicant in Singapore can take the form of oral leniency statements. The Leniency Guidelines 2016 provide that undertakings can offer information relating to a suspected infringement by way of an oral corporate statement. Oral corporate statements will be recorded and transcribed at the CCCS's premises. Where an oral corporate statement is made, the applicant and/or its legal representatives will be given the opportunity to verify the accuracy of the CCCS's transcript.[20]

10.4.5 Grant of Conditional Immunity or Leniency

When the CCCS is satisfied that the conditions for conditional immunity or leniency have been met, it will issue a letter to the applicant confirming the grant of conditional immunity or leniency. The letter will state the conditions and continuing obligations that the applicant has to meet to maintain its conditional immunity or leniency. Failure to abide by the conditions and obligations may lead to the CCCS revoking the grant of conditional immunity or leniency.[21]

10.4.6 Scope of Protection

Where the CCCS uncovers information that it considers to be the subject of a separate infringement falling outside of the scope of the leniency granted, the leniency received by an applicant will not extend to the separate infringement.

If the applicant failed to comply with the terms on which conditional immunity or leniency was granted, or made a false declaration or gave false information to the CCCS at any point in time, the CCCS can revoke the grant of conditional immunity or leniency. If the CCCS is minded to revoke the grant of conditional immunity or leniency, the applicant will be notified in writing and given an opportunity to make representations.[22] If the CCCS revokes the grant of conditional immunity or leniency (or if a leniency applicant withdraws its leniency application), leniency or immunity may be available to the next-in-line applicant. It is likely (albeit

[20] Ibid., para. 5.10.
[21] Ibid., para. 5.12.
[22] Ibid., para. 11.2.

untested) that the withdrawal of a leniency application could only be practically done before the issuance of a final decision by the CCCS.

10.5 Leniency Submissions and Domestic Discovery

While information such as written submissions and supporting documents provided by any immunity or leniency applicants may also potentially be included in the CCCS's inspection files to which defendants are granted access, it is understood that the CCCS does not grant access to files by third parties seeking damages, pursuant to Section 89 of the Singapore Competition Act, which requires the CCCS to withhold such confidential information.

There may be a possibility for a third-party claimant, pursuing a future claim against an undertaking or defendant based on rights of private action arising out of a CCCS infringement decision, pursuant to Section 86 of the Singapore Competition Act, to apply in the context of such civil proceedings for the following:

1. Discovery against one or more defendants to a CCCS infringement decision (that is, against the undertakings subject to an infringement decision by the CCCS, and who were granted access to inspection files by the CCCS) to require the defendants to furnish copies of documents taken or copied by these defendants from the CCCS's inspection files.
2. Third-party discovery against the CCCS to require the CCCS to disclose the documents in its inspection files, or any document withheld from the inspection files.

This issue of whether the leniency statements and documents, as submitted to the CCCS pursuant to a leniency application, are discoverable in a right of private action remains untested. Unlike jurisdictions such as the United States and Australia[23], the right of private action in Singapore exists by way of a follow-on action, which precludes independent standalone action by claimants. In Singapore, for a civil claim based on a right of private action, the court will be bound by the infringement decision of the CCCS, and any findings of the infringement will be accepted as final and conclusive; the civil claim will not involve a decision on liability but the appropriate remedy and quantum of damages (if applicable). Discovery

[23] United States of America Clayton Antitrust Act, Section 4, 15 U.S.C. Section 15; Competition and Consumer Act 2010 No. 51 of 1974 of the Commonwealth of Australia, Section 82.

will be determined in accordance with Order 24 of the Rules of Court,[24] which governs the discovery process in a civil proceeding. To date, there have not been any claims in civil proceedings in Singapore courts under a right of private action by third parties arising from infringement decisions by the CCCS. Accordingly, the possibility of civil litigants applying for discovery against infringing undertakings or the CCCS (or both), and which documents and submissions are discoverable, remains untested.

10.6 Leniency in Practice

In recent years there has been a notable increase in the number of publicised instances of parties applying for immunity or leniency under the CCCS's leniency programme. The CCCS notes that it has more than thirty leniency cases involving more than sixty leniency applicants.[25] As of 30 June 2021, the leniency programme had led to the issuance of infringement decisions and the impositions of financial penalties in nine cases. This amounts to more than 50 per cent of all cartel infringement decisions issued by the CCCS to date.

The CCCS notes that the rise of leniency applications may be attributable to a number of factors, such as the perception of the CCCS as an active and rigorous enforcer, a growing level of awareness of the CCCS's leniency programme and trust in the way in which the CCCS administers the programme.[26]

10.6.1 International Cartel Cases

Large financial penalties were imposed by the CCCS against the infringing parties in the three international cartel cases thus far, notwithstanding that the financial penalties had also been reduced for the immunity and/or leniency applicants across these three cases. Significantly, it is observable that entities are filing for leniency in Singapore as a proxy for amnesty from regulators of Southeast Asia, the majority of which have antitrust regimes but not necessarily leniency programmes.

[24] Supreme Court of Judicature Act (Chapter 322, Section 80), Rules of Court (Rev. Ed. 2014) (Rules of Court).

[25] See OECD, 'Roundtable on Challenges and Co-ordination of Leniency Programmes – Note by Singapore', DAF/COMP/WP3/WD(2018)19 (2018), para. 5. Retrieved from www.oecd.org/daf/competition/challenges-and-coordination-of-leniency-programmes.htm.

[26] Ibid., para. 6.

In *Ball Bearings*,[27] the CCCS received leniency applications in 2011–2012 that related to anti-competitive agreements in respect of an autoparts international cartel, in particular the sales, distribution and prices of ball and roller bearings to aftermarket customers in Singapore. Following investigations, the CCCS issued infringement findings in respect of a single continuous infringement that took place during the period from at least 1998 (seven years before the Singapore Competition Act came into force on 1 January 2006). In particular, the CCCS found that a parent company can be held jointly and severally liable for an infringement of Section 34 of the Singapore Competition Act committed by its subsidiary company, where the parent company exercises decisive influence on the subsidiary company's commercial conduct at the time of the infringement. The leniency programme was applied and the CCCS imposed financial penalties totalling S$9.31 million (approximately US$6.89 million).

In *Air Freight Forwarders*,[28] the CCCS became aware in 2011 that international freight forwarders may have been involved in anti-competitive activity that had an impact in Singapore, and made inquiries with freight forwarders. The CCCS subsequently commenced its investigation in July 2012 pursuant to multiple leniency applications received following the inquiries. The CCCS issued infringement findings in respect of the conduct that took place prior to November 2007, four years before the CCCS first made inquiries with freight forwarders. The leniency programme was applied and the CCCS imposed financial penalties totalling S$7.15 million (approximately US$5.29 million).

In *Aluminium Electrolytic Capacitors*,[29] the CCCS's investigations revealed a consistent and regular pattern of communication between the infringing undertakings, from at least 1997 until 25 March 2013. This marked the longest potential duration of infringement that the CCCS had investigated since its inception. In the infringement decision itself, the CCCS found that three of the infringing undertakings were parties to a single continuous infringement for more than seven years, while the remaining undertakings

27 CCS 700/002/11: Notice of Infringement Decision in relation to the supply of ball and roller bearings (27 May 2014).

28 CCS 700/003/11: Notice of Infringement Decision in relation to the provision of air freight forwarding services for shipments from Japan to Singapore (11 December 2014) (*Air Freight Forwarders*).

29 CCS 700/002/13: Notice of Infringement Decision issued by CCS in relation to the market for sale, distribution and pricing of Aluminium Electrolytic Capacitors in Singapore (5 January 2018).

were party to the single continuous infringement for just over three years. The first in line to apply for leniency received total immunity from financial penalties, while the other leniency applicants were also awarded a discount in accordance with their position in the leniency queue. The total financial penalties amounted to S$19.55 million (approximately US$14.47 million), one of the highest in the CCCS's history, even after discounts for leniency.

10.6.2 Other Notable Domestic Cartel Cases

In *Electrical and Building Works*,[30] the leniency programme was applied and the CCCS imposed financial penalties totalling S$187,592.94 (approximately US$132,000).

In *Electrical Services and Asset Tagging Services*,[31] the leniency programme was applied and the CCCS imposed financial penalties totalling S$626,118 (approximately US$465,550).

In the infringement decisions mentioned above:

1. The first-in leniency applicant received full immunity from fines.
2. The subsequent leniency applicants received reductions in the financial penalty (amount of reduction not disclosed in the CCCS's published decisions).

In *Hotel Room Accommodation*,[32] the leniency programme was applied and the CCCS imposed financial penalties totalling S$1,522,354 (approximately US$1.12 million) against four parties. The first-in leniency applicant in this case did not receive full immunity from fines because it only came forward after the CCCS exercised its formal powers of investigation under Section 63 of the Singapore Competition Act. Accordingly, the first-in leniency applicant was awarded an undisclosed reduction in penalty.

In *Fresh Chicken Distributors*, the leniency programme was applied and the CCCS imposed financial penalties totalling S$26,948,639 (approximately US$19.87 million; which were subsequently reduced to S$20,111,163, approximately US$14.79 million) against thirteen fresh

[30] CCS 500/001/09: Notice of Infringement Decision in relation to collusive tendering (bid-rigging) in electrical and building works (4 June 2010).

[31] CCS 700/003/15: Notice of Infringement Decision in relation to bid-rigging of tenders in Singapore for electrical services and asset tagging services (28 November 2017).

[32] CCCS 700/002/14: Notice of Infringement Decision in relation to the exchange of confidential corporate customer information in the provision of hotel room accommodation in Singapore (30 January 2019) (*Hotel Room Accommodation*).

chicken distributors. The first-in leniency applicant in this case did not receive full immunity from fines because it only applied for leniency after the CCCS began its investigations. Accordingly, the first-in leniency applicant was awarded an undisclosed reduction in penalty.

A point of interest to note in *Fresh Chicken Distributors* was the way the leniency programme was applied. The CCCS issued notices of the PID to the parties on 8 March 2016 and the parties submitted written and oral representations to the CCCS. Thereafter, on 27 September 2016, the CCCS informed the parties that further investigations needed to be done based on the parties' earlier representations to the CCCS, and it was at this point in time that the parties were informed of the continued availability of leniency. As a result, four parties successfully applied for leniency. After further investigations, the CCCS sent notices of the supplementary PID to the parties on 21 December 2017.[33]

In *Building, Construction and Maintenance Tenders*,[34] the leniency programme was applied and the CCCS imposed financial penalties totalling S$32,098 (approximately US$23,500) against three parties. The first-in leniency applicant did not receive full immunity from fines because (1) it only came forward after the CCCS exercised its formal powers of investigation under Section 63 of the Singapore Competition Act; (2) it was considered by the CCCS to be an initiator and coordinator of the bid-rigging arrangements; (3) it did not fully cooperate with the CCCS's investigation; and (4) it did not provide very useful information in relation to the investigation. The ultimate reduction in the financial penalty provided to the first-in applicant was not publicly disclosed.

In the CCCS's most recent decision, *Swimming Pools and Other Water Features Maintenance Services*,[35] the leniency programme was applied and the CCCS imposed financial penalties totalling S$419,014 (approximately US$308,100) against the three parties. The first-in leniency applicant did not receive full immunity from fines because it only applied for leniency after the CCCS began its investigations. Accordingly, the first-in leniency applicant was awarded an undisclosed reduction in penalty.

[33] CCCS 500/7002/14: CCCS Penalises Fresh Chicken Distributors for Price-fixing and Non-compete Agreements (12 September 2018), paras. 61–68 (*Fresh Chicken Distributors*).

[34] CCCS 500/7003/16: Notice of Infringement Decision in relation to bid rigging of building, construction and maintenance tenders (4 June 2020) (*Building, Construction and Maintenance Tenders*).

[35] CCCS 700/002/14: Notice of Infringement Decision in relation to the provision of maintenance services for swimming pools, spas, fountains and water features (14 December 2020) (*Swimming Pools and Other Water Features Maintenance Services*).

10.6.3 Interaction between Leniency and Mitigation

Another point to note in *Fresh Chicken Distributors* is how the CCCS has treated cooperation as a mitigating factor, when leniency has already been granted. In previous decisions, the CCCS has consistently rejected cooperation as a valid mitigating factor given that cooperation is a pre-condition for leniency.[36]

In contrast, in *Fresh Chicken Distributors*, cooperation was considered a valid mitigating factor despite leniency already having been granted for the leniency applicants; a reduction in penalty was granted for three of the leniency applicants for their cooperation.[37]

It is unclear why the CCCS chose to consider cooperation as a mitigating factor in *Fresh Chicken Distributors*. One possible reason is because the parties were told to apply for leniency only after the first PID was issued and the CCCS might have been accounting for the cooperation the parties provided before they applied for leniency. However, this contrasts with the earlier decision in *Air Freight Forwarders*. In that case, the leniency applicants argued that mitigation should be awarded on top of the leniency discount because they began cooperating even before applying for leniency.[38] The CCCS declined to grant any extra cooperation discount in mitigation because (1) there is no reason to grant an extra cooperation discount in addition to a leniency discount given that cooperation is a pre-condition for leniency, and (2) their cooperation was already accounted for in the leniency discount.

The subsequent decisions of *Hotel Room Accommodation*, *Building, Construction and Maintenance Tenders* and *Swimming Pools and Other Water Features Maintenance Services* seem to be in line with the previous decisions, in so far as the CCCS declined to consider cooperation as a mitigating factor because it was already considered for the purposes of the leniency discount.[39]

10.7 Role of Counsel in Leniency Applications in Singapore

Counsel plays a vital role in multiple aspects when it comes to leniency applications in Singapore.

[36] See the following cases: *Aluminium Electrolytic Capacitors*, *Electrical and Building Works*, *Ball Bearings*, *Air Freight Forwarders* and *Electrical Services and Asset Tagging Services*.

[37] *Fresh Chicken Distributors*, paras. 563, 576 and 665.

[38] *Air Freight Forwarders*, para. 698.

[39] *Hotel Room Accommodation*, para. 613; *Building, Construction and Maintenance Tenders*, paras. 166, 180 and 191; *Swimming Pools and Other Water Features Maintenance Services*, paras. 195 and 208.

First and foremost, counsel will identify situations where leniency is worth pursuing, and will draw the possibility of a leniency application to the attention of the client. The CCCS has noted that awareness of the availability and requirements for leniency applications is still lacking in Singapore. According to a stakeholder perception survey conducted by the CCCS in 2019, only 6.4 per cent of businesses surveyed had heard of the CCCS's leniency programme.[40] Moreover, even where a business is aware of the leniency programme, it may be tempting to wish to initiate the programme out of caution, prior to the true exposure to a competition law violation being properly determined through an assessment of the facts. Initiating the programme means that the applicant admits that the cartel conduct has occurred and potentially opens the door for follow-on private damages claims, which are matters on which guidance of experienced counsel should be sought.

Secondly, counsel can help ensure applicants comply with the conditions for leniency as set out in the Leniency Guidelines 2016. For example, to secure a marker, an applicant is expected to define the market in which the cartel activity occurred and detail the impact of the conduct on the identified relevant markets in Singapore.[41] The concept of a relevant market may not be easily accessible to a leniency applicant without experience with competition law. As the CCCS notes in its Guidelines on Market Definition, defining a relevant market often requires 'an assessment of the various types of evidence and the exercise of judgement'.[42] The CCCS notes that it has had situations where investigated undertakings fail to identify the correct entities or articulate the conduct for which they are applying for leniency.[43] There is a real risk that leniency applicants may fail to meet these requirements if they are not properly advised.

The consequences of not complying with the conditions of leniency can be potentially severe. The CCCS can withdraw a leniency applicant's marker. The CCCS can also revoke the grant of conditional immunity/ leniency or leniency.[44]

[40] See CCCS, 'Executive Summary: CCS Stakeholder Perception Survey Results 2019' (November 2020). Retrieved from www.cccs.gov.sg/resources/publications/cccs-stakeholder-perception-survey/cccs-stakeholder-perception-survey-results-2019.

[41] Leniency Guidelines 2016, para. 5.5.

[42] CCCS, 'CCCS Guidelines on Market Definition' (2007), para. 2.10.

[43] See OECD, 'Roundtable on Challenges and Co-ordination' (n. 25 above), para. 33.

[44] See Leniency Guidelines 2016, para. 11.2.

In *Electrical Services and Asset Tagging Services*,[45] one of the leniency applicants failed to adhere to the condition of 'continuous and complete co-operation' as well as the condition that it 'unconditionally admit to the conduct for which leniency is sought' under the Leniency Guidelines 2016, because it persistently denied liability for initiating the bid rigging; this was in contrast to what it initially submitted in its leniency application. Accordingly, the CCCS reduced the leniency discount offered to it.[46]

Thirdly, it is noteworthy that Singapore has four national languages (English, Mandarin Chinese, Tamil and Malay) and investigated parties are not always fluent in English, the language in which the CCCS conducts its affairs. This results in counsel serving an important role in ensuring that signed statements provided by interviewees are fully understood, along with the implications of any statements therein.

Fourthly, competition investigations in Singapore can often involve international cartels, and thus different competition law regimes. It is frequently critically important to assess how the submission of a leniency application in one jurisdiction may have implications in another jurisdiction (or the associated rights of defence available in that other jurisdiction).

10.8 International Cooperation

10.8.1 Singapore's Economy

Singapore is one of the most open economies in the world. In the Global Competitiveness Report 2019, Singapore ranked first in the world in the report's Global Competitiveness Index 4.0.[47] Singapore has close economic ties with neighbouring countries in Southeast Asia. It is part of the ten-nation Association of Southeast Asian Nations (ASEAN), which established the ASEAN Economic Community (AEC) on 31 December 2015. The AEC aims to integrate Southeast Asian economies into a single market and production base. ASEAN currently has a combined gross domestic product of US$3.2 trillion, making it the fifth largest economy in

[45] Case No. CCS 700/003/15: Notice of Infringement Decision in relation to bid-rigging of tenders in Singapore for electrical services and asset tagging services (28 December 2017).

[46] Ibid., para. 291.

[47] See World Economic Forum, 'The Global Competitiveness Report Index 4.0 2019 edition (Singapore)' (2019). Retrieved from http://reports.weforum.org/global-competitiveness-report-2019/economy-profiles/#economy=SGP.

the world. Within ASEAN, Singapore is the largest exporter and importer. Singapore accounted for 27.5 per cent of ASEAN's exports and 25.8 per cent of ASEAN's imports in 2019.[48]

With no natural hinterland and being open (importing approximately 90 per cent of goods), Singapore is particularly susceptible and vulnerable to the anti-competitive effects of global and local cartels. Therefore, Singapore needs to pursue its own competition enforcement, with the aid of foreign competition bodies, to protect its markets and consumers.

10.8.2 Overview of Singapore's International Cooperation

The Singapore Competition Act, in Sections 87 and 88, provides a mechanism by which the CCCS may enter into arrangements with foreign competition bodies to, inter alia, provide assistance and furnish to each other information required by the other party for the purpose of performing its functions. The Singapore Competition Act also provides that the CCCS need not furnish any information to a foreign competition body pursuant to such arrangements unless, as a requirement, a written undertaking is obtained from the foreign competition body that it will comply with the terms specified in the requirement.

According to the CCCS, it has entered into various Regional Cooperation Agreements (RCAs) that promote international cooperation for effective competition enforcement.[49] The RCAs can be broadly classified into non-competition-specific RCAs and competition-specific RCAs.

The non-competition-specific RCAs refer to Singapore's multilateral and bilateral free trade agreements (FTA) that have chapters pertaining to competition. The provisions in the competition chapter of FTAs commonly require the signatories to exchange information and cooperate in the development of any new competition measures. Currently, Singapore has about sixteen FTAs with a competition chapter. In 2018, Singapore entered into the Comprehensive and Progressive Trans-Pacific Partnership Agreement (CPTPP) with ten other partners. The CPTPP contains a competition chapter that highlights the need for cooperation to enable effective competition law enforcement. More recently, in

[48] See ASEAN Secretariat, 'ASEAN Key Figures 2020' (2020), pp. 39 and 50. Retrieved from www.aseanstats.org/publication/akf_2020.

[49] OECD, 'Regional Competition Agreements: Benefits and Challenges – Contribution from Singapore', DAF/COMP/GF/WD(2018)75 (2018).

2019 Singapore signed the Eurasian Economic Union–Singapore Free Trade Agreement (EAEUSFTA) with Armenia, Belarus, Kazakhstan, Kyrgyzstan and Russia, and in 2020 the Regional Comprehensive Economic Partnership (RCEP) with fourteen other partners. While the EAEUSFTA and RCEP have yet to enter into force, each of them similarly contains a competition chapter that highlights the need for cooperation between the relevant authorities to enable effective competition law enforcement.

Competition-specific RCAs refer to agreements with different competition authorities that usually take the form of a Memorandum of Understanding (MOU) or a Memorandum of Cooperation (MOC). Singapore currently has three MOU/MOCs – one with the Japan Fair Trade Commission since July 2017, one with Indonesia's Commission for the Supervision of Business Competition since August 2018, and more recently one with the Competition Bureau Canada since 17 September 2019. The MOU/MOCs enhance cooperation between the respective competition authorities through the mutual notification of enforcement activities, the provision of an avenue for exchange of information and the coordination of enforcement activities, while recognising the need for each authority to comply with its domestic laws.

In addition to RCAs, the CCCS also utilises informal cooperation mechanisms, such as informal dialogues, to facilitate information sharing. For example, it is understood that the CCCS holds frequent dialogues with the Australian Competition and Consumer Commission and the New Zealand Competition Commission to facilitate general information sharing between the agencies. The CCCS also engages the international community by participating regularly in international conferences and workshops on cartel enforcement held by the Organisation for Economic Co-operation and Development, the International Competition Network, the ASEAN Expert Group on Competition, and Brazil, Russia, India, China and South Africa (i.e. the BRICS nations).

International cooperation can be especially important when investigating cartel cases. The CCCS has engaged in both regional and international cooperation with other competition authorities and regulatory bodies when investigating international cartels with cross-jurisdictional elements. This is done on a case-by-case basis. Instances of such international cooperation include, among others:

1. Sharing information to coordinate dawn raids for evidence preservation.

2. Sharing general information such as theories of harm and general categories of information between the competition authorities. Information is shared to the extent that such information is not confidential, and where waivers have been granted to the CCCS to discuss the matter with other authorities and vice versa.

In sharing information, the CCCS takes into account information provided by leniency applicants, bearing in mind the differences in how each relevant jurisdiction operates, such as the possibility of private actions, discovery obligations that a leniency applicant could be subject to and whether the jurisdiction operates a civil or criminal regime.

The changes in the Leniency Guidelines 2016 could usher in a chapter of enhanced cooperation with other international agencies. In particular, paragraph 2.2 of the Leniency Guidelines 2016 requires a leniency applicant to grant an appropriate waiver of confidentiality in respect of any jurisdiction where the applicant has also applied for leniency or any other regulatory authority that it has informed of the conduct, thus eliminating the risk of confidentiality issues hampering international cooperation.

10.9 Reform

There are no known upcoming revisions to the leniency programme currently under consideration.

In terms of enforcement priorities, the CCCS is embracing its new consumer protection role. In the CCCS's annual report FY19/20[50], the Chief Executive of the CCCS, Ms Sia Aik Kor, noted that the CCCS is closely monitoring the motoring and beauty industries, which have been consistently ranked among the top three industries with the highest number of complaints received by the Consumers Association of Singapore in 2018 and 2019.

Additionally, the CCCS has indicated that it intends to focus on key sectors such as digital platforms, transport and hospitality. In line with this objective, the CCCS published, in 2019, a market study on the online travel booking sector in Singapore and a discussion paper on data portability in collaboration with the Personal Data Protection Commission of Singapore, and in 2020 a market study on e-commerce platforms.

[50] See CCCS, Annual Reports, 'Promoting Competition Protecting Consumers (FY 2019/20)' (2020), p. 6. Retrieved from www.cccs.gov.sg/media-and-publications/publications/in-house-publications/annual-reports.

11

The Leniency Programme in Malaysia's Competition Regime

A Critical Evaluation

CASSEY LEE

11.1 Introduction

Cartel activities – which include coordinated efforts to restrict competition by fixing prices, allocating market share and preventing market entry – are legally prohibited in many competition law regimes. Historically, such activities can be very difficult to detect and prosecute. Due to their illegality and harsh sanctions against them, cartel activities are often undertaken in secrecy to avoid any public scrutiny and attention from competition authorities. Since the 1990s, leniency programmes have become an important tool for competition agencies to tackle cartel activities. Such programmes have proven to be effective in some countries that have implemented them. However, a leniency programme is, in itself, not a sufficiently effective tool to combat cartel activities. A number of factors could affect the efficacy of a leniency programme. These may include the internal design of the leniency programme per se, such as the incentives offered to participants. External factors such as the sanctions on cartel activities, the independence of the competition agency and the political climate could affect the decision to utilise a leniency programme.

For a newly established competition regime, such as the one in Malaysia, being a latecomer in competition law implementation can be advantageous due to the opportunities to learn from the experiences of more mature competition authorities. This includes the design of leniency programmes. However, there might be other factors that could diminish the efficacy of its leniency programme due to its domestic institutional environment. Malaysia's competition law was gazetted in 2010 and the country's competition agency began implementing its leniency programme in 2014. Even though the leniency guidelines have been in existence for more than seven years at the time of this writing, there is little information and study on whether the leniency programme in Malaysia's competition regime has been effective or not. This study aims to fill this knowledge gap by examining and critically evaluating the leniency programme in Malaysia's competition regime.

The outline of this chapter is as follows. Section 11.2 will provide a background on the cartel provisions and leniency programme in Malaysia's competition regime. Section 11.3 will examine the design of the country's leniency programme by comparing it with best-practice standards and the research literature. Section 11.4 will look at how politics and institutions can affect the effectiveness of the country's leniency programme. Section 11.5 provides some evidence on the business community's perception of the quality of institutions in Malaysia in terms of courts and corruption. Section 11.6 concludes.

11.2 Cartel Provisions and Guidelines on Leniency in the Competition Act 2010

Malaysia is a relative newcomer to competition law.[1] The country's competition law, the Competition Act 2010 (CA2010), was gazetted in June 2010 and came into force in January 2012. The enforcement agency for the CA2010 is the Malaysia Competition Commission (MyCC), which was established with the enactment of the Competition Commission Act 2010 (CCA2010). The MyCC began its operations in June 2011.

11.2.1 Cartel Provisions in the Competition Act

Cartel activities are prohibited under Section 4 of the CA2010. The section states that a horizontal agreement between enterprises that has 'the goal or effect [of] significantly preventing, restricting or distorting competition' is legally prohibited (see Box 11.1). The list of cartel activities that are prohibited under Section 4(2) includes price fixing and allocation of market shares. In addition, Section 4(2) also covers activities that limit or control other aspects of business activities such as production, market access, technological development, investment and bid rigging.

[1] For a history of competition law and policy in Malaysia, see Lee, C., 'Malaysia', in Brooks, D. and Evenett, S. (eds.), *Competition Policy and Development in Asia* (London: Palgrave, 2005) 197; Lee, C., 'Competition Law Enforcement in Malaysia: Some Recent Developments' (2014) 51 *Malaysian Journal of Economic Studies* 77.

BOX 11.1: SECTION 4 OF THE COMPETITION ACT 2010 – PROHIBITED HORIZONTAL AND VERTICAL AGREEMENT

4. (1) A horizontal or vertical agreement between enterprises is prohibited insofar as the agreement has the object or effect of significantly preventing, restricting or distorting competition in any market for goods or services.

(2) Without prejudice to the generality of subsection (1), a horizontal agreement between enterprises which has the object to –

(a) fix, directly or indirectly, a purchase or selling price or any other trading conditions;

(b) share market or sources of supply;

(c) limit or control –

(i) production;

(ii) market outlets or market access;

(iii) technical or technological development; or

(iv) investment; or

(d) perform an act of bid rigging, is deemed to have the object of significantly preventing, restricting, or distorting competition in any market for goods or services.

(3) Any enterprise which is a party to an agreement which is prohibited under this section shall be liable for infringement of the prohibition.

The prohibition against cartel activities is not per se illegal. Section 5 of the CA2010 provides circumstances where the infringement of the prohibition can be relieved. These include (1) the existence of significant identifiable technological, efficiency or social benefits; (2) benefits that could not reasonably have been provided by the parties to the agreement without the agreement; (3) the detrimental effect of the agreement on competition being proportionate to the benefits provided; and (4) the agreement not allowing the enterprise concerned to eliminate competition completely in respect of a substantial part of the goods or services. In addition, the circumstances stated in Section 5 can also lead to an individual exemption (Section 6) or block exemption (Section 8).

11.2.2 Cartel Procedures

The investigation and enforcement procedures for cartel activities are similar to those found in other competition regimes. They begin with an investigation by the MyCC. If the MyCC is convinced that a case can be made, it issues a proposed decision. The targeted enterprises are then given time to make written representation to the MyCC. The MyCC follows this up with an invitation to the targeted firms to make an oral representation. Once this stage is completed, the MyCC issues a decision that includes sanctions. The targeted enterprise can make an appeal to the Competition Appeal Tribunal, which will then conclude the process by undertaking a judicial review.

11.2.3 Sanctions on Cartels

Sections 40 and 61 of the CA2010 provide the general sanctions for the infringement of the Act (including cartel activities).

Section 40(4) states that the financial penalty imposed on enterprises that have infringed the Act should not exceed 10 per cent of their worldwide turnover over the period during which the infringement occurred. The ceiling for financial penalties is provided in Section 61 of the Act, which states that if the offender is a corporate body, the fine is:

1. For the first instance – a fine of up to but not exceeding RM5 million; and
2. For subsequent offences – a fine up to but not exceeding RM10 million.

The corresponding fines for non-corporate bodies are:

1. For the first instance – a fine up to but not exceeding RM1 million or imprisonment for a term not exceeding five years or both; and
2. For subsequent offences – a fine not exceeding RM2 million or imprisonment for a term not exceeding five years or both.

The financial sanctions were further clarified with the publication of the Guidelines on Financial Penalties in November 2014. In the Guidelines, two key objectives are guiding the determination of financial penalties, namely (1) the seriousness of the infringement, and (2) deterrence of anti-competitive acts. The computation of the financial penalty is determined by nine factors, namely (1) seriousness of infringement, (2) turnover, (3) duration of infringement, (4) impact of infringement, (5) degree of fault, (6) role of enterprise, (7) recidivism, (8) existence of a compliance programme, and (9) penalties imposed in similar cases. Finally, the amount of the financial penalty paid by enterprises can be reduced if they are granted leniency for cooperating with the MyCC. This is discussed next.

11.2.4 Leniency Programme

The leniency programme in Malaysia's competition regime is incorporated in Section 41 of the Competition Act 2010 (see Box 11.2). The two key features of the provisions on leniency are (1) the maximum reduction of any penalties is 100 per cent, and (2) there are no limits on the number of enterprises that can be granted leniency. The actual percentage of penalty reduction depends on the order in which the enterprises come forward to cooperate with the MyCC and the stage of the investigations. Section 41(2)(c) provides further flexibility to the MyCC on what other circumstances are relevant – which certainly can include bringing to its attention infringements that were not previously detected.

The Guidelines on Leniency Regime (Guidelines) was published by MyCC in October 2014 to provide further clarification and guidance on its leniency programme. A key emphasis of the Guidelines is that the enterprise(s) seeking leniency can only do so after it has (they have) admitted infringement of the Act. In addition, the Guidelines also emphasise the importance of the significance of assistance provided by the enterprise(s) seeking leniency. The

BOX 11.2: SECTION 41 OF THE COMPETITION ACT 2010 – LENIENCY REGIME

41. (1) There shall be a leniency regime, with a reduction of up to a maximum of one hundred percent of any penalties which would otherwise have been imposed, which may be available in the cases of any enterprise which has –
   (a) admitted its involvement in an infringement of any prohibition under subsection 4(2); and
   (b) provided information or other form of co-operation to the Commission which significantly assisted, or is likely to significantly assist, in the identification or investigation of any finding of an infringement of any prohibition by any other enterprises.

(2) A leniency regime may permit different percentages of reductions to be available to an enterprise depending on –
   (a) whether the enterprise was the first person to bring the suspected infringement to the attention of the Commission;
   (b) the stage in the investigation at which –
      (i) an involvement in the infringement was admitted; or
      (ii) any information or other co-operation was provided;
   (c) any other circumstances which the Commission considers appropriate to have regard to.

MyCC retains flexibility in interpreting the significance of the cooperation. Another key feature of the leniency regime programme highlighted in the Guidelines is that enterprises that initiated the cartel (i.e. the ringleaders) or coerced other enterprises to participate in the cartel activity are not eligible for 100 per cent reduction in financial penalties (item 2.7). The Guidelines also provide detailed information on the marker system used.

In terms of reduction in financial penalties, the Guidelines provide a clearer picture of who is eligible for such leniency. Such an enterprise would be one that has admitted involvement in a cartel that the MyCC has no knowledge of (item 3.4). However, the Guidelines do indicate that the MyCC can offer a 100 per cent penalty reduction in other circumstances (item 3.7) – which can be interpreted to include cases under investigation (rather than unknown cartels), especially at the early stages (item 3.9). 'Other circumstances' could also involve cooperation that would enhance successful investigation and prosecution. This is clarified in item 8.1, which states that the granting of leniency is initially of a 'conditional' nature. The grant of leniency becomes unconditional only if all the conditions of the conditional grant of leniency and infringement decision are met. The conditions for the grant of conditional leniency are fairly exhaustive (item 8.4 of the Guidelines). They include admission of involvement in infringement, provision of significant assistance, ceasing and desisting of infringing activities, full disclosure of cartel participation, continuing cooperation with the MyCC, ceasing destruction of any relevant documents, non-harassment and non-intimidation of others to participate in the cartel and non-disclosure of the leniency grant.

Finally, it should be noted that the granting of leniency to an enterprise does not immunise the enterprise from civil proceedings by parties that suffered from the act of infringement. This implies that any admission of infringement and cooperation may reduce financial penalties, but this may be offset by losses from civil proceedings. Thus, the lack of immunity from private enforcement for enterprises involved in a leniency programme may deter enterprises from participating in the programme.

11.2.5 Cartel Cases and the Operation of the Leniency Programme in Malaysia

Since the CA2010 came into force in January 2012, there has been a total of eight cartel cases involving the infringement of Section 4(2) with a proposed decision and decision (see Table 11.1).

Table 11.1 *Cases with decisions under Section 4(2) of the Competition Act 2010*

Date of decision	Section	Case	Status
6 December 2012	4(2)(a)	Cameron Highlands Floriculturist Association (CHFA) Penalty: RM20,000 if CHFA fails to undertake remedial actions	Decision issued
31 March 2014	4(2)(b)	Malaysian Airline System Berhad, AirAsia Berhad and AirAsia X Sdn Bhd Penalty: RM10 million (The Competition Appeal Tribunal set aside the penalty on 5 February 2016)	Decision issued but appeal successful
30 January 2015	4(2)(a)	Twenty-four ice manufacturers in Kuala Lumpur, Selangor and Putrajaya Penalty: RM283,600	Decision issued
12 February 2015	4(2)(a)	Fifteen members of the Sibu Confectionery and Bakery Association Penalty: RM247,730	Decision issued
1 June 2016	4(1), 4(2)(a)	One IT service provider and four container depot operators Penalty: RM645,774 (Note: Appeal by Prompt Dynamics Sdn Bhd was dismissed on 3 March 2017)	Decision issued
8 February 2018	4(2)(a)	Seven tuition and day-care centres Penalty: RM33,068.85	Decision issued
14 September 2020	4(2)(a)	General Insurance Association of Malaysia and its 22 members. Penalty: RM173,655,300	Decision Issued
26 July 2021	4(2)(a)	Seven warehouse operators at Port Klang Penalty: RM1,043,012.52	Decision Issued

Source: Author's compilation based on MyCC public statements.

As mentioned above, detailed guidelines on the MyCC's leniency programme were only published in October 2014, more than two and a half years after the CA2010 came into force. Thus, the first two cartel cases are unlikely to involve the use of its leniency programme. For the remaining six cases, based on publicly available information, a leniency application was noted in only one case involving price fixing by seven tuition and day-care centres. The utilisation of the leniency programme for each of these six cases is discussed based on public documents from the MyCC.

1. Price fixing by ice manufacturers. A total of twenty-four enterprises were involved. Of these, reductions on financial penalties were given to eleven enterprises for cooperating with the MyCC by providing additional information. There is, however, no indication that the reductions in financial penalties were due to leniency.
2. Price fixing by Sibu Confectionery and Bakery Association. Fifteen firms were involved, but no reductions due to leniency were documented. There were reductions in penalties for a few enterprises, but this was due to enterprises not increasing their prices.
3. Price fixing by an information technology service provider and four container depot operators. No reductions in financial penalties by the MyCC were documented in this case. This implies that leniency was not granted to any of the firms.
4. Price fixing by seven tuition and day-care centres. The final infringement decision has been issued. One of the enterprises did apply for leniency. However, this application was rejected by the MyCC on two grounds: the leniency application took place at an advanced stage of the investigations and made no significant contribution to the investigations; and the applicant was an instigator of the price-fixing agreement.
5. Price fixing by twenty-two enterprises in the insurance industry. The final infringement decision was issued by the MyCC. A 25 per cent discount and moratorium on payment of penalty were given to the enterprises due to the Covid-19 pandemic. However, there was no mention of the application of leniency in this case.
6. Price fixing by seven warehouses in Port Klang. One enterprise was given a 20 per cent discount on penalty due to admission of guilt. There is no mention of leniency as a mitigating factor in the case.

To sum up, based on publicly available information, the leniency programme has not been utilised very frequently in cartel cases in Malaysia. There is only one recorded case of a leniency application in the cartel cases and this was rejected. The under-utilisation of the leniency programme in cartel cases in Malaysia leads to the question of whether this is due to the deterrence effect or whether there are any deficiencies in the design of the programme or other external factors that compromise its efficacy.

Deterrence reduces the number of cartel activities.[2] Most of the cases investigated under Section 4(2) were initiated by media reports. In the case involving a leniency application, investigations were initiated by complaints by a customer (buyer). Given that none of the cartel cases was detected by the use of a leniency programme, it is unlikely that the leniency programme has had a deterrence effect on cartel activities. The issue of the design of the leniency programme is, therefore, examined in the next two sections.

11.3 Analysing the Design of Malaysia's Leniency Programme

In the literature on leniency policies, the two developments that are generally regarded as significant advancements in leniency policy implementation are the United States (US) Department of Justice's (DOJ) revision of its leniency programme in 1993 and the European Commission's (EC) introduction of its leniency programme in 1996. The EC's programme was subsequently revised in 2002 and 2006. Both these two developments provided the momentum for other countries to adopt leniency programmes.

The work of the International Competition Network (ICN) was also crucial in assisting competition agencies in designing their leniency programmes. ICN, for example, came up with the Anti-Cartel Enforcement Manual (ICN Manual) in 2009 with a chapter on best practices in the drafting and implementation of leniency policy.[3] These developments without doubt influenced the design of Malaysia's leniency programme. This is clear from a comparison between the ICN Manual's recommendations updated in 2014 and the MyCC's leniency programme. One example is the best practices on the marker system in the ICN Manual. Most of these best practices can be found in the MyCC's leniency programme.

[2] Jenny, F., 'Foreword', in Beaton-Wells, C. and Tran, C. (eds.), *Anti-cartel Enforcement in a Contemporary Age: Leniency Religion* (Oxford: Hart Publishing, 2015), v.

[3] ICN, 'Chapter 2: Drafting and Implementing an Effective Leniency Policy' (2014). Retrieved from www.internationalcompetitionnetwork.org/portfolio/leniency-program.

It might therefore be useful to analyse the MyCC's leniency programme from the perspective of the ICN Manual. The ICN Manual lists three elements that are important pre-requisites for an effective leniency policy.[4] How does the MyCC's leniency programme compare with the best practices outlined by the 2014 ICN Manual?

The first pre-requisite relates to the credibility of the enforcement agency in terms of its commitment and ability to detect and prosecute cartels. However, there is some endogeneity here, as the performance of a competition agency in terms of detecting and prosecuting cartels depends partly on the efficacy of the leniency policy. The MyCC has clearly developed some credibility in enforcement as it has issued decisions in cartel cases. Before the insurance industry case, most of these cases had involved relatively small financial penalties.

The second pre-requisite is that the sanctions imposed must be substantial enough (the ICN uses the term 'significant') to make leniency attractive to cartel members. The financial penalty for infringement under the CA2016 and the MyCC Guidelines is 10 per cent of total revenues up to a maximum of RM5 million. The 10 per cent threshold is similar to the financial penalty under the European Union (EU) competition regime. However, given that Malaysia's domestic market is smaller than that of the EU and the US, the RM5 million ceiling could be significant and sufficient.

Finally, the third pre-requisite is transparency and certainty in the operation of a leniency policy. The degree of transparency and certainty of the MyCC's leniency programme are unclear. The procedures as outlined by its Guidelines are fairly detailed, but the agency retains substantial discretion in implementing its leniency programme (see the discussion above). Such discretionary powers, while providing some flexibility, may create uncertainties. However, such uncertainties can be reduced over time if the MyCC is able to demonstrate – through effective enforcement – the value of the leniency programme. Thus, building up a credible enforcement reputation is absolutely essential.

Beyond these broad assessments of Malaysia's leniency programme, there are other, more specific elements of the programme that might be compared to findings from the theoretical and empirical research literature on an optimal leniency programme. However, as noted by Giancarlo Spagnolo, the theoretical literature does have limitations that arise from the need to make restrictive assumptions for tractable models of optimal

[4] Ibid., pp. 5–6, sub-section 2.3.

leniency policy.[5] Nevertheless, such models are still useful to highlight how specific elements of leniency programmes work. These elements are discussed below.

Zhijun Chen and Patrick Rey argue that it is optimal to offer leniency before and after investigations have begun (especially when the prospects of successful prosecution are significantly enhanced by it).[6] In the latter case, the offer of leniency should only be made to the first informant. This is because the reduction in expected penalty for the first informant exceeds any penalty reductions that can be secured before investigations are started. Subsequent informants – who will receive lower penalty reductions – may not be sufficiently incentivised to report. Malaysia's leniency programme departs from this theoretical finding as it offers leniency not only to the first reporter but to others as well. However, it is difficult to say whether doing so is sub-optimal, because the value of subsequent leniency applications (to the MyCC) may lie in the additional information that is needed to prosecute a cartel. This is covered in the EU's leniency policy as well.[7]

Another element that is discussed in the theoretical literature is the treatment of ringleaders. The MyCC's guidelines on leniency state that cartel ringleaders are not eligible for 100 per cent reduction in financial penalties. As noted by the ICN Manual,[8] this feature can be found in some leniency programmes in some countries. The theoretical literature on optimal leniency programmes does not provide a definitive answer to the question of whether excluding the ring leader from 100 per cent leniency is a good practice or not. Bruce Kobayashi's work on plea bargaining implies that ringleaders tend to have the most information on cartels.[9] Therefore, they should be incentivised to defect (apply for leniency) in order to maximise the probability of successful prosecution of the cartel. However, as noted by Spagnolo, ringleaders are also the parties that benefit from the cartel and lose the most from defecting.[10] The cost–benefit

[5] Spagnolo, G., 'Leniency and Whistleblowers in Antitrust', in Buccirosi, P. (ed.) *Handbook of Antitrust Economics* (Cambridge, MA: MIT Press, 2008), 259.

[6] Chen, Z. and Rey P., 'On the Design of Leniency Programs' (2013) 56(4) *Journal of Law and Economics* 917.

[7] Spagnolo, 'Leniency and Whistleblowers in Antitrust' (n. 5 above), p. 281.

[8] ICN, 'Drafting and Implementing an Effective Leniency Policy' (n. 3 above), p. 9.

[9] Kobayashi, B. H., 'Deterrence with Multiple Defendants: An Explanation for Unfair Plea Bargains' (1992) 23(4) *Rand Journal of Economics* 507.

[10] Spagnolo, 'Leniency and Whistleblowers in Antitrust' (n. 5 above), p. 282.

calculus for ring leaders to defect is likely to be affected by a number of factors, including (1) the share of gains enjoyed by the ring leader in the cartel, (2) the distribution of information among cartel leaders, and (3) the penalties incurred if prosecution is successful.

Finally, the MyCC's leniency guidelines specifically state that the leniency programme does not immunise a successful applicant for leniency from civil proceedings (under Section 64 of the CA2010) initiated by individuals who have suffered from the infringement. The lack of such immunisation from civil proceedings could reduce the incentives for enterprises to participate in the leniency programme.

To sum up, the leniency programme in Malaysia appears to be underutilised in the cartel cases that have been investigated by the MyCC. Drawing from best practices as well as the research literature, there could be a number of reasons underlying this situation. Another possibility that is important but often taken as exogenous in the research literature is the political and institutional environment. This is explored next.

11.4 Effectiveness of the Leniency Programme in Malaysia: The Role of Politics and Institutions

It is possible that the efficacy of a leniency programme may also depend on the political and institutional environment. In the literature on the judiciary and politics, for example, there are links between politicians and judges. For example, politicians may be involved in the selection, promotion and disciplining of judges.[11]

From an institutional perspective, the MyCC is formally (de jure) an independent regulatory agency established through the CCA2010. It is, however, de facto quasi-independent due to a number of factors. First, it receives an annual financial allocation from the Government of Malaysia. This allocation amounted to RM6.9 million or 90 per cent of its total income in 2018. Second, under the CCA2010, all members of the Commission are appointed by the Prime Minister upon the recommendation of the Minister of Domestic Trade and Consumer Affairs. In 2021, four of the ten commissioners of the MyCC are senior bureaucrats from ministries.

The influence of politics on independent regulatory commissions in Malaysia can be seen from the way in which political changes can bring about changes in these regulatory commissions. Barisan Nasional (BN) – the

[11] Jacob, H., Blankenburg, E., Kritzer, H. M., Provine, D. M. and Sanders, J., *Courts, Law and Politics in Comparative Perspective* (New Haven: Yale University Press, 1996).

ruling coalition party that has ruled since Malaysia achieved independence in 1957 – was defeated in the country's general elections on 9 May 2018. This political change was followed by changes in the leadership of independent regulatory commissions or, in some cases, the closure of such commissions. In the case of the MyCC, its former commission chairman (appointed in April 2017 for a three-year term), who was a member of parliament under the BN government, was replaced on 5 September 2018. Another regulatory commission, the Land Public Transport Commission, was abolished in 2018. These developments do suggest that the appointment of regulatory commissions (at least in the past) is not politically neutral. Otherwise such appointments would have been robust against changes in political regimes.

Has the quasi-independence of the MyCC affected the design and implementation of its leniency programme? This is a difficult question to answer. The structure of its leniency programme does follow many of the best practices as encapsulated in the ICN Manual and the leniency programmes in other countries and regions (e.g. the EU's leniency programme). Thus, it is unlikely that the MyCC's quasi-independent status has compromised the design of its leniency programme.

Given the close nexus between politics and regulatory commissions in the country, the public perception of the credibility of these commissions could be affected by the overall state of governance in the country. One related and important area of governance is anti-corruption. The Whistleblower Protection Act 2010 (WPA2010) plays a similar role to leniency in competition law. In the case of WPA2010, Section 7(1) of the Act provides immunity to whistleblowers from civil and criminal proceedings. The enforcement agency for anti-corruption in the country is the Malaysian Anti-Corruption Commission (MACC), which was established through the MACC Act 2009. The significance of whistleblowing can be seen in Table 11.2, which provides a summary of MACC's enforcement statistics from 2013 to 2019.

The statistics in Table 11.2 indicate that the number of whistleblowers in Malaysia is very small. The number of whistleblowers accounts for less than 1 per cent of the total information received on corruption. This could be attributed to at least two key weaknesses in the WPA2010,[12] the oversight role played by the minister and the potential for ministerial

[12] Leong, C., 'A Critical Look into the Whistleblower Protection Act 2010', Policy IDEAS No. 36 (2017). Retrieved from https://ideas.org.my/wp-content/uploads/2021/04/PI36-Whistleblower-Protection.pdf.

Table 11.2 *Enforcement statistics from the Malaysian Anti-Corruption Commission*

	2012	2013	2014	2015	2016	2017	2018	2019
Information on corruption	5,496	4,027	2,954	2,892	3,417	3,816	4,396	4,442
Investigation papers opened	NA	976	919	982	985	863	833	1,039
Investigation papers completed (1 year)	35	796	781	NA	NA	NA	NA	951
Arrests	701	509	552	842	939	879	894	1,101
Total whistle-blowers seeking protection	35	6	15	8	44	46	76	50
Total whistle-blowers protected	29	6	10	7	42	44	71	47

NA, not available.
Source: MACC, Annual Reports, 2013–2019.

intervention in the implementation of the Act. In addition, the Act also applies to cases where the disclosure of improper conduct may be prohibited by other laws such as the Official Secrets Act (for public agencies) and Financial Services Act 2013 (for financial institutions).

Aside from these weaknesses, the credibility of enforcement agencies could also be affected by the public's perception of the independence and fairness of the governance system in Malaysia. Two high-profile cases have damaged the credibility of enforcement agencies. The first is the National Feedlot Corporation (NFC) scandal, which involved misuse of funds in a government-funded project. The whistleblower in this case was subsequently sentenced to jail for thirty months for exposing confidential banking information, which is prohibited under the Banking and Financial Institutions Act (Bafia). The case against the NFC executive chairman was withdrawn by the then Attorney General Apandi Ali due to lack of strong evidence.

The second case is corruption involving the Malaysian state fund 1MDB. In June 2017, the US DOJ filed civil forfeiture complaints to seek the forfeiture and recovery of about US$540 million that was misappropriated from 1MDB. The Attorney General of Malaysia (Abdul Gani Patail), who led the investigation into 1MDB, was replaced in July

2017. His replacement, Apandi Ali, subsequently cleared the then Prime Minister Najib Razak (who was also the de facto leader of the United Malays National Organisation, UMNO).

Both the NFC and 1MDB scandals attracted public attention. Though the investigations were terminated under the UMNO-led BN government, the two cases were subsequently revisited after the ruling coalition BN lost the general elections in May 2018. The new government formed by the Pakatan Harapan (PH) coalition subsequently replaced a number of key high-level positions such as the Chief Justice, Attorney General, Commissioner of MACC, Judicial Appointments Commissioners and chairman of the MyCC.

The political and institutional environment for competition agencies is most likely to be an important factor in assessing the efficacy of competition law enforcement in general and its leniency programme more specifically. However, it is challenging to find direct evidence on how the leniency programme in Malaysia's competition regime is affected by this factor. In other words, it is difficult to tell whether the deterioration in overall governance in Malaysia in the past has discouraged cartel members from using the MyCC's leniency programme to defect. This is one area of research that requires further work.

11.5 Perceptions of Businesses on Courts and Corruption

The quality of the institutional environment can determine the efficacy of a leniency programme. There is no publicly available information (based on surveys) on businesses' perceptions of the leniency programme in Malaysia. However, there is information on businesses' perceptions of courts and corruption, which can be an indirect measure of the quality of institutions in Malaysia. This is based on the World Bank's 2015 Enterprise Survey for Malaysia, which covers 1,000 firms from the manufacturing and services sectors.[13]

11.5.1 Courts

In the survey, firms were asked to indicate their response to the statement that 'the court system is fair, impartial and uncorrupted'. Close to one-third (32 per cent) of the respondents indicated that they disagree or

[13] World Bank, 'Malaysia – Enterprise Survey 2015' (2017). Retrieved from https://microdata.worldbank.org/index.php/catalog/2804.

Table 11.3 *Business perception of the court system*

	Frequency	Per cent	Cumulative
'The court system is fair, impartial and uncorrupted'			
Don't know (spontaneous)	15	1.5	1.5
Does not apply	57	5.7	7.2
Strongly disagree	67	6.7	13.9
Tend to disagree	250	25.0	38.9
Tend to agree	472	47.2	86.1
Strongly agree	139	13.9	100.0
Total	1,000	100.0	
'To what degree are courts an obstacle to the current operations of this establishment?'			
Don't know (spontaneous)	31	3.1	3.1
Does not apply	139	13.9	17.0
No obstacle	242	24.2	41.2
Minor obstacle	248	24.8	66.0
Moderate obstacle	230	23.0	89.0
Major obstacle	80	8.0	97.0
Very severe obstacle	30	3.0	100.0
Total	1,000	100.0	

Source: World Bank's Enterprise Survey 2015 – Malaysia

strongly disagree with this statement (Table 11.3). About 61 per cent agreed or strongly agreed with the statement. Firms were also asked the extent to which courts are an obstacle to the current operations of their establishment (Table 11.3). The proportion of respondents indicating courts to be a major and very severe obstacle to their business was 11 per cent.

11.5.2 Corruption

On the issue of corruption, firms were asked in the survey about whether informal gifts or payments were expected or requested when they applied for an operating licence (Table 11.4). Due to the sensitivity of the question, only a quarter of the firms surveyed responded. Of these, 22 per cent answered in the affirmative. When asked indirectly whether corruption was an obstacle to the current operations of their business, about 10 per cent of the respondents indicated that corruption was a major or very severe obstacle.

Table 11.4 *Business perception of corruption*

	Frequency	Per cent	Cumulative
'In reference to application for an operating license, was an informal gift or payment expected or requested?'			
Don't know (spontaneous)	13	5.00	5.00
Refusal (spontaneous)	16	6.15	11.15
Yes	57	21.92	33.08
No	174	66.92	100.00
	260	100.00	
'To what degree is corruption an obstacle to the current operations of this establishment?'			
Don't know (spontaneous)	35	3.5	3.5
Does not apply	63	6.3	9.8
No obstacle	250	25.0	34.8
Minor obstacle	294	29.4	64.2
Moderate obstacle	254	25.4	89.6
Major obstacle	75	7.5	97.1
Very severe obstacle	29	2.9	100.0
Total	1,000	100.0	

Source: World Bank's Enterprise Survey 2015 – Malaysia

Overall, the survey revealed that a significant proportion of businesses surveyed do have negative perceptions of the quality of institutions in terms of courts and corruption. While these findings cannot be used to argue that businesses have low trust in the leniency programme, it does provide an indication of the perception of businesses of the overall institutional environment within which the programme operates. The change in government following the general elections in May 2018 heighted expectations for institutional reforms (including the renewal of regulatory and legal reforms) that can further strengthen competition regulation and law.[14] However, the PH government was toppled in February 2020 following the defections of several politicians in the PH coalition. This ushered in a period of political instability in subsequent months. At the time of writing (September 2021), senior political leaders from UMNO have returned to power and have signed a memorandum of understanding with PH that

[14] The reform processes began in 2010 but may have subsequently lost momentum. See OECD, *Implementing Good Regulatory Practice in Malaysia* (Paris: OECD Publishing, 2015) for a description of these early reforms.

includes an agreement to uphold the independence of the judiciary. This was deemed by many to be a key commitment given the ongoing corruption cases in the courts involving senior UMNO leaders.

11.6 Conclusion

Malaysia's competition regime is fairly new. The CA2010 only came into force in January 2012 and the MyCC's detailed guidelines on its leniency programme were not published until October 2014. Since then, only six cases involving cartel activities have been investigated and finalised. To the author's knowledge and based on publicly available documents, just one cartel case investigated by the MyCC involved a leniency application. This was the cartel case involving price fixing by seven tuition and day-care centres in 2017. In this case, the leniency application was rejected. Overall, the leniency programme in Malaysia appears to be under-utilised despite being carefully designed based on best practices in other countries and from the ICN. That leaves the question of why the leniency programme for competition law has not been utilised more extensively. This could be due to design issues, such as too much discretionary power for the MyCC and a lack of immunisation from civil proceedings in the leniency grant. It could also be due to political and institutional factors, such as the de facto oversight from the government and spillovers from deterioration in the country's state of governance. The perceptions of the business community on the quality of institutions in terms of courts and corruption do indicate that institutional reforms are likely to be needed to further enhance the environment within which competition law enforcement and, more specifically, the leniency programme operates. The change of government following the general elections in May 2018 fuelled expectations for institutional reforms aimed at improving the quality of institutions in the country. However, these expectations were dashed following the toppling of the PH government and the months of political instability that ensued amid the Covid-19 pandemic.

12

Hong Kong's Revised Leniency Policy and Its Potential to Deter Cartels

SANDRA MARCO COLINO*

12.1 Introduction

Hong Kong may have been late in adopting competition law, but its first leniency policy for cartel investigations arrived remarkably soon. The city's first cross-sector competition legislation, the Hong Kong Competition Ordinance (HKCO), was adopted in June 2012 and entered into full effect in December 2015.[1] A month earlier, in November 2015, the Hong Kong Competition Commission (HKCC or Commission) published the Leniency Policy for Undertakings Involved in Cartel Conduct (Leniency Policy for Undertakings).[2] By contrast, it took the United States (US) Department of Justice (DOJ) eighty-eight years from the adoption of the Sherman Act in 1890 to introduce the country's – and the world's – first such policy.[3] On the other side of the Atlantic, the European Commission's earliest Leniency Notice dates back to 1996,[4] almost forty years after the Treaty of Rome planted the seed of the European Union's (EU) competition regime.[5]

* The work described in this chapter was substantially supported by a grant from the General Research Fund of the Research Grants Council of the Hong Kong Special Administrative Region (SAR), China (Project No CUHK 14600718). I am grateful to Brent Snyder for his helpful comments and insights. All errors are mine alone.

1 Hong Kong SAR, Competition Ordinance, Ordinance No 14 (2012) A1347 (HKCO).

2 HKCC, 'Leniency Policy for Undertakings Engaged in Cartel Conduct' (November 2015). Retrieved from www.compcomm.hk/en/legislation_guidance/policy_doc/files/Leniency_Policy_Eng.pdf (2015 Leniency Policy).

3 The current US leniency policies are Department of Justice, Corporate Leniency Policy (10 August 1993). Retrieved from www.justice.gov/atr/file/810281/download; and Department of Justice, Individual Leniency Policy (10 August 1994). Retrieved from www.justice.gov/sites/default/files/atr/legacy/2006/04/27/0092.pdf.

4 European Commission, 'Commission Notice on Non-imposition or Reduction of Fines in Cartel Cases', O.J. C207/4 (1996) (1996 Leniency Notice).

5 Treaty establishing the European Economic Community (25 March 1957). It has been modified on several occasions. The current version is known as the Treaty on the Functioning of the European Union [2012] OJ C326/47.

The HKCC, whose staff includes members with experience working in established antitrust jurisdictions, can be said to have had 'last-mover advantage' – that is, the benefit of hindsight that US and EU enforcers did not enjoy.[6] By the time the Hong Kong legislation entered into force, international experience strongly suggested that a mechanism to break the trust between cartel members was a must-have in the fight against collusion.[7] Leniency encourages cartel members to blow the whistle on the illegal activity they are involved in, by offering them a 'reward – usually immunity, or a partial reduction in the penalty or penalties they would normally face for partaking in collusion – in exchange for the voluntary disclosure of information that serves as evidence of the existence of the cartel'.[8] The eagerness to possess this tool is an accurate reflection

[6] The first Chief Executive Officer (CEO) of the HKCC (2014–2017), the late Stanley Wong, had practised and enforced competition law in multiple countries, including Canada and Ireland. It was under his leadership that the first Leniency Policy for Undertakings was adopted. Rose Webb was the next CEO (2016–2017) and she possessed extensive experience in Australia. Other members of the HKCC have previously worked in the United Kingdom, US, France, Portugal and Belgium (in the European Commission).

[7] There is abundant literature on leniency policies and it will be cited throughout the chapter. See, e.g., Apesteguia, J., Dufwenberg, M. and Selten, R., 'Blowing the Whistle' (2007) 31 *Economic Theory* 143; Aubert, C., Rey, P. and Kovacic, W., 'The Impact of Leniency Programs on Cartels' (2006) 24 *International Journal of Industrial Organization* 1241; Beaton-Wells, C. and Tran, C. (eds.), *Anti-Cartel Enforcement in a Contemporary Age: Leniency Religion* (Oxford: Hart Publishing, 2015); Beaton-Wells, C., 'The Politics of Cartel Criminalization: A Pessimistic View from Australia' (2008) 29 *European Competition Law Review* 3; Borrell, J.-R., Jiménez, J. L. and García, C., 'Evaluating Antitrust Leniency Programs' (2004) 10 *Journal of Competition Law and Economics* 107; Brenner, S., 'An Empirical Study of the European Corporate Leniency Program' (2009) 27 *International Journal of Industrial Organization* 639; Chen, Z. and Rey, P., 'On the Design of Leniency Programs' (2013) 56 *Journal of Law and Economics* 917; Choi, J. P. and Gerlach, H., 'Global Cartels, Leniency Programs and International Antitrust Cooperation' (2012) 30 *International Journal of Industrial Organization* 528; Harrington, J. E. and Chang, M.-H., 'Endogenous Antitrust Enforcement in the Presence of a Corporate Leniency Program' (30 November 2013). Retrieved from https://bepp.wharton.upenn.edu/files/?whdmsaction=public:main.file&fileID=5147; Motta, M. and Polo, M., 'Leniency Programs and Cartel Prosecution' (2003) 21 *International Journal of Industrial Organization* 347; Rey, P., 'On the Use of Economic Analysis in Cartel Detection' in Ehlermann, C.D. and Atanasiu, I. (eds.) *Competition Law Annual 2006: Enforcement of Prohibition of Cartels* (Oxford: Hart Publishing, 2007), 81; Rodríguez, A. E. and Menon, A., *The Limits of Competition Policy: The Shortcomings of Antitrust in Developing and Reforming Economies* (The Hague: Wolters Kluwer, 2010); Stephan, A., 'An Empirical Assessment of the European Leniency Notice' (2009) 5 *Journal of Competition Law and Economics* 537.

[8] Marco Colino, S., 'The Perks of Being a Whistleblower: Designing Efficient Leniency Programs in New Antitrust Jurisdictions' (2017) 50 *Vanderbilt Journal of Transnational Law* 535, p. 541.

of the HKCC's determination to focus on cartel activity, considered the 'supreme evil of antitrust',[9] when enforcing the law.[10] As of December 2020, all but one of the cases the HKCC has brought before the Hong Kong Competition Tribunal (HKCT or Tribunal) relate to collusion.[11] In fact, in January 2020 the HKCC announced that it had entered into its first ever leniency agreement,[12] in the context of the *Quantr* case.[13] The policy is thus no longer a mere theoretical possibility. It has actually led to proceedings, and even a finding of infringement and a fine.

Brent Snyder, who was the HKCC's Chief Executive Officer (CEO) from September 2017 until November 2020, has emphasised that '[s]ince 1993, leniency programmes have been the most effective tool to detect, investigate and prosecute international cartels'.[14] As the former Deputy Assistant Attorney General of the Antitrust Division of the DOJ, Snyder has first-hand knowledge of the world's pioneer leniency programme. Under the original US policy, full immunity was only available on a discretionary basis, and before an investigation had been triggered. Unsurprisingly, it remained virtually dormant.[15] In 1993, the policy was amended so that the first company to report a cartel not yet identified by the authorities would

[9] This is how the US Supreme Court described collusion in *Verizon Communications Inc.* v. *Law Offices of Curtis V Trinko, LLP*, 540 US 398 (2004) 407–8.

[10] Leniency is considered '[t]he single most significant development in cartel enforcement'. See Hammond, S. D., 'The Evolution of Criminal Antitrust Enforcement over the Last Two Decades' (Presentation at 24th Annual National Institute on White Collar Crime, ABA Criminal Justice Section and ABA Center for Continuing Legal Education, Miami, 25 February 2010), p. 1. Retrieved from www.justice.gov/atr/speech/evolution-criminal-antitrust-enforcement-over-last-two-decades. See also Fox, E. and Crane, D., *Global Issues in Antitrust and Competition Law* (Toronto: Thomson Reuters, 2010), p. 75.

[11] The non-cartel case, announced in December 2020, relates to a potential abuse of substantial degree of market power, and constitutes the first ever attempt to enforce the Second Conduct Rule of the HKCO. See case CTEA3/2020 *Competition Commission* v *Linde HKO Limited, Tse Chun Wah and Linde GmbH* (nyd).

[12] HKCC Press Release (22 January 2020). Retrieved from www.compcomm.hk/en/media/press/files/20200122_ENG_PR_Competition_Commission_takes_IT_cartel_conduct_case_to_Competition_Tribunal.pdf.

[13] Case CTEA1/2020 *Competition Commission* v *Quantr Limited and Cheung Man* Kit [2020] HKCT 10 (*Quantr*).

[14] Snyder, B., 'Leniency Programmes: Brent Snyder Shares Tips on Effective Leniency Programmes', OECD Competition Division (20 August 2018). Retrieved from www.youtube.com/watch?v=dJSNoWD0vb8.

[15] Spratling, G. R., 'The Experience and Views of the Antitrust Division' (Address at the US Sentencing Commission Symposium: Corporate Crime in America: Strengthening the 'Good Citizen' Corporation, 8 September 1995) in Ewing, K. P. (ed.), *Competition Rules for the 21st Century: Principles from America's Experience*, 2nd ed. (The Hague: Kluwer Law, 2006), 623, p. 623.

be automatically granted leniency. Leniency would further be made available in some cases once an investigation is ongoing.[16] The following year, a leniency policy for individuals was introduced for company employees who furnish the DOJ with information on their employers' collusive activities.[17] From then onwards, leniency has proven to be a crucial antitrust asset:

> By 2010, there were twenty times more [leniency] applications than there were under the original policy, and 90 percent of the $5 billion paid in penalties for antitrust violations between 1996 and 2010 was obtained in the context of investigations that involved leniency requests. In fact, in 1999 alone, the total amount of the fines imposed was higher than the sum of all the penalties levied during the entire prior 109-year history of U.S. antitrust enforcement.[18]

These accomplishments, supported by numerous studies with encouraging results,[19] have led to the adoption of similar programmes in more than fifty jurisdictions.[20] Under Snyder, Hong Kong's leniency system was reformed, becoming more closely aligned with that of the US. The principal changes were introduced in two stages. First, in 2019, the HKCC published its Cooperation and Settlement Policy for Undertakings Engaged

16 US Department of Justice, Corporate Leniency Policy (n. 3 above).

17 US Department of Justice, Leniency Policy for Individuals (n. 3 above).

18 Marco Colino, 'The Perks of Being a Whistleblower' (n. 8 above), p. 556.

19 Empirical studies include Miller, N. H., 'Strategic Leniency and Cartel Enforcement' (2009) 99 *American Economic Review* 750; Klein, G., 'Cartel Destabilization and Leniency Programs – Empirical Evidence' (Zentrum für Europäische Wirtschaftsforschung, ZEW Discussion Paper No 10-107, 2010). Retrieved from www.econstor.eu/bitstream/10419/44455/1/645296945.pdf; Zhou, J., 'Evaluating Leniency with Missing Information on Undetected Cartels: Exploring Time-Varying Policy Impacts on Cartel Duration' (GESY Discussion Paper No 353, University of Munich, April 2011). Retrieved from https://epub.ub.uni-muenchen.de/13201/1/353_01.pdf. Experimental studies are similarly positive. See, e.g., Apesteguia, J., Dufwenberg, M. and Selten, R., 'Blowing the Whistle' (2007) 31 *Economic Theory* 143; Hinloopen, J. and Soetevent, A. R., 'Laboratory Evidence on the Effectiveness of Corporate Leniency Programs' (2008) 39 *RAND Journal of Economics* 607; Dijkstra, P. T., Haan, M. A. and Schoonbeek, L., 'Leniency Programs and the Design of Antitrust: Experimental Evidence with Free-Form Communication' (2020) 59 *Review of Industrial Organization* 13. Retrieved from https://doi.org/10.1007/s11151-020-09789-5.

20 Hammond, 'The Evolution of Criminal Antitrust Enforcement' (n. 10 above); UNCTAD, 'Competition Guidelines: Leniency Programmes' (22 June 2016). Retrieved from https://unctad.org/system/files/official-document/ditcclp2016d3_en.pdf. The US, EU and Canada are typically considered the 'Big Three' corporate leniency policies. See O'Brien, A., 'Leadership of Leniency', in Beaton-Wells and Tran, *Anti-Cartel Enforcement in a Contemporary Age* (n. 7 above), p. 19.

in Cartel Conduct (Cooperation Policy),[21] with penalty reductions for undertakings willing to cooperate but who are not the first to blow the whistle, and a leniency plus scheme offering additional reductions to undertakings under investigation who report additional cartels they may be part of.[22] Second, in April 2020, changes to the original Leniency Policy for Undertakings were announced, opening the door to leniency agreements even when an investigation is already underway, and sparing certain leniency beneficiaries from damages claims.[23] Simultaneously, a brand new Leniency Policy for Individuals was published, offering protection to past and current employees of corporate cartelists.[24]

This chapter assesses the special design and characteristics of Hong Kong's revised leniency policy, and discusses its suitability to tackle the city's cartels. The analysis largely reveals a thorough, sharply devised tool with significant potential, but somewhat hampered by the HKCO's shortcomings. To explore the merits of the system, the chapter consists of six sections. Following this introduction, Section 12.2 looks at the general framework of the city's competition legislation. Thereafter, Section 12.3 discusses cartels in Hong Kong and the HKCC's activity against cartels to date. Section 12.4 focuses on the details of the leniency policy, and a critical discussion of these is carried out in Section 12.5. Section 12.6 concludes.

12.2 Background: General Aspects of the Hong Kong Competition Ordinance

Before delving into the analysis of Hong Kong's leniency policy, this section will cover the principal features of the city's first cross-sector competition legislation. The HKCO contains three core substantive rules. The First Conduct Rule (FCR) prohibits agreements and concerted practices between undertakings, as well as decisions by associations of undertakings, that have as their object or effect the prevention, restriction or distortion of competition.[25] The Second Conduct Rule (SCR) targets single-firm conduct, and condemns the abuse of a substantial degree of market power

[21] HKCC, 'Cooperation and Settlement Policy for Undertakings Engaged in Cartel Conduct' (April 2019). Retrieved from www.compcomm.hk/en/legislation_guidance/policy_doc/files/Cooperation_Policy_Eng.pdf (Cooperation Policy).

[22] Ibid., Section 4.1.

[23] See Section 12.4 below.

[24] Ibid.

[25] HKCO, Part 2, Division 1, Subdivision 1, Section 6.

by means of conduct with an anti-competitive object or effect.[26] The Merger Rule (MR) prohibits mergers that may substantially lessen competition, but only applies to mergers between telecoms licensees.[27]

The HKCC, set up in 2013, is Hong Kong's antitrust watchdog. Its main enforcement task is to look into potential infringements, and therefore under the city's competition law it is vested with wide investigatory powers, including the power to request documents and to conduct dawn raids.[28] After an investigation, the HKCC may decide there was no infringement, or it may issue a warning notice, and even require the undertaking under scrutiny to accept commitments.[29] If the company refuses, or the HKCC feels that commitments are not enough to address the issue at stake, then the HKCC may bring proceedings before the HKCT. The HKCC is also entrusted with the adoption of guidelines, the development of completion advocacy initiatives and conducting market inquiries.

Wide-ranging penalties may be imposed for breaches of the HKCO.[30] The HKCT may order a person or an undertaking 'to pay to the Government a pecuniary penalty of any amount it considers appropriate'.[31] These fines are nonetheless capped at 10 per cent of the Hong Kong turnover for each year of infringement, for a maximum of three years.[32] In June 2020, the HKCC published its Policy on Recommended Pecuniary Penalties.[33] A four-step process is recommended to determine the amount of fines: first, the base amount is calculated; second, aggravating and mitigating factors are weighed in; third, the 10 per cent cap is applied; and fourth, any cooperation arrangements, including leniency, are taken into consideration. It should be noted, however, that only the HKCT has the power to impose fines, and it is not bound by the guidance issued by the HKCC. According to the HKCO, however, the HKCT must consider factors such as the nature and extent of the violation, any consequential loss or damage, the circumstances and recidivism, when

26 Ibid., Part 2, Division 2, Subdivision 1, Section 21.

27 Ibid., Schedule 7, Part 2, Section 3.

28 Ibid., Sections 129–131.

29 Ibid.

30 See Marco Colino, S., 'Punishing Cartel Behaviour: Means to Encourage Compliance with the Hong Kong Competition Ordinance', in Cheng, T., Marco Colino, S. and Ong, B. (eds.), *Cartels in Asia: Law and Practice* (The Hague: Wolters Kluwer, 2015), 315, p. 315.

31 HKCO, Section 93(1).

32 Ibid., Section 93(3).

33 HKCC, 'Policy on Recommended Pecuniary Penalties' (June 2020). Retrieved from www.compcomm.hk/en/legislation_guidance/policy_doc/files/Policy_on_Recommended_Pecuniary_Penalties_Eng.pdf.

deciding on the specific amount.[34] In addition to fines, the HKCO contains the possibility of seeking a director disqualification for breaches of the main substantive provisions.[35] Imprisonment is reserved for certain procedural breaches.[36]

It should also be noted that there are no standalone private rights of action.[37] Therefore, any damage claims must necessarily stem from follow-on actions, based on an infringement that has already been confirmed by the HKCT. The Tribunal may also deal with appeals relating to the HKCC's decisions granting exemptions, exclusions, commitments and, importantly for the purposes of this study, also leniency agreements.

For the purposes of this chapter, the FCR is particularly relevant and deserves further scrutiny. The EU-inspired wording of the provision potentially catches a very wide range of joint practices, and the law is crystal clear that hard-core cartels (specifically price fixing, market sharing and customer allocation, output restrictions and bid rigging) not only constitute a violation, but also amount to serious anti-competitive conduct.[38] This has important practical implications. For instance, warning notices will not be issued before taking action.[39] Moreover, the de minimis rule,[40] which excludes agreements of lesser significance from the scope of the law, will not apply.[41] The Guideline on the First Conduct Rule (Guideline FCR) specifically states that cartels are considered to have an anti-competitive object,[42] confirming that an effect on competition is not required for collusion to be unlawful.[43] As a result, the efficiency considerations of the HKCO are 'unlikely' to come into play.[44]

[34] HKCO, Section 93(2).

[35] Ibid., Sections 101–105.

[36] Ibid., Part 3, Division 4; Part 8, Sections 125 and 128; Part 10, Division 3, Sections 151 and 151C; and Part 12, Division 4.

[37] Ibid., Sections 110–112.

[38] HKCO, Section 2.

[39] Ibid., Section 82.

[40] Ibid., Schedule 1. Agreements, decisions by associations of undertakings or concerted practices where the combined turnover of the parties is HK$200 million or less are considered of lesser significance.

[41] HKCC, 'Guideline on the First Conduct Rule' (27 July 2015), para 5.2. Retrieved from www.compcomm.hk/en/legislation_guidance/guidance/first_conduct_rule/files/Guideline_The_First_Conduct_Rule_Eng.pdf.

[42] Ibid., para. 3.7.

[43] Ibid., para. 3.5.

[44] Ibid., para. 4.4. Efficiency considerations can be found in HKCO, Schedule 1.

12.3 Cartels in Hong Kong

12.3.1 Collusion before the Introduction of Cross-Sector Competition Legislation

Prior to the entry into force of the HKCO, only cartels in the telecommunications and broadcasting sectors were illegal. The Telecommunications Ordinance and the Broadcasting Ordinance contained sector-specific competition law provisions.[45] They were rarely ever used, and were repealed when the HKCO became effective. The Telecommunications Authority (TA), which was entrusted with their application, failed to adopt a hands-on approach to enforcement. The only collusive activity ever investigated took place in 2000, when every licensed mobile telephone operator individually announced an increase of between 20 and 25 per cent in the cost of all its service plans. Even more alarmingly, all the competitors were to implement the price spike on the same date. During the investigation, the companies justified their behaviour, asserting that they had experienced losses in previous years and were trying to recoup them. They even admitted to holding joint discussions about pricing prior to making the announcement. While this should have been more than enough to establish a punishable breach of the Telecommunications Ordinance, the TA did not impose any penalties.[46] Similarly, the Hong Kong courts displayed disappointing tolerance for some of the most blatant cases of collusion. For example, in the *Chan Wai Yip* case, a bid-rigging scenario was not deemed to be unlawful.[47]

12.3.2 Cartel Investigations under the HKCO

Some of Hong Kong's markets possess features that make collusion not only easy, but even likely. These are markets difficult to penetrate with high concentration levels, inelastic demand and homogeneous end

[45] Telecommunications Ordinance (Cap 106), Sections 7K and 7L, and Broadcasting Ordinance (Cap 562), ss. 13 and 14. See Williams, M., 'Seeds of Its Own Destruction: Hong Kong's Dysfunctional Competition Policy' (2006) 1 *Journal of Business Law* 52.

[46] This case is covered, inter alia, in Marco Colino, S., 'A History of Competition: The Impact of Antitrust on Hong Kong's Telecommunications Markets' (2019) 29 *Fordham Journal of Intellectual Property, Media and Entertainment Law* 931, p. 956; Ping, L. and Chen, E., 'Competition Policy under Laissez-Faireism: Market Power and Its Treatment in Hong Kong' (2002) 21 *Review of Industrial Organization* 145.

[47] *HKSAR* v *Chan Wai Yip and others* [FACC No. 4 of 2010].

products.[48] The permissive attitude towards cartels prior to the introduction of the HKCO would have made cartels highly enticing for the players in those markets. It is no surprise, therefore, that the HKCC has put this kind of activity at the top of its enforcement agenda. In addition to the cases that have been brought before the HKCT to date, the HKCC's Enforcement Policy expressly states that the watchdog 'will accord priority to those cases which involve' certain types of conduct, among which cartels are the first to be listed.[49] Cartel cases are easier to win than others that require extensive effects analysis and reliance on complex economic theories, and therefore they offer newly established competition agencies an opportunity to go on a winning streak if incidences of collusion are targeted at the outset.

The HKCC's cartel work took off in 2016, with the publication of two reports: one relating to the practices of trade associations,[50] and another based on a market study[51] of the residential building renovation and maintenance market.[52] In the former, the HKCC insisted on the need to avoid price recommendations, fee scales and any restrictions on price competition between the members of the associations.[53] The latter found that bid rigging was likely to be a common occurrence in the renovation industry.[54] Also in 2016, the Commission required the Hong Kong Newspaper Hawker Association to go back on a recommendation it made to its members relating to a minimum retail price for certain brands of cigarettes.[55]

48 See Ivaldi, M., Jullien, B., Rey, P., Seabright, P. and Tirole, J., 'The Economics of Tacit Collusion' (Final Report for the Directorate General for Competition, European Commission, IDEI, March 2003). Retrieved from http://ec.europa.eu/competition/mergers/studies_reports/the_economics_of_tacit_collusion_en.pdf.

49 HKCC, 'Enforcement Policy' (2015), para. 3.5. Retrieved from www.compcomm.hk/en/legislation_guidance/policy_doc/files/Enforcement_Policy_Eng.pdf.

50 HKCC, 'Report on Trade Associations in Hong Kong and the Competition Ordinance' (March 2016). Retrieved from www.compcomm.hk/en/media/reports_publications/files/TA_project_report_EN.pdf (Report on Trade Associations).

51 Section 130 of the HKCO enables the HKCC to conduct market studies 'into matters affecting competition in markets in Hong Kong'.

52 HKCC, 'Report on Study into Aspects of the Market for Residential Building Renovation and Maintenance' (May 2016). Retrieved from www.compcomm.hk/en/media/press/files/Report_on_market_study.pdf (Building Renovation and Maintenance Report).

53 Report on Trade Associations, p. 5.

54 Building Renovation and Maintenance Report.

55 HKCC Press Release, 'Competition Commission Welcomes Quick Rectification by the Hong Kong Newspaper Hawker Association on Retail Price of Branded Cigarettes' (31 May 2016). Retrieved from www.compcomm.hk/en/about/public_notices/files/HKNHA_20160531_e.pdf.

In 2017, a report on the auto-fuel market, the result of another market study, was published. This report denounced, inter alia, parallel pricing practices on the part of the oil companies.[56]

Thus far, only the residential building renovation and maintenance market study has led to proceedings. This may be in part due to the low likelihood of finding substantial evidence of collusion when conducting such an investigation,[57] and also in part due to the (possibly consequential) lack of recent market studies. No reports were published during Snyder's time as CEO. However, the value of this important instrument should not be written off. By closely examining specific markets, antitrust watchdogs can instil fear in those companies that might be breaching the law. The pressure should push them towards reporting and applying for leniency. After all, studies suggest that fear plays a greater role in the decision to cooperate with the competition authorities than scrupulous cost–benefit analyses.[58]

As of 2020, a total of seven cases have been brought before the HKCT, of which six relate to collusion. The long-awaited first case was announced on 23 March 2017, and was the outcome of an investigation into the bid-rigging practices of five information technology (IT) companies. According to the HKCC, Nutanix Hong Kong Limited (Nutanix), British Telecom Hong Kong Limited (BT), SiS International Limited (SiS), Innovix Distribution Limited (Innovix) and Tech-21 Systems Limited (Tech-21) acted in contravention of the FCR in relation to a tender issued by the Hong Kong Young Women's Christian Association (YWCA) for the supply and installation of a new IT server system.[59] Having previously agreed on the 'winner' of the tender, the bids submitted by the others effectively amounted to dummy bids. The HKCC sought a declaration of infringement and the imposition of financial penalties on the undertakings. Two years later, on 17 May 2019, the HKCT found that a contravention of the FCR had indeed taken place.[60] However, SiS was not

[56] The HKCC did not conclude that this was necessarily a consequence of price coordination, since parallel pricing can also indicate vigorous competition. HKCC, 'Report on Study into Hong Kong's Auto-fuel Market' (May 2017), p. 59. Retrieved from www.compcomm.hk/en/media/press/files/Full_Report_Auto_fuel_Market_Study_Report_Eng.pdf.

[57] Wils, W. P. J., 'The Use of Leniency in EU Cartel Enforcement: An Assessment after Twenty Years' (2016) 39 *World Competition* 327.

[58] Ibid., pp. 343–46.

[59] Case CTEA 1/2017 *Competition Commission* v. *Nutanix and Others* [2019] HKCT 2 (*Nutanix*).

[60] Ibid.

considered to be part of the bid-rigging practices, since the employee who had been partaking in the collusive arrangements did not have authority to bind the company, and his superiors were unaware of his conduct.[61] At the time of writing, the specific amount of the fines was yet to be determined.

The second case arrived shortly after the first. On 14 August 2017, the HKCC announced that it had commenced proceedings against ten construction and engineering companies, namely W Hing Construction Co. Ltd, Sun Spark Construction Ltd, Mau Hang Painting & Decoration Co., Tai Dou Building Contractor, Kam Kee Machine Electrical Iron Works Co. Ltd, Hip Yick Construction Co., Tai Wah Civil Engineering, Wai Sun Iron & Decoration Co., Wide Project Engineering & Construction Co. and Luen Hop Decoration Engineering Co. Ltd.[62] Following an investigation, it found that the undertakings had engaged in price fixing and market sharing in relation to the renovation of a public housing estate in the Kwun Tong area of Hong Kong. On 17 May 2019, the HKCT agreed with the HKCC and declared that an infringement had occurred.[63] A year later, on 29 April 2020, it applied the maximum fines available under the HKCO to all the companies involved in the cartel (that is, 10 per cent of local turnover per year of infringement, up to a maximum of three years).[64] This was the first time the HKCT had ever applied a penalty for a breach of the HKCO.

A further case involving collusion in relation to the provision of renovation services was brought on 6 September 2018 against the companies Goldfield N&W Construction Co. Ltd (Goldfield), Kam Kwong Engineering Co. Ltd (Kam Kwong) and Pacific View Engineering Limited (Pacific View).[65] These were the first proceedings launched after Snyder became CEO, and signalled a new era with regard to the imposition of penalties. On this occasion, the Commission did not just seek a declaration of infringement and corporate fines for the pricing and customer arrangements, but also individual pecuniary penalties and even a director disqualification order.[66] It was in the context of this

61 Ibid.

62 Case CTEA 2/2017 *Competition Commission* v. *W Hing Construction Company Ltd and Others* [2019] HKCT 3 and [2020] HKCT 1 (*W Hing*).

63 *W Hing* [2019].

64 *W Hing* [2020].

65 Case CTEA1/2018 *Competition Commission* v *Kam Kwong Engineering Company and Others* [2020] HKCT 3 (*Kam Kwong*).

66 Ibid.

case that, in July 2020, the HKCT adopted the so-called Carecraft procedure,[67] which aims to facilitate the settlement of disputes by allowing the disposal of proceedings by consent.[68] The application of this procedure implies that the HKCT will have to decide whether to make a director disqualification order based on the agreed facts presented by the parties.

A third investigation into the same sector led to another case, announced on 3 July 2019. According to the HKCC, the companies Fungs E & M Engineering Co. Ltd, Yee Hing Metal Shop, Cheung Min (trading as Accord Construction & Decoration Co.), Hing Shing Construction Co., Luen Hop Decoration Engineering Co. Ltd (Luen Hop) and Dao Kee Construction Co. Ltd engaged in customer allocation and price coordination in relation to public housing located once again in Kwun Tong.[69] In addition to corporate and individual fines, and two director disqualification orders, the HKCC also pursued an 'order that these decoration contractors and individuals be restrained or prohibited from entering into or participating in any anti-competitive agreements in respect of any renovation projects under the HKHA's Decoration Contractor System'.[70] In October 2020, the HKCT adopted its first ever director disqualification order against the director of Luen Hop.[71]

On 20 January 2020, the HKCC opened proceedings against Quantr Ltd (Quantr).[72] In 2017, the undertaking colluded with a competitor in the context of a bid for the procurement of IT services for Ocean Park Corporation, which owns one of the city's main theme parks. Nintex, the software provider, was also investigated for participating in the illegal conduct through the acts of a former employee. It agreed to resolve the matter by taking steps to ensure compliance and accepting an infringement notice, making this the first case in which such a notice was ever issued by the HKCC. Importantly, it is also the first case where leniency

[67] The name of the procedure derives from the case in which it was originally formulated, *Re Carecraft Construction Co. Ltd* [1994] 1 WLR 172.

[68] *Kam Kwong*.

[69] Case CTEA1/2019 *Competition Commission* v. *Fungs E & M Engineering Company Limited and Others* (nyd).

[70] HKCC Press Release (3 July 2019). Retrieved from www.compcomm.hk/en/media/press/files/20190703_Competition_Commission_takes_renovation_cartel_case_to_Competition_Tribunal_eng_PR.pdf.

[71] Case CTEA1/2019 *Competition Commission* v. *Fungs E & M Engineering Company Limited and Others* [2020] HKCT 9.

[72] *Quantr*.

was successfully granted. Quantr's co-bidder applied, seemingly met all the requirements to qualify for leniency, and a leniency agreement was offered under Section 80 of the HKCO.[73] No action has been taken against the company, which has not been named. On 3 November 2020, the HKCT handed down its judgment on the case, finding that an infringement of the FCR had indeed taken place. Quantr was ordered to pay a modest fine of HK$37,702 (less than US$5,000), and the rest of the penalties sought were suspended on the condition that the companies involved conduct competition compliance programmes for their staff. As a consequence, no director disqualification was imposed. The unusual speed with which this case was decided is a consequence of the fact that the HKCC and the companies under investigation 'reached agreement to resolve both the liability and relief portions of the proceedings by consent, and did so at an early stage, saving both sides significant time and costs'.[74]

The most recent cartel case, launched on 20 March 2020, relates to a possible cartel in the textbook market.[75] TH Lee Book Co. Ltd, Commercial Press (Hong Kong) Ltd and Sino United Publishing (Holdings) Ltd allegedly colluded in relation to textbooks for primary and secondary schools in Hong Kong. While their conduct was agreed to and entered into before the HKCO came into force, it continued after the law became effective. The HKCC is seeking a declaration of contravention, corporate and individual pecuniary fines, and a director disqualification order.[76]

12.4 Hong Kong's Leniency Policy

12.4.1 Leniency in the HKCO

Section 80 of the HKCO explicitly vests the HKCC with the power to offer leniency:

1) The Commission may, in exchange for a person's co-operation in an investigation or in proceedings under this Ordinance, make an agreement (a 'leniency agreement') with the person, on any terms it

[73] See Section 12.4 below.

[74] HKCC Press Release (3 November 2020). Retrieved from www.compcomm.hk/en/media/press/files/EN_PR_IT_case_judgment.pdf.

[75] Case CTEA2/2020 *Competition Commission* v. *TH Lee Book Company Limited and Others* (nyd) (*Textbook Cartel*).

[76] Ibid.

considers appropriate, that it will not bring or continue proceedings under Part 6 for a pecuniary penalty in respect of an alleged contravention of a conduct rule against –

(a) if the person is a natural person, that person or any employee or agent of that person;
(b) if the person is a corporation, that corporation or any officer, employee or agent of the corporation;
(c) if the person is a partner in a partnership, that partnership or any partner in the partnership, or any employee or agent of the partnership; or
(d) if the person is an undertaking other than one referred to in paragraph (a), (b) or (c), that undertaking or any officer, employee or agent of the undertaking, in so far as the contravention consists of the conduct specified in the agreement.

2) The Commission must not, while a leniency agreement is in force, bring or continue proceedings under Part 6 for a pecuniary penalty in breach of that leniency agreement.

It is thus possible for the Commission to enter into leniency agreements with natural persons and corporations alike, and leniency in non-cartel investigations is not ruled out – the law refers generally to the 'contravention of *a* conduct rule'.[77] The wording of this provision would suggest that leniency is limited to 'pecuniary penalties' and cannot cover director disqualification orders. However, as seen below, the HKCC has opted for a broad interpretation of Section 80, and successful applicants will also be spared from disqualification.[78] The impact of this on the success of leniency could be significant. The prospect of having this severe individual penalty looming over leniency applicants could certainly discourage them from coming forward with information.

The HKCC may terminate leniency agreements in accordance with Section 81 of the HKCO, which states:

1) The Commission may terminate a leniency agreement if –
   (a) the other party to the agreement agrees to the termination;
   (b) it has reasonable grounds to suspect that the information on which it based its decision to make the agreement was incomplete, false or misleading in a material particular;

[77] HKCO, Section 80, emphasis added.

[78] See Section 12.4.2 below.

(c) the other party to the agreement, or if the agreement was made by a person as an officer, employee or agent of an undertaking, that undertaking has been convicted of an offence under Part 3; or
(d) it is satisfied that the other party to the agreement, or if the agreement was made by a person as an officer, employee or agent of an undertaking, that undertaking has failed to comply with the terms of the agreement.

2) The Commission may terminate a leniency agreement by giving notice in writing to the other party to the agreement and to any other person who appears to the Commission to be likely to benefit from the agreement, stating –
(a) the date of the termination; and
(b) the reasons for the termination.
3) A notice under subsection (2) must specify the period within which representations may be made to the Commission about the proposed termination.
4) The period specified for the purpose of subsection (3) must be a period of at least 30 days beginning after the day on which the notice is given.
5) Before terminating a leniency agreement, the Commission must consider any representations about the proposed termination that are made to it.

Section 81 thus vests the HKCC with the power to cancel a leniency arrangement only under the specific circumstances listed above.

12.4.2 The Competition Commission's Leniency Policies

Having explored the HKCO's leniency provisions, it is now time to discuss the policies adopted by the HKCC in keeping with that basic framework. Reference is made to 'policies' in plural given that, since 2020, there is a policy for undertakings and another for individuals. Both are fleshed out below.

12.4.2.1 Leniency Policy for Undertakings

In November 2015, a month before the HKCO became fully effective, the HKCC published its original Leniency Policy for Undertakings.[79]

[79] 2015 Leniency Policy.

A revised version was announced in April 2020,[80] aimed at enhancing 'the effectiveness and transparency of [the HKCC's] leniency programme' so as to improve cartel deterrence.[81] Unless specified otherwise, the discussion here relates to the modified guidance.

Scope While the HKCO does not limit leniency to collusive practices,[82] the Leniency Policy for Undertakings only contemplates resorting to leniency in investigations relating to cartels,[83] defined as 'agreements and/or concerted practices between two or more undertakings which consist of (i) fixing, maintaining, increasing or controlling the price for the supply of goods or services, (ii) allocating sales, territories, customers or markets for the production or supply of goods or services, (iii) fixing, maintaining, controlling, preventing, limiting or eliminating the production or supply of goods or services, or (iv) bid-rigging'.[84] This does not mean that it is impossible to be granted a leniency agreement in the context of other violations. However, such cases are not covered by the Leniency Policy for Undertakings,[85] and therefore there is currently no certainty as to the conditions under which immunity could be arranged beyond cartels.

To be offered a leniency agreement by the HKCC, it is imperative that the applicant has not coerced others into participating in the collusion, and is not the 'clear single ringleader' of the cartel.[86] This wording does not entirely close the door on leniency for companies with a prominent role in the unlawful coordination, as long as they are not the only evident instigator. Moreover, the undertaking must have 'taken prompt and effective action to terminate its participation in the cartel conduct',[87] unless the HKCC asks that it continue to be involved so as to provide assistance in the investigation, or to prevent raising suspicion among the rest of the

80 HKCC, 'Leniency Policy for Undertakings Engaged in Cartel Conduct' (April 2020). Retrieved from www.compcomm.hk/en/legislation_guidance/policy_doc/files/Leniency_Policy_Undertakings_E.pdf (Leniency Policy for Undertakings).

81 Deacons, 'Competition Commission Revises Leniency Policy for Undertakings and Introduces New Leniency Policy for Individuals' *Lexology* (24 April 2020). Retrieved from www.lexology.com/library/detail.aspx?g=3ad6f2b9-c39b-4b13-a100-9e8a3a65c0af.

82 See Section 12.4.1 above.

83 Leniency Policy for Undertakings, Section 1.3.

84 Ibid., Section 1.3(a).

85 Ibid., p. 1, which states that '[t]his Policy does not preclude the Commission from entering into a leniency agreement in circumstances other than those provided for in it'.

86 Ibid., Section 2.15(b).

87 Ibid., Section 2.15(c).

cartel members.[88] It is also necessary to ensure 'full and truthful disclosure'; to protect confidentiality; to adopt or maintain a compliance programme; and to continue 'full and truthful cooperation' with the HKCC.[89]

Types of Corporate Leniency Since 2015, leniency has been available to the first undertaking to come forward with information about a cartel before an investigation has been opened. A novelty of the 2020 revision is that it is now possible to seek leniency even if the HKCC is already looking into the conduct. The former is known as type 1 leniency, while the latter is type 2.[90] In both cases, the HKCC vows not to issue proceedings before the HKCT against the successful applicant 'in relation to the reported conduct'.[91] However, in type 2 cases, the HKCC may issue an infringement notice, which requires the applicant to admit to contravening the FCR.[92] On the basis of the notice, it will be possible to pursue follow-on damage claims before the HKCT.

The fact that damages may have to be paid by whistleblowers can act as an obstacle for leniency applications, since they may end up 'expos[ing] the applicant to follow-on actions'.[93] This is likely to be reason why successful type 1 leniency applicants are shielded from damages claims under the revised policy. Regardless of the type of leniency, of course, no penalties of any kind will be sought against the beneficiaries.[94] Any leniency granted would extend to current and possibly even former employees and officers and partners of the beneficiary, if they 'fully and truthfully cooperate with the Commission'.[95]

Termination of the Leniency Agreement In line with Section 81 of the HKCO, the Leniency Policy for Undertakings gives the HKCC considerable discretion to terminate leniency agreements,[96] provided that 'it has reasonable grounds to suspect that that party has at any time knowingly provided false or materially incomplete information to the

88 Ibid., note 12.
89 Ibid., Sections 2.15(a), (d), (e) and (f).
90 Ibid., Section 1.3(d).
91 Ibid., Section 1.3(e).
92 Ibid., Section 2.15(g). See also *Quantr*.
93 Carabine, N., Wan, E., Huckerby, M. and Wilkinson, J., 'Hong Kong Competition Commission's Enforcement and Leniency Policies' (18 December 2015). Retrieved from https://read01.com/AJxj8.html#.YpNvdujP25c.
94 HKCO, Section 93.
95 Leniency Policy for Undertakings, para. 1.3(f).
96 Ibid., Section 3.

Commission or has otherwise failed to comply with the terms of the leniency agreement'.[97] The threat of losing immunity might exert pressure on the companies to observe the arrangement; however, it also increases uncertainty. This is more concerning considering that, if leniency is terminated, not only can the undertaking face proceedings before the HKCT,[98] but also any information it previously provided 'may be retained by the Commission and used as evidence against that undertaking and other participants in the cartel conduct'.[99] It is thus in the interest of a company that has succeeded in attaining leniency to ensure that the agreement is not in any way jeopardised.

Cooperation and Leniency Plus The Leniency Policy for Undertakings only allows 'the first cartel member who meets all the requirements for receiving leniency and enters into a leniency agreement' to benefit from its scope.[100] Until 2019, this meant there was no official policy towards undertakings that, while willing to cooperate, did not win the race to leniency. The 2015 policy referred to potential reductions in the fines sought and other perks for companies not qualifying for leniency,[101] provided that they approached the HKCC 'in a timely manner seeking to cooperate' and put forward 'significant evidence regarding the cartel conduct'.[102] However, the HKCT would not be bound by the HKCC's recommendations with regard to financial penalties, and the extent to which the fines eventually imposed on these companies would be reduced was entirely uncertain.[103]

Important changes in this respect arrived on 29 April 2019, when the HKCO published its Cooperation and Settlement Policy for Undertakings Engaged in Cartel Conduct (Cooperation Policy).[104] Relying on this new instrument, undertakings that are not the first to come forward may enter into a cooperation agreement with the HKCC, and may attain a reduction of up to 50 per cent of the penalties recommended to the HKCT, as well as a commitment from the HKCC 'not to take any proceedings against any current and former employees, officers, partners and agents

97 Ibid., para. 3.1.
98 Ibid., para. 3.3.
99 Ibid., para. 3.4
100 Ibid., para. 1.2.
101 2015 Leniency Policy, Section 4.2.
102 Ibid., Section 4.4.
103 Leniency Policy for Undertakings, Section 4.5.
104 Cooperation Policy.

of the undertaking provided that they fully and truthfully cooperate with the Commission'.[105] The discounts are calculated on a case-by-case basis, with reference to three general bands,[106] and then adjusting the amount taking into consideration the timing, nature, value and extent of the cooperation.[107] A requirement for entering into a cooperation agreement is that an Agreed Factual Summary, fleshing out the settled facts, be included.[108]

The Cooperation Policy further introduced leniency plus, by virtue of which undertakings cooperating with the HKCC that disclose the existence of a separate cartel can benefit from an additional reduction of up to 10 per cent off the recommended pecuniary penalty for the first cartel.[109] The exact discount will depend on a number of factors, including the significance of the second cartel and the strength of the evidence provided.[110]

Confidentiality Issues Sections 125–127 of the HKCO cover the preservation of confidentiality in investigations and proceedings. Accordingly, Section 4 of the Leniency Policy for Undertakings discusses the confidentiality obligations of both the leniency applicant and the HKCC. The former must 'keep confidential the fact of the investigation, its application for leniency ... and the terms of any leniency agreement entered into with the Commission', unless disclosure is required by law or specific consent for disclosure has been granted.[111]

The HKCC's confidentiality obligations are a delicate matter. In order to be able to implement a successful leniency policy, it is crucial that applicants feel protected from exposure in other jurisdictions. This is particularly important given the relatively low financial penalties applicable in Hong Kong: it would not make much sense to admit to collusion in order to be spared from modest fines if the information disclosed can be used elsewhere to impose a more severe punishment. Under Section

105 Ibid., Section 1.2(e).

106 The Cooperation Policy refers to specific bands of recommended discounts 'based on the order in which undertakings express their interest to cooperate'. For band 1, the discount would be between 35 and 50 per cent, for band 2 between 20 and 40 per cent, and for band 3 up to 25 per cent. Cooperation Policy, Section 3.3.

107 Ibid., Section 3.5.

108 Ibid., Sections 1.2(c), 2.7 and 2.8.

109 Ibid., Section 4.1.

110 Ibid., Section 4.3.

111 Leniency Policy for Undertakings, Section 4.1.

125 of the HKCO, the HKCC is under a general obligation 'to preserve and aid in preserving the confidentiality of any confidential information'. The Leniency Policy for Undertakings reiterates that duty,[112] but it is not absolute. Section 126 of the CO contains a list of exceptions to the protection of confidentiality, and in the context of leniency the HKCC 'reserves the right to use and disclose Leniency Material with appropriate confidentiality protections in its investigations and any proceedings'.[113]

Despite this prospect, the revised Leniency Policy for Undertakings insists that 'it is the Commission's policy not to release Leniency Material', and the competition watchdog will even 'firmly resist, on public interest immunity and other applicable grounds, requests for Leniency Material'.[114] This is much more emphatic than the previous wording in the 2015 version, which simply referred to the HKCC's 'best endeavours' to protect confidentiality.[115] Moreover, whereas the original policy did not specify the circumstances under which information could be shared,[116] it is now clear that it will only be in order to comply with the law or a court order, with the leniency applicant's consent, or relating to information that is already public.[117] While the possibility of disclosure remains, it is now clear that it is rather unlikely that information relating to leniency applications will be released. These clarifications are thus invaluable for the prospect of convincing cartel members to blow the whistle.

Application Process The Leniency Policy for Undertakings refers to six stages in a successful leniency application. The first involves requesting a marker. Markers are common in other jurisdictions (including the US), and have the purpose of securing 'an initial indication that leniency is available to an identified leniency candidate while it gathers more information to support its leniency application'.[118] The marker system

112 Ibid., Section 4.3.

113 Ibid., Section 4.4.

114 Ibid.

115 2015 Leniency Policy, Section 5.6.

116 There was instead a reference to the HKCC, 'Guideline: Investigations' (27 July 2015). Retrieved from www.compcomm.hk/en/legislation_guidance/guidance/investigations/files/Guideline_Investigations_Eng.pdf. See 2015 Leniency Policy, Section 5.5.

117 Leniency Policy for Undertakings, Section 4.4.

118 Mobley, S. and Denton, R. (eds.), *Global Cartels Handbook—Leniency: Policy and Procedure* (Oxford: Oxford University Press, 2011), p. 392.

constitutes a way to safeguard a place in the leniency queue until proof of the collusive activity the applicant wants to blow the whistle on.[119]

In Hong Kong, it is possible to make an initial consultation anonymously either by phone or by email, with the applicant obliged to explain 'that it has uncovered information or evidence suggesting its participation in possible cartel conduct'.[120] No admission of liability is required at this stage,[121] but the information provided must cover 'the broad nature of the cartel', including 'the affected industry, product(s) and/or service(s), the general nature of the conduct and the time period'.[122] Once the HKCC has looked into the matter and determined that a marker is available, if the undertaking wants to apply, it will have to reveal its identity[123] and provide some preliminary information including the names of the other companies and 'key individuals' involved in the collusion, the time and geographical scope, a description of the conduct and, if it is a cross-border cartel, whether other authorities are also scrutinising the activity.[124] A novelty of the 2020 version of the Leniency Policy for Undertakings is that, in the event that the marker is already taken, undertakings are encouraged to collaborate with the HKCC under the terms of the Cooperation Policy.[125] Cooperation is a requirement for staying in the queue for the marker in case it becomes available.[126]

The second stage comes in the event that a marker has been attained and involves perfecting that marker. This is done through a proffer process,[127] during which the information provided by the undertaking must be expanded to include 'a detailed description of the cartel conduct and its functioning', providing 'information about its duration and participants, the products or services affected by it, the names of persons involved in the conduct' as well as the evidence it possesses on the collusion.[128] The time frame will be determined by the HKCC, but it will

[119] See, e.g., Favart, M., 'Belgium', in Buhart, J. (ed.), *Leniency Regimes*, 4th ed. (London: Sweet & Maxwell, 2012), 36, p. 36.

[120] Leniency Policy for Undertakings, Section 2.3.

[121] Ibid.

[122] Ibid.

[123] Ibid., Sections 2.5 and 2.7.

[124] Ibid., Section 2.7.

[125] Cooperation Policy.

[126] Leniency Policy for Undertakings, Section 2.6.

[127] Ibid., Section 2.9.

[128] Ibid., Section 2.11.

usually be a minimum of thirty calendar days and may be extended.[129] In order to reinforce the protection of confidentiality and put potential applicants at ease, the Leniency Policy for Undertakings offers reassurance that, in the event that a leniency agreement is not eventually entered into, the information provided in the proffer will not be used as evidence.[130] However, the HKCC retains the right to use the powers vested in it by the HKCO to obtain information in order to request what was revealed in the proffer.[131]

The third stage involves entering into the leniency agreement, which will be offered to the undertaking 'based on the proffer and any additional information provided'.[132] It is drafted according to the template that can be found in Annex A of the Leniency Policy for Undertakings. The fourth stage is compliance with that agreement. For the HKCC, this requires not bringing proceedings against the undertaking, its partner in any potential partnerships and its current officers or employees. In some cases, the Commission may agree to additionally protect agents, as well as former officers, employees and partners. The leniency beneficiary is obliged to maintain 'complete, truthful and continuous cooperation with the Commission throughout its investigation and any ensuing enforcement proceedings before the Tribunal or other courts in relation to that conduct'.[133]

The fifth stage is triggered by follow-on claims relating to the collusion that the leniency applicant helped uncover.[134] If they arise, then the HKCC is in a position to issue an infringement notice in order to allow the HKCT to award damages.[135] However, such notices may only be issued against type 2 leniency applicants, since the revised policy protects type 1 agreements from exposure to follow-on actions.[136] The process culminates with the sixth stage; that is, a letter from the HKCC confirming the fulfilment of all the conditions for leniency.[137] This might be once an infringement notice has been issued by the HKCC, or when litigation before the courts has concluded.[138]

[129] Ibid., note 11 and Section 2.12.
[130] Ibid., Section 2.13.
[131] Ibid. and HKCO, Section 41.
[132] Leniency Policy for Undertakings, Section 2.14.
[133] Ibid., Section 2.16.
[134] Ibid., Section 2.17.
[135] Ibid.
[136] Ibid.
[137] Ibid., Section 2.18.
[138] Ibid.

12.4.2.2 Leniency Policy for Individuals

The Leniency Policy for Individuals Involved in Cartel Conduct (Leniency Policy for Individuals) is a novelty of the 2020 reform.[139] It offers new hope in the battle against collusive practices, particularly when considered in the context of the new trend, kicked off by the *Kam Kwong* case,[140] of seeking individual sanctions for cartels. The modest corporate penalties available under the HKCO might not be enough to break the trust between cartelists, but the fear of personal fines and director disqualification orders might just make employees turn against the companies they work for, and they may be in a position to provide the coveted proof of collusion. Indeed, the HKCC explains that the Leniency Policy for Individuals is 'designed to provide a strong, transparent, and predictable incentive for an individual to stop their involvement in cartel conduct and to report the conduct'.[141]

Scope The Leniency Policy for Individuals is unsurprisingly limited to *individuals*[142] involved in *cartel conduct*.[143] With regard to the first boundary, which relates to the subjects of the policy, the person seeking leniency must not be the ringleader or have coerced others to enter into the cartel.[144] In addition to being the first individual to come forward, they must also apply before a marker has been granted to an undertaking in the context of the Leniency Policy for Undertakings, following the procedure described above.[145] Moreover, they are required to cooperate with the HKCC throughout the investigation.[146] As for the conduct affected, violations of the HKCO that do not amount to collusion cannot benefit from leniency.[147]

Termination of the Leniency Agreement Much like the Leniency Policy for Undertakings, the Leniency Policy for Individuals refers to Section 81

[139] HKCC, 'Leniency Policy for Individuals Involved in Cartel Conduct' (April 2020). Retrieved from www.compcomm.hk/en/legislation_guidance/policy_doc/files/Leniency_Policy_Individuals_E.pdf.

[140] *Kam Kwong*.

[141] Leniency Policy for Individuals, para. 1.1.

[142] Ibid., para. 1.2(b).

[143] Ibid., para. 1.2(a).

[144] Ibid., para. 1.2(c).

[145] See Section 12.4.2.1 above.

[146] Leniency Policy for Individuals, para. 1.2(f).

[147] Ibid., para. 1.2(a). The definition of cartel given here is identical to that in the Leniency Policy for Undertakings.

of the HKCO, relating to the termination of the leniency agreement. The HKCC explains that it will only take the nuclear option 'if it has reasonable grounds to suspect that that party has at any time knowingly provided false or materially incomplete information to the Commission or has otherwise failed to comply with the terms of the leniency agreement'.[148] The individual will be given an opportunity to address the HKCC's concerns before termination.[149] The stakes to avoid it are high, given that proceedings against the former leniency beneficiary might ensue, and the information provided might be used against them.[150]

Confidentiality The confidentiality conditions of the Leniency Policy for Individuals are virtually identical to those of the Leniency Policy for Undertakings. After recognising the applicant's obligations in this regard,[151] the HKCC discusses its own duties. The secrecy of leniency applications and related documents is guaranteed within the boundaries of the law, and in particular of Section 126 of the HKCO. However, the HKCC reiterates that it is not its practice to release leniency material, and that it will 'firmly resist' requests in this regard. Like in the Leniency Policy for Undertakings, the exceptions to this position are requests by a tribunal or an obligation under the law, where permission has been granted by the applicant, and situations in which the information is in the public domain.[152]

Application Process The application process established for individuals resembles the one laid down for undertakings. However, instead of six stages, there are only five. Follow-on actions do not affect leniency applications made ad personam, and therefore the fifth stage of the system used in corporate leniency cases is not relevant here. The remainder of the process is the same.

12.5 Effectiveness of Hong Kong's New Leniency System

The above changes certainly raise expectations about the future prospect of leniency in Hong Kong. In this section, the potential value of the system

[148] Ibid., para. 3.1.
[149] Ibid., para. 3.2.
[150] Ibid., paras. 3.3 and 3.4.
[151] Ibid., para. 4.1.
[152] Ibid., para. 4.4.

is discussed, taking into account both quantitative and qualitative criteria. Particular attention is paid to the impact of the reforms on the aspects considered crucial for success, namely the strength of the punishment cartelists face if they do not come forward, the risk of getting caught and subsequently the risk of getting caught and penalised, and the transparency of the tool.[153]

12.5.1 *The Quantity of Applications as an Indicator of Success*

At first sight, a single successful leniency application in the first five years of enforcement of the HKCO does not appear to suggest that the policy has been tremendously effective. The rather insignificant fine imposed as a result of the proceedings triggered by the evidence obtained intensifies the feeling of disappointment.[154] A look at the international arena is not much more encouraging. In recent years, some of the legal systems with highly regarded leniency programmes have been reporting a significant drop in leniency requests.[155] Is it then incongruous to be insisting on the importance for Hong Kong of a policy that might be falling into disuse?

Before concluding that leniency is of limited value, it is worth considering the reasons for the decline registered in jurisdictions such as the EU and the US. The plunge recorded by the European Commission coincides with the entry into force of the Damages Directive,[156] suggesting that the heightened fear of exposure to civil litigation is what may be dissuading leniency applicants.[157] Businesses are right to be concerned about damages claims. By way of example, after obtaining leniency for the information provided to the European Commission about the airfreight cartel,[158] Lufthansa was sued by Deutsche Bahn for €1.76 billion in damages.[159]

153 Fox and Crane, *Global Issues in Antitrust and Competition Law* (n. 10 above), p. 78.

154 *Quantr*.

155 Petkoski, D., Sánchez-Calero, P. and Bello, A., 'Reduction in Leniency; Drop in Enforcement?' *Lexology* (15 August 2019). Retrieved from www.lexology.com/library/detail.aspx?g=62d7c2fb-a154-40a5-989e-465e0c5da31c.

156 Directive 2014/104/EU of the European Parliament and of the Council of 26 November 2014 on certain rules governing actions for damages under national law for infringements of the competition law provisions of the Member States and of the European Union [2014] OJ L349/1.

157 See Cauffmann, C., 'The Interaction of Leniency Programmes and Actions for Damages' (2011) 7 *Competition Law Review* 181.

158 European Commission Decision of 9 November 2010, case COMP/39258 – Airfreight C(2010) 7694 final.

159 Burns, J., 'Lufthansa Reaches Settlement with Deutsche Bahn to End Cargo Cartel Dispute', *Cargo Airports & Airline Services* (28 August 2019). Retrieved from www.caasint.com/db-and-lufthansa-reach-settlement-to-end-cartel-legal-dispute.

In the US, the DOJ has been experiencing a general decrease in enforcement activity, which could be related to what has been described as 'cyclical' criminal enforcement, as well as a potential reduction of infringements as a consequence of deterrence.[160] In fact, a fall in leniency applications would be consistent with an effective policy that not only detects cartels, but also discourages their formation. William Kovacic has insisted that measuring the success of leniency by the number of applications is erroneous, since ultimately there should be fewer cartels rather than more convictions.[161]

In light of the above observations, it is not entirely fair to compare the issues of a policy that is just beginning to take off with those currently affecting other analogous yet more mature systems. Without a doubt, one of the most notable problems facing leniency arrangements in general is convincing cartelists that it is in their interest to break the trust and admit to being part of a highly profitable, unlawful activity. This will naturally be true also for Hong Kong.[162] In order to overcome this hurdle, it is necessary for the authorities to focus on creating a tangible fear of detection. As Snyder has acknowledged, 'the best way to make leniency attractive is to prove you can and will detect and prosecute cartels even without a leniency applicant'.[163] In this sense, the cartel cases brought before the HKCT (discussed earlier) would be the first vital step towards an effective strategy against collusion.[164] If successful, there should be an increase in the number of leniency applications within the next few years.

160 Ibid.

161 Kovacic, W. E., 'A Case for Capping the Dosage: Leniency and Competition Authority Governance', in Beaton-Wells, C. and Tran, C., *Anti-Cartel Enforcement in a Contemporary Age* (n. 7 above), 123, p. 130. See also Bigoni, M., Fridolfsson, S.-O., Le Coq, C., and Spagnolo, G., 'Fines, Leniency and Rewards in Antitrust' (2011) 43 *RAND Journal of Economics* 368, p. 369.

162 See, e.g., Nylander, J., 'Why Hong Kong Needs a Whistleblowing Policy', *Forbes Asia* (14 August 2015). Retrieved from www.forbes.com/sites/jnylander/2015/08/14/why-hong-kong-needs-a-whistleblowing-policy/#218c460f71f5; Michael, B., 'Hong Kong Needs a Whistle-blower Law for Better Governance and Business Practices, Researcher Says', *South China Morning Post* (11 August 2015). Retrieved from www.scmp.com/news/hong-kong/law-crime/article/1848274/hong-kong-needs-whistle-blower-law-better-governance-and.

163 Connolly, R., 'Some Comments from Brent Snyder, Former Antitrust Division Criminal Deputy, as the Head to the Hong Kong Competition Commission', *Cartel Capers* (12 July 2017). Retrieved from http://cartelcapers.com/blog/comments-brent-snyder-former-antitrust-division-criminal-deputy-heads-hong-kong-competition-commission.

164 See Section 12.3 above.

12.5.2 *Qualitative Assessment of the Revised Policy*

Looking beyond the numbers, the 2020 amendment of the leniency policy addresses many of the shortcomings of the original. Already since 2019, thanks to the Cooperation Policy, those who are not the first to report are able to obtain certain rewards when they come forward.[165] The revised Leniency Policy for Undertakings further recognises the enticing possibility of obtaining immunity when an investigation is already underway.[166] The modification ought to help the HKCC speed up the process of gathering all the necessary evidence to prove the existence of collusion. Perhaps more significantly, the assurance that leniency applicants will not be exposed to damage claims is crucial, as the European experience shows.[167] It does raise questions as to whether all of the victims of the cartel will see the harm they have suffered repaired. In principle, those injured by the leniency beneficiary ought to have the possibility of issuing a recovery action against the rest of the cartelists, based on the principle of joint and several liability. As a consequence, cartel members that do not attain leniency are likely to see their damages bills increase, a development that might make coming forward with information more appealing.

The new policy places more emphasis on the lengths the HKCC is willing to go to in order to preserve confidentiality. Even though it is not possible to grant absolute protection,[168] the HKCC insists that it will 'firmly resist' disclosure requests,[169] and the circumstances under which information might be shared are narrow and clearly fleshed out.[170] This clarity is certainly welcome, but it remains to be seen whether it will be enough to put the minds of potential applicants at ease. Still, no antitrust system offers absolute confidentiality protection.[171] The Hong Kong policy is as

165 Cooperation Policy.

166 See Section 12.4.2.1 above. Clarification regarding the treatment of those providing information in the context of ongoing investigations had been requested by the HKCA in its 'Comments on the Draft Leniency Policy' (2015). Retrieved from www.compcomm.hk/en/enforcement/consultations/past_consultations/files/S16_Hong_Kong_Competition_Association.pdf.

167 See Section 12.5.1 above. See also Vedder, H., 'The Kone Case and the Lifts Cartel – an Upward Effect on Prices and Effectiveness?' *European Law Blog* (19 June 2014). Retrieved from http://europeanlawblog.eu/?p=2397, discussing the negative impact of exposure to damages claims on the incentive to report.

168 Hong Kong Competition Ordinance, Section 126 and Leniency Policy for Undertakings, Section 4.4.

169 Ibid.

170 Leniency Policy for Undertakings, Section 4.4.

171 See, e.g., case C-360/09 *Pfleiderer AG* v. *Bundeskartellamt* [2011] ECR I-5161 or case C-536/11 *Bundeswettbewerbsbehörde* v. *Donau Chemie AG and others* [2013] 5 CMLR 19.

tight as it can be in this regard. It does however effectively require a written confession, which could be of concern for those thinking of reporting.

Some important question marks remain. For example, it is unclear what 'coercing' others to join the cartel means. Since it is a matter that would rule out both corporate and individual leniency, it would be helpful to understand what the HKCC considers to amount to coercion.[172] Also, the guidance says nothing about the application of Section 80 of the HKCO beyond cartels, meaning that it is currently unrealistic to expect leniency requests relating to any other kinds of violations.[173] The HKCC's powers to terminate leniency agreements, both for undertakings and individuals, continue to be broad.[174] However, this also serves to put pressure on applicants to use their best endeavours to avoid termination.

Undoubtedly, the biggest challenges facing the policy are, on the one hand, the lack of convergence between leniency systems (meaning uncertainty as to whether a company is the first to file in all relevant jurisdictions)[175] and, on the other hand, the modesty of the corporate fines envisaged by the HKCO for anti-competitive conduct.[176] The best way to address this would be to modify the law, but naturally this is not something in the hands of the HKCC. For the time being, the threat of individual fines and director disqualification orders needs to continue to be emphasised. Since 2017, the HKCC has indeed made use of these harsher penalties, and the fact that the HKCT has now actually imposed them is a welcome development in this regard. The other avenue worth exploring would be increasing the incentive of leniency by offering positive rewards (i.e. a recompense) to applicants, like Korea does.[177]

12.6 Conclusion

From the very beginning of Hong Kong's competition law history, the HKCC has had its eyes set on building a workable leniency policy to

[172] See HKCA, 'Comments on the Draft Leniency Policy' (n. 167 above).

[173] Ibid.

[174] Leniency Policy for Undertakings, paras. 3.1, 3.3 and 3.4.

[175] The book this chapter is part of serves to highlight the differences between Asian leniency regimes.

[176] See Section 12.2 above.

[177] Stephan, A., 'Is the Korean Innovation of Individual Informant Rewards a Viable Cartel Detection Tool?' in Cheng, Marco Colino and Ong, *Cartels in Asia* (n. 30 above), 109, p. 109. On the merits of positive rewards, see Spagnolo, G., '*Divide et Impera*: Optimal Leniency Programs', Stockholm School of Economics (2005) Retrieved from http://ftp.zew.de/pub/zew-docs/veranstaltungen/rnic/papers/GiancarloSpagnolo.pdf.

combat collusion. Its efforts are certainly commendable, and – at least on paper – they appear to have paid off. Undertakings and individuals can apply for leniency, may be rewarded even if they are not the first to report and/or the cartel they are involved in is already under investigation, and those undertakings blowing the whistle on a cartel that was previously unknown to the Commission will not face damages claims. Remarkable efforts have also been made to convince potential applicants that the information they provide will be treated as confidential, save under very specific circumstances. Whether or not this potentially powerful weapon will effectively lead to greater cartel detection and deterrence is less clear. The limitations of the competition legislation it stems from, particularly the low financial corporate fines envisaged, might diminish the attractiveness of blowing the whistle to escape punishment. It is hoped that the legislator will address these shortcomings in the not too distant future. In the meantime, the HKCC has demonstrated it has the will and the power to bring down the city's cartels, and it now has the support of a robust leniency policy in this endeavour.

13

The Leniency Programme under the Indian Competition Law

NIKITA KORADIA, KIRAN MANOKARAN AND JUHI HIRANI

13.1 Introduction

Cartels have historically been regarded as the most pernicious anti-competitive offence. They have the potential to have a significant adverse impact on the competition and yet remain elusive. Anti-competitive agreements are often entered into between competitors under clandestine circumstances. The Competition Commission of India (CCI) observed that agreements restraining competition are generally made in 'smoke filled rooms' and often lack a formal/written agreement.[1] Further, establishing the existence of a cartel seldom happens through direct evidence. The enforcement agency predominantly relies on parallel behaviour of the competing enterprises viewed in conjunction with a collection of circumstantial evidence, known as 'plus factors',[2] to prove the existence of a cartel. Thus, detection of cartels is an arduous and expensive process.

The concept of leniency in competition law emerged precisely to remedy these drawbacks. Cartels are widely regarded as unstable on account of their individual members' desire to earn more than the rest and their propensity to cheat. Leniency programmes typically capitalise on this trait and incentivise cartel members to break ranks and disclose vital information that would enable the enforcement agency to crack down on the cartels, in exchange for leniency. Owing to the nascency of the leniency programme in India, there is still a lack of clarity on the leniency programme itself and its collateral impact on other aspects of the competition law, such as private enforcement and inter-agency cooperation.

1 CCI, Suo Moto Case No. 01 of 2019, In re: Alleged anti-competitive conduct by Maruti Suzuki India Limited (MSIL) in implementing discount control policy vis-à-vis dealers.

2 CCI, MRTP Case: RTPE No. 20 of 2008, All India Tires Dealers Federation vs. Tire Manufacturers (MRTP Case: RTPE No. 20 of 2008).

In this chapter, we explore the legal framework of the leniency programme in India as developed in Article 46 of the Competition Act 2002 (Competition Act)[3] and the Competition Commission of India (Lesser Penalty) Regulations 2009 (LPR)[4] (Section 13.2). We also analyse the jurisprudential trends in the decisions passed by the CCI under the Competition Act and the LPR. This allows us to highlight the shortcomings of the existing system of administering the leniency programme (Section 13.3). We further critically discuss interconnected concepts. First, the interaction between the leniency programme and private enforcement is dealt with. This will be done with the closely related aspect of confidentiality (Section 13.4). Second, as some changes to the Competition Act are contemplated, the leniency programme will be discussed in its possible interaction with administrative sanctions, leniency plus, settlement and commitments (Section 13.5). As more and more cartels operate in a cross-border setting, the leniency programme will be discussed against the context of inter-agency cooperation (Section 13.6).

13.2 Legal Framework of the Leniency Programme in India

13.2.1 Section 46 of the Competition Act 2002 as the Basis for the Leniency Programme

In India, the power and mechanism to administer a leniency programme are provided under Section 46 of the Competition Act. This provision is further elaborated in the LPR. Accordingly, the CCI is empowered to impose a lesser penalty on any persons involved in a cartel if they make a full, true and vital disclosure in respect of the alleged violations. While normally the CCI may impose a penalty up to three times an enterprise's profits or 10 per cent of its turnover, whichever is higher, for each year of cartelisation,[5] the LPR permits a reduction in penalty up to 100 per cent to the first applicant, up to 50 per cent to the second applicant and up to 30 per cent to the subsequent applicants.[6]

[3] The Competition Act, 2002, to which the President accorded assent in January 2003. Retrieved from www.cci.gov.in/sites/default/files/cci_pdf/competitionact2012.pdf (Competition Act).

[4] CCI Notification, 'The Competition Commission of India (Lesser Penalty) Regulations, 2009 (No. 4 of 2009)' (2009). Retrieved from www.cci.gov.in/sites/default/files/regulation_pdf/Lesser%20Penalty%20Regulations%20with%20Amendments.pdf (LPR).

[5] Competition Act, Section 27(b).

[6] LPR, Regulation 4.

13.2.2 *Eligibility for the Lesser Penalty*

In order to be eligible for the lesser penalty, an applicant is required, in addition to making vital disclosure, to cease further participation in the cartel, unless otherwise directed by the CCI, and to offer complete cooperation with the investigation, including supplying all relevant information, documents and evidence, and refrain from suppressing or destroying information and documents that may contribute to the establishment of a cartel.[7] Though initially only enterprises were permitted to file applications under the LPR, a 2017 amendment permitted even individuals to file for lesser penalty applications.[8]

13.2.3 *Process of the Lesser Penalty Application*

The process of applying for a lesser penalty is provided under Regulation 5 of the LPR. An applicant desirous of disclosing information is required to file a 'marker' with the Secretary of the CCI, whereby it expresses its intention to disclose vital information relating to the existence of a cartel. Upon receipt of such an expression of interest the Secretary would place the matter before the CCI for determination of the priority status, which would then be intimated to the applicant. The applicant must submit a written application, along with the information and evidence relating to the existence of the cartel, as stipulated in the Schedule to the LPR, within a period of fifteen days. The priority in which the applications are received is vital, because unless the first application has been evaluated, the CCI would not take up subsequent applications for consideration. There is, however, no limitation prescribed in the LPR as to the maximum number of markers or applications that can be entertained.

13.2.4 *Quantification of the Lesser Penalty*

As per Regulation 4 of the LPR, only the first applicant is eligible for a reduction in penalty up to 100 per cent. In order to qualify for the first priority status, the applicant must be the first to make a vital disclosure by submitting evidence enabling the CCI to form a prima facie opinion regarding the existence of a cartel. Regulation 2 (1)(i) of the LPR defines

[7] Ibid., Section 3.

[8] Ibid., Section 2(1)(b) and Note 1. In Note 1, it is stated that the amendment is the result of an amendment of the Competition Act in 2017.

'vital disclosure' to mean full and true disclosure of information or evidence by the applicant to the CCI, which is sufficient to enable the CCI to form a prima- facie opinion about the existence of a cartel or which helps to establish the contravention of the provisions of Section 3 of the Competition Act. The subsequent applicants can be further demarcated into 'second priority' and 'third priority', who may be granted a reduction up to 50 per cent and 30 per cent, respectively. The qualifying criterion for subsequent applicants is that the information disclosed should provide significant added value to the evidence already in the possession of the CCI or the Director General (DG). The explanation to Regulation 4(b) of the LPR has defined 'added value' to mean the extent to which the evidence provided enhances the ability of the CCI or the DG, as the case may be, to establish the existence of a cartel.

The quantification of reduction in penalty is at the sole discretion of the CCI. In exercising its discretion, the CCI takes into consideration the following factors:[9]

- The stage at which the applicant comes forward with the disclosure.
- The evidence already in the possession of the CCI.
- The quality of the information provided by the applicant.
- The entire facts and circumstances of the case.

In addition to the above, the applicant is required to extend full cooperation to the CCI and the DG. The CCI is at liberty to refuse a reduction in penalty if the applicant fails to cooperate up to the completion of the proceedings.[10] A reduction in penalty can also be refused if the CCI determines, after providing the applicant with an opportunity for a hearing, that the applicant has not made vital disclosure or has provided false evidence.

13.3 Judicial Trends and Concerns in Administering a Lesser Penalty

13.3.1 Lack of Strong Advocacy and Visibility

Though the LPR were notified in 2009,[11] the concept of leniency had not gained much impetus in India. With the first known leniency application

[9] LPR, Regulation 3(4).

[10] Competition Act, Section 46(3).

[11] The regulations were notified on 13 August 2009.

being filed in 2013[12] and the first decision on such an application passed in 2017,[13] the leniency programme in India was off to a slow start. Therefore, up until 2017 there were no decisions under the LPR that could suggest the judicial trends followed by the CCI in adjudicating leniency applications. The volume of leniency applications filed in the past eleven years of the programme's existence has been very low and to date, the CCI has passed only around thirteen decisions based upon a leniency application. This could ostensibly be for two reasons: there is a need for (a) stronger advocacy and awareness as to the existence of the leniency programme; and (2) a swift and consistent approach of the CCI in deciding on leniency applications.

Disclosures made under leniency applications are nothing short of a confession on the part of the applicants about engaging in anti-competitive conduct that would normally entail enormous legal consequences. An applicant in so choosing to apply for leniency also braves the repercussions of breaking its relationship with the other members of the cartel. Finally, there is also the factor of the reputation of the enterprise when it comes forward to confess that it has been part of a cartel. Given the high stakes and risks involved in making disclosures as required by the leniency programme, it is natural for an applicant to hesitate and exercise caution while applying for a lesser penalty under the LPR. To prompt more enterprises to take the bold step forward, the leniency programme must evince a high level of trustworthiness and consistency. This can be achieved through stronger advocacy in order to increase awareness of the programme and to offer reasonable certainty in the minds of the applicants by being consistent in its adjudication of lesser penalty applications.

13.3.2 Consistency in the Treatment of First Priority Applications

In terms of awarding a lesser penalty to the first applicant, the CCI has been consistent in its approach of awarding a 100 per cent reduction if the first applicant made a vital disclosure enabling the CCI to form a prima facie opinion regarding the existence of a cartel and, especially, if such

12 The earliest recorded date of a lesser penalty application was on 11 January 2013, which was filed by the second and third opposite parties on 11 January 2013 in CCI, Suo Motu Case No. 02 of 2013, In Re: Cartelization in respect of tenders floated by Indian Railways for supply of Brushless DC Fans and other electrical items.

13 CCI, Suo Motu Case No. 03 of 2014, In Re: Cartelization in respect of tenders floated by Indian Railways for supply of Brushless DC Fans and other electrical items, was decided on 18 January 2017.

disclosure was the basis of initiating an investigation. The first applicants in the *Battery* case,[14] the *Sports Broadcasters* case,[15] the *Batteries Manufacturer* case,[16] the *EPS System* case[17] and the *Beer Market* case[18] were all awarded a 100 per cent reduction in penalty, which was also extended to some of their employees. In all of these cases, one of the members of the cartel came forward with vital disclosure as to the existence and operation of the cartel that formed the basis of the CCI's investigation. In other words, the CCI did not have the required intelligence to form a prima facie case and commence the investigation until it was in receipt of the vital documents and evidence disclosed by the applicant. Consequently, the first applicant in all these cases enjoyed a 100 per cent reduction in penalty imposed by the CCI.

In the *Brushless DC Fans* case[19] and the *Nagrik Chetna Manch* case,[20] the first applicants were awarded a reduction of only 75 per cent and 50 per cent, respectively, since they came forward with the disclosure only after the DG had already commenced its investigation. The CCI noted that when the application was made by the first applicant, the CCI was already in possession of adequate evidence to form a prima facie view regarding the existence of a cartel in contravention of the provisions of Section 3 of the Competition Act.[21] The difference in quantum can be attributed to the stage at which the disclosure was made after the commencement of the investigation, since in the *Brushless DC Fans* case the DG issued notice on 8 January 2015 and the first applicant filed its leniency application on 13 January 2015 disclosing vital information,[22] whereas in the *Nagrik Chetna Manch* case, the first applicant filed its application at a much later stage of

14 CCI, Suo Motu Case No. 02 of 2016, In Re: Cartelization in respect of zinc carbon dry cell batteries market in India.

15 CCI, Case No 2 of 2013, In Re: Cartelization by broadcasting service providers by rigging the bids submitted in response to the tenders floated by Sports broadcasters.

16 CCI, Suo Motu Case No. 03 of 2017, In Re: Anticompetitive conduct in the Dry-Cell Batteries Market in India (*Dry-Cell Batteries Market*).

17 CCI, Suo Motu Case No. 07 (01) of 2014, In Re: Cartelization in the supply of Electric Power Steering Systems (*EPS Systems*).

18 CCI, Suo Motu Case No. 06 of 2017, In Re: Alleged anti-competitive conduct in the Beer Market in India.

19 CCI, Suo Motu Case No. 03 of 2014, In Re: Cartelization in respect of tenders floated by Indian Railways for supply of Brushless DC Fans and other electrical items (*Brushless DC Fans*).

20 CCI, Case No. 50 of 2015, Nagrik Chetna Manch vs. Fortified Security Solutions and others (*Nagrik Chetna Manch*).

21 *Brushless DC Fans*, para. 7.10; *Nagrik Chetna Manch*, para. 102.

22 *Brushless DC Fans*, para. 7.1.

the investigation.[23] Therefore, the approach of the CCI can be reasonably predicted when the disclosure is vital and enables the CCI to form a prima facie case. This can be a strong motivating factor for inducing members of a cartel to be the first to apply for leniency.

13.3.3 *Inconsistencies in the Treatment of Subsequent Applications*

The CCI, however, has been rather inconsistent in adjudicating subsequent applications. Unlike the first applicant, which is adjudicated on the basis of vital disclosure, the strength of the subsequent applications is determined in the basis of significant added value, which is a very subjective criterion. As to what type of disclosures would have significant added value to the investigation, this is entirely at the discretion of the CCI, having regard to the information and evidence already at its disposal. This also impacts the quantification of the reduction in penalty awarded to subsequent applicants, which adds to the uncertainty of the applicants. In the *Battery* case,[24] the second and third applicants were awarded 30 per cent and 20 per cent reduction, respectively, whereas in the *EPS Systems* case[25] the second applicant was granted a 50 per cent reduction. In stark distinction between the *Battery* case and the *Solid Waste Processing* case,[26] the CCI had arrived at identical findings with respect to the quality of disclosure and cooperation extended by the subsequent applicants and yet refused to grant any reduction in the latter case. The CCI in the *Battery* case observed that the evidence submitted by the subsequent applicants did not result in significant added value and yet granted a reduction in penalty on the count that it had provided 'genuine, full, continuous and expeditious cooperation during the course of investigation'.[27] However, in the *Solid Waste Processing* case, despite recording that the subsequent applicants supported the investigation and extended full cooperation, the CCI had not granted any reduction in penalty.[28] Yet again in the *M/s Alis Medical Agency* case,[29] the CCI granted one of the opposite parties a reduction of 40 per cent of the penalty

23 *Nagrik Chetna Manch*, paras. 3–5.

24 *Dry-Cell Batteries Market*.

25 *EPS Systems*.

26 CCI, Suo Motu Case No. 03 of 2016, In re: Cartelization in Tender Nos. 21 and 28 of 2013 of Pune Municipal Corporation for Solid Waste Processing (*Solid Waste Processing*).

27 *Dry-Cell Batteries Market*, para 10.3.

28 *Solid Waste Processing*, para. 92.

29 CCI, Case No. 65, 71, 72 of 2014 & 68 of 2015, In Re: M/s. Alis Medical Agency and Federation of Gujarat State Chemists & Druggists Associations & 6 ors.

on account of its cooperation during the investigation, despite there being no lesser penalty applications filed by any of the parties. This lack of consistency in determining what conduct and disclosures could secure a reduction in penalty for subsequent applicants could potentially deter applicants from coming forward to seek leniency, thus diminishing the programme's efficacy. There is a need for greater clarity as to what could be construed to have 'significant added value' under the LPR.

13.3.4 Confusing Standards

Curiously, in some cases there have been leniency applications filed by applicants disclosing that they have been a part of a cartel where the CCI dismissed the proceeding, as it did not find adequate evidence in favour of the existence of a cartel. In both the *Flashlights Market* case[30] and the *Bearings (Automotive and Industrial)* case,[31] the CCI observed that the applicants did not disclose adequate evidence to establish an infringement under Section 3 of the Competition Act, despite the DG's investigation report finding in favour of the existence of a cartel. In the *Anti-Vibration Rubber Products* case,[32] neither the DG nor the CCI found a positive case as to the existence of a cartel, despite the disclosure made by the leniency applicant. Thus, unclear and inconsistent standards for awarding a lesser penalty could result in impeding full and frank disclosures from entities. Unless the leniency regime demonstrates a certain degree of consistency and predictability, enterprises engaging in cartelisation may not risk disclosure.

13.4 Interaction with Private Enforcement

13.4.1 Private Enforcement through Follow-on Actions

Private enforcement is a mechanism to try competition law suits either parallel to public enforcement suits or as follow-on suits. Private enforcement can act as a complement to costly detection of anti-competitive conduct by the public agencies.

[30] CCI, Suo Motu Case No. 01 of 2017, In Re: Alleged Cartelisation in Flashlights Market in India (*Flashlights Market*).

[31] CCI, Suo Motu Case No. 07 (02) of 2014, In Re: Cartelisation in the supply of Bearings (Automotive and Industrial).

[32] CCI, Suo Motu Case No. 01 of 2016, In Re: Cartelisation in the supply of Anti-Vibration Rubber Products and Automotive Hoses to Automobile Original Equipment Manufacturers.

Private enforcement's confluence with the Indian competition landscape is not new, yet remains unexplored and untouched.[33] Section 53N of the Competition Act deals with standing in private enforcement cases and it allows any enterprise or individual or government enterprise or local authority to institute a suit for compensation before the competition appellate authority only as a follow-on action once public adjudication is done by the CCI or the appellate authority.[34] The section remains silent on the issue of whether private enforcement can be instituted in the appellate court in case an appeal is preferred to the Supreme Court. However, it can be notably inferred that the follow-on claims of compensation must be restricted until such a time as the Supreme Court finds on the contravention. The Competition Law Review Committee (CLRC) has recommended allowing compensation claims to be filed post determination by the Supreme Court regarding the contravention.[35] Section 53N of the Competition Act does not acknowledge standalone compensation claims and also restricts the jurisdiction of any other courts to determine compensation claims arising from antitrust wrongs.

13.4.2 Private Enforcement Disincentivises Leniency if Not Well Regulated

13.4.2.1 Clarity on the Height of Damages Required

The presence of private enforcement disincentivises leniency applications.[36] Leniency applicants risk paying damages even though their penalty

[33] As yet no cases have gone to trial under Section 53N of the Competition Act. In total nine cases have been filed that are in abeyance. See Rathi, S. and Seth, R., 'Awards for Compensation in Antitrust: The Road Less Travelled in India' *CPI Competition Policy International* (23 April 2020). Retrieved from www.competitionpolicyinternational.com/awards-for-compensation-in-antitrust-the-road-less-travelled-in-india.

[34] 'A claim for compensation can be initiated before the NCLAT only if there is a finding by the CCI or the NCLAT that the provisions of the Competition Act have been contravened. Private antitrust actions can therefore only be initiated under Section 53N of the Competition Act following a finding of antitrust infringement against an enterprise by the CCI or the NCLAT.' Sharma, M. M., 'Private Antitrust Litigation in India: Overview' (2019). Retrieved from https://uk.practicallaw.thomsonreuters.com/w-021-3374?transitionType=Default&contextData=(sc.Default)&firstPage=true.

[35] Ministry of Corporate Affairs, Government of India, 'Report of Competition Law Review Committee' (2019), p. 96. Retrieved from www.ies.gov.in/pdfs/Report-Competition-CLRC.pdf.

[36] Knight, T. and Claire, C. S., 'Reconciling the Conflict: Antitrust Leniency Programs and Private Enforcement' (Working Paper, 2019). Retrieved from https://people.clas.ufl.edu/thomasknight/files/KnightSteClaire.pdf.

in the public enforcement system has been reduced.[37] Antitrust scholars claim that there is an inherent conflict between private enforcement and successful leniency applications.[38] However, the proposition that application for leniency and a private enforcement system are inherently in conflict might not always be true, as has been claimed by some scholars.

The scholars against this proposition claim that a proper well-regulated private enforcement system might incentivise applicants to come forward and apply for leniency. This can be achieved by granting better protection to leniency applicants from damages, for example by restricting joint and several liability or by preventing the disclosure of information obtained through the leniency process.[39]

Section 53N(3) of the Competition Act states:

> The Appellate Tribunal may … pass an order directing the enterprise to make payment … as compensation for the loss or damage caused to the applicant as a result of any contravention … committed by such enterprise: Provided that the Appellate Tribunal may obtain the recommendations of the CCI before passing an order of compensation.

The main aim of competition law damages in India is to compensate the victims, as can be inferred from the language of the Competition Act.[40] This inference can also be drawn since it provides for compensation only to the extent of loss and damage caused and does not provide for exemplary or punitive damages, and therefore a private competition law damages claim might not necessarily be deterrent in nature, unlike in the United States (US) where it provides for treble damages.[41] The word 'compensation' has not been defined in the Competition Act and hence must be attributed a meaning in common parlance as meaning to make good the loss. To induce leniency applications, the height of damages provided under Section 53N of the Competition Act should not be restricted to the general definition of compensation, which means to make good the loss. Section 53N of the Competition Act mentions the height of damages to be

[37] Juška, Ž., 'The Effectiveness of Antitrust Collective Litigation in the European Union: A Study of the Principle of Full Compensation' (2018) 49 *IIC* 63.

[38] Buccirossi, P., Marvão, C. and Spagnolo, G., 'Leniency and Damages' (Stockholm Institute of Transition Economics, SITE Working Paper No. 32, 2015). Retrieved from www.econstor.eu/bitstream/10419/204743/1/site-wp0032.pdf.

[39] Ibid.

[40] Ibid.

[41] Cavanagh, E. D., 'The Private Antitrust Remedy: Lessons from the American Experience' (2010) 41 *Loyola University Chicago Law Journal* 629.

equal to the foreseeable loss suffered by the party due to the wrongdoing. This height might not be dissuasive enough for cartelists to come forward, since the penalty is not very high. The higher penalty coupled with proportional immunity or minimised liability to the participants who come forward and treble damages or punitive damages for other co-cartelists would incentivise leniency applications.[42]

Furthermore, the Competition Act states that the only qualification in determination of compensation by the appellate authority would be to seek recommendation from the CCI on the height of compensation.[43] This lack of clarity on how much compensation may be awarded disincentivises leniency applicants and discretion on the part of the CCI to award compensation on a case-by-case basis gives further room for speculation by the wrongdoer regarding its lability. For successful leniency applications, transparency and predictability[44] among the applicants is of the utmost importance. The Competition Act must provide clear guidelines on the height of compensation to be awarded in cases of competition law damages to bring more transparency with respect to the liability of the wrongdoers. This certainty would help the wrongdoers in desisting from cartel activities in the first place. Moreover, certainty about the height of compensation would also allow the leniency applicant to weigh the benefits of leniency if extended to private enforcement versus getting caught, if the damages provided are treble or exemplary.[45]

13.4.2.2 Essential to Protect the Leniency Applicant from Multiple Damages

There is no clarity on whether the wrongdoer who has applied for leniency under Section 46 of the Competition Act will be granted immunity from damages under Section 53N of the Competition Act. For the private enforcement tool to be effectively used with the leniency tool, there should be clear guidelines on the immunity of the leniency applicant from the damages awarded under Section 53N of the Competition Act.

42 Buccirossi, Marvão and Spagnolo, 'Leniency and Damages' (n. 38 above).

43 Competition Act, Section 53N.

44 ICN, 'Guidance on Enhancing Cross-Border Leniency Cooperation' (2020). Retrieved from www.internationalcompetitionnetwork.org/wp-content/uploads/2020/07/CWG-Leniency-Coordination-Guidance.pdf.

45 Buccirossi, P., Marvão, C. and Spagnolo, G., 'Leniency, Damages, and EU Competition Policy' *VOX[EU], CEPR* (14 July 2015). Retrieved from https://voxeu.org/article/leniency-damages-and-eu-competition-policy.

The Act must be amended to extend the immunity provision of the leniency applicant to damages under any other provision of the Competition Act. This model can instead induce the filing of leniency applications, since the leniency application would now protect them from multiple suits and multiple damages. Contrastingly, in the European Union (EU) Damages Directive,[46] the liability of the leniency applicant is restricted to indirect purchasers or providers, and to the extent that full compensation could not be obtained from other cartelists. The idea behind not completely immunising the leniency applicant is that they also must not be remitted of liability under the special liability regime; instead they should be provided with clear guidelines on their liability and minimise it as far as possible so that it does not act as a disincentive for them to self-report.[47]

India can adopt similar measures to bring more clarity to the liability that could be attached to self-reporting entities. If the goal of private enforcement is predominantly to compensate the victims, then absolving the leniency applicant absolutely from all liability might not further this goal. The CCI in that case can minimise the liability of the leniency applicant to the extent of its direct purchasers.[48] However, since there is no jurisprudence in India with respect to private enforcement, it remains to be seen how the appellate authority and the CCI regulate these cases.

In relation to joint and several liability, it could be said that the existence of such liability[49] among cartel participants might dissuade the filing of leniency applications, since even if the applicant is granted immunity under the lesser penalty regulation and the same immunity is not extended to private enforcement, the applicant's incentive to apply for leniency will be counterbalanced by its obligation to pay damages.[50] The Competition Act does not provide for joint and several liability under the public

[46] Directive 2014/104/EU of the European Parliament and of the Council on certain rules governing actions for damages under national law for infringements of the competition law provisions of the Member States and of the European Union, OJ L 349, p. 1 (EU Damages Directive).

[47] ICN Cartel Working Group, 'Development of Private Enforcement of Competition Law in ICN Jurisdictions' (2019). Retrieved from www.internationalcompetitionnetwork.org/wp-content/uploads/2019/07/CWG_Privateenforcement-2019.pdf.

[48] The author contends that indirect purchasers should not be allowed to sue under this mechanism, since it would weaken the private enforcement system and thereby weaken the incentive to apply for leniency. It has been explored in the antirust standing section.

[49] Joint and several liability means that all cartelists shall be equally liable towards the victims and each victim shall have the right to claim all its loss from each liable party. Buccirossi, Marvão and Spagnolo, 'Leniency, Damages, and EU Competition Policy' (n. 45 above).

[50] Ibid.

enforcement mechanism. The CCI, while levying a penalty under Section 27 of the Competition Act, imposes individual penalties. However, there is no clarity under Section 53N of the Competition Act with regard to whether the cartelists will be jointly and severally liable for private antirust wrongs. Even though it could be inferred from Section 27 of the Competition Act that the cartelist will not be jointly and severally liable, Section 53N of the Competition Act should be amended to bring more clarity.

Joint and several liability could be introduced in India in line with the Hungarian model, where the immunity recipient is only liable to its direct and indirect purchasers and suppliers.[51] However, the Hungarian model should be applied in the Indian context only to the extent of direct purchasers and suppliers, considering the diversified density in terms of the Indian population. The Hungarian model does not allow other victims to seek redress from the immunity recipient, with the only exception that the other victims could not obtain full compensation from the co-cartelists, which is very unlikely.[52] The co-cartelists' ability to claim from the immunity recipient under joint and several liability is limited to the victims of the recipient only and not beyond, and hence incentivises leniency. The model that India adopts is yet to be seen; however, it is beyond time that certainty and transparency must be brought into the legislation and little discretion is given to the regulator.

13.4.3 *Standing in Private Enforcement Cases*

Section 53N of the Competition Act has given a very wide antitrust standing to claim compensation by any person or enterprise who can prove that they have suffered any injury due to anti-competitive activity. It does not differentiate between direct and indirect purchasers. Instead, Section 53N of the Competition Act has left it to the appellate authority to determine if there is a correlation between the harm caused due to the anti-competitive

[51] Kovacs, M. and Turi, A., 'Competition: Leniency after the Antitrust Damages Directive in Hungary: A Compromise between Private and Public Interests?' *CEE Legal Matters* (1 August 2018). Retrieved from https://ceelegalmatters.com/hungary/8971-competition-leniency-after-the-antitrust-damages-directive-in-hungary-a-compromise-between-private-and-public-interests. Even in the US under the Antitrust Criminal Penalty Enhancement & Reform Act (ACPERA), the civil liability of the leniency applicant is restricted to the portion of actual damages the claimant has suffered due to the illegal conduct of the leniency applicant specifically, and applicants should not be jointly and severally liable.

[52] ICN Cartel Working Group, 'Development of Private Enforcement' (n. 47 above); Buccirossi, Marvão and Spagnolo, 'Leniency, Damages, and EU Competition Policy' (n. 45 above).

activity and the compensation claimed. This allows even a person including an end consumer to institute a compensation claim against the wrongdoer. It also does not address the passing-on defence and hence it can be presumed that this is not available under the Indian competition law. The absence of a passing-on defence might lead to overcompensation to the direct purchasers, who might have already passed on the overcharge to the downstream consumers. However, the presence of it might lead to uncertainty in calculating the height of compensation to be paid to indirect purchasers, who might be extremely scattered and hence not all of them would bring suits and most often would not want to indulge in litigation. This would also affect the expected cost that the infringing firm has to pay for its illegal anti-competitive behaviour.[53] Moreover, the direct purchasers would have better resources and evidence to prove the claim vis-à-vis an indirect purchaser.[54] Therefore, the presence of a passing-on defence would weaken the deterrent effect of private enforcement, as it may decrease the expected cost the infringing firm has to pay and increase the litigation cost, duplication of evidence collection and so on. A more predictable model for a stronger private enforcement system would be to not allow the passing-on defence. A stronger private enforcement system coupled with more certainty with regard to the height of the penalty imposed on the wrongdoer, along with greater protection to the leniency applicant, would incentivise leniency.[55]

13.4.4 Guaranteeing Confidentiality Regarding the Leniency Dossier

It is well understood that a damages claim can have chilling effects on potential leniency applicants coming forward. As the disclosure of the information filed by the leniency applicant forms the basis for such private claims, it is important for the watchdog to limit the confidential information available for filing such follow-on actions.[56] In cases

[53] Landes, W. M. and Posner, R. A., 'Should Indirect Purchasers Have Standing to Sue under the Antitrust Laws? An Economic Analysis of the Rule of Illinois Brick' (1979) 46 *University of Chicago Law Review* 602.

[54] Knight, T. and de Weert, W., 'On Implementing Private Damages in European Competition Cases' (Working Paper, 2015). Retrieved from https://people.clas.ufl.edu/thomasknight/files/PrivateDamages.pdf.

[55] Ibid.

[56] Brusick, P., 'Competition Guidelines: Leniency Programmes' (2016). Retrieved from https://unctadmena.org/wp-content/uploads/2018/12/Competition-Guidelines_Leniency-Programmes_EN.pdf (UNCTAD Leniency Guidelines).

where the access to information in the leniency documents is readily available, it could lead to a disadvantageous situation for the leniency applicant being on the radar of the plaintiffs to a private enforcement suit, which would only act as a deterrent to the whistleblowers. Therefore, it is recommended that there should be rules in place governing the disclosure of the information in the leniency application in order to ensure that any such disclosure does not disincentivise the willingness of cartelists to voluntarily submit any information, including self-incriminating evidence.[57]

The confidentiality regime has undergone a progressive change in recognising the need to provide due protection to certain sensitive information obtained from leniency applicants, along with allowing the parties access to certain information to exercise their right of defence during the investigation proceedings.

In India, confidentiality of the parties is safeguarded under three legal provisions:

- Section 57 of the Competition Act.
- Regulation 35 of the Competition Commission of India (General) Regulations, 2009 (General Regulations).
- Regulation 6 and 6A of the LPR.

While the first two provisions are general in nature, the third provision, the LPR, specifically lays down the extent of confidentiality granted in leniency cases.

As per Regulation 6 of the LPR, the CCI and the DG shall treat the identity of the leniency applicant and the information, documents and evidence furnished by the leniency applicant as confidential. However, the same may be disclosed by the CCI and DG in the following circumstances:

- When such a disclosure is required by law.
- When the leniency applicant has agreed to such a disclosure in writing.
- When there has been public disclosure by the leniency applicant.

By means of an amendment to the LPR,[58] where the leniency applicant has not agreed to the disclosure of the information, documents and evidence furnished by him or her and where such a disclosure to another

[57] OECD, 'Challenges and Co-ordination of Leniency Programmes – Background Note by the Secretariat', DAF/COMP/WP3(2018)1 (2018). Retrieved from https://one.oecd.org/document/DAF/COMP/WP3(2018)1/en/pdf.

[58] LPR, Regulation 6.

party is necessary for investigation purposes, the DG has been granted the power to disclose the same to another party after recording the reasons in writing and seeking the prior approval of the CCI. The amendment is silent on certain aspects such as the extent of the information to be disclosed by the DG, the right of the leniency applicant to be informed before such a disclosure, and whether an opportunity is given to the whistle-blower to contest such a disclosure before the CCI. Such a residuary power bestowed upon the DG may undermine the principles of natural justice and invite a significant risk of exposure for the leniency applicant.

The non-confidential version of the information, documents and evidence furnished by the leniency applicant can be inspected by the parties after the release of the investigation report of the DG. However, these parties should not disclose the information, documents and evidence so obtained other than for the purposes of legal proceedings.[59] The Supreme Court has also confirmed the order of the Delhi High Court directing the CCI to provide the non-confidential version of the documents and information submitted by the leniency applicant to the requesting parties, on the grounds that such parties under the guise of confidentiality cannot be denied any evidence, after redacting the confidential information, for preparing their defence case.[60]

However, the contents of the leniency application that are accorded confidentiality are treated separately from the information and evidence collected by the DG from the leniency applicant as part of its investigation, to which such a confidential status is not extended. It has been clarified that confidentiality on such evidence can only be in terms of Section 35 of the General Regulations.[61]

The wide residuary power given to the DG to waive confidentiality granted in circumstances as it may deem fit can act as a deterrent for potential leniency applicants to cooperate with the CCI to facilitate cartel detection. Such a cherry-picking application of confidentiality could be antithetical to the objectives of a leniency programme.[62]

[59] Ibid., Section 6A.

[60] *Competition Commission of India and another* vs. *Forech India Limited*, Special Leave to Appeal (C) No(s) 9018–9019 of 2020.

[61] *Nagrik Chetna Manch*.

[62] ICN, 'Good Practices for Incentivising Leniency Applications' (2019). Retrieved from www.internationalcompetitionnetwork.org/wp-content/uploads/2019/05/CWG-Good-practices-for-incentivising-leniency.pdf.

Much like its EU counterpart,[63] in order to balance the rights of all the parties to the leniency proceeding, CCI has allowed the creation of confidentiality rings where the information, including the confidential information, is disclosed only within a defined category of individuals.[64] The creation of confidentiality rings is not inscribed in the LPR, however, and is merely a law of precedent. The CCI has also introduced[65] the setting-up of a confidentiality ring and levying a monetary penalty in case of any disclosure otherwise. However, in order to clear the mire of the confidentiality regime in leniency cases, such regularisation also needs to be extended to the extant LPR in order to bridge the gap between the provision and application of confidentiality rings.

Even though there have been significant efforts by the competition authorities to monitor the extant confidentiality regime in cases of leniency, there are various concerns looming over present and potential leniency applicants, such as reputational loss and commercial claims, due to wide information disclosure in leniency orders. Therefore, in cases where no violation is established[66] by the CCI despite a leniency application being filed, the order published should ensure minimal disclosure of confidential information.

In order to enhance the trust of leniency applicants, the CCI could consider policy safeguards such as the possibility for oral leniency applications to limit information leaks.[67] It is recommended that there should be a clear confidentiality policy enabling a mechanism to process the information received from a leniency applicant. The EU guidance on confidentiality claims[68] and the EU Damages Directive[69] are cogent examples of such a mechanism, listing several measures such as redactions, confidentiality rings, appointing experts to access certain confidential information concerned by a disclosure request to produce summaries of the information in a non-confidential form, closed hearings and restriction of the access to court records. The protection of confidential information regime in India

63 European Commission, 'Communication on the Protection of Confidential Information by National Courts in Proceedings for the Private Enforcement of EU Competition Law', C 242/01 (2020), paras. 51–56.

64 *EPS Systems.*

65 The Competition Commission of India (General) Amendment Regulations 2022, Regulation 35.

66 *Flashlights Market.*

67 UNCTAD Leniency Guidelines.

68 ICN, 'Good Practices for Incentivising Leniency Applications' (n. 62 above).

69 EU Damages Directive, p. 1.

lacks a concrete stipulation like the rules of the EU Damages Directive, according to which the national courts can never order the disclosure of leniency statements and settlement submissions for the purpose of actions for damage. Adoption of similar provisions in the Indian regime would help strike the right balance between public and private enforcement.

13.5 Improving the Leniency Programme through Interaction with Other Laws

13.5.1 Incentivising Leniency Applications through Administrative Sanctions

The incentive to file for leniency can be enhanced if there are strong sanctions in place from which applicants could be immunised if they make a vital disclosure regarding the existence of an anti-competitive activity. The Competition Act, under Section 48(1), raises a presumption of wrongdoing against every person who is responsible for conducting the affairs of a company involved in anti-competitive activity. Therefore, if there are strong civil sanctions coupled with administrative sanctions in place, individuals would be more incentivised to defect from the illegal behaviour and run for immunity. Indian competition law does not provide for administrative sanctions like disqualification of individuals. The provision for disqualification of directors or officers in charge falls squarely within the purview of the Companies Act 2013 (Companies Act).

Section 62 of the Competition Act provides, however, that the provisions of the Competition Act are in addition to any other law in force, and Section 21A of the Competition Act allows the CCI to make cross-reference to a statutory authority on an issue raised during the proceedings or on which the CCI proposes to take steps that fall within the sole prerogative of that statutory authority. A director disqualification can be ordered for infringement of competition law by cross-referring the disqualification under the Companies Act. If leniency under Section 46 of the Competition Act is granted for such an administrative sanction also, the individuals will be incentivised to defect from the cartel for the fear of being disqualified[70] and come forward to file for leniency.

[70] CCI, Case No. 28 of 2014, *Mr. KP. K. Krishnan* vs. *M/s Alkem Laboratories and Another Srinivas et al.* (2018). This was one of the only cases in which a disassociation order was passed against the two officials who were directly in charge of the operations of the company. CCI has yet not passed a disassociation order as part of individual sanctions.

The underlying presumption on which this is based is the higher the legal penalty cost associated with the detection of anti-competitive activity, the higher the incentive of the wrongdoers to defect from the cartel and come forward.[71]

13.5.2 Rethinking the Interaction with Public Procurement

Public procurement markets in India are qualified by limited suppliers or alternative bidders and complex laws, thereby restricting competition in the market to a few. The regulatory or institutional conditions such as licensing and other restrictions such as inter alia minimum capital requirements further limit competition in the market, making it more prone to collusion.[72] The CCI has been extremely proactive in uncovering bid-rigging cases and has imposed steep penalties.[73] However, stricter enforcement policies may induce leniency in public procurement cases, such as debarment or suspension of bidders and public officials who have been found contravening the Competition Act. For instance, the US Federal Acquisition Regulation permits debarment of contractors suspected of violating competition laws and recording of a judgment violating competition law is a valid ground for debarment.[74] The CCI in all the bid-rigging cases has passed a combination of cease-and-desist orders and penalties. However, no provision exists either under the Competition Act or under various rules such as the General Financial Rules 2017 (GFR) that governs central procurement regarding debarment for violation of competition laws. Rule 151 of the GFR permits debarment from bidding for violation of the Prevention of Corruption Act 1988 or for committing an act punishable under the Indian Penal Code 1860.[75] To make leniency more attractive, the GFR could be amended to extend debarment for competition law violations. Extending the immunity under leniency to such debarment would induce wrongdoers to come forward.

71 Koradia, N., Manokaran, K. and Saeed, Z., 'Algorithmic Collusion and Indian Competition Act: Suggestions to Tackle Inadequacies and Naivety', in Van Uytsel, S. (ed.), *The Digital Economy and Competition Law in Asia* (Singapore: Springer, 2021), 127, p. 127.

72 OECD, 'Roundtable on Collusion and Corruption in Public Procurement', DAF/COMP/GF(2010)6 (2010). Retrieved from www.oecd.org/competition/cartels/46235884.pdf.

73 CCI, Suo Motu Case No. 02 of 2011, In re: Aluminium Phosphide Tablets Manufacturers.

74 48 Code of Federal Regulations, § 9.407-2(a)(2), Causes for Suspension: Violation of Federal or State Antitrust Statutes Relating to the Submission of Offers. In relation to the EU, EU Damages Directive, Article 57(4).

75 Ministry of Finance, Department of Expenditure, 'General Financial Rules 2017' (2017), Rule 151. Retrieved from https://doe.gov.in/sites/default/files/GFR2017_0.pdf.

13.6 Upcoming Challenges for the Leniency Programme

13.6.1 Settlements and Commitments

Settlement and commitment agreements allow the otherwise lengthy enforcement litigation to be expedited, increase the deterrence and detection rate and facilitate better deployment of the regulator's resources to deal with other cases. The Indian competition law does not have a defined settlement regime. However, it was recognised that there is a need to introduce settlement provisions in India and the CCI has a power to pass such settlement orders under Section 27 of the Competition Act.[76] The draft Competition (Amendment) Bill 2020 (Draft Bill) introduces the settlement and commitment provisions in Section 48A and Section 48B of the Competition Act respectively. The Draft Bill entails that any person can file for settlement[77] after the DG submits its investigation report but before the order of the CCI, whereas the party can offer a commitment[78] after an order for investigation has been made but before the DG has submitted its investigation report. The primary difference between the stage in which a settlement and a commitment can be offered is that a settlement may be offered after the CCI, on the basis of the DG report, opines that there is a contravention of the provisions of the Competition Act and a detailed inquiry would thus be required. Such a contravention is not established when a party offers a commitment; that is, before the DG submits its investigation report. Therefore, any party applying for settlement could appear to implicitly admit its guilt. Hence the absence of an express clarification vis-à-vis whether any party offering a settlement or a commitment will be construed to admit its guilt could deter such parties from entering into such agreements.

Moreover, these provisions only apply to an alleged charge under Section 3(4) and Section 4 of the Competition Act – that is, in the cases of vertical agreements and abuse of dominance, respectively – and do not apply in the case of horizontal agreements. In order to attain procedural efficiencies, it is essential that leniency and settlement provisions should complement and not be exclusive of each other. It is suggested that the settlement provisions be applied to cartel cases as well, wherein the benefits under both

[76] *The Tamil Nadu Film Exhibitors Association* vs. *Competition Commission of India*, [2015] 132 SCL 274 (Madras).

[77] Competition (Amendment) Bill 2020, Section 48A (Competition Bill). A version of the Competition Bill can be retried from www.taxmanagementindia.com/file_folder/folder_5/Draft_Competition_Amendment_Bill_2020.pdf.

[78] Competition Bill, Section 48B.

settlement and leniency would be cumulative. An example could be drawn from the EU, where the reduction of fines for leniency applicants is much more than the standard 10 per cent settlement reduction.[79] This fosters a balance where a standard settlement reduction is attractive to enter into a settlement procedure and small enough in comparison with the benefits to file for a leniency application, thus making them complementary to each other.[80] Additionally, in order to further foster cooperation and escape the lengthy timelines involved in an enforcement litigation, allowing parties to enter into settlement even before the conclusion of an investigation at a much earlier stage – as in the US, where the Antitrust Division of the Department of Justice follows a more streamlined early settlement process of not bringing further charges against the alleged party in exchange for waiver of the party's procedural rights to trial and appeal, along with substantial and ongoing cooperation in providing documents and evidence.[81] This could further benefit both the parties and the CCI, and thus facilitate advancement from the rudimentary enforcement mechanisms.

13.6.2 Leniency Plus

Leniency plus is a tool that allows enterprises who could not obtain complete immunity through the leniency policy to disclose to the Commission information on the existence of another cartel in a different market and cooperate with the Competition Agency on its working. In return, the applicant not only gets immunity from its participation in the second cartel, but also gets a substantial additional reduction[82] in its sanctions for its participation in the first cartel.[83] It is a tool to detect cartels aimed at multimarket cartelists.[84] Leniency plus was introduced in the US leniency programme in the

[79] European Commission, 'Antitrust: Commission Introduces Settlement Procedure for Cartels – Frequently Asked Questions', MEMO/08/458 (2008). Retrieved from https://ec.europa.eu/commission/presscorner/detail/fr/MEMO_08_458.

[80] OECD, 'Policy Roundtables: Leniency for Subsequent Applicants', DAF/COMP(2012)25 (2012). Retrieved from www.oecd.org/daf/competition/Leniencyforsubsequentapplicants2012.pdf.

[81] O'Brien, A., 'Cartel Settlements in the U.S. and EU: Similarities, Differences & Remaining Questions' (Presentation at 13th Annual EU Competition Law and Policy Workshop, Florence, 6 June 2008). Retrieved from www.justice.gov/atr/speech/cartel-settlements-us-and-eu-similarities-differences-remaining-questions.

[82] US Department of Justice, *Antitrust Division Manual*, 5th ed. (2014), p. III-102. Retrieved from www.justice.gov/atr/file/761166/download.

[83] Martyniszyn, M., 'Leniency (Amnesty) Plus: A Building Block or a Trojan Horse?' (2015) 3(2) *Journal of Antitrust Enforcement* 391.

[84] Enterprises that operate in several different product markets.

1990s and is intertwined with and inseverable from penalty plus. Penalty plus means that if an enterprise does not take the benefit of leniency plus and at a later stage the enterprise's involvement is uncovered in a different cartel, the failure to disclose its involvement to such a prohibited agreement will be considered as an aggravating sentencing factor.

The Competition Act does not provide for a leniency plus tool for the detection of cartels. However, this has been proposed under the Draft Bill. A self-standing leniency plus might not serve the intended purpose of inducing leniency applications, since the absence of disclosure of another cartel would not be met by any unwanted consequences and therefore would not incentivise leniency applicants to disclose another cartel. For the effective implementation of leniency plus, it must be introduced as a plus package with penalty plus. Therefore, the Indian competition law must be amended to include leniency plus coupled with penalty plus for enhancing the effectiveness of the leniency programme.

13.6.3 Withdrawal of Leniency Applications

Currently, there is no provision in the Indian competition law regime enabling the withdrawal of a leniency application by the applicant. However, the CLRC report recognises situations in which an application for leniency is filed initially during the discovery of internal documents, but pursuant to a detailed investigation, the applicant may want to withdraw it in cases where it determines that it has not been involved in the cartel. Therefore, the Draft Bill provides for an amendment to the existing Section 46 of the Competition Act; that is, a provision for a lesser penalty to allow withdrawal of an application by any leniency applicant. However, the provision does not elaborate on the manner and time of such withdrawal of an application. The withdrawal does not prevent the Commission and the DG from using the evidence submitted by the leniency applicant for the purpose of prosecution under the Competition Act. Countries such as the UK[85] and Brazil[86] also provide for withdrawal

[85] Office of Fair Trading, 'Applications for Leniency and No Action in Cartel Cases: OFT's Detailed Guidance on the Principles and Process', OFT1495 (2013). Retrieved from https://assets.publishing.service.gov.uk/government/uploads/system/uploads/attachment_data/file/284417/OFT1495.pdf.

[86] Ministry of Justice, Administrative Council for Economic Defense (CADE), 'Guidelines: Cade's Antitrust Leniency Program' (updated 2020). Retrieved from https://cdn.cade.gov.br/Portal/centrais-de-conteudo/publicacoes/guias-do-cade/guidelines-cades-antitrust-leniency-program-2020.pdf.

of a leniency application and could be used as good examples for detailed provisions on the manner of treatment of the information submitted by the leniency applicant. In order to encourage applicants to come forward, it is recommended that the LPR incorporate provisions such as in Brazil, where upon the withdrawal of the application, the information submitted by the leniency applicant is to be kept confidential, all the documents will be returned to the applicant and the Commission should not be allowed to use the information for initiating any investigations.

13.7 Inter-agency Cooperation

Cooperation with both domestic as well as international agencies facilitates improvement in the tools and techniques of cooperation, better channelling of resources by reducing the multiplicity of work, reduction in costs of business and risks of divergent outcomes, along with streamlining the investigation process. Such cooperation not only aids in smooth competition assessment, but also in designing appropriate remedies.

It is essential that robust coordination is established between the CCI and other sectoral regulators to better favour leniency applicants in a manner that will incentivise applicants to apply for leniency, while evaluating their potential liabilities with other sectoral regulators.[87] Therefore, it is suggested that immunity granted for violation of Section 3(3) of the Competition Act shall also be extended to violations under any other law, to cover situations where the gravity of the penalty for violation under any other law might act as a disincentive for potential leniency applicants to come forward.

Section 18 of the Competition Act permits the CCI to enter into any memorandum or arrangement with any foreign agency to perform its duties under the Competition Act. Subsequently, the CCI has entered into memoranda of understanding with the following international agencies:[88]

- Federal Trade Commission (FTC) and Department of Justice (DOJ), US.
- Director General Competition, EU.
- Federal Antimonopoly Service (FAS), Russia.

87 ICN, 'Guidance on Enhancing Cross-Border Leniency Cooperation' (n. 44 above).

88 OECD, 'Annual Report on Competition Policy Developments in India', DAF/COMP/AR(2020)45 (2020). Retrieved from https://one.oecd.org/document/DAF/COMP/AR(2020)45/en/pdf.

- Australian Competition and Consumer Commission (ACCC).
- Competition Bureau (CB), Canada.
- Competition authorities of the BRICS nations, i.e. the Federative Republic of Brazil, the Russian Federation, the People's Republic of China and the Republic of South Africa.

Additionally, the CCI has also been engaged in coordination with other jurisdictions through memberships of international organisations such as the International Competition Network (ICN), Competition Committee of the Organisation for Economic Co-operation and Development (OECD) and the United Nations Conference on Trade and Development (UNCTAD), in order to get exposure to best practices worldwide.[89]

13.8 Conclusion

The CCI is a relatively recent regulator in the field of competition law. Though the Competition Act came into effect in 2009, it has not seen the jurisprudence on leniency advancing with the requisite pace. Additionally, the inconsistency in its judicial approach on the reduction of penalty, belated recognition of leniency for individuals, absence of stronger tools for detection of cartels, absence of administrative sanctions for competition law violations and indeterminate imposition of quantum of penalty for competition law infringement has made leniency an ineffective tool for the detection of cartels. Recent years have seen an upsurge in leniency cases, but for effectively curbing the menace of cartels, the leniency tool must be updated with more predictability, transparency and effectiveness. The Competition Act must be amended to make leniency more attractive by increasing the sanctions associated with cartels, emphasising more on individual sanctions and therefore inducing individual leniency, reducing discretion in the quantum of leniency being awarded to various participants, strengthening the private enforcement system and protecting the disclosure of information by the applicant. There needs to be more certainty in the decisional practices of the CCI, which should further the goal of stronger leniency enforcement in India.

[89] Ibid.

14

Cartel Defection in the Philippines through Leniency

Incentives Jeopardised by Discretionary Decision-Making Power

ALIZEDNEY M. DITUCALAN AND STEVEN VAN UYTSEL

14.1 Introduction

After twenty-five years of discussion, the Philippine Congress passed a new competition law in 2015.[1] This competition law, Republic Act 10667, alternatively known as the Philippine Competition Act (PCA),[2] is the consolidated product of substitute House Bill 5286 of the House of Representatives and substitute Senate Bill 2282 of the House of the Senate during the 16th Congress of the Republic of the Philippines.[3] The PCA took effect on 8 August 2015.

In a nutshell, the PCA mandates the creation of a national competition authority called the Philippine Competition Commission (PCC). The PCC will 'implement the national competition policy'[4] of the government. As a quasi-judicial body, it has 'original and primary jurisdiction over the enforcement and implementation'[5] of the PCA. In addition, the PCA acknowledges that criminal enforcement is done by the Office

1 See Ditucalan, A. M., 'Institutional Design of Philippine Competition Law' (2018) 8 *KLRI Journal of Law and Legislation* 27.

2 Republic Act 10667, an Act Providing for a National Competition Policy Prohibiting Anti-Competitive Agreements, Abuse of Dominant Position and Anti-Competitive Mergers and Acquisitions, Establishing the Philippine Competition Commission and Appropriating Funds Therefor (21 July 2015). Retrieved from www.officialgazette.gov.ph/2015/07/21/republic-act-no-10667 (Philippine Competition Act or PCA).

3 Ditucalan, 'Institutional Design of Philippine Competition' (n. 1 above), p. 36.

4 PCA, Section 5.

5 Ibid., Section 12.

for Competition within the Department of Justice (DOJ-OFC) for criminal prosecution and through private parties for civil actions.[6] A leniency programme is among features to assist the enforcement of the PCC and the DOJ-OFC.

The general framework of the leniency programme of the Philippines is outlined in Section 35 of the PCA.[7] This Section gives the PCC and the DOJ-OFC the authority to adopt more detailed implementation rules. The PCC did so in 2018.[8] The DOJ-OFC followed in 2020.[9] As of 2021, there were no cases related to any of the leniency programmes. It can be questioned whether such cases will arrive soon. This is not because of a lack of incentives. The leniency programmes are conceptualised in such a way that if one immunity has been forgone, there is another chance to obtain immunity. The problem is, though, that the enforcement agencies often have discretion not to grant immunity. This discretionary power also exists in relation to the applications for reduction. Therefore, and this will be the argument in this chapter, it could be said that the Philippine leniency programmes try to incentivise cartel participants to come forward with information regarding the anti-competitive conduct, but that the incentives are veiled in an unpredictable and non-transparent enforcement procedure. This may negatively impact the whole leniency regime.

The chapter is structured as follows. Section 14.2 will describe Section 35 of the PCA, which is the provision in the law offering the basis for developing leniency programmes in the Philippines. The different leniency programmes and the types of leniency offered are detailed in Section 14.3. In Section 14.4, we deal with the actual leniency application and show how much discretion the enforcement agencies have in judging these leniency applications. Section 14.5 concludes.

[6] Ibid., Sections 13 and 45.

[7] Ibid, Section 35.

[8] PCC, 'Rules of the Leniency Program of the Philippine Competition Commission' (2018). Retrieved from www.phcc.gov.ph/wp-content/uploads/2018/12/Leniency-Rules-Clean-Version.pdf (Rules of the Leniency Program). The Rules of the Leniency Program were promulgated on 27 December 2018 and took effect on 16 January 2019.

[9] 'Rules Implementing the Criminal Provisions of Republic Act No. 10667, Otherwise Known as the Philippine Competition Act (PCA)' (2020). Retrieved from www.doj.gov.ph/files/2020/DC/DC%20016%20Rules%20Implementing%20the%20Criminal%20Provisions%20of%20RA%2010667%20or%20The%20Philippine%20Competition%20Act(1).pdf (Criminal Implementation Rules).

14.2 Section 35 of the PCA, the Basis for the Philippine Leniency Programme

14.2.1 Corporate and Individual Leniency under the PCC's Leniency Programme

Section 35 of the PCA is mainly written with the PCC in mind. This section starts out by stating that the PCC will develop a leniency programme. This leniency programme will cover immunity from suit and reduction of fine. Section 35 of the PCA further mentions that the leniency programme should be available to any entity that has participated in horizontal anti-competitive agreements, such as price fixing and bid rigging, and market allocation and output restriction.[10]

The reference to 'entity' has caused controversy. In Section 4(h) of the PCA, we can read that an entity is 'any person, natural or juridical, sole proprietorship, partnership, combination or association in any form, whether incorporated or not, domestic or foreign, including those owned or controlled by the government, engaged directly or indirectly in any economic activity'.[11] It could be questioned, when the entity is a juridical person, whether Section 35 of the PCA gives competence to the PCC to deploy a separate leniency programme addressed at corporate officials. In other words, should the leniency programme embrace the option for the 'current and former director, officer, trustee, partner, employee, or agent of a juridical person'[12] to apply for leniency?

During the Bicameral Conference, Rep. Rufus B. Rodriguez addressed this issue and stated:

> The individual whistleblower is not envisioned in this particular section. If you can see, this is coming from the EU and it is about cartel really, we have cartels, it's two or more, it cannot be one … what we're talking here, are entities, and one entity coming out itself as an entity, not as an individual ….[13]

The PCC has neglected this understanding of Section 35 of the PCA. The Rules of the leniency programme enable corporate officials to apply for leniency. However, there is an important limitation. Corporate officials

10 PCA, Section 35. This section is limited to in scope to horizontal agreements as defined in Section 14(a) and (b) of the PCA.

11 Ibid., Section 4.

12 Rules of the Leniency Program, Section 2, para. 2.

13 Records of the Bicameral Conference Committee on the Disagreeing Provisions of House Bill No. 5286 and Senate Bill No. 2282, pp. 25–26.

can only apply for leniency when they are liable for an anti-competitive horizontal agreement.

What is the importance of the limitation? It excludes corporate officials from applying for leniency when the anti-competitive agreement would be subject to an administrative fine. Indeed, the PCA seems to impose only criminal liability on corporate officials. This can be deduced by interpreting Section 29 in combination with Section 30 of the PCA. The former does not make any reference to corporate officials, while the latter explicitly states that incarceration only applies to individuals, whether or not they belong to a juridical entity.[14]

This broad interpretation of entity may make sense. The PCA does impose criminal sanctions, but has no strict division of power over the criminal proceedings. The PCC can initiate a criminal proceeding, but so can the DOJ-OFC. Therefore, the PCC had to address the relationship between its leniency application and corporate officials. By offering the possibility of carving out individuals from the corporate leniency programme,[15] which can be deduced from the fact that a corporate leniency application only applies to those corporate officials coming forward together with the juridical entity, the PCC had to offer one more safety net for the corporate officials. Leniency applications submitted by corporate officials will be treated separately from the application of the juridical entity. This means that anything affecting the corporate leniency application will not necessarily affect the individual leniency application.[16]

It is generally understood that offering leniency to individuals may offer an extra incentive for the race to the enforcement agencies. However, it is also possible that the corporate officials do not possess the necessary evidence to successfully apply for leniency. If they do, the juridical entity may not necessarily be willing to fully disclose their evidence of the anti-competitive agreement. Furthermore, it is conceivable that former employees may use the leniency programme to retaliate against their former employer.

The corporate officials are further protected by offering them the possibility to submit joint applications, an option that is not open for juridical entities.[17]

[14] PCA, Section 30, where it is determined that, in case of a juridical person, 'the penalty of imprisonment shall be imposed on its officers, directors, or employees holding managerial positions, who are knowingly and willfully responsible for such violation'.

[15] Rules of the Leniency Program, Section 8, para. 2.

[16] Ibid., paras. 3 and 4.

[17] Ibid., Section 9.

14.2.2 Leniency under the DOJ-OFC's Leniency Programme

Section 35 of the PCA also acknowledges that the DOJ-OFC can set up a leniency programme. Therefore, the provision stipulates in its last paragraph that, if a preliminary investigation is pending before the DOJ-OFC, leniency or immunity may be granted by that office.

The ability to grant leniency has been elaborated in a circular containing the Rules Implementing the Criminal Provisions of the Republic Act No. 10667, Otherwise Known as the Philippine Competition Act (Criminal Implementation Rules). Rule IV of the Criminal Implementation Rules lays out the DOJ-OFC's leniency programme.

The DOJ-OFC's leniency programme has two components: granting immunity from suit and recognising immunity from suit.[18] The former alludes to a new leniency application that has to be submitted to the DOJ-OFC, while the latter refers to an immunity from suit that is granted by the PCC.

This unique situation of having a double-layered leniency programme will be attractive to watch develop. It has to be seen whether this kind of institutional design of the leniency programme will optimally complement competition law enforcement. One practical advantage of this model is that it provides more doors for cartel participants to come forward through. However, this model may be counterintuitive and counterproductive to the race to the competition agency. Because of the multiple chances to apply for leniency, cartel participants may only come forward when they see that the investigation is making progress. In fact, the cartel participants may only come forward when there are already reasonable grounds for a full administrative proceedings or when evidence warrants the filing of a criminal complaint before the DOJ-OFC.

Moreover, this model could present an odd situation wherein the PCC rejects an application for leniency, but subsequently the DOJ-OFC grants such an application. Theoretically, the DOJ-OFC is not bound by the negative appraisal of facts by the PCC. Submitting another application will render the DOJ-OFC's leniency programme a de facto appellate body for leniency applications denied by the PCC, and this at the moment that the case is forwarded to the DOJ-OFC for preliminary investigation. If this reading is correct, this de facto appeal will complement the actual appeal provided for in Section 12 of the Criminal Implementation Rules.

[18] Criminal Implementation Rules, Rule IV, Section 1.

This Section offers an appeal procedure before the Office of the Secretary of Justice for DOJ-OFC leniency applications that have been denied or, if conditionally accepted, will later be revoked.

14.2.3 Leniency beyond Administrative Fines

The leniency that can be provided under Section 35 of the PCA is either immunity from suit or reduction of fines. By stating this, any leniency programme in the Philippines will have a broader coverage than most of the leniency programmes deployed in Asia. Most of the leniency programmes in Asia, even in countries that have criminal provisions, do not extend beyond administrative fines.[19]

The Rules of the Leniency Program acknowledge the dual scope. The PCC's leniency programme offers both immunity from suit and reduction of fines. Immunity from suit should be understood broadly. It covers both administrative and criminal proceedings. However, according to Section 1 of the Rules of the Leniency Program, immunity from suit will also cover civil proceedings, on the condition that these proceedings are 'initiated by the PCC on behalf of the affected parties and third parties'.[20] Hence, independent civil proceedings, initiated by any person who suffers direct injury,[21] can be directed at all firms infringing the law, even the one that has been granted immunity from suit.

The scope of the leniency programme of the Criminal Implementation Rules is by nature more limited than the leniency programme of the PCC. The DOJ-OFC is only occupied with criminal proceedings, due to which the immunity from suit is limited to that kind of proceedings. Since this kind of proceedings could lead to both criminal fine and imprisonment, the immunity from suit will cover both. Note, however, that the DOJ-OFC's leniency programme will neither create the possibility of reduction nor acknowledge the reduction granted by the PCC.

[19] See, e.g., Van Uytsel, Chapter 5 this volume; Choi, Chapter 7 this volume.

[20] Rules of the Leniency Program, Section 1, para. 2. Note that 'the Competition Act authorises the PCC to institute civil suits. PCA, Section 12(a). Unfortunately, the law does not prescribe the requirements for, or the procedure leading to, such civil action on the part of the PCC. Indeed, it fails to even state what relief the PCC would be entitled to demand in such civil suits.' See Prodigalidad, P.-A. T. and Ocampo, C. L. D., 'Philippines', in Gotts, I. K. and Schwartz, K. S. (eds.) *The Private Competition Enforcement Review*, 14th ed. (London: Law Business Research, 2021) 192.

[21] PCA, Section 45.

14.3 Different Types of Leniency and Their Conditions

14.3.1 Leniency before or after Fact-Finding or Preliminary Inquiry

Leniency applications by participants to anti-competitive agreement may be submitted in the following stages: (1) before fact-finding or preliminary inquiry; or (2) after fact-finding or preliminary inquiry. When the leniency is submitted prior to fact-finding or preliminary inquiry, the leniency applicant will obtain immunity from suit when all application requirements are complied with. After fact-finding or preliminary inquiry, there are two options. If there is still no information available on a particular entity, that entity could obtain immunity from suit (discretionary immunity). In any other situation, the PCC can only grant a reduction of the fine.

The terminology of fact-finding and preliminary inquiry has not always been used to distinguish different stages of the leniency application process.[22] It should be recalled that the original text under section 7 of Senate Bill No. 2282 and under section 25 of House Bill No. 5286 made reference to investigation throughout the provision that now constitutes Section 35 of the PCA. However, during the meetings of the Bicameral Conference Committee discussing the contradictory provisions, the word 'investigation' was replaced with the words 'fact-finding or preliminary inquiry' to make it clear and consistent with Section 31 of the PCA. During the deliberations of the bicameral committee, one of the members also asked why the proposed provision had 'or' between fact-finding and preliminary inquiry. The reason was not clarified, but it can be derived from the exchanges of the members that fact-finding and preliminary inquiry come at different stages or time frames and the two are not interchangeable. Fact-finding is a prelude to a preliminary inquiry.[23]

Despite this discussion in the *travaux préparatoires* of the PCA, an argument could be made that fact-finding is synonymous with preliminary inquiry or that fact-finding and preliminary inquiry are interchangeable. The Rules of Procedure of the PCC use fact-finding in the explanation of the preliminary inquiry. Section 2(1) of the Rules of Procedure states that fact-finding and preliminary inquiry share the same purpose and that is to 'ascertain whether there are reasonable grounds to conduct a

[22] See Records of the Bicameral Conference Committee on the Disagreeing Provisions of House Bill No. 5286 and Senate Bill No. 2282, pp. 16–20; Rep. Tinio's question, ibid., p. 20; question of Sen. Aquino to Rep. Gutierrez, ibid., p. 20; statement of Rep Cua, ibid., p. 21.

[23] See question of Sen. Aquino to Rep. Gutierrez, ibid., pp. 20–21.

Full Administrative Investigation'. If this is the purpose, the difference in timeline between fact-finding and preliminary inquiry may not be that important. What matters is the time when the PCC takes cognisance of an infringement.

14.3.2 Immunity and Reduction under the PCC's Leniency Programme

For immunity from suit, the entity must meet the following conditions described in Section 3 of the Rules of the Leniency Program:[24] (1) at the time the entity comes forward, the PCC has not received information about the activity from any other source, whereby the phrase any other source means an 'entity that has been granted conditional immunity';[25] (2) upon the entity's discovery of illegal activity, it took prompt and effective action to terminate its participation therein; (3) the entity reports the wrongdoing with candour and completeness and provides full, continuing, and complete cooperation throughout the investigation; and (4) the entity did not coerce another party to participate in the activity and clearly was not the leader in, or the originator of, the activity.

The restricted interpretation of any other source in Section 3 of the Rules of the Leniency Program could have a remarkable outcome. An entity may still qualify for immunity from suit even if the PCC has already obtained information prior to the start of a fact-finding or preliminary inquiry. Moreover, in the PCC's Leniency Program: Frequently Asked Questions document, it is also noted:

> the benefit of immunity from suit is available until it is granted to an entity. Hence, in case the first qualified entity is only granted reduction of fines, the second qualified entity may be granted immunity from suit if it submitted the Marker Request Form prior to the start of Preliminary Inquiry, or at the discretion of the PCC if the Marker Request Form was submitted after the start of the Preliminary Inquiry.[26]

For discretionary immunity, which can be applied for after the PCC has commenced a fact-finding or preliminary inquiry, the following conditions must be met by the leniency applicant: (1) the entity reports the

[24] These requirements are a repetition of the requirements set out in Section 35 of the PCA.

[25] Rules of the Leniency Program, Section 3(a).

[26] PCC, 'Leniency Program: Frequently Asked Questions (FAQs)' (2019), p. 8. Retrieved from www.phcc.gov.ph/wp-content/uploads/2020/09/Leniency-Program-FAQs-09302020_final.pdf (FAQs)

wrongdoing with candour and completeness and provides full, continuing and complete cooperation throughout the investigation; (2) the entity did not coerce another party to participate in the activity and clearly was not the leader in, or the originator of, the activity; (3) the entity took prompt and effective action to terminate its participation in the illegal activity; (4) at the time the entity comes forward, the PCC does not have evidence against the entity that is likely to result in a sustainable conviction; and (5) the PCC determines that granting leniency would not be unfair to others.[27] The problem with this form of immunity is the discretion afforded to the PCC.[28] This discretion is further exacerbated by not determining unfairness.

A reduction of the administrative fine can be applied for after the PCC has received information or after a fact-finding or preliminary inquiry has begun. The conditions for obtaining reduction are similar to the ones applicable to discretionary immunity. There is one additional requirement: the applicant must be the first one to come forward and qualify for reduction or the first one to qualify after a previous grant of conditional reduction has been revoked.[29]

14.3.3 Immunity under the DOJ-OFC's Leniency Programme

The leniency programme of the DOJ-OFC has two elements. On the one hand, the DOJ-OFC may grant immunity from suit. On the other hand, the DOJ-OFC has to recognise any immunity from suit granted by the PCC. Since the conceptualisation of the latter has been described above, here we will address the requirements put forward in the Criminal Implementation Rules.

Section 2 of the Criminal Implementation Rules stipulates that an applicant for immunity from suit needs to take the following conditions into consideration: (1) prompt and effective termination of the illegal anti-competitive conduct and this must be done upon discovery; (2) submission of the application during the preliminary investigation; (3) submission of evidence that could lead to a sustainable conviction; (4) disclosure of the wrongdoing with candour and completeness and providing full, continuing and complete cooperation throughout the preliminary investigation; (5) no coercion or instigation of another entity to

[27] Rules of the Leniency Program, Sections 3 and 4.

[28] Ibid., Section 4.

[29] Ibid.

participate in the anti-competitive conduct and the applicant must not have been the leader or originator of such conduct; and (6) no reporting of false, misleading or malicious information to the PCC or the DOJ-OFC. Just like in the case of discretionary immunity or the reduction of a fine under the PCC's leniency programme, the DOJ-OFC has the possibility of rejecting an immunity application on the grounds of fairness. What these grounds may be is not stipulated in the Criminal Implementation Rules.

14.4 The Actual Leniency Application

14.4.1 Securing a Marker

A prospective applicant for leniency may, at its own option, visit the Leniency Committee of the PCC for initial contact.[30] This preliminary step is merely limited to questions relating to the PCC's leniency programme and does not lead to the initiation of a leniency application. This initial contact is not available under the DOJ-OFC's leniency programme.

Both leniency programmes in the Philippines, whether it is that of the PCC or the DOJ-OFC, starts with securing a marker. Whereas the Rules of the Leniency Program in Section 5 stipulate that 'an entity seeking the benefits of the Leniency Programme may request for a marker from the PCC at any time prior to the commencement of adjudication on the anti-competitive agreement that it intends to report', the FAQs document of the PCC states that 'an application under the Leniency Program begins with a request for a marker'.[31]

This is in line with the leniency programme under the DOJ-OFC. This leniency programme stipulates that a respondent will submit a marker request form in order to start the immunity application. This would suggest that the request for a marker is the triggering point of the leniency application. In short, the request for a marker is contemporaneous with the application for leniency. This may be different from EU or US practice,[32] where a formal application can be submitted without going through the marker process. However, it is not so different from Japan, where a simplified application procedure serves the purpose of a marker.[33]

Because a marker is contemporaneous with the application for leniency, the applicant must be ready to disclose in the request for a marker

[30] FAQs, p. 11.
[31] Ibid.
[32] Balasingham, Chapter 2 this volume.
[33] Van Uytsel and Uemura, Chapter 6 this volume.

detailed information relating to the nature of the cartel activities, products or services (price fixing, output restriction or market allocations) or procurement or projects (bid rigging) involved; the geographical areas affected; the entities involved in the agreement; the individuals involved in the agreement and their name, job title or position; the terms of the agreements between entities or competitors; other agreements; the applicant's involvement or participation; and the effectivity or period of the cartel activity.[34]

The mere submission of the marker request form will protect the applicant's place in the queue under the DOJ-OFC leniency programme.[35] The PCC will issue a written receipt of the request for a marker. This written marker document will indicate the date and time the request was made and the description of the illegal activity reported. Once the marker is obtained or issued to the applicant, the applicant is given an initial period of thirty days to gather and submit information and evidence about the reported anti-competitive agreement.[36] The period of thirty days is reduced to ten days in the DOJ-OFC leniency programme if the complaint to this office is made by the PCC.[37] Only the marker obtained from the PCC can be extended. However, the PCC seems to have discretion as to whether to grant an extension and how long it will extend.[38]

Before the marker period expires, the leniency applicants need to perfect their marker. This will be done by submitting additional information and evidence focusing on (1) the entities involved in the alleged anti-competitive agreement; (2) the affected products and services; (3) the affected geographical area(s) or territory(ies); (4) the duration of the alleged anti-competitive agreement; and (5) the nature of the alleged anti-competitive agreement.[39] Whereas the information just mentioned is parallel for both the PCC's and the DOJ-OFC's leniency programmes, both have specific information requirements as well. The PCC requests the applicant to also state the reason why the entity is eligible under the leniency programme and information on any past leniency applications within and outside the

34 For the PCC's marker request form, PCC, 'Leniency Marker Request Form'. Retrieved from www.phcc.gov.ph/leniency-application. For the marker system under the DOJ-OFC leniency programme, see Criminal Implementation Rules, Rule IV, Section 3(a).

35 Criminal Implementation Rules, Rule IV, Section 3(b).

36 Rules of the Leniency Program, Section 5(a). See also Criminal Implementation Rules, Rule IV, Section 3(b).

37 Criminal Implementation Rules, Rule IV, Section 3(b).

38 Rules of the Leniency Program, Section 5(a).

39 Ibid., Section 5(b); Criminal Implementation Rules, Rule IV, Section 3(c).

Philippines.[40] The DOJ-OFC is more explicit in demanding the submission of all pieces of evidence in the applicant's possession, especially the evidence contemporaneous to the anti-competitive conduct, and whatever is relevant in relation to that evidence, including how it has been obtained.[41]

Even though it could appear that the above information is the same information that must be indicated or disclosed in the marker request form, it should be emphasised that perfecting the marker requires the submission of evidence. This evidence is not required when requesting the marker.

The creation of a specific list may be criticised. The American Bar Association noted that such a list may 'in practice significantly increase the effective burden associated with obtaining immunity by requiring (or expecting) too much, too soon (immediately at the time of an application). The additional burden in the quantum of evidence necessary to meet the immunity threshold may have unintended consequence of, in effect, slowing the race to the enforcement authority that leniency programmes are designed to foster'.[42] However, the experience of Japan shows that this should not necessarily be the case. The detailed guidance that the Japanese leniency programme provides to the leniency applicant has by no means delayed the race to the Japanese enforcement agency.[43]

Under the DOJ-OFC leniency programme, the marker has to be requested during the preliminary inquiry. The PCC's leniency programme enables the cartel participants to apply for leniency prior to the commencement of adjudication.[44] The adjudication commences when the Enforcement Office files the Statement of Objections.[45] It is obvious that this provision has to be read in concert with Sections 3 and 4 of the PCA and leads to the conclusion that such a late request for a marker can only mean that it will be a marker to obtain a reduction from the fine.

[40] Rules of the Leniency Program, Section 5(b).

[41] Criminal Implementation Rules, Rule IV, Section 3(c).

[42] 'Comments of the ABA Section of Antitrust Law and Section of the International Law in Response to the Commission of the European Communities' Request for Public Comment on the Draft Commission Notice on Immunity from Fines and Reduction in Fines in Cartel Cases' (November 2006), pp. 5–6. Retrieved from https://ec.europa.eu/competition/cartels/legislation/files_leniency_consultation/aba.pdf.

[43] Van Uytsel, S., 'Anti-Cartel Enforcement in Japan: Does Leniency Make the Difference?' in Beaton-Wells, C. and Tran, C. (eds.), *Anti-Cartel Enforcement in a Contemporary Age: Leniency Religion* (Oxford: Hart Publishing, 2015), 81, p. 81.

[44] Rules of the Leniency Program, Section 5.

[45] PCC, 'Rules of Procedure of the Philippine Competition Commission' (2017), Section 2.11. Retrieved from www.phcc.gov.ph/2017-rules-of-procedure.

The Rules of the Leniency Program do indeed not limit the application for a marker to the first applicant. Any leniency applicant needs to go through the marker procedure in order to apply for leniency. Since the PCC's leniency programme allows for the possibility of moving up in the application queue if others fail in their application, applying the marker to everyone is a necessity. The question is whether a marker still makes sense at a stage when the investigation is about to close and thus the PCC has been investigating the case for several weeks.

14.4.2 Conditional Leniency

Upon perfecting the marker, the enforcement agencies continue to evaluate the submitted evidence. The evaluation standards differ between the leniency programmes of the DOJ-OFC and the PCC. Both enforcement agencies will look at the quality of the information. The DOJ-OFC will check whether the information and evidence support the existence of an infringement.[46] The PCC will ascertain whether the information and evidence enable the PCC to carry out targeted investigation on the alleged anti-competitive agreement or offer a sufficient basis for initiating adjudication through the filing of a Statement of Objection.[47]

The Criminal Implementation Rules do not provide any further information on the process of judging the quality of the information and evidence. The Rules of the Leniency Program, to the contrary, do. Section 6 of the Rules of the Leniency Program explicitly mentions that it is within the discretion of the PCC to decide whether the information and evidence fulfil the standard of either allowing a targeted inspection or offering a sufficient basis for initiating adjudication. This formulation shows again that there was no intention of the PCC to provide a transparent and predictable process for leniency applicants.

Denial of conditional leniency will prevent the PCC from using the self-incriminating information and evidence,[48] unlike the DOJ-OFC.

[46] Criminal Implementation Rules, Rule IV, Section 6(a).

[47] Rules of the Leniency Program, Section 6.

[48] Rules of the Leniency Program, Sections 6 and 7. A similar principle applies to the withdrawal of the leniency application before conditional leniency is granted or denied. Note that denial of conditional leniency and its rendering the information and evidence useless for the PCC is not ironclad, as the Enforcement Office is not precluded from continuing the investigation or from using the same as evidence. If the application is abandoned prior to the denial or grant of a conditional leniency and no written notice is given to the Committee, the documents and information may be used by the PCC.

Instead, the DOJ-OFC offers the opportunity to appeal the decision denying conditional leniency. This procedure happens before the Office of the Secretary of Justice.[49]

14.4.3 Continued Cooperation until the End of Either the Administrative and Civil Case or the Criminal Case

Conditional leniency does not free the leniency applicants.[50] A set of conditions apply until the administrative case has reached its end.[51] If the PCC has also instituted a civil case, the leniency application only becomes final when a decision is taken in that case.[52] This can be substantially later than the administrative case. Leniency applications submitted to the DOJ-OFC will only become final when the criminal case is decided.[53] In the meantime, the leniency applicants need to continue cooperating with the enforcement agencies.

A lack of cooperation will lead to a revocation of the conditional leniency.[54] Such will be the case if there is a failure to appear at any meeting on the part of current and former employees called in by the enforcement agencies; a failure to submit information and evidence that comes into the possession of the leniency applicant; or a failure to deliver testimony or sworn statements for the administrative, criminal and/or civil case. The submission of false information or the destruction or concealment of information will have the same effect on the conditional leniency. So will the disclosure of the leniency application or any of its content lead to the revocation of the conditional leniency. Once conditional leniency has been revoked, all the information and evidence submitted by the applicant may be used in evidence against it and to third parties.[55]

Finally, the identity of an entity applying for leniency, as well as of those granted leniency, conditional or otherwise, shall be confidential, unless

[49] Criminal Implementation Rules, Rule IV, Section 12.

[50] For the PCC, Rules of the Leniency Program, Section 6(c); for the DOJ-OFC, Criminal Implementation Rules, Rule IV, Section 7.

[51] Rules of the Leniency Program, Section 13.

[52] FAQs, p. 13.

[53] Criminal Implementation Rules, Rule IV, Section 7.

[54] For the PCC, Rules of the Leniency Program, Section 7; for the DOJ-OFC, Criminal Implementation Rules, Rule IV, Section 8.

[55] Ibid. Individual corporate officials can keep the protection of the leniency programme if leniency is denied to the juridical person. For the PCC, Rules of the Leniency Program, Section 8; for the DOJ-OFC, Criminal Implementation Rules, Rule IV, Section 9.

the PCC determines such sworn testimony or sworn statement is necessary for a case filed by the PCC in relation to the reported violation.[56] The DOJ-OFC has no provisions on confidentiality.

14.5 Conclusion

Leniency is an efficient enforcement tool for competition agencies in combatting cartels that are very difficult to prosecute because of the sophistication and secrecy involved in such a practice. The basic goal of this tool is to attract cartel participants to defect from the cartel arrangement in exchange for immunity from suit or reduction of fine. For a relatively young competition agency that lacks the resources and expertise in detecting and prosecuting moneyed cartels, a leniency programme offers the advantage of enabling investigations without using many resources. It is however worth pointing out that in order to be attractive to cartel participants, a leniency programme must have clear and predictable rules. In the absence of clear and predictable rules, cartel participants may not recognise the incentive of racing to the enforcement agency.

Against this background and the observations made above, there are some issues that are worth highlighting in this conclusion.

The leniency programmes in the Philippines are generous. The leniency programme of the PCC offers immunity that covers both administrative and criminal cases and some civil cases. Moreover, immunity is available no matter whether the PCC is aware or unaware of the cartel. For those who cannot obtain immunity, they can apply for a sanction reduction. However, the reduction applicants can be granted immunity if the immunity applicants fail in this endeavour. Even if immunity has not been applied for when the PCC undertakes the investigation, there is still a possibility of applying for immunity to the DOJ-OFC. A denial of this application can still be appealed.

Despite the incentive structure to defect from a cartel, there are a few elements that may jeopardise an application. First, the position of employees is not fixed, as they can be excluded from a leniency application. Furthermore, the PCC has broadened its discretionary power. Immunity in cases where the PCC is aware of the cartel depends on the discretion of the PCC. Reduction always depends on the discretion of the

[56] Rules of the Leniency Program, Section 10.

PCC. Conditional leniency is contingent upon a discretionary decision of the PCC. The DOJ-OFC undermines its incentive of immunity by making conditional leniency not automatic and thus dependent upon its discretion. These ever-returning discretionary decision-making powers of the enforcement agencies will reduce the transparency and predictability of leniency programmes. Eventually, this may affect the race to the enforcement agency's door.

15

The Absence of a Leniency Programme in Thai Competition Law

PLOYKAEW PORANANOND*

15.1 Introduction

The year 2017 saw the enactment of the new Trade Competition Act of 2017 (2017 Act), which repealed the Trade Competition Act of 1999 (1999 Act). It marked Thailand's third attempt at adopting competition law statutes. The first foray was the Price Control and Antimonopoly Act of 1979, whose primary goals were price control of goods and services and monopoly control. These goals were in opposition to each other. The first objective aimed to control the price of listed goods and services, while the second aimed to support market competition. Due to technical difficulties, only the price control provisions were enforced. It would later be replaced by the 1999 Act, which was enacted during the financial-sector reconstruction in the aftermath of the Asian financial crisis of 1999. It is unfortunate that the statute was originally connected to a package of measures introduced to deal with the consequences of the Asian financial crisis;[1] competition itself was not a priority in the reforms, since most of them were related to financial-sector reconstruction. On the surface, the statute contained all the substantive competition provisions found in most competition law statutes, namely abuse of dominant position, merger control and anti-competitive agreements. It also contained a provision prohibiting unfair competition, as well as a unique trade policy provision prohibiting restrictions on international trade for personal consumption. The statute

* Special gratitude must be extended to Mr Kanoknai Thawonphanit, School of Law, Thammasat University, and Ms Nithinee Thongtae, School of Law, Chiangrai Rajabhat University, without whom this chapter would not have seen the light of day.

[1] Flatters, F., 'Thailand and the Crisis: Roots, Recovery and Long-Run Competitiveness', in Woo, W. T., Sachs, J. D. and Schwab, K. (eds.), *The Asian Financial Crisis Lessons for a Resilient Asia* (Cambridge, MA: MIT Press, 2000) 257; Thailand, Letter of Intent (14 August 1997).

established the primary competition law enforcement agency called the Trade Commission, under the purview of the Ministry of Commerce, and the Office of Trade Competition Commission acting as its secretariat body. The Trade Commission has investigated and considered ninety-five cases over its eighteen years of implementation,[2] based primarily on complaints received. There was no record of adjudication decisions.

The new 2017 Act is regarded as the reform statute with the objective to modernise Thai competition law. Nonetheless, the 2017 Act only brought limited change, since it preserves the same substantive provisions as its predecessor. The preserved provisions include abuse of dominant position, merger control and restrictive agreements. The reform is more evident in the institutional structure of the Trade Competition Commission (the Commission) and the Office of Trade Competition Commission (the Office). The new 2017 Act attempts to grant independence to the Office by extracting it from the Ministry of Commerce and transforming it into an independent organisation directly under the Constitution. In doing so, the 2017 Act admits that the principle of independence is at the core of competition authorities.[3] However, the formation of the new Commission is unlikely to be devoid of interference. Indeed, the 2017 Act insists that the Commissioners are appointed by the Prime Minister from a list selected and nominated by a committee composed of high-level bureaucrats, representatives of big business associations and a consumer representative.[4] Other changes include abandoning the universal application of criminal sanctions to all violations of competition law, including administrative fines for less serious violations, and introducing a two-court system. Consequently, the Intellectual Property and International Trade Court, a specialised court of justice, has jurisdiction in all criminal and civil damages[5], while the Administrative Court has jurisdiction over administrative orders of the Commission.[6]

Despite introducing reform of the national competition law, a feature of the 2017 Act is the continued absence of a leniency programme.

[2] Office of Trade Competition Commission, 'Summary of Complaints Statistic' (24 June 2021). Retrieved from https://tcct.or.th/view/1/Summary_of_complaint_statistics/TH-TH (in Thai).

[3] UNCTAD, 'The Role of Competition Policy in Promoting Economic Development: The Appropriate Design and Effectiveness of Competition Law and Policy', (TD/RBP/CONF.7/3, 2010). Retrieved from https://unctad.org/en/Docs/tdrbpconf7d3_en.pdf.

[4] Thailand Trade Competition Act, Section 11.

[5] Ibid., Section 26.

[6] Ibid., Sections 52–62.

Detection and punishment of cartels have long been difficult endeavours for many competition authorities, both regional and national.[7] A leniency programme is understood as the granting of immunity from penalties or the reduction of penalties for competition law violations in exchange for cooperation with the competition law enforcement authorities.[8] This omission is especially jarring against the backdrop of the rising number of jurisdictions adopting leniency policies in support of enforcement activities relating to cartel-related conduct.[9]

This chapter will explain the difficulties in incorporating a leniency programme into Thailand's competition law and its eventual exclusion from the modernised 2017 Act. It starts with some general background information on the current competition law regime in Section 15.2. It then retraces, in Section 15.3, the steps leading to the omission of a leniency programme from the 2017 Act. Section 15.4 describes the alternative measures adopted in place of a leniency programme.

15.2 Background on Thai Competition Law

The goals of competition law that traditionally figured in the nota bene of previous laws inexplicably disappeared from the 2017 Act. In place of the goals, the new statute states that the reasoning behind this modernised bill is to overcome past obstacles preventing the enforcement of competition law. Specifically, the absence of autonomy and independence of the previous competition agency are regarded as the principal causes preventing the regulation of free and fair competition. One can infer then that the new goal of Thai competition law is 'the protection of free and fair competition'.[10] The combination of economic and social goals may create conflict and when that occurs, the economic goal is often expected to be circumvented for the benefit of other goals.[11] Installing multiple goals of

7 Cauffman, C., 'The Interaction of Leniency Programmes and Actions for Damages' (2011) 7 *Competition Law Review* 181.

8 Wils, W. P. J., 'Leniency in Antitrust Enforcement: Theory and Practice' (2007) 30 *World Competition* 25.

9 Hammond, S. D., 'The Evolution of Criminal Antitrust Enforcement over the Last Two Decades' (Presentation at 24th Annual National Institute on White Collar Crime, ABA Criminal Justice Section and ABA Center for Continuing Legal Education, Miami, 25 February 2010).

10 Thailand Trade Competition Act, N.B.

11 Lee, C. and Fukunaga, Y., 'Competition Policy Challenges of Single Market and Production Base' (ERIA Discussion Paper Series, 2013).

competition law is usually politically motivated.[12] Perhaps its true purpose is to ensure that there will always be a legitimate political vehicle available to give expression to social goals.[13] Nonetheless, the indecisiveness reflected in the goals of competition law set the tone for the Thai competition law.

This section is organised as follows: it will begin with an analysis of the institutional design of the competition law agency in accordance with the 2017 Act, followed by an explanation of the substantive provisions of the law.

15.2.1 Institutional Design

A new institutional design is the main feature of Thailand's revised competition law. The law allows the establishment of an independent Commission. This institutional formation follows the integrated agency model, with the Commission assuming an investigative and enforcement role. A decision made by the Commission is subject to judicial review. The 2017 Act also introduces a two-court system: the Intellectual Property and International Trade Court is a specialised court of justice having jurisdiction in all criminal and civil damages,[14] while the Administrative Courts have jurisdiction over administrative orders of the Commission.[15]

The focus on the agency's independence is especially tailored to overcome the history of non-enforcement of the previous competition law regime. There are several contributing factors behind this non-enforcement[16]; nevertheless, interference from the government is singled

[12] Rodriguez, A. and Menon, A., *The Limits of Competition Policy: The Shortcomings of Antitrust in Developing and Reforming Economies* (Alphen aan den Rijn: Wolters Kluwer, 2010), p. 98.

[13] Ibid.

[14] Thailand Trade Competition Act, Section 26.

[15] Ibid.

[16] Ranging from a deficit in democracy, cronyism, absence of competition culture, irregular meeting of the Commission, to the country's economy with close ties between business and politics. See, e.g., Chantara-Opakorn, A., 'Thailand Competition Law and Its Implication on International Mergers and Acquisition' (2000) 18 *Wisconsin International Law Journal* 591; Thanitcul, S., 'Competition Law in Thailand: A Preliminary Analysis' (2002) 1 *Washington University Global Studies Law Review* 171; Paopongsakorn, N., 'The New Competition Law in Thailand: Lessons for Institutional Building' (2002) 21 *Review of Industrial Organization* 185; Williams, M., 'Competition Law in Thailand: Seeds of Success or Fated to Fail?' (2004) 27 *World Competition* 459; Nikomborirak, D., 'The Political Economy of Competition Law: The Case of Thailand' (2006) 26 *Northwestern Journal of International Law & Business* 597; McEwin, I. and Thanitcul, S., 'Thailand', in

out as the main factor.[17] In one instance, an ex-commissioner hinted that the Commission received direct instructions from the Minister of Commerce.[18] Consequently, the 2017 Act seeks to separate the competition agency from political influence by extracting it from the Ministry of Commerce. The new Commission is now an independent agency under the Constitution.

This revised institutional design is in accordance with the general understanding of the principle of independence, which is long regarded as the core of any institutional design of competition authorities.[19] Ideally, competition authorities should be insulated from 'political and budgetary interference'.[20] In addition, there is a direct correlation between an agency's independence and its improved enforcement.[21] Therefore, it should not come as a surprise that the independence of the national competition agency is seen as the primary solution to overcome obstacles in the enforcement of competition law in Thailand. Interestingly, the only independence from which the Commission seeks refuge is political influence, more specifically governmental influence. Nonetheless, some doubts linger over whether this new legal status of the competition agency is sufficient to grant the Commission actual independence, since the 2017 Act itself provides that the seven members of the Commission are nominated by the Prime Ministry based on the recommendation made by the Nomination Committee consisting of five Permanent Secretaries of different Ministries, the Secretary of the National Economics and Social Development Board, the Secretary of the Consumer Protection Board, the Chairman of the Thai Chamber of Commerce and the Chairman of the

Williams, M. (ed.), *The Political Economy of Competition Law in Asia* (Cheltenham: Edward Elgar, 2013), 251; Nikomborirak, D., 'The Political Economy of the Competition Regimes in Thailand and Korea: A Comparison', in Lewis, D. (ed.) *Building New Competition Law Regimes: Selected Essays* (Cheltenham: Edward Elgar, 2013), 110; Thaipublica, '12 Years of Failure to Enforce the Thai Trade Competition Act (An Interview with the Ex-Commissioner Pornapa Thaicharoen 2012)' (2012). Retrieved from http://thaipublica.org/2012/02/competition-act-12-enforcement-has-failed (in Thai).

17 Nikomborirak, D., 'Banana Matters and Monopoly' (2014). Retrieved from http://thaipublica.org/2015/05/tdri-11-5-2558 (in Thai).

18 Thaipublica, '12 Years of Failure' (n. 16 above).

19 UNCTAD, 'The Role of Competition Policy' (n. 3 above).

20 Khemani, S. and Dutz, M., 'The Instruments of Competition Policy and Their Relevance for Economic Development', in Frischtak, C. R. (ed.), *Regularities Policies and Reform: A Comparative Perspective* (New York: World Bank, 1995), 16.

21 Ma, T.-C., 'Competition Authority Independence, Antitrust Effectiveness, and Institutions' (2010) 30 *International Review of Law & Economics* 226.

Federation of Thai Industries.[22] It is evident that the concern for independence does not extend to the nomination process. In September 2018, Thailand finally appointed its first Commission under the 2017 Act.[23] Most of the seven Commissioners are former government officers, with two members from academia in the field of economics, and one member with a background in the business sector.[24]

15.2.2 Substantive Provisions

To understand the shape of a competition law, one must first strive to understand the reach of its application. Hence, defining *undertaking*, the subject of the application of competition law, is a crucial step. Thai competition law is applicable to undertakings in 'agriculture, industry, commerce, finance, insurance, and services and shall include other undertakings as prescribed by Ministerial Regulations'.[25] The language here focuses on the economic sector in which the undertaking engages. It means that the 2017 Act will be applicable to all undertakings participating in economic activity, with no regard to the undertaking's legal status or denomination. This shifts the focus to the nature of the activity of the undertaking. As long as the activity is considered economic, competition law will apply. This formulation bears a certain similarity to European Union (EU) competition law, where the term 'undertaking' is defined by case law as 'every entity engaged in an economic activity, regardless of the legal status of the entity and the way in which it is financed'.[26] Thailand introduces some limitations to the application of its competition law. It shall not apply to a central or local administration; a state-owned enterprise necessary for public security, public interest or utilities; a farmers' group or cooperative society; or undertakings under specific sectoral regulations with competition

[22] Thailand Trade Competition Act, Section 11.

[23] Cabinet Resolution, 4 September 2018.

[24] Order of the Prime Minister No. 350/2561 Regarding the Appointment of Chairperson, Deputy Chairperson, and Commissioners in the Trade Competition Commission (27 December 2018). Somkiat Tankrittiwat was an independent committee member of Adamas Incorporation Public Company Limited; Isranews Agency, 'Adamas the Main Co-Contractor of the Ministry of Tourism and Sports Worth 250 M. Now with 109 M. in Debt' (2014). Retrieved from www.isranews.org/isranews-scoop/33198-adm.html (in Thai).

[25] Thailand Trade Competition Act, Section 5.

[26] *Höfner and Elser* v. *Macroton GmbH* (ECR I-1979) para. 21; *Poucet and Pistre* v. *Assurances Générales de France* (ECR I-637) para. 17; *Fédération Française des Sociétés d'Assurance* v. *Ministry of Agriculture and Fisheries* (ECR I-4013) para. 14.

law provisions.[27] The state-owned enterprise exception can be confusing considering that, by definition, state-owned enterprises are created to fulfil the functions of public security, public interest or public utilities. It is therefore likely that most state-owned enterprises will be exempted from the application of competition law.

Thai competition law contains three principal prohibitions: abuse of dominant position, anti-competitive agreement and merger control. Dominant position is defined as a position obtained by an undertaking, both individually or collectively, when its market share and turnover are beyond the criteria set by the Commission.[28] The possession of dominant position in the relevant market in itself is not a violation of competition law unless it is accompanied by abuse. Additionally, behaviours classified as abuse of dominant position are unfair price fixing, unfair condition fixing, unreasonable restriction to services and goods below the demand of the market, and unreasonable interference with another undertaking.[29]

Regarding the prohibition of anti-competitive agreement, this prohibition can be divided into two categories: horizontal and vertical anti-competitive agreement. Horizontal anti-competitive agreements, or hard-core cartels, are universally considered to be undesirable.[30] Therefore, all the competition laws around the world prohibit horizontal collaboration outright without allowing any reasonable defences,[31] since it is assumed that this type of agreement outweighs any possible pro-competitive justifications.[32] This resonates well with the general belief that cartels are bad and must be regulated. The 2017 Act defines horizontal agreements as all agreements resulting in monopoly, reduction or limitation of competition, which are per se illegal.[33] The prohibited behaviours include direct or indirect price fixing, product or service limitation, bid rigging and geographical division. On the other hand, vertical anti-competitive agreements are agreements resulting in monopoly, reduction or limitation of competition. They commonly include price (minimum or maximum resale price maintenance) and non-price restraints (exclusive territorial or customer arrangements, exclusive

[27] Thailand Trade Competition Act, Section 4.

[28] Ibid.

[29] Ibid.

[30] Fox, E. and Crane, D., *Global Issues in Antitrust and Competition Law* (St Paul, MN: West Publishing, 2010), p. 5.

[31] Rodriguez and Menon, *The Limits of Competition Policy* (n. 12 above), p. 87.

[32] Sheth, M., 'Formulating Antitrust Policy in Emerging Economies' (1997) 86 *Georgetown Law Journal* 451.

[33] Thailand Trade Competition Act, Section 54.

dealings, tie-ins, selective distribution and quantity forcing).[34] The prohibited vertical behaviours are agreements that monopolise, reduce or restrict competition in a market, which can take the form of price fixing, product and service restriction or market allocation if the agreement is entered into by non-competitors in the same market.[35] The list expands to include other non-price restrictions including quality reduction, non-price maintenance and exclusive dealings. The 2017 Act accepts some countervailing benefits as justifications for anti-competitive vertical restraints, including technological or economic development and technology transfer.[36] However, these are appreciated by the Commission according to the rule of reason test, provided that the agreement in question does not create monopoly, substantially limit competition or have a negative impact on consumers.[37]

The term 'merger' is chosen in the 2017 Act to encompass mergers among producers, sellers, producers and sellers or service providers, involving acquisition of all or part of the assets or stocks both directly and indirectly of another business in order to control its policy, business administration, direction or management, and joint ventures.[38] The 2017 Act broadly defines concentration to encompass all levels of concentration of undertakings as long as it results in the extinction of one undertaking and the birth of a new undertaking. Thai merger control is divided into two regimes. First, a mandatory post-merger notification for mergers that substantially lessen competition in the relevant market must be done within seven days of the completion of the merger.[39] The language is a direct installation of the US antitrust substantial lessening of competition test.[40] Second is a mandatory pre-merger notification for mergers resulting in a monopoly or dominant position in the market. This type of test has already been abandoned by the EU competition law in favour of the significant impediment to effective competition test.[41]

[34] OECD, *Trade and Competition Policies for Tomorrow* (Paris: OECD Publishing, 1999), p. 43.

[35] Thailand Trade Competition Act, Section 55.

[36] Ibid., Section 56.

[37] Ibid.

[38] Ibid., Section 51.

[39] Ibid., Section 52.

[40] The Clayton Act, 15 U.S.C. §§ 12–27, 29 U.S.C. §§52–53.

[41] Council Regulation (EC) No 139/2004 on the Control of Concentrations between Undertakings art. 2(2). The previous criterion of dominant position has been reduced to a mere example of significant impedance of effective competition. However, dominant position has not completely been erased from the EU Merger Regulation. It still appears in the regulation as a prime indication of concentration between undertakings incompatible with the common market.

For the pre-merger notification, the Commission must decide within ninety days from the notification date, with no more than a fifteen-day extension. Thailand's choice in dividing merger control into two regimes is a peculiar one. It is commonly understood that a pre-emptive review of a merger is less costly and less complicated than attempting to deconcentrate an anti-competitive concentration that has already been realised.[42] Thailand's choice to preserve both pre- and post-merger control adds to the business cost and complication in the enforcement of the law. The justification for this dual regime is likely born out of necessity, namely to facilitate business concentrations that do not seriously affect the economy or consumers' general interest and to prevent them from undergoing long and arduous control by the Commission. The Commission considers the efficiency defence on the basis of valid business-related necessity and the benefit in supporting an undertaking. Here again, the rule of reason shall apply. No efficiency defence shall apply if a merger severely damages the economy or negatively impacts the essential benefits that consumers are entitled to.[43]

With many alterations and innovations in the 2017 Act aiming at finally bringing about actual enforcement of competition law, it is incongruous that it is willing to exclude a leniency programme.

15.3 Explaining the Absence of a Leniency Programme in Thai Competition Law

It is uncontested that Thailand's choice not to include a leniency programme in its competition law stands in stark contrast to the global trend.[44] In particular, the trend of enacting a leniency programme in Southeast Asia has been well noted,[45] possibly because a leniency programme is regarded as an essential tool in identifying and prosecuting

42 Furse, M., *The Law of Merger Control in the EC and the UK* (Oxford: Hart Publishing, 2007).

43 Thailand Trade Competition Act, Section 52.

44 See Crumplar, T., 'An Alternative to Public and Victim Enforcement of the Federal Securities and Antitrust Laws: Citizen Enforcement' (1975) 13 *Harvard Journal on Legislation* 76; Kovacic, W., 'Private Monitoring and Antitrust Enforcement: Paying Informants to Reveal Cartels' (2001) 69 *George Washington Law Review* 766; Engstrom, D., 'Whither Whistleblowing? Bounty Regimes, Regulatory Context, and the Challenge of Optimal Design' (2014) 15 *Theoretical Inquiries in Law* 605.

45 Shiau, D. and Chen, E., 'Emerging Trends in Leniency Regimes in Southeast Asia – How These Impact on Multi-Jurisdiction Leniency Strategy' (2017) 38 *European Competition Law Review* 165.

cartels.[46] Moreover, it appears that adopting a leniency programme was discussed at length in the Drafting Committee, before being ultimately dropped from the reformed law.

15.3.1 *A Leniency Programme: Desired by the Enforcers*

There is compelling evidence that among all the competition law enforcement measures, effective anti-cartel enforcement is by far the most important determinant of positive productivity growth of a jurisdiction.[47] However, this anti-cartel enforcement can be difficult to execute due to the high standard of proof required; this is especially true in jurisdictions whose criminal law requires the standard of beyond a reasonable doubt.[48] In their fact-finding mission to obtain proof, competition authorities generally first attempt to detect the cartel themselves through market monitoring. However, the judiciary often deems such economic evidence insufficient to prove the existence of a cartel.[49] Competition authorities can also try to surmise the existence of cartels from third parties' complaints. This measure relies on a basic desire for revenge among competitors.[50] Perhaps the best method of collection of information and evidence is when the sources are undertakings or individuals who have participated in the cartel themselves.[51] This method is particularly useful in price-fixing cartels, which tend to be secretive in nature. The undertakings that have committed the violations and their staff may be the only ones holding the information that the competition authorities need in order to detect and punish.[52] It is precisely this last method that inspired the creation of leniency programmes.

[46] Schmidt, J., 'Keeping US Courts Open to Foreign Antitrust Plaintiffs: A Hybrid Approach to the Effective Deterrence of International Cartels' (2006) 31 *Yale Journal of International Law* 211.

[47] Buccirossi, P., Ciari, L., Duso, T., Spagnolo, G. and Vitale, C., 'Competition Policy and Productivity Growth: An Empirical Assessment' (2013) 95 *Review of Economics and Statistics* 1324.

[48] Harding, C., Beaton-Wells, C. and Edwards, J., 'Leniency and Criminal Sanctions in Anti-Cartel Enforcement: Happily Married or Uneasy Bedfellows?' in Beaton-Wells, C. and Tran, C. (eds.), *Anti-Cartel Enforcement in a Contemporary Age: Leniency Religion* (Oxford: Hart Publishing, 2015), 233.

[49] Wils, 'Leniency in Antitrust Enforcement' (n. 8 above).

[50] Baker, D., 'The Use of Criminal Law Remedies to Deter and Punish Cartels and Bid-Rigging' (2001) 69 *George Washington Law Review* 693.

[51] Wils, 'Leniency in Antitrust Enforcement' (n. 8 above).

[52] Ibid.

A leniency programme is an enforcement tool aimed at facilitating both deterrence and detection of cartels.[53] It seeks to modify the rules prescribing penalties for illegal cartel behaviours. The modifications exist either in the non-imposition or the reduction of the penalties.[54] By granting lenient treatment in exchange for information, a leniency programme gives incentives to undertakings participating in an illegal cartel activity to withdraw from this activity and provide necessary intelligence to competent competition authorities. Giving its usefulness in anti-cartel enforcement, a leniency programme is often regarded as 'the single most important tool for cartel detection, prosecution, and deterrence'.[55] Moreover, a leniency programme has a beneficial side effect of engendering distrust among cartel participants. To properly create and sustain a successful cartel, all the participants have to equally benefit from increased profits. To discourage defection among participants, extensive mechanisms are put in place that may involve monitoring and handing out reward or punishment. In order to entice cartel participants to deviate from their agreed collusion, a leniency programme must elevate the benefit of defection in their eyes. Usually this is done progressively by first making it harder for cartel participants to reach agreement, diminishing trust among them, and ultimately increasing the need for costly monitoring.[56] Consequently, the cartel would then become too costly to maintain.

It is unsurprising that Thai competition law authorities would find the various benefits of a leniency programme attractive. They too cannot avoid the difficulties in anti-cartel enforcement. The 2017 Act firmly states that participating in hard-core cartels, such as price fixing, goods or services fixing, bid rigging, geographical allocation resulting in monopoly, and reducing or limiting competition,[57] falls under criminal sanction not

[53] Van Uytsel, S., 'Anti-Cartel Enforcement in Japan: Does Leniency Make the Difference?' in Beaton-Wells, C. and Tran, C. (eds.), *Anti-Cartel Enforcement in a Contemporary Age: Leniency Religion* (Oxford: Hart Publishing, 2015), 81.

[54] See Spagnolo, G., 'Optimal Leniency Programs' (Fondazione Eni Enrico Mattei, Working Paper 42.2000, 2000). Retrieved from https://papers.ssrn.com/sol3/papers.cfm?abstract_id=235092; Landeo, C. M. and Spier, K. E., 'Optimal Law Enforcement with Ordered Leniency' (2020) 63 *Journal of Law and Economics* 71.

[55] ICN, 'Trends and Developments in Cartel Enforcement' (Presentation at the 9th Annual ICN Conference, Istanbul, 29 April 2010). Retrieved from www.internationalcompetitionnetwork.org/wp-content/uploads/2018/05/CWG_TrendsReport.pdf.

[56] Spagnolo, G., 'Divide et Impera: Optimal Leniency Programmes' (Stockholm School of Economics, CEPR Discussion Paper No. 4840, 2004). Retrieved from https://papers.ssrn.com/sol3/papers.cfm?abstract_id=716143.

[57] Thailand Trade Competition Act, Section 54.

exceeding two-year imprisonment and/or an amount of a fine not exceeding 10 per cent of total turnover of the year in which the violation has occurred.[58] The criminal sanction attached to this prohibition of competition law elevates the standard of proof required, perhaps to a height that may be just out of reach of the Commission. Past competition law enforcement experiences revealed no adjudication cases born out of the Commission's cartel investigation, despite it periodically receiving complaints on the issue. These complaints underscore the challenges the Commission faced when gathering evidence of collusion based on the testimony of whistle-blowers.

Haunted perhaps by the ghost of the non-enforcement of the previous law, the Office of Trade Competition Commission was in support of the inclusion of some form of a leniency programme in the new statute. It proposed the following inclusion to the Drafting Committee:

> *The Commission may decide to grant immunity or reduction in administrative fine in accordance with section 79 to undertakings who are not the principal, instigator, or supporter of the violation of section 54 admitting to their participation in the violation of section 54 and providing important information or cooperating with the Office of Trade Competition Commission in providing clues or facilitating the investigation process in accordance with section 54.*
>
> The [leniency programme]'s rules, procedures, and conditions shall be in accordance with the Commission Notice.[59]

The proposal targeted both violation by a single undertaking and collective violation. It concerned the provision of intelligence and evidence, as well as other means of facilitating the Commission's investigative process. There does not seem to be any indication regarding the preference for a pre- or post-investigation process. Nonetheless, it is clear that the proposal favoured giving an extensive discretionary power to the competition agency.

Perhaps conscious of the fact that a leniency programme needs to anticipate the likelihood that cartel participants will defect from the cartel, it was decided that the leniency programme needed to be supplemented with guarantees that leniency would only be granted if certain procedural rules were fulfilled. The authorities also proposed a draft leniency programme guideline imposing conditions in granting leniency. The proposed leniency programme contains the following design features:

[58] Ibid., Section 72.

[59] Emphasis added.

- Undertakings shall not submit false evidence or witness.
- Undertakings shall fully cooperate by submitting any additional evidence or witness as requested by the Office of Trade Competition Commission.
- Undertakings shall not reveal their leniency programme application.

Furthermore, the proposed guideline excluded the leaders or participants who forced other undertakings to join the cartel or cease certain behaviours in accordance with the cartelistic agreement. The Commission will hold the power to grant a reduction in administrative fine in a manner that is in accordance with the future Commission's Notice. However, this power does not extend to the granting of immunity. Regarding the imprisonment sanction, the Office of Trade Competition Commission will submit a memorandum expressing its opinion not to prosecute the first undertaking to report and apply for the leniency programme to the Office of the Attorney General. This memorandum will serve only to communicate the Commission's intention to grant leniency so as not to interfere with the Office of the Attorney General's exclusive discretionary power regarding the criminal enforcement procedure.

15.3.2 A Leniency Programme: Denied by the Drafting Committee

There were many reasons to reject the inclusion of a leniency programme, chief among which was the argument that a leniency programme can be strategically used to punish rivals and, in some extreme cases, even to help strengthen collusion.[60] Undertakings may intentionally participate in a cartel, only to document all the evidence against other participants and report the cartel to competition authorities in order to apply for a leniency programme later. In this regard, the benefits of a leniency programme are distorted and reduced to a simple 'revenge game'.[61] Doubts have also been cast regarding the trustworthiness of such undertakings in such a high-stakes investigation as criminal enforcement of cartels.[62] Yet none of these arguments was used by the Drafting Committee. Instead, the Drafting Committee rejected the leniency programme proposal in three cascading steps.

[60] Sokol, D. D., 'Cartels, Corporate Compliance, and What Practitioners Really Think about Enforcement' (2012) 78 *Antitrust Law Journal* 201; Harding, Beaton-Wells and Edwards, 'Leniency and Criminal Sanctions' (n. 48 above).

[61] Baker, D., 'The Use of Criminal Law Remedies to Deter and Punish Cartels and Bid-Rigging' (2001) 69 *George Washington Law Review* 693.

[62] Harding, Beaton-Wells and Edwards, 'Leniency and Criminal Sanctions' (n. 48 above).

The first step was to subtly exclude immunity from the proposed leniency programme. While a leniency programme was extensively discussed at this stage, it was done under the reductive denomination of measures to reduce penalty, indicating that immunity was never a part of the policy. Moreover, during the discussion, the representative from the Office of the Attorney General was quick to object to the Commission's power to offer immunity from penalties, citing constitutional restrictions. Indeed, the 2017 Thailand Constitution states that the trial and adjudication of cases are the exclusive powers of the courts.[63] This particular claim ignores the function of a leniency programme at the investigation stage, as well as conflating the power to enter a plea with the power to issue a criminal sanction; the latter is indeed an exclusive judicial power. Nevertheless, the claim was not refuted, and the Drafting Committee agreed to avoid interfering with the judicial power.

The Drafting Committee then proceeded to reduce the scope of application of the leniency programme to only soft-core cartels. Under the 2017 Act, agreements considered as soft-core cartels are:[64]

- Agreements between non-competitors in the same market fixing price of goods and services, or allocating geographical areas of operation.
- Agreements reducing the quality of goods or services.
- Exclusive agreements.
- Agreements prescribing certain sale or production contracts that result in monopoly, reduction or restriction of competition in the market.

Participating in soft-core cartels only carries the sanction of an administrative fine not exceeding 10 per cent of the turnover of the year in which the offence was committed.

The decision to exclude undertakings participating in hard-core cartels from the leniency programme greatly hindered its efficiency. As mentioned above, a leniency programme is designed to aid in the detection and collection of evidence against cartelists who escape the detection of the competition authorities' market monitoring. Hard-core cartels, in particular, are difficult to detect since they are not usually concluded through written agreements, but rather through physical meetings, telephone calls or any other secretive means. It is hard for competition

[63] Constitution of the Kingdom of Thailand, Section 188.

[64] Thailand Trade Competition Act, Section 55.

authorities to obtain such evidence without it being voluntarily provided by the cartelists themselves. Furthermore, it is argued that a leniency programme functions well in tandem with the harshness of cartel sanctions.[65] Indeed, past experiences of the US and the EU have shown that increasing sanctions 'have made leniency even more attractive'.[66] In other words, a leniency programme becomes more attractive as the threat of sanction becomes more threatening. By eliminating harsher sanctions against hard-core cartels,[67] the Drafting Committee successfully undermined the effectiveness of the leniency programme.

Finally, reinforcing the effort of excluding hard-core cartels from the leniency programme, the Drafting Committee eliminated all criminal sanctions from the leniency programme, citing potential conflicts with the Code of Criminal Procedure (CCP). More specifically, it claimed that granting the power to the Commission to offer reduction in criminal sanction in a leniency programme is in direct violation of the exclusive judicial power to order criminal sanctions, citing Sections 37 and 38 of the CCP. However, Section 37 of the CCP simply states the different ways in which criminal cases can be settled, while Section 38 of the CCP extensively grants the power to settle the case after the fine has been paid to competent officials. The latter allows competent officials to fix the amount of the appropriate fine. Regardless of the legal fact, this motion was affirmed, and the proposed leniency programme was left with only the reduction of financial penalty.

Perhaps a better explanation for the persistent refusal of a leniency regime lies in Thai legal culture, which only confers the power to reduce criminal penalty to the discretionary power of the courts. It follows that the Drafting Committee was reluctant to act against this traditional role through the adoption of more innovative tools like a leniency programme. The Drafting Committee was not convinced by the accepted knowledge that leniency can waive or reduce any penalties that can be

65 Werden, G., Hammond, S. D. and Barnett, B., 'Detection and Deterrence of Cartels: Using All the Tools and Sanctions' (2011) 56 *Antitrust Bulletin* 207; Baker, D., 'Why Is the United States So Different from the Rest of the World in Imposing Serious Criminal Sanctions on Individual Cartel Participants?' (2011) 12 *Sedona Conference Journal* 301.

66 Nicolosi, C., 'No Good Whistle Goes Unpunished: Can We Protect European Antitrust Leniency Applications from Discovery?' (2011) 31 *Northwestern Journal of International Law & Business* 225.

67 Thailand Trade Competition Act, Section 72. The sanction for participating in a hard-core cartel shall not exceed two years' imprisonment and/or a fine not exceeding 10 per cent of the turnover of the year in which the offence was committed.

imposed or sought by the competition authorities, either financial fines and/or imprisonment.[68]

The proposed leniency programme was then left with only a reduction in financial penalty, which in turn got conflated with existing powers to reduce administrative fines. This marked the end of the discussion on a leniency programme and its subsequent disappearance from the adopted reform. The current Section 79 of the 2017 Act merely states:

> For all offences under this Act, the Commission shall have the power to settle cases. In executing such power, the Commission may assign the Secretary-General to act on the Commission's behalf.
>
> When the alleged person pays the fine for the amount of settlement within the required period, it shall be deemed that the case is terminated under the provisions of the Code of Criminal Procedure.
>
> The amount of fine to settle cases shall be determined according to criteria, methods, and conditions prescribed in the Commission's notification.

15.4 The Proposed Alternative to a Leniency Programme in Thai Competition Law

For many competition authorities in the world, leniency has become the principal instrument of competition law enforcement against hard-core cartels.[69] Its main objective is to incite undertakings participating in cartelistic behaviour to cease their cartelistic activities and provide necessary information regarding the cartel to competent competition authorities. In this regard, a leniency programme is deemed an indispensable tool, because without it the detection and collection of evidence against cartels are practically impossible.[70] It is even admitted that successful anti-cartel enforcement discourages cartels while effectively combatting those that nonetheless emerge.[71] The question thus arises of how Thailand competition law chooses to proceed in the absence of a leniency programme. This will come to define Thailand's anti-cartel enforcement. This section aims to examine the measures made available in the absence of a leniency programme before evaluating the effectiveness of such measures.

68 See, Wils, W. J. P., 'Is Criminalization of EU Competition Law the Answer?' (2005) 28 *World Competition* 117.

69 Marvão, C. and Spagnolo, G., 'What Do We Know about the Effectiveness of Leniency Policies? A Survey of the Empirical and Experimental Evidence' in Beaton-Wells and Tran, *Anti-Cartel Enforcement in a Contemporary Age* (n. 48 above), 57.

70 ICN, 'Trends and Developments in Cartel Enforcement' (n. 55 above).

71 O'Fiachain, B., 'The Criminal Cartel Offence: Considerations for Effective Enforcement' (2017) 17 *UCD Law Review* 36.

The purpose of a leniency programme is to aid with the detection and information gathering on collusive activities by providing full or partial immunity from the penalty imposed. The Korean experience has advocated for the effectiveness of such a tool since the information gathered through a leniency programme has assisted in expediting the investigations of the national competition authority.[72] In the absence of such a tool, Thailand has to resort to other measures in pursuit of the detection and collection of evidence against cartelistic behaviours. Mindful of Thailand's own constitutional and criminal procedural limitations, the Drafting Committee opted for a recognisable tool with underwhelming success in identifying and prosecuting cartels.

15.4.1 *Comparable Incentive*

The purpose of a leniency programme is to aid with the detection and information gathering on collusive activities by offering the incentive of immunity or reduction in penalty imposed. When the Drafting Committee chose to exclude a leniency programme from the 2017 Act, it needed a convincing alternative measure to help overcome the difficulty in obtaining information regarding cartelistic behaviours. Such a measure is found in an existing traditional tool, which is the Commission's power to fix and adjust the appropriate amount of a fine.[73] Ostensibly, this measure offers the reduction in financial penalty similar to that of a leniency programme. The Commission wishes to use such a measure to entice whistle-blowers to come forward with information that is nearly impossible to gather due to its secretive nature.

The 2017 Act grants the Commission the power to prescribe administrative sanctions to undertakings found to be in violation of competition law provisions including abuse of dominant position, merger, soft-core cartel and unfair competition. In particular with regard to participants in a soft-core cartel, Section 82 of the 2017 Act allows the Commission to fix the amount of administrative fine not exceeding 10 per cent of the total turnover of the year in which the offence has been committed.[74] Additionally, Section 72 of the 2017 Act prescribes criminal sanction not exceeding two years of imprisonment and/or a fine not exceeding 10 per cent of the

[72] Koh, S. and Jeong, J., 'The Leniency Program in Korea and Its Effectiveness' (2014) 10 *Journal of Competition Law & Economics* 161.

[73] Thailand Trade Competition Act, Sections 73–75.

[74] Ibid., Section 82.

turnover in the year of the offence in the case of hard-core cartels. In a case where the offence was committed in the first year of business operation, the maximum fine shall be reduced to one million Baht (approximately US$30,500). These provisions were later precisely reiterated in the Notice of the Competition Commission on the Calculation of Fine[75] without any change or addition.

The Commission has a large margin of appreciation in setting the fine. With regard to soft-core cartels, the Commission may set any amount of administrative fine provided the amount does not exceed 10 per cent of the turnover of the year in which the offence was committed by the undertaking.[76] In the case of hard-core cartels, the Commission can recommend criminal sanction not exceeding two years' imprisonment and/or a fine not exceeding 10 per cent of the turnover of the year in which the offence was committed.[77] If the cartelistic conduct occurred during the first year of business of the undertaking, the Commission may disregard the turnover criteria and impose a fine not exceeding one million Baht (approximately US$30,500). This extension of the power of the Commission is certainly in accordance with Section 38 of the CCP, which grants competent officials the power to fix the amount of an appropriate financial fine to settle a case. In addition to these limitations, the Commission must also take into consideration the seriousness of the offence committed when fixing the amount of the fine.[78] In this regard, as a strong incentive, the Commission is free to offer a reduced fine to undertakings coming forward with useful information on cartelistic behaviours.

The extensive discretionary power of the Commission is accompanied by its policy of valuing confidentiality over transparency. The identity of the undertakings under investigation is never revealed. This anonymity policy extends to the publication of the Commission decision, in which the names of the undertakings are only disclosed unofficially in the news or informal interviews. Furthermore, the Commission decision is rarely publicised in its entirety. Only press releases averaging between two and four pages are released to the public, with only mentions of the sanction administered without any explanation regarding the application of competition law or the calculation of the fine. A good example of how the Commission freely uses its discretionary power to set a fine can be

[75] Notice of the Competition Commission on the Calculation of Fine, Article 11.

[76] Thailand Trade Competition Act, Section 82.

[77] Ibid., Section 72.

[78] Ibid., Section 85.

seen in its decision against an energy drink (later informally revealed as M150),[79] in which the Commission found the undertaking to be in violation through abuse of its dominant position in the energy drink market in Thailand under the 1999 Act. Many key pieces of information were absent from the publicised decision, namely how the market was defined, the calculation of market share, the identities of other players in the same market, and details on the anti-competitive conduct that qualifies as 'abuse'. It can be deduced from the 1999 Act itself that the undertaking likely retains over 50 per cent of the market and has sales turnover of more than one billion Baht (approximately US$30 million). Because the violation of abuse of dominant position under Thai competition law, both the 1999 and the 2017 versions, carries criminal sanction, the Commission forwarded the findings to the public prosecutor in February 2019, seven months after its decision. Nonetheless, the Commission reached a settlement with the undertaking and imposed a fine of six million Baht (approximately US$183,000) on the company, and another six million Baht (approximately US$183,000) on the company's director. The settlement was widely publicised as a landmark decision of the Commission without revealing the calculation behind the fine.

15.4.2 *Incomparable Result*

The examples of other jurisdictions in this book have attested to the effectiveness of a leniency programme in aiding in the detection and collection of evidence against cartelistic activities. Korea, for instance, reports that such a policy plays an important role in speeding up the investigations of its national competition authority.[80] While Thailand has successfully implemented an alternative measure focused on offering a reduction in sanction in exchange for intelligence and evidence against cartel participants, doubts still remain as to whether such a measure is a comparable replacement for a leniency programme. Indeed, it is believed that the effectiveness of a leniency programme is due to three important factors: adequate threat of sanction, predictable behaviour of participants in the cartel and continued successful enforcement of competition law. The sanction for participating in illegal cartel activity should outweigh the profit gained to incite cooperation with the national competition agency. A violation can be deterred if the value of a sanction imposed, such as a

[79] Decision of Competition Commission (1 August 2018).

[80] Koh and Jeong, 'The Leniency Program in Korea and Its Effectiveness' (n. 72 above).

fine, exceeds the expected gain associated from the violation adjusted by the probability that the sanction will be imposed.[81] It has to make cooperating with the agency more appealing and worthwhile than the negative consequences of straying from illegal business partners. It follows that the possibility of betrayal among cartelists would incite suspicion and distrust among them.[82] Such uncertainty and fear would eventually make cartels less appealing. However, such an impact relies heavily on the effectiveness of the enforcement of competition law.[83] Without examples of prior decisive decisions against cartels by the national competition authority, any new measure would fail to deliver.

In the case of Thailand, these factors are simply not present. The offer of a reduction in fine cannot imitate the attractiveness of an effective leniency programme, since it cannot lure undertakings to voluntarily provide information and evidence of cartels. In general, a competition law–related investigation commences after the reception of a voluntary anonymous complaint. A year after the enactment of the 2017 Act, the Commission had received two complaints of cartelistic conduct.[84] There were only twenty-eight complaints of alleged anti-competitive agreements made throughout the eighteen years of the previous competition law.[85] Most of the cartel investigations based on the complaint were dropped on the recommendation of the Secretariat. The low number of cases indicates the underwhelming success of the alternative measures to a leniency programme.

There are currently two noteworthy decisions taken by the Commission in recent years. The first one is a landmark pioneer case of a decision made based on the new Act, where the Commission fined provincial fruit wholesalers 25,000 Baht (approximately US$760) for unfair trade. The fine was based on the sales turnover of the wholesalers and was reduced because the wholesalers had cooperated with the investigation. Neither the turnover nor the calculation used in deciding the reduced fine was communicated to the public. It is possible that the Commission reached this number after negotiation with the interested parties. Another notorious case is

[81] Calvani, T. and Calvani, T. H., 'Cartel Sanctions and Deterrence' (2011) 56(2) *Antitrust Bulletin* 185.

[82] O'Fiachain, 'The Criminal Cartel Offence' (n. 71 above).

[83] Van Uytsel, S., 'A Comparative US and EU Perspective on the Japanese Antimonopoly Law's Leniency Program' (2008) 75 *Hosei Kenkyu* F1.

[84] Office of Trade Competition Commission, 'Summary of Complaints Received from 2018 – August 2019' (24 June 2021). Retrieved from https://tcct.or.th/view/1/Summary_of_complaint_statistics/TH-TH (in Thai).

[85] Ibid.

the highest fine decision by the Commission to date, discussed above, in which an energy drink manufacturer (M150) and its CEO were found to be in violation of the 1999 Act for abuse of dominant position and fined twelve million Baht (approximately US$366,000) in total. Since abuse of dominant position carries a criminal penalty under both the 1999 Act and the 2017 Act, the Commission submitted the case to the public prosecutor, but a settlement between the undertakings and the Commission was reached before any decision was made by the public prosecutor. Here as well, neither the turnover nor the calculation used in deciding the reduced fine was communicated to the public. Both decisions, while marking an important advancing step in the enforcement of competition law in Thailand, also demonstrate an incredible level of discretionary power and opacity on the part of the Commission. In a general scenario, the demonstration of such power would create a high level of uncertainty among undertakings, which would consequently affect the national competition authority's credibility. This is not the case for Thailand. Because these decisions were made in light of close to two decades of non-enforcement of competition law, they were welcomed with open arms and denote the Commission's willingness to make a mark in history. The public perception of the enforcement of competition law is currently favourable.

15.5 Conclusion

This chapter retraced the story of how a leniency programme was regrettably omitted from the 2017 Act. To fill the void left by such an absence, the 2017 Act offers a known tool as an alternative measure to a leniency programme, which is the Commission's discretionary authority to freely fix the fine. Similar to a leniency programme, this ability also aims to incite voluntary participation from undertakings engaged in cartelistic behaviours. However, it cannot imitate the same level of incentive offered by a leniency programme. The primary cause for this ineffectiveness is linked to the effectiveness of the Commission's prior decisions. Since a decision with a severe criminal penalty does not exist in Thailand's history of a competition law regime, participants in cartels do not fear prosecution. Therefore, the benefit from participating in such illegal activity far outweighs the risk of getting denounced by peers or getting caught by the Commission. The low number of cases investigating cartels attests to this statement. The intended alternative measure thus failed to fill the vacuum left by the abandonment of a leniency programme in Thai competition law.

PART IV

Concluding Remarks

16

Leniency Programmes in Asia

Convergence, Divergence and Distinctiveness

STEVEN VAN UYTSEL, MARK FENWICK
AND YOSHITERU UEMURA

16.1 Introduction

The United States (US) initiated the first leniency programme in 1978. An amended version of 1993 triggered other countries to follow the US example. However, not all these leniency programmes were identical. The one developed in the European Union (EU) diverged to a great degree. Detailed studies of international organisations into the conceptualisation of leniency programmes to establish international guidelines basically confirmed the trend set out by the US and the EU. The common ground between leniency programmes is relatively small, only extending to elements that are essential to make up a leniency programme. The way these essential elements are elaborated or implemented often differs across the different leniency programmes, resulting in diverse suggestions in the international guidelines. This basically still forces any country wanting to draw up a leniency programme to further research existing leniency programmes for what the benefits or pitfalls could be of conceptualisation choices.

This book gathers such insights by studying the experiences of Hong Kong, India, Japan, Malaysia, People's Republic of China (China), Philippines, Republic of China (Taiwan), Republic of Korea (Korea), Singapore and Thailand. The lesson to be drawn from these experiences is similar to the trend described in the international guidelines. There is convergence among the Asian leniency programmes, but only on a limited number of core elements. This means that divergence is the main characteristic of Asian leniency programmes. However, many of these divergences are subtle, meaning that the core elements, which are shared among all the Asian leniency programmes, are differently implemented.

Other differences give a distinctive flavour to the leniency programme, by adding something that does not exist in most other Asian leniency programmes. Some of these distinctive features may even be characterised as unique. It should also be pointed out that for some of the countries investigated, most obviously Thailand, this distinctiveness is very apparent. Unlike all the other researched countries, Thailand has not implemented a leniency programme at all.

It is the intention of this concluding chapter to map out this shifting landscape of convergence, divergence and distinctiveness. A schematic overview is given in the Appendix to this chapter.

The chapter is structured as follows. Section 16.2 identifies the general belief of Asian countries in the need to have a leniency programme for the enforcement of their respective anti-cartel provisions. Despite this belief, very few jurisdictions have made active use of their leniency programme. In Section 16.3, we make the observation that leniency programmes in Asia are embedded in the respective competition laws and not in soft law documents. A detailed comparison between the different leniency programmes in Asia is provided in Section 16.4. That section is divided into three parts. One relates to the broad structure of leniency programmes, a point where they seem to converge. The next one deals with the subtle difference within this broad structure. Finally, we introduce some of the unique characteristics that have developed in the various Asian leniency programmes.

16.2 A General Belief in the Necessity of a Leniency Programme

16.2.1 Early Adoption of Leniency Programmes in Asia

There is a belief in Asia that leniency programmes are an essential instrument for the enforcement of the anti-cartel provisions of their respective competition laws. Ten different Asian countries with a competition law regime in place have been discussed. Nine out of the ten now have a leniency programme. When we take into consideration that only three countries, Japan, Korea and Taiwan, had a fully functioning competition law in place three decades ago, the omnipresence of leniency programmes is remarkable. The US and the EU, for example, were operating their respective competition laws for much longer before they turned to leniency programmes as an instrument to assist in enforcement. In the US, it took nearly nine decades before the first leniency programme was devised. If we take the first successful leniency programme into consideration, it took more than a century for the US to implement one. The EU experimented with the enforcement of its competition law for four decades before a leniency programme was adopted.

Why, then, were most Asian countries so eager to make the switch much faster?

There is no doubt that the apparent success of the US and the EU in taking decisions based upon leniency applications influenced many enforcement agencies. When presenting the ratio between the number of cartels depending on a leniency application and the ones not depending on a leniency application, both the US and the EU could show a balance in favour of the former. Furthermore, the sanctions imposed on cartels gradually increased as the leniency programmes allowed the full extent of cartels to be uncovered more effectively. Japan, an early adopter of a leniency programme in Asia, has shown a similar result. Moreover, Japan's advocacy for a leniency programme was also based on efficiency reasons. Leniency programmes allowed the Japan Fair Trade Commission (JFTC) to terminate the investigation in record time.

The success of a leniency programme could also be deduced from guidelines issued by international organisations. While the Organization for Economic Co-operation and Development's (OECD) report only theoretically informed the Asian countries about the positive effects of a leniency programme, many of the Asian enforcement agencies could experience at first hand how leniency was advocated for within the framework of the International Competition Network (ICN). Even though ICN only released its guidelines on leniency programmes in 2009, the discussion, in which the Asian enforcement agencies could participate, had already been going since 2004. The Member States of the Association of Southeast Asian Nations (ASEAN) found that the experts advising them on writing a competition law recommended a leniency programme for the enforcement of the anti-cartel provisions. This recommendation, though, was not supported with any reference to the beneficial effects of having such a programme. The initiative of the United Nations Conference on Trade and Development (UNCTAD) was most likely too late to show the relevance of leniency programmes, as most researched Asian leniency programmes were adopted by the time UNCTAD issued its guideline in 2016.

16.2.2 *Early Adoption of a Leniency Programme: A Good Decision?*

International guidelines have held that certain elements should be in place prior to the introduction of a leniency programme. Two of these elements are high sanctions and an active enforcement agency. The former could, in theory, be addressed in the competition law itself. The latter requires a time element, namely a period in which the enforcement agency can show that it is functioning properly.

Some observations could be made in relation to Asia. First, few of the Asian countries had a well-developed competition law by the time that leniency programmes were promoted. Some of these competition laws were more actively enforced than the others. Japan was enforcing its competition law mainly against bid rigging. The Korean enforcement agency was recognised as aggressive. Thailand had no enforcement record at all. The sanctions could probably be higher in all these countries. Second, the majority of Asian countries still had to adopt a competition law by the time that leniency programmes were endorsed as effective instruments for the enforcement of anti-cartel provisions.

Combining the preliminary thoughts from the international guidelines with these observations might lead to the conclusion that a leniency programme would make sense for Japan and Korea, and maybe Taiwan. The enforcement focus in Japan was on bid rigging, a specific form of price fixing and something for which leniency programmes were designed. The aggressive character of the enforcement agency could also justify the early adoption of a leniency programme in Korea. Japan could show a positive enforcement record after the adoption of the leniency programme. This was especially so in relation to real price-fixing agreements and international big-rigging agreements in private procurement projects. In contrast, Korea, the first Asian country to enact a leniency programme only one year after the EU introduced its leniency programme, did not succeed in turning its initial leniency programme into a success. This shows that the story about pre-requisites is not as simple as the international guidelines might lead us to believe.[1] Japan demonstrates that, in an interconnected world where cartels are increasingly active across borders, the adoption of a leniency programme may make sense even in the absence of high sanctions. Korea illustrates that aggressiveness is not sufficient if the leniency programme does not offer transparent and predictable outcomes.

Should a leniency programme then be introduced together with the first competition law? The enforcement results of the Asian leniency programmes, many of which were adopted at the same time as the respective competition laws, are mixed. Hong Kong and Singapore both implemented their respective leniency programme at the same time they implemented their competition

[1] KFTC, 'Cartel Leniency Program in Korea' (2009), slide 8. Retrieved from https://ftc.go.kr/DATA/download/eng/Quick_Link/Leniency%20Program%20of%20Korea.pdf.

laws. Both countries had on average one cartel-related decision per year. Hong Kong could only link one decision to a leniency application, while Singapore could do so for a little over half of its decisions. Malaysia adopted its leniency programmes a few years after the enactment of its competition law. Over a period of eleven years, seven cartel-related investigations were conducted and only one could be linked to a leniency application. From all the countries that had a longer history of competition law enforcement, such as Japan, India, Korea and Taiwan, only India and Taiwan have a relatively low number of decisions based upon their respective leniency programmes.

Although the abovementioned data are silent on the quality of the leniency applications and the range of the sanctions for infringing the law, a tentative conclusion can nevertheless be drawn. New competition law regimes should not refrain from adopting a leniency programme. However, if the decision is made to adopt one, two elements should be given particular consideration. First, the leniency programme should be enacted without any obvious design flaws and, if such a design flaw is discovered, it should be rectified as quickly as possible. Second, when implementing a leniency programme in a competition-unfriendly environment, the enforcement agency may need to invest heavily in awareness raising regarding the scale and scope of the anti-competitive conduct. If the political economy prevents a move in either direction, it may be better to abstain from implementing a leniency programme.

Thailand would seem to exemplify this. Thailand has had a fully fledged competition law on paper since 1999, but its enforcement remained non-existent. The Office of Trade Competition Commission, the enforcement agency in Thailand, investigated ninety-five cases. However, not a single one of the ninety-five investigations led to an adjudication. Introducing a leniency programme in such an environment risks becoming a futile exercise. Cartel participants would not be wary of the law nor of its enforcer. Continuing the infringement would be much more profitable as the likelihood of an enforcement action seems low. Yet the decision not to create a leniency programme was not based on such reasoning. The drafting committee used the incompatibility of a leniency programme with the Thai legal order to justify the rejection of a leniency programme.

16.3 Leniency Programmes in Asia Are Embedded in the Law

Leniency programmes in Asia share one element that offsets them from the early adopters of leniency programmes in the US and the EU. The US and the EU developed their leniency programmes as soft law instruments, while the researched Asian countries have all embedded at least one article in their respective competition laws that is attributed to the leniency programmes.

The US leniency programme was developed in a policy statement of the Antitrust Division of the Department of Justice. The European Commission incorporated its leniency programme in a notice. Both a policy and a notice are non-binding legal instruments. These 'rules of conduct which, in principle, have no legally binding force but which nevertheless may have practical effects'[2] have their origin in the flexible rules prescribing the sanction for infringing the anti-cartel provisions of their respective competition laws. The laws prescribing the sanction only stipulated the maximum sanction that could be applied.

In the US, for example, the Sherman Act determines that the penalty for an infringement is 'up to $100 million for a corporation and $1 million for an individual, along with up to 10 years in prison'.[3] The rules on sanctioning an infringement of European competition law have been elaborated in a Regulation of the Council of the EU. The one that is currently in force is Council Regulation (EC) No 1/2003 of 16 December 2002 on the implementation of the rules on competition laid down in Articles 81 and 82 of the Treaty.[4] Article 23(2) of this Regulation formulates the right to impose a fine. At the same time, however, this Article instructs that the fine can be anything up to 10 per cent of the total turnover of the preceding business year. The Regulation further states, in Article 23(3), that the gravity and the duration of the infringement shall be one consideration for fixing the amount of the fine.

There have been no guidelines on whether to follow the US or EU example and work out a leniency programme in a non-binding legal instrument. In fact, none of the researched Asian countries actually followed this example. If the substantive leniency programme is not inscribed in the competition law itself, then at least the competition law has a provision empowering the enforcement authorities to elaborate one. Japan and Korea are countries that have most of their leniency programme regulated in their respective competition law. The only elements that are further

[2] Snyder, F., 'The Effectiveness of European Community Law: Institutions, Processes, Tools and Techniques' (1993) 56 *Modern Law Review* 19, p. 32.

[3] Sherman Act, Section 1 (Title 15 of the US Code, Chapter 1 (Monopolies and Combinations in Restraint of Trade)).

[4] Council Regulation (EC) No 1/2003 of 16 December 2002 on the implementation of the rules on competition laid down in Articles 81 and 82 of the Treaty, OJ L 1, 4.1.2003. Retrieved from https://eur-lex.europa.eu/legal-content/EN/ALL/?uri=celex%3A32003R0001.

developed in soft law instruments in these countries are the procedural rules. All the other countries, including Singapore, China, India, Taiwan, Malaysia and the Philippines, empower their respective enforcement agencies to implement a leniency programme in their respective competition law. These countries included both substantive and procedural rules of their respective leniency programmes in a soft law instrument. Very often these countries were restrained in the writing of their leniency programme by general standards set forward in the competition law.

There is an obvious advantage in creating a leniency programme in a soft law instrument. Even though the experimentation with leniency programmes may have been finished in the US, with its first and last change in 1993, and the EU, with its second and last change in 2006, the experimentation in Asia with the leniency programme may not yet be over. Several of the Asian countries have recently made changes to their respective leniency programmes. The question is whether this is going to be the last time that changes will be made. The more that the leniency programme deviates from what has been tried elsewhere, the more uncertain it will be that the changes made will give the hoped-for results. It could be argued that some of the necessary changes could have been implemented more swiftly if the leniency programmes were implemented in a soft law instrument.

The choice of a soft law instrument might, however, create too much flexibility for an enforcement agency. If the leniency programme was to be embedded in a non-binding instrument, there is a risk that an enforcement agency would not obey the leniency programme to the letter. That this risk is real is shown by two examples of countries that have most of their respective leniency programme developed in a soft law instrument. It has been well documented that the words of the early leniency programme applicable to price-related infringements of the Chinese Antimonopoly Law were not important for the higher officials of the National Development and Reform Commission. The Competition and Consumer Commission of Singapore has actively indicated that leniency is still available to cartel participants. Such 'nudging' is also not excluded in China. Thailand, though it does not have a leniency programme, seems to provide too much scope for flexibility in cooperation between business and regulators.

Despite these considerations, the choice between hard law and soft law will also be determined by the political economy of a country. Japan, for example, was constrained in developing its leniency programme as a soft law instrument outside its Antimonopoly Law. Japan has had a tradition of not attributing discretionary powers to its administrative enforcement agencies. The JFTC, as an administrative agency, was thus not given the power to determine the size of the sanction. In line with this, the legislator determined fixed sanctions for each infringement in the competition law itself. The JFTC simply had to mathematically apply these sanctions. With the implementation of a leniency programme, the risk arose that the JFTC would manipulate the sanctions. To avoid that risk, however, the only option was to make the leniency programme part of the competition law and, again, determine how the JFTC should mathematically apply a formula to reduce the sanction in the case that a cartel was reported.

16.4 Asian Leniency Programmes Compared

16.4.1 Subtle Differences within a Broader Converging Structure of Asian Leniency Programmes

16.4.1.1 Identical Scope, but Differences among the Eligibility Criteria

Leniency programmes were designed to assist the enforcement agencies in their fight against one type of competition law infringement: hard-core cartels. A hard-core cartel is a horizontal agreement among competitors to fix price. These agreements can be divided into several sub-categories: pure price fixing, bid rigging, production reduction or territorial division. Currently, all Asian countries limit their leniency programmes to hard-core cartels. This is the consequence either of limiting the leniency programme to the sanctions applicable to hard-core cartels or of the explicit statement of this limitation at the beginning of the leniency programme. In the past, there used to be only one exception. The earliest leniency programmes in China used to also apply to vertical price-fixing agreements.

All researched Asian competition laws punish the infringers of the anti-cartel provision with a financial sanction. It should thus not come as a surprise that the leniency programmes are focused on this financial sanction. This limited scope is achieved by linking the leniency programme directly to the provisions prescribing the sanctions. In Hong Kong, however, the lenient treatment only indirectly applies to the financial sanction. The lenient treatment implies that no court proceeding will be commenced against the infringer, with the consequence that no sanction can be applied. The Philippines has a similar system for the first cartel participant that applies for leniency prior to an investigation. It should be noted that some countries, like Japan, Korea and the Philippines, also have criminal sanctions applicable to hard-core cartels. Legally speaking the leniency programme does not extend to criminal sanctions in Japan and Korea. However, there is an informal practice in both Japan and Korea not to refer the first successful leniency applicant to the prosecutor's office if a decision is made to pursue a criminal investigation by the respective enforcement agencies. In the Philippines, it has been recognised that leniency given to a cartel participant by the Philippine Competition Commission (PCC) will be recognised in a criminal proceeding. Furthermore, if no leniency has been obtained before the PCC, a separate leniency procedure exists for the criminal procedure. This has to be obtained from the Office of Competition of the Department of Justice.

Not all cartel participants are eligible to apply for leniency. Ringleaders are eligible to apply for leniency in all jurisdictions. However, if a firm can be singled out as the leader, this corporation will not be eligible for leniency in Hong Kong. The same would be the case in Malaysia for the ringleader that also organised the cartel. In China and the Philippines, ringleaders are only eligible for reduction and not immunity. Originators are not eligible for leniency in Malaysia and Hong Kong. They are eligible in Singapore, China and the Philippines, but only for reduction. Other countries do not put restrictions on originators. Coercers, corporations that have forced a firm to join the cartel or prevented a firm from leaving the cartel, are subject to restrictions in most countries. Korea, Japan, Taiwan, Malaysia and Hong Kong exclude a coercer from the leniency programme. Singapore, China and the Philippines allow the coercer to apply for reduction but not for immunity. India does not put any restriction on a coercer, who thus can fully enjoy the benefits of a leniency programme.

Two important features can be distilled from this. First, there is a widespread belief that criminal sanctions can disrupt a leniency programme. However, informal arrangements can be sufficient to prevent such disruption. Second, most countries prioritise efficiency concerns, understood as obtaining as much information about the cartel as possible, over fairness concerns, understood as preventing key players in a cartel from enjoying lenient treatment when the law is enforced. One explanation for this choice could be the difficulty of applying the concepts to a factual situation. Only for a coercer do fairness considerations seem to be more important than efficiency concerns. It is necessary, however, that the concept of coercer can be proven with substantial evidence.

16.4.1.2 Different Criteria Separating Two Phases of a Leniency Programme

Leniency programmes are split into two phases: pre- and post-investigation. It is important to know in which phase you are applying for leniency. If it is not the incentive structure that is different, then it is the quality of the evidence that is different. It is thus important for a potential leniency applicant to know in which phase the application is going to be submitted.

All countries that were investigated position the start of the investigation as the point dividing the two phases in a leniency programme. However, the start of an investigation is interpreted differently across Asia.

Japan has one of the most objective standards for this determination: the start of an investigation coincides with the dawn raid. The Philippines put forward the fact-finding or preliminary inquiry as the start of the investigation. The rules clarify that such an inquiry starts with the receipt of a complaint or a referral by another agency.

The standard in other countries is less transparent. In Singapore and Hong Kong, the decision to start an investigation is the standard, as a complaint does not necessarily provide a reasonable cause to suspect an infringement. India, though using the different terminology of a prima facie case, also implements the decision to investigate as the standard to differentiate the various phases. China, Taiwan and Malaysia look at the moment at which the cartel becomes known to them, making awareness the standard.

Korea is special because it does not make a distinction between pre- and post-investigation phases. The first applicant who complies with the conditions will get immunity, while the second always gets 50 per cent. It is not important whether the investigation has started or not.

The international guidelines discussed do not provide any guidance on how to deal with these differences. However, it could be said that the more difficult it is for the leniency applicant to ascertain in which phase a leniency application will be submitted, the more there is a need to have a procedure allowing potential applicants to anonymously consult with the enforcement agencies. Equally, it is important that the enforcement agencies do not retract any information given during these informal consultations.

16.4.1.3 Immunity, But Not for All First Applicants

Lenient treatment is available for the first cartel participant to defect and successfully report the existence of the cartel to the enforcement authorities. There is no exception in Asia to this observation. As long as the leniency application is made prior to the start of an investigation, the lenient treatment is immunity. There are three exceptions. China, India and the Philippines have the flexibility to give less than immunity to the first applicant prior to the investigation. Whereas the Competition Commission of India (CCI) has full discretion to give whatever reduction to whomever applies first, the State Administrator for Market Regulation (SAMR) and the PCC have to give respectively up to 80 per cent or 80 per cent when the first leniency applicant is the organiser (China), the leader or the originator (India) or the coercer (China and India). It is not immediately clear from practice, however, what the effect is of the exceptions to the immunity offer. Full discretion, based upon experimentation in the US and the EU, may have a negative effect on leniency applications.

When a decision is made to apply for immunity prior to an investigation, the applicant may not have all documents to hand. To provide enough time, but still allow the applicant to position itself for the most lenient treatment possible, a marker system has been created. All researched Asian leniency programmes have a marker procedure. Yet the procedure to obtain and perfect the marker differs slightly across the different countries. Some, like Korea, Japan and the Philippines, have a simplified application, in which a brief description of the cartel has to be given. The PCC, however, aims to obtain more information during the marker application than Korea and Japan. However, this is an objective that does not need to be completed up until the real leniency application is submitted. Others, like Singapore, India, Taiwan, Malaysia and Hong Kong, just require the applicant to contact the responsible person within the enforcement agency. Also the timing to perfect the marker differs between the jurisdictions. The jurisdictions with a simplified application procedure as a marker, which are Korea, Japan and the Philippines, together with China and Malaysia, have a period fixed by law to perfect the marker. This period varies between 15 and 30 days. Some allow for an extension to 60 days, whereby the granting of such an extension is at the discretion of the agency. In Singapore, Taiwan and Hong Kong, countries in which the marker has to be granted by the enforcement agency, the same agency has the power to decide the time within which the marker has to be perfected. The possibility for extension allows more and better information to be obtained from the first applicant. However, extending the period for too long may jeopardise the leniency procedure, especially if the leniency applicant needs to terminate its participation in the cartel.

Another standard that differs slightly among the Asian jurisdictions is the information that needs to be submitted in order to obtain immunity. The information requirement is different depending on whether it is immunity prior to or after an investigation. Prior to an investigation, the main standard is to require the submission of information that allows an investigation to start. This information requirement can be found in Singapore, China, Taiwan and Malaysia. However, both China and Taiwan refine the just-mentioned information requirement with the requirement of also submitting unknown information. The remaining jurisdictions, Korea, Japan, India, Hong Kong and the Philippines, require, in one way or another, information to be submitted to establish the infringement. While Korea and Hong Kong use an abstract formulation to obtain this kind of information, Japan and the Philippines list the required information in the regulation implementing the leniency programme. The risk with this kind of procedure is that firms may be offering only the minimum. The Indian leniency programme incorporates a subjective element by stating that the information needs to be vital to allow a prima facie opinion on the existence of a cartel. The latter may require further explanation of the CCI in order not to scare leniency applicants.

It is possible that the first firm only defects after the start of the investigation. Also in these cases, the first applicant can receive immunity in all Asian countries except Japan. Japan only offers a reduction to leniency applicants once the investigation has started. The immunity offered in other Asian countries is not necessarily automatic. Singapore, China and India can offer up to 100 per cent, albeit that the bottom line is 80 per cent in China and 0 per cent in Singapore and India. The criteria to offer something lower than immunity depend on the value of the information. In Hong Kong and Malaysia, the first applicant will either get full immunity or nothing at all. Immunity will be denied in Hong Kong if there is a reasonable belief that the leniency applicant will not comply with the leniency conditions. The decision in Malaysia depends on the value of the information and the timing of reporting. The Philippine situation is different still. Immunity from the fine is automatic, but immunity from suit is only offered at the discretion of the PCC. The PCC will make a decision based on the lack of evidence against the applicant and fairness reasons. A leader, originator or coercer will only receive a reduction. It is obvious that the enforcement agencies have much more discretion in this phase of the leniency programme. To keep the leniency programme attractive, some guidelines may be necessary. Eventually, informal contact or hypothetical applications could limit the discretion given in this phase.

Once an investigation has started, many jurisdictions use a different information requirement, since the enforcement agencies already have information and, from an enforcement efficiency point of view, unknown information is desirable. This is expressed in various ways. Korea requests information that substantiates the cartel's existence. China, India and Taiwan have a similar perspective by asking for information to prove the existence of a cartel. Singapore and Malaysia require value-added information, albeit that in Singapore it needs also to be significant. Hong Kong sticks to its requirement of asking for a detailed cartel description, while the Philippines elaborates in its regulation the information that needs to be submitted. Technically speaking, the latter does not require new information. However, the PCC can deny immunity on fairness reasons and it is conceivable that submitting no new information could be unfair.

16.4.1.4 Generosity of a Leniency Programme Revealed in the Reductions Offered to Subsequent Leniency Applicants

All researched leniency programmes, except in Hong Kong, offer the possibility of some form of lenient treatment to cartel participants successfully defecting subsequent to the first one. However, the number of cartel participants that can obtain leniency and the degree of leniency for these subsequent applicants vary from jurisdiction to jurisdiction.

Korea and the Philippines limit the availability of reduction to the second applicant. China and India offer leniency to second and third applicants, even though China can expand the number of applicants based on the severity of the case. Taiwan's leniency programme is open to up to four applicants, while Japan, Singapore and Malaysia accept an unlimited number of applications. There is no golden rule on how many cartel participants should be eligible for leniency. Japan, for example, has experimented with increasing the number of eligible firms. While originally allowing three firms to apply, then increasing it to five firms, the current Japanese leniency programme now allows an unlimited number of firms to apply. Looking at the other changes to the Japanese leniency programme, each subsequent leniency applicant should be subject to extra information requirements. As this is not the case in Japan, where the second and third leniency applicants can still submit information similar to the first applicant, Japan had to devise an extra layer to its leniency programme forcing each and every subsequent leniency applicant to submit as much information as possible.

The order of the subsequent applications is determined by the order of application in Korea, Japan, Taiwan and Malaysia. Singapore, China and India take the value of the information into consideration to determine who will be the subsequent leniency applicant. The Philippines does not look only at the order of applications and the value of the information, but also at the role played and the timing of the submission.

The degree of lenient treatment differs depending on the system used in each of the countries. Only Japan and the Philippines explicitly employ a system of reduction whereby the degree is determined by whether the leniency application was made prior to or after the start of an investigation. Prior to an investigation, the degree of reduction tends to be higher than afterwards. Furthermore, the Philippines reduces the degree of reduction if the leniency applicant was the leader, the originator or the coercer. In the other countries, the start of the investigation does not impact the degree of lenient treatment. Korea, which has the simplest system, offers a 50 per cent reduction to the second applicant. India gives importance to the order of application, whereby the second will be entitled to a higher upper limit of reduction. However, the value of the information will finally decide the actual degree of reduction. Singapore and Malaysia follow the latter part of the Indian system. The degree of reduction is fluid and not a priori decided. Several factors will contribute to deciding the degree of reduction, among which are order of application, timing of submitting the application, quality of the information and level of cooperation. A mix of the different systems can be found in China and Taiwan, whereby the order of application will determine the band of reduction, but within each band a further decision has to be made on the actual level of reduction.

For reductions, the requirement for information resembles the one applicable to immunity applications in the post-investigation stage. In order to be meaningful for the investigation, most leniency programmes aim for submitting extra information. The exceptions are Japan for the second and third applicants and the Philippines. Applicants for reduction can submit the information required by the regulation constituting the leniency programme. The other countries seek extra information. From the fourth leniency applicant, Japan seeks unknown information. China also sees value in unknown information, but does not exclude information that can give extra value to already known information. The latter information requirement seems to be prevalent in India, Taiwan and Malaysia.

16.4.1.5 Greatest Convergence among the Conditions Applicable to Asian Leniency Programmes

The application for lenient treatment can only be successful if various conditions are met. Some of the conditions are similar across the different Asian leniency programmes. The ones that are similar do not directly relate to the information that has to be submitted. Once a leniency application has been made, all leniency programmes demand continuous cooperation. Frank disclosure, sometimes referred to as the obligation to submit true information, is also present in all the researched leniency programmes. A slightly different situation arises with regard to the obligation to abstain from destroying or concealing evidence and information from the moment the decision has been made to apply for leniency. All jurisdictions, except Hong Kong, impose such a condition. Also typical for the leniency programmes is the obligation to terminate participation in the cartel. This obligation is automatic and can only be reversed by an explicit order of the enforcement agency. Taiwan, though, is the exception. The Taiwanese leniency programme has an obligation to keep participating in the cartel until an explicit order is given to terminate. The obligation to keep the leniency application confidential from other cartel participants and other third parties is generally present in all leniency programmes, except for the Indian one. Leniency applicants are obliged to disclose foreign leniency applications in Singapore, China and the Philippines. This obligation does not exist in the other researched countries.

16.4.1.6 Confidentiality

The international guidelines have stressed the need to be wary about the potential for private damages actions following a decision based on a leniency application. To protect the leniency programme, the international guidelines suggest keeping the leniency dossier confidential. Such a guideline is valuable for jurisdictions with a vibrant private enforcement regime. In Asia, according to the contributions, this is not the case and this is despite legislative efforts to stimulate private enforcement in several jurisdictions.[5] In this situation, the confidentiality of the leniency dossier is mostly untested.

Some jurisdictions extend the confidentiality beyond the leniency dossier. Taiwan and the Philippines also guarantee the confidentiality of the

[5] Korea and Taiwan have implemented treble damages for private actions in competition law cases.

identity of leniency applicants. This is not an absolute right to confidentiality. But as in relation to the leniency dossier, it has been untested as to when the identity of the leniency applicant will be revealed. Japan offers an incentive to leniency applicants in bid-rigging cases to publish their identity on the JFTC website. Publicity around their identity will reduce the period during which they are barred from participating in public procurement projects by half.

Leniency applicants are further required to keep their application secret from other cartel participants. This obligation is to be found in all countries. It prevents the possibility of other cartel participants destroying evidence.

16.4.2 Distinctive Elements in the Asian Leniency Programmes

Besides this general convergence and subtle differences, there are also some points of distinctiveness in Asian leniency. Some of these distinctive points exist from the adoption of the leniency programme. Other distinctive points have been created after experimentation with a leniency programme. Hong Kong has, from its early stage, chosen to limit its leniency programme to the first applicant. Thailand compensates for the lack of a leniency programme with a possibility to mitigate the sanction based upon active cooperation with the enforcement agency. Japan has altered its leniency programme due to which a part of the reduction is fixed and another part negotiable. Singapore has created a fast-track procedure that is complementary to the leniency programme. Korea, Singapore and Hong Kong have a leniency plus programme.

Hong Kong distinguishes itself from the other leniency programmes by only providing immunity as an incentive for a leniency application. However, there is still a possibility to reduce the sanction by cooperating with the enforcement agency during the investigation. The first three cartel participants, none of whom has applied for leniency, that cooperate with the enforcement agency can be granted a certain degree of reduction. Whether the reduction is given depends on the approval of the Competition Tribunal.

Offering a reduction of the financial sanction for actively cooperating with the enforcement agency, and this without reporting the cartel to the enforcement agency, is the main strategy in Thailand. This strategy is the result of the deliberate decision not to establish a leniency programme. As with Hong Kong, however, the reduction in return for cooperation operates in a more discretionary setting.

The unique feature of Japan's leniency programme is its division into a two-step procedure for subsequent leniency applicants. This procedure implies that an applicant applies for leniency. This leniency application can be complemented with an application for negotiation on the evidence that can be submitted. In doing so, the reduction of the leniency programme can be aggregated with a reduction under the negotiation process. The latter reduction depends on the information the leniency applicant can provide to the JFTC. The total reduction of leniency programme and the negotiation can be more than could have been received under the leniency programme of 2005 and 2009. It is obvious that this feature was created to facilitate the JFTC's investigation by improving the quality of the information.

Singapore has created a fast-track procedure. This was done to assist the CCCS in achieving a more effective and efficient enforcement. Whether or not a case will be handled according to the fast-track procedure is a discretional decision of the CCCS, though the investigated parties can suggest that they are open to this procedure. If the CCCS decides to follow the fast-track procedure, the relevant enterprises have to admit their liability for the infringement. It is possible that the CCCS starts this procedure after having received a leniency application. The leniency programme and the fast-track procedure are thus not mutually exclusive. It is possible for a leniency applicant to benefit both from the reduction of the leniency programme and the fast-track procedure. The fast-track procedure can be stopped at any stage by the CCCS, but also by the parties involved in this procedure.

Korea, Singapore and Hong Kong have decided to create a leniency plus programme. 'Leniency plus', originally conceptualised as 'amnesty plus' in the US, enables a firm 'who is unable to secure complete immunity under the leniency policy, to cooperate with an antitrust agency with regard to operation of another cartel on an unrelated market'.[6] The benefit a firm can enjoy from doing so is 'immunity in relation to its participation in the second cartel (under the leniency policy), but also from an additional reduction of sanctions for its involvement in the first investigated illegal practice (hence the "plus")'.[7] Korea follows this traditional understanding of leniency plus. The leniency plus applicant can receive an additional reduction up to 100 per cent depending on the size of the subsequently disclosed cartel, and up to immunity for the second cartel.

[6] Martyniszyn, M., 'Leniency (Amnesty) Plus: A Building Block or a Trojan Horse?' (2015) 3(2) *Journal of Antitrust Enforcement* 391.

[7] Ibid., p. 393.

Hong Kong adds a slight twist to this traditional understanding, because it does not offer leniency to subsequent applicants. This is compensated by the possibility to cooperate with the Hong Kong Competition Office and formalise this in a cooperation agreement. To increase the incentive to cooperate, leniency plus allows an additional 10 per cent to be obtained on top of the reduction achieved in the cooperation agreement, and this in return for reporting on a different cartel for which immunity can be obtained. Singapore combines the Korean and Hong Kong approaches. Leniency plus in Singapore can be obtained either if the firm has applied for leniency – which is the Korean approach – or is enjoying a reduction as a mitigating factor due to its cooperation with the CCCS – which is the Hong Kong approach. In the second market, the leniency plus applicant can obtain immunity or reduction.

16.5 Concluding Remarks

Research on the Asian leniency programmes has revealed experimentation. Not a single leniency programme that has been researched in this book is identical to any other, and many deviate from what the US and the EU have developed. Moreover, on a national level, even the original designs of the oldest leniency programmes have evolved based on the experience of regulators.

The experimentation with leniency programmes can be explained from a political economy perspective. Japan had to create a leniency programme devoid of any power for the JFTC because of lobbying, misunderstanding of the concept by the political elite and a rigid existing legal framework. This resulted in a highly transparent and predictable leniency programme. However, while highly beneficial for cartel participants, such a leniency programme, especially if leniency is available to more than one cartel participant, is draining the resources of the enforcement agency by accumulating unmeritorious leniency applications. This conclusion and a generally changing legal environment made it possible for Japan to rethink its leniency programme by 2019. Similarly, China, confronted with a power struggle over the competence to enforce its competition law, could not do anything else than split it over three agencies. With two different agencies in charge of cartel-related conduct, two different leniency programmes developed. After a few years of experimenting with this setting, China decided to merge the leniency programmes into one. However, before this was completed, the decision had been made to bring all consumer- and market-related government powers under one agency. This facilitated the working out of a single leniency programme. A loose stance towards cartels may have been the driving force for creating a leniency programme with a lot of discretion for the Malaysian enforcement agency. Unpredictable leniency programmes may, as studies and real-life experiments in the US and the EU have shown, not be attractive for cartel participants to use. Thailand exemplifies the opposite. Rather than forcing the conceptualisation of a leniency programme in a certain direction, the political economy simply prevented such a programme from coming into existence.

Other experimentation can be brought back to enforcement results. Korean scholars were able to identify the strategic use of their leniency programme, whereby large firms would set up cartels and then apply for leniency. In this scheme, smaller firms were facing severe sanctions. Eventually, many of them had to leave the market. This finding triggered a series of changes to prevent strategic use of the leniency programme. Among these changes were a five-year exclusion for recidivists from the leniency programme and excluding participants of a two-party cartel from the leniency programme. On the other side, there is now research on whether leniency plus could result in strategic abuse and, if so, whether changes to its conceptualisation are required. Japan decided to overhaul its leniency programme to avoid unmeritorious leniency applications, applications that were filed but did not contribute anything new to the investigation.

Achieving better enforcement has also provided an additional reason for experimentation. In Taiwan, it was found that the enforcement agency needed more financial resources to establish a more aggressive enforcement policy, one of the necessary pre-requisites for an effective leniency programme. For that purpose an antitrust fund was established, allowing the Taiwan Fair Trade Commission to take a certain percentage from the financial sanctions it imposes. Outside of the actual leniency programme, some of the enforcement agencies experimented with nudging. China, but also Singapore, has given an indication to cartel participants that leniency is still available.

Cross-fertilisation by expertise from abroad can be seen as the reason for experimentation in Hong Kong. Leaving aside whether the original leniency programme was successful or not, a revision was implemented when the Hong Kong Competition Commission was under the supervision of CEO Brent Snyder. As former Deputy Assistant Attorney General of the Antitrust Division of the Department of Justice, he had experienced the success of the US leniency programme. With that knowledge, he introduced a US-like leniency programme in Hong Kong, one applicable to corporations, one applicable to individuals. This makes Hong Kong, besides the Philippines, the only two countries offering leniency to individuals.

Whether all the experimentation evolved into good results is yet to be seen. The use of the leniency programme in China for vertical agreements was much criticised and controversial. Despite the criticism, the leniency programme was often used in a vertical context in China.[8] Since the adoption of the new leniency programme in 2019, China has aligned the scope of its leniency programme to a more conventional setting and limited it to horizontal price-fixing agreements. This evolution is notable, especially since the use of leniency programmes in a vertical context seems to make sense when algorithms and artificial intelligence are finding their way into price-setting strategies. It is in the enforcement of the EU law against manufacturers of consumer electronics that this has become apparent.

Despite an apparently bright future, leniency programmes may need to evolve to respond to algorithms and artificial intelligence as facilitators of cartels. Moreover, enforcement agencies may need to develop new incentive structures for cases in which institutional investors holding shares in common in competing firms act as orchestrators of collusion.[9] It is conceivable that institutional investors will influence price-related strategies and that not all competing firms may be aware that they are implementing this type of collusion.[10] Probably little is to be expected from leniency programmes in this context. The incentive structure of a leniency programme is geared towards a financial benefit for the defecting cartel participant and not the orchestrator.

[8] Vietnam is currently the only Asian country in whose competition law the possibility is inscribed to extend a leniency programme to vertical agreements.

[9] It should be understood that this hypothesis does not include the hypothesis holding that common ownership, whereby several institutional investors hold a small share in competing firms, will have a unilateral effect on the price. For this kind of debate, see, e.g., Azar, J., Schmalz, M. C. and Tecu, I., 'Anticompetitive Effects of Common Ownership' (2018) 73 *Journal of Finance* 1513; Elhauge, E., 'The Growing Problem of Horizontal Shareholding' (2017) 3 *Antitrust Chronicle* 1; Azar, J., Raina, S. and Schmalz, M. C., 'Ultimate Ownership and Bank Competition' (2016). Retrieved from https://ssrn.com/abstract=2710252; Elhauge, E., 'Horizontal Shareholding' (2016) 129 *Harvard Law Review* 1267. On the possibility of common shareholding contributing to collusion, see OECD, 'Common Ownership by Institutional Investors and Its Impact on Competition –Background Note by the Secretariat', DAF/COMP(2017)10 (2017), pp. 20–21. Retrieved from https://one.oecd.org/document/DAF/COMP(2017)10/en/pdf; Rock, E. B. and Rubinfeld, D. L., 'Common Ownership and Coordinated Effects' (New York University School of Law, Law & Economics Research Paper Series, Working Paper No. 18–40, 2018). Retrieved from www.law.nyu.edu/sites/default/files/Rock%20and%20Rubinfeld%20II%20SSRN-id3296488.pdf.

[10] Rock and Rubinfeld, 'Common Ownership and Coordinated Effects' (n. 9 above), pp. 16–19.

Appendix

Schematic Overview of the Leniency Programmes from Korea, Japan, Singapore, China, India, Taiwan, Malaysia, Hong Kong and the Philippines

	Korea	Japan	Singapore	China	India	Taiwan	Malaysia	Hong Kong*	Philippines**
First implemented	1996	2005	2006	2007	2009	2012	2014	2015	2015
Latest version	2016 (2020 takes effect)	2019	2016	2019	2017	2015	2014	2020	2018
Law	Article 22-2 MRTFA	Article 7-2 AMA	–	Article 46 AMA	Article 46 CA	Article 35 TFTA	Section 41 CA	Section 80 HKCO	Section 35 RA 10667
Regulation	Enforcement Decree Leniency Notice	Rules on Reporting the Facts and Submitting the Materials Regarding Immunity from or Reduction of Surcharges	CCCS's Guidelines on Lenient Treatment	SAMR Guidelines for the Application of the Leniency Programme to Horizontal Monopoly Agreements	Competition Commission of India (Lesser Penalty) Regulations	Regulations on Immunity and Reductions of Fines in Illegal Concerted Action Cases	Guidelines on Leniency Regime	Leniency Policy for Undertakings Engaged in Cartel Conduct	Rules of the Leniency Programme of the Philippine Competition Commission
Scope	Surcharge	Surcharge	Financial penalty	Financial penalty	Financial penalty	Administrative penalty	Financial penalty	Commencing a proceeding	Commencing a suit or administrative fine
Marker system	√	√	√	√	√	√	√	√	√
Eligible for marker	First applicant	First applicant	First applicant (queue possible)	First applicant	First applicant	First applicant	Any applicant	First applicant	Anyone who is eligible to apply for leniency
Order determined by	Date of simplified application	Date of email (or fax) of simplified application	CCCS	Date of applying for leniency	Secretary of CCI	TFTC	Leniency officer	HKCO	Date and time of making the request
Time of perfecting	15 days (extension to 60 days)	20 days	Case by case	30 days (extension to 60 days at judgement of SAMR)	15 days	Case by case	30 days (extension at discretion of leniency officer)	Case by case	30 days (extension at discretion of Commission)

Written application	√	√	√	√	√	√	√	√	√
Method	Post, fax or email	Email or fax	Online, email or post	Email, fax or post	Email or fax	Registered mail or in person	Email, post or in person on the spot	Telephone or email	In person, registered mail, private courier or email
Oral application	Possible (recorded by KFTC)	Exception (recorded by JFTC)	Possible (recorded)	√	Possible (followed by a written one)	Possible (recorded)	–	Possible (recorded)	Not explicitly excluded (the entity must provide information)
Prior informal consultation possible	–	√	√	√ (In writing or orally)	–	–	√	√	√
Scope of eligibility	2	Unlimited	Unlimited	3 (Extension possible)	3	4	Unlimited	1	3
Ringleader	√	√	√	√ (For reduction/ guidelines mention 'organise')	√	√	√ (No if instigator)	– (Clear single)	√ (But not for immunity or full reduction)
Coercer	–	–	√ (Only up to 50%)	√ (But only for reduction)	√	–	–	–	√ (But not for immunity or full reduction)
Instigator	√	√	√ (Only up to 50%)	√ (But only for reduction; guidelines mention 'organise')	√	√	–	–	√ (But not for immunity or full reduction)

(cont.)

	Korea	Japan	Singapore	China	India	Taiwan	Malaysia	Hong Kong	Philippines
Recidivist	– (Within 5 years after receiving leniency)	√	√	√	√	√	√	√	√
Two-member cartel	–	√	√	√	√	√	√	√	√ (Fairness could trump this possibility)
General conditions									
Admit the infringement	√	–	√	–	–	–	√	–	–
Cooperation	Faithfully (continuous and sincere)	Upon request	Continuous and complete	√	Fully and continuously	Promptly upon request	Continuous	Continuous	Continuing, full and genuine
Full disclosure	√	–	√	√	√ (Vital)	–	√	√	√
Frank (true) disclosure	√	√	√	√	√ (Vital)	√	√	√	√
No destruction of evidence	√	√	(Full and frank disclosure)	√	√	√	√	–	√
Keep application confidential	√ (Expression of sincere cooperation)	–	√	√ (But waiver by SAMR possible)	–	√	√	√	√
Cease infringement	√	√	√	√	√	–	√	√	√
Authorisation to continue	√	–	√	√	√	Automatic (until told to cease)	√	√	–

Disclosure of foreign leniency applications	–	–	√	√	–	–	–	–	√
Adopt a compliance programme	–	–	–	–	–	–	–	√	–
Voluntary reporting	√	–	–	–	–	√	–	–	–
Possibility to add new conditions	–	–	–	√ (No conduct that affects investigation)	–	–	√	–	–
Pre-investigation immunity	√	√	√	√	√	√	√	√	√
Eligible	First applicant	First applicant	First applicant	First applicant	First applicant	First applicant	First applicant	First applicant	First applicant
Automatic (upon complying with conditions)	If the cartel is unknown or no information available to substantiate the cartel	√	√ (If no sufficient information to establish the existence of a cartel)	√ (Unless organiser or coercer, who will receive no less than 80% reduction)	– (Up to 100% immunity)	√ (If cartel is unknown or no investigation has started)	– (Admit the infringement and cartel unknown to MACC)	– (Reasonable grounds for non-compliance with conditions)	√ (Unless the applicant is a leader, originator or coercer or the cartel's existence has been reported)
Information	Substantiate the cartel's existence	Available information	Information to commence an investigation	Unknown information enabling initiating a case or launching an investigation	Vital to allow a prima facie opinion on the existence of a cartel	Unknown information enabling to start an investigation	Identify an infringement; or start an investigation	Detailed description of the cartel	Information prescribed in the rules on leniency

(cont.)

	Korea	Japan	Singapore	China	India	Taiwan	Malaysia	Hong Kong	Philippines
Additional protection	Criminal referral (Article 71 MRTFA) Corrective measures (Article 21 MRTFA)	Criminal referral (informal)	–	–	–	–	–	Follow-on damages actions	Criminal sanction (recognition of immunity)
Substitute for information	–	–	–	–	–	–	Cooperating significantly to assist the identification or investigation of the infringement	–	–
Post-investigation immunity	√	–	√	√	√	√	√	√	√
Eligible	First applicant	–	First applicant	First applicant	First applicant	First applicant	First applicant (in theory)	First applicant	First applicant
Automatic	√	–	–	–	–	√	–	–	–
(upon complying with the conditions)			Up to 100%	Between 80% and 100% immunity	Up to 100% immunity		(Depends on timing of reporting and value of information)	(Reasonable grounds re non-compliance with conditions)	(Discretion of the Commission, which looks at the lack of evidence against the applicant and the fairness of granting leniency)
Information	Substantiate the cartel's existence	–	Significant added value sufficient to issue an infringement decision	Information enabling the establishment of a monopoly agreement	Vital to establishing an infringement	Proving the culpability of the cartel	Value-added information to identify the infringement	Detailed description of the cartel	Information prescribed in the rules on leniency

Additional protection	Immunity or reduction of corrective measures	–	–	–	–	Corporate representatives	–	–	–
Reduction	√	√	√	√	√	√	√	–	√
Eligible	Second applicant	Unlimited	Unlimited	Up to 2, but unlimited in severe cases (discretion of SAMR to decide what is severe)	2 applicants	Up to 4 applicants	Unlimited	–	First applicant who is a coercer, leader or originator, first applicant and second applicant
Degree of reduction	50%	50%	Up to 50%	Between 30% and 50% Between 20% and 30% No more than 20%	Up to 50% (second) Up to 30% (third)	30%–50% 20%–30% 10%–20% 10% or less	Up to 99%	–	100% 80% 45% 65% 35% 50% 25%
Reduction automatic	√	√	–	–	–	–	–	–	–
Basis for calculating the degree of reduction or band attribution	Order of application	Order of application	Timing of reporting, evidence known to CCCS, quality of information	Value of information	Value of information	Order of application	Order of application, value of information, date of application, other cooperation	–	Order of application, role of applicant, timing of application (prior to or after start of investigation)

(cont.)

	Korea	Japan	Singapore	China	India	Taiwan	Malaysia	Hong Kong	Philippines
Information	Substantiate cartel	Information available (2nd to 3rd applicants; or Unknown information (4th to ~ applicants)	Useful to issue an infringement decision	Greater probative effect, supplementary probative value, unknown information proving monopoly agreement, unknown information confirming probative value of other information	Significant added value	Significantly help the investigation or contribute to the probative value of the already existing information	Value-added information helping to identify the infringement	–	Information prescribed in the rules on leniency
Additional protection	Discretionary mitigation of corrective measures	–	–	–	–	Corporate representatives	–	–	–
Reduction for cooperation outside leniency	–	√	–	–	–	–	–	√	–
Combinable with leniency	–	√	–	–	–	–	–	–	–
Degree of reduction	–	Before investigation: up to 40 % After investigation: up to 20 %	–	–	–	–	–	35%–50% 20%–49% Up to 25%	–
Basis for band attribution	–	Order of application and value of information	–	–	–	–	–	Order of application	–
Automatic	–	Agreement with JFTC	–	–	–	–	–	Approval of Competition Tribunal	–

Leniency Plus	√ (But immunity/ reduction also applies to initial cartel)	–	√ (Immunity for newly disclosed cartel)	–	In the draft law	–	–	√ (Only reduction for newly disclosed cartel)	–
Fast-track procedure	–	–	√ (Extra reduction)	–	–	–	–	–	–
Antitrust fund	–	–	–	–	–		–	–	–

* The schematic overview only covers the corporate leniency programme of Hong Kong.

** The schematic overview only covers the leniency programme of the Philippine Competition Commission.

Note: Thailand does not have a leniency programme. However, it provides a reduction of sanction based upon the cooperation of the investigated cartel participant with the enforcement agency.

AMA, Antimonopoly Act; CA, Competition Act; CCCS, Competition and Consumer Commission of Singapore; CCI, Competition Commission of India; HKCO, Hong Kong Competition Ordinance; JFTC, Japan Fair Trade Commission; KFTC, Korean Fair Trade Commission; MACC, Malaysian Anti-Corruption Commission; MRTFA, Monopoly Regulation and Fair Trade Act; RA, Republic Act; SAMR, State Administration for Market Regulation; TFTA, Taiwan Fair Trade Act; TFTC, Taiwan Fair Trade Commission.

BIBLIOGRAPHY

Ae, J., 'Japan: Draft Guidelines on Amendment to the Antimonopoly Act: Reduction System for Cooperation and Attorney–Client Privilege' (2020). Retrieved from https://globalcompliancenews.com/japan-draft-guidelines-released-on-amendment-to-the-antimonopoly-act-reduction-system-for-cooperation-and-attorney-client-privilege-20200504

Agamben, G., *The State of the Exception* (Chicago: University of Chicago Press, 2003)

Albrecht, S., *Die Anwendung von Kronzeugenregelungen bei der Bekämpfung internationaler Kartelle* (Baden-Baden: Nomos, 2008)

Aldaba, R. M. and Sy, G. S., 'Designing a Cooperation Framework for Philippine Competition and Regulatory Agencies' (Discussion Paper Series No. 2014-31, 2014). Retrieved from https://pidswebs.pids.gov.ph/CDN/PUBLICATIONS/pidsdps1431.pdf

American Antitrust Institute, 'Comments of the American Antitrust Institute Prepared for the Antitrust Division Roundtable on the Antitrust Criminal Penalty Enhancement and Reform Act' (31 May 2019). Retrieved from www.justice.gov/atr/page/file/1168666/download

Anthony, G. (ed.), *Values in Global Administrative Law* (Oxford: Hart Publishing, 2011)

Antimonopoly Commission of the State Council, 'Guidelines for the Application of the Leniency Programme to Horizontal Monopoly Agreement Cases' (2019). Retrieved from http://gkml.samr.gov.cn/nsjg/fldj/202009/t20200918_321856.html (in Chinese)

Apesteguia, J., Dufwenberg, M. and Selten, R., 'Blowing the Whistle' (2007) 31 *Economic Theory* 143

Arbault, F. and Peiró, F., 'The Commission's New Notice on Immunity and Reduction of Fines in Cartel Cases: Building on Success' (2002) 2 *Competition Policy Newsletter* 15

Argenton, C., Geradin, D. and Stephan, A., *EU Cartel Law and Economics* (Oxford: Oxford University Press, 2020)

Ariga, M. and Rieke, L. V., 'The Antimonopoly Law of Japan and Its Enforcement' (1964) 39 *Washington Law Review* 437

ASEAN, *ASEAN Regional Guidelines on Competition Policy* (Jakarta: ASEAN Secretariat, 2010). Retrieved from www.asean.org/wp-content/uploads/images/2012/publications/ASEAN%20Regional%20Guidelines%20on%20Competition%20Policy.pdf

ASEAN Secretariat, 'ASEAN Key Figures 2020' (2020). Retrieved from www.aseanstats.org/publication/akf_2020/

Aubert, C., Rey, P. and Kovacic, W., 'The Impact of Leniency Programs on Cartels' (2006) 24 *International Journal of Industrial Organization* 1241

Ayres, I. and Braithwaite, J., *Responsive Regulation* (Oxford: Oxford University Press, 1996)

Azar, J., Raina, S. and Schmalz, M. C., 'Ultimate Ownership and Bank Competition' (2016). Retrieved from https://ssrn.com/abstract=2710252

Azar, J., Schmalz, M. C. and Tecu, I., 'Anticompetitive Effects of Common Ownership' (2018) 73 *Journal of Finance* 1513

Baker & McKenzie, 'Introduction of a Bargaining System to Japanese Criminal Procedure' (2018). Retrieved from www.bakermckenzie.co.jp/wp/wp-content/uploads/ClientAlert_180921_Japanese_Plea_Barganing_System_E.pdf

Baker, D., 'Why Is the United States So Different from the Rest of the World in Imposing Serious Criminal Sanctions on Individual Cartel Participants?' (2011) 12 *Sedona Conference Journal* 301

Baker, D., 'The Use of Criminal Law Remedies to Deter and Punish Cartels and Bid-Rigging' (2001) 69 *George Washington Law Review* 693

Balasingham, B., *The EU Leniency Policy: Reconciling Effectiveness and Fairness* (Alphen aan de Rijn: Wolters Kluwer, 2017)

Baldwin, R., Cave, M. and Lodge, M., *Understanding Regulation* (Oxford: Oxford University Press, 2012)

Barlund, I. M. H., *Leniency in EU Competition Law* (Alphen aan de Rijn: Wolters Kluwer, 2020)

Barnett, T., 'Criminal Enforcement of Antitrust Laws: The U.S. Model', in Hawk, B. (ed.), *Annual Proceedings of the Fordham Competition Law Institute: International Antitrust Law & Policy* (New York: Fordham University Press, 2007) 1

Bauer, G. and Wagner, R., 'Resale Price Maintenance in the Digital Age' (2018). Retrieved from http://competitionlawblog.kluwercompetitionlaw.com/2018/08/23/resale-price-maintenance-digital-age

Beaton-Wells, C., 'The ACCC Immunity Policy for Cartel Conduct: Due for Review' (2013). Retrieved from https://papers.ssrn.com/sol3/papers.cfm?abstract_id=2316556

Beaton-Wells, C., 'Immunity for Cartel Conduct: Revolution or Religion? An Australian Case Study' (2014) 2 *Journal of Antitrust Enforcement* 126

Beaton-Wells, C., 'Leniency Policies: Revolution or Religion', in Beaton-Wells, C. and Tran, C. (eds.), *Anti-Cartel Enforcement in a Contemporary Age: Leniency Religion* (Oxford: Hart Publishing, 2015) 3

Beaton-Wells, C., 'The Politics of Cartel Criminalization: A Pessimistic View from Australia' (2008) 29 *European Competition Law Review* 3

Beaton-Wells, C. and Tran, C. (eds.), *Anti-Cartel Enforcement in a Contemporary Age: Leniency Religion* (Oxford: Hart Publishing, 2015)

Becker, G. 'Crime and Punishment: An Economic Approach' (1968) 76 *Journal of Political Economy* 169

Beeman, M. L., *Public Policy and Economic Competition in Japan: Change and Continuity in Antimonopoly Policy, 1973–1995* (Abingdon: Routledge, 2002)

Bell, R. B. and Millay, K., 'The Corporate Leniency Program: Did the Antitrust Division Kill the Goose that Laid the Golden Eggs?' (2018) 33 *Antitrust* 80

Berzins, M., 'Wrestling with Cartels: The Emergence of Competition Laws, Anti-Cartel Enforcement and a Leniency Programme in Japan' (2008) 8(1) *International Journal of Knowledge, Culture & Change Management* 15

Bhattacharjea, A. and De, O., 'Cartels and the Competition Commission' (2012) 47(35) *Economic and Political Weekly* 14

Bigoni, M., Fridolfson, S.O., Le Coq, C. and Spagnolo, G., 'Fines, Leniency, Rewards and Organized Crime: Evidence from Antitrust Experiments' (IFN Working Paper No. 738, 2008). Retrieved from www.ifn.se/wfiles/wp/wp738.pdf

Bigoni, M., Fridolfson, S. O., Le Coq, C. and Spagnolo, G., 'Fines, Leniency and Rewards in Antitrust' (2011) 43 *RAND Journal of Economics* 368

Billiet, P., 'How Lenient Is the EC Leniency Policy? A Matter of Certainty and Predictability' (2009) 30 *European Competition Law Review* 14

Black, J. 'Forms and Paradoxes of Principles-based Regulation' (2009). Retrieved from http://eprints.lse.ac.uk/23103/1/WPS2008-13.pdf

Black, J, Hopper, M. and Bland, C., 'Making a Success of Principles-Based Regulation' (2007) 1 *Law & Financial Markets Review* 191

Bloom, M., 'Despite Its Great Success, the EC Leniency Programme Faces Great Challenges', in Ehlermann, C. D. and Atanasiu, I. (eds.), *European Competition Law Annual 2006: Enforcement of Prohibition of Cartels* (Oxford: Hart Publishing, 2007) 546

Borrell, J.-R., Jiménez, J. L. and García, C., 'Evaluating Antitrust Leniency Programs' (2014) 10 *Journal of Competition Law and Economics* 107

Borrell, J.-R., Jiménez J. L. and Ordóñez-de-Haro, J. M., '25 Years of Leniency Programs: A Turning Point in Cartel Prosecution' (2019) 1(2) *Competition Policy International Antitrust Chronicle* 1. Retrieved from http://diposit.ub.edu/dspace/bitstream/2445/154157/1/693856.pdf

Borrell, J.-R., Jiménez, J. L. and Ordóñez-de-Haro, J. M., 'The Leniency Programme: Obstacles on the Way to Collude' (2015) 3 *Journal of Antitrust Enforcement* 149

Braithwaite, J. and Drahos, P., *Global Business Regulation* (Cambridge, UK: Cambridge University Press, 2000)

Brenner, S., 'An Empirical Study of the European Corporate Leniency Program' (2009) 27(6) *International Journal of Industrial Organization* 639

Brisset, K. and Thomas, L., 'Leniency Program: A New Tool in a Competition Policy to Deter Cartel Activity in Procurement Auctions' (2004) 17 *European Journal of Law and Economics* 5

Brumfield, N. A., Gidley, J. M., Zhang, Z. A. and Ying, Y., 'China Merges Antitrust Enforcement Agencies into One, as Its Anti-Monopoly Law Approaches 10th Anniversary' (2018). Retrieved from www.whitecase.com/sites/whitecase/files/files/download/publications/china-merges-antitrust-enforcement-agencies-into-one-samr.pdf

Brusick, P., 'Competition Guidelines: Leniency Programmes' (2016). Retrieved from https://unctadmena.org/wp-content/uploads/2018/12/Competition-Guidelines_Leniency-Programmes_EN.pdf

Buccirossi, P., Marvão, C. and Spagnolo, G., 'Leniency and Damages' (Stockholm Institute of Transition Economics, SITE Working Paper No. 32, 2015). Retrieved from www.econstor.eu/bitstream/10419/204743/1/site-wp0032.pdf

Buccirossi, P., Marvão, C. and Spagnolo, G., 'Leniency, Damages, and EU Competition Policy', *VOX^EU, CEPR Policy Portal Vox* (14 July 2015). Retrieved from https://voxeu.org/article/leniency-damages-and-eu-competition-policy

Buccirossi, P., Ciari, L., Duso, T., Spagnolo, G. and Vitale, C., 'Competition Policy and Productivity Growth: An Empirical Assessment' (2013) 95 *Review of Economics and Statistics* 1324

Bucy, P. H., 'Civil Prosecution of Health Care Fraud' (1995) 30 *Wake Forest Law Review* 720

Buretta, J. and Terzaken, J., 'Chapter 32: United States', in Buretta, J. and Terzaken, J. (eds.), *The Cartels and Leniency Review* (London: Law Business Research, 2018) 346

Buretta, J. and Terzaken, J. (eds.), *The Cartels and Leniency Review* (London: Law Business Research, 2018)

Burns, J., 'Lufthansa Reaches Settlement with Deutsche Bahn to End Cargo Cartel Dispute', *Cargo Airports & Airline Services* (28 August 2019). Retrieved from www.caasint.com/db-and-lufthansa-reach-settlement-to-end-cartel-legal-dispute

Burris, S., Drahos, P. and Shearing, C., 'Nodal Governance' (2005) 30 *Australian Journal of Legal Philosophy* 1

Cai, J., 'Public Antitrust Enforcement of Resale Price Maintenance in China: A Crusade or Discrimination?' (2016) 42 *Brooklyn Journal of International Law* 1

Callies, G. P. and Zumbansen, Z. *Rough Consensus and Running Code: A Theory of Transnational Private Law* (Oxford: Hart Publishing, 2010)

Callon, M., Lasoumes, P. and Barthe, Y., *Acting in an Uncertain World: An Essay on Technical Democracy* (Cambridge, MA: MIT Press, 2009)

Calvani, T. and Calvani, T. H., 'Cartel Sanctions and Deterrence' (2011) 56 *Antitrust Bulletin* 185

Carabine, N., Wan, E., Huckerby, M. and Wilkinson, J., 'Hong Kong Competition Commission's Enforcement and Leniency Policies' (18 December 2015). Retrieved from https://read01.com/AJxj8.html#.YpNvdujP25c

Carle, J., Lindeborg, P. and Segenmark, E., 'The New Leniency Notice' (2002) 23 *European Competition Law Review* 265

Cassese, S., 'Administrative Law without the State? The Challenge of Global Regulation' (2005) 37 *New York University Journal of International Law and Politics* 663

Castberg, A. D., 'Prosecutorial Independence in Japan' (1997) 16(1) *Pacific Basin Law Journal* 38

Cauffman, C., 'The Interaction of Leniency Programmes and Actions for Damages' (2011) 7 *Competition Law Review* 181

Cavanagh, E. D., 'The Private Antitrust Remedy: Lessons from the American Experience' (2010) 41 *Loyola University Chicago Law Journal* 629

CCCS, 'CCCS Practice Statement on the Fast Track Procedure for Section 34 and 47 Cases 2016' (2016). Retrieved from www.cccs.gov.sg/-/media/custom/ccs/files/legislation/legislation-at-a-glance/cccs-guidelines/cccs-fast-track-procedure-for-section-34-and-section-47-cases.pdf

CCCS, 'FAQ: Approach CCCS for Leniency or Reward' (2018). Retrieved from www.cccs.gov.sg/faq/approaching-cccs-for-leniency-or-reward

Chantara-Opakorn, A., 'Thailand Competition Law and Its Implication on International Mergers and Acquisition' (2000) 18 *Wisconsin International Law Journal* 591

Chen, A. C. M., 'Due Process and Transparency Requirements for Investigating Competition Cases in Taiwan', in Sokol, D. D. and Guzman, A. T. (eds.), *Antitrust Procedural Fairness* (Oxford: Oxford University Press, 2019) 88

Chen, A. C. M., 'The LCD Cartel: Impacts and Implications for the Competition Policy of Taiwan', in Charbit, N. and Ramundo, E. (eds.), *William E. Kovacic Liber Amicorum: An Antitrust Tribute Volume II* (New York, Institute for Competition Law, 2014) 325

Chen, A. C. M., 'Political, Economic and Legal Driving Forces Shaping the Developmental Contours of Competition Law: The Experience of Taiwan', in Van Uytsel, S., Hayashi, S. and Haley, J. (eds.), *Research Handbook on Asian Competition Law* (Cheltenham: Edward Elgar, 2020) 81.

Chen, A. C. M., 'The Taiwan Fair Trade Commission Imposes Record Fines on Independent Power Producers for Collectively Refusing to Adjust the Rate for Wholesale Electricity' (2013) *e-Competitions – National Competition Laws Bulletin* No. 52502

Chen, C. and Soltes, E. 'Why Compliance Programmes Fail and How to Fix Them', *Harvard Business Review* (March 2018). Retrieved from https://hbr.org/2018/03/why-compliance-programmes-fail

Chen, J. and Harrington, J. E., 'The Impact of the Corporate Leniency Program on Cartel Formation and the Cartel Price Path' (Center for International Research on the Japanese Economy, Working Paper No. CIRJE-F-358, 2005). Retrieved from https://repository.upenn.edu/cgi/viewcontent.cgi?article=1155&context=bepp_papers

Chen, R., 'Legal Informality and Human Capital Development in China', in Liebman, B. L. and Milhaupt, C. J. (eds.), *Regulating the Visible Hand? The Institutional Implications of Chinese State Capitalism* (Oxford: Oxford University Press, 2016) 151

Chen, T. and Liu, L., 'Antitrust Alert: Taiwan Strengthens Its Fair Trade Law' (2011). Retrieved from www.jonesday.com/en/insights/2011/12/antitrust-alert--taiwan-strengthens-its-fair-trade-law

Chen, Z. and Rey, P., 'On the Design of Leniency Programs' (2013) 56(4) *Journal of Law and Economics* 917

Cheng, T. K., *Competition Law in Developing Countries* (Oxford: Oxford University Press, 2020)

Cheng, T. K., 'Hong Kong Competition Law and Legal Transplant', in Van Uytsel, S., Hayashi, S. and Haley, J. (eds.), *Research Handbook on Asian Competition Law* (Cheltenham: Edward Elgar, 2020) 168

Cheong, M. F., Teoh, J. B. C. and Khoo, E. L. E., 'Legal Transplant: Giving Life to Malaysia's Competition Regime', in Van Uytsel, S., Hayashi, S. and Haley, J. (eds.), *Research Handbook on Asian Competition Law* (Cheltenham: Edward Elgar, 2020) 181

Chia, S. Y., 'The ASEAN Economic Community: Progress, Challenges, and Prospects' (ADBI Working Paper 440, 2013). Retrieved from www.adb.org/publications/asean-economic-community-progress-challenges-andprospects

Choi, J. P. and Gerlach, H., 'Global Cartels, Leniency Programs and International Antitrust Cooperation' (2012) 30 *International Journal of Industrial Organization* 528

Choi, N., 'Problems of Leniency Programs in International Cartels and the Direction to Improve the Programs' (2013) 28 *Journal of Korean Competition Law* 85 (in Korean)

Choi, Y. S., 'Competition Laws and Policies against International Cartels in Northeast Asia: International Cooperation for Effective Enforcement', in Cheng, T., Marco Colino, S. and Ong, B. (eds.), *Cartels in Asia: Law & Practice* (Hong Kong: Wolters Kluwer Law & Business, 2015) 133

Choi, Y. S., 'The Evolution of Fair and Free Competition Law in the Republic of Korea', in Van Uytsel, S., Hayashi, S. and Haley, J. (eds.), *Research Handbook on Asian Competition Law* (Cheltenham: Edward Elgar, 2020) 65

Choi, Y. S., 'The Issue of Information Exchanges Regarding Price under Competition Law: Comments on the Supreme Court's Judgment on the *Ramen* Cartel from a Comparative Perspective' (2016) 35 *Soongsil Law Review* 1

Choi, Y. S., 'The Rule of Law in a Market Economy: Globalisation of Competition Law in Korea' (2014) 15 *European Business Organization Law Review* 419

Choi, Y. S. and Heinemann, A., 'Competition and Trade: The Rise of Competition Law in Trade Agreements and Its Implications for the World Trading System' (2020) 43(4) *World Competition* 521

Clarcke, J. L. and Evenett, S. J., 'Deterrent Effects of National Anti-Cartel Laws: Evidence from International Vitamins Cartel' (2003) 48 *Antitrust Bulletin* 689

Cleary, W. B., 'The Law of Criminal Procedure in Contemporary Japan (2)' (1991) 41(4) *Hokkaido Law Review* 512

Colignon, R. A. and Usui, C., *Amakudari: The Hidden Fabric of Japan's Economy* (Ithaca, NY: Cornell University Press, 2003)

Connolly, R., 'Some Comments from Brent Snyder, Former Antitrust Division Criminal Deputy, as the Head to the Hong Kong Competition Commission', *Cartel Capers* (12 July 2017). Retrieved from http://cartelcapers.com/blog/comments-brent-snyder-former-antitrust-division-criminal-deputy-heads-hong-kong-competition-commission

Connor, J. M., 'Global Antitrust Prosecutions of International Cartels: Focus on Asia' (2008). Retrieved from https://editorialexpress.com/cgi-bin/conference/download.cgi?db_name=IIOC2008&paper_id=13

Connor, J. M., *Global Price Fixing*, 2nd ed. (Berlin: Springer, 2007)

Connor, J. M. and Helmers, C. G., 'Statistics on Modern Private International Cartels, 1990–2005' (American Antitrust Institute AAI Working Paper No. 07-01, 2007). Retrieved from https://papers.ssrn.com/sol3/papers.cfm?abstract_id=944039

Connor, J. M. and Miller, D., 'Determinants of EC Antitrust Fines for Members of Global Cartels' (6 March 2013). Retrieved from http://papers.ssrn.com/sol3/papers.cfm?abstract_id=2229358

Crampton, P. and Reynolds, G., 'Leniency Programmes in Competition Law', in Dhall, V. (ed.), *Competition Law Today – Concepts, Issues, and the Law in Practice* (Oxford: Oxford University Press, 2007) 113

Crane, D., 'Why Leniency Does Not Undermine Compensation', in Beaton-Wells, C. and Tran, C. (eds.), *Anti-Cartel Enforcement in a Contemporary Age: Leniency Religion* (Oxford: Hart Publishing, 2015) 263

Crumplar, T., 'An Alternative to Public and Victim Enforcement of the Federal Securities and Antitrust Laws: Citizen Enforcement' (1975) 13 *Harvard Journal Legis* 76

Dabbah, M. M., *International and Comparative Competition Law* (Oxford: Oxford University Press, 2010)

DavisPolk, 'Update on Establishment of Single Antitrust Agency in China' (Client Memorandum, 2018). Retrieved from www.davispolk.com/sites/default/files/2018-10-24_china_consolidates_antitrust_powers_into_single_agency.pdf

Deacons, 'Competition Commission Revises Leniency Policy for Undertakings and Introduces New Leniency Policy for Individuals', *Lexology* (24 April 2020). Retrieved from www.lexology.com/library/detail.aspx?g=3ad6f2b9-c39b-4b13-a100-9e8a3a65c0af

Delrahim, M., 'Winds of Change: A New Model of Incentivizing Antitrust' (11 July 2019). Retrieved from www.justice.gov/opa/speech/assistant-attorney-general-makan-delrahim-delivers-remarks-new-york-university-school-1-0

Deng, F. and Zhang, Y., 'Interview with Xu Kunlin, Director General of the Bureau of Price Supervision and Anti-monopoly under the National Development and Reform Commission of the People's Republic of China' (2014) 13 *Antitrust Source* 1. Retrieved from www.edgewortheconomics.com/media/publication/61_Fei_Deng_Interview_with_DG_Xu_Kunlin_of_Chinas_NDRC.pdf

Dijkstra, P. T., Haan, M. A. and Schoonbeek, L., 'Leniency Programs and the Design of Antitrust: Experimental Evidence with Free-Form Communication' (2020) 59 *Review of Industrial Organization* 13. Retrieved from https://doi.org/10.1007/s11151-020-09789-5

Ditucalan, A. M., 'Institutional Design of Philippine Competition Law' (2018) 8 *Korean Legislation Research Institute Journal of Law and Legislation* 27

Ditucalan, A. M., 'The Philippine Competition Law Dilemma: US-EU Fusion to Tension', in Van Uytsel, S., Hayashi, S. and Haley, J. (eds.), *Research Handbook on Asian Competition Law* (Cheltenham: Edward Elgar, 2020) 233

Dodoo, N., 'A New Dawn for Cartel Enforcement in China', in Emch, A. and Ng, W. (eds.), *Wang Xiaoye: The Pioneer of Competition Law in China – Liber Amicorum* (New York: Institute for Competition Law, 2019) 67

Dokei, T., Nakajima, H. and Onoki, T., 'New Bill: Expansion for Leniency and Fines under the Japan Anti-Monopoly Act' (2019). Retrieved from www.jdsupra.com/legalnews/new-bill-expansion-for-leniency-and-24551

Drahos, P., *The Global Governance of Knowledge: Patent Offices and Their Clients* (Cambridge, UK: Cambridge University Press, 2000)

Editorial Board, 'China's NDRC Uses Leniency Program to Uncover and Punish Cartel Members' (2012). Retrieved from https://blogs.orrick.com/antitrust/2012/12/03/chinas-ndrc-uses-leniency-program-to-uncover-and-punish-members-of-cartel

Editorial Board, 'Interview with Wu Zhenguo, Director General, Anti-Monopoly Bureau of the State Administration for Market Regulation (SAMR), People's Republic of China', *Antitrust Source* (June 2021). Retrieved from www.samr.gov.cn/xw/zj/202107/P020210707589294998827.pdf

Eichenwalt, K., *The Informant: A True Story of Greed, Conspiracy, and Whistleblowing* (London: Portobello Books, 2009)

Eichner, A. W., 'Battling Cartels in the New Era of Chinese Antitrust Enforcement' (2012) 47 *Texas International Law Journal* 587

Elhauge, E., 'The Growing Problem of Horizontal Shareholding' (2017) 3 *Antitrust Chronicle* 1

Elhauge, E., 'Horizontal Shareholding' (2016) 129 *Harvard Law Review* 1267

Ellis, C. J. and Wilson, W. W., 'What Doesn't Kill Us Makes Us Stronger: An Analysis of Corporate Leniency Policy' (2001). Retrieved from www.researchgate.net/publication/2498536_What_Doesn't_Kill_us_Makes_us_Stronger_An_Analysis_of_Corporate_Leniency_Policy

Emch, A., 'Chinese Antitrust Institutions: Many Cooks in the Kitchen' (2014) 10 *Competition Policy International* 217

Emch, A. and Hao, Q., 'The New Chinese Anti-Monopoly Law – An Overview', (eSapience Center for Competition Policy, 2007). Retrieved from www.sidley.com/~/media/files/publications/2007/11/the-new-chinese-antimonopoly-law-an-overview/files/view-pdf/fileattachment/newchineseantimonopolyenglish.pdf

Engstrom, D., 'Whither Whistleblowing? Bounty Regimes, Regulatory Context, and the Challenge of Optimal Design' (2014) 15 *Theoretical Inquiries in Law* 605

Epstein, R. A., 'Curbing the Abuses of China's Anti-Monopoly Law: An Indictment and Reform Agenda' (2014). Retrieved from https://sls.gmu.edu/cpip/wp-content/uploads/sites/31/2014/04/Curbing-the-Abuses-of-Chinas-Anti-Monopoly-Law.pdf

European Chamber of Commerce in China, 'Press Release: European Chamber Releases Statement on China AML-Related Investigations' (13 August 2014). Retrieved from www.europeanchamber.com.cn/en/press-releases/2132/european_chamber_releases_statement_on_china_aml_related_investigations

European Commission, 'Antitrust: Commission Fines Six LCD Panel Producers €648 Million for Price Fixing Cartel' (8 December 2010). Retrieved from https://ec.europa.eu/commission/presscorner/detail/es/IP_10_1685

European Commission, 'Commission Notice on Immunity from Fines and Reduction of Fines in Cartel Cases', O.J. C45/3 (2002)

European Commission, 'Commission Notice on Immunity from Fines and Reduction of Fines in Cartel Cases', O.J. C298/17 (2006)

European Commission, 'Commission Notice on Non-imposition or Reduction of Fines in Cartel Cases', O.J. C207/4 (1996)

European Commission, 'Competition: Revised Leniency Notice – Frequently Asked Questions' MEMO/06/469 (7 December 2006)

European Commission, 'Press Release: Commission Fines ADM, Ajinomoto, Others in Lysine Cartel' (7 June 2000). Retrieved from https://ec.europa.eu/commission/presscorner/detail/en/IP_00_589

European Commission, 'Press Release: Commission Fines Eight Companies in Graphite Electrode Cartel' (18 July 2001). Retrieved from http://europa.eu/rapid/press-release_IP-01-1010_en.htm?locale=en

European Commission, 'Press Release: Commission Imposes Fines on Vitamin Cartels' (21 November 2001). Retrieved from http://europa.eu/rapid/press-release_IP-01-1625_en.htm

European Commission, 'White Paper on Modernisation of the Rules Implementing Articles 85 and 86 of the EC Treaty', OJ C132/1 (1999)

European Commission, *XXVIth Report on Competition Policy 1996* (Brussels: Office for Official Publications of the European Communities, 1997)

Favart, M., 'Belgium', in Buhart, J. (ed.), *Leniency Regimes*, 4th ed. (London: Sweet & Maxwell, 2012) 36

Feess, E. and Walzl, M. 'Corporate Leniency Programs in the EU and the USA' (German Working Papers in Law and Economics, Working Paper No. 24, 2003). Retrieved from http://papers.ssrn.com/sol3/papers.cfm?abstract_id=384740

Fenwick, M., 'The Multiple Uncertainties of Corporate Criminal Law', in Fenwick, M. and Wrbka, S. (eds.), *Legal Certainty in a Contemporary Context* (Singapore: Springer, 2016) 148

Fenwick, M., 'The New Corporate Criminal Law and Transnational Legal Risk', in Fenwick, M. and Wrbka, S. (eds.), *Flexibility in Modern Business Law* (Singapore: Springer, 2016) 149

Fenwick, M., Kaal, W. A. and Vermeulen, E. P. M., 'Regulation Tomorrow: What Happens When Technology Is Faster Than the Law?' (2017) 6(3) *American University Business Law Review* 561

Fenwick, M., McCahery, J. A. and Vermeulen, E. P. M., 'Fintech and the Financing of SMEs and Entrepreneurs: From Crowdfunding to Marketplace Lending', in Cumming, D. and Hornuf, L. (eds.), *The Economics of Crowdfunding: Startups, Portals & Investor Behavior* (London: Palgrave Macmillan, 2016) 103

Fenwick, M., Siems, M. and Wrbka, S. (eds.), *The Changing Meaning of Legal Certainty in Contemporary Comparative and Transnational Law* (London: Hart Publishing, 2019)

Fenwick, M., Van Uytsel, S. and Wrbka, S. (eds.), *Networked Governance and the Law* (Singapore: Springer, 2014)

Fenwick, M., Van Uytsel, S. and Ying, B., *Regulating Fintech in Asia: Global Context, Local Perspectives* (Singapore: Springer, 2020)

Fenwick, M. and Vermeulen, E. P. M., 'The Future of Finance: Why Regulation Matters', in Liaw, K. T. (ed.), *The Routledge Handbook of Fintech* (New York: Routledge, 2020) 38

Fenwick, M. and Vermeulen, E. P. M., 'The New Firm: Staying Relevant, Unique & Competitive' (2015) 16 *European Business Organization Law Review* 595

Financial Conduct Authority, 'Regulatory Sandbox' (2015). Retrieved from www.fca.org.uk/publication/research/regulatory-sandbox.pdf

Fine, R. A., 'Plea Bargaining: An Unnecessary Evil' (1987) 70 *Marquette Law Review* 615

Flatters, F., 'Thailand and the Crisis: Roots, Recovery and Long-Run Competitiveness', in Woo, W. T., Sachs, J. D. and Schwab, K. (eds.), *The Asian Financial Crisis Lessons for a Resilient Asia* (Cambridge, MA: MIT Press, 2000) 257

Foster, A. L., 'Navigating the Unique Features of China's Competition Landscape' (2017) 31(2) *Antitrust* 79

Fox, E., 'Linked-In: Antitrust and the Virtues of a Virtual Network', in Lugard, P. (ed.), *The International Competition Network at Ten: Origins, Accomplishments and Aspirations* (Antwerp: Intersentia, 2011) 105

Fox, E. and Crane, D., *Global Issues in Antitrust and Competition Law* (St Paul, MN: West Academic Publishing, 2010)

Funahashi, K., 'International Cooperation to Crack International Cartels – Japanese Successes and Failures' (2004). Retrieved from www.jftc.go.jp/en/policy_enforcement/speeches/2004_files/internationalcartel1.pdf

Furse, M., *Antitrust Law in China, Korea and Vietnam* (Oxford: Oxford University Press, 2009)

Furse, M., *The Criminal Law of Competition in the UK and in the US* (Cheltenham: Edward Elgar, 2012)

Furse, M., *The Law of Merger Control in the EC and the UK* (Oxford: Hart Publishing, 2007)

Garret, B. L., *Too Big to Jail: How Prosecutors Compromise with Corporations* (Boston, MA: Harvard University Press, 2016)

Gerber, D., *Global Competition: Law, Markets, and Globalization* (Oxford: Oxford University Press, 2010)

Geverola, A. and Rigburg, K., 'A Changing Landscape: The DOJ Antitrust Division's Use of Deferred Prosecution Agreements', *Arnold & Porter, Enforcement Edge Blog* (12 August 2021). Retrieved from: www.arnoldporter.com/en/perspectives/blogs/enforcement-edge/2021/08/doj-antitrust-division-use-of-deferred

Ghoshal, V. and Sokol, D. D., 'The Evolution of U.S. Cartel Enforcement' (2014) 57 *Journal of Law & Economics* 51

Ghosal, V. and Sokol, D. D., 'The Rise and (Potential) Fall of U.S. Cartel Enforcement' (2020) 2 *University of Illinois Law Review* 471

Government Accountability Office, 'Criminal Cartel Enforcement: Stakeholder Views on Impact of 2004 Antitrust Reform Are Mixed, But Support Whistleblower Protection' (Report to Congressional Committees, GAO-11-916, July 2011). Retrieved from www.gao.gov/assets/gao-11-619.pdf

Griffin, J. M., 'The Modern Leniency Program after Ten Years – A Summary Overview of the Antitrust Division's Criminal Enforcement Program' (Presentation at the American Bar Association Annual Meeting, San Francisco, 12 August 2003). Retrieved from www.justice.gov/atr/public/speeches/201477.htm

Gu, M. and Yu, Sh., 'Better Late Than Never: NDRC Publishes Full Decisions on Zhejiang Car Insurance Cartel Case – Analysis of NDRC's Antitrust Law Enforcement Approach' (2014). Retrieved from www.chinalawvision.com/2014/09/competition-law-anti-monopoly-law/better-late-than-never-ndrc-publishes-full-decisions-on-zhejiang-car-insurance-cartel-case-analysis-of-ndrcs-antitrust-law-enforcement-approach

Haley, J. O., 'Japanese Antitrust Enforcement: Implications for United States Trade' (1991) 18 *Northern Kentucky Law Review* 335

Hamaguchi, Y. and Kawagoe, T., 'An Experimental Study of Leniency Programs' (RIETI Discussion Paper Series 05-E-003, 2003). Retrieved from www.rieti.go.jp/jp/publications/dp/05e003.pdf

Hammond, S. D., 'Cornerstones of an Effective Leniency Program' (Presentation at the ICN Workshop on Leniency Programs, Sydney, 22–23 November 2004). Retrieved from www.justice.gov/atr/speech/cornerstones-effective-leniency-program

Hammond, S. D., 'Detecting and Deterring Cartel Activity through an Effective Leniency Program' (Presentation at the International Workshop on Cartels, Brighton, 21–22 November 2000)

Hammond, S. D., 'The Evolution of Criminal Antitrust Enforcement over the Last Two Decades' (Presentation at the 24th Annual National Institute on White Collar Crime, ABA Criminal Justice Section and ABA Center for Continuing Legal Education, Miami, 25 February 2010). Retrieved from www.justice.gov/atr/speech/evolution-criminal-antitrust-enforcement-over-last-two-decades

Hammond, S. D., 'An Update of the Antitrust Division's Criminal Enforcement Program' (Presentation at the ABA Section of Antitrust Law Cartel Enforcement Roundtable, Washington, DC, 16 November 2005)

Han, K. J., 'Cartel Leniency Program and Cartel Enforcement in South Korea' (2015) MPA/MPP Capstone Projects 225. Retrieved from https://uknowledge.uky.edu/mpampp_etds/225

Han, M., Huang, C., van Opstal, C., Wong, J., Seet, J. and Liang, X., 'Antitrust China 2020 Annual Review' (2020). Retrieved from www.fangdalaw.com/wp-content/uploads/2021/01/ANTITRUST-CHINA-2020-ANNUAL-REVIEW.pdf

Harding, C., Beaton-Wells, C. and Edwards, J., 'Leniency and Criminal Sanctions in Anti-Cartel Enforcement: Happily Married or Uneasy Bedfellows?' in Beaton-Wells, C. and Tran, C. (eds.), *Anti-Cartel Enforcement in a Contemporary Age: Leniency Religion* (Oxford: Hart Publishing, 2015) 233

Harding, C. and Joshua, J., *Regulating Cartels in Europe*, 2nd ed. (Oxford: Oxford University Press, 2010)

Harrington, J. E., Jr, 'Optimal Corporate Leniency Programs' (2008) 56(2) *Journal of Industrial Economics* 215

Harrington, J. E., Jr, *The Theory of Collusion and Competition Policy* (Cambridge, MA: MIT Press, 2017)

Harrington, J. E., Jr and Chang, M.-H., 'Endogenous Antitrust Enforcement in the Presence of a Corporate Leniency Program' (30 November 2013). Retrieved from https://bepp.wharton.upenn.edu/files/?whdmsaction=public:main.file&fileID=5147

Harris, H. S. Jr, Wang, P. J., Zhang, Y., Cohen, M. A., and Evrard, S. J., *Anti-Monopoly Law and Practice in China* (Oxford: Oxford University Press, 2011)

Harris, S., 'Korea', in Sokol, D. D., Crane, D. A. and Ezrachi, A. (eds.), *Global Antitrust Compliance Handbook* (Oxford: Oxford University Press, 2014) 24.01

Hayashi, S., 'The 2013 Amendment to the Antimonopoly Act – Procedural Fairness under Japanese Competition Law' (2015) 39 *Journal of Japanese Law* 89

Heng, J. and Ping, L., 'China's Anti-Monopoly Law and the Role of Economics in Its Enforcement' (2020) 6(3) *Russian Journal of Economics* 219. Retrieved from https://rujec.org/article/56362

Hetzel, P., *Kreunzeugenregelungen im Kartellrecht* (Baden-Baden: Nomos, 2004)

Hinloopen, J. and Soetevent, A. R., 'Laboratory Evidence on the Effectiveness of Corporate Leniency Programs' (2008) 39 *RAND Journal of Economics* 607

HKCA, 'Comments on the Draft Leniency Policy' (2015). Retrieved from www.compcomm.hk/en/enforcement/consultations/past_consultations/files/S16_Hong_Kong_Competition_Association.pdf

HKCC, 'Cooperation and Settlement Policy for Undertakings Engaged in Cartel Conduct' (April 2019). Retrieved from www.compcomm.hk/en/legislation_guidance/policy_doc/files/Cooperation_Policy_Eng.pdf

HKCC, 'Enforcement Policy' (2015). Retrieved from www.compcomm.hk/en/legislation_guidance/policy_doc/files/Enforcement_Policy_Eng.pdf

HKCC, 'Guideline: Investigations' (27 July 2015). Retrieved from www.compcomm.hk/en/legislation_guidance/guidance/investigations/files/Guideline _Investigations_Eng.pdf

HKCC, 'Guideline on the First Conduct Rule' (27 July 2015). Retrieved from www.compcomm.hk/en/legislation_guidance/guidance/first_conduct_rule/files/Guideline_The_First_Conduct_Rule_Eng.pdf

HKCC, 'Leniency Policy for Individuals Involved in Cartel Conduct' (April 2020). Retrieved from www.compcomm.hk/en/legislation_guidance/policy_doc/files/Leniency_Policy_Individuals_E.pdf

HKCC, 'Leniency Policy for Undertakings Engaged in Cartel Conduct' (November 2015). Retrieved from www.compcomm.hk/en/legislation_guidance/policy_doc/files/Leniency_Policy_Eng.pdf

HKCC, 'Policy on Recommended Pecuniary Penalties' (June 2020). Retrieved from www.compcomm.hk/en/legislation_guidance/policy_doc/files/Policy_on_Recommended_Pecuniary_Penalties_Eng.pdf

HKCC, 'Press Release: Competition Commission Takes IT Cartel Conduct Case to Competition Tribunal' (22 January 2020). Retrieved from www.compcomm.hk/en/media/press/files/20200122_ENG_PR_Competition_Commission_takes_IT_cartel_conduct_case_to_Competition_Tribunal.pdf

HKCC, 'Press Release: Competition Commission Takes Renovation Cartel Case to Competition Tribunal' (3 July 2019). Retrieved from www.compcomm.hk/en/media/press/files/20190703_Competition_Commission_takes_renovation_cartel_case_to_Competition_Tribunal_eng_PR.pdf

HKCC, 'Press Release: Competition Commission Welcomes Judgment in IT Cartel Conduct Case' (3 November 2020). Retrieved from www.compcomm.hk/en/media/press/files/EN_PR_IT_case_judgment.pdf

HKCC, 'Press Release: Competition Commission Welcomes Quick Rectification by the Hong Kong Newspaper Hawker Association on Retail Price of Branded Cigarettes' (31 May 2016). Retrieved from www.compcomm.hk/en/about/public_notices/files/HKNHA_20160531_e.pdf

HKCC, 'Report on Study into Aspects of the Market for Residential Building Renovation and Maintenance' (May 2016). Retrieved from www.compcomm.hk/en/media/press/files/Report_on_market_study.pdf

HKCC, 'Report on Study into Hong Kong's Auto-Fuel Market' (May 2017). Retrieved from www.compcomm.hk/en/media/press/files/Full_Report_Auto_fuel_Market_Study_Report_Eng.pdf

HKCC, 'Report on Trade Associations in Hong Kong and the Competition Ordinance' (March 2016). Retrieved from www.compcomm.hk/en/media/reports_publications/files/TA_project_report_EN.pdf

Hollman, H. M. and Kovavic, W. E. 'The International Competition Network: Its Past, Current and Future Role', in Lugard, P. (ed.), *The International Competition Network at Ten: Origins, Accomplishments and Aspirations* (Antwerp: Intersentia, 2011) 51

Hollman, H. M., Kovavic, W. E. and Robertson, A. S., 'Building Global Antitrust Standards: The ICN's Practicable Approach' in Ezrachi, A. (ed.), *Research Handbook on International Competition Law* (Cheltenham: Edward Elgar, 2012) 89

Hölzel, N., *Kronzeugenregelungen im Europäischen Wettbewerbsrecht: Ermittlungsinstrument unter Reformzwang* (Halle: Universitätsverlag Halle-Wittenberg, 2011)

Hovenkamp, H., *Federal Antitrust Policy: The Law of Competition and Its Practice*, 6th ed. (St Paul, MN: West Academic, 2020)

Howard, A., 'The Draft Directive on Competition Law Damages – What Does It Mean for Infringers and Victims?' (2014) 35 *European Competition Law Review* 51

Huang, Y. and Zhang, Z. 'Study on Frontier Issues and the Future of Regulations over Monopoly Agreements in China', in Faure, M. G. and Zhang, X. (eds.), *Competition Policy and Regulation* (Cheltenham: Edward Elgar) 45

Ibáñez Colomo, P., 'Article 101 TFEU and Market Integration' (2016) 12(4) *Journal of Competition Law & Economics* 749

ICN, 'About the ICN' (2018). Retrieved from www.internationalcompetitionnetwork.org

ICN, 'Anti-Cartel Enforcement Manual – Chapter 2: Drafting and Implementing an Effective Leniency Policy' (2014). Retrieved from www.internationalcompetitionnetwork.org/portfolio/leniency-program

ICN, 'Checklist for Efficient and Effective Leniency Programmes' (2017). Retrieved from www.internationalcompetitionnetwork.org/wp-content/uploads/2018/09/CWG_LeniencyChecklist.pdf

ICN, 'Good Practices for Incentivising Leniency Applications' (2019). Retrieved from www.internationalcompetitionnetwork.org/wp-content/uploads/2019/05/CWG-Good-practices-for-incentivising-leniency.pdf

ICN, 'Guidance on Enhancing Cross-Border Leniency Cooperation' (2020). Retrieved from www.internationalcompetitionnetwork.org/wp-content/uploads/2020/07/CWG-Leniency-Coordination-Guidance.pdf

ICN, 'ICN's Vision for Its Second Decade' (2011). Retrieved from www.internationalcompetitionnetwork.org/wp-content/uploads/2018/07/ICN2dDecade2011.pdf

ICN, 'Memorandum on the Establishment and Operation of the International Competition Network' (2001). Retrieved from www.internationalcompetitionnetwork.org/wp-content/uploads/2019/07/ICNMemo_on_Establishment.pdf

ICN, 'Trends and Developments in Cartel Enforcement' (Presentation at the 9th Annual ICN Conference, Istanbul, 29 April 2010). Retrieved from www.internationalcompetitionnetwork.org/wp-content/uploads/2018/05/CWG_TrendsReport.pdf

Inoue, A., *Antitrust Enforcement in Japan – History, Rhetoric and Law of the Antimonopoly Act*, 2nd ed. (Tokyo: Dai-Ichi Hoki, 2019)

Inoue, A., *The Leniency Practice: Protect Your Company against the Rough Seas of Competition* (Tokyo: Lexis Japan, 2006) (in Japanese)

Inoue, A., 'The Recent Amendment of the Japanese Antimonopoly Law' (2006) 1(1) *Japan Business Law Review* 4

Irie, G. and Matsushima, T., *Cartel Regulation and Leniency: Research on and Practical Use of the Reduction and Immunity of the Surcharge System* (Tokyo: Sankyouhouki, 2014) (in Japanese)

Ishida, H. and Hara, E., 'Japan: Cartels' (2014) 2014 *Asia-Pacific Antitrust Review* 110

Isranews Agency, 'Adamas the Main Co-Contractor of the Ministry of Tourism and Sports Worth 250 M. Now with 109 M. in Debt' (27 September 2014). Retrieved from www.isranews.org/isranews-scoop/33198-adm.html

Italianer, A., 'Fighting Cartels in European and the US: Different Systems, Different Goals' (2013). Retrieved from http://ec.europa.eu/competition/speeches/text/sp2013_09_en.pdf

Ivaldi, M., Jullien, B., Rey, P., Seabright, P. and Tirole, J., 'The Economics of Tacit Collusion' (Final Report for the Directorate General for Competition, European Commission, IDEI, March 2003). Retrieved from http://ec.europa.eu/competition/mergers/studies_reports/the_economics_of_tacit_collusion_en.pdf

Iwase, K., 'The Role of Competition Policy in Economic Partnership Agreements' (Lecture at the 12th Technical Training Course on the Antimonopoly Act and Competition Policy, Osaka and Tokyo, 22 August–22 September 2005). Retrieved from www.jftc.go.jp/eacpf/05/jicatext2/0916Rol.pdf

Iyori, H., 'A Comparison of U.S.-Japan Antitrust Law: Looking at the International Harmonization of Competition Law' (1995) 4 *Pacific Rim Law & Policy Journal* 59

Iyori, H. and Uesugi, A., *The Antimonopoly Laws and Policies of Japan* (Washington, DC: Federal Legal Publications, 1994)

Jacob, H., Blankenburg, E., Kritzer, H. M., Provine, D. M. and Sanders, J., *Courts, Law and Politics in Comparative Perspective* (New Haven: Yale University Press, 1996)

Jaspers, J. D., 'Leniency in Exchange for Cartel Confessions' (2020) 17(1) *European Journal of Criminology* 106

Jenny, F., 'Foreword', in Beaton-Wells, C. and Tran, C. (eds.), *Anti-Cartel Enforcement in a Contemporary Age: Leniency Religion* (Oxford: Hart Publishing, 2015) v

Jephcott, M., 'The European Commission's New Leniency Notice—Whistling the Right Tune' (2002) 23 *European Competition Law Review* 378

JFTC, 'Concerning the Enforcement Status of the Antimonopoly Law Infringement Cases of the Fiscal Year 2020' (5 May 2021). Retrieved from www.jftc.go.jp/houdou/pressrelease/2021/may/210526.html (in Japanese)

JFTC, 'Enactment of the Act to Amend the Antimonopoly Act' (2019). Retrieved from www.jftc.go.jp/en/pressreleases/yearly-2019/June/19061907.html

JFTC, 'Public Announcement Regarding Businesses to Which the System for Reduction of or Immunity from the Surcharge Applied' (2021). Retrieved from www.jftc.go.jp/dk/seido/genmen/kouhyou/index.html

JFTC, 'Rules on Reporting and Submission of Materials Regarding Immunity from or Reduction of Surcharges (Fair Trade Commission Rule No. 7 of 2005)' (2005). Retrieved from www.jftc.go.jp/en/legislation_gls/antimonopoly_rules_files/immunityH21.pdf

JFTC, 'Rules on Reporting the Facts and Submitting the Materials Regarding Immunity from or Reduction of Surcharges (Fair Trade Commission Rule No. 3 of 2020)' (2020). Retrieved from www.jftc.go.jp/en/legislation_gls/201225001.pdf

Johnson, C. A., *Japan: Who Governs? The Rise of the Developmental State* (New York: W. W. Norton, 1995)

Johnson, C. A., *MITI and the Japanese Miracle – The Growth of Industrial Policy, 1925–1975* (Stanford: Stanford University Press, 1982)

Jolly, R. L. and Prescott, J. J., 'Beyond Plea Bargaining' (2020). Retrieved from https://ssrn.com/abstract=3579226

Jung, Y. and Chang, S. W., 'Korea's Competition Law and Policies in Perspective: Symposium on Competition Law and Policy in Developing Countries' (2005–2006) 26 *Northwestern Journal of International Law & Business* 687

Juška, Ž., 'The Effectiveness of Antitrust Collective Litigation in the European Union: A Study of the Principle of Full Compensation' (2018) 49 *International Review of Intellectual Property and Competition Law* 63

Kaal, W. A. and Vermeulen, E. P. M., 'How to Regulate Disruptive Innovation: From Facts to Data' (2017) 57 *Jurimetrics: The Journal of Law, Science, and Technology* 169

Kameoka, E., *Competition Law and Policy in Japan and the EU* (Cheltenham: Edward Elgar, 2014)

Kang, W., 'Fully Rethinking Cartel Offence in Terms of Substantive and Constitutional & Procedural Law' (2020) 176 *Justice* 113 (in Korean)

Kecsmar, K. and Keidel, A., 'Shaping the EU Leniency Programme: The Recent Approach Adopted by EU Courts' (2015) 6(8) *Journal of European Competition Law & Practice* 556

Keidanren, N., 'Proposal of Nippon Keidanren Regarding Revision of the Antimonopoly Act Enforcement Systems' (5 September 2005). Retrieved from www.keidanren.or.jp/english/policy/2003/088.html

Kennedy, K. C., *Competition Law and the World Trade Organisation: The Limits of Multilateralism* (London: Sweet & Maxwell, 2001)

Keohane, R. and Nye, J. S., Jr, *Power and Independence: World Politics in Transition* (Boston, MA: Little Brown, 1977)

KFTC, '2019 White Paper' (24 October 2019). Retrieved from www.ftc.go.kr/www/cop/bbs/selectBoardList.do?key=191&bbsId=BBSMSTR_000000002318&bbsTyCode=BBST01 (in Korean)

KFTC, 'Cartel Leniency Program in Korea' (2009). Retrieved from https://ftc.go.kr/DATA/download/eng/Quick_Link/Leniency%20Program%20of%20Korea.pdf

KFTC, 'Policy Area: Competition – Cartel'. Retrieved from www.ftc.go.kr/eng/contents.do?key=502

KFTC, 'Press Release: Amendment to the MRFTA Was Passed by the Congress' (9 December 2020). Retrieved from www.ftc.go.kr/www/selectReportUserView.do?key=10&rpttype=1&report_data_no=8868 (in Korean)

KFTC, 'Public Notification on the Implementation of the Leniency Programme Including Corrective Measures for Voluntary Reporters, etc. of Illegal Cartel Conduct' (Notification No. 2021–72, amended 10 June 2021)

Khemani, S. and Dutz, M., 'The Instruments of Competition Policy and Their Relevance for Economic Development', in Frischtak, C. (ed.), *Regularities Policies and Reform: A Comparative Perspective* (Washington, DC: World Bank, 1995) 16

Kingsbury, B., Krisch, N. and Stewart, R. B., 'The Emergence of Global Administrative Law' (2005) 68 *Law and Contemporary Problems* 15

Kjaer, P., *Between Governing and Governance: On the Emergence, Function and Form of Europe's Post-National Constellation* (Oxford: Hart Publishing, 2010)

Klein, G. J., 'Cartel Destabilization and Leniency Programs – Empirical Evidence' (ZEW Discussion Paper No. 10–107, Zentrum für Europäische Wirtschaftsforschung, 2010). Retrieved from www.econstor.eu/bitstream/10419/44455/1/645296945.pdf

Klein, J. I., 'The War against International Cartels: Lessons from the Battlefront' (Presentation at Fordham Corporate Law Institute 26th Annual Conference on International Antitrust Law & Policy, New York, 14 October 1999). Retrieved from www.justice.gov/atr/speech/war-against-international-cartels-lessons-battlefront

Knight, T. and Claire, C. S., 'Reconciling the Conflict: Antitrust Leniency Programs and Private Enforcement' (Working Paper, 2019). Retrieved from https://people.clas.ufl.edu/thomasknight/files/KnightSteClaire.pdf

Knight, T. and de Weert, W., 'On Implementing Private Damages in European Competition Cases' (Working Paper, 2015). Retrieved from https://people.clas.ufl.edu/thomasknight/files/PrivateDamages.pdf

Kobayashi, B. H., 'Deterrence with Multiple Defendants: An Explanation for Unfair Plea Bargains' (1992) 23(4) *Rand Journal of Economics* 507

Kobayashi, B. H., 'Symposium: Antitrust, Agency, and Amnesty: An Economic Analysis of the Enforcement of Antitrust Laws against Corporations' (2001) 69 *George Washington Law Review* 715

Koh, S. and Jeong, J., 'The Leniency Program in Korea and Its Effectiveness' (2014) 10 *Journal of Competition Law & Economics* 161

Koma, F., Inoue, A. and Ae, J., 'Japan', in Mobley, S. R. and Denton, J. (eds.), *Global Cartels Handbook: Leniency: Policy and Procedure* (Oxford: Oxford University Press, 2011) 317

Komesar, N. K., *Law's Limits: The Rule of Law and the Supply and Demand of Rights* (Cambridge, UK: Cambridge University Press, 2001)

Kon, S. and Barcroft, A., 'Aspects of the Complementary Roles of Public and Private Enforcement of UK and EU Antitrust Law: An Enforcement Deficit?' (2008) 1(1) *Global Competition Litigation Review* 11

Koradia, N., Manokaran, K. and Saeed, Z., 'Algorithmic Collusion and Indian Competition Act: Suggestions to Tackle Inadequacies and Naivety', in Van Uytsel, S. (ed.), *The Digital Economy and Competition Law in Asia* (Singapore: Springer, 2021) 127

Kovacic, W. E., 'A Case for Capping the Dosage: Leniency and Competition Authority Governance', in Beaton-Wells, C. and Tran, C. (eds.), *Anti-Cartel Enforcement in a Contemporary Age: Leniency Religion* (Oxford: Hart Publishing, 2015) 123

Kovacic, W. E., 'Private Monitoring and Antitrust Enforcement: Paying Informants to Reveal Cartels' (2001) 69 *George Washington Law Review* 766

Kovacs, M. and Turi, A., 'Competition: Leniency after the Antitrust Damages Directive in Hungary: A Compromise between Private and Public Interests?' *CEE Legal Matters* (1 August 2018). Retrieved from https://ceelegalmatters.com/hungary/8971-competition-leniency-after-the-antitrust-damages-directive-in-hungary-a-compromise-between-private-and-public-interests

Kroes, N., 'Taking Competition Seriously – Anti-Trust Reform in Europe' (Presentation at the International Bar Association/European Commission Conference 'Anti-trust Reform in Europe: A Year in Practice', Brussels, 10 March 1999). Retrieved from http://europa.eu/rapid/press-release_SPEECH-05-157_en.htm

Kum, C. H., Yoon, H. and Park, Y. J., 'In Brief: Cartel Immunity and Leniency Programmes in South Korea', *Lexology* (28 November 2020). Retrieved from www.lexology.com/library/detail.aspx?g=620d0f61-bf8c-4f79-b45b-a457c1330018

Kurita, M., 'Effectiveness and Transparency of Competition Law Enforcement – Causes and Consequences of a Perception Gap between Home and Abroad on the Anti-Monopoly Act Enforcement in Japan' (2004) 3 *Washington University Global Studies Law Review* 387

Kwon, N., 'An Economic Analysis of Leniency in Korea' (2010) 18(4) *Korean Journal of Industrial Organization* 41 (in Korean)

Kwon, O. and Seo, J., *Antitrust Law*, 3rd ed. (Paju: Bobmunsa, 2018) (in Korean)

Lande, R. and Davis, J., 'Comparative Deterrence from Private Enforcement and Criminal Enforcement of the U.S. Antitrust Laws' (2011) 37 *Brigham Young University Law Review* 315

Landeo, C. M. and Spier, K. E., 'Optimal Law Enforcement with Ordered Leniency' (2020) 63 *Journal of Law and Economics* 71

Landes, W. M, 'Optimal Sanctions for Antitrust Violations' (1983) 50 *University of Chicago Law Review* 652

Landes, W. M. and Posner, R. A. 'Should Indirect Purchasers Have Standing to Sue under the Antitrust Laws? An Economic Analysis of the Rule of Illinois Brick' (1979) 46 *University of Chicago Law Review* 602

Lane, E., *Lobbying and the Law* (Los Angeles: University of California Press, 1964)

Lee, C., 'Competition Law Enforcement in Malaysia: Some Recent Developments' (2014) 51 *Malaysian Journal of Economic Studies* 77

Lee, C., 'Malaysia', in Brooks, D. H. and Evenett, S. J. (eds.), *Competition Policy and Development in Asia* (London: Palgrave, 2005) 197

Lee, C. and Fukunaga, Y., 'Competition Policy Challenges of Single Market and Production Base' (ERIA Discussion Paper Series, 2013).

Lee, H., Kim, K.-W. and Ha, M.-H., 'Needs and Devices to Protect Statements of Cartel Leniency Applicants from U.S. Discovery' (2010) 22 *Journal of Korean Competition Law* 338 (in Korean)

Lee, H. W. and Choi, Y. J., 'How the New Leniency Program in Korea Affect Cartel Formation and Cartel Detection?' (2014) 32(2) *Korean Journal of Economic Studies* 99 (in Korean)

Lee, K. J., 'Measures to Enhance the Effectiveness of Leniency Programs' (2018) 31(4) *Commercial Cases Review* 249 (in Korean)

Lee, M. H., 'Recent Developments in the Treatment of Collusion by Korean Courts' (2005) 4(2) *Journal of Korean Law* 115

Leong, C., 'A Critical Look into the Whistleblower Protection Act 2010' (Policy IDEAS No. 36, 2017) Retrieved from https://ideas.org.my/wp-content/uploads/2021/04/PI36-Whistleblower-Protection.pdf

Leslie, C. R., 'Editorial: Antitrust Leniency Programmes' (2011) 7 *Competition Law Review* 175

Leslie, C. R., 'Antitrust Amnesty, Game Theory, and Cartel Stability' (2006) 31 *Journal of Corporation Law* 453

Levy, N. and O'Donoghue, R., 'The EU Leniency Programme Comes of Age' (2004) 27 *World Competition* 75

Li, C., *Chinese Politics in the Xi Jinping Era: Reassessing Collective Leadership* (Washington, DC: Brookings Institution Press, 2016).

Li, G. and Young, A., 'Competition Laws and Policies in China and Hong Kong: A Tale of Two Regulatory Journeys' (2002) 7 *Journal of International Trade Law and Policy* 186

Liang, D. 'China', in Campbell, N. (ed.), *Cartel Regulation 2021* (London: Law Business Research, 2021) 74. Retrieved from https://mcmillan.ca/wp-content/uploads/2021/02/2021_Cartel-Regulation_book_secured.pdf

Liao, T. and Li, B. 'Antitrust Dawn Raids in China: On the Tenth Anniversary of Chinese Antitrust Enforcement' (2018) 10 *China Antitrust Law Journal* 1

Lieber, J. B., *Rats in the Grain: The Dirty Tricks and Trials of Archer Daniels Midland* (New York: Hachette Book Group, 2002)

Linklaters, 'Order of the State Administration for Industry and Commerce No. 53' (2010). Retrieved from www.linklaters.com/pdfs/mkt/london/1a.pdf

Lowe, P., 'Setting Enforcement Priorities at European and National Level Post Modernization' (Presentation at the VIII Treviso Conference, Treviso, 22 May 2008). Retrieved from http://ec.europa.eu/competition/speeches/text/sp2008_17_en.pdf

Lowe, P., 'What's the Future for Cartel Enforcement' (Presentation at the Understanding Global Cartel Enforcement, Brussels, 11 February 2003). Retrieved from http://ec.europa.eu/competition/speeches/text/sp2003_044_en.pdf

Lugard, P. (ed.), *The International Competition Network at Ten: Origins, Accomplishments and Aspirations* (Antwerp: Intersentia, 2011)

Lynch, N. E., 'Immunity in Criminal Cartel Investigations: A US Perspective' (2011). Retrieved from www.lw.com/presentations/immunity-in-criminal-cartel-investigations-us-perspective

Lynch, N. E. and Fox, K., 'How ACPERA Has Affected Criminal Cartel Enforcement' (11 August 2011). Retrieved from https://m.lw.com/thoughtLeadership/how-acpera-affects-criminal-cartel-enforcement

Ma, J., *Competition Law in China: A Law and Economics Perspective* (Heidelberg: Springer, 2019)

Ma, J. and Sokol, D. D. 'Procedural Fairness in Chinese Antitrust', in Sokol, D. D. and Guzman, A. T. (eds.), *Antitrust: Procedural Fairness* (Oxford: Oxford University Press, 2019) 71

Ma, T.-C., 'Competition Authority Independence, Antitrust Effectiveness, and Institutions' (2010) 30 *International Review of Law & Economics* 226

Maclachlan, P. L., *Consumer Politics in Postwar Japan: The Institutional Boundaries of Citizen Activism* (New York: Columbia University Press, 2002)

Maher, I. and Papadopoulos, A., 'Competition Agency Networks around the World', in Ezrachi, A. (ed.), *Research Handbook on International Competition Law* (Cheltenham: Edward Elgar, 2012) 60

Marco Colino, S., 'A History of Competition: The Impact of Antitrust on Hong Kong's Telecommunications Markets' (2019) 29 *Fordham Journal of Intellectual Property, Media and Entertainment Law* 93

Marco Colino, S., 'The Perks of Being a Whistleblower: Designing Efficient Leniency Programs in New Antitrust Jurisdictions' (2017) 50 *Vanderbilt Journal of Transnational Law* 535

Marco Colino, S., 'Punishing Cartel Behaviour: Means to Encourage Compliance with the Hong Kong Competition Ordinance', in Cheng, T., Marco Colino, S. and Ong, B. (eds.), *Cartels in Asia: Law and Practice* (The Hague: Wolters Kluwer, 2015) 315

Martina, M., 'EU Lobby Piles in on Foreign Criticism of China's Antitrust Enforcement', Reuters (9 September 2014). Retrieved from www.reuters.com/article/uk-china-antitrust-eu/eu-lobby-piles-in-on-foreign-criticism-of-chinas-antitrust-enforcement-idUKKBN0H40SB20140909

Martina, M., 'Exclusive: Tough-Talking China Pricing Regulator Sought Confessions from Foreign Firms', Reuters (20 August 2013). Retrieved from https://jp.reuters.com/article/idINL4N0GK18M20130822

Martina, M. and Miller, M., '"Mr. Confession" and His Boss Drive China's Antitrust Crusade', Reuters (15 September 2014). Retrieved from www.reuters.com/article/us-china-antitrust-ndrc-insight-idUSKBN0HA27X20140915

Martyniszyn, M., 'Leniency (Amnesty) Plus: A Building Block or a Trojan Horse?' (2015) 3(2) *Journal of Antitrust Enforcement* 391

Marvão, C., 'Challenges and Co-ordination of Leniency Program – Note by Catarina Marvão – Background Materials for the Meeting of OECD Competition Committee' (2018). Retrieved from https://one.oecd.org/document/DAF/COMP/WP3/WD(2018)32/en/pdf

Marvão, C. and Spagnolo, G., 'Leniency Inflation, Cartel Damages and Criminalization' (29 June 2021). Retrieved from https://ssrn.com/abstract=3180685.

Marvão, C. and Spagnolo, G., 'What Do We Know about the Effectiveness of Leniency Policies? A Survey of the Empirical and Experimental Evidence', in Beaton-Wells, C. and Tran, C. (eds.), *Anti-Cartel Enforcement in a Contemporary Age: Leniency Religion* (Oxford: Hart Publishing, 2015) 57

Mason, C., *The Art of the Steal* (New York: Berkeley Publishing Group, 2005)

Matake, Y., 'Recent Developments Regarding Attorney–Client Privilege' (2019). Retrieved from www.noandt.com/ja/publications/2019/documents/competitionandantitrust_no11.pdf

Matsushita, M., 'The Antimonopoly Law of Japan', in Graham, E. M. and Richardson, J. D. (eds.), *Global Competition Policy* (New York: Columbia University Press, 1997) 151

Mayer Brown, 'Vietnam Competition Law: Key Changes in 2019' (2018). Retrieved from www.mayerbrown.com/-/media/files/perspectives-events/publications/2019/02/vietnam_competition_law_key_changes_in_2019.pdf

McEwin, I. and Thanitcul, S., 'Thailand', in Williams, M. (ed.), *The Political Economy of Competition Law in Asia* (Cheltenham: Edward Elgar Publishing, 2013) 251

McMillan, J., 'Dango: Japan's Price Fixing Conspiracies' (1991) 3(3) *Economics and Politics* 201

Michael, B., 'Hong Kong Needs a Whistle-Blower Law for Better Governance and Business Practices, Researcher Says', *South China Morning Post* (11 August 2015). Retrieved from www.scmp.com/news/hong-kong/law-crime/article/1848274/hong-kong-needs-whistle-blower-law-better-governance-and

Miller, N. H., 'Strategic Leniency and Cartel Enforcement' (2009) 99 *American Economic Review* 750

Ministry of Corporate Affairs, Government of India, 'Report of Competition Law Review Committee' (2019). Retrieved from www.ies.gov.in/pdfs/Report-Competition-CLRC.pdf

Misawa, M., 'An Overview of Problems Concerning Political Donations in Japan' (2008) 21(2) *Columbia Journal of Asian Law* 161

Mobley, S. and Denton, R. (eds.), *Global Cartels Handbook – Leniency: Policy and Procedure* (Oxford: Oxford University Press, 2011)

Mogaki, M., 'The Transforming Japanese State and Governance in Antimonopoly Regulation' (2014). Retrieved from www.psa.ac.uk/sites/default/files/conference/papers/2014/201404%20PSA%20Conference%20(Mogaki).pdf

Mogaki, M., *Understanding Governance in Contemporary Japan: Transformation and the Regulatory State* (Manchester: Manchester University Press, 2019)

Monti, M., 'Fighting Cartels Why and How? Why Should We Be Concerned with Cartels and Collusive Behaviour?' (Presentation at 3rd Nordic Competition Policy Conference, Stockholm, 11–12 September 2000). Retrieved from http://europa.eu/rapid/press-release_SPEECH-00-295_en.htm

Morita, M. K., 'Structural Impediments Initiative: Is It an Effective Correction of Japan's Antimonopoly Policy' (1991) 12 *University of Pennsylvania Journal of International Law* 742

Motta, M. and Polo, M., 'Leniency Programs and Cartel Prosecution' (2001) 21 *International Journal of Industrial Organization* 347

Murakami, M., *The Japanese Antimonopoly Act* (Tokyo: Shouji Houmu, 2003)

Nakano, M., *The Policy-Making Process in Contemporary Japan* (London: Palgrave Macmillan, 1997)

Nakazawa, T. and Weiss, L. W., 'The Legal Cartels of Japan' (1989) 34 *Antitrust Bulletin* 641

Nambu, T., 'A Successful Story: Leniency and (International) Cartel Enforcement in Japan' (2014) 5(4) *Journal of European Competition Law & Practice* 158

Nayoung, K. and Yungsan, K., 'Who Confesses for Leniency: Evidence from Korea' (2016) 12(2) *Journal of Competition Law & Economics* 351

NDRC, 'Order No. 7: Rules on Anti-Price Monopoly' (29 December 2010). Retrieved from www.gov.cn/flfg/2011-01/04/content_1777969.htm (in Chinese)

Ng, W., *The Political Economy of Competition Law in China* (Cambridge, UK: Cambridge University Press, 2018)

Nicolosi, C., 'No Good Whistle Goes Unpunished: Can We Protect European Antitrust Leniency Applications from Discovery?' (2011) 31 *Northwestern Journal of International Law & Business* 225

Nikomborirak, D., 'Banana Matters and Monopoly' (2014). Retrieved from http://thaipublica.org/2015/05/tdri-11-5-2558 (in Thai)

Nikomborirak, D., 'The Political Economy of Competition Law: The Case of Thailand' (2006) 26 *Northwestern Journal of International Law & Business* 597

Nikomborirak, D., 'The Political Economy of the Competition Regimes in Thailand and Korea: A Comparison', in Lewis, D. (ed.), *Building New Competition Law Regimes: Selected Essays* (Cheltenham: Edward Elgar Publishing, 2013) 110

Ning, S., Yin, H. and Peng, K., 'China', in Varney, C. A. and Terzaken, J. (eds.), *The Cartels and Leniency Review* (London: Law Business Research, 2017) 57

Noonan, L., 'Banks Face Pushback over Surging Compliance and Regulatory Costs', *Financial Times* (28 May 2015). Retrieved from www.ft.com/content/e1323e18-0478-11e5-95ad-00144feabdc0#axzz3jN2kPKMc

Nylander, J., 'Why Hong Kong Needs a Whistleblowing Policy', *Forbes Asia* (14 August 2015). Retrieved from www.forbes.com/sites/jnylander/2015/08/14/why-hong-kong-needs-a-whistleblowing-policy/#218c460f71f5

O'Brien, A., 'Leadership of Leniency', in Beaton-Wells, C. and Tan, C. (eds.), *Anti-Cartel Enforcement in A Contemporary Age: Leniency Religion* (Oxford: Hart Publishing, 2015) 17

O'Brien, A., 'Cartel Settlements in the U.S. and EU: Similarities, Differences & Remaining Questions' (Presented at 13th Annual EU Competition Law and Policy Workshop, Florence, 6 June 2008). Retrieved from www.justice.gov/atr/speech/cartel-settlements-us-and-eu-similarities-differences-remaining-questions

Obsteiner, T., 'International Antitrust Litigation: How to Manage Multijurisdictional Leniency Applications' (2013) 4(1) *Journal of European Competition Law & Practice* 16

O'Connell, J., 'Rabbit, Revisited – Antitrust Enforcement in China' (2014) 28(2) *Antitrust* 6

Oded, S., 'Leniency and Compliance: Towards an Effective Leniency Policy in the Chinese Anti-Monopoly Law', in Faure, M. G. and Zhang, X. (eds.), *The Chinese Antimonopoly Law* (Cheltenham: Edward Elgar, 2013) 142

OECD, 'Annual Report on Competition Policy Developments in India', DAF/COMP/AR(2020)45 (2020). Retrieved from https://one.oecd.org/document/DAF/COMP/AR(2020)45/en/pdf

OECD, 'Best Practice Roundtables on Competition Policy' (2021). Retrieved from www.oecd.org/daf/competition/roundtables.htm

OECD, 'Challenges and Co-ordination of Leniency Programmes' (2018). Retrieved from www.oecd.org/daf/competition/challenges-and-coordination-of-leniency-programmes.htm

OECD, 'Challenges and Co-ordination of Leniency Programmes – Background Note by the Secretariat', DAF/COMP/WP3(2018)1 (2018). Retrieved from https://one.oecd.org/document/DAF/COMP/WP3(2018)1/en/pdf

OECD, 'Competition and the Use of Markers in Leniency Programmes' (2014). Retrieved from www.oecd.org/daf/competition/markers-in-leniency-programmes.htm

OECD, 'Executive Summary of the Roundtable on Challenges and Co-ordination of Leniency Programmes' (2018). Retrieved from https://one.oecd.org/document/DAF/COMP/WP3/M(2018)1/ANN2/en/pdf

OECD, 'Fighting Hard Core Cartels: Harm, Effective Sanctions and Leniency Programmes' (2002). Retrieved from www.oecd.org/competition/cartels/1841891.pdf

OECD, *Implementing Good Regulatory Practice in Malaysia* (Paris: OECD Publishing, 2015)

OECD, 'Policy Roundtables: Leniency for Subsequent Applicants', DAF/COMP(2012)25 (2012). Retrieved from www.oecd.org/daf/competition/Leniencyforsubsequentapplicants2012.pdf

OECD, 'Private Remedies' (2011) 11(2) *OECD Journal: Competition Law and Policy* 11

OECD, 'Recommendation of the Council Concerning Effective Action against Hard Core Cartels', C(98)35/FINAL (25 March 1998). Retrieved from https://legalinstruments.oecd.org/public/doc/193/193.en.pdf

OECD, 'Recommendations and Best Practices on Competition Law and Policy' (2021). Retrieved from www.oecd.org/daf/competition/recommendations.htm

OECD, 'Regional Competition Agreements: Benefits and Challenges – Contribution from Singapore', DAF/COMP/GF/WD(2018)75 (2018). Retrieved from https://one.oecd.org/document/DAF/COMP/GF/WD(2018)75/en/pdf

OECD, 'Report on Leniency Programs to Fight Hard Core Cartels', Document DAFFE/CLP (27 April 2001)

OECD, 'Resolution of the Council Concerning the Committee of Experts on Restrictive Business Practices and Amending Its Name and Terms of Reference', C(87)138(Final) (2020). Retrieved from https://oecdgroups.oecd.org/Bodies/ShowBodyView.aspx?BodyID=1673&Lang=en

OECD, 'Roundtable on Challenges and Co-ordination of Leniency Programmes – Note by Singapore', DAF/COMP/WP3/WD(2018)19 (2018). Retrieved from www.oecd.org/daf/competition/challenges-and-coordination-of-leniency-programmes.htm

OECD, 'Roundtable on Challenges and Co-ordination of Leniency Programmes – Note by Taiwan', DAF/COMP/WP3/WD(2018)20 (5 June 2018). Retrieved from https://one.oecd.org/document/DAF/COMP/WP3/WD(2018)20/en/pdf

OECD, 'Roundtable on Challenges and Co-ordination of Leniency Programmes – Note by the United States', DAF/COMP/WP3/WD(2018)33 (23 May 2018). Retrieved from https://one.oecd.org/document/DAF/COMP/WP3/WD(2018)33/en/pdf

OECD, 'Roundtable on Collusion and Corruption in Public Procurement', DAF/COMP/GF(2010)6 (2010). Retrieved from www.oecd.org/competition/cartels/46235884.pdf

OECD, *Trade and Competition Policies for Tomorrow* (Paris: OECD Publishing, 1999)

Office of Fair Trading, 'Applications for Leniency and No Action in Cartel Cases: OFT's Detailed Guidance on the Principles and Process', OFT1495 (2013). Retrieved from https://assets.publishing.service.gov.uk/government/uploads/system/uploads/attachment_data/file/284417/OFT1495.pdf

Office of Trade Competition Commission, 'Summary of Complaints Received from 2018–August 2019' (24 June 2021). Retrieved from https://tcct.or.th/view/1/Summary_of_complaint_statistics/TH-TH (in Thai)

O'Fiachain, B., 'The Criminal Cartel Offence: Considerations for Effective Enforcement' (2017) 17 *University College Dublin Law Review* 36

O'Kane, M., *The Law of Criminal Cartels: Practice and Procedure* (Oxford: Oxford University Press, 2009)

Ong, B., 'Competition Law and Policy in the ASEAN Region: Origins, Objectives and Opportunities', in Ong, B. (ed.), *The Regionalisation of Competition Law and Policy within the ASEAN Economic Community* (Cambridge, UK: Cambridge University Press, 2019) 1

Ong, B., 'Competition Law in Singapore: The First Decade', in Van Uytsel, S. Hayashi, S. and Haley, J. (eds.), *Research Handbook on Asian Competition Law* (Cheltenham: Edward Elgar, 2020) 151

Paopongsakorn, N., 'The New Competition Law in Thailand: Lessons for Institutional Building' (2002) 21 *Review of Industrial Organization* 185

Park, S., 'Key Issues and Implications of the Leniency Policy' (2018) 116 *Justice* 301 (in Korean)

Park, S. B., 'Practical Issues and Proposed Solutions for the Current Leniency Program' (2012) 26 *Journal of Korean Competition Law* 3

Park, S. B., 'Practical Issues in the Enforcement of Leniency Program in Korea' (2015) 15 *Journal of Korean Law* 73

Parthasarathy, S., *Competition Law in India* (Alphen aan de Rijn: Wolters Kluwer Law & Business, 2011)

Pelkmans, J., *The ASEAN Economic Community: A Conceptual Approach* (Cambridge, UK: Cambridge University Press, 2016)

Petkoski, D., Sánchez-Calero, P. and Bello, A., 'Reduction in Leniency; Drop in Enforcement?' *Lexology* (15 August 2019). Retrieved from www.lexology.com/library/detail.aspx?g=62d7c2fb-a154-40a5-989e-465e0c5da31

Ping, L. and Chen, E., 'Competition Policy under Laissez-Faireism: Market Power and Its Treatment in Hong Kong' (2002) 21 *Review of Industrial Organization* 145

PLC Cross-Border Handbooks, *Competition: Volume 2 – Leniency* (Toronto: Practical Law Company, 2008)

Poapongsakorn, N., 'The New Competition Law in Thailand: Lessons for Institution Building' (2002) 21(2) *Review of Industrial Organization* 185

Poranakond, P., *Competition Law in the ASEAN Countries: Regional Law and National Systems* (The Hague: Wolters Kluwer, 2018)

Prodigalidad, P.-A. T. and Ocampo, C. L. D., 'Philippines', in Gotts, I. K. and Schwartz, K. S. (eds.), *The Private Competition Enforcement Review*, 14th ed. (London: Law Business Research, 2021) 192

Rathi, S. and Seth, R., 'Awards for Compensation in Antitrust: The Road Less Travelled in India', *CPI Competition Policy International* (23 April 2020). Retrieved from www.competitionpolicyinternational.com/awards-for-compensation-in-antitrust-the-road-less-travelled-in-india

Rey, P., 'On the Use of Economic Analysis in Cartel Detection', in Ehlermann, C. D. and Atanasiu, I. (eds.), *Competition Law Annual 2006: Enforcement of Prohibition of Cartels* (Oxford: Hart Publishing, 2007) 81

Reynolds, M. and Anderson, D., 'Immunity and Leniency in EU Cartel Cases: Current Issues' (2006) 27 *European Competition Law Review* 82

Riley, A., 'Cartel Whistleblowing: Toward an American Model' (2002) 9 *Maastricht Journal of European and Comparative Law* 67

Riley, A., 'The Modernisation of EU Anti-Cartel Enforcement: Will the Commission Grasp the Opportunity?' (CEPS Special Report, January 2010)

Rock, E. B. and Rubinfeld, D. L., 'Common Ownership and Coordinated Effects' (New York University School of Law, Law & Economics Research Paper Series, Working Paper No. 18–40, 2018). Retrieved from www.law.nyu.edu/sites/default/files/Rock%20and%20Rubinfeld%20II%20SSRN-id3296488.pdf

Rodriguez, A. E. and Menon, A., *The Limits of Competition Policy: The Shortcomings of Antitrust in Developing and Reforming Economies* (Alphen aan den Rijn: Wolters Kluwer, 2010)

Sabel, C. and Zeitlin, J., 'Learning from Difference: The New Architecture of Experimentalist Governance in the EU' (European Governance Papers No. C-07-02, 2002)

Salemme, E., *Enforcing European Competition Law through Leniency Programmes in the Light of Fundamental Rights: With an Overview of the US Leniency Programme* (Baden-Baden: Nomos, 2019)

Sandhu, J. S., 'The European Commission's Leniency Policy: A Success?' (2007) 28(3) *European Competition Law Review* 148

Schaede, U., *Cooperative Capitalism: Self-Regulation, Trade Associations, and the Antimonopoly Law in Japan* (Oxford: Oxford University Press, 2000)

Schmidt, J., 'Keeping US Courts Open to Foreign Antitrust Plaintiffs: A Hybrid Approach to the Effective Deterrence of International Cartels' (2006) 31 *Yale Journal of International Law* 211

Schroll, G., *Der Einfluss interner und externer Faktoren auf die Effektivität der Kronzeugenprogramme der EU-Kommission und des Bundeskartellamtes* (Bern: Peter Lang, 2012)

Sharma, M. M., 'Private Antitrust Litigation in India: Overview' (2019). Retrieved from https://uk.practicallaw.thomsonreuters.com/w-021-3374?transitionType=Default&contextData=(sc.Default)&firstPage=true

Sharot, T., 'The Optimism Bias' (2011) 21(23) *Current Biology* R941

Shenefield, J. H., 'The Disclosure of Antitrust Violations and Prosecutorial Discretion' (1978) 48(1) *Antitrust Law Journal* 463

Sheth, M., 'Formulating Antitrust Policy in Emerging Economies' (1997) 86 *Georgetown Law Journal* 451

Shiau, D. and Chen, E., 'Emerging Trends in Leniency Regimes in Southeast Asia – How These Impact on Multi-Jurisdiction Leniency Strategy' (2017) 38 *European Competition Law Review* 165

Shi, S.-H. and Chuang, C.-F., 'The Study on the Implementation Effectiveness of Leniency Policy of Other Countries' (Research Project Report Commissioned by the TFTC, November 2017)

Shinagawa, T. and Iwanari, H., *Reduction and Immunity from the Surcharge under the Antimonopoly Law* (Tokyo: Koutori Kyoukai, 2010) (in Japanese)

Shiraishi, T., *Dokusen Kinshi Hou [The Antimonopoly Law]* (Tokyo: Yuhikaku Publishing, 2006)

Shry-Hau, S., 'A Comparison of the Effectiveness and Efficacy of the Leniency Program: What Can Taiwan Learn from the Success Stories of the USA, Germany and Korea?' (2018) 26 *Fair Trade Quarterly* 115

Simmons, I. and O'Rourke, K., 'Reflections on Cartel Enforcement' (2012) 27(1) *Antitrust* 33

Simpson, S., *Corporate Crime, Law & Social Control* (Cambridge, UK: Cambridge University Press, 2002)

Slaughter, A.-M., *A New World Order* (Princeton: Princeton University Press, 2012)

Slaughter, A.-M., 'The Real New World Order' (1997) 47 *Foreign Affairs* 183

Snyder, B., 'Leniency Programmes: Brent Snyder Shares Tips on Effective Leniency Programmes' (OECD Competition Division, 20 August 2018). Retrieved from www.youtube.com/watch?v=dJSNoWD0vb8

Snyder, F., 'The Effectiveness of European Community Law: Institutions, Processes, Tools and Techniques' (1993) 56 *Modern Law Review* 19

Soderbergh, S., *The Informant* (Los Angeles: Warner Bros Pictures, 2009)

Sokol, D. D., 'Cartels, Corporate Compliance, and What Practitioners Really Think about Enforcement' (2012) 78 *Antitrust Law Journal* 201

Son, Y.-H., 'Discussion over Abolishment of Exclusive Complaint Right under the Monopoly Regulation and Fair Trade Act' (2018) 32(4) *Business Law Review* 225 (in Korean)

Spagnolo, G., '*Divide et Impera*: Optimal Leniency Programs' (Stockholm School of Economics, CEPR Discussion Paper No. 4840, 2004). Retrieved from https://papers.ssrn.com/sol3/papers.cfm?abstract_id=716143

Spagnolo, G., '*Divide et Impera*: Optimal Leniency Programs' (Stockholm School of Economics, 2005) Retrieved from http://ftp.zew.de/pub/zew-docs/veranstaltungen/rnic/papers/GiancarloSpagnolo.pdf

Spagnolo, G., 'Leniency and Whistleblowers in Antitrust', in Buccirosi, P. (ed.), *Handbook of Antitrust Economics* (Cambridge, MA: MIT Press, 2008) 259

Spagnolo, G., 'Optimal Leniency Programs' (Fondazione Eni Enrico Mattei, Working Paper 42.2000, 2000). Retrieved from https://papers.ssrn.com/sol3/papers.cfm?abstract_id=235092

Spratling, G. R., 'The Corporate Leniency Policy: Answers to Recurring Questions' (Presentation at the ABA Antitrust Section Spring Meeting, Washington, DC, 1 April 1998)

Spratling, G. R., 'Detection and Deterrence: Rewarding Informants for Reporting Violations' (2001) 69 *George Washington Law Review* 798.

Spratling, G. R., 'The Experience and Views of the Antitrust Division – Address at the US Sentencing Commission Symposium: Corporate Crime in America: Strengthening the 'Good Citizen' Corporation, 8 September 1995', in Ewing, K. P. (ed.), *Competition Rules for the 21st Century: Principles from the America's Experience*, 2nd ed. (The Hague: Kluwer Law, 2006) 623

Spratling, G. R., 'Making Companies an Offer They Shouldn't Refuse' (Presentation at the 35th Annual Symposium on Associations and Antitrust, Washington, DC, 16 February 1999)

Stephan, A., 'An Empirical Assessment of the 1996 Leniency Notice' (ESRC Centre for Competition Policy and the Norwich Law School, Working Paper No. 05–10, 2005). Retrieved from https://papers.ssrn.com/sol3/papers.cfm?abstract_id=911592

Stephan, A., 'An Empirical Assessment of the European Leniency Notice' (2008) 5 *Journal of Competition Law & Economics* 537

Stephan, A., 'The EU Method of Antitrust Enforcement', in Healey, D., Jacobs, M. and Smith, R. (eds.), *Research Handbook on Methods and Models of Competition Law* (Cheltenham: Edward Elgar, 2020) 391

Stephan, A., 'Is the Korean Innovation of Individual Informant Rewards a Viable Cartel Detection Tool?' in Cheng, T., Marco Colino, S. and Ong, B. (eds.), *Cartels in Asia: Law and Practice* (The Hague: Wolters Kluwer, 2015) 109

Stephan, A. and Nikpay, A., 'Leniency Decision-Making from a Corporate Perspective: Complex Realities', in Beaton-Wells, C. and Tran, C. (eds.), *Anti-Cartel Enforcement in a Contemporary Age: Leniency Religion* (Oxford: Hart Publishing, 2015) 139

Stephan, A. and Nikpay, A., 'Leniency Theory and Complex Realities' (CCP Working Paper 14–8, 2014). Retrieved from https://papers.ssrn.com/sol3/papers.cfm?abstract_id=2537470

Stucke, M. E., 'Am I a Price Fixer? A Behavioral Economics Analysis of Cartels', in Beaton-Wells, C. and Ezrachi, A. (eds.), *Criminalising Cartels: Critical Studies of an International Regulatory Movement* (Oxford: Hart Publishing, 2011) 263

Stucke, M. E., 'Greater International Convergence and the Behavioral Antitrust Ambit', in Ezrachi, A. (ed.), *Research Handbook on International Competition Law* (Cheltenham: Edward Elgar, 2014) 158

Suurnäkki, S. and Tierno Centella, M., 'Commission Adopts Revised Leniency Notice to Reward Companies That Report Hard-Core Cartels' (2007) 1 *Competition Policy Newsletter* 7

Suwazono, S., *The 2005 Amendments of the Antimonopoly Law – An Article-by-Article Commentary of the New Surcharge System and the Hearing/Criminal Investigation System* (Tokyo: Shojihoumu, 2005) (in Japanese)

Suwazono, S., 'A Japanese View of Competition Law Enforcement', *InformaConnect* (21 November 2016). Retrieved from https://informaconnect.com/a-japanese-view-of-competition-law-enforcement.

Suzuki, K., *Competition Law Reform in Britain and Japan: Comparative Analysis of Policy Networks* (Oxford: Routledge, 2002)

Suzuki, M., 'Japan' (2010) 32(2) *Antitrust* 37

Svetiev, Y., *Experimentalist Competition Law and the Regulation of Markets* (Oxford: Hart Publishing, 2020)

Svetiev, Y., 'Partial Formalization of the Regulatory Network' (2010). Retrieved from http://papers.ssrn.com/sol3/papers.cfm?abstract_id=1564890&download=yes

Svetiev, Y. and Wang, L., 'Competition Law Enforcement in China: Between Technocracy and Industrial Policy' (2016) 79(4) *Law and Contemporary Problems* 187. Retrieved from https://scholarship.law.duke.edu/cgi/viewcontent.cgi?article=4807&context=lcp

Swaak, C. and Arp, D., 'A Tempting Offer: Immunity from Fines for Cartel Conduct under the European Commission's New Leniency Notice' (2003) 24 *European Competition Law Review* 9

Takeshima, K., 'Leniency Programme and Bid Riggings in Public Sector – Enforcement Experiences in Japan' (2007). Retrieved from www.jftc.go.jp/en/policy_enforcement/speeches/2007/saicsymposium2007.html

Terakawa, Y., 'International Exchange of Information between Competition Authorities: Update on Recent Bilateral Developments in Japan' (Presentation at 5th International Cartels Workshop, Brussels, 1–3 October 2003). Retrieved from https://dl.ndl.go.jp/view/download/digidepo_1254664_po_terakawa_icw_031003.pdf?contentNo=1&alternativeNo=

Tett, G., *Fool's Gold: The Inside Story of J.P. Morgan and How Wall St. Greed Corrupted Its Bold Dream and Created a Financial Catastrophe* (New York: Free Press, 2010)

Teubner, G., *Dilemmas of Law in the Welfare State* (London: De Gruyter, 1986)

Thaipublica, '12 Years of Failure to Enforce the Thai Trade Competition Act (An Interview with the Ex-Commissioner Pornapa Thaicharoen' (4 February 2012). Retrieved from http://thaipublica.org/2012/02/competition-act-12-enforcement-has-failed

Thanitcul, S., 'Competition Law in Thailand: A Preliminary Analysis' (2002) 1 *Washington University Global Studies Law Review* 171

Thanitkul, S., 'Competition Law in Thailand: In Transition to an Operational Law', in Van Uytsel, S., Hayashi, S. and Haley, J. (eds.), *Research Handbook on Asian Competition Law* (Cheltenham: Edward Elgar, 2020) 118

Tuan, N. A., 'A Review of Ten Years of Enforcement: Challenges and Prospects of the Vietnamese Cartel Regime', in Cheng, T., Marco Colino, S. and Ong, B. (eds.), *Cartels in Asia: Law and Practice* (Hong Kong: Wolters Kluwer Law & Business, 2015) 211

Uesugi, A., 'The Japanese Leniency Programme – One Year In' (2007) 21 *Antitrust* 79

Uesugi, A., 'A Leniency Programme à la Japonnaise – How It Is Going to Be Enforced' (2005). Retrieved from www.jftc.go.jp/en/policy_enforcement/speeches/2005_files/051116uesugi_aba.pdf

Uesugi, A., 'How Japan Is Tackling Enforcement Activities against Cartels' (2005) 13 *George Mason Law Review* 349

Uesugi, A., 'Japan's Cartel System and Its Impact on International Trade' (1986) 27 *Harvard International Law Review* 389

UNCTAD, 'About UNCTAD' (2021). Retrieved from https://unctad.org/about

UNCTAD, 'About UNCTAD: History' (2021). Retrieved from https://unctad.org/about/history

UNCTAD, 'About UNCTAD-MENA' (2018). Retrieved from https://unctadmena.org/about

UNCTAD, 'Competition Guidelines: Leniency Programmes' (22 June 2016). Retrieved from https://unctad.org/system/files/official-document/ditcclp2016d3_en.pdf

UNCTAD, 'Sixth United Nations Conference to Review all Aspect of the Set of Multilaterally Agreed Equitable Principles and Rules for the Control of Restrictive Business Practices' (2010). Retrieved from https://unctad.org/meeting/sixth-united-nations-conference-review-all-aspect-set-multilaterally-agreed-equitable

UNCTAD, 'The Role of Competition Policy in Promoting Economic Development: The Appropriate Design and Effectiveness of Competition Law and Policy', TD/RBP/CONF.7/3 (2010). Retrieved from unctad.org/en/Docs/tdrbpconf7d3_en.pdf

UNCTAD, 'UNCTAD MENA Programme 1st Annual Review Meeting' (2017). Retrieved from http://unctad.org/en/pages/MeetingDetails.aspx?meetingid=1386

USC US-China Institute, 'Decision of the Central Committee of the Communist Party of China on Some Major Issues Concerning Comprehensively Deepening the Reform, November 12, 2013' (12 November 2013). Retrieved from https://china.usc.edu/decision-central-committee-communist-party-china-some-major-issues-concerning-comprehensively

US Department of Justice, *Antitrust Division Manual*, 5th ed. (2014). Retrieved from www.justice.gov/atr/file/761166/download

US Department of Justice, 'Corporate Leniency Policy' (1993). Retrieved from www.justice.gov/atr/file/810281/download

US Department of Justice, 'Frequently Asked Questions about the Antitrust Division's Leniency Program and Model Leniency Letters' (2017). Retrieved from www.justice.gov/atr/page/file/926521/download

US Department of Justice, 'Individual Leniency Policy' (1994). Retrieved from www.justice.gov/atr/individual-leniency-policy

Utton, M. A., *Cartels and Economic Collusion: The Persistence of Corporate Conspiracies* (Cheltenham: Edward Elgar, 2011)

Van Barlingen, B., 'The European Commission's 2002 Leniency Notice after One Year of Operation' (2003) (2) *Competition Policy Newsletter* 16

Van Barlingen, B. and Barennes, M., 'The European Commission's 2002 Leniency Notice in Practice' (2005) 3 *Competition Policy Newsletter* 6

Van den Bergh, R. J. and Camesasca, P. D., *European Competition Law and Economics: A Comparative Perspective*, 2nd ed. (Cheltenham: Edward Elgar, 2006)

Van den Bergh, R. and Faure, M. 'Critical Issues in the Enforcement of the Anti-monopoly law in China: A Law and Economics Perspective', in Faure, M. G. and Zhang, X. (eds.), *Competition Policy and Regulation: Recent Developments in China, the US and Europe* (Cheltenham: Edward Elgar, 2011) 54

Van Uytsel, S., 'Adopting Competition Law in Asia: An Increasingly Complex Reality', in Van Uytsel, S., Hayashi, S. and Haley, J. (eds.), *Research Handbook on Asian Competition Law* (Cheltenham: Edward Elgar, 2020) 2

Van Uytsel, S., 'Am I a Bid Rigger? How Bureaucrats Came within the Focus of Regulating Bid Rigging in Japan' (Presentation at the 13th Asian Competition Forum, Hong Kong, 11 and 12 December 2017).

Van Uytsel, S., 'Anti-Cartel Enforcement in Japan: Does Leniency Make the Difference?' in Beaton-Wells, C. and Tran, C. (eds.), *Anti-Cartel Enforcement in a Contemporary Age: Leniency Religion* (Oxford: Hart Publishing, 2015) 81

Van Uytsel, S. 'A Comparative US and EU Perspective on the Japanese Antimonopoly Law's Leniency Program' (2008) 75 *Hosei Kenkyu* F1

Van Uytsel, S., 'The Hybridization of Competition Law Enforcement: Some Lessons from Japan's Introduction of the Leniency Program' (ASLI Working Paper Series, Working Paper Series No.027, 2012)

Van Uytsel, S., 'The International Competition Network, Its Leniency Best Practice and Legitimacy: An Argument for Introducing a Review System', in Fenwick, M., Van Uytsel, S. and Wrbka, S. (eds.), *Networked Governance, Transnational Business and the Law* (Berlin: Springer, 2014) 185

Van Uytsel, S., 'Leniency under the Japanese Antimonopoly Law: Towards the End of the Cartel Archipelago?' in Cheng, T., Marco Colino, S. and Ong, B. (eds.), *Cartels in Asia: Law and Practice* (Hong Kong: Wolters Kluwer Law & Business, 2015) 67

Van Uytsel, S., 'The Proliferation of Competition Law in Asia: From Forced Adoption to an Integration Project', in Van Uytsel, S., Hayashi, S. and Haley, J. (eds.), *Research Handbook on Asian Competition Law* (Cheltenham: Edward Elgar, 2020) 25

Van Uytsel, S. and Ying, B., 'Delayed Leniency Applications – The Unfortunate But Predictable Outcome of the Flexible Leniency Policies under the Chinese Antimonopoly Law', in Fenwick, M. and Wrbka, S. (eds.), *Flexibility in Modern Business Law: A Comparative Assessment* (Singapore: Springer, 2016) 91

Vande Walle, S., 'Competition and Competition Law in Japan: Between Skepticism and Embrace', in Dowdle, M. W., Gillespie, J. and Maher, I. (eds.), *Asian Capitalism and the Regulation of Competition: Towards a Regulatory Geography of Global Competition Law* (Cambridge, UK: Cambridge University Press, 2013) 123

Vande Walle, S., 'Deterrence of Antitrust Violations: Do Actions for Damages Matter in Japan?' (2012) 2 *Asian Journal of Law and Economics* 3

Vande Walle, S., 'The Saitama Saturday Club Case: Political Meddling, Public Opinion, and Antitrust Enforcement in Japan at a Turning Point' (2013) 36 *Journal of Japanese Law* 143

Varian, H. R., *Intermediate Microeconomics*, 9th ed. (New York: W.W. Norton, 2020)

Vedder, H., 'The Kone Case and the Lifts Cartel – An Upward Effect on Prices and Effectiveness?' *European Law Blog* (19 June 2014). Retrieved from http://europeanlawblog.eu/?p=2397

Veljanovski, C., 'Cartel Fines in Europe – Law, Practice and Deterrence' (2007). Retrieved from http://ssrn.com/abstract=920786

Voss, K., 'Between Enforcement and Regulation: A Study of the System of Case Resolution Mechanisms Used by the European Commission in the Enforcement of Articles 101 and 102 TFEU' (Doctoral Thesis, Stockholm University, 2019)

Wahyuningtyas, S. Y., 'Challenges in Combating Cartels, 14 Years after the Enactment of Indonesian Competition Law' (2014) 7(10) *Yearbook of Antitrust and Regulatory Studies* 279

Wahyuningtyas, S. Y., 'Indonesian Competition Law: Up for Renewal', in Van Uytsel, S., Hayashi, S. and Haley, J. (eds.), *Research Handbook on Asian Competition Law* (Cheltenham: Edward Elgar, 2020) 100

Wakui, M., *Antimonopoly Law: Competition Law and Policy in Japan* (Bury St Edmunds: Arima Publishing, 2008)

Wakui, M., 'Bid Rigging Initiated by Government Officials: The Conjuncture of Collusion and Corruption in Japan', in Cheng, T., Marco Colino, S. and Ong, B. (eds.), *Cartels in Asia: Law and Practice* (The Hague: Wolters Kluwer, 2015) 41

Walsh, D. J., 'Carrots and Sticks – Leniency and Fines in EC Cartel Cases' (2009) 30(1) *European Competition Law Review* 30

Wanandi, Y., 'ASEAN's Past and the Challenges Ahead: Aspects of Politics and Security', in Tay, S. S. C., Estanislao, J. P., Soesastro, C. (eds.), *Reinventing ASEAN* (Singapore: ISEAS, 2001) 25

Wang, K., Yang, M. and Zhang, D., 'China's New State Administration for Market Regulation: What to Know and What to Expect', *Ropes & Gray Alert* (2018). Retrieved from www.ropesgray.com/en/newsroom/alerts/2018/04/Chinas-New-State-Market-Regulatory-Administration-What-to-Know-and-What-to-Expect

Wang, M.-Y., 'Analysis and Review of Leniency Policy and Reward Programs' (2016) 25 *Fair Trade Quarterly* 127

Wang, P., Zhang, Y. and Xue, Q., 'Combination of China's Three Antitrust Enforcement Agencies May Bring More Aggressive Enforcement over Long Run' (June 2018). Retrieved from www.jonesday.com/en/insights/2018/06/combination-of-chinas-three-antitrust-enforcement

Wang, X., *The Evolution of China's Anti-Monopoly Law* (Cheltenham: Edward Elgar, 2014)

Wang, X., 'Retrospectives and Prospects of China's Anti-Monopoly Law', in Van Uytsel, S., Hayashi, S. and Haley, J. (eds.), *Research Handbook on Asian Competition Law* (Cheltenham: Edward Elgar, 2020) 209

Wang, X. and Su, J., *Competition Law in China* (Alphen aan de Rijn: Wolters Kluwer, 2012)

Warin, F. J. and Jaffe, P. E., 'The Deferred-Prosecution Jigsaw Puzzle: A Modest Proposal for Reform; (2005) 19 *Andrews Litigation Report* 3

Weber Waller, S., 'Towards a Constructive Public-Private Partnership to Enforce Competition Law' (2006) 29 *World Competition* 367

Werden, G., 'Deterrence and Detection of Cartels: Using All the Tools and Sanctions' (Presentation at the ABA Center for Continuing Legal Education, Miami, 1 March 2012)

Werden, G., Hammond, S. and Barnett, B., 'Detection and Deterrence of Cartels: Using All the Tools and Sanctions' (2011) 56 *Antitrust Bulletin* 207

Whelan, P., 'Criminal Cartel Enforcement in the EU: Avoiding a Human Rights Trade-Off', in Beaton-Wells, C. and Ezrachi, A. (eds.), *Criminalising Cartels: Critical Studies of an International Regulatory Movement* (Oxford: Hart Publishing, 2011) 217

Whelan, P., *The Criminalization of European Cartel Enforcement: Theoretical, Legal, and Practical Challenges* (Oxford: Oxford University Press, 2014)

Whish, R. and Bailey, D., *Competition Law*, 10th ed. (Oxford: Oxford University Press, 2021)

White, L. J., 'Lysine and Price Fixing: How Long? How Severe?' (2001) 18 *Review of Industrial Organization* 23

Williams, M., 'Cartel Prohibition and the Search for Deterrent Penalties: The United States, the European Union, Australia and China Compared', in Healey, D., Jacobs, M. and Smith, R. (eds.), *Research Handbook on Methods and Models of Competition Law* (Cheltenham: Edward Elgar, 2020) 116

Williams, M., 'Competition Law in Thailand: Seeds of Success or Fated to Fail?' (2004) 27 *World Competition* 459

Williams, M., 'Leniency Policy with Chinese Characteristics', in Beaton-Wells, C. and Tran, C. (eds.), *Anti-Cartel Enforcement in a Contemporary Age: Leniency Religion* (Oxford: Hart Publishing, 2015) 33

Williams, M., 'Seeds of Its Own Destruction: Hong Kong's Dysfunctional Competition Policy' (2006) 1 *Journal of Business Law* 52

Williams, R., 'Cartels in the Criminal Law Landscape', in Beaton-Wells, C. and Ezrachi, A. (eds.), *Criminalising Cartels: Critical Studies of an International Regulatory Movement* (Oxford: Hart Publishing, 2011) 311

Wils, W. P. J., 'Is Criminalization of EU Competition Law the Answer?' (2005) 28 *World Competition* 117

Wils, W. P. J., 'Leniency in Antitrust Enforcement: Theory and Practice' (2007) 30 *World Competition* 25

Wils, W. P. J., 'The Use of Leniency in EU Cartel Enforcement: An Assessment after Twenty Years' (2016) 39(3) *World Competition* 327

Woodall, B., *Japan under Construction: Corruption, Politics, and Public Works* (Berkeley: University of California Press, 1996)

Woodall, B., 'The Logic of Collusive Action: The Political Roots of Japan's Dangō System' (1993) 25(3) *The Journal of Comparative Politics* 297

World Bank, 'Malaysia – Enterprise Survey 2015' (2017). Retrieved from https://microdata.worldbank.org/index.php/catalog/2804

World Economic Forum, 'The Global Competitiveness Report Index 4.0 2019 edition (Singapore)' (2019). Retrieved from http://reports.weforum.org/global-competitiveness-report-2019/economy-profiles/#economy=SGP

Wu, S., Hsieh, Y. and Wu, W.-H., 'Leniency Programme in Taiwan: The Impact of a "Whistle-Blower" System in Eastern Culture'. (2013). Retrieved from www.leeandli.com/Att/Profile/Euromoney%20-%20Taiwan%20competition.pdf

Xu, Sh. and Tao T., 'Monopoly Agreements, Trade Associations and Competition Culture in China', in Cheng, T., Marco Colino, S. and Ong, B. (eds.), *Cartels in Asia: Law and Practice* (Hong Kong: Wolters Kluwer Law & Business, 2015) 255

Xue, Q. and Yang, X. 'Anti-Cartel Law and Enforcement in China: A Survey', in Emch, A. and Stallibras, D. (eds.), *China's Anti-Monopoly Law: The First Five Years* (The Hague: Wolters Kluwer, 2013) 83

Yang, M.-Ch., 'Competition Law and Policy of the Republic of Korea' (2009) 54(3) *Antitrust Bulletin* 621

Yi, S.-S. and Jung, Y., 'A New Kid on the Block: Korean Competition Law, Policy, and Economics' (2007) 3(2) *Competition Policy International* 153. Retrieved from www.researchgate.net/profile/Sang-Seung-Yi/publication/227387454_A_New_Kid_on_the_Block_Korean_Competition_Law_Policy_and_Economics/links/0046351d02a6080bb1000000/A-New-Kid-on-the-Block-Korean-Competition-Law-Policy-and-Economics.pdf?origin=publication_detail

Yoshikawa, S., 'Fair Trade Commission vs. MITI: History of the Conflicts between the Antimonopoly Policy and the Industrial Policy in Post War Period of Japan' (1983) 15 *Case Western Reserve Journal of International Law* 489

Ysewyn, J. and Kahmann, S., 'The Decline and Fall of the Leniency Program in Europe' (2018) 1 *Concurrence* 44

Yu, X., Jiang, H. and Ling, Z., 'How Does the Leniency Program Apply to Monopoly Agreement Cases? Highlights of the Relevant Antitrust Guidelines' (2020) (in Chinese). Retrieved from www.sohu.com/a/415223549_120051855

Yun, S.-U. and Song, J.-H., 'Practical Issues of the Current Leniency Program' (2009) 20 *Journal of Korean Competition Law* 263 (in Korean)

Zetzsche, D. A., 'Regulating a Revolution: From Regulatory Sandboxes to Smart Regulation' (2017) 23 *Fordham Journal of Corporate and Financial Law* 31

Zhang, A. H., *Chinese Antitrust Exceptionalism: How the Rise of China Challenges Global Regulation* (Oxford: Oxford University Press, 2021)

Zhang, A. H., 'Bureaucratic Politics and China's Anti-Monopoly Law' (2014) 47(3) *Cornell International Law Journal* 671

Zhang, A. H., 'Commentary: Why Did China Wait So Long to Crack Down on Alibaba?' (4 February 2021). Retrieved from www.channelnewsasia.com/commentary/chinese-tech-giant-alibaba-jack-ma-regulation-ant-300791

Zhang, A. H., 'The Role of Media in Antitrust: Evidence from China' (2018) 41 *Fordham International Law Journal* 473

Zhang, A. H., 'Strategic Public Shaming: Evidence from Chinese Antitrust' (2017). Retrieved from https://papers.ssrn.com/sol3/papers.cfm?abstract_id=2943268

Zhang, C. and Sun, S., 'What Determines Antitrust Fines in China?' (2019) 40 *European Competition Law Review* 47

Zhang, X. and Zhang, V. Y., 'New Developments in China's Competition Policy against Monopolistic/Collusive Agreements', in Faure, M. and Xu, G. (eds.), *Economics and Regulation in China* (Abingdon: Routledge, 2013), 109

Zhang, Z. and Wu, B., 'Governing China's Administrative Monopolies under the Anti-Monopoly Law: A Ten-Year Review (2008–2018) and Beyond' (2018). Retrieved from https://papers.ssrn.com/sol3/papers.cfm?abstract_id=3294291

Zhiyue, B., 'Commentary: Why China's US$2.8 Billion Fine Is a Huge Relief for Alibaba' (14 April 2021). Retrieved from www.channelnewsasia.com/commentary/china-fine-alibaba-billions-monopoly-behaviour-jack-ma-215146

Zhou, J., 'Evaluating Leniency with Missing Information on Undetected Cartels: Exploring Time-Varying Policy Impacts on Cartel Duration' (GESY Discussion Paper No 353, University of Munich, April 2011). Retrieved from https://epub.ub.uni-muenchen.de/13201/1/353_01.pdf

Zingales, N., 'European and American Leniency Programmes: Two Models towards Convergence' (2008) 5(1) *Competition Law Review* 5

Zisler, A., 'The Work of the OECD Committee of Experts on Restrictive Business Practices' (1974) 19 *Antitrust Bulletin* 289

INDEX

www.ingramcontent.com/pod-product-compliance
Lightning Source LLC
LaVergne TN
LVHW011657200926
848484LV00004B/968
* 9 7 8 1 0 0 9 1 5 2 7 0 9 *